Sheena Sumarat

PRACTICAL LOGIC

An Antidote for Uncritical Thinking

D0166056

PRACTICAL LOGIC

An Antidote for Uncritical Thinking

FIFTH EDITION

Douglas J. Soccio
Shasta College
and
Vincent E. Barry
Bakersfield College

Harcourt Brace College Publishers
Fort Worth   Philadelphia   San Diego   New York   Orlando   Austin   San Antonio
Toronto   Montreal   London   Sydney   Tokyo

Publisher	**Earl McPeek**
Acquisitions Editor	**David Tatom**
Product Manager	**Steve Drummond**
Developmental Editor	**Pam Hatley**
Project Editor	**Elaine Richards**
Art Director	**Pat Bracken**
Production Manager	**Diane Gray**

Cover photo: Pat Bracken

ISBN: 0-15-503036-1
Library of Congress Catalog Card Number: 97-73101

Copyright © 1998, 1992, 1988, 1980, 1976 by Holt, Rinehart and Winston

All rights reserved. No parts of this publication may be reproduced or transmitted in any form or by any means, electronic or mechanical, including photocopy, recording, or any information storage and retrieval system, without permission in writing from the publisher.

Requests for permission to make copies of any part of the work should be mailed to: Permissions Department, Harcourt Brace & Company, 6277 Sea Harbor Drive, Orlando, Florida 32887-6777.

Address for orders:
Harcourt Brace College Publishers
6277 Sea Harbor Drive
Orlando, FL 32887-6777
1-800-782-4479

Address for editorial correspondence:
Harcourt Brace College Publishers
301 Commerce Street, Suite 3700
Fort Worth, TX 76102

Web site address:
http://www.hbcollege.com

Harcourt Brace & Company will provide complimentary supplements or supplement packages to those adopters qualified under our adoption policy. Please contact your sales representative to learn how you can qualify. If as an adopter or potential user you receive supplements you do not need, please return them to your sales representative or send them to: Attn: Returns Department, Troy Warehouse, 465 South Lincoln Drive, Troy, MO 63379.

Printed in the United States of America

7 8 9 0 1 2 3 4 5 6   039   9 8 7 6 5 4 3 2 1

For Mike,
my brother and mentor,
with love and admiration
—*DJS*

We would like to open this preface to the fifth edition of *Practical Logic: An Antidote to Uncritical Thinking* with a special note of appreciation and gratitude to our loyal users. Given today's crowded textbook marketplace, we feel particularly honored that our modest book has been so well-received.

We have tried to keep *Practical Logic, Fifth Edition,* flexible enough to be adaptable to a variety of teaching styles while improving its virtues: clarity, accessibility, respect for real life, and good humor. We have, we hope, smoothed out rough spots without making major alterations in a text that will be 25 years old in 2001.

The focus of this fifth edition revision can be summed up in two words: *enhance pedagogy.*

About The Fifth Edition   To quote from the 1980 preface to the second edition of *Practical Logic:* "There was a time when, to paraphrase Gertrude Stein, logic was logic was logic. If two students who had taken introductory logic courses at different institutions chanced to meet, they shared conversational ground. 'Undistributed middle,' 'existential import,' and 'truth table' were familiar landmarks on the landscape of logic. But things have changed."

Judging by the wide variety of introductory texts, the soup of introductory critical thinking courses is even thicker than it was in 1980, before the term critical thinking gained the cachet it has today. Texts range from the comprehensive little-bit-of-everything bibles of traditional logic courses to slim critical thinking texts. Courses range from those that emphasize formal logic—the *science* of logic as it were, to those stressing critical thinking—the *art* of logic.

Drawing from both approaches, this fifth edition of *Practical Logic: An Antidote For Uncritical Thinking* continues the evolution of the seeds planted in 1976: hitting the mark between rigor (the science of logic) and accessibility and usefulness (the art of logic). *Practical Logic, Fifth Edition,* offers instructors some middle ground between the extremes of a very traditional, formalistic approach and an exclusively informal approach.

In making the difficult decisions of what to include and exclude, what to expand and what to reduce, we have, as in the past, relied on the experiences and advice of instructors, students, and reviewers. We have chosen to improve and refine *Practical Logic's* most effective and useful features: clear, realistic, relevant, everyday examples; user-friendly tone; and ample pedagogical aids.

The principal changes in this edition relate to content and structure from a pedagogical standpoint. Alterations have been made that enhance the coherence, clarity, accuracy and thoroughness of the overall text as well as of individual sections. The structure of the text has been streamlined and integrated, whenever possible following an intuitive, natural pattern. We think these alterations in structure and content have resulted in a pedagogically superior introductory logic text that we characterize as a *logical approach to critical thinking.*

Our fifth edition changes were made with an eye to our basic respect for the needs, interests, and abilities of today's students—people pursuing a variety of goals. *Practical Logic, Fifth Edition,* is clear, precise, and rigorous. This edition feels "natural" because its chief goal is to help students enhance their thinking and evaluative skills by fostering respect for *rational discourse:* the giving and receiving of reasons according to commonly agreed upon standards of verification, for the purpose of distinguishing truth from falsehood, appearance from reality, and mere opinion from informed opinion.

New to the Fifth Edition   Exercises have been updated, reordered, and improved, particularly the early exercises involving cogency and argument recognition, and fallacy exercises involving ambiguity and language. Early discussions of the importance of background knowledge in critical thinking combine with the new section on rational discourse to anticipate and minimize common sources of student-instructor frustration centering on misconceptions regarding differences between justified (informed) opinions and mere (top-of-the-head) opinions.

The chapter "Sophistries and Pseudoscience," now Chapter 14, has been moved to the last section of the text, Part Five: Evaluating Arguments. This relocation reflects our experience that this material is best treated after the chapters on induction, cause, and fallacies. Many instructors do this already. The new chapter order allows for better cross-referencing and provides a rich source of causal fallacies, begged questions and the like, for the assessment of modern-day sophistries.

Longtime users will immediately note that we have dropped the treatment of extended arguments to make room for the return of Venn diagrams in a new, streamlined appendix. Instructors and students have pointed out that for many students, and especially for visual learners, Venn diagrams offer a quick, clear picture of the relationship between the premises and conclusion of standard-form categorical syllogisms. The new, stand-alone appendix is clear enough to be seamlessly integrated into the treatment of categorical syllogisms, assigned to selected students for extra credit, or generally recommended as an additional teaching aid.

The entire text has been carefully polished. A number of fallacy definitions have been clarified and tightened to prevent confusion and sharpen distinctions. Revised material includes:

Chapter 1: Basic Anatomy   The fifth edition opens with improved explanations of "The Importance of Form and Content," and "Cogency," and a new section, "A Word About Being Well Informed," that immediately link the text to today's social climate via a brief discussion of the nature and benefits of rational discourse. Exercises have been updated and now include a new and more realistic "Stretching Exercise." The revised Chapter 1 is compassionately encouraging without being hokey or preachy. Revisions are intuitive and accessible.

Chapter 2: Recognition, Function, and Scope of Arguments   This material benefits from an enhanced discussion of argument recognition that addresses and acknowledges the naturalness of certain common sources of early frustration for many students. The new section, "A Word About Logic Exercises," anticipates and defuses some student anxiety over the need to interpret and justify answers to logic exercises.

Chapter 5: Careless Language Use   A revised discussion of "Questionable Premises and Ambiguity" underscores the link between language and logic and anticipates material in the next chapter.

Chapter 6: Inattention to Subject Matter   A clarified treatment of "Questionable Premises and Errors of Assumption" sharpens important distinctions within the basic category of fallacies of relevance and helps students distinguish among similar fallacies. The fallacy previously known as Invincible Ignorance has been renamed Willed Ignorance to better reflect the nature of this commonplace error in reasoning.

Chapter 7: Categorical Syllogisms   New material on obversion, conversion, and contraposition provides additional ways for students to infer relations among standard-form categorical propositions, and new exercises offer quick, valuable opportunities for student success.

Chapter 10: Inductive Reasoning and Generalizations   An amplified discussion of the significance of distinguishing between possibilities and probabilities clarifies one of the most common errors of everyday reasoning.

Chapter 11: Statistical Arguments   Fresh examples of the Concealed Evidence fallacy include those from the added category of "apples to oranges" comparisons. New material rounds out the examination of significant, deceptive marketing ploys.

Chapter 14: Sophistries and Pseudoscience   This unique and timely chapter benefits from its new location, after the treatment of fallacies, induction, and causality. The treatment of predictive power and falsifiability has been significantly improved.

Appendix: Venn Diagrams   "Back by popular demand," Venn diagrams provide an excellent visual representation of validity and the relationship between premises and conclusions in categorical syllogisms. Using a unique crescent-ellipse approach, this appendix provides students with a satisfying adjunct to the rules for validity that govern categorical syllogisms. Presenting Venn diagrams as an appendix maximizes instructor flexibility without intruding on the core text.

The Instructor's Manual for the fifth edition includes the solutions to those exercises not answered in the text and a test bank. These simple, but thorough, basic tests can be great time-savers as stand-alone tests or as supplements to instructor-prepared tests.

Acknowledgments   As our list of indebtedness grows, it becomes impossible to acknowledge all those who have had a hand in shaping *Practical Logic*. The list must always begin with countless students who have resisted, cajoled, and coerced us so that we have had to learn from them about teaching logic. We would also like to thank the reviewers of this edition: Dave Wolff, Big Bend Community College; Patrick Lippert, North Idaho College; Kenneth Stern, The State University of New York at Albany; Bernie Allen, West Virginia University—Parkersburg; W. Mark Cobb, Pensacola Junior College; and Stephen Thomassin, Ventura College. We offer special thanks to Pam Hatley at Harcourt Brace College Publishers for her courtesy, kindness, and encouragement. We are also grateful to David Tatom's continuing interest in *Practical Logic*, to Elaine Richards for her oversight of this project, and to Steven Baker and Betsy Ener for their careful proofing of the manuscript.

Doug Soccio reaffirms his gratitude to Vince Barry for the opportunity to become part of a text with which he fell in love almost 22 years ago.

Doug also expresses gratitude and love, for the patience, support, good humor, and hard work his wife Margaret contributed to this revision.

CONTENTS

PART ONE   ARGUMENTS AND CASES   1

CHAPTER 1   BASIC ANATOMY   3

Cases   5
  Arguments as Cases   7
Parts of an Argument   8
The Importance of Form and Content   10
Cogency   12
  Reasonableness   12
  Relevancy   13
  Sufficiency   14
A Word about Being Well Informed   15
A Word of Encouragement   16
A "Stretching" Exercise   17
Summary   17
Summary Exercises   18

CHAPTER 2   RECOGNITION, FUNCTION,
                AND SCOPE OF ARGUMENTS   19

Explanations and Nonarguments   20
The Best Way to Recognize Arguments Is from Context   22
Signal Words and Phrases   23
A Word about Logic Exercises   24
Abbreviated Arguments   28
Functions of Argument   29
The Scope of Argument   32
Summary   34
Summary Exercises   35
Additional Exercises   35

PART TWO   THINKING CRITICALLY
               ABOUT ARGUMENTS   41

CHAPTER 3   THE PUBLIC DIMENSION   43

Critical Thinking   45
Knowledge, Belief, and Truth   48
  Belief   48
  Truth   50
    Truth Is Not Relative   50

Sources of Knowledge   **52**
  Senses   52
  Reason   54
  Authority   54
    Determining the Reliability of Authority   55
Subjective and Objective Claims   **57**
Evaluating Evidence Objectively   **59**
  Physical Conditions   60
  Sensory Acuity   60
  Necessary Background Knowledge   60
  Objectivity   61
  Supporting Testimony   61
Reasonableness and Relevancy Reconsidered   **61**
The Fallacy of Unknowable Fact   **62**
The Fallacy of Provincialism   **63**
The Fallacy of Argument from Ignorance   **64**
Fallacies of Authority   **67**
  The Fallacy of False Authority   67
  The Fallacy of Positioning   68
  The Fallacy of Traditional Wisdom   69
  The Fallacy of Popularity   70
Summary   **73**
Summary Exercises   **75**
Additional Exercises   **76**

CHAPTER 4   THE PERSONAL DIMENSION   79
Emotions and Reasons   **80**
Human Needs   **82**
  Physical Needs   82
  Emotional Needs   83
Defense Mechanisms   **83**
  Scapegoating   84
  Projection   85
  Introjection   86
  Denial   87
  Rationalizing   88
  Prejudging   89
  Stereotyping   89
Summary   **91**
Summary Exercises   **91**
Additional Exercises   **92**

CHAPTER 5   CARELESS LANGUAGE USE   95
Language and Experience   **96**
Informative and Persuasive Language   **98**
  Objective Connotation   99
  Subjective Connotation   99

Doublespeak   **102**
    Euphemism as Doublespeak   104
    Jargon as Doublespeak   107
    Buzzwords as Doublespeak   109
    Puffery as Doublespeak   110
    Gobbledygook   112
Ambiguity and Argument   **115**
Questionable Premises and Ambiguity   **116**
    Equivocation   116
    Amphiboly   117
    Composition   120
    Division   121
Summary   **122**
Summary Exercises   **123**
Additional Exercises   **124**

CHAPTER 6   INATTENTION TO SUBJECT MATTER   128

Reliance on Emotion   **128**
    Personal Attack   129
        Character Assassination   130
        Circumstantial Personal Attack   131
        Tu Quoque   133
    Two Wrongs Make a Right   133
        Common Practice   135
    Mob Appeal   135
        Bandwagon Appeal   137
        Snob Appeal   138
    Pity   139
    Fear   141
Reliance on Diversion   **145**
    Red Herring   145
    Ridicule   146
    Straw Argument   147
Questionable Premises and Errors of Assumption   **151**
    Begging the Question   153
        Circular Reasoning   154
    Loaded Epithets   154
    Complex Question   155
    Dismissal   156
    Willed Ignorance   157
Summary   **160**
Summary Exercises   **162**
Additional Exercises   **163**

PART THREE DEDUCTIVE
ARGUMENTS 169

CHAPTER 7 CATEGORICAL SYLLOGISMS 171

Validity 171
Categorical Propositions 172
 Propositional Form 174
 Distribution 177
 The Simplified Square of Contradiction 180
 Existential Import 182
 Obversion, Conversion, and Contraposition 183
Standard-Form Categorical Syllogisms 185
 Form 187
 Spotting the Conclusion 188
Rules of Validity 191
Validity and the Cogency Criteria 199
Summary 200
Summary Exercises 202
Additional Exercises 203

CHAPTER 8 RECONSTRUCTING ARGUMENTS 205

Translating Categorical Propositions Into Standard Form 206
 Arguments with Logical Equivalencies 206
 Propositions Containing Singular Terms 207
 Propositions Containing Adjectival Phrases 208
 Propositions Lacking the Verb *To Be* 208
 Propositions Containing Irregular Quantifiers 209
 Propositions Lacking Subject or Predicate Terms 209
 Propositions Using *Only* and *None But* 210
 Propositions Containing Two Statements: Affirmative and Negative 211
The Enthymeme 215
The Sorites 218
Rational Reconstruction and Validity 222
 Principle of Charity 222
 Three Steps to Rational Reconstruction 223
 Four Things To Do in Reconstruction 226
  Relevant Reconstruction 226
  Self-Supporting Reconstruction 227
  Appropriate Strength of Reconstruction 228
  Contextually Accurate Reconstruction 229
Summary 232
Summary Exercises 233
Additional Exercises 233

CHAPTER 9   ADDITIONAL SYLLOGISMS   235

Disjunctive Syllogisms   **236**
Conditional Syllogisms   **239**
  Pure Conditional Syllogism   242
The Dilemma   **244**
  Dilemmas and Cogency   245
  The Counterdilemma   246
Summary   **249**
Additional Exercises   **251**

PART FOUR   INDUCTIVE ARGUMENTS   253

CHAPTER 10   INDUCTIVE REASONING AND GENERALIZATIONS   255

Induction and the Sufficiency Criterion   **256**
  Sufficiency and Quality   258
Inductive Generalization   **259**
  Strong Inductive Generalizations   260
  Weak Inductive Generalizations   261
  Statistical Generalizations   261
  Induction and Strong Generalizations   262
Possibilities and Probabilities   **263**
Reliable Inductive Generalizations   **264**
  Comprehensiveness   265
  Size   265
  Randomness   266
  Margin for Error   266
Inductive Fallacies   **269**
  Hasty Conclusion   269
    Anecdotal Evidence   271
    Accident   272
    Guilt by Association   272
Summary   **274**
Summary Exercises   **276**
Additional Exercises   **276**

CHAPTER 11   STATISTICAL ARGUMENTS   279

Studies, Surveys, Polls   **281**
  Studies   281
  Polls and Surveys   283
Statistics and Fallacies   **286**
  The Fallacy of Biased Sample   286
    The Pollster   286
    The Sampling Technique   286
    The Respondent   287

The Fallacy of Equivocation   290
    Verbal   290
    Weasel Words   291
    Visual   292
The Fallacy of Biased Question   295
The Fallacy of Ambiguous Question   297
The Fallacy of False Dilemma   298
The Fallacy of Concealed Evidence   299
    Nonstatistical   300
        Apples to Oranges   303
    Statistical   304
Summary   307
Summary Exercises   309
Additional Exercises   309

CHAPTER 12   ANALOGICAL ARGUMENTS   314

The Value of Analogical Arguments   315
Analogical Arguments and the Cogency Criteria   319
    Number of Entities Involved   319
    Number of Relevant Likenesses   319
    Number and Nature of Differences   319
Faulty Analogy   323
Summary   326
Summary Exercises   326
Additional Exercises   326

CHAPTER 13   CAUSE   331

The Idea of Cause   332
Causal Concepts   334
    Necessary Cause   334
    Sufficient Cause   334
    Necessary and Sufficient Cause   335
    Contributory Cause   335
Methods for Establishing Probable Cause   336
    Agreement   337
    Difference   338
    Joint Method of Agreement and Difference   339
    Concomitant Variation   340
Correlations and Causes   341
Fallacies of Causation   346
    Post Hoc Fallacy   347
        Magical Thinking   348
    Slippery Slope Fallacy   348
    Oversimplification Fallacy   349
Causal Arguments and the Cogency Criteria   352
Summary   352
Summary Exercises   354
Additional Exercises   354

PART FIVE   EVALUATING ARGUMENTS   365

CHAPTER 14   SOPHISTRIES AND PSEUDOSCIENCE   367

Predictive Power and Falsifiability   368
The New Sophists and their Sophistries   370
  Psychological Sophistry   372
  Success Sophistry   374
  Spiritual and Psychic Sophistry   377
    Tricks of the Trade   377
    Electronic Wizardry   378
    Selective Cures   379
    Concealing Wealth   380
    Crossroads Pitch   380
    Multiple Predictions   380
    Vague Prediction   381
    Causal Confusion   382
Pseudoscience   384
Summary   388
Summary Exercises   389
Additional Exercises   389

CHAPTER 15   NORMATIVE AND NONNORMATIVE ARGUMENTS   392

Evaluating Arguments: The Basic Procedure   393
Fallacies and Defense Mechanisms Covered in the Text   394
  Defense Mechanisms   395
  Fallacies of Meaning   395
  Fallacious Reliance on Emotion   395
  Fallacious Reliance on Diversion   395
  Fallacious Reliance on Assumption   395
  Fallacies Connected with Induction   395
  Fallacies of Authority   395
  Formal (Deductive) Fallacies   396
Cogency, Knowledge, and Truth   396
  An Extended Example   398
Values and Value Judgments   403
  Normative and Nonnormative Statements   403
Normative Arguments   406
  Is It Possible To Evaluate Normative Claims for Reasonableness?   407
    Language Clarification   409
    1. Personal Preference   409
    2. Social Preference   410
    3. Conformity with Principle, Standard, or Law   411
  Evaluation   413
    1. Pseudojustification   414
    2. Minimum Adequacy Requirements   416

Summary   **419**
Summary Exercises   **419**
Additional Exercises   **420**

APPENDIX   VENN DIAGRAMS   **425**
Venn Diagrams   **425**
Diagramming Specific Propositions   **428**
Diagramming Categorical Syllogisms   **430**
Crescents and Ellipses   **433**
   Spotting Crescents and Ellipses   433
   Diagramming Propositions with X   434
Using Venn Diagrams To Test for Validity   **435**
   Arguments with Two Particular Premises   440
   Arguments Containing Mixed Premises   443
Reviewing What We Have Learned   **445**
   Diagramming an A Minor Premise   445
   Diagramming an A Major Premise   446
   Diagramming an O Minor Premise   446
   Diagramming an O Major Premise   446
   Diagramming an E Minor or Major Premise   447
   Diagramming an I Minor or Major Premise   448
Eight Steps for Testing Validity with Venn Diagrams   **448**
Using Venn Diagrams To "See" Syllogistic Fallacies   **449**
Reinforcing Exercises   **451**

Glossary   **453**
Answers to Selected Exercises   **463**
Index   **497**

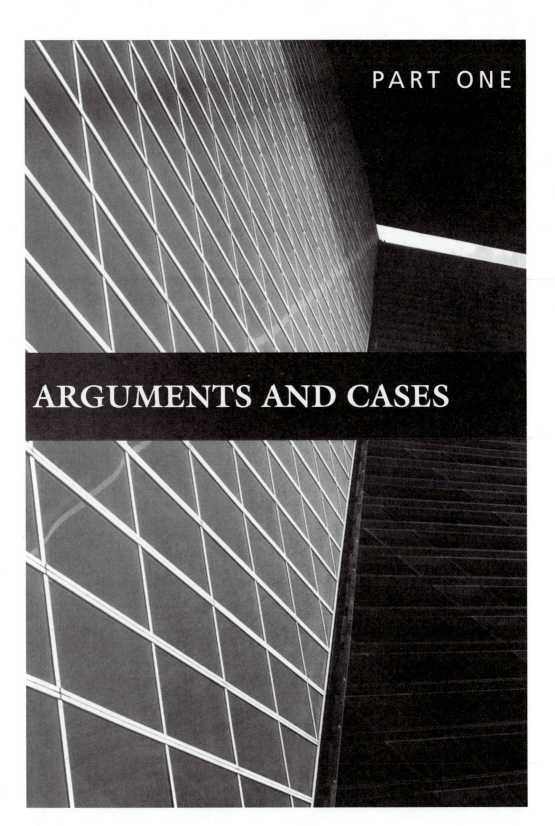

PART ONE

ARGUMENTS AND CASES

CHAPTER 1

Basic Anatomy

. . . all our dignity lies in thought. Let us strive, then, to think well.

BLAISE PASCAL

Do you ever get the feeling that everyone's trying to sell you something?

"I realized my own potential by reading *Dianetics,*" you hear an attractive young woman tell you in a television commercial. Then she adds, "Buy it. Read it. Use it."

Before you can digest that pitch, another voice exhorts, "Energize your love life!" It goes on to reassure you that "You can have as much love as you want once you discover how to tap the incredible energy of your inner sexuality!" And to discover how to do that, "You ought to know about a wonderfully helpful new book. . . ."

Bored with television, you open a magazine to find an ad that asks, "Can't find a pair of jeans to fit? Inseams too short? Rises too low?" [If so,] "Try a pair of Wranglers." Opposite that ad is one for Nike shoes that simply says, "Just do it." And on the following pages. . . .

There's no point in going on. Everywhere somebody has something to sell, whether in politics, business, education, religion, sports, or entertainment; you name it, someone has it—a product, a belief, a candidate, a pastime, even a mate. It's little wonder that many today feel angry, confused, and frustrated.

So how do you handle it all? Which of the claims for your loyalty do you accept? Which do you reject as just more blooming, buzzing confusion?

Once asked what it takes to be a successful writer, Ernest Hemingway replied, "A good crap detector." Crude? Perhaps. What he meant was an ability to separate the authentic from the phoney, the real from the illusory, the significant from the trivial, the artistic from the merely clever.

Well, it's not only the writer who needs that capacity. Everyone does—especially today. Lacking it, we can do little more than surrender, go along with our own exploitation—or, perhaps, withdraw from society altogether.

Neither choice is attractive. We need a middle position that allows us to recognize the sensible and reject the nonsensical. We need to sift and filter the input that bombards us daily. We must so refine our powers of perception and judgment that we can distinguish the legitimate claim from the bogus, the appeal we should accept from the one we should ignore. In short, we need a good "crap detector."

Perhaps you've noticed how over the last few years there has been growing public dissatisfaction with the widespread lack of civility in public discourse. Employers complain about job candidates' lack of critical reasoning skills. Educational institutions at every level now require some critical thinking courses for graduation. We wouldn't be surprised if you're reading this book in a course designed to fulfill just such a requirement. Clearly, we need effective critical thinking skills. Critical thinking skills do more than just help us make wiser choices in our private lives; they are also vital civic virtues. Casting an informed ballot or making a reasonable determination as a juror are just two obvious examples of instances when being good citizens requires having a good "crap detector." The criminal case of *California v. Simpson* (the "O.J. Simpson case") drew national attention to the difficulty many of today's courts face in finding unbiased, clear-thinking individuals capable of serving on juries.

Too often, television and radio talk shows and "discussion" panels seem to consist of two or more people talking at once, making rude comments and "in-your-face" gestures, of agitated participants who don't appear to be listening to what others have to say.

Of course, the most important issues confronting us deserve careful consideration and discussion. Yet today's most socially significant issues—euthanasia, abortion, welfare reform, affirmative action, censorship, same-sex marriages—are precisely the sort of topics that most often trigger intense, personal reactions of the kind that make critical assessment difficult, if not impossible. We think that there is a much better alternative to endless bickering and dogmatic assertions of righteousness, an alternative that respects persons and ideas: *rational discourse.*

Rational discourse is the giving and receiving of reasons, according to commonly agreed-upon standards of verification, for the purpose of distinguishing truth from falsehood, appearance from reality, and mere opinion from informed opinion. Its ultimate goal is to separate truth from falsehood and appearance from reality, as much as is humanly possible. Participating in rational discourse requires, among other things: 1) a willingness to consider all sides of an issue; 2) desire and willingness to avoid being controlled by bias; 3) respect for appropriate expertise without succumbing to uncritical dependency on authorities and experts; 4) ongoing effort to stay well informed; and 5) the mental maturity to avoid taking legitimate criticism personally.

One good way to develop or refine skills necessary to participate in rational discourse is through the study of logic and critical thinking.

Logic is the study of the rules of correct argument, and critical thinking is the careful assessment of both logical and nonlogical claims. In this opening chapter, we begin to refine our powers of perception and judgment. We take the first steps toward shoring up our intellectual defenses, toward arming ourselves against the

THE LOCKHORNS

"WE HAVEN'T BEEN TALKING FOR FIVE MINUTES AND YOU'RE ALREADY RESORTING TO LOGIC!"

Reprinted with special permission of King Features Syndicate.

onslaught of the inane. We move toward so improving our reasoning that we exercise significant control over our lives.

Specifically, this chapter focuses on what an argument is. By the time we've completed the chapter, we'll have taken the first step toward making sense of things, toward constructing our own "crap detector."

One other thing: In our eagerness to stress the usefulness of clear, critical thinking in helping us increase control over our lives, we don't mean to imply that this is critical thinking's sole function. Logic and critical thinking also have what we can term an aesthetic dimension. Thinking logically is fun, and at times even elegant. Although you may not be able to appreciate this now or in the early stages of your study, at some point you'll probably glimpse the "beauty" of thinking logically and reasoning well.

CASES

As noted above, we are bombarded by efforts to sell us things: ideas, products, services, beliefs, even relationships. We also try to sell ourselves: stop smoking, lose weight, don't have children yet, and so on. We experience—and use—a variety of persuasive techniques and strategies in these efforts. These include logical reasons, factual claims, causal connections, powerful words and phrases, humor, personal loyalties or group affiliations, authoritative pronouncements, promises of friendship or threats of separation—or worse. In other words, *we construct a case for or against something.*

A case consists of all the elements used to persuade someone (including ourselves) of something. A case is more than just facts and reasons, though a *good* case must include them. We constantly make cases. Think, for example, of any instance in which you did everything you could think of to persuade someone of something. Perhaps in disputing the accuracy of a police officer's radar gun, you also appealed to his pity to avoid getting a ticket. And when that failed, you mentioned that you were the mayor's cousin. Again, maybe after giving your still-reluctant daughter excellent reasons for studying, you switched tactics and "reminded" her of the Nintendo set she wanted for her birthday by saying something like this, "Gosh, I hope we don't have to use the money I was going to buy the Nintendo set with to pay for a tutor."

In other words, you made a *case* against receiving a ticket, and a *case* for your daughter to study. And we've all probably seen movie and television lawyers use logic, tricks, humor, anger, feelings of revenge and disgust, as well as technical evidence to win their cases.

Cases don't have to include logical reasons; they can consist of threats or promises. Sometimes, a case provides a powerful motive for its conclusion, without providing *logical* evidence. If your daughter begins to cry when you threaten not to buy her the Nintendo set, you may be unable to resist her case. And it is a case. If she knows that you are easily swayed by tears, then she may have good reason to suspect that crying will get you to retract your demand that she study. Your second case, the one she is reacting against, may be summarized this way: "You should study because you want a Nintendo set, and I will not buy you one unless you study." Her countercase looks something like this: "I will cry and suffer loudly and dramatically if you make me study and don't buy me the Nintendo set—like you promised. And you hate it when I cry and you feel guilty when you disappoint me by not keeping your word. Therefore, you should buy me the Nintendo whether or not I study."

Neither you nor your daughter need to express every part of your cases in words. An emotional subtext is often an important component of these informal, everyday cases. Even though your daughter has not included logical reasons as part of her case, she may have offered you strong personal motives for accepting it—depending on your personality and state of mind at the time. Similarly, the strength of your case will depend on your daughter's assessment of your willingness to carry through on your threat, and the strength of her desire for a Nintendo set. You and your daughter have used two common ploys in making cases: appeals to fear and pity (see Chapter 6). Technically, appeals to emotions are not logical reasons. In fact, logicians classify these two emotional appeals as *errors in reasoning.* Yet they often work.

This observation teaches us something important about cases: Cases do not always involve logic. They may (and they often do), but they need not. But because we are reasoning beings, most of us respond to reason, or even the appearance of reason. Further, most of us don't like to think of ourselves as being purely emotional and arbitrary in our choices. We like to think of ourselves as basing our decisions on reasons and evidence. In short, logic. Consequently, most cases claim to present logical evidence for their point of view. Even when cases make emotional appeals, they often imply or state that these emotions are reasons for accepting their point of view.

Thus it is important to distinguish the *apparent case* from the *actual case.* Sometimes we offer reasons that "look good" and give our cases the appearance of rationality when in fact the power of the case comes from its emotional subtext. To repeat, cases need not contain any logical appeal at all, though most cases will—or at least will try to look like they do.

Obviously not all cases can be good because some are contradictory. Sometimes we must decide, not unlike a jury, between competing cases. Should we accept our parents' case and go to college, or should we accept our sweetheart's case and get married? Is that church's case for how to interpret the Bible better than this one's? Should I rely on conventional treatment for my cancer or go to a foreign clinic specializing in nutritional cures?

Because the issues involved are so often vital, we need to find reliable ways of analyzing cases. And because cases can become quite complex, we need a way to determine which elements are relevant and which are not. Fortunately, most (if not all) cases share common features. Once we grasp these basic elements, we will be able to apply certain rules and guidelines to cases under scrutiny, and thereby make the process of evaluation much more manageable and reliable. We will be able to make the most reasonable judgment possible given the particular case in question. We will be able to *decide* and *choose* rather than just *react* or *guess*.

In ordinary usage, we often interchange the words "cases" and "arguments," as in "Dad makes a good argument (i.e., *case*) for going to college" or "Dr. Butcher's case (i.e., *argument*) for surgery leaves me unconvinced." Our interchangeability of these terms is understandable and often correct because many cases imply arguments. And every argument can be considered a case that someone is making for something. But as logicians use the term "argument," not every case contains an argument.

Let's consider the relationship between cases and arguments more closely.

Arguments as Cases

In the study of logic and critical thinking, *an argument is a group of truth claims intended or understood to provide support (evidence) for another truth claim*. *Truth claims*, as the term reminds us, are statements asserting something to be true. Depending on what is asserted, truth claims may be either true or false. Logicians use the terms *proposition, statement,* and *assertion* when referring to truth claims.

In general terms, an argument consists of a truth claim combined with reasons for accepting the claim. For a group of propositions to be an argument, then, one of them must be understood as being supported by the others. Here's an example: "Mothers are females. Jane's a mother. Therefore, Jane's a female." These three statements are truth claims or propositions. The order in which they are presented, combined with the word "therefore," reveals the *intention,* or *understanding* of the arguer. The statement "Jane's a female" is to be understood as being supported by the first two statements. In other words, the first two statements supposedly make a "logical case" for the third statement. In more technical terms, the first two propositions are claimed to entail, or logically guarantee, the third proposition. This means that if the first two statements are taken as true, then, logically speaking, the third statement must also be taken as true. To accept the first two statements while rejecting the third would be self-contradictory. Taken as a group, then, these three statements comprise an argument. We could combine all these statements into a single sentence: "Because (1) mothers are females and (2) Jane's a mother, therefore (3) Jane's a female." We still have an argument. An argument, then, can be a group of statements that take the form of individual sentences or merely a single sentence.

STUDY HINT
Pay Attention to Key Terms

One of the best ways to get off to a good start in your study of logic is to think of learning logic as if you were learning a foreign language. When key terms are introduced they will be identified by *italics*. They will also be included in the glossary. Sometimes, as you will see in this chapter, these key terms are familiar words but with more precise definitions. It is helpful to pay extra attention to these terms right away. Try to see how their new definitions are different from the ways in which we usually use these terms.

Example: Logical arguments are not the same things as disagreements, disputes, or quarrels. How are they different?

PARTS OF AN ARGUMENT

In speaking of arguments, logicians give special names to their basic components. (We've already learned that truth claims are technically referred to as propositions, statements, or assertions.) The terms *premise* and *conclusion* are used to distinguish the claim being supported in an argument from the claims being offered as providing that support. *The premises of an argument are the support statements. The conclusion of an argument is the statement being supported.*

Thus, in the argument "All mothers are females. Jane is a mother. Therefore Jane is a female," the first two propositions are the premises and the third is the conclusion. Similarly, in the argument "Marie ought to be hired for the job because she has qualifications superior to all the other applicants," "Marie ought to be hired" is the conclusion, and "she has qualifications superior to all the other job applicants" is the premise. Notice from these two examples that premises and conclusions can occur anywhere in the argument. Premises don't have to appear at the beginning; conclusions don't have to appear at the end.

The premises of an argument constitute the evidence offered to prove the truth of the conclusion. Premises and conclusions must always be propositions. In other words, the parts of an argument are propositions (statements with truth value) arranged in a certain relationship. One of these is the proposition whose truth value we are interested in supporting (the conclusion). The other propositions are statements that we hope will show that the conclusion is indeed true (the premises). Premises, then, are statements whose truth value is presumably already established. They're used to "make the case" for the conclusion.

In the argument "All mothers are female. Jane is a mother. Therefore Jane is a female," the first two propositions are the premises and the third is the conclusion. So arranged, the premises, which presumably are true, are intended to establish the truth of the conclusion.

In the argument "All mothers are females. Jane is a female. Therefore Jane is a mother," once again the first two propositions are premises and the third is the conclusion. Here again, the conclusion is claimed to be demonstrated by the presumably true premises.

Notice how we can have two completely different arguments using exactly the same propositions. The difference is in *how the propositions are used:* whether they are treated as evidence or as conclusions. Although both arguments contain the same information, the internal relationship of the parts of the arguments is different. The first example is logically acceptable whereas the second one is flawed. (We will discuss the qualities of good arguments as we proceed, but you might want to stop a moment and analyze these two examples to see how you think they differ logically.)

STUDY HINT
Not All Propositions Are Premises or Conclusions

The important thing to understand is that a premise is *any* proposition *used as evidence* in a logical argument. A conclusion is *any* proposition whose truth value we are *attempting to establish* by means of a logical argument. *Premise* and *conclusion* are relative terms. The very same proposition may be a premise in one argument and the conclusion in another.

Consider this example: "Because all logic students are bright people, Marie must be bright, since Marie is a logic student." Here we notice that the middle proposition (Marie must be bright) is the conclusion whereas the first and third propositions are the premises. The stated order of propositions is not what determines how they function in an argument. *Whether a proposition is a premise or a conclusion is determined by how it is used, not by where it happens to occur in the passage.*

It is possible to express the very same argument in a number of ways:

1. Because Marie is a logic student, and because all logic students are bright, Marie must be bright.

2. Marie must be bright. After all she is a logic student, and we know that all logic students are bright.

3. It follows logically that because Marie is a logic student she must be bright, since all logic students are bright.

Although each of these expressions of the same argument varies in stated order, the conclusion and premises remain the same.

THE IMPORTANCE OF FORM AND CONTENT

All arguments contain two distinct components: a logical shape or structure known as their *logical form* (or *logic* for short), and the specific *content* of their premises and conclusion. The strongest arguments contain only true statements arranged in a logically appropriate form. Arguments fail to establish their conclusions if (1) they contain false, ambiguous or meaningless premises or conclusions; or (2) if their logical structure is flawed. Although we will study content and logical structure in depth shortly, it is crucial to get a clear sense of the basic relationship between the content and logic of arguments now.

As noted, the purpose of an argument is to *demonstrate, establish, prove, and/or show* that a particular conclusion is true. To do this, arguments provide evidence or grounds in the form of premises. Thus each argument consists of a relationship between its premises and its conclusion. Premises and conclusions are claims about what is true (or false). The actual determination of which claims are true or false usually depends on more than logical factors. (The exceptions are certain technical propositions that express logical relationships and rules.)

The claim that "Kutras must be male because Kutras is a bachelor" is based on the meaning of "bachelor," not logic. Claims such as "Cigarette smoking is a leading cause of lung cancer," or "You can't get AIDS from casual contact," must be verified by appeals to scientific and statistical evidence. Different kinds of claims, then, require different kinds of verification. The complete assessment of an argument or case often requires that we verify factual claims.

As important as it is that arguments contain only true propositions, containing only true propositions is not enough to render an argument acceptable. Consider this obviously flawed argument which contains all true propositions.

> **All human beings are mortal.**
> **Madonna is a human being.**
> **Madonna is a rock 'n' roll singer.**

This example fails as an argument because the conclusion, though true, goes beyond the information provided by the premises, which are also true. Anyone deciding that Madonna is a rock 'n' roll singer based *only* on the information provided by these premises will have reasoned poorly.

Whenever we make or accept an argument, we are asserting that the premises provide "enough evidence" to warrant accepting the conclusion. In other words, making or accepting an argument always involves the assertion that the premises are capable of *establishing* the truth of the conclusion. That is a more complicated assertion than merely claiming that the conclusion is true. Making or accepting an argument includes asserting (explicitly or implicitly) that the truth of the conclusion has been demonstrated or proven—given the truth of the premises.

The logical component of arguments is sometimes compared to a computer. Given a body of information (data), a computer can process questions. But, generally speaking, a computer is in no position to evaluate the truth of the data fed it. A computer simply takes the information given and draws conclusions from it. The reliability of these conclusions depends on two factors: the accuracy of the information used to derive them and the program which we are using. If we put good data into a flawed program, we will receive unreliable conclusions. If we put faulty data into a good program, we will also receive unreliable conclusions. And, obviously, if we put faulty data into a flawed program, we will receive unreliable conclusions.

Faulty data can be compared to false or unclear content in an argument. And a flawed program is analogous to bad logical form. Good arguments require (1) clear, true content (2) arranged in appropriate logical form. *Evaluation of argumentative cases involves attention to both form and content according to certain criteria.* Clearly the study of logical structure alone is not very practical if it is possible for correctly structured arguments to produce unreliable conclusions based on faulty content. By the same token, it is not particularly helpful to learn how to collect true propositions (facts) if we are unable to discern the relationships and implications among them.

Any argument with acceptable content and form has enough force or strength that it will, or should, win the assent of a reasonable person. In a word, it compels our agreement. Let's agree to call such an argument *cogent*. When we construct arguments, we're attempting to formulate *cogent* ones. And when we evaluate other people's arguments, we're testing for cogency. In brief, we want to ensure that arguments have acceptable form and content—that they're cogent.

But under what conditions exactly is an argument cogent—does it have acceptable form and content? How do we know that our own arguments and those of others are cogent? In a real sense, our entire study will be an extended answer to the question of cogency. We can take the first steps toward this answer by introducing three criteria of cogency that will occupy us, in one way or another, throughout our study of logic: reasonableness, relevancy, and sufficiency.

Before considering these notions, let's acknowledge that different terminology is used to talk about arguments. For example, the word *valid* has been used to mean "legal," "true," "logical," "correct," and so on. The word *argument* has been used to mean "dispute," "debate," "fight," "disagreement," or logical argument. Good arguments have been called "good," "sound," "cogent," "acceptable," "reasonable," "justified," and so on. In order to sharpen your reasoning skills and refine your understanding of logical argument, make it a practice to distinguish the technical use of terms in this text from other uses of the same terms. What counts most is that you understand the concepts to which our use of terms apply, so that we have common understanding. Do not be sidetracked or hindered because we use a term in a way you're not used to. You are developing a precise technical vocabulary—a most important part of logical and critical thinking. With care, you will be able to zero in on the meanings behind key terms when you encounter them used in differing ways. But your success as logic students depends, in part, on mastering the terminology as well as the concepts presented in this text.

COGENCY

A cogent argument is one that compels agreement because of the acceptability of its content and form. Another, and perhaps simpler, way to say this is that a cogent argument has *reasonable* and *relevant* premises that are *sufficient* to support the conclusion.

Reasonableness

An argument meets the reasonable criterion if there is known good evidence for the truth of all its premises and no known evidence against their being true.

An argument's premises are reasonable if those qualified to assess the premises accept them as being true. This is a modification of the so-called appeal to the rational person. The "rational person" referred to here is a concept, not an actual individual. *The appeal to the rational person asserts that when determining the basic reasonableness of an argument we ask the following hypothetical question: Would a disinterested rational person possessing relevant knowledge and expertise accept these premises as true? If the answer is yes, then the premises are reasonable.*

One important function of the reasonable criterion is to help us separate our personal biases and limits from a critical assessment of an argument. Philosophers and logicians have struggled for centuries over the concept of the "rational person." They are aware of the danger of assuming that the way *we* think is rational and of uncritically dismissing those who disagree with us as irrational or unreasonable. There probably never will be an absolutely pure way to determine reasonableness. But we can often determine unreasonableness.

Suppose that an argument contains the premise "The Earth is not flat." By now, the sciences have so soundly established the truth of that claim that rejecting it is evidence that a person is not reasonable *in regard to that issue.* An argument will always lack cogency if its premises cannot be accepted by a "rational person." This is not necessarily as arbitrary a criterion as you might think. Remember that the "rational person" must be disinterested, that is, must not be blinded by a personal need to accept or reject any point of view, and must possess relevant knowledge and experience. (In Chapter 3 we'll explore some of the more important aspects of evaluating who is or is not qualified to evaluate different kinds of evidence.)

However, the fact that an argument meets the reasonableness criterion is no guarantee that it is cogent. The reasonableness criterion only applies to the probable truth of the premises. We must also consider how the premises relate to the conclusion.

Relevancy

An argument meets the relevancy criterion if its premises provide evidence that is logically, factually, or causally related to establishing the conclusion as it is formulated.

Consider the kind of arguments implied in political campaigns. For example, many people refuse to vote for someone discovered to have had an extramarital affair. If the argument against candidate X goes "X has cheated on his/her spouse. Therefore X will make a bad governor," the premise is not obviously relevant to the conclusion. Indeed, historical evidence suggests that some of our most able leaders were also adulterers. Similarly, a person's gender, race, or religion is not relevant to determinations of competence, trustworthiness, or intelligence. But arguments and cases often contain logically irrelevant appeals to emotion and taste. Some irrelevancies are quite subtle, some are deeply ingrained habits of thinking, and many are widely persuasive. We will be on the lookout for them from now on.

The issue of what is relevant can be tricky. For example, one of the reasons that character issues like the one in the preceding case of candidate X continue to arise in political campaigns is because many people think that marital fidelity is relevant to whether or not a candidate will make a good governor. In technical, complex, or controversial cases, the issue of relevancy may require specialized expertise to determine whether the evidence offered satisfies the relevancy criterion. Controversial cases are those in which qualified experts disagree. For example, a controversial 1994 book about intelligence argued that race and gender are relevant factors for determining intelligence.[1] Social and biological scientists remain divided on the issue of the relevance of these factors.

Further complicating the issue of relevancy is the fact that we often use the term *relevant* to mean "personally interesting" or "useful in a practical endeavor." This is what students often mean when they complain that their courses aren't "relevant." So we need to be extra attentive when scrutinizing arguments and cases for relevancy. We want to take special precautions to ensure that the premises offered as evidence for a conclusion are logically, factually, or causally relevant to establishing that specific conclusion's truth.

We do not want to be sidetracked into accepting premises that "feel relevant" but fail to bear directly on the conclusion. Avoiding this pitfall will take practice, and in some cases we will disagree with one another. When relevance is not immediately obvious, the burden of showing relevancy falls upon the arguer. For example, suppose you complain to your logic instructor that you can't

---

1. See Richard J. Herrnstein and Charles Murray, *The Bell Curve: Intelligence and Class Structure in American Life* (New York: The Free Press, 1994).

understand why you're doing poorly on tests, since you do so well on the homework, and your instructor asks if you drink lots of coffee while you do homework. You might wonder what drinking coffee has to do with taking tests. Your instructor could show relevancy by explaining that "Educational psychologists have shown that students have the highest rates of knowledge retrieval when their biochemical brain states are roughly the same as when they learned new material or skills. Drinking lots of coffee at home and very little before logic class might be contributing to your diminished performance on tests."

Of course, even if being coffee-deprived before tests turns out to be relevant to your problem, it may not be all that's affecting your test grades, because even true (reasonable), relevant premises are not necessarily adequate evidence for establishing the truth of a conclusion. No matter how reliable the individual pieces of evidence, there must also be a sufficient amount of evidence.

STUDY HINT
Logical v. Psychological Relevancy

The intensity with which a belief is held does not reflect the reliability of the belief. Sincerity is of limited evidentiary value. Psychological relevancy is not the same as logical relevancy. Neither truth value nor cogency are functions of the sincerity, integrity, or intelligence of the arguer or the critic.

Sufficiency

*An argument meets the sufficiency criterion when its premises, **taken as a whole**, provide enough evidence to support the conclusion.*

Consider this type of argument: "I have owned two Fords and they both fell apart. Therefore, Fords are poorly made." The premises are reasonable and relevant. But the arguer's limited experience is insufficient to draw any conclusion about the reliability of Ford automobiles as a whole. Concluding that you gave me the flu because you are the last person I touched before I developed a fever, is another example of reasoning that violates the sufficiency criterion, although it satisfies both the reasonableness and relevancy criteria.

To sum up: An argument that meets the sufficiency criterion may not be cogent because, in order to meet the sufficiency criterion, an argument need not provide reasonable premises for its conclusion. An argument must, however, meet the relevancy requirement in order to meet the sufficiency requirement. That is, sufficiency implies relevancy. An argument that meets either or both of the reasonableness and relevancy criteria may still lack sufficient evidence to sustain its conclusion.

A good way to understand this is to consider legal cases. The rules and procedures that govern the admission of evidence and testimony of witnesses are designed to ensure that the first two criteria are met. Technical claims, for example, must be supported by qualified experts. This requirement ensures that they are reasonable. The judge must make sure that all evidence and testimony is relevant to the case. Next the judge or jury must decide if the reasonable, relevant evidence allowed is sufficient to support a guilty verdict against the defendant. In other words, is the evidence sufficient or not?

Consider this argument:

> **All mothers are female.**
> **Margaret is a female.**
> **Margaret is a mother.**

The premises are reasonable and relevant to establish the conclusion, but they are obviously not sufficient. *Cogency* is a function of all three criteria: *sufficiency*, *reasonableness*, and *relevancy*.

Determining the sufficiency of any argument's premises varies with how tight a connection the argument asserts between its premises and conclusion. Some arguments attempt to make an airtight case for their conclusions; they're called *deductive* arguments. Other arguments attempt to establish their conclusions with a relatively strong degree of probability; they're called *inductive* arguments. As you can well imagine, different rules and standards apply to each kind of argument. We will devote considerable time to both kinds of arguments in Part Three and Part Four.

A WORD ABOUT BEING WELL INFORMED

Applying the cogency criteria requires interpretation, evaluation, and judgment on a case by case basis. We must *decide* whether or not a proposition is reasonable, whether premises are sufficient to establish their conclusions, and so forth. Our decisions are influenced by our life experiences and background beliefs. *Background beliefs are our current opinions about moral values, politics, religion, society, the natural world, and the like.*

We must be careful not to base our background beliefs on untested assumptions, biased or outdated sources, or unqualified "experts." When we lack a reliable knowledge base for our background beliefs, our ability to assess a case or analyze an argument is necessarily limited. We might be able to assess the logical structure of an argument, but we will not be able to determine cogency if we lack the resources to determine relevancy, reasonableness, and sufficiency—determinations that sometimes require specialized experience, education, or skill.

We can, however, see to it that we are well-informed by reading a daily newspaper, by making effective use of our television viewing, by reading a weekly newsmagazine, and by reading a variety of nonfiction books and magazines from a broad array of perspectives.

There is little merit in expressing uninformed, "off the top of the head" reactions (they're barely even opinions). There is even less merit in scrutinizing arguments and cases when we don't have the experience or knowledge to make *informed* judgments.

FRANK AND ERNEST reprinted by permission of Newspaper Enterprise Association, Inc.

A WORD OF ENCOURAGEMENT

Whew! If you're a typical introductory logic or critical thinking student, all these criteria and terms may seem hazy or "mushed together" at this stage. That's to be expected. There's a lot to learn here, and so far we've been talking about arguments and critical thinking in general and abstract ways. As we begin to study specific examples, you'll soon find yourself having the "aha experience" on a regular basis. The "aha experience" is the pleasure that comes from realizing a practical application of a concept learned in class, from seeing an example of something covered in class pop up in your "real life." So don't jump to any hasty conclusions about your ability to succeed in or enjoy your logic studies just yet. Doing so would be a form of reasoning error known as *a hasty conclusion* (covered in Chapter 10).

It is much too soon to expect to be able to apply the cogency criteria with any confidence. Remember that you have an entire academic term (plus a lifetime) to become a more polished reasoner. Your task at this early stage is to begin watching for arguments and making tentative analyses of them. Practice looking for the main point or conclusion. Try to identify conclusions. "Play" with the cogency criteria. Make it a habit to use technical language to talk and *think* about arguments. Be alert to the kinds of claims people make and the nature of the evidence they provide (or fail to provide). But don't, after only one chapter, worry about feeling a bit overwhelmed.

And if you're already excited, just wait. It gets even better.

A "STRETCHING" EXERCISE

Use the following sets of exercises to get into the swing of thinking carefully and critically. Prepare thoughtful responses using your new understanding of arguments, cases, and cogency. It is especially helpful to discuss your reasoning. Your instructor may want you to do this in small study groups in class, or in writing. If at all possible, find a study partner who will discuss this (and subsequent) exercises with you. Logic is, among other things, a skill in communication, and there is no substitute for practice.

A. Make the best cases you can for the following.

1. College textbooks should be provided free to all students, regardless of income level.

2. Admission to specific state colleges and universities should be decided by a random selection process from a pool of all college-qualified applicants. No state-financed colleges or universities should be allowed to be more selective than any others.

3. Movie ratings (G, PG, R, X) should be abolished.

4. Private companies should be allowed to hire and fire anyone they want to without government interference.

5. Abortion is murder.

B. Make the best case you can against the above proposals.

C. Analyze the cases you constructed in A and B according to the cogency criteria.

D. Were you able to make equally strong cases both for and against these five proposals? Do you think that the facts or truth limit whether or not you can make equally strong cases for or against a claim? To what extent do you think personal knowledge, beliefs, and temperament influence the ability to argue in either direction? Discuss fully.

SUMMARY

In this chapter we learned that logic is the study of correct argument. An argument is a group of truth claims intended or understood to provide support for another truth claim. Truth claims may be either true or false. Logicians refer to truth claims as propositions, statements, or assertions. The terms *conclusion* and *premise* are used to distinguish the claim being supported in an argument from the claims being offered as providing that support. The premises of an argument are the support statements. The conclusion of an argument is the statement being supported.

We learned that rational discourse is the giving and receiving of reasons, according to commonly agreed upon standards of verification, for the purpose of distinguishing truth from falsehood, appearance from reality, and mere opinion from informed opinion.

We learned that arguments are often buried in cases. A case consists of all of the elements used to get someone (including ourselves) to accept a conclusion. Although not every case we make is an argument, all arguments can be considered cases that we're attempting to make.

We learned that cogent arguments compel agreement because of the acceptability of their form (logic) and content (truth value). A cogent argument has reasonable premises for which there is known good evidence (and no equally good counterevidence). The premises of a cogent argument are logically, factually, or causally related to establishing its conclusion. Lastly, the premises of a cogent argument, taken as a whole, provide enough evidence to support the conclusion; they are sufficient.

Summary Exercises

1. What is a logical argument? What's the best way to identify logical arguments?

2. What is the difference between an argument and a case?

3. What's meant by cogency?

4. Name and briefly explain the three criteria for cogency.

5. Give your own examples of arguments that violate each of the three criteria for cogency.

CHAPTER 2

Recognition, Function, and Scope of Arguments

One unerring mark of the love of truth is not entertaining any proposition with greater assurance than the proofs it is built upon warrant.

JOHN LOCKE

In Chapter 1 we noted that for a group of propositions to be an argument, one (called the conclusion) is understood or intended to be supported by the others (called premises). Logical arguments attempt to demonstrate or establish the truth of *problematic* claims (known as conclusions) based upon statements (called premises) which are presumed to be true or *unproblematic*.

Problematic is technical shorthand for saying "the truth of the statement is in doubt"; *unproblematic,* on the other hand, means "the truth is *not* in doubt." Attempting to "demonstrate" or "establish" that a statement is true is also known as "offering evidence" for it. The truth of the conclusion, then, is what is being "demonstrated" by the evidence-statements known as premises. This special relationship between the premises and conclusion of an argument is known as an *evidentiary* or *logical relationship*.

In critical and logical analysis, we treat statements as problematic for purposes of verifying them, strengthening our understanding of them, or simply testing our skill at constructing cogent arguments. In certain cases, we genuinely do not know if a claim is true or false. Once there is enough good evidence to *prove* that a claim is true (or false), that claim is no longer considered problematic.

With practice and experience, you will refine the ability to distinguish problematic claims from unproblematic ones. For now, remember that whether a statement is being treated as problematic or unproblematic is a matter of intention and context. For our purposes, *problematic* does not mean merely "doubted by someone." Rather, *a statement is problematic when: (1) the truth of the statement is not taken for granted* (treated as obviously true), and *(2) evidence is offered to show that it is true.* In other words, *an attempt to prove that a statement is true indicates that it is problematic.*

EXPLANATIONS AND NONARGUMENTS

In contrast to arguments, *explanations, elaborations, and other nonarguments treat the truth as unproblematic.* For instance, explanatory statements attempt to show *why* something is true; they do not attempt to prove *that* it is true. The statement "Logic class has been expanded to two sections because of increased enrollment," takes for granted *that* the class has been expanded and explains *why*. The assertion "Margaret looks better since she got married," offers an explanation—not a proof—of why Margaret looks better; it takes for granted that she looks better. Presumably, there is no doubt in the asserter's mind that the logic class has been expanded to two sections and that Margaret looks better. Both claims are treated as unproblematic.

In order to determine whether or not a passage contains an argument, we need to know whether or not it's intended to demonstrate a claim or merely to assert, explain, or elaborate a claim. But this can be difficult if the originator of the passage is unavailable. There is always the possibility that what appears to be an explanation is really intended as an argument. Because people do not always reason clearly, we cannot simply assume that whenever proof is lacking or insufficient we do not have arguments. If we do that, then the only arguments we ever discover will be cogent! By the same token, we should not assume that everything that might somehow, under some interpretation, possibly be an argument is, therefore, an argument.

One of the most frustrating things for beginning logic students is, ironically, recognizing arguments. Some of this difficulty simply "comes with the territory" of learning new concepts and skills. But some of the confusion comes from other sources. Because we are bombarded by so many deliberate attempts to palm off clichés, emotional pitches, appeals to emotions and personal biases, as if they were good reasons for buying this product, voting for so-and-so, watching this show, initially we find it difficult to switch gears and start looking carefully and critically at the cases presented.

Cases typically are meant to persuade us; but they are not necessarily intended to present good and sufficient reasons for their claims. Too often their main purpose is to get us to buy, believe, or choose something. Thus they are geared to *work*. Because we like to believe that we make rational choices, advertisements, inducements, and other forms of persuasion are sometimes presented in the trappings of logic. At other times, emotional, patriotic, religious, sexual, or lifestyle appeals disguise the weak arguments at the heart of the persuader's case.

All of this conspires to confuse us—which is often the intention. A confused, uncritical consumer of ideas, beliefs, and products is much easier to persuade

"WILL YOU MAKE YOUR CLOSING
ARGUMENT SO WE CAN GET TO SLEEP?"

Reprinted with special permission of King Features Syndicate.

than a clear, critical thinker. In our efforts to improve our critical- and logical-thinking skills, we should work to develop an increased awareness of arguments. This awareness amounts to a heightened sensitivity to the presence of arguments and occurs for most of us as a natural consequence of studying this material. Others may have to work at it a bit, but like any skill, it can be improved with effort and desire. As this ability increases, logic and critical thinking become fun.

Now we should offer a friendly word of caution. As we shall see below, the best way to recognize arguments is from context. Unfortunately, it's been our experience as logic teachers, that a common "side effect" of studying logic is a tendency to see arguments everywhere: logic books and teachers may inadvertently convey the message that anything anyone claims must be scrutinized. Many students report their frustration over the inadequate arguments and reasons their friends and families resort to. As they learn about specific errors of reasoning, some budding logicians begin "correcting" those around them by analyzing practically everything as if it were intended as an argument.

Learning how we used to accept poor arguments and pseudoarguments (cases designed to appear as if they present evidence when they do not) may trigger an initial overreaction. We suddenly spot arguments everywhere. A middle ground is clearly preferable to either extreme: uncritical unawareness to the presence of arguments or hypercritical analysis of anything that might under the remotest possibility be an argument.

Compounding this confusion is the fact that the *best way to identify arguments is from the context in which they occur*. No text can do justice to the variety and subtlety of the contexts in which arguments naturally occur without telling elaborate stories to set the stage. In what follows, look for general patterns and clues. Remember that sometimes whether or not something is an argument is a matter of reasonable disagreement. In such cases, be prepared to make your own argument showing that your conclusion, "Yes, this is an argument," or "No, this is not an argument," is reasonable.

THE BEST WAY TO RECOGNIZE ARGUMENTS IS FROM CONTEXT

Context refers to the "environment" surrounding statements and claims. One element of this environment is "rhetorical context": elements leading up to and following a passage. These are such things as place, purpose, and certain key expressions. Place: Does the passage occur in an advertisement, in a court of law, over coffee? Purpose: Is someone trying to sell us something, a cause, a product, an idea? Phrases: Terms such as *it follows that, since,* and *so we must conclude that* strongly suggest the presence of an argument. In other words, we must learn to recognize the surroundings in which arguments are most likely to occur.

The intention or purpose of the author of a passage is extremely important in recognizing arguments. (Don't let the term *passage* mislead you. Some passages are written, but many are spoken or thought.) Is the most likely purpose one of proving or showing that something is true by offering evidence in its support? If so, we count the passage as an argument. If the most likely purpose is simply to state a fact, convey information, explain something, elaborate on a theme, or express emotion, we probably do not have an argument.

In a complicated passage, many of these functions may be present. Indeed, in real life, we usually enmesh our arguments in cases, which can include an array of explanations, expressions of strong feelings, and other "nonlogical" matters. These are analogous to the color of paper or style of print used in a book or to the accent and vocal qualities of a speaker. They are often powerful influences on what and how we think—as they are meant to be. But strictly speaking, nonlogical expressions are not part of the argument; they are not evidence that can logically support a conclusion. We will study many of these factors as we look at the influences of language on logic, at bad arguments called *fallacies,* and the psychological elements that influence our reasoning. Our present task, however, is to be as clear as we can about exactly what logical arguments are and then to practice recognizing them.

Often, we will have to infer what we think someone else probably meant. Not only is that fair, it is unavoidable. When we are listening to the radio or reading something, for example, we cannot ask the author whether or not he or she is arguing. So we must make our own best assessment. If, upon careful reflection, a passage seems to be an argument, we evaluate it according to the standards of good reasoning that we are currently learning.

Developing contextual sensitivity is a skill. Some of us have a natural knack for it; others must develop it. In all cases, however, it is a skill that can be developed or refined with some practice. One of the smartest things you can do early in your logical studies is to start wondering about things you read and hear everyday. Ask yourself: Is this an argument? Why—or why not? Don't worry about being absolutely correct (that expectation isn't reasonable). Instead, concentrate on what clues you can uncover to support your own conclusion that this is or is not an argument.

You will probably discover that you spontaneously begin to notice that logical arguments can occur practically anywhere. One of the most exciting things about beginning logic is the common student reaction: "Wow! All of a sudden I see arguments all over the place." Even television commercials become entertaining as we see them in this context. The number of arguments will not change; our awareness of them will. And believe it or not, that new awareness is a very valuable skill. It helps us deal more effectively with life, and it makes life more interesting.

STUDY HINT
Distinguish Arguments from Nonarguments
in Terms of Purpose and Intention

When trying to decide if a particular group of propositions is an argument, ask yourself if it is intended to prove or demonstrate the truth of something about which there is ignorance or disagreement. If the answer is yes, treat the passage as an argument. If, on the other hand, the passage amplifies, clarifies, or somehow completes an idea whose truth is not being questioned, do not treat it as an argument.

With persistence and proper guidance, most of us can become better thinkers than we are today. In the beginning, distinguishing arguments from nonarguments may seem frustrating. Don't despair.

There are some guidelines that will help us. Among the most helpful are the so-called signal words. Let's look at these.

SIGNAL WORDS AND PHRASES

*A signal word or phrase alerts us to the **possible** presence of a premise or conclusion.* We have a vast array of such words in English. Among the conclusion signals are *so, thus, therefore, consequently, it follows that, as a result, hence, finally, in conclusion,* and similar words. Among the premise signals are *since, as, because, for, inasmuch as, for the reasons that,* and the like. Although helpful in recognizing arguments—their premises and conclusions—signal words are no substitute for contextual analysis. In fact, these words can be downright misleading inasmuch as they don't always indicate the presence of an argument.

To see how misleading these words can be, recall the earlier distinction we drew between arguments and explanations. Arguments attempt to establish the truth of a proposition; explanations take the truth of a proposition for granted and offer information to account for it. Thus we saw that the statement "Marie looks better since her vacation" is an explanation. In contrast, "Marie ought to be hired for the job since she has qualifications superior to all the other applicants" is an argument. Yet the word *since* appears in both statements. In the first, *since* serves as a temporal connective; that is, it merely shows a time connection between two events. In the second statement, *since* functions as a logical connective. It signals a reason, a premise, which is offered to justify the truth of a proposition, a conclusion. Thus there are two different uses of *since*—one in an explanation, the other in an argument. The only way to differentiate between the two functions of *since* and other such words is from context.

COMMON SIGNAL WORDS AND PHRASES

Conclusion Indicators	Premise Indicators
accordingly	as
as a result	assuming that
consequently	because
entails that	for
finally	for the reason that
hence	given that
in conclusion	if
implies that	in view of the fact
it follows that	inasmuch as
now we can see that	owing to
proves that	since
shows that	
so	
then	
therefore	
thus	

The lesson is simple but important. Yes, signal words are useful in helping us recognize arguments, their premises and conclusions. But blindly relying on them can lead us astray. It can make us mistake an argument for a nonargument.

A WORD ABOUT LOGIC EXERCISES

Learning to think critically and evaluate arguments according to the three criteria for cogency is similar to getting professional training to help fine-tune a skill we already have. If you've ever taken golf or tennis or baseball lessons after you've already played for a while, or typing lessons after hunting and pecking for years, you may have noticed an interesting—and common—phenomenon: as you learn to do things properly, "by the book," your skill *temporarily* worsens.

What seems to happen is that in the process of paying attention to how we stand or hold a ball or club or racquet, or type with all ten fingers after using only two, initially we become distracted and lose our timing. We feel awkward and self-conscious. Our attention is divided between doing something and monitoring how we're doing it. Often we performed fairly well, perhaps exceptionally well, on our own, and this sudden, temporary sense of confusion is frustrating. It may tempt us to go back to our old ways. Yet, if our trainers and coaches know what they are doing, we will ultimately improve our efficiency and performance as a result of drills, repetitive exercises, and very careful attention to the smallest detail.

In some ways, learning to refine our reasoning skills is similar. You already analyze arguments and cases, pointing out "You're being inconsistent" or "That doesn't follow at all" or "Now you're jumping to conclusions," and so forth. In order to learn how to think even more logically—to refine your thinking skills— it will be necessary to be more alert, more detailed, and more precise than you probably have needed to be before—or in all candor will need to be most of the time. In other words, it is necessary to "overtighten the bow."

Just as an athlete may not need to play a pickup game of playground basketball with the same intensity and rigor he would call upon in tournament play, you will not always need to be as precise as you will during the process of learning to use new tools of analysis. But just as the athlete does need to be able to call on professional skill and ability in tournament play, you can benefit from having the ability to call on more refined critical thinking skills in the real-life equivalent of "tournament play": when the stakes are high and cases are presented to you involving important matters.

A most important part of learning to evaluate arguments is, naturally enough, actually evaluating them. Consequently, we have provided approximately 1300 exercises for you in this text. For some exercises, more than one answer or explanation is plausible—provided you can make a cogent case for each. For other exercises, only one answer is correct. Just because more than one plausible answer is possible, however, it does not follow that any answer is acceptable. Some answers, explanations, and interpretations will clearly be wrong.

Why are we telling you this now? By telling you what to expect, we hope you will not be surprised or unduly discouraged when you feel as if all the details and precision demanded of you are unrealistic. They serve an important purpose. We also want you to have realistic expectations about the exercises which will help you apply your new knowledge and turn it into skill: Expect to have to do some interpreting, some figuring out—some *analysis*. Be prepared to support any answer with a cogent case.

What makes an answer to an exercise acceptable, what does a cogent explanation involve? A cogent explanation is *detailed*. It is not vague, overly general, or evasive. In other words, a cogent explanation is *specific*. It points out exactly where an argument goes wrong and why. A cogent explanation *uses technical terminology when appropriate, and uses it correctly*. Lastly and obviously, a cogent explanation satisfies the three criteria for cogent arguments.

There's no way to learn a skill without practice. And there's no way to practice any skill at any level without making mistakes. But mistakes become our allies when they reveal areas that need improvement. Mistakes and the fear of mistakes become our enemies when they discourage us from trying at all, or when we are so defensive that we cannot learn from an analysis of them.

When you are tempted to resist doing the exercises or are tempted to resist providing detailed, cogent explanations, it might help to remind yourself that you're "overtightening the bow" for good reasons. Logic is color blind, age blind, gender blind, appearance blind, status blind: it seeks only cogent arguments, only strong cases. You have as much right and as much chance to provide these as anyone else.

EXERCISE 2-1 *

NOTE: Exercises marked with * are either all or partially answered in the back of the book.

This exercise will help you become more familiar with the relationship between the premises and conclusions of arguments. Assume that the following passages are arguments. Using signal words, other language clues, and your own judgment, identify their premises and conclusions. It may help you to set up each argument according to the following format.

> Premise
> Premise
> Premise...
> Conclusion

Note: Logicians often use this form to reveal an argument's basic structure. The line is read as "thus" or "therefore," or any conclusion indicator of your choice. Here's an example of putting an argument into this form.

Argument: If all men are ball players, then no women are ball players, since no women are men.

Using the signal words for premise (if, since) and conclusion (then), we rearrange the argument as follows:

> **All men are ball players.**
> **No women are men.**
> **No women are ball players.**

1. No apples can be blue, since no food is blue, and all apples are food.

2. Some logic students are enjoying this exercise, though no logic students are thrilled by it, because no one who is enjoying this exercise is thrilled by it.

3. Anyone who can write a logic book is a genius. Anyone who can understand a logic book is a greater genius. Therefore, logic students are smarter than logic book writers, since logic students can understand logic books.

4. If some parties lead to trouble, and all trouble should be avoided, then some parties should be avoided.

5. Obviously J.R.'s married; he's wearing a ring.

6. If people should be paid comparable salaries for comparable work, then since women are people, they should be paid the same salaries as men when they do the same work.

7. Everything must have a cause. Nothing can cause itself. Clearly, then, the universe must have a cause.

8. If everything must have a cause, then God must have a cause. After all, God's something.

9. If all rocks are minerals, then, since no minerals are tasty, some rocks are not tasty.

10. Look, it's pretty obvious: first, rock music becomes more and more crude; then it becomes satanic; next, kids start listening to it; then they commit suicide. Rock music leads to teen suicides.

11. If I marry Natasha, then Julie will be hurt. When Julie is hurt, she goes on the warpath. When Julie goes on the warpath, she is a terror to behold. Since I hate beholding terror, I guess it follows that I had better not marry Natasha.

12. It's not fair to make U.S. taxpayers bail out savings and loan institutions that have failed because of greedy managers. But that's exactly what Congress is doing. Therefore, what Congress is doing is not fair.

13. Since more than half of all automobile accidents involve drivers under 25, it follows that drivers under 25 are probably a greater driving risk than those older than 25.

14. Smith missed work today. He must be ill because he only misses work when he's ill.

15. The presidential candidate that Maine selects usually indicates the one who'll be elected. So it's safe to say, "As Maine goes, so goes the nation."

16. Every class I've taken so far has had an even male-female distribution. So, the student population of this college is evenly divided between males and females.

17. If the president stands for reelection, he'll surely be elected. Anyone who thinks the president won't run again just doesn't understand politics or political ambition. So, it's clear who the next president will be: the present incumbent.

18. Sandy was either present or she knows someone who was present. If she was present, she knows more than she's admitting. If she knows someone who was present, she knows more than she's admitting. Either way, Sandy knows more than she's admitting.

19. The chances that there are atmospheric conditions similar to Earth's elsewhere in the universe are very high. So extraterrestrial life probably exists.

20. This argument is valid because its premises logically entail its conclusion, and any argument whose premises logically entail its conclusion is valid.

ABBREVIATED ARGUMENTS

Both cases and arguments can be presented in an abbreviated form. That is, they do not always state or express premises or conclusions. Consider this simple example: "You're going to die since you're a human being." As stated, the conclusion, "You're going to die," does not follow from the single premise (signaled by the word "since"), "you're a human being." When a premise or conclusion is not stated, it is suppressed, or implied. It is implicit rather than explicit. In our example, the suppressed premise is "All human beings are going to die." Thus, the complete argument is as follows:

> (All human beings are going to die.)
> You're a human being.
> _____
> You're going to die.

As a rule, premises or conclusions are omitted when they are obvious—at least in the opinion of the person making the case or argument. When the suppressed or missing component is truly "obvious," as in the example above, this presents no problem. But in more complex cases, unscrupulous persuaders may present inadequate cases or faulty arguments hoping that their audiences will uncritically assume that they establish their desired conclusions. Even with the best of intentions, abbreviated arguments remain problematic, for until all the evidence is clearly expressed, or until the conclusion is explicitly formulated, we cannot assess the cogency of the argument before us.

EXERCISE 2-2 *

The following arguments are abbreviated. Using the same form as the example above, identify what you think is the most likely suppressed premise or conclusion. Show the suppressed proposition in parentheses. Here's an example:
Argument: Anyone who buys a hamburger at Joe's is a fool, and I'm no fool.

> Anyone who buys a hamburger at Joe's is a fool.
> I'm no fool.
> _____
> (I don't buy hamburgers at Joe's.)

Hint: Don't overlook the very obvious. Initially you may think that an argument is complete. Treat each of these as abbreviated. Some needed piece of information is missing. Without it, the argument cannot be cogent. (Even with it, the argument may not be cogent, but we're only interested in filling in the missing piece.) With practice, your sense of what's missing will sharpen. This is a difficult exercise, but worthwhile.

1. It follows that no bears wear hats, since only people wear hats.

2. T.R. must be a woman, since T.R. is Eileen's sister.

3. Don't eat that, it's poison.

4. Mom won't like Yellowstone National Park because of the crowds.

5. If Bill Clinton knows how to run this country, then I'm a monkey's uncle.

6. The Cubs can't win the pennant since they lack power hitters.

7. If Polly's going to the party, then I'm staying home.

8. No one is allowed without a ticket, and you don't have a ticket, so . . .

9. Over 1,000,000 sold.

10. You can't know how I feel. Only the lonely know how I feel.

11. You must have murdered Bozo the Clown, since only another clown could've gotten close enough to kill him.

12. You only hurt the ones you love, so don't worry, I can't hurt you.

13. If God can prevent evil, but doesn't, then He's cruel. If God would like to prevent evil, but can't, then He's not all-powerful. God is not cruel.

14. If there's an afterlife, then I'll learn about the mysteries of the universe. If there's no afterlife, I'll sleep the dreamless sleep.

15. Chick's Cleaner uses only 100 percent natural ingredients, while our competitors' use artificial ingredients.

FUNCTIONS OF ARGUMENT

All arguments share a common purpose of providing rational evidence for the truth of their conclusions. Beyond this, however, when arguments occur as part of a case they may be used for a variety of other purposes. Three of the most common uses to which arguments are put are *demonstration, refutation,* and *explanation.*

The primary purpose of an argument is to demonstrate the truth of a problematic claim.

A problematic claim, recall, is one whose truth is as yet unproven or whose truth is not yet known to the arguer's audience. The arguer's audience includes the arguer when argument is used as a rational process of discovery. In such cases, we often speak of "reasoning" something out or "figuring it out." *Reason is defined as the capacity to draw conclusions based on evidence.* Argument is used to demonstrate the truth of a problematic claim when a group of accepted or established propositions (premises) are put together allowing us to draw inferences from them.

For example, a detective may have already established the following:

1. Cooney died between 12 AM and 2 AM.

2. Cooney weighed 290 pounds.

3. Cooney's body was carried across a sand dune.

4. Fetters publicly threatened the victim.

5. Hinshaw privately threatened the victim.

6. Vargas professed love for the victim.

7. Each of the suspects had strong motives for killing Cooney.

8. There was only one set of footprints on the sand.

9. All other suspects have been cleared. One of these three killed Cooney.

So far, the detective only knows that any one or all of the suspects could have killed Cooney. But as more information is discovered, our rational detective begins to draw conclusions:

10. Vargas was on live television from 10 PM until 4 AM the night of Cooney's demise.

Transitional Conclusion A:
Vargas could not have committed the murder.

11. Hinshaw had back surgery two days before the murder.

Transitional Conclusion B:
Hinshaw could not have carried Cooney's body over the dune.

Ultimate Conclusion C:
Based on A and B, Fetters killed Cooney.

In the process of putting these propositions together, the detective drew two intermediary or transitional conclusions from the evidence. These two conclusions then became unproblematic (assuming all the other evidence in the chain is true) and were used as premises in a new argument to yield a main or ultimate conclusion.

In this example the detective used a series of arguments to demonstrate the innocence of Hinshaw and Vargas and the guilt of Fetters.

Often when we speak of proving this or that we mean demonstrating the truth or falsity of a problematic claim.

A second important use of argument involves the refutation of problematic claims.

Here's an example by contemporary philosopher John Hospers of a refutation of the idea that all moral values are relative. Note how Hospers makes his case without laying out his arguments in a formal way:

> If what the majority of a society or group approves is *ipso facto* right in that society, how can there be any such thing as moral improvement? If someone in a headhunting society were convinced that headhunting was cruel, barbarous, and wrong and proceeded to share these sentiments with his chieftain, the relativistic chieftain would reply, "But the majority in our tribe considers it right, so it *is* right." In a society in which most people cheated the government on their income tax, it would be right to do so, though it would no longer be right once the percentage of cheaters dropped below 50. If ethical relativism is correct, it is clearly impossible for the moral beliefs of a society to be mistaken because the certainty of the majority that its beliefs were right would prove that those beliefs *were* right for that society at that time. The minority view would therefore be mistaken, no matter what it was. Needless to say, most people who state that "in morals everything is relative" and who proceed to call themselves ethical relativists are unaware of these implications of their theory.[2]

Hospers reveals what he sees as the absurdity of ethical relativism in a clear but informal manner. His argument is designed to refute another's position by revealing a perhaps overlooked and undesired consequence of holding it.

Notice how arguing can function as a *process* involving both demonstration and refutation. Indeed, the process of searching for the truth rests on the continual demonstration and refutation of claims in light of new knowledge, new experiences, and improved reasoning skills.

Arguments and explanations can overlap when a passage offers reasons for believing a claim in the process of explaining how it came to be true.

Consider the case of Maureen and Michel. In the process of explaining why he does not want to marry her, Michel also presents Maureen with his reasons for believing that marriage is a bad idea: "Let me explain, Maureen. You are only twenty years old and I am eighty. You want to have children and I already have 12. You believe in God and I am an atheist. A marriage must be based on common interests, shared values, and romantic compatibility. We have few interests in common. Our basic values differ. I have no interest in romance. Your friends find mine stodgy and dull. Mine find yours loud and silly. Therefore we should not marry."

Is this an explanation or an argument? Clearly it is both. Explanations often include reasons for believing a claim. When they do, we should analyze them for reasonableness, relevancy, and sufficiency. In other words, when an explanation

---

2. John Hospers, *Human Conduct: Problems of Ethics,* Shorter Ed. (New York: Harcourt Brace Jovanovich, 1972), p. 37 ff.

provides reasons, we should treat it as an argument. This will prevent us from uncritically accepting the conclusion contained in the explanation.

Although we do not want to arbitrarily lump explanations and arguments together, when a passage contains both an explanation and an argument, we are best served by applying critical and logical standards to it.

EXERCISE 2-3

Study any arguments you found in Exercise 2-1 to see whether they are demonstrations, refutations, explanations, or some combination. Be prepared to explain your conclusion with reasons.

THE SCOPE OF ARGUMENT

The scope of argument is as wide as human interests. Arguing, in our technical sense, differs from the everyday notion of arguing. In everyday terms, "to argue" is to disagree, to fight, get angry or hurt. The kind of arguing we are studying is also called reasoning. If we distinguish *reasoning*, the process of drawing conclusions from evidence, from other forms of thinking, then we will get a fuller picture of the scope of argument. We "argue" in the sense of constructing and evaluating arguments *whenever we combine accepted (unproblematic) truths in order to infer additional ones.* We "argue" when we refute claims with reasons, or when we weigh alternatives. We argue alone just by reasoning, or publicly through conversation, articles, speeches, and so forth.

Anti-smoking, anti-drinking, and anti-drug campaigns are examples of arguments made on the *personal dimension.* Personal arguments appeal to our hopes and fears. Another aspect of the personal dimension of argument involves evaluating arguments according to the personal characteristics of their advocates. Uncritically accepting a claim because the initiator of the argument is someone we admire falls into this category. So does uncritically rejecting a claim because the person making it is of a certain color, gender, age, size, or because he or she is poor or unattractive, and so on. Throughout our study of argument we will encounter a number of fallacies (errors in reasoning) which involve inappropriate use of personal factors—our own or others.

Political campaigns and debates are the most obvious examples of the political scope of argument. In fact, however, *political arguments* occur daily: in casual conversation, during legislative sessions, whenever an agency or business must turn to the government for money or support. Political issues are among our most important. They include the allocation of limited resources, affirmative action guidelines, educational policies, health care, shelter for the poor, international relations, and so on.

Moral values concern each of us. Moral values concern human conduct, and what is considered good or bad, right or wrong. Because these are so closely intertwined with values, *moral arguments* can be especially difficult. Because moral claims involve and influence the very basic aspects of life, they warrant special scrutiny.

It is perhaps more difficult here than anywhere else to find unproblematic premises. For example, the argument, "Lying is wrong because we have a moral obligation to follow God's law and God forbids lying," is only acceptable to people who already believe in following God's commandments. Since the Ten Commandments forbid lying, people who *already* believe that they are divinely ordered need no additional reasons to support their belief. People who do not believe in the Ten Commandments do not have this reason to accept the claim "Lying is wrong."

Similar problems occur in other moral arguments because establishing moral premises is so difficult. Yet the alternative to moral reasoning is chaos and anarchy. As difficult as moral argumentation can be, it is worth every effort, for even when consensus is absent, the process of reasoning helps us understand and clarify what we believe and at least postpones the use of force.

Legal arguments are a special category. The law attempts to set carefully defined standards of evidence and proof. Criminal cases are decided by the standard of "reasonable doubt," and civil cases by that of a "preponderance of the evidence." Within these guidelines, strict rules apply pertaining to what is accepted as relevant. Juries and judges are called "triers of fact" in legal terminology to show that the function of a trial is to examine evidence bearing on the problematic issue before the court: Formal legal accusations, indictments, and civil claims are treated as problematic until a trier of fact evaluates the evidence offered by both sides. Both sides present a series of arguments to make their cases. The trier of fact sifts though these arguments and the verdict is the ultimate conclusion in a string of arguments and counterarguments.

In practice, arguments may involve these and other areas (e.g., religious, scientific, economic). Complex issues such as abortion certainly do. For example, before we can reasonably determine whether or not abortion is murder, we need to determine whether or not the fetus is a person. To do that we need to determine what makes a person a person. Once (if) we agree on what makes a person a person, we must decide whether all persons have equal rights. If we determine that they do not, then we must determine how to weigh conflicting rights. We must also make political decisions: Whose beliefs should determine the law? We must make legal choices: What should the law be? This is only a sketch of the complexity of this single issue.

One way to deal with complexity is to opt out of the rational arena, to refuse to engage in what philosophers call *rational discourse, the use of reason to order, clarify, and identify truth claims.* The problem with doing so is that the only alternative to rational discourse is force or some form of manipulative persuasion. When people cannot or will not reason with one another, the only way to resolve disagreements is to make one side give way—as through economic power, the force of numbers, or violence. When people are forced to give way without being rationally convinced, they tend to harbor resentments and wait for an opportunity to exert force themselves.

Perhaps many (most?) of us are unwilling to reason about some cherished beliefs. We may be unable to seriously consider any other point of view. But most of us seem to be basically reasonable. If we were not, we would not be so upset when we are shown to be contradicting ourselves or to hold inconsistent beliefs.

That we get angry means that we are uncomfortable with contradictions and inconsistencies. This suggests that we already value being rational. Who among us is honestly indifferent to being illogical? While we may sometimes *be* illogical, we tend to believe that our beliefs are supported by reason—by cogent arguments.

Logic and argument have a hook in most of us whether we like it or not. The ancient Greeks believed that the essence of being human is the capacity to reason. Although they may have oversimplified things, they were right to the extent that whatever else we are, we are reasoning beings. The scope of argument is the whole range of human endeavor. The scope of argument is the scope of reason. A rational person demands good reasons where reasons are relevant and appropriate. A rational person avoids both the excesses of a rigid reliance on reason and logic and an uncritical acceptance or rejection of claims based on moods, hunches, or custom.

EXERCISE 2-4

Consider the arguments you found in Exercise 2-1 from the standpoint of the scope of argument. For each one, determine whether it is primarily personal, political, moral, legal, or some combination of these. Be prepared to explain your conclusion with evidence.

SUMMARY

In this chapter we learned that the essential difference between arguments and nonarguments is intention or purpose. Arguments attempt to demonstrate or establish the truth of problematic claims, known as conclusions. This special relationship between the premises and the conclusion is known as an evidentiary or logical relationship.

We also learned that recognizing arguments is a learnable skill. Because so many of the claims we encounter are meant to persuade us *by any means that work*, we are often deliberately misled and confused about what constitutes reasonable evidence for believing claims. This may make recognizing arguments somewhat difficult at first. To improve our skills, we rely on context—the best way to recognize arguments—and signal words and phrases. These are words and phrases which often indicate the presence of an argument by identifying the evidentiary relationship between premises and their conclusion. They do not guarantee the presence of argument, but suggest it.

We briefly reviewed three common uses of argument: demonstration, refutation, and explanation. The uses of argument are not exclusive, and all three may appear in extended arguments.

We learned that the scope of argument is as wide as human interest, and that arguing is the same thing as reasoning. Among the important areas in which reasoning functions, we have identified the personal, political, moral, and legal. The full scope of argument, however, is the scope of reason, and in complex cases, these various areas often intermingle.

Lastly, we noted the importance of rational discourse, and discovered how ingrained is the desire to be rational. This suggests that arguing (reasoning) is common to the human condition, even though good reasoning is difficult, and disagreements among well-intentioned, reasonable people are common.

Summary Exercises

1. What is meant by a *problematic* claim?

2. What is meant by an *unproblematic* claim?

3. List as many premise indicators as you can without referring back to the text.

4. List as many conclusion indicators as you can without referring back to the text.

5. Are the premises of an argument problematic? Explain why or why not.

6. Distinguish between arguments and explanations.

7. Why is it important to recognize arguments?

8. What is rational discourse? Why is it important?

9. Discuss what you see as some of the major cultural and social factors that might inhibit the development of rational discourse. Be specific.

10. Suggest some plausible ways to encourage rational discourse. Be specific.

ADDITIONAL EXERCISES*

A. Decide which of the following you think are arguments and which you think are nonarguments. The important point here is to understand *why* you think a passage is or is not an argument. Try to determine *a plausible context* for each passage; look for signal words and see how they are used, and distinguish premises from conclusions when you think you've spotted an argument. Be prepared to defend your answers with arguments.

1. She is upset today because of the terrible accident.

2. Jones cannot be the murderer because he was miles away when the crime occurred.

3. The flight has been delayed by bad weather.

4. We must begin to develop alternative energy sources, for our existence as an autonomous nation is at stake.

5. Most doctors want to set their own fees. Therefore, doctors are natural opponents of socialized medicine.

6. Nobody will take advice, but everybody will take money. Clearly, then, money is better than advice.

7. Political dissenters have no place in our society, for those who criticize and disrupt a nation are its enemies.

8. There's no good reason for a fence around a cemetery. After all, those inside can't get out, and those outside don't want to get in.

9. I've read enough of what you've written to know you'll understand what I'm going to say.

10. "You can fool all of the people some of the time, and some of the people all the time, but you cannot fool all the people all of the time." Abraham Lincoln

11. "I think, therefore I am." René Descartes

12. "[E]ven if we admit that societies often hold different ethical principles, this does not mean that there are no correct or true principles. To take a parallel case, we know that societies and cultures frequently hold different beliefs about the nature of the world and the things that are on it. This does not mean that the different beliefs are all correct or that the choice among them is arbitrary or due to upbringing." Ronald Munson, *Intervention and Reflection: Basic Issues in Medical Ethics,* 3rd Ed. (Belmont, Cal.: Wadsworth, 1988).

13. It's unwise to exceed the posted speed limit, for statistics indicate that speeders have a greater chance of having accidents than those who don't speed.

14. I don't think I'm going to the party. I have too much homework to do.

15. We could put our extra money into a simple savings account, or into some long-term investment. The advantage of a savings account is that we can get the money out quickly and easily. The disadvantage is that savings accounts pay pretty low interest. The advantage of a long-term investment is a good rate of interest. Given our budget, we may need to use any money we try to save. I guess we'd better give up the higher interest rate and settle for quick access.

16. You should definitely wear the green shirt. I like you so much better in green.

17. They're letting too many students into college. In the first place, there aren't enough teachers for required courses. This means that classes are crowded and even then some students can't get in. Crowded classes make it harder to learn, and more students drop out. Having to wait two or three years to get into English 1A frustrates some students, and they drop out. Other students cannot afford to spend a few extra years in college waiting for openings in required courses. So, the more students

they let into college, the more they lose. Yep, they're letting too many students into college.

18. If you really loved me, you'd go out and buy me a hot fudge sundae. But you won't go, so I guess you don't really love me.

19. Whether we survive depends on whether we can solve internal problems. History indicates that nations divided against themselves don't last long.

20. The ultimate motivation for hostility lies in the impulse to destroy. We don't destroy to live, then, but live to destroy.

21. The United States is spending too much money on education. If we can't defend ourselves, what good are millions of dead educated people? We should, clearly, spend more on defense than on education.

22. DONNA: I'm all for capital punishment.
DICK: Why's that?
DONNA: Because it deters crime.
DICK: Oh, I don't know.
DONNA: What do you mean? I can give you a book full of statistics to prove it does.

23. PHIL: Women should be allowed to have an abortion on demand.
DIXIE: I don't think so. That could lead to some really bizarre events, such as aborting a fetus in the eighth month simply because the mother wants to take a vacation.
PHIL: But if the state doesn't allow women to have abortions when they want them, then it's violating their basic freedom to do with their bodies what they want.

24. JACK: There should be considerably more government control of advertising. Otherwise, consumers are going to be increasingly harmed and victimized.
JERYL: But don't you realize that such intervention is an insult to the whole concept of free enterprise? No, I say there should be far less government policing of advertising, inasmuch as every government intervention injures the free enterprise system.

25. ". . . You have been at your club all day, I perceive."
"My dear Holmes!"
"Am I right?"
"Certainly, but how—"
". . . A gentleman goes forth on a showery and miry day. He returns immaculate in the evening with the gloss still on his hat and his boots. He has been a fixture, therefore, all day. He is not a man with intimate friends. Where, then, could he have been? Is it not obvious?" (Arthur Conan Doyle, "The Hound of the Baskervilles")

B. Here are 15 arguments. The conclusions have been underlined for you. Study each argument carefully. It may help to set up each argument in the format you used in Exercise 2-1. Decide whether or not you think each argument is cogent. If you decide that an argument is uncogent, explain which of the cogency criteria it fails to meet. If you are uncertain whether or not an argument is cogent, explain why it is difficult to tell. *This exercise is more difficult than the ones you've done so far, but is well worth extra effort.* Your answers will, of course, depend partly on your general background knowledge, and partly on what you've learned so far. At this early stage of your logic studies, the reasons you give for your answers are as important as the answers themselves. Try to think in terms of the strength of the evidence being offered for the conclusion. Ask yourself: "Is the evidence offered *strong enough* to support the claim being made (underlined portion)?"

This is a good exercise to discuss in class or with a study partner.

1. I've eaten at this restaurant twice a month for fourteen years, and never had bad service or food. Any restaurant that is consistent is rare. Therefore, <u>this must be one of the best restaurants in the area</u>.

2. All women need someone to nurture and care for. And since this includes women in prison, <u>women in prison need someone to nurture and care for</u>.

3. Countless millions of people believe that the Bible is divinely inspired. If that many people believe in it, <u>it cannot be just a human achievement</u>.

4. Using drugs would only affect the user if society would just back off and quit making drugs illegal. <u>Laws against drugs are the source of our drug problem</u>.

5. It is always best to err on the side of caution. And since we don't know for sure whether or not the fetus is a human being at the moment of conception, we can't be sure whether or not abortion is murder. Just in case it is, <u>abortion should be illegal</u>.

6. Look, I know it's not fashionable to think this way in the 1990s, but <u>I just don't believe that women are as competent as men</u>. I'm over fifty years old, and I come from a family with six women in it. I've worked with hundreds of women over the years.

7. <u>You owe it to yourself to see *Twister*</u>, it's the most exciting, popular movie of the summer.

8. We hate to take your property, Ms. Musick, but the country has a legal right to appropriate property for the common good. And your house is sitting on the only large-enough parcel of land suitable for the new county hospital. Since the old hospital was too small even before it burned down, and since the county has both a legal and social obligation to provide hospital services for those who cannot afford private care, <u>we must take your property</u>.

9. I don't have any duty to cook my own supper, and I can afford to eat out, and I want to eat out, <u>so I'm going to do it</u>.

10. Look, we all know that everybody cheats in college. Nobody gets hurt as long as you don't cheat on important classes in your major. Your GPA goes up, you get financial aid, you're happy. Your family's proud. The college gets tuition money. Your professors get big classes and keep their jobs. <u>Therefore, cheating in college is a social benefit</u>.

11. If gay people just quit being promiscuous, <u>the AIDS epidemic would disappear</u>, since sexual promiscuity causes AIDS, and more gay people have AIDS than straight people.

12. <u>Suicide and mercy killings are sins</u>, because only God has the right to decide life and death.

13. If I pay my rent, then I can't afford gasoline for my car, which is on empty now. If I can't buy gasoline, I can't get to work. If I can't get to work, I'll be fired. If I'm fired, I won't be able to pay my rent. Therefore, <u>if I pay my rent I won't be able to pay my rent</u>!

14. I can't put my finger on it, but <u>I know Jolene's a crook</u>. Just look at her sneaky expression.

15. <u>College expenses are ridiculous</u>. I just spent $200 on textbooks in ten minutes.

PART TWO

THINKING CRITICALLY
ABOUT ARGUMENTS

CHAPTER 3

The Public Dimension

No one is as wrong as the man who knows all the answers.

THOMAS MERTON

People hold a wide array of interesting and inconsistent beliefs. Some of us believe that the Bible is the infallible word of God, others insist that it is not. A famous actress wrote a best-selling book in which she claimed that "she" floated high above her body, attached only by a thin silver cord, and nearly reached the moon. Millions of people apparently believe her. Some people still believe the Earth is flat; others insist that we are living inside of a great hollow sphere. Scientists claim to know that the Earth is spherical and we are living on its surface. A supermarket commercial states, "Our computers have randomly chosen two hundred items from a carefully selected list of one thousand products. Then we compared our prices with those at X and Y for the same two hundred items. The result is clear: our prices are consistently lower."

On what bases should we accept or reject such claims? With so many seemingly sincere, intelligent, and decent people disagreeing about the Bible, the Koran, the Book of Mormon, and so on, how can a thoughtful observer accept or reject any group's claims to infallibility or superiority? Could the actress have had an "out-of-body experience"? Are such experiences literally true, or are they just colorful ways of talking? How can we decide? Who can we ask? What does the commercial really tell us? How were the one thousand items chosen? Are they typical of the products most of us regularly purchase? Could they have been carefully chosen because these specific items are known to be priced higher at competitors' stores? If that's the case, then the "random selection" of two hundred products from a carefully limited larger list is bogus, since what we really have is a random selection from a biased sample. How can we find out?

We can begin by learning to think more carefully. By asking more relevant questions. By suspending our judgment until we have reasonable, relevant, and sufficient reasons upon which to accept or reject a claim. In order to do this, it's useful to view arguments as having public and personal dimensions.

The public dimension of an argument, which we'll consider in this chapter, *consists of the objective properties of its logic and content, and the objective criteria relevant to presenting and analyzing cases. Objective properties are independent of any individual's moods, biases, limits, and knowledge.* The truth value of most claims depends on facts, not on the subjective states of individuals. Logical cogency is also objective. It is a function of whether or not an argument meets the criteria of reasonableness, relevancy, and sufficiency.

The actual determination of what is true is complex and often messy. There is room for disagreement, and some philosophers and scientists argue that objective knowledge is not possible, because every idea, inference, and perception is influenced by the person who has them. This is an interesting and subtle argument at its best. But we would do well to proceed as if objective knowledge were possible—or at least as if relatively objective knowledge is possible for a number of important reasons.

One of the most common stumbling blocks to clear thinking is lack of objectivity. We tend to favor some beliefs over others for personal reasons, and if we are not careful may allow our uncritically accepted preferences to distort our thinking. We may have difficulty rejecting ideas to which we have devoted considerable time and effort. In short, we may simply *want* some claims to be true and others to be false.

Our information may come from biased sources or be incomplete. We may base decisions on family loyalty or patriotic feelings without carefully analyzing the claims involved. Whether or not pure objectivity is possible, we can often recognize the difference between subjective, personally distorted thinking, and cooler, more objective reasoning—at least in others. As we shall see, by bringing argument analysis into the public dimension, we benefit from a variety of perspectives. We are better able to abstract what is rationally cogent and persuasive from what is not, and to distinguish fact from opinion.

Equally important, it is obvious that we do have impersonal, objective knowledge. Simple examples are found in arithmetic: $3 + 5 = 8$ for Buddhists, Christians, Muslims, atheists, men, women, Americans, Russians. Scientists *do know* many things, such as the operation of certain chemicals on the human body. They know that a certain chemical will affect a person's blood count regardless of his or her religious beliefs, level of education, and so on.

Over 2,000 years ago, two of the finest thinkers in ancient Athens quarreled over the issue of whether or not knowledge has a public dimension. One of them (a man named Protagoras) believed that truth is relative. That is, he believed that truth is nothing more than a matter of opinion—what we believe to be true *is* true to us (while we believe it). In other words, all opinions are true. The other thinker, Socrates, was the first great Western philosopher. Socrates disagreed with Protagoras. But how to show Protagoras the error of his ways? Here is a considerably simplified paraphrase of one of Socrates' encounters with Protagoras:

PROTAGORAS: All opinions are true.

SOCRATES: *I* believe that your opinion is false. By your own position, my opinion is true. Therefore, if your opinion is true, then it is false! Since that is a contradiction, you must be confused—and wrong.

Socrates' *reductio ad absurdum* of this version of Protagoras's view is crucial to our purposes.[3] Even extreme relativists and subjectivists *argue*. They try to *demonstrate* that their views are cogent. But notions such as truth, cogency, and so forth, are meaningless if any claim is true just because someone believes it to be. Further, our behavior indicates that we believe in a public dimension of knowledge. We avoid toxic materials, we walk on the moon, and use scientific discoveries to eliminate birth defects or improve fertility rates. In other words, experience teaches that some opinions are better than others and that some are—at the very least—more likely to be true than false, whereas others are—at the very least—quite likely to be false. This is Socrates' point, which he makes in typical Socratic fashion—by closely examining what Protagoras said. Such critical thinking at once reflects and reveals the public dimension of argument and reasoning.

CRITICAL THINKING

Critical thinking is the conscious and deliberate scrutiny of cases and arguments to determine whether or not they meet the criteria of reasonableness, relevancy, and sufficiency. Although the application of these criteria sometimes invites multiple interpretations, they are, in theory, objective and public in nature. The activity of critical thinking in large part aims to expose this objective and public aspect of argument. These criteria, in turn, shape the activity of critical thinking. Thus, when Socrates responds to Protagoras he is implicitly subjecting his antagonist's claim to one litmus test of cogent argument: reasonableness. In fact, Protagoras's claim fails this test. It's self-contradictory.

Curiously, one of the first tasks facing a critical thinker is learning how to think critically about thinking critically. That means that we must learn to be selective about how carefully we scrutinize claims. To cite a simple example, it is more important to thoroughly evaluate claims about where to invest our savings than it is to evaluate competing claims about which brand of ice cream tastes better or which is the greatest team in the NBA. A reasonable person, as we noted elsewhere, demands sufficient reasons where reasons are appropriate. But a reasonable person does not treat every claim with equal seriousness since clearly not every claim involves important issues.

Another thing to remember about critical thinking is that it is not the same as "hairsplitting" and "nitpicking." A person who challenges practically every assertion with "Prove it!" or "How do you know?" is not going to be very effective in ascertaining the truth. Besides annoying others, and perhaps causing them to become defensive and resistant to reasoning, these excessive individuals lack a clear sense of priorities. In other words, they lack a hierarchy of values and principles to aid them in their search for truth. It may also be that some of these

---

3. A *reductio ad absurdum* is an argument that shows that a particular claim or line of reasoning is absurd, contradictory, or generates an unacceptable result.

persons are not really interested in the truth so much as in showing off or demonstrating others' errors.

In any case, because the search for truth requires public testing of claims, consistently alienating others limits our social circle. Yet we want it to include individuals of many beliefs and backgrounds, for this assures us that our ideas—and theirs—will get a fair hearing. Strong arguments will survive the ongoing test of a marketplace of ideas. Weak ones will not. If we limit our intellectual interaction to those just like us, we diminish our opportunities to hear alternative views presented by those who hold them. We fail to consider all the relevant evidence.

Critical thinkers have a healthy dose of skepticism. That is, critical thinkers do not take claims at face value. For example, before accepting the claims in a book on nutrition or marriage, a critical thinker will want to know something about the author's qualifications. If a neighbor says vitamin E builds muscle mass, a critical thinker will ask, courteously of course, "Where did you learn that?"

There is a sense in which critical thinking involves what we might call *intellectual maturity.* That is, critical thinking takes effort. It requires discipline. It requires a willingness to risk offending others by asking questions. It may require doing research. It may involve risking long-standing relationships when evidence leads us to new religious or political views.

It is no exaggeration to say that critical thinking takes courage. Uncritical thinking is often characterized by reflex trust or distrust, and takes things at face value. Critical thinking requires a conscious decision to suspend judgment, to question comfortable beliefs, and to entertain the possibility of adopting new ones if that is where the evidence leads. This can be threatening.

Is critical thinking worth it? Obviously we think so. The alternative is indifference to the truth. There is no other way to put it. It is one thing to be unaware and quite another to deliberately decide not to think carefully. By learning some of the basic principles of logic and critical thinking, you will acquire tools that you may use or may not use. We are betting that you will use them and even find the process exciting. In fact, our experience is that many students report becoming almost addicted to critical thinking during the course of a semester or quarter. Besides, critical thinking is like many other skills: Describing it makes it sound much more complicated than it is.

If pressed to give a list of characteristics of "critical thinking," we'd certainly include the following:

1. application of the criteria of reasonableness, relevancy, and sufficiency to all important claims;

2. distinguishing what is important from what is not according to regularly reevaluated principles;

3. careful attention to the meanings of terms;

4. balanced use of relevant expertise;

5. unwillingness to accept any claim that is inconsistent with our own carefully analyzed experience;

6. careful assessment of motives (our own and others);

7. respect for conflicting views when they are reasonably defended;

8. refusal to take legitimate criticism of arguments personally;

9. asking interrelated and relevant questions;

10. a willingness to be moved by reason;

11. being open to the possibility of error;

12. willingness to suspend judgment until sufficient evidence is found; and

13. objectivity.

In contrast to critical thinking, uncritical thinking asks too few or inappropriate questions. It accepts sweeping generalities without qualifying them, and confuses personal feeling with objective verification. Uncritical thinking tends to be vague, lacking attention to details, and emotion-based. It also trivializes or ignores important patterns and logical connections. In short, uncritical thinking is characterized by:

1. unwillingness to consider the possibility of being wrong;

2. confusing arguments with those who advocate them;

3. taking criticism of arguments personally;

4. indifference to evidence;

5. drawing hasty conclusions based on limited personal experience;

6. contempt for those holding conflicting views;

7. fear or contempt for other cultures;

8. impatience with questions;

9. inappropriately dogmatic assertions of absolute certainty;

10. hostility to reasonable demands for evidence; and

11. inability to distinguish qualified expertise from mere authority.

From this list, we can see that uncritical thinking tends to be *partial* in two ways. First, it is simply inadequate. It bases conclusions on limited or biased sources, as when, say, a Buddhist derives all of his ideas about Christianity from Buddhist sources (or vice versa). Second, uncritical thinking is partial to certain persons, values, dogmas, without subjecting them to objective evaluation.

The antidote for uncritical thinking involves objectivity, learning how to ask important, perhaps difficult questions, and a willingness to suspend judgment and live without absolute certainty. It also involves demanding evidence of ourselves, subjecting our own beliefs to critical scrutiny. In short, the antidote for uncritical thinking involves a commitment to knowledge and truth.

KNOWLEDGE, BELIEF, AND TRUTH

What *does* it mean to say you know something? Most of us go through life claiming all sorts of knowledge. Few ever seriously wonder what it means to know something. When you or I claim to *know* that the sun is about 93 million miles from Earth or that a human first walked on the moon in the summer of 1969, just what do we mean?

Although the meaning of knowledge is a highly philosophical question, it's nonetheless important in our study of logic. Just think about it: Even the simplest argument expresses knowledge; for example, "Since every apple I've tasted from this bag is sour, every apple in the bag must be sour." The speaker claims to know that (1) a number of apples are sour and that (2) all apples in the bag are sour. Obviously the person knows (1) in a different sense from (2). You might say that the speaker can be certain about the apples tasted but not certain about the untasted ones. Yet the person claims to *know* both.

Whenever we formulate arguments, we are claiming to know something, premises, on the basis of which we claim to know something else, conclusions. Thus, any argument implies knowledge.

We can look at the connection between knowledge and argument in another way. Recall that we should be compelled only by cogent arguments, ones that meet the three basic criteria: reasonableness, relevancy, and sufficiency. Thus, we should accept the apple argument only if it's cogent. But this presumes that we *know* when an argument is cogent. In other words, in accepting an argument as cogent, we are, in effect, claiming to *know* that it meets the three criteria. So whenever you accept an argument as cogent, you are as much making a claim to knowledge as you are when you say, "I know that the sun is 93 million miles from the Earth" or "I know that a human first walked on the moon in the summer of 1969." To accept an argument as cogent is to say, "I *know* that this argument is cogent."

Both the contents and the ultimate evaluation of arguments, then, are comprised of assertions of knowledge. This is why the meaning of knowledge is fundamental to a study of argument. When we ask, "What does it mean to *know* something?" we are not merely waxing philosophical. We are asking a question, the answer to which will help us sharpen our ability to analyze arguments, both in theory and in practice.

Any claim to knowledge implies at least three things: belief, truth, and justification in the form of evidence. Indeed, *we may define knowledge as justified, true belief.* Lacking an understanding of belief, truth, and justification, we invite fallacies into argument. So in addition to explaining these three things, we'll also be considering some informal fallacies that result from a misunderstanding or an ignorance of belief, truth, and justification.

Belief

Belief refers to a person's attitude or opinion toward a claim. Thus, Agent Fox Mulder, a character on the television show *The X Files, believes* that extraterrestrial life exists; the chemist Linus Pauling *believed* that vitamin C could prevent the common cold. You and I might hold beliefs that correspond or clash with one or both of these beliefs.

There are several ways to understand what "believes" means in such cases. Let's consider Mulder's belief. One way to speak of his belief is to say that Mulder regards the statement "Extraterrestrial life exists" as being true. Another way is to say that Mulder has a high degree of confidence in the truth of the statement that extraterrestrial life exists. Either way of understanding belief statements is fine for our purposes. The key thing is that belief refers to an attitude that someone has toward a statement, that is, a proposition. And, of course, an attitude may be correct *or* incorrect. Our beliefs may be erroneous. Maybe extraterrestrial life does not exist. Or maybe vitamin C cannot cure the common cold: Beliefs about things are at base subjective or personal, although obviously they are at times made public.

Now, the connection between knowledge and belief is that when we claim to know something, we believe it. When we *know* something, we are not just guessing, musing, or speculating. "I know that *P*" (where *P* stands for *any* proposition, such as "Extraterrestrial life exists," "Vitamin C can cure the common cold," "I will be laid off") implies "I believe *P*" (that is, "I believe that extraterrestrial life exists," and so on).

Just imagine what you'd think if someone said, "I know that the Earth is spherical, but I don't believe it" or "I know that humans have visited the moon, but I don't believe it." You'd think it odd, to say the least. How can someone *know* something, but not believe it? They can't.

Of course there are times, as when expressing emotion, that we say things such as "I know the President has been assassinated, but I don't believe it!" or "I know that I'm looking at pictures of the planet Saturn, but I don't believe it!" But these are rhetorical utterances. We don't intend to be taken literally. What we ordinarily mean is "Intellectually I know *P*, but emotionally I find it hard to accept *P*."

Since knowledge implies belief, where there is no belief, there can be no claim to knowledge. Thus, if a man does not believe he will be fired, he cannot be said to know that he will be fired. Even if subsequently he is fired, at most it could be said later that he should have known but never that he did know.

STUDY HINT

It is possible to believe something without knowing it, but it is not possible to know something without also believing it.

At the same time, *mere belief is not sufficient for knowledge*. Simply because a man believes he will be fired doesn't mean he actually will be fired. Similarly, simply because Mulder believes that extraterrestrial life exists doesn't mean that extraterrestrial life in fact exists; simply because Pauling believed that vitamin C can cure the common cold doesn't mean that vitamin C can actually cure it. No, knowledge implies something else—truth.

Truth

To say you know is to imply not only belief but also truth. If Mulder claimed to *know* that extraterrestrial life exists, he would be implying not only that he believes it but also that it is, in fact, the case. Although the distinction between belief and truth may seem obvious, many people confuse them.

When we term a proposition true, we mean that the proposition describes an actual state of affairs. By a "state of affairs," we simply mean some event, condition, or circumstance. Obviously, there are many states of affairs in the world. For example, if you're taller than 5 feet, that's a state of affairs; if the air temperature at present is 60 degrees or above, that's a state of affairs; if the current U.S. President is a Republican, that's a state of affairs. A true proposition, then, describes some actual state of affairs. The state of affairs doesn't have to exist only in the present; it may have occurred in the past or will occur in the future. The following are examples of true propositions: "Washington, D.C., is the capital of the United States," "George Washington was the first U.S. President," "Water boils at 212 degrees Fahrenheit at sea level," "A spirochete causes syphilis." A false statement, in contrast, is one that does not describe a state of affairs. Just negate the four preceding examples and you'll have false statements.

The essential difference between a truth and a belief, then, is that a true statement reports an actual state of affairs, whereas a belief statement reports *what someone thinks* is a state of affairs. To illustrate, the propositions "Deanna has cancer" and "I believe Deanna has cancer" report two different states of affairs. The first reports what is purportedly the case; the second reports what someone thinks is the case. Notice that there is nothing contradictory about the first statement being false and the second true. The truth of any belief statement depends simply on whether the speaker is accurately reporting the *belief.* The truth of "Deanna has cancer," in contrast, depends on whether Deanna actually has cancer—and that needs to be determined publicly through appropriate testing.

It should be obvious that no amount of believing Deanna has cancer will alter one iota whether she actually has the disease. But we often think and act as if belief does, in fact, mean truth. And because beliefs are relative, we sometimes assume that truths are as well. Thinking this way, we can do irreparable damage to the public aspect of argument by effectively foreclosing objective evaluation of premises.

Truth Is Not Relative

When we ignore the difference between belief and truth, we're likely to assume that truth is relative. When we speak of the relativity of truth, we generally mean that persons themselves determine at least some truths and that these truths may vary from individual to individual. The error of this position takes root in a misunderstanding of what truth is.

Remember that truth is a characteristic of a proposition that's present when the proposition describes an actual state of affairs. Thus, "Humans have visited the moon" describes an actual state of affairs. That state of affairs is *independent* of what any one of us thinks or believes about it. It has a public dimension. Humans have either visited the moon or they have not. In this instance, humans have visited the moon. That's a fact, and *facts are not relative, although beliefs certainly are*. Put another way, *facts are not arguable*, but *opinions* about facts are.

What if the statement "Humans have visited the moon" were made before the summer of 1969, when the first person visited the moon? Then the statement would be false. But be careful. This doesn't mean that truths change, that what was not true yesterday may be true today. The error in thinking so arises from a failure to see that we must always evaluate propositions within their contexts. In part this means we must take into account *when* the propositions are expressed. A proposition expressed before July 20, 1969, about humans visiting the moon is an altogether different proposition from one uttered today, even though the sentences' words and syntax remain constant. What we have here are two propositions, and one, uttered prior to July 20, 1969, was, *is*, and always will be, false. The other, uttered after July 20, 1969, *is*, and always will be, true. The meaning of a proposition, and therefore its truth value, cannot be separated from its context, including its historical context. Failing to realize this, we fall into the error of thinking that truth changes, that what may be true today may be false tomorrow, or that what's false today may be true tomorrow. Not fully understanding the meaning and nature of truth can also lead to a common informal fallacy, the argument from ignorance.

STUDY HINT

The truth itself is not relative, but belief is. This is why it sometimes *appears* as if the truth (fact) itself changes, when in fact our beliefs (opinions) have changed.

EXERCISE 3-1 *

A. Would you require anything more than the speaker's word before accepting the following propositions as true? That is, which express knowledge? belief?

1. I think I've got a cavity in a back molar.

2. I have a cavity in a back molar.

3. The restaurant is two blocks west of here.

4. The restaurant, I believe, is two blocks west of here.

5. Something tells me it's going to rain tomorrow.

6. I'm going to be sick.

B. Why would you agree or disagree with the following?

1. Until we know which it is, a proposition is neither true nor false. For example, since we don't know whether there is life in outer space, the proposition "There is life in outer space" is neither true nor false.

2. A proposition may be true at one time but not another, as with "The United States is made up of 48 states." That proposition was true in 1950 but is not true now.

3. Sometimes a claim may be true *about* one person but not *about* another, as with the proposition "I am 6 feet tall."

4. Sometimes a proposition may be true *for* one person but not true *for* another, as with the sign that reads "Persons under 21 not admitted." Since I'm over 21, the statement is not true *for* me.

5. If you can't disprove a proposition, it's logical to consider that proposition true. For example, since no one can disprove the existence of ghosts, it makes sense to assume that ghosts exist.

SOURCES OF KNOWLEDGE

Philosophers and logicians have long been attentive to the issue of the sources of knowledge. They have inquired into where we get the beliefs we hold and whether there is one single source of knowledge or many sources. If there are many sources, they have wondered if some are more reliable than others. In modern discussions, philosophers usually recognize three sources of knowledge: senses, reason, and authority. We'll briefly examine each of these. Keep in mind that understanding these sources provides insights into the foundations of the premises of arguments. It also sharpens our ability to evaluate those premises, to determine whether they support their conclusions.

Senses

A primary source of knowledge is our outer senses. We know it's raining because we can *see* and *feel* the rain, maybe even *hear* it. We know that a food has spoiled because we can *smell* its stench; we know that milk has gone bad because we can *taste* its sour flavor. We can call such knowledge sense knowledge.

Philosophers sometimes debate the reliability of such sense knowledge. They wonder whether the five senses are dependable sources. To see why some people question the reliability of the senses, think about what a pencil in a glass of water looks like. It appears to be bent, but of course isn't. Or consider that when we drive up a hill on a hot day, we see what appears to be a pool of water at the top. Or perhaps as a child you were frightened by what looked like a menacing figure on your bedroom wall but in reality was no more than your father's over-coat. What about things like this? Do they show that the senses are unreliable sources of knowledge?

Our preceding examples seem to suggest that our five outer senses can be deceived, that they are not always dependable sources of knowledge. Before assuming this, *consider for a moment how many times you were actually taken in by such illusions.* Probably no more than once. Even though the pencil appears bent each time you see it in a glass of water, you are no longer fooled. You have learned to see through the illusion. This suggests that it is not the senses that mislead us, but our interpretations of the information the senses provide. Such perceptual errors, then, are more accurately termed *interpretive* or *judgmental errors.* Because we didn't wait until we received more information—which would have resulted from pulling the pencil from the glass of water, driving to the wet spot, turning on the light switch in the bedroom—we jumped to a conclusion.

So we can say that the senses are reliable sources of knowledge. It is in interpreting what these senses receive that we may commit judgmental errors and later express these errors in propositions and arguments.

One way to ensure that our judgments are accurate is to open them to public verification. *By public verification we mean that almost anyone wanting to could verify the claim.* If someone tells us it's raining we can verify this for ourselves. If someone tells us that the soup is too hot to drink, we can find out for ourselves. Such claims stem from sense experiences. Any of us—assuming that our outer senses are functioning adequately—can verify them. Statements that are open to public verification are mainstays as argument premises.

EXERCISE 3-2

For which of the following propositions are reports of inner senses adequate sources of verification? For which are they not? Which, if any, need public verification? Explain.

1. I've got a toothache.

2. I have a cavity in a rear molar.

3. The person over there has a toothache.

4. I feel the presence of Jesus.

5. "Eureka!" ("I've got it." That is, "I have the solution to this problem.")

6. Every morning about this time I get terribly depressed.

7. I just know I've got high blood pressure.

8. You're lying.

9. I know you love me, even if you won't admit it.

10. The reason I like art so much is that I was a painter in a past life.

Reason

In general, reason is the capacity for rational thought, judgment, or discrimination. For our purposes, let's define reason as *the capacity to draw conclusions from evidence*. Reason, together with the senses, is a chief source of knowledge. We know a little bit about reason from our introductory remarks in Chapters 1 and 2.

In most cases, reason alone is not sufficient to establish the truth of an argument's premises. To get at truth we must make careful appeals to the world of experience—that is, we must often leave pure reason and go to other areas—physics, chemistry, biology, social science, history—in order to find out if the premises are reporting actual states of affairs.

Authority

Authority refers to *an expert other than ourselves*. Authority is a most common secondary source of knowledge. We say that authority is a *secondary* source of knowledge because we must rely on other people's observations and trust their technical judgment. Just think about everything you know based on authority: World history, the state of your health, the condition of your car, the direction of the economy, the events of the day, the weather—the list goes on and on. Indeed, without reliance on authority, we would know very little of what we ordinarily take for granted. In fact, when you start thinking about how great a role authority plays in what you know, you can't help feeling a little nervous. After all, taking something on authority implies an act of trust. We just hope our trust hasn't been misplaced.

Since the time of Gutenberg's printing press, the printed word has been our most authoritative source of knowledge. What's between two covers, centered on a page and facing us in clear, bold print smacks of truth. We trust it. In many instances our trust is rewarded; we learn the truth. With the increase in publishing, however, with the great number of ghostwritten books, and with the staggering economic possibilities of contemporary publications, we'd better be skeptical about automatically accepting the written word as a reliable source of knowledge.

In the area of self-improvement books alone, for example, there is an ever-increasing barrage of publications, all making some claim to the truth. Many contradict others. Thus, for the physical-fitness buff there are authoritative sources that hold daily exercise as the key to long and healthful lives; other people espouse Mark Twain's dictum: Whenever you feel like exercising, just lie down until the feeling passes. For those concerned with their figures, there are high-protein, liquid, and low-carbohydrate diets allowing us to eat as much as we want; other sources would enforce meager food consumption with all the rigor of a medieval monastery. And for those who think their sex lives unexciting, there are manuals making sex sound as mechanically predictable as tuning a car; others maintain that continual sexual bliss is rare, if at all possible.

Determining the Reliability of Authority

How do we determine when authority is a reliable source of knowledge? First and obviously, *we should ensure that the authority is just that—an expert in the field*. Perhaps the grossest violation of this principle is the practice of endorsements, all-pervasive in advertising. Enlisting the support of celebrities to sell products that have nothing to do with the celebrities' areas of expertise is a fallacious appeal to authority, a practice we'll say considerably more about shortly.

Even when we're sure the authority is indeed an expert in a directly related area, we should not accept the viewpoint unquestioningly; often even the experts are divided. As a second criterion, then, *we should ensure a consensus of expert opinion*. Take, for example, the major 1973 Supreme Court ruling on obscenity. By a margin of only one vote, the court found that obscenity should be determined by community standards and not by some universally applied standard stressing the social redemption of a body of work. If we argue that we *know* this ruling is best because the Supreme Court has decided it, our appeal to experts ignores dissenting opinions of equal experts. Recognizing that such striking discord exists even among experts, we should realize that what we have is not knowledge but a belief that, at least for a time, is law. Understanding this point might make us less vulnerable to the uneasiness many people complain of in a modern society that's constantly shifting, changing, and rearranging; treating such positions as truths we *know* exposes us to degrees of insecurity hardly tolerable when these "truths" change. Obviously, authorities agree on many points: All agree that water boils at 212 degrees Fahrenheit at sea level; that Caesar was assassinated on the Ides of March in 44 BC; that George Washington was the first president of the United States. In basing our claims to knowledge of such things on the recorded word of scientists and historians, we're certainly within our rights. But where there is genuine disagreement among authorities on, for example, matters of health, we should suspend our claim to knowledge and realize that the best we can hold is a well-informed belief and opinion. Realizing this, we remain open to contradictory evidence.

Third, even in cases where the experts agree, we should ask ourselves, *"Can I find out for myself?"* This is a crucial question. It's asking whether we could discover—given the time, interest, energy, and resources—this knowledge for ourselves, firsthand. With some authoritative claims, this presents no problem. Thus, we can boil water to find out if in fact it does boil at 212 degrees Fahrenheit at sea level; we can drop a large rock and a penny from the same height to see if mass affects the speed of a falling body; we can spray arsenic on insects to see if it's a poison. Of course we hardly ever do these things to prove the truth of such propositions because it would be a waste of our time.

What about instances in which we cannot have a direct sense experience and in which unaided reason is insufficient, as in "Lincoln was assassinated"; "Napoleon was defeated by Wellington at Waterloo"; "The Battle of Hastings occurred in AD 1066"? In these cases we should easily be able to conceive of someone not so different from ourselves who could have had a direct sense experience of the claim. Then we should weigh corroborative sense experience—that is, identical sense experiences that other eyewitnesses have had. Under no circumstances should we maintain that in the last analysis the primary justification for holding that Lincoln was assassinated is that "it says so in the history books." Someone must have witnessed it or enough of the circumstances surrounding it to give the claim its ultimate and primary foundation.

In summary, faced with a barrage of arguments and opinions, unable to check out all facts for ourselves, we must often rely on *authority as a secondary source of knowledge*. There are dangers in relying on authority as a source of knowledge. Yet if we never did, we'd know very, very little. How do we know when to lend faith to the statements of a particular authority? We must ask ourselves: Is the authority a recognized expert in the field? Do the authorities in the field agree? Can we check the claims of authority for ourselves? This last criterion underscores an important fact to remember: Authority may never be the primary source of knowledge. Ultimately knowledge must be based on the senses or reason or both.

EXERCISE 3-3 *

Which of the following propositions would you feel confident to take on authority? Explain why or why not.

1. $E = MC^2$

2. Hell exists (meaning the preternatural abode of evil and not, as Sartre suggests, "other people").

3. Many theologians believe that hell exists.

4. This Bible says that hell exists.

5. Sugar causes tooth decay.

6. The Earth was once visited by astronaut-gods.

7. The U.S. Declaration of Independence was adopted on July 4, 1776.

8. Mercy killing is moral.

9. The *Mona Lisa* is an outstanding painting.

10. Democracy is the best form of government.

11. The Vietnam War was a necessary evil.

12. The Iran-Contra scandal is the result of a flawed presidential management style.

13. Taking the Shah of Iran into the United States caused Iranian students to seize the U.S. embassy in Teheran.

14. The crash of the space shuttle *Columbia* was due to faulty O-rings on the booster rockets.

SUBJECTIVE CLAIMS AND OBJECTIVE CLAIMS

A subjective claim is a proposition whose truth value is dependent on the unique knowledge, beliefs, and experiences of a specific individual. An objective claim is a proposition whose truth value is independent of any specific individual's unique knowledge, beliefs, or experiences. For example, the proposition "It's uncomfortably warm in this room" is subjective because its truth value depends on the individual asserting it. Distinguish this from a proposition such as "The temperature of this room is 98 degrees Fahrenheit." In the first example, the individual's preferences, physical condition, and so forth, are essential components of the proposition. In the second example, the inner experiences of the person making the claim are irrelevant to it.

We want to use special care not to confuse subjective and objective claims. We must also use special care in assessing the truth value of subjective claims. This is not usually a matter of great difficulty when we are aware that a claim is subjective: "I really enjoyed the concert" or "I don't feel well" are clearly subjective. Often, however, subjective claims are presented in a fashion that suggests they are objective and independent of the observer making them.

This misrepresentation occurs most often when we express evaluations in art, morality, politics, religion, and other areas of controversy. Rather than saying, "Boy! I really like Coca-Cola a lot more than Pepsi-Cola," we might say, "Coke is better than Pepsi." This second way of expressing a subjective claim deletes any reference to the individual making it, and hence obscures its subjective nature. Thus the impression given is that we are making a factual assertion about Coke and Pepsi when in fact we are reporting a personal preference. (For a more complete discussion of value judgments and logic see Part Five, "Evaluating Arguments.")

There is nothing wrong with subjective claims as such, but when treated as if objective, we often waste time and effort disputing their truth value. Suppose that your friend says, "The Chicago Cubs are a great baseball team." If this claim means, "I like the Chicago Cubs a great deal," its truth value is a function of her feelings. If, on the other hand, she means that considering such things as the earned run averages of the Cubs' pitchers, the overall rate of fielding errors per game, the win-loss record of the club, paid attendance averages, and so on, her claim is objective. In the second case, its truth value is independent of any individual. In the first case, however, its truth value is dependent on a specific individual—her. We would, of course, treat the two types of claims differently in our analysis.

With experience, we can learn to recognize disguised subjective claims. If we do not, we are likely to engage in pointless wrangles of the "Is so!" "Is not!" variety. The treatment of subjective claims and evaluative judgments is so important that it is treated in a separate chapter in Part Five. At this point, we want to be clear about the difference between subjective and objective claims so that we can apply appropriate standards of evaluation to the knowledge claims we encounter.

STUDY HINT

A claim is subjective when its truth value cannot be determined without considering the knowledge, attitudes, moods, and feelings of the person making it. We should develop a sensitivity to subjective claims disguised as objective claims. The best way to do this is to demand clarity, precision, information about frames of reference, and other pertinent factors when we suspect that an apparently objective claim is actually subjective.

EXERCISE 3-4

Analyze each of the following claims and determine whether it is *most likely* objective or subjective. (If both possibilities are reasonable, recast the original statements into two new ones: one clearly objective and the other clearly subjective.)

1. *Hamlet* is the greatest drama ever written in the English language.

2. This soup is awful!

3. $2 \times 2 = 6$.

4. Homosexuality is wrong.

5. One-third of all teenage marriages are the result of unexpected pregnancies.

6. This room is too small for a class of 100 students.

7. This room is too big for a literature class. Its size makes it difficult to establish good rapport with students.

8. The Smiths' house is orange.

9. You've got to be really sick to like that movie!

10. Pornography is really sick.

11. I feel the presence of Jesus.

12. Terrorism is morally wrong.

13. Christians believe in the divinity of Jesus.

14. St. Joseph is the capital of Missouri.

15. Say what you will, Mozart's music is superior to Beethoven's.

16. Among tribes of the Northeast Coast, the death of a family member demands the killing of a stranger.

17. I don't think that plan will work.

18. Wow! *Ace Ventura* is the funniest movie ever made!

19. *Chez Barre* is the only place to eat if you want truly fine food.

20. You know you're ruining little Lester the way you spoil him.

21. No two ways about it: Oldsmobile makes the finest mid-size sedan available for under $15,000.

22. I just don't like that guy. There's something weird about him. I'm getting bad vibes.

23. This logic text is lousy.

24. I love you.

25. You're the kindest person I've ever known.

EVALUATING EVIDENCE OBJECTIVELY

In general, a claim to knowledge is warranted when there is enough of the right kind of evidence to support it. Just when is this? That is, when—under what conditions—can I assume that I have *enough of the right kind of evidence* to accept an objective claim as justified?

In answering this question it's helpful to recognize that an essential ingredient in evidence is what scientists call an *observation*. Whenever scientists weigh something, measure it, take its temperature, and record findings, they are making observations. These observations frequently serve as a basis for the evidence in a subsequent argument. Thus your family doctor concludes that you have a flu on the basis of observations made about your condition. Similarly, Fox Mulder might conclude that extraterrestrial life exists, and Linus Pauling might have concluded that vitamin C can prevent the common cold, on the basis of observations they made. Therefore the question of sufficiency of evidence for a claim to knowledge is bound up with observations.

When may we accept an observation as correct? When we have satisfied ourselves about the conditions under which the observation was made and about the ability of the observer. Specifically, there are five key things to think about in evaluating observations:

1. the physical conditions under which the observations were made;

2. the sensory acuity of the observer;

3. the necessary background knowledge of the observer;

4. the objectivity of the observer; and

5. the supporting testimony of other observers.

Let's briefly consider each of these as well as some fallacies of relevance that arise in connection with them.

Physical Conditions

Physical conditions refer to the conditions under which the observations were made. For example, if your doctor diagnosed your condition solely on the basis of a telephone conversation with you, that diagnosis would be seriously in doubt. Contrast that with a diagnosis reached after a complete physical examination. In the latter case, the conditions under which the observations were made are much more conducive to a correct claim than a diagnosis reached under the conditions of a telephone conversation.

Sensory Acuity

Sensory acuity refers to the sensory abilities of the observer. Some people can see and hear better than others; some have a more sharply developed sense of smell and taste, even of touch. Observations must always be evaluated in the light of the observer's ability to have made the observations.

In science, where precise measurements are crucial, instruments heighten the observer's sensory acuity. As a result, in evaluating the reliability of scientific investigations where exact measurements of height, weight, volume, and temperature are crucial, we must evaluate the accuracy of the instruments as well as the sensory abilities of the persons making the observations.

The technological extension of the human senses can be decisive in providing enough of the right kind of evidence to justify a conclusion. The classic example is probably found in the invention of the telescope, which allowed so many of the claims of the so-called Copernican revolution to be confirmed. In our own time, we can point to things such as the *Pioneer XI* spacecraft, which journeyed into outer space and, with the aid of marvelously sophisticated cameras, confirmed, for example, that Saturn is girded with radiation.

Necessary Background Knowledge

Necessary background knowledge refers to what an observer must already know in order to make a reliable observation. For example, a layperson is unlikely to have the necessary background to diagnose cancer. We may have the ability to observe the presence of a lump or to notice a change in a wart or mole, but the actual, technical diagnosis of cancer requires highly technical background knowledge in the field of pathology.

We needn't go far today to see how often this condition is violated. Celebrities are paid large sums to endorse automobiles, political candidates, and weight-loss products sight unseen. More often than not, these endorsers lack the necessary background knowledge to make their endorsements credible. We'll say considerably more about this later in this chapter. For now, it's enough to recognize that we must make sure that observers have the necessary background knowledge to make claims based on their observations.

Objectivity

Objectivity refers to the quality of viewing ourselves and the world without distortion. As noted earlier, none of us can be absolutely objective because, hard as we may try, we will always view things through the lens of our experiences, assumptions, and emotions. The best we can do is to become aware of these biases and minimize their impact on our observations. The same applies to how we evaluate the observations that make up the premises of other people's arguments.

Be aware of people's frames of references, their "taken-for-granteds." This doesn't mean that you should automatically dismiss the view of someone who may have a vested interest in a case. Rather you should be aware of how their loyalties, their built-in biases, may be coloring their observations and, as a result, coloring the evidence they present for a conclusion. Failing to do this, you easily can swallow, and of course formulate, all sorts of bogus arguments. And, of course, we should also be aware of our own frames of reference. In important matters, we should take nothing for granted.

Supporting Testimony

Supporting testimony refers to the observations of other observers that tend to support the evidence presented. For instance, a UFO report made by a lone observer has a lower rate of credibility than one supported by two or twenty or two hundred observers.

Additionally, the quality of evidence also depends on the extent to which supporting observations have met the previously stated four conditions. Reports of a miracle from six members of a devoutly religious family will have less credibility than if they were supported by the observations of some skeptical nonbelievers. Depending on other factors, an alibi supplied by a spouse in a criminal proceeding has less credibility than an alibi supported by strangers. A mass of biased, ill-informed, or muddled supporting testimony adds little if any weight to evidence for a claim.

REASONABLENESS AND RELEVANCY RECONSIDERED

We earlier identified the public dimension of an argument with the objective properties of its logic and content—in other words with the three criteria for a cogent argument: reasonableness, relevancy, and sufficiency of premises to support the conclusion. An argument that has reasonable and relevant premises sufficient to support its conclusion is cogent.

Often we think we've provided such premises when we haven't. Instead we've offered only the *appearance* of a reasonable or relevant premise. When we do this, our reasoning is flawed and our argument is fallacious. In logic a *fallacy* is an incorrect argument—incorrect because it flouts one or more of the three "public" criteria for a cogent argument.

One reason we argue fallaciously pertains directly to our discussion about the public dimension of argument. In brief, we can get so emotionally caught up in the case we're trying to make that we forget or downplay the fact that ordinarily our audience is not ourselves, but someone else. We cannot expect this "someone else" to blindly accept our claims or to share our own degree of conviction. Indeed, if they're rational individuals, they will examine what we say very carefully. And when they do, they probably will be applying—in an informal, intuitive sort of way—the three criteria that make a good argument.

In short, arguments are typically formulated for a public (i.e., someone other than oneself) who will assess them, or should, in an objective manner. As a result, the evidence offered needs a solid basis in reason and fact. This means that arguers need to separate what they *believe* from what they know, and ensure that their sources of knowledge are reliable. When they're careless in these matters, they inevitably court fallacies by violating one or another of the criteria of a cogent argument.

Let's see how.

THE FALLACY OF UNKNOWABLE FACT

When an argument contains premises based on observations that are questionable because of unfavorable physical conditions, inadequate sensory acuity, or a lack of necessary background knowledge, the argument commits the fallacy of unknowable fact. *The fallacy of unknowable fact is an argument that contains premises that are unknowable, either in principle or in this particular case.*

What's unknowable obviously cannot be verified and is therefore not reasonable support for a conclusion. The most common kind of unknowable fact fallacy is the one that consists of a claim that *in principle* is knowable, but probably is unknowable in this particular case. For example, the makers of Fleischmann's margarine once claimed, "Every 15 seconds a doctor recommends Fleischmann's margarine." Now, even if this claim is knowable in principle (and you could easily argue that it isn't), it is highly unlikely that the makers of Fleischmann's knew this for a fact. Just think what it would take to determine this fact—how much time, money, and personnel would have to be involved. Lacking the details of how Fleischmann's arrived at this observation, we'd best treat it as an unknowable fact, and not draw any conclusion from it, such as: "I should use Fleischmann's."

An unknowable fact is sometimes signaled by a glaring inconsistency. Here, for example, is an excerpt from a Jack Anderson column, which deals with a so-called secret meeting held by business leaders, purportedly to kill the proposed Consumer Protection Agency. In reading the selection, keep in mind that the meeting was, by Anderson's own characterization, *secret*. What he reports presumably is intended to support a claim that big business is deliberately attempting to undercut the effectiveness of the Consumer Protection Agency.

> Armstrong Cork's blunt-spoken Emmett, who presided over the secret sessions, was not interested in a compromise that would satisfy both sides. He just wanted to bury

the Consumer Protection Agency. "The better the bill," he snorted, "the worse it is for us." Another participant also rejected any concessions, warning the assembled business tycoons to remember the "Trojan Horse" story. . . . Still another warned that the White House would throw its full weight behind the bill because, "There is a big need for a White House victory, and this could well be it." The assembled tycoons agreed to make a last-ditch effort to defeat the consumer bill.

Some secret meeting! Actually, how secret could it have been when the column is replete not only with what apparently happened but with verbatim quotes, snorts, and warnings. If in fact the meeting was secret, it's doubtful that the columnist would know in such detail what went on. Notice that Anderson is not only reporting what occurred but is also characterizing the mood and identifying strategy. Was Anderson actually there? Did he have a source who attended the meeting? If so, did that source accurately record those quotes? These are important questions because the "facts" reported are advancing the conclusion that big business is conspiring to "kill" the Consumer Protection Agency. Readers can easily be seduced by these "facts" because the thesis is altogether plausible; indeed it's probably most consistent with what business perceives as its own best interests. The thesis may even be accurate. But what concerns us as students of logic are the supposed facts that are advancing that thesis, and in particular how these can be verified.

THE FALLACY OF PROVINCIALISM

When an argument lacks objectivity, it frequently commits the fallacy called provincialism. *Provincialism is an argument or mind-set that views things exclusively in terms of group loyalty.* People who argue by appeal to provincialism insist on seeing the world through the eyes of the group with which they identify. Thus, a salesperson who argues that you should buy a domestic car rather than import because "it's only the American thing to do," is appealing to provincialism. Even if this is a relevant point, it is not in and of itself adequate to support the conclusion, because there are other factors pertinent to the selection of a car. Thus an appeal to provincialism will, at the least, always violate the sufficiency criterion.

Some years ago, many Americans were perfectly comfortable when the United States bombed Libya, apparently hoping to destroy Moammar Gadhafi and/or his terrorist associates. Their reasoning apparently went like this: "It is all right to bomb Libyan women, children, and other noncombatants because we must stop terrorism." Of course one of our objections to terrorism is that it involves the indiscriminate killing of innocent people. But what *we* do is "different."

We are often more than eager to help other countries with internal problems—Haiti, Bosnia, and so forth—yet preciously guard our own right to self-determination. The "Yes, but they are different" rationale is the tip-off to a provincial attitude. The white man who will hire only white men and the woman who will hire only women are loyal to a group. So is the family who always sides with Sister whenever she has a fight with her husband.

Athens in the fifth century BC was a masculine-dominated, chauvinistic society, in which homosexual friendships between male members of the citizenry were accepted as "the highest form of friendship." Today's history or philosophy students sometimes criticize the ancient Athenians by applying a twentieth-century, Judeo-Christian, American standard. When this is pointed out, some students insist on applying this standard anyway. By insisting on applying the moral standard of their group to an ancient, pagan culture, they exhibit a form of provincialism. Other students are *only* interested in issues directly tied to their group. They take—or avoid—courses in Black History, Women's Studies, Western Civilization, and so on, for provincial reasons, not to broaden their knowledge. One of the more disturbing aspects of the widely-watched O. J. Simpson criminal trial of 1994–1995 was the fear that jurors would base their deliberations solely on their racial or ethnic loyalties.

Sometimes the group identified with is considerably smaller, perhaps a professional or occupational group. Thus an economist might argue, "The present administration deserves very low marks because it's quite clear that it knows nothing about introductory economics." Here a judgment about the administration's competence is made exclusively in terms of economics, the author's field. Similarly, an educator might favor the reinstitution of the military draft because it will help sagging college enrollments (the assumption being that many potential draftees will seek to avoid the draft by enrolling or will gain the wherewithal to attend college later). Again, the arguer sees things exclusively through the lens of a particular group. Whenever we reduce a complex decision to matters of loyalty to one issue—abortion, gay rights, animal rights, taxes—we run the risk of thinking provincially.

THE FALLACY OF THE ARGUMENT FROM IGNORANCE

The argument-from-ignorance fallacy is an argument that confuses a lack of proof (ignorance) with a refutation. Such an argument violates the relevancy criterion because it shifts the burden of proof from the argument to the person making the argument. It claims that because the person can't prove—or disprove—the conclusion, the opposite conclusion must be true. A more callous disregard of the meaning of truth would be difficult to find.

We can see a good example of this fallacy in a running debate between Ken and Pete over the existence of God. Pete believes in God; Ken doesn't. But they rarely get far in their discussion because inevitably Pete claims, "Since you can't disprove God exists, then He must." In response Ken insists that on the contrary, because Pete can't prove the existence of God, God must not exist. Both positions are arguments from ignorance. Our inability to disprove a conclusion doesn't make it true; neither does our inability to prove a conclusion make it false.

In fact, the argument from ignorance is popular. Here are other current examples:

WILMA: Life in outer space doesn't exist because nobody has ever proved that it does.

SLIM: Who has ever proved that people have souls? Nobody. That proves that the whole concept of souls is just a religious superstition.

B.J.: Pot can't lead to hard-core drug addiction, for nobody has ever demonstrated that it can.

SWEENEY: These so-called psychics have never established a scientific basis for their concepts. So this whole question of psychic phenomena is silly. The fact is that so-called psychic experiences have no basis in science.

STUDY HINT

A lack of evidence is exactly that: a lack of evidence. Therefore our opponent's lack of evidence is not in and of itself a sufficient reason for us to reject the truth of the conclusion, although it is grounds for rejecting the cogency of the *argument*.

Each argument reveals that the arguer is misinformed about the nature of truth. There are lots of propositions which are false that we can't refute; likewise, there are lots of statements which are correct that we can't prove. Our inability to prove or refute a statement does not in and of itself warrant a conclusion about that statement's truth, although it would be relevant in helping us, together with other factors, to decide whether or not to *believe* something. Thus, if after repeated investigations, no causal connection between contracting AIDS and hugging has ever been established, that's certainly evidence to help support a *belief* that there may be, in fact, no causal connection. But it is not enough to warrant the conclusion that there is, in fact, no causal connection (because one has never been established). Perhaps tomorrow or the day after, maybe in the next series of experiments, such a connection will be discovered.

EXERCISE 3-5 *

Analyze the following for the presence of the fallacies of argument from ignorance, provincialism, and unknowable fact.

1. BETH: I'm prepared to accept the claim that astronaut-gods visited Earth a long time ago.
   BRAD: Really?
   BETH: Sure. Nobody has come up with any conclusive evidence that they didn't.

2. JIM (rushing around to open the car door for Susan): Here, let me get that for you.
   SUSAN: That's not necessary. I'm perfectly capable of opening my own door.

JIM: No, I insist: It's the least I can do to show that chivalry isn't dead—it's just asleep.

3. Newspaper column: Russian deployment of troops in Afghanistan was strictly a diversionary tactic to conceal their number-one priority, which remains expansion in Europe and Asia.

4. GENERAL: War has always been with us, Captain, and will continue to be.
   CAPTAIN: That's fortunate.
   GENERAL: I'll say it is. Otherwise we'd be out of a job.

5. Ad: Every ninety seconds, somewhere in America, someone reaches for a MacDingle's fishburger. Isn't it about time you joined them?

6. CONSUMER: The rising price of gas is really putting the pinch on my budget.
   AUTO DEALER: Well, you know these inflated fuel prices aren't really that bad. They'll probably get us all into fuel-efficient cars.
   CONSUMER: You carry some of them don't you?
   AUTO DEALER: *Some* of them? That's our whole line.

7. BARBARA: This new incident at Three Mile Island has really got me thinking about the dangers of commercial nuclear power plants.
   TOD: Oh, I wouldn't worry about that. My dad says the dangers are greatly exaggerated.
   BARBARA: He works for a power company, doesn't he?
   TOD: Uh-huh.
   BARBARA: Well, he should know then.

8. LADY BIRD JOHNSON (explaining why she joined the women's movement in support of the Equal Rights Amendment): People whom I respect and believe in and like were part of it. Particularly my two daughters—they thought it was right.

9. CAROLYN: Vitamin E really improves your sex life.
   JEANNINE: Oh, I don't know. I've never read anything that really establishes that.
   CAROLYN: Well, it's improved mine, I can tell you.
   JEANNINE: Who's to say it was the vitamin E? Maybe other things were involved.
   CAROLYN: Maybe so, but until somebody can convince me what they are, I'm going to go right on believing it's the vitamin E.

10. EUGENE: I never vote for a candidate who's not anti-abortion, regardless of his or her stand on anything else.

11. According to James Ussher, sixteenth-century Anglican archbishop, and Dr. John Lightfoot, seventeenth-century chancellor of St. Catherine's College in Cambridge, creation occurred exactly 5,985 years ago, at 9 AM London time, October 23, 4004 BC.

12. It's perfectly obvious: The universe must have had a beginning.

13. The Russians have never been able to prove that they are not conducting secret weapons tests. And since they can't, we can sure figure out why: They're conducting 'em!

14. ATTORNEY: Your Honor, please make the witness answer my question: Did you see your brother shoot at Mr. Hatfield?
    WITNESS: Judge, I can't answer that. We McCoys always stick together—no matter what.

15. Sign: "This is a Christian business."

FALLACIES OF AUTHORITY

The Fallacy of False Authority

The fallacy of false authority is an argument that violates any of the criteria for a legitimate appeal to authority. Thus, if an argument uses as an expert a person who in fact is not an expert in the appropriate field, if there is not a consensus of expert opinion, or if we could not—even in theory—verify the claim for ourselves, the argument offers as a premise something that is irrelevant to the issue at hand.

Without doubt the most common examples of false authority are found in product endorsements. Constantly we are bombarded by celebrities selling products about which they know as little as any of us, in some cases a lot less. But because of their names and reputations, they earn whopping fees for merchandising. Thus sports stars push everything from coffeemakers to panty hose. Hollywood stars hawk everything from pickup trucks to political candidates.

Among today's most effective—and highly paid—examples of this questionable use of celebrity-as-super-salesperson are athletes. In 1995, Shaquille O'Neal's endorsements were estimated at $12 million. The Shaq's endorsements include Reebok, Pepsi, autographed trading cards, basketballs, and shoes, a Shaq Fu videogame and Shaq Attack pinball game, Shaq toy action figures for Kenner Toys, a Spaulding Shaq signature series of balls and backboard, NBA home videos, and more. But the most highly paid celebrity athlete of recent years, particularly after his spectacular 1995 comeback from retirement, is Michael Jordan. Jordan's 1995 endorsements were conservatively estimated at $30 million. Among Jordan's endorsements are Nike's Air Jordan shoes and posters, Hanes underwear, Ball Park Franks, Rayovac batteries and chargers, Wheaties cereal, and McDonald's fast food.[4]

Cybil Shepard and Bruce Willis, formerly the two glamorous, "exciting" stars of the television show "Moonlighting," have sold hair products and wine

---

4. *Newsweek*, May 1, 1995.

coolers, respectively. Shepard is now doing ads for Mercedes-Benz. Former Oakland Raider Lyle Alzado sold subscriptions to *Sports Illustrated.* Wrestling "baddie" King Kong Bundy sold computers. Mickey Spillane and Rodney Dangerfield sell beer. Candice Bergen and Jonathan Price battle it out in the "long-distance wars," pitching long-distance phone service. We've had James Coburn for MasterCard and Angela Lansbury, Robert Duvall, and Karl Malden, at one time or another, touting various credit cards.

Lindsay Wagner is at the front of a long line of actors and personalities selling cars: James Garner for Mazda, Ricardo Mantalban for Chrysler Cordoba, Telly Savalas for Toyota, even Grace Jones and Adam Ant for Honda motor scooters. Rod Stewart crooned, "You're in my heart, you're in my soul," to a Mercury. Back in "the old days" of the 1950s and 1960s Milton Berle and Bob Hope would've sold us the gas: Texaco.

To our list we add Brooke Shields in her tight denim trousers, Janet Jackson, Linda Evans, Catherine Deneuve, Joan Collins, Jacqueline Bisset, Martha Raye, Rosemary Clooney, Edward Hermann, and the venerable John Houseman—all selling something, trying to cash in on their images: beauty, glamour, sophistication, whatever. The hawkers change over the years, to reflect the culture heroes of the times. But the song is the same.

The Fallacy of Positioning

A contemporary variation on the false appeal to authority has become so popular that it invites a special designation: the fallacy of positioning. *The fallacy of positioning is an argument that tries to capitalize on someone else's earned reputation to sell something or to enhance our own status.* But, of course, the reputation of another is ordinarily irrelevant to establishing one's own reputation. Here's how positioning works.

Suppose a car-rental agency such as Avis advertises "We're the world's second largest car-rental agency. Since we're second, we must try harder." The car-rental agency here positions itself next to the leader, presumably Hertz, thus allowing it through transference to be identified with the most successful competitor. Goodrich has used this technique masterfully with its claim "We're the ones without the blimp," thus reminding us of a well-identified tire manufacturer, Goodyear.

Positioning creates a spot in the prospective buyer's mind for a company, a spot that includes not only the company's image but its competitor's as well. It's based on the assumption that the mind has become an advertising battleground. To be successful, a manufacturer must relate to what's already in the mind, what is fixed as authoritative. Thus, although RCA and General Electric failed in trying to directly buck IBM in the computer industry, the smaller ads for Apple Macintosh computers show an officeful of laughing, interested people clustered around Macintosh computers while IBM computers sit ignored. Honeywell succeeded by using the theme of "the other computer company." 7-Up®, realizing that half the soft drinks sold are colas, successfully waged an "Uncola" cam-

© Tribune Media Services, Inc. Reprinted with permission.

paign. Finally, here are two manufacturers of copy machines that have gone after Xerox's top position in the field:

Ad for Pitney Bowes: "We don't have to make Xerox look bad to look good."
Ad for Toshiba: "O.K. Xerox, Try and copy this."

On a personal level, name dropping, frequenting prestigious shops and restaurants, using high-status brands, or living in an exclusive neighborhood *in order to impress others* are commonplace variants of positioning. Such practices attempt to take advantage of what's called the *halo effect,* an enhanced social reputation due to proximity to an individual, group, or locale of high prestige. During the 1992 presidential campaign, both George Bush and Bill Clinton repeatedly alluded to Harry S. Truman, whose reputation was at an all-time high due to the reassessment of contemporary historians and the publication of David McCullough's bestselling biography *Truman.*

The Fallacy of Traditional Wisdom

Fallacious appeals to authority can take yet another form: the appeal to traditional wisdom. *The fallacy of traditional wisdom is the argument that uses the past to justify claims made in the present.* Thus, in answer to a student's question about why students must be tested, a teacher replies, "Why, students have been taking tests since the first school was built. That should tell you something about the value of tests and why you need to take them." Actually, the fact that students have always taken tests says nothing at all about their value or why students should continue to take them. The appeal is strictly to tradition to justify a practice in the present. Now, if reasons were forthcoming to show the wisdom of this tradition, fine. In offering them, the arguer, in effect, would be providing relevant evidence for the tradition of testing, rather than merely asking the audience to accept her own (or even their own) preferred custom.

A former U.S. senator once committed the fallacy of traditional wisdom in justifying his opposition to the Equal Rights Amendment to the Constitution. Said the late Senator Sam Ervin (D–N.C.):

> I tell them, "Why ladies, any bill that lies around here for forty-seven years without getting any more support than this one has got in the past obviously shouldn't be passed at all. Why, I think that affords most conclusive proof that it's unworthy of consideration."[5]

Ervin's argument may be persuasive for an anti-ERA audience, but it does not offer *relevant proof*, because the fact that a bill has languished around Congress for forty or four-times-forty years does not show that it's unworthy of consideration. What are the *reasons* for its historic neglect?

The fact is that using tradition as the exclusive determinant of a present course is not only foolish—it is potentially dangerous. By such logic, women still wouldn't be allowed to vote, blacks still wouldn't be allowed to eat in the restaurants of their choice, and sex education still wouldn't be taught in many places other than street corners and back alleys.

Common phrases that often invite an appeal to traditional wisdom are *the Founding Fathers, the earliest settlers, from time immemorial, tried and true, the lessons of history, it says so in, look at the record,* and others. Beware of them. Learn from tradition, but don't be enslaved by it.

The Fallacy of Popularity

Finally, a fallacious authority may take the form of an appeal to popularity. *The fallacy of popularity is an argument that tries to justify something strictly by appeal to numbers.* Thus, a bookseller tries to persuade you to buy a recent publication on the basis that *everyone* is reading it, or *thousands of copies* have already been sold. So what? Why should *you* read it? Maybe there are good reasons for reading the book, maybe there aren't. Like traditional wisdom, popularity substitutes for reasons. Not knowing what the reasons are, we can't evaluate them.

Be cautious of the fashionable. Whatever's sought by many for a period of time frequently becomes the vehicle for fallacies of popularity. Thus, today what's "natural" is "in"; what's "artificial" is "out." Shrewd advertisers recognize this. They pitch their ads to this popular sentiment, hoping to reach a wide and sympathetic audience for their products. Also they hope to profit by associ-

---

5. Quoted in Howard Kahane, *Logic and Contemporary Rhetoric* (Belmont, Cal.: Wadsworth, 1976), p. 11.

ation with what appears to be a broadly held value. This practice is currently being investigated and new laws have been passed as to who can claim "natural."

The appeal to popularity is common outside advertising. President Lyndon Johnson once replied to American and European critics of his Vietnam War policy by pointing out that almost every country in Asia wanted the United States to remain militarily engaged in Vietnam. Did this justify our engagement there? Again, Johnson was known for carrying agreeable poll results in his pocket and using these to wall himself off from criticism. Both Johnson and Nixon used their overwhelming election "mandates" to justify policies that had become extremely unpopular and that caused both presidents great personal anguish and embarrassment. To an extent, President Bush seems to have followed the same script with respect to a constitutional amendment to protect the American flag. And many members of Congress, when answering criticism of Congress's resounding vote to ban television blackouts of home football games providing tickets are sold out several days in advance, simply replied, "How many Americans do you think are upset?"

In concluding this section, let's repeat that appeals to authority are legitimate when:

1. the authorities are genuine experts in the pertinent field;

2. there is a consensus of authoritative opinion; and

3. we can, at least in theory, verify the claims for ourselves.

In the absence of any of these criteria, an argument that appeals to an expert commits the fallacy of false authority. Fallacious appeals to authority, however, may occur in a variety of other ways as well: by positioning, by appealing to traditional wisdom, by relying on popularity.

EXERCISE 3-6

Identify the fallacies (false authority, positioning, traditional wisdom, popularity) in the following passages.

1. JOE: You know, I think I'm going to start banking at First Federal.
   JILL: Why's that?
   JOE: Well, I saw Spike Lee do a commercial for them the other day. I figure a guy as successful as he is must know something about saving money.

2. REPORTER: Sir, there's been a lot of talk recently about migrant workers and particularly about how they are not receiving due process under the law.
   DISTRICT ATTORNEY: Well, I don't for a minute deny that there have been abuses. But you must remember that's how we do things in this state. I don't say it's right, mind you, but that's the way it's done.

3. Ad for Subaru: "Subaru and Mercedes, two of the finest engineered cars around. One sells for eight times the price of the other. The choice is yours."

4. Ad for insurance company: "We were founded just a couple of years after the U.S. Constitution was signed, and by the same kind of people who signed the Constitution."

5. FRANK: You know, I think all political parties should be entitled to TV time and not just the major ones.
   WINNIE: I don't see that at all. The major parties represent the significant viewpoints. The other parties don't.
   FRANK: Why do you say that?
   WINNIE: Well, by far the vast majority of Americans belong to the Republican or Democratic parties. So what those parties have to say is obviously important.

6. Ad for Equitable Life Assurance Society (written below a 1950-vintage picture of a father helping his son with his homework): "Nobody Else Like You Service. We stole the idea from your father." [Equitable has another, identical ad, except that Mama has replaced Papa.]

7. JOYCE: No TANG for me. I'd prefer something more nutritious.
   GEORGE: More nutritious? Don't you realize that NASA chose TANG for its astronauts?

8. BILL: There's no question that humans are inherently aggressive.
   JUNE: I disagree.
   BILL: If you do, you'll have to disagree with some pretty heavy thinkers, such as Darwin and Lorenz and Ardrey. As for me, their endorsement of the aggressionist view offers pretty good evidence for it.

9. JERRY: Educated people can't really believe in God any more.
   RITA: I disagree. I know plenty of educated people who hold deep religious beliefs.
   JERRY: Either they're faking them or they're not educated. For, as Freud pointed out in his *The Future of an Illusion,* religious belief is simply impossible for educated people today.

10. STAN: There's no question that the Golden Rule is a sound moral principle.
    STU: Why do you say that?
    STAN: Because it's basic to every system of ethics ever devised. I mean you can go back thousands and thousands of years and see some variation of the Golden Rule in society. Everybody has adopted it in one form or other.

11. PETE: Reincarnation explains why some of us have good lives and others have difficulties.

KEN: I'm not sure. I don't see any good evidence to support belief in reincarnation.

PETE: Oh, yeah? Well, just the other day I saw Shirley MacLaine on the "Phil Donahue Show," and she explained it. In fact, she's even written two books about psychic phenomena, among other things. And they certainly wouldn't let her publish them if she didn't know what she was talking about.

12. STUDENT: I don't see why we have to have a term paper in this class. We write enough essays for you to evaluate us.

    PROFESSOR: Term papers have always been part of college courses. They must be valuable learning aids to have withstood the test of time.

13. I know God must exist. For all recorded history billions of people have believed in some type of deity. If the vast majority of humankind has believed in God, who are we to doubt?

14. It is obvious that God does not exist, my biology teacher told me so, and she's a Ph.D.

15. The number-one selling small truck in America today!

16. Kids ought to have jobs! I had a job when I was in school, and my daddy had jobs. So you, my boy, should have a job, too.

17. JOAN: I feel sorry for kids today.

    DORIS: Why's that?

    JOAN: Well, all these single-parent "families." You know, that's not really a family. The family has always been Mom, Dad, and the kids. That's the way it's supposed to be.

18. ROSS: I'm getting a divorce.

    JIM: Why?

    ROSS: My therapist says that my marriage is unworkable, and he oughta know. He's an expert in marital relations.

19. GEORGE: Yep, I get to turn in my paper late. Barbara gave me permission, you know.

    RICH: Barbara?

    GEORGE: You know! Dr. Boyce. Oh, that's right, you don't know her well enough to call her Barbara.

20. But Mom! You've got to get me Jordache jeans, Nike shoes, and Opium perfume. All the other girls have them.

SUMMARY

In this chapter we learned about the public dimension of arguments. The public dimension of an argument consists of the objective properties of its logic and content, and the objective criteria relevant to presenting and analyzing cases. We also learned that an argument's cogency is an objective property, and not determined by personal belief or degree of emotional conviction.

Next, we distinguished between critical and uncritical thinking. We characterized critical thinking as the conscious and deliberate scrutiny of cases and arguments to determine whether or not they meet the criteria of reasonableness, relevancy, and sufficiency. In contrast to critical thinking, uncritical thinking asks too few or inappropriate questions. It accepts sweeping generalities without qualifying them, and confuses personal feeling with objective verification.

We also examined knowledge. It's important to be clear on what we mean in claiming to know something because both the content and our ultimate evaluation of arguments are comprised of assertions of knowledge. Knowledge implies belief, truth, and justification. Belief refers to a person's attitude toward a particular statement. Truth is characteristic of a proposition that describes an actual state of affairs. Ignoring the difference between belief and truth sometimes leads us to the erroneous assumption that truth is relative. Truth is *not* relative; beliefs are. Not understanding the nature and meaning of truth can lead us to confuse the relationship of the arguer to the argument. This in turn can result in a failure to distinguish between an argument's evidence, its cogency, and our own attitude toward it. In other words, we overlook the fact that cogency is an objective characteristic of an argument.

The third ingredient of knowledge, justification, refers to the nature of the evidence to support a conclusion, which depends on having enough of the right kind of evidence. What constitutes enough of the right kind of evidence, in turn, depends on the kind of statement we're dealing with. We've learned to distinguish between objective statements, in which the assumptions, experiences, and beliefs of the person making them are irrelevant, and subjective statements, whose truth value does depend on the subjective values and experiences of the individual who asserts them. Objective statements, which need justification outside ourselves—that is, in the world—raise the most serious questions of what constitutes enough of the right kind of evidence to warrant a claim of knowledge. The question of sufficiency of evidence is tied up with observations, which underlie the premises of arguments. We can accept observations as correct when we satisfy ourselves about the conditions under which they were made and about the abilities of the observer. Specifically, five key considerations should be introduced in evaluating observations and evidence:

1. the physical conditions under which the observations were made;

2. the sensory acuity of the observer;

3. the background knowledge of the observer;

4. the objectivity of the observer; and

5. the supporting testimony of others.

This chapter dealt with three important sources of knowledge: the senses, reason, and authority. The senses and reason are primary sources of knowledge.

Generally speaking, what we term "perceptual errors" are actually judgmental errors. One way to ensure that our judgments are accurate is to expose them to public verification. Reason is the capacity to draw conclusions from evidence. Authority, another source of knowledge, refers to an expert outside ourselves. In determining the correctness of an appeal to authority, we must ensure that the authority is in fact an expert in the field, that there is a consensus among the authorities, and that we can—at least in theory—verify the claim for ourselves. In the absence of any of these criteria, an argument commits the fallacy of false appeal to authority. Celebrity endorsements of products almost always rely on false appeal to authority. False authority has several variations. One is the fallacy of positioning, an argument that tries to capitalize on the earned reputation of a leader in a field to sell something or to enhance the arguer's reputation. For example, Toshiba copy machines' ad reads, "O.K. Xerox, Try and copy this." Another variation is the fallacy of traditional wisdom, an argument that uses the past to justify claims made in the present. For example, Senator Sam Ervin dismissed the Equal Rights Amendment on the ground that it had lain around Congress for forty years which, according to Ervin, was proof that the proposal was unworthy of consideration. A last variation is the fallacy of popularity, an argument that tries to justify something strictly by appeal to numbers. For example, arguing for the purchase of a book because it's a best-seller.

We also learned to identify three common fallacies that result from failing to apply critical thinking to the analysis of what constitutes sufficient, reasonable, relevant evidence for a conclusion. The fallacy of the argument from ignorance confuses an opponent's inability to disprove a conclusion as proof of the conclusion's correctness. We used the example of insisting that vitamin C cures the common cold because no one has proven that it doesn't. The fallacy of unknowable fact is an argument that contains a premise which is unknowable either in a particular case or in principle. An example of a fact that's unknowable in a particular case is Fleishmann's claim that "Every 15 seconds a doctor recommends Fleishmann's margarine." The fallacy of provincialism is an argument that exclusively views things in terms of loyalty to a group. An economist who argues that an administration is inept solely on the basis of its economic policy would commit the fallacy of provincialism.

Summary Exercises

1. Explain the difference between critical and uncritical thinking. Be specific and give examples of each.

2. What is meant by the public dimension of argument?

3. Students sometimes say, "I know the answer to that question but I just can't think of it." Is it possible to "know" an answer and not be able to think of it? Why or why not?

4. Restate the student proposition in 3. in unambiguous fashion.

5. In your own words, reproduce Socrates' *reductio* of Protagoras's assertion that the truth is relative.

ADDITIONAL EXERCISES*

Identify the fallacies, if any, in the following passages. Choose from false authority, positioning, traditional wisdom, popularity, argument from ignorance, unknowable fact, and provincialism. Be prepared to support your claim with a cogent argument.

1. FERRIS: I really think we should terminate our mutual defense treaty with Taiwan.
   MARILYN: But a large portion of the Congress doesn't agree.
   FERRIS: The president does.
   MARILYN: So what? The Congress represents the people. And if a majority of representatives think we shouldn't, that's the will of the people and the wise thing to do.

2. JUDY: Of course God exists.
   JUD: How can you be so sure?
   JUDY: Simple—every theologian says so.

3. SAM: There's little question that the Earth is about 93 million miles from the sun.
   SUE: I agree. After all, astronomers agree on that.

4. BART: You know, we really have to get rid of all these protective tariffs.
   LIL: But they protect domestic manufacturers.
   BART: Says you. I just finished an economics text that says protective tariffs only protect inefficiency.

5. CAROL: The United States should get out of the United Nations.
   CARL: I don't think that sort of isolationism is wise.
   CAROL: Well, I can see you've forgotten the warnings of the Founding Fathers against entangling alliances.

6. Julie Nixon, reacting to nationwide moral outrage at the content of the presidential Watergate-related transcripts: "I don't see how you can be shocked by the transcripts. It is a human being reacting to a situation where he saw all his dreams crumbling down around him and trying to weigh everything, to explore every alternative. To my mind I think that would have been the only human and natural thing to do." (*Los Angeles Times,* May 12, 1974, p. 12)

7. Al Pollack, owner of The Shadows restaurant, reacting against the proposed San Francisco "truth in advertising" ordinance to require restaurant owners to identify food prepared off the premises and then frozen: Three-quarters or seven-eighths of the people who come into my place . . . don't give a good goddamn. (*Los Angeles Times,* July 4, 1974, p. 11)

8. Ad for Avis Rent-A-Car Systems, Inc.: "Avis features cars engineered by Chrysler."

9. "Can you put 2 and 2 together? Then use this Free Information Stamp to learn how you can add NEW INCOME, NEW PRESTIGE, NEW SECURITY to your life. (Flyer advertisement from International Accountants Society)

10. Ad for Circus Masters Vitamins: NBA Players Association use and recommend Walgreen Vitamins.

11. Ad for Winston cigarettes: "Winston's Down Home Taste!"

12. JOE: Boy, those Muslim terrorists really burn me up. There's just no excuse for terrorism of that sort.
    JEAN: I tend to agree. But I suppose that some of them might truly believe that God—or Allah as they prefer—wants them to wage jihad, or holy war.
    JOE: So what? They're heathens.

13. I don't care what you say.

14. This country is controlled by a few very powerful, very wealthy businessmen. They decide who gets elected, what gets into the news, what gets to Congress. And the most horrible thing about it is that nobody knows they exist. They are so clever and so powerful, no one can ever come up with proof of their influence. It's frightening.

15. Of course he's the best. He's my son!

16. DR. FROID: You see, you wrecked your mother's car last night as a way of punishing your mother.
    PATIENCE: I don't understand. It was just an accident. I wasn't mad at my mother.
    DR. FROID: Not consciously. Consciously, you are afraid to acknowledge your anger. So you have repressed it.
    PATIENCE: But I don't feel angry.
    DR. FROID: Of course not. We are never aware of our unconscious feelings while they are unconscious.

17. The sixth grade's better than the fifth grade, nyah, nyah! Everything we do is better.

18. CHAIRPERSON: The chair recognizes Ms. Malone.
    MS. MALONE: Thank you. As a psychologist, I would like to point out that the issue of drug abuse is primarily a psychological one. Thus we should look to a solution in that direction.
    CHAIRPERSON: The chair recognizes Chief Parker.
    CHIEF PARKER: Thanks. With all due respect to Ms. Malone, let me point out that the real consequences of drug abuse are felt in our legal system: courts, jails, and most of all at the level of the cop on the beat.
    CHAIRPERSON: Reverend Edwards?

Rev. Edwards: Thank you. And let me say that I agree with both Ms. Malone and Chief Parker—up to a point. What we're all overlooking, however, is, I'm afraid, the crux of the whole problem: America is suffering from a spiritual and religious crisis.

19. Joyce: I just read an article about how the quality of air can be a factor in lung cancer.
    Jim: You don't believe everything you read, do you?
    Joyce: No, but I'm inclined to believe that.

20. Ad for Ronson razors: "Take it from Ronson there is no better Flexible Head Shaving System than ours. Who do you think Schick took it from?"

21. Clint Eastwood justifying the film role he does: "A guy sits alone in a theater. He's young and he's scared. He doesn't know what he's going to do with his life. He wishes he could be self-sufficient, like the man he sees up there on the screen, somebody who can look out for himself, solve his own problems. I do the kind of roles I'd like to see if I were still digging swimming pools and wanted to escape my problems." (*Time,* January 9, 1978, p. 48)

22. "Goodrich—we're the ones without the blimp."

23. Boy! I didn't realize that you were so important. Just look at the size of this office—and right next to the president's.

24. I don't like this idea of another major political party. The Republicans and Democrats are plenty. I mean, we've done okay with just two parties for over 200 years, haven't we?

25. Rush Limbaugh's book must be great. Millions of copies were sold in the first few months it was in print.

26. Junior: I think I want to major in poetry.
    Dad: Poetry? Are you nuts? What kind of job can you hope to get? Take it from me. Go into business. Look at how successful I am. I ought to know.
    Junior: You're right, Dad. You've sure made a lot of money. I guess you do know what you're talking about.

27. Joe: Hey, be careful. You'll pull a muscle exercising that way.
    Joan: What's wrong with the way I'm exercising?
    Joe: Well, Cindy Crawford says that you should do it like this.
    Joan: What does she know?
    Joe: She's an expert. She's made a videotape and an audiotape, she's written about exercising, and she's stayed in excellent shape herself.

CHAPTER 4

The Personal Dimension

He who knows others is learned;
he who knows himself is wise.

CHUANG-TZU

Recall that the public dimension of an argument consists of the objective properties of its logic and content, and the objective criteria relevant to presenting and analyzing cases. This means that logical cogency is independent of our moods, biases, limits, and knowledge. Cogency is a function of whether or not an argument meets the objective (i.e., public) criteria of reasonableness, relevancy, and sufficiency.

The actual determination of cogency can be complex because it involves judgments about truth, as well as about reasonableness, relevancy, and sufficiency. Thus there is room for disagreement about the cogency of a given argument. This is especially true in controversial areas where there is as yet no established, generally accepted, unproblematic body of evidence supporting one side or other, and in areas involving value judgments. We see this today in discussions concerning affirmative action, abortion, euthanasia, the environment, and capital punishment, to cite only a few examples.

If we fail to remember that cogency is an objective characteristic of an argument, we may fall into the trap of confusing evidence that satisfies us individually with the objective quality of that evidence. One of the most common stumbling blocks to clear thinking occurs because we naturally tend to favor some beliefs over others for personal reasons. If we are not careful, we may allow our uncritically accepted preferences to distort our thinking. We may also have difficulty rejecting some ideas because we simply *want* them to be true, or are so overcome by strong emotions that we can't reason clearly.

It is helpful not to lose sight of the following facts:

1. *Persons* make arguments.

2. Persons are not computers or "logic machines," not "Mr. Spocks" or "Datas."

3. All sorts of personality (nonlogical) factors affect the arguments we make, and also affect our capacity to evaluate arguments.

4. So, even though in theory it's the public dimension (the three criteria) that defines cogent arguments, in practice arguments arise in a very complex milieu that includes important personal concerns.

These personal factors can be both a source of inspiration (e.g., when we become outraged over some unjust policy or practice) and a source of confusion, distraction, and even irrationality (e.g., when we're so angry that we can't think straight, or resort to violence, or even break down).

We see, then, that personal factors can be important "extralogical" influences bearing on critical thinking skills because, although they may be logically irrelevant to a particular claim, they can be *personally relevant*. One of the major pitfalls is to ignore or dismiss the personal dimension of reasoning. Any practical study of logic and argument must include a look into this powerful influence on so much of our thinking. If we fail to do this, we run the risk of creating a false impression of the relationship between logic and personal motivation.

Thinking does not occur in a vacuum. We reason for various motives: to learn the truth, to persuade others, to learn more about the world or ourselves, to discover patterns and relationships, and so forth. The very formidable thinker David Hume said "Reason is and ought to be the slave of the passions." He did not mean that emotions and strong desires ought to blindly control us, but that reasoning is a tool best used in full awareness of a complex set of desires and needs. Clear thinking can help us sort out conflicting desires; it can help us distinguish wants from needs; it can help us identify and arrange our values in a hierarchical way.

Logic and emotions are not inevitably in opposition; rather, properly understood, they are complementary and enable us to live the best possible lives. In this chapter, we'll take a look at some of the most common sources of confusion and error that can occur when certain personal factors inhibit our ability to think clearly and critically; so our focus will be on problems stemming from the personal dimension of thinking. It's equally important, however, not to think of the public and personal dimensions of argument as being mutually opposed to one another.

Let's begin by distinguishing between emotions and reasons.

EMOTIONS AND REASONS

Emotions lack truth value; they are neither true nor false. Claims (propositions) about emotions, on the other hand, are either true or false. For example, the claim "Smith is angry" is either true or false, whereas anger is an emotion Smith may or may not have experienced. If we fail to take adequate note of the distinction between an emotion and a claim about an emotion, we will inevitably confuse emotions with reasons.

When emotions are confused with reasons, the intensity of our feelings and the sincerity with which we hold our beliefs can become substitutes for logical evidence. Thus a sincere atheist offers as "evidence" for the claim that there is no God the intensity with which the conviction is held. The atheist is in turn "refuted" by the sincere theist who "simply knows with all my heart" that God exists.

To the detached, objective thinker, the intensity with which an individual holds a belief is irrelevant to its truth value. As we learned in Chapter 3, knowledge is justified true belief—and sincerity and intensity tell us more about the believer than about the belief. Sincerity and intensity are aspects of the personal dimension of argument. Truth and cogency, however, are part of the public dimension.

STUDY HINT

Emotions lack truth value; only propositions have truth value. Psychological conviction, in and of itself, is not proof of the truth of any belief. We must distinguish reasons from feelings, logical evidence from psychological sincerity.

It's important to our critical thinking skills that we do not confuse *psychological conviction* with *logical cogency*. Where reasons are appropriate, good reasons should be demanded. Ironically, clear thinking may be most helpful where it is most difficult: when we face problems, especially personal problems which involve strong, often conflicting, feelings and values, or which involve deeply held beliefs and biases. It is precisely during periods of intense feeling that we are most likely to forget or refuse to think clearly. It is in just such times of emotional intensity that we are most prone to rationalizing the conclusions we deeply desire, or most tempted to offer some other faulty justification based solely on how we feel about something or what we desire the truth to be.

In practice, arguments tend to be presented as part of a case. Arguments offer reasons for accepting the truth of their conclusions. But cases often include more than just logical evidence. They include rhetorical devices, appeals to emotions or group loyalty, and so forth. In other words, cases go beyond the public dimension and appeal to more than the three criteria for cogency.

The nonlogical components of a case can be powerfully persuasive even when the argument lacks cogency. Because we are not merely reasoning beings, we are not always convinced by even the best arguments. (Indeed, a cynic might assert that we are rarely convinced by objective evidence.) In any case, we rarely encounter pure arguments, stripped of all rhetorically persuasive embellishments. The arguments we are called upon to evaluate in real life are often clouded by nonlogical, emotional appeals.

Even though *in theory* the public aspects of arguments are readily apparent, *in practice* they are often overlooked. In many instances, persuaders deliberately attempt to distract us from critical assessment of their arguments. Then, too, reacting is quicker and easier than analyzing. Political speeches, advertisements and commercials, sales pitches, seductions, and their like include both deliberate and unplanned psychological factors.

In every case or dispute two psychologies are always involved: our own and the arguer's. What is *psychologically sufficient and relevant* to either of us is not necessarily *logically sufficient or relevant*. And just as there is a difference between belief and truth, there is a clear difference between *feeling* that a statement is reasonable and its actually being so. Effective thinking and analysis requires surefootedness along the interface of the logical and the *psycho*logical. This is no more apparent than when basic needs intersect with rational thought.

HUMAN NEEDS

All living organisms have needs that must be satisfied if the organism is to survive. Human beings function in varying degrees of well-being and satisfaction according to how well a complex set of needs are met and integrated. Satisfaction of needs bears directly on the ability to think critically. A need will not just disappear because we choose to ignore it or are incapable of satisfying it. If it remains unfulfilled, we may experience such distress or unhappiness that our thinking and perceiving skills are seriously impaired.

We've all probably had times when we were too depressed or excited or angry to concentrate. Or we may have been too tired or even too hungry. We might be in love or going through a difficult separation and find that we are easily distracted by our feelings. Such periods are common to the human condition, and we often recognize their causes and expect them to pass. But there are also times when people are completely unaware (unconscious) of the extent to which their thinking skills are impaired due to some physical, mental, or emotional condition.

It is important to be aware of the basic needs which must be met in order to think critically and clearly. When these needs are unmet to a significant degree, they impair our thinking skills. They may even impair our senses. For convenience, we can distinguish between two basic categories of needs: physical and emotional.

Physical Needs

Clearly our first-order needs are essentially physiological: we need food, water, air, physical activity, rest, and so forth, in order to maintain our biochemical balance. Included in our list of physical needs are things such as a need for shelter, an instinct to avoid pain, and so forth. Unmet physical needs have immediate and often dramatic effects on our thinking abilities, which in turn affect our ability to satisfy other needs.

Perhaps you have suffered through a lecture in a classroom so hot or cold that you were virtually unable to concentrate on anything but your own discomfort. Then, too, there are all those afternoon logic students who erroneously conclude that they cannot think logically when the chief cause of poor comprehension is not too little gray matter, but too much lunch too close to class time. In other words, blood that could be rushing oxygen to excited brain cells is, instead, aiding in the digestion of two burritos or an avocado-and-sprout pizza.

Too much noise, too little sleep, poor nutrition, and other physical factors all contribute to a diminished ability to perceive clearly and to think well. When these needs are poorly satisfied, we suffer from various forms of discomfort or dysfunction that affect our abilities to concentrate, to identify, to remember, and to organize—all crucial analytic skills (which are discussed in detail throughout our text). Unmet physical needs have a direct bearing on sensory acuity, and can severely distort our assessment of evidence.

Emotional Needs

We also require a certain emotional equilibrium. A most basic emotional need seems to be the need for security and trust. Closely related to this is the need to receive and give love. Psychologist Abraham Maslow says that the need for love is as evident as the need for iodine or vitamin C.[6] In *Creative and Critical Thinking,* Moore, McCann, and McCann suggest that our basic emotional needs include the following: affection, group acceptance, approval, autonomy, achievement, prestige, service to others, conformity to conscience, and self-growth.[7]

You might ask: What does love have to do with critical thinking? Unmet emotional needs can distort our perspective by causing us to focus exclusively or predominantly on whatever we lack. If we feel unloved, we may be so lonely or hungry for affection that we are easily swayed by personable salespeople, or convinced to donate money to deceptive organizations. Seeing only what we want to see, we may fail to critically scrutinize the seductive claims of people who are kind to us.

Unmet needs of any sort can result in defense mechanisms.

DEFENSE MECHANISMS

A defense mechanism is a strategy designed to support a favored self-concept despite contradictory fact. Our self-concept consists of the impression we have of the kind of person we are. A defense mechanism is actually a complex set of behavioral, emotional, and intellectual habits working together to "defend" a favored concept of ourselves.

In this context, the term "favored" is value-neutral in that it simply means "selected over others." The favored, defended self-concept need not be a healthy

---

6. Abraham Maslow, *Toward a Psychology of Being,* 2d ed. (New York: D. Van Nostrand, 1968), p. 23.

7. W. Edgar Moore, Hugh McCann, and Janet McCann, *Creative and Critical Thinking* (Boston: Houghton Mifflin Company, 1985), pp. 368–75.

or accurate one; we might, for example, hold a false concept of ourselves as incompetent or inferior. Individuals suffering from the psychological disorder anorexia nervosa, for instance, view themselves as obese regardless of their actual weight. Their "favored" self-concept is that they are overweight. No objective evidence alters this favored self-concept. On the other hand, a favored self-concept might be one that insists on viewing the self as great or magnificent despite objective evidence of only modest ability.

The important point here is that defense mechanisms, by their very nature, are opposed to our search for cogent arguments. Defense mechanisms are *rationalizations* used to find and/or create "evidence" to support a preselected conclusion. By contrast, *reasoning* has as its goal the acceptance of *whatever* conclusion the evidence legitimately supports.

STUDY HINT

Rationalizing has as its goal the support of a desired conclusion *regardless of the actual evidence*. *Reasoning* has as its goal cogent arguments.

When, for whatever reasons, we hang on to an inadequate, distorted, inaccurate self-concept, we have also developed defense mechanisms designed to support a particular vision of ourselves, others, and the world, in a way that reinforces the distorted self-concept. Because our basic consideration in all decisions is how to protect the favored self-concept, everything is evaluated in light of its potential to support or refute this particular point of view.

Defense mechanisms always involve a particularly dangerous attitude known as *willed ignorance*. We'll meet it again in Chapter 6, but it will be helpful to take a quick look at it here. As the phrase suggests, ignorance is lack of knowledge, *willed* because a person in this state says or thinks, "I don't care what anybody says, I am going to think X." Example: "I don't care what anybody says, I know kissing causes AIDS." All defense mechanisms can be characterized as following this pattern: "I don't care what anybody says, what new facts are discovered, or whether my reasoning is cogent, I will always believe X."

Let's consider three of the more common techniques available that foster defensive distortions.

Scapegoating

Scapegoating is the defense mechanism that singles out an innocent individual or group to blame for some undesired condition.

Here's an example: Rather than consider the possibility that his teaching methods are ineffective, Mr. Christopher blames his poor reputation on the influx of single mothers into college classes. In fact, he even blames high divorce rates (his own included) and increased drug use and higher taxes on single mothers—just the way Hitler and his Nazis blamed most of post–World War I Germany's troubles on Jews and other "inferior types."

Here are some more examples of scapegoating: "Every time the Democrats begin to get things in pretty good shape, the Republicans mess them up." At some companies, low morale is conveniently blamed on the boss, when it is in fact the product of more complex factors than one person's frailties.

A young white male might be able to assuage any hint of self-doubts about himself by blaming his failure to get a job on "affirmative action." Uncritically defending a concept of himself as highly capable and desirable, but cheated and abused by affirmative action laws, may make him feel good for the moment—but it will discourage him from honest introspection and assessment of his skills in light of the current job market. Without an objective, rational analysis of his actual circumstances, talents, and the like, he is apt to fail to identify a solution to his real problem: he needs more schooling, retraining, whatever.

Note how such scapegoating requires that we prejudge and stereotype others, that we "leap to conclusions" based on distortions of facts, that we oversimplify. In other words, in addition to whatever cultural and personal influences lead us to scapegoat, we cannot resort to scapegoating without also falling into reasoning errors.

Projection

Projection is the defense mechanism that attributes to others undesirable traits similar to those which we find in ourselves.

Projection can act as a barrier between our favored self-concept and some undesirable trait of ours that could threaten or destroy that self-concept. This form of projection is often accompanied by intolerance, judgmentalism, and hostility. For example, deceptive and dishonest people often indiscriminately see others as untrustworthy. Hostile and defensive people tend to see acts of aggression everywhere, interpreting accidental bumps in the store or lane changes on the freeway as deliberate personal attacks.

Very selfish people, for instance, require and demand a great deal of attention. When they fail to get enough attention, they have two basic choices: either assess circumstances critically and objectively, and realize that their needs are excessive, or fight to retain a self-concept of themselves as selfless, decent people. Excessively selfish people often choose the latter. What conclusion follows from this faulty premise? That other people are not giving them their fair share of attention. Thus, in their projections, it is other people who appear selfish.

Projection is commonly—but not always—accompanied by extreme, unwarranted hostility, resentment, or aggression. As the rest of the world keeps challenging our defense mechanisms with better reasoned alternative views, facts that do not support our favored self-concept, and with an alarming consistency among those who challenge us, we become more combative, more defensive: hostile, resentful, aggressive.

Projection, like other defense mechanisms, requires distortion of facts, inaccurate perceptions, and reliance on insufficient evidence and irrelevant assertions.

Introjection

Introjection is the defense mechanism in which we uncritically internalize the values, beliefs, and experiences of others.

We may introject the values of our parents, our political party or church, friends, and so forth. Introjection almost always inhibits our ability to perceive and think for ourselves. When introjected beliefs substitute for our own actual experience, the price we pay is a diminished ability to assess conditions accurately or draw our own conclusions, since we must repress, distort, or deny our own perceptions, experiences, and judgments in favor of someone else's.

Members of cults have been known to introject the values of the cult or its charismatic leader to such an extent that they no longer experience things as they are—rather they "see" whatever the official position dictates. The child who introjects a parent's attitudes toward men or women may never see the other sex objectively. Introjection differs from influence: introjected values interfere with perception, judgment, and reality testing.

We've seen a few of the ways that defense mechanisms make life momentarily bearable at a price that can get pretty steep over the long run because they require a distortion of evidence, even a denial of our own experiences, judgments, and beliefs. These may create extreme hostility or aggression in us, as we become increasingly sensitive to even the slightest threat to our carefully balanced rationalizations. In Chapter 6 we'll study fallacies centered on personal attacks and mob appeals, both of which cater to supporting a favored self-concept. Entire groups can succumb to this form of uncritical persuasion.

A good defense against defensive mechanisms includes clear, critical-thinking skills. But in order to think as well as possible, we must also avoid the stumbling blocks to clear thinking which function as methods of distortion: denial, rationalizing, prejudging, and stereotyping.

EXERCISE 4-1 *

Discuss and explain the following scenarios in terms of scapegoating, projection, and introjection.

SCENARIO 1: Bud hates what he sees as his dad's bullying behavior of Dad's employees. Bud regularly pushes his little brother Buster around.

SCENARIO 2: The president of the Coalition for Clean Thoughts works very hard to remove *Playboy* and *Penthouse* magazines from local stores. He tries to have them replaced with *Clean Living* and *Wholesome Hobbies.* He is especially angry at the "liberal establishment" and "secular humanists" for wanting to "enforce their morals on the rest of us."

SCENARIO 3: After two weeks of law school, an excited Melvin begins to smoke a pipe—just like his favorite professor, Professor Kingfish. Over the semester, Melvin finds out what brand of tobacco Kingfish smokes, and begins to read everything Kingfish ever wrote. By the end of the term, Melvin's a devout Libertarian, just like Kingfish.

SCENARIO 4: Kay, a second-generation Irish-American, is frustrated. She hasn't had a good job in over 18 months, when automation made her old job obsolete. She's especially annoyed because of the large influx of Latino and Asian immigrants. Kay is convinced that foreigners are taking jobs away from "loyal, real Americans."

SCENARIO 5: Frustrated by her conviction for resisting arrest for slapping a police officer, Zsa Zsa Gabor accuses the press of being unfairly aggressive and hostile for dwelling on the issue.

Denial

Psychological denial is a defense mechanism that protects a favored self-concept by refusing to acknowledge the existence or nature of some unpleasant circumstance.

Many of us are aware that alcohol and drug abusers often deny their problems. What's not so commonly recognized is the extent to which the friends and families of substance abusers also deny the degree and power of the addiction. They assert that the addictive behavior is "not that big of a deal," that it is "caused by marital problems," that "everybody gets a little stoned now and then," and so forth. What such reactions deny, for example, is that many people who have marital or family problems do not abuse drugs, or that most people do not get cited for driving under the influence, and so on.

In some of its most serious cases, denial is manifest in victims of spousal abuse who insist that their abuser is kind and loving despite clearly contradictory evidence. On a perhaps less-serious scale, we see denial in those individuals who insist on the efficacy of astrological predictions notwithstanding clear cases of failed and/or vague predictions. On a national scale, our failure to adequately address environmental problems, shortages of water, and energy, involve denial. We see denial in the ever-faithful followers of political or religious figures who

Calvin and Hobbes   by Bill Watterson

Calvin and Hobbes © 1992 Watterson. Distributed by Universal Press Syndicate. Reprinted with permission. All rights reserved.

are openly proven to have lied or embezzled money or falsified credentials. The list of examples is endless.

Clearly we cannot be effective thinkers if we deny and distort the objective nature or consequences of what's going on around us. Denial is the psychological impetus behind fallacies of dismissal, which involve simply refusing to acknowledge the seriousness of an issue or diverting attention to something less threatening. Denial is also a common accompaniment of willed ignorance (which is explained in Chapter 6).

Rationalizing

Rationalizing is the defense mechanism that presents bogus reasons as justification for a favored conclusion. When we reason we draw conclusions from evidence. When we rationalize, by contrast, we have already decided on a favored conclusion, and offer false reasons to justify accepting it. We do not subject it to critical scrutiny or attempt to objectively evaluate it.

The evidence offered as part of a rationalization may be reasonable. That is, it may be acceptable to others and on its face. But the reasons offered are technically irrelevant, and hence insufficient to advance their conclusion, because they are not the *real* reasons we have for holding the conclusion. For example, a business owner might rationalize hiring a relative by citing his or her employment record. And it may be a perfectly adequate record. But if the owner based the hiring decision on other facts, the reasons *offered* for hiring the relative constitute a rationalization. If another employer has secretly decided only to hire (or not to hire) persons of a certain race, age, or appearance, then any other reasons offered to the public are rationalizations.

The essential difference between reasoning and rationalizing is one of intention. If our purpose is to see where the evidence leads or what it demonstrates, we are reasoning. If, rather, our real purpose is to find reasons to support a conclusion we insist upon holding, we are rationalizing—even if the reasons

Calvin and Hobbes   by Bill Watterson

Calvin and Hobbes © 1993 Watterson. Distributed by Universal Press Syndicate. Reprinted with permission. All rights reserved.

are good. Rationalizing presents reasons to the public dimension, which, in fact, are not the real reasons we have for accepting or rejecting a conclusion. It is helpful to realize that rationalizations are often spotted by others. Rationalizations only provide public face-saving, at best, and they often fail to do even that.

The basic problem with rationalizations, from our perspective, is that they encourage errors of assumption. This is an important species of poor reasoning that results from treating problematic claims as if they are unproblematic. We simply *assume*, without demonstration, that a claim is true, and then proceed to use it to justify further claims. Since any reasonable analysis of an argument requires careful scrutiny of its premises, any practice which discourages or avoids testing of assumptions is uncritical.

Prejudging

A prejudice is a conclusion arrived at prior to pertinent experience or independent of evidence.

In other words, we make up our minds before we have sufficient evidence to draw our conclusion. Racial, sexual, and religious prejudices are unfortunately common. And yet it is also common to discover that many highly prejudiced individuals have had virtually no personal experience with the objects of their prejudgments. Indeed, prejudice thrives on limited contact with its object.

Anti-Semitism flourishes even among people who have never knowingly met a Jew. Strong negative prejudices against Christian fundamentalists flourish in academic circles among seemingly well-educated intellectuals who don't know any fundamentalists. This list, too, could go on and on. Prejudices function as defense mechanisms by arbitrarily restricting what counts as evidence.

Stereotyping

Stereotyping is a form of prejudice that occurs when we overlook an individual's unique qualities by viewing him or her only according to a rigid preconception.

When stereotyping occurs, we tend to expect certain behavior patterns—and to convince ourselves of their occurrence regardless of their actual presence. A white racial bigot, for example, might have a stereotyped picture of all blacks as being lazy. Thus, he keeps track of every time his black neighbor's yard badly needs mowing (which in reality is not often) because this confirms his stereotype. He overlooks all those times his neighbor's yard is well cared for, as well as ignoring the fact that his own yard is much more poorly cared for. Acknowledging these facts weakens the stereotyped pictures he holds of blacks and of himself. Meanwhile, his black neighbor holds a stereotyped view of Hispanics. She notices every discourtesy her Mexican American neighbor commits while overlooking the fact that her own daughter's Hispanic kindergarten teacher has paid special attention to the child in order to help her overcome a slight stuttering problem.

When exceptions to cherished stereotypes are pointed out, we tend to invoke various forms of bad arguments to defend the stereotype and thus maintain our favored self-concept. Here, as always, the price for distortion is high. We fail in the search for truth.

EXERCISE 4-2 *

Identify any instances of denial, rationalizing, prejudging, or stereotyping you find in the following.

1. NEIGHBOR: Aren't you worried that Teddy's been arrested again? This is the fourth time, isn't it?
   MOM: Fifth. But, no, I'm not worried. He's just an exuberant kid. You know how it is with teenagers.

2. EBENEEZER: How'd you do in logic class?
   JACOB: I flunked. But it was a lousy class anyway.
   EBENEEZER: I though you said you really liked Ms. Demorgan.
   JACOB: That was before I realized what a lousy teacher she is. I'm actually glad I flunked—anybody who passed that class had to kiss up to old Demorgan. Yeah! Now that I think about it, I'm real glad I flunked.

3. The story goes that upon being denied membership in an "exclusive" country club because he was Jewish, Groucho Marx said: "I won't belong to any club that would have me as a member."

4. MAUREEN: I bet you're sorry you didn't wait two weeks to buy that stereo at Joe's, now that the same thing's on sale for 40 percent off.
   KEN: Not at all. I've gotten to use it for an extra couple of weeks.

5. BUBBA: Geez, I wish we didn't have to hire women firefighters.
   TAB: Who knows, they might be just fine. Why don't you give 'em a chance?
   BUBBA: Hey, man, come off it. They're gonna be all muscles with short hair, and they're gonna hate men and stuff. That's the way these feminists are.
   TAB: You ever meet a real live feminist, Bubba?
   BUBBA: Don't haf'ta. I know what they're like before I meet 'em.

6. Yeah? Well I'm glad you don't like me 'cause I don't like you either. I only asked you out 'cause I felt sorry for you.

7. Look, for now I want to smoke. Do you mind? Smoking keeps me calm, helps keep my weight down. If I really wanted to quit I would.

8. Anorexic teenage girls see themselves as fat no matter what their real weight is.

9. I'm getting depressed just thinking about studying my logic. I know what I need: I'll go on a picnic to unwind. Let's see. Where's that picnic basket? Gotta go to the store, get the car lubed. . . .

10. I'm sorry my assignment's not ready, but I forgot the due date.

SUMMARY

In this chapter we've seen some of the "nonlogical" factors that bear on critical thinking in real life. Among the major nonlogical factors, which influence our thinking, are basic human needs. These include physical and emotional needs. Physical needs are the most basic needs of all, and they include physiological requirements for survival and health, the need for shelter, and other physical factors that affect us. Emotional needs include giving and receiving affection, approval, achievement, prestige, and conformity to a group.

We learned about defense mechanisms, strategies designed to support a favored self-concept despite contradictory fact. The defense mechanisms covered are:

1. Scapegoating: the process of singling out an innocent individual or group to blame for some undesired condition.

2. Projection: the process of attributing to others traits which we find undesirable in ourselves.

3. Introjection: a process in which we internalize the values, beliefs, and experiences of others.

4. Psychological denial: refusal to acknowledge the true existence or nature of some unpleasant circumstance.

5. Rationalization: "reasons" are constructed for the sole purpose of justifying a desired conclusion.

6. Prejudging: arriving at a conclusion prior to pertinent experience.

7. Stereotyping: overlooking an individual's unique qualities by viewing him or her only according to a rigid preconception.

Although cogency is an objective (i.e., public) quality of an argument, we must be careful not to overlook the personal dimension in which arguments arise. We must be especially wary of the ever-present possibility of distortion resulting from unmet needs or reliance on defense mechanisms, which can preclude objective evaluation of premises according to their reasonableness, relevancy, and sufficiency to support their conclusion.

The public and personal dimension of argument are interconnected in a fundamental way. Even though an argument's cogency is part of its public dimension, we must determine whether or not the premises of an argument meet the three criteria for cogency. Precisely because we do not want to evaluate arguments on strictly subjective grounds, we must remain sensitive to the potential for interference from unmet needs and defense mechanisms.

Summary Exercises

NOTE: In addition to learning a little more about ourselves, discussing the material in this chapter can be entertaining as we laugh at some of the common foibles that beset most of us. Without diminishing the serious side of defense mechanisms, distortions, and the like, you might find it helpful and enjoyable to discuss the following questions with other readers of *Practical Logic.* If you do, it is probably best to keep personal examples on the light side.

1. Discuss some of the specific ways clear thinking is inhibited by emotional factors.

2. What plausible strategies can you suggest to avoid the need for defense mechanisms?

3. See if you can identify three or four ways in which you might improve your grades by taking better care of your physical needs. You might, for example, modify the place in which you usually study: Is it comfortable? quiet? too quiet? too warm or cold? Are there other physical conditions (in yourself or your environment) that might be beneficially modified in a way that will enhance your critical-thinking skills?

4. Provide one or two examples of your own scapegoating, introjection, and projection.

5. Denial is one of the most serious concepts in this chapter. Can you think of any cases of denial in your own life? If yes, how did you finally come to realize that you had been denying some aspect of reality? In any case, how can we best protect ourselves against succumbing to denial? Discuss.

6. Do you think that rationalizing always makes us uncomfortable, or is it possible that some rationalizations actually work? Discuss.

ADDITIONAL EXERCISES

Scrutinize the following situations. Identify the likely presence of any of these aspects of the personal dimension: unmet physical or emotional needs, scape-goating, projection, introjection, psychological denial, and rationalization. Your analyses will necessarily be speculative, so be prepared to explain your thinking.

1. Sal's always chiding Pete about Pete's physical condition. Pete's over-weight and rarely exercises. Pete goads Sal about the fact that Sal has not read a book in over a year.

2. Sylvia notices a slight lump on the back of her neck. She decides it's probably a cyst and forgets about it.

3. Pastor Richards, the activist leader of the local anti-abortion coalition, hates the Muslims. He says, "Muslims are fanatics. They try to force their religious beliefs on the rest of the world."

4. Tim is trying to write a sociology essay while his roommate Tad is prac-ticing the drums.

5. Joann's dad is an alcoholic. Joann knows that if it weren't for her dad, her life would be fine.

6. Les is a liberal. He despises the way conservatives are trying to censor pornography, rock 'n' roll, and even textbooks. He's often been heard to say, "Freedom of speech and expression. That's what this country is founded on. Lose that and you lose everything." Les was recently arrested for getting carried away while demonstrating against granting a permit for a rally to the local chapter of the American Nazi Party. He was quoted in the paper as saying while led to jail: "Nobody should have to listen to that garbage. Freedom of speech doesn't include the right to be degenerate or immoral, or to offend the values of the community!"

7. Asked how he felt about losing an unusually hard-fought, expensive campaign for the Senate, ex-Senator Fiskew replied, "Now I'll have time to be with my family. My family's always been the most important thing in my life. I've served the people of this great state for six terms, I could use a rest. I'm glad I lost, actually."

8. Hubbard was enjoying his new car quite a bit—until his brother said that he'd be afraid to travel on the freeway in such a small vehicle. Now Hubbard's uneasy, too.

9. Molina has lots of important homework due tomorrow morning. It's two weeks before Hanukkah and Christmas, and she wants to make fudge treats for her friends. She decides that she won't be able to concentrate on homework because she's so excited about the holidays. She makes the fudge.

10. Trish always takes over an hour to get ready for school. She tries to look attractive to the boys in her class, and goes out of her way to flatter them. She is annoyed at the way Elvira is always flirting. She told her mom, "Ooh, I hate Elvira! Every time I'm talking to a cute guy she butts in. All she cares about are boys, boys, boys. And she's shameless. Always dressed up and flirting. I can't stand it when girls are like that!"

11. J. Birch hates the way the Russian Communists still get involved in the internal affairs of other countries. He can't stand the way they won't stay out of other countries' business. That's why he's enlisted in the U.S. Army. He's hoping he'll get to go fight in Central America.

12. Recalling the old Lionel model train set he had as a child, Chester ordered a train set from the Sunday supplement. It looked great in the picture. When he received his set, however, it was much smaller than he expected, and made of low-grade plastic. When his wife expressed disappointment, Chester said, "Hey, this is better than the old sets. It's small enough to store easily, it's lightweight, and we don't have to worry about it if the grandkids bust it up. I'm glad I ordered it."

13. Nora's having trouble with her Spanish test—the most important test of the year. Nora's vision seems to be blurring, her palms are sweaty, and she can't concentrate, even though she's well prepared for the test.

14. Marsha's been upset since she learned that her new office mate—whom she's yet to meet—is from Georgia. "How could they do that," she moaned, "put a bigot in my office. You know how prejudiced Southern white males are."

15. Irving's a bit worried about how well he's doing in logic class, but he's never stopped by Professor Oscar's office to pick up his graded tests.

Careless Language Use

The limits of my language mean the limits of my world.
LUDWIG WITTGENSTEIN

Who defines the terms wins the arguments.

CHINESE PROVERB

Throughout this study of logic, we have seen again and again the importance of the formulation of a premise or conclusion, not only to the cogency of an argument, but to the very meaning of its premises and conclusions. Logical thinking cannot be separated from language. Arguments, after all, are groups of *propositions*. Propositions are assertions or statements that express some claim to truth. On this fundamental level, logic requires language. If a sentence is vague or ambiguous, that is, if it lacks a clear, precise meaning, then it can't be evaluated. If it can't be evaluated, then it cannot be assumed to be reasonable. Thus careless or misleading language use renders arguments suspect, and makes application of the cogency criteria difficult or impossible.

What is language? For our purposes, we can consider language to consist of a body of words with standardized meanings, and the rules which govern their usage. Language, then, consists of a *system* of symbols (words) and rules for their usage. By standardizing the meanings and usage of words, we are able to communicate ideas and emotions. If words could mean anything anyone wants, or if there were no order to how words are used, then obviously communication would be impossible.

In Chapter 3 we learned the importance of the public dimension to knowledge claims and logical analysis. Language is the tool we use to put arguments into the public dimension, to frame them for necessary scrutiny. We need language to demonstrate, prove, or disprove claims. Language is also the chief tool we use to express feelings. This makes language a most powerful means of persuasion.

Aristotle classified human beings as rational animals, but a good case can be made that we are more social than rational. To the extent that we are social animals, the linguistic dimension of argument takes on added significance. We respond to emotionally powerful appeals, basing our opinions on the images and moods associated with differing claims.

If we wish to be practical critical thinkers, we need to learn to separate irrelevant emotional appeals from logical evidence, and to spot evasive, misleading, or empty claims. We need to recognize the power and effects of language on argument (and subsequently on thinking and behaving). Virtually every pitch made to us—from attempts to seduce, marry, or sell us something to those intended to convict or convert us—includes a linguistic dimension. One of the worst mistakes we can make is to take for granted this aspect of the argumentative case.

LANGUAGE AND EXPERIENCE

Language is not neutral. It does more than reflect our sense of reality: it helps create it. Language not only reports what we see, but actually influences and shapes our ideas and experiences. It's as if we see what we say.

In recent years, the impact language has on a person's subsequent experience of things has attracted the attention of many philosophers, linguists, and semanticists (scholars primarily interested in the connection between language and one's experience of reality). The appropriate literature from these fields suggests that language can provide a kind of script or map for people to follow in how they think about and experience the world.

The simplest examples of this point can be seen in the impact of words with high emotive value. For example, words such as *politician, crisis, corpse, abortion, atheist, motherhood, liberation,* and *sex* deliver an emotional wallop to many people. Often our feelings are so identified with such words that their mere mention sets off an emotional reaction. The reaction may be positive or negative.

The implications of language's impact on thought and subsequent experience are far-reaching. For example, once-polite words such as *Negro* and *colored* have rapidly vanished from contemporary American language usage. With these words have disappeared their mental associations of segregation and inferiority. *Negro* and *colored* have been replaced by *black*, a descriptive term as neutral as *white* or *red*. But neutrality in this instance is a comparative victory in the blacks' struggle for equality. Hence, *black* represents semantic, if not social and economic, equality with *white*. And because it does not produce the mental images of separation and inferiority that *Negro* and *colored* did, it will affect our perceptions differently. The result will help create a new reality, as will the more recent *African American*. This is already happening and is laying the basis for new assumptions about race relations—assumptions that in turn form the bases for thinking, reasoning, and arguing. For example, *Hispanic* and *Latino* are replacing *Mexican American; Native American* is increasingly used in place of *American Indian;* and *people of color* is being used to refer to nonwhites in general. Some philosophers use the term *womanist* instead of *feminist*. Each of these linguistic shifts reflects and influences cultural and value shifts.

Just as language can give us insight into individuals, so it can reveal information about groups. Has it ever occurred to you, for example, that we have only one word for snow and for camel? It probably hasn't. In fact, now that you have thought about it you might be inclined to ask. So what? How many words for snow and camel do you need? Lots, if you're an Eskimo or an Arab.

In fact, Eskimos have a separate word for each kind of snow: soft snow, hard-packed snow, slushy snow, wind-driven snow. An Arabian has over five thousand different words for camels that point up the most minute differences of age, sex, and body structure. Similarly, although English precisely distinguishes among the multitude of flying things in our experience—birds, airplanes, kites, blimps, rockets, skydivers—Hopi, a Native American language, has just one noun for everything airborne other than birds. Likewise, Zulus have words for white cow and red cow but none for plain old cow. And aborigines of Central Brazil have no word for parrot or palm but many words for the different varieties of parrots and palms in their experience.

The point is simple: The language of a people reflects how they see and think about things. It reveals their assumptions, biases, and interests; it discloses what's important and what's trivial in their lives.

So developing a sensitivity to language and its usage can help foster invaluable insights into ourselves and others. Such insights can be extremely helpful in understanding and analyzing arguments, in uncovering their hidden assumptions, in detecting their errors.

Consider for example, the title *Ms.*, which offers mental associations distinctly different from *Mrs.* or *Miss.* The latter terms make a point of a woman's marital status. Moreover, *Mrs.* alters a woman's most intimate identification label, her name, by merging it with her husband's. Language here reveals long-standing cultural biases: The male, we seem to have assumed, has an identity, the female does not—she must borrow hers from his. The result? He receives more name recognition than she, and what receives recognition is usually what is thought important. *Ms.* balances this recognition somewhat by giving the woman a title that—like the man's—leaves marital status unannounced. Such changes are likely to affect the way we think and the way we experience the world. To those born into a society that exclusively uses *Ms.* to denote any female, such notions as the following might come more easily than if that society were using *Mrs.* or *Miss:*

1. that marriage does not mean the sacrifice of the woman's personality on the altar of male egotism;

2. that the husband-wife relationship is not one of employer-employee;

3. that the marriage contract may be a commercial debasement of a unique psychophysical relationship that union between a man and a woman should foster;

4. that this psychophysical relationship might just as easily be pursued outside marriage as in; and

5. that the unmarried woman is not by definition a failure.

Naturally, language alone will not bring about these new attitudes, but it can help create a fertile soil in which such attitudes grow. And, to repeat, our attitudes usually form the assumptions from which we do much of our reasoning.

INFORMATIVE AND PERSUASIVE LANGUAGE

Language can be used to convey information in as objective and neutral a way as possible and it can be used to persuade. It can function to provide facts and details, but also to *interpret* those facts and details. In any argument analysis, it is crucial to distinguish informative language from persuasive language. Strictly speaking, arguments contain only informative language (propositions). Cases, on the other hand, often contain persuasive language as well. In extreme instances, cases may contain *only* persuasive language. In order to properly analyze arguments, we need to distinguish informative language from persuasive language.

Informative language expresses cognitive meaning. As the name implies, cognitive meaning conveys information by reporting facts, describing events, characteristics, and so forth. Informative language is the language of propositions: it asserts truth claims, and is thus appropriate for logical argument. As the name suggests, *persuasive language aims to convince us of something.* It aims to *change* our minds or our feelings or both. Indeed, sometimes our feelings change because our minds change, and sometimes our minds change with our feelings; so persuasive language often appeals to both intellect and emotion.

When persuasive language appeals to reason, it consists chiefly of language conveying cognitive meaning. But when persuasive language appeals to emotions, it has *emotive meaning.* Words with emotive meaning are "loaded" or "charged": they convey positive or negative feelings. *Emotive language, then, is any word or phrase that arouses moods and feelings.*

STUDY HINT

Emotive language is language used for the primary purpose of evoking emotions in order to influence thoughts, actions, or beliefs.

We expect and appreciate emotive language in sermons, inspirational speeches, moments of condolence or affection, times of anger and frustration, and so on. Emotive language only becomes a problem when it interferes with clear thinking or is used to deceive and manipulate. As critical thinkers, we must be especially wary of arguments presented in emotive language. In the hands of a master, emotive language can be so subtle, so effective that we fail to recognize its presence. When this happens, we may believe that we are making rational decisions when in fact we are being emotionally manipulated.

This doesn't at all mean that emotive language has no place in communication. Some of our greatest literature glitters with emotive expression. It's just that in argument, we should minimize—if not avoid—its use altogether. Otherwise we're apt to throw reason to the winds. Also, we should be suspicious of any argument that tries to persuade us primarily on the basis of emotionally loaded words and phrases. If there are sound reasons for a position, we have a right to hear them. Indeed, we should demand them. In their absence, in the presence of emotive language, we should assume that someone is trying to manipulate our emotions to gain adherence to a position. Even well-intentioned arguers can unwittingly use emotive language if they don't pay close attention to a word's meaning. And audiences can be suckered into accepting all sorts of shoddy claims if they lack sensitivity to the implications of certain words and phrases. In large part, then, we can avoid being either a victim or abuser of emotive language by learning some basics about the connotations of words.

Objective Connotation

Meaning sometimes refers to a term's connotation, which can be either objective or subjective. *The objective connotation (or intension) of a term is the collection of properties common to all (and only) those things to which the term refers.* Thus the connotation of *chair* is "a piece of furniture used to sit on." As with definitions, in an objective connotation we ordinarily place the term being defined in a class of similar terms (pieces of furniture) and then show how it differs (used to sit on). Depending on the term, we may need to specify a number of increasingly precise differences. For example, a couch is also a piece of furniture used to sit on, so we may need to specify dimensions or other factors to get an acceptable definition.

Subjective Connotation

There is another kind of connotation that is of crucial importance to our study of language. *The subjective connotations of a term include the moods, images, attitudes, and values commonly or individually associated with it.* For example, we might objectively define the term *law students* as "all those individuals currently studying legal practices and procedures for the purpose of becoming licensed lawyers." But suppose that to you the term *law student* immediately calls to mind aggressive individuals willing to do anything to get into and graduate from law school. Strictly speaking, that's not part of the objective meaning of the term. On the other hand, it is the *associated meaning* you have somehow acquired for or derived from the term.

In addition to objective connotations, then, many words acquire associative meanings. The number *1* has different subjective connotations for most of us than does *13*. *Blue* has come to be associated with emotional depression, *red* with anger or a "hot" temperament.

A young man may rankle at being called *Bobby* and insist on being called *Bob* because to him (and often to others) *Bob* has more adult associations than *Bobby*. We can all think of countless examples of various terms that actually denote the same object but in ways that reflect widely divergent values, moods, and images.

Farcus

by David Waisglass
Gordon Coulthart

11-14
© 1995 Farcus Cartoons/dist. by Universal Press Syndicate   WAISGLASS/COULTHART

**"You're only being suspended — it's not
like being fired or anything."**

Farcus © 1995 Farcus Cartoons. Distributed by Universal Press Syndicate. Reprinted with permission. All rights reserved.

The very same medical procedure can, for example, be "described" as "an abortion," "the termination of pregnancy," "medical intervention in gestation," or "murdering the baby." Obviously, the emotional impact of the different descriptions varies markedly. That is why people with different beliefs speak differently. To one person, the procedure is "seen as" a murder, whereas to another the very same thing is "seen as" the simple termination of a pregnancy.

Consider the importance of subjective connotation to a northern California abortion trial in 1990. The trial set new legal ground by being the first in California to allow anti-abortion protestors to defend trespassing and blocking access to an abortion clinic with what is known as a "necessity defense." A necessity defense argues that breaking the law is demanded by one's firm conviction that a much greater wrong will occur if the law is not broken. In this case, the protestors argued that they had moral and religious obligations to prevent "baby killing." The protestors' necessity defense held that violating laws of trespass was a necessary lesser evil than standing "politely" by while "baby killing" took place.

Their lawyer had run into legal difficulties in other cases for continually, and often against judges' explicit orders, referring to abortionists, their staffs, and prosecutors as "baby killers" and referring to legal abortions as "murders." He also referred to abortionists and those who prosecuted his clients as "murderers" and "accessories to murder." He referred to aborted fetuses as "corpses" and medical instruments as "weapons." The lawyer knew and acknowledged the power of his carefully chosen words. He felt they were necessary to making his case.

What we see here is just one example of the powerful effects of subjective connotations on perception and, often, behavior. The misuse of emotive language occurs when these associations are used to evoke emotions for the purposes of persuasion in a fashion that (1) makes it more difficult to think clearly because emotions are raised before an opportunity for reflection, (2) distorts events in a manner favorable to those attempting to influence us, and (3) deliberately avoids making clear assertions that can be rationally analyzed.

EXERCISE 5-1

1. Discuss possibly differing values and views of reality expressed by each of the following pairs of words, phrases, or names.

   a. my wife / the wife

   b. instructor / professor

   c. gal / woman

   d. Indian / Native American

   e. building / skyscraper

   f. bright / gifted

   g. cheap / inexpensive

   h. chairperson / chairman

   i. want / need

   j. punish / discipline

   k. Hillary Clinton / Hillary Rodham Clinton

   l. Cassius Clay / Muhammad Ali

   m. Jerry Rivers / Geraldo Rivera

2. Do you think any description is ever neutral? Discuss why or why not.

3. Provide and analyze a current example of a controversy or disagreement in which each side insists on using language that favors its values and position.

4. If you are fortunate enough to be studying logic during an election campaign, analyze the worldview and values suggested by the key words and phrases used by candidates.

5. Do you think that people's names affect the way they think of themselves and, subsequently, how they behave? Illustrate.

6. In correcting a small child, an English, Italian, or Greek speaker will often say, "Be good." A French speaker will say, "Be wise"; a Scandinavian, "Be friendly"; a German, "Be in line"; a Hopi Indian, "That is not the

Hopi way." Discuss what difference each directive might make in a child's view of the world. Are values involved? If so, what values? What are the long-range implications of associating behavior with these values?

7. An older logic student once objected to the examples used in the discussion of how language reflects how we see things. She pointed out that when she was a child, "colored" was a term of respect. She added that since that was the way she was taught, using the word "black" in place of "colored" felt awkward to her. She claimed that she was not prejudiced, but that she was going to continue to use "colored." She thought that insisting on changing the language was unfair to her generation. She had similar reservations about "Ms." Analyze her viewpoint. Do you agree or disagree? Explain.

8. Comment on this claim: "Social change cannot occur without a new vocabulary." Do you agree or not? Explain.

9. In his book *In the Spirit of Crazy Horse,* Peter Mathiessen writes that during the 1975 clash between the Federal Bureau of Investigation (FBI) and the American Indian Movement (AIM), the press referred to two or three small Indian cabins and tents as an "armed camp" and "Tent City." AIM, however, referred to the area as a "spiritual encampment," and the men who lived there, previously referred to as "skins," "bros," and "warriors," became known as "People's Defenders." Discuss the value differences reflected in these language differences. Peter Mathiessen, *In the Spirit of Crazy Horse* (New York: Viking Press, 1991), p. 197.

DOUBLESPEAK

When we become overly concerned with persuasion, we not only tend to sacrifice informative language for emotive, but also tend to misuse language in a variety of ways. For convenience, we can group these common misuses of language under the popular heading of *doublespeak.*

In his book of the same title, William Lutz defines *doublespeak* this way:

> Doublespeak is language that pretends to communicate but really doesn't. It is language that makes the bad seem good, the negative appear positive, the unpleasant appear attractive or at least tolerable. Doublespeak is language that avoids or shifts responsibility, language that is at variance with its real or purported meaning. It is language that conceals or prevents thought; rather than extending thought, doublespeak limits it.[8]

---

8. William Lutz, *Doublespeak* (New York: Harper & Row, 1989), p. 1. The discussion that follows is based on this excellent and informative book.

Reprinted with special permission of King Features Syndicate.

Doublespeak is a way of appearing to say one thing, but actually *not* saying it. This is why it's called doublespeak: It is two-faced in the way a lie is two-faced. Doublespeak is all around us, and we spot it regularly. Many instances of doublespeak are funny or merely annoying, as when we say "sanitation engineer" instead of trash collector, or "at this point in time" instead of now.

Sometimes, however, doublespeak is serious and deadly. Lutz cites the 1982 case of St. Mary's Hospital in Minneapolis as an example of deadly doublespeak. An anesthetist turned a wrong knob during a cesarean section delivery and killed the mother and unborn child with a fatal dose of nitrous oxide. The hospital referred to it as a *therapeutic misadventure*. A husband's life forever scarred, a mother and her baby dead, all were swept away as a "therapeutic misadventure." In 1977, the Pentagon referred to the projected deaths of tens of millions of civilians who might happen to live near a site chosen for a neutron-bomb blast as *collateral damage*.

Doublespeak is as old as history. In his account of the Gallic Wars, Julius Caesar characterized the especially brutal and bloody defeat of Gaul as "pacifying" Gaul. When traitors had been executed in ancient Rome, their executions were genteelly announced with the phrase "they have lived." Capital punishment was described as "taking notice of a man in the ancestral manner."

By obscuring the actual events or actions to which it refers, doublespeak appears to say something other than it actually does. It manipulates emotions by obscuring facts. We just don't feel as bad about a "therapeutic misadventure" as we do about malpractice or incompetence. By presenting misleading cognitive content, doublespeak tricks us into drawing incorrect conclusions. Our reasoning cannot be cogent if it is based on false, unclear, or misleading premises.

Given the proliferation of doublespeak in today's world, we need to learn to spot it and to determine what's really being said (and done) before we can make informed decisions. A good way to begin this sensitization is to become familiar with doublespeak's various guises. Here is a handful.

Euphemism as Doublespeak

A euphemism is an inoffensive or positive word or phrase used to avoid facing or acknowledging a harsh, unpleasant, or distasteful reality. Examples include *passing away* for *dying*, or *fibbing* for *lying*.

Sometimes euphemisms are used in a benign, sociable way to avoid hurting others' feelings, or as a matter of respect or delicacy. In such cases, euphemisms are not meant to deceive, but to comfort, or at least to minimize hurt. This is why we might say, "I am so sorry at your loss," instead of, "Too bad your father died." We and the bereaved both certainly know that someone has died. The intention here is compassionate, not deceptive or manipulative. Similarly, when we excuse ourselves to use the *bathroom* or *restroom*, when no bathing or resting facilities are present or desired, we are not trying to deceive others about our purpose, but to politely explain a momentary absence. We should not consider such uses of euphemism as doublespeak, even though they do obscure their subject.

We determine the presence of doublespeak much like we do that of argument—by intention and context. When the intent of a word, phrase, or passage is to evade responsibility, deceive, or manipulate, it is doublespeak. For example, in 1977, the Pentagon tried to get funding for a neutron bomb attached to a bill before Congress by referring to the bomb as a "radiation enhancement device." This artfully crafted euphemism is clearly doublespeak.

Even the most well-intentioned uses of euphemism require caution, for the purpose of any euphemism is to obscure, not to reveal. Reality gets buried under euphemism; it's difficult to see. Indeed, an excessive use of euphemistic language can lead to a failure to act and think responsibly. Sometimes reality is harsh. It remains harsh whether we like it or not.

For instance, refusing to talk or think about sex in clear terms can lead to unhappiness and irresponsibility. Describing infidelity as a "love affair" glosses over the reality of lies and deception. Equating sexual intercourse with *making love* glosses over the impersonal quality of a one-night sexual encounter and makes it seem like something it is not. It might be interesting to speculate on what—if any—effect clear speaking would have on our current epidemic of unwanted teen pregnancies, sexually transmitted disease, and high abortion rates. *Spending the night* or *sleeping with* someone distorts not only the actual purposes of sexual encounters, but the emotions and consequences that purely sexual relationships and encounters often generate. Some psychologists even advocate

"Look, I'd rather be free, too, but at least we're not in a zoo anymore."

Drawing by Mankoff; © 1993 The New Yorker Magazine, Inc.

using the phrase "falling" or "being in *lust*" as a more honest substitute for "falling" or "being in *love*," when the primary relationship is sexual.

STUDY HINT

The *primary* purpose of euphemism is to gloss over something that troubles us because we view it as unpleasant or threatening.
   We should be wary of euphemisms in discussing important matters, because their function is to conceal rather than to reveal.

   Euphemisms used in advertising are best treated as doublespeak, since with rare exceptions, the chief purpose of advertising is not informative, but persuasive; not revealing, but concealing and altering.
   Consider these examples: Ads for laxatives often avoid the offensive *constipation* for the more polite *irregularity*. ("When irregularity strikes, reach for. . . .") Even tampon advertisements are scrupulous in avoiding their reason for existence: menstruation. Instead, their makers talk in hushed terms of "that time of

© Grimmy Inc., Distributed by Tribune Media Services. Reprinted with permission.

the month"; their appeals rely more often on fear and embarrassment than on hygiene. Hence, the main problem with euphemism in argument is that when we feel that a word is offensive, we are inclined to talk around the word and what it represents. In doing this, we permit arguments to assume all kinds of erroneous appeals. Consider this:

> Why not do something about your problem breath before you don't even have a best friend who wouldn't tell you about it? Use FRESH—the mouthwash for those who want to keep their best friends and *make* a lot more.

Can you spot the euphemism in this ad? It's *problem breath*. Precisely what does this phrase mean? Since it doesn't say "temporary bad breath," we can't assume that the ad refers to the scent that onions, garlic, and the like leave in our mouths. *Problem breath* seems to mean a chronic, persistent foulness of breath that resists normal hygienic practices such as tooth brushing. But is such a problem a breath problem? More likely the problem originates in the esophagus or stomach and signals a far more serious condition than the euphemism *problem breath* would indicate. We are led to make mistaken assumptions about the origin of the problem and thus to another mistaken assumption—that the advertised product can cure it.

EXERCISE 5-2 *

Give the noneuphemistic, but polite (not slang), equivalent of the following expressions:

1. to pass away

2. to go to the bathroom

3. make love

4. in a family way

5. senior citizen

6. powder room

7. to terminate an employee

8. to terminate with extreme prejudice

9. the dearly departed

10. a woman's time of the month

11. to lay off an employee

12. not our best employee

13. financial difficulties

14. roommates

15. to appropriate

16. to subdue a suspect

17. to stretch the truth

18. wealthy

19. not what I expected

20. being a little slow

EXERCISE 5-3

Find five or more advertisements that capitalize on euphemisms in their appeals. Translate the euphemistic language into straightforward language. Do the ads lose their appeal? Discuss why or why not.

Jargon as Doublespeak

Jargon is the specialized, technical language of a trade, profession, or membership, such as those of doctors, lawyers, educators, auto mechanics, firefighters, police officers, and so on.

Properly used, jargon allows members of a group to communicate rapidly and precisely. For example, when logicians speak of a valid argument, the single word *valid* tells us that the argument is deductive, that its premises entail the conclusion with logical certainty, and that nothing has been said about the truth of the premises. Learning the technical meaning of that one word allows us to communicate efficiently in a kind of precise shorthand. Weight lifters, chefs, plumbers, data processors, and so on, enjoy similar precision and efficiency when they employ their group's jargon. The ability to use jargon not only can enhance our understanding, it may be a condition of full membership in a specific group. We become professional when we learn to employ professional language.

But jargon, like euphemism, can be as misused as doublespeak. When technical language is used outside of the group, it no longer communicates clearly; it tends to obscure. How helpful would it be to announce to the nonlogician members of your family, "That's a fallacious argument because it commits the post hoc fallacy?" Not very, if they've never heard of post hoc. One reason people use jargon outside of the group is to impress nonexperts. It makes us—so we think—appear intelligent, superior; it shows that we know more than they do. This last assumption is flawed, for we may only know more terms than they do. Mom may be a better critical thinker than her logician daughter even though she hasn't the jargon to express herself like a trained logician.

Jargon used before a nontechnical audience should be treated as doublespeak because jargon's proper use is always within a specialized group, or to train people to become members of the group. Jargon as doublespeak is designed to make the simple appear complex, or the merely ordinary appear to be special.

Here's an example of jargon as doublespeak: On May 9, 1978, a plane crashed while trying to land in Pensacola, Florida. Three of the 52 passengers were killed. The airline, National Airlines, made an after-tax profit of $1.7 million that year from the insurance settlement following the accident. Although this resulted in a per-share dividend of $.18 for stockholders, the company had to deal with a problem: explaining the $1.7 million in its legally mandated annual report to stockholders—without revealing that one of its planes crashed. The company solved its problem by using legal jargon in a report delivered to a general audience.

In law, the loss of property through theft, accident, or condemnation is called "involuntary conversion." The annual report accounted for the $1.7 million as the result of involuntary conversion. The use of that phrase was not intended to communicate clearly, but to conceal from the vast majority of stockholders what really happened. Officials could technically claim to have told the truth; however, their use of a phrase they could reasonably expect most of their audience not to understand is doublespeak. "Involuntary conversion" lacks the emotional punch and clarity of "fatal plane crash."

Remember that language consists not just of words, meanings, and structural rules. It also consists of context. Using precise terms out of context changes them to imprecise terms. Doublespeakers often add insult to injury by hiding behind a narrowly interpreted sense of what's being said. Some people refer to this trait as being "cash-register honest." Cash-register honesty involves making a show of telling small truths such as "Excuse me, clerk, but you've given me a quarter too much change," while lying or deceiving on a larger scale (say, shoplifting a carton of cigarettes). Doublespeakers like National Airlines can always claim to have told the exact, precise, literal truth. But by doing so in unexpected ways, or out of context, they mislead most of their audience.

In fact, if we had to choose one word to characterize jargon as doublespeak, it would be *vague*. To be vague is to be imprecise. A word is vague when its meaning is obscure and blurred, when it lacks enough specificity to allow us to determine its truth value. This usually results when the connection between the word and what it's supposed to stand for is uncertain.

STUDY HINT

The misuse of jargon occurs when technical terms are used outside of the field to which they belong and/or for purposes of impressing without clarifying.

There is a proper and valuable use of jargon. Indeed, most special fields require a precisely defined jargon for purposes of quick, accurate communication. However, terms that may be clear and precise in one context may be unclear and misleading in another.

Example: We have already learned some helpful logical jargon: valid, cogent, and the like.

Maybe at times we'd rather not be understood; many persons in public life seem to be so predisposed. But most of us probably want to be understood most of the time. And we'd like to be understood, not *mis*understood. When we use language in such a way that it can mean more than one thing, we court misunderstanding. In fact, careless language leads to specific errors in argument. These we'll consider in the next chapters. However, it's fitting here to take a brief look at three forms of the misuse of jargon that can hinder clear thinking—indeed, that are often deliberately used for just that purpose.

Buzzwords as Doublespeak

The expression *buzzwords* has been attributed to Edmund G. "Jerry" Brown, Jr., a former governor of California. Brown was referring to the use of words that, although vague, ambiguous, and often devoid of content in a particular context, have a dynamic, exciting "feel" to them. They generate a kind of "buzz," but mean nothing.

Buzzwords are vague words and phrases that create an impression of action, dynamism, and vitality but that are devoid of content, that is, convey no meaning. Examples include the *misuse* of expressions such as *exciting concept, meaningful interchange, new coalition,* and *moral majority.* The use of such terms does not necessarily imply the presence of buzzwords. We must always take context and intention into account. Both are important.

Terms that create a "buzz" one season may be dated the next. Buzzwords must be constantly changed: They need to be perceived as "fresh" and "exciting"—two still overused buzzwords.

When a talk show host on a stale TV show says, "We have an exciting show for you folks tonight," *exciting* is probably a buzzword. In political circles, the vague expression *tax reform* has been used as a buzzword. Terms like *democracy, wonderful, marvelous, beautiful,* even *God,* are prime candidates for buzzwords.

Buzzwords make us feel good; they make us feel alert, dynamic, part of something exciting and vibrant, without actually saying much at all. In other words, they substitute exciting feelings for meaningful communication.

Thomas Sowell, a Fellow of Stanford University's Hoover Institute and a news columnist, goes so far as to say, "This may go down in history as the era when buzzwords replaced thinking. Like other organs that shrink from lack of use, the human brain may get smaller and smaller with the passing of generations."[9] Sowell cites *diversity* as an example of an emerging buzzword. He notes that in its decision in the case of Metro Broadcasting versus FCC, the United States Supreme Court used the term *diversity* 21 times (not counting its variants *diverse* and *diversification*). Sowell points out that none of the uses was defined or supported with evidence of any sort. Sowell adds that colleges no longer have racial "quotas" to meet, instead they must have "diversity." Yet we are never exactly sure what *diversity* means—only that it sounds good to some people.

And as is true in so many cases of doublespeak, buzzwords are used to encourage us to feel that the speaker agrees with us in a vague way so that he or she can avoid making any specific commitment. The advantages of buzzwords for those who use them are that exciting language can substitute for cogent reasoning, and the less specific a claim, the more difficult it is to criticize—not because it is well supported but because there is nothing there to analyze. Buzzwords are commonly used to obscure the fact that little is actually being done. They sell the promise of action.

Puffery as Doublespeak

Puffery is an old term. One of the meanings of *puff* is "to inflate with air or pride." *Puffery is the use of obscure, technical, or complex words and grammar for the purpose of inflating the content of a claim.* In other words, puffery is a snow job.

For example, some academic administrators now refer to students as "educational consumers." This sounds more impressive than the common word *students*. It also tells us something about how these administrators view students, education, and their role in it.

One tip-off to puffery is that two words are used when one will do, three are even better, and so on. Best of all, the words should be impressive. (No, the correct use of jargon by your professors is not puffery—though professors have been known to succumb to the tendency to impress and dazzle their students with pretentious language. When the purpose is to impress rather than to communicate clearly puffery is present—even among professors.)

In a brochure for a $29.95 "Limited Edition" pocket watch, we find this: "Designed in the traditional style of the finely crafted pocket watches carried by people of taste and distinction for centuries, each of these true collector's items

---

9. Thomas Sowell, "Today's brainless buzzwords don't say what they really mean," *Redding Record Searchlight*, July 29, 1990.

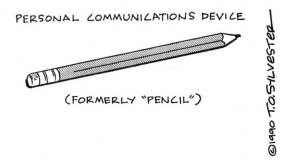

PERSONAL COMMUNICATIONS DEVICE

(FORMERLY "PENCIL")

©1990 T.O.SYLVESTER

is also a fine quartz-accurate chronometer. . . ." What does it mean to say "designed in the traditional style of finely crafted pocket watches"? Does it mean that these watches are themselves finely crafted? It *might*—but then again, it might not. This "might or might not" is the charm of vagueness (assuming your wish is to obscure, not to reveal). We are, it seems, meant to *assume* that this is a finely crafted watch.

Interestingly enough, however, in the three enclosures that accompany this colorful brochure, not one single word is mentioned about any warranty for the watch. Is that perhaps a hint? What exactly is it to "design" something "in the traditional style of finely crafted pocket watches"? Does "design" mean "thought out," crafted by watchmakers, manufactured? And what is "quartz-accurate"? Is it the same thing as highly accurate? It *might be* (there's that vagueness again)— but it might not be. Aren't many of those inexpensive watches given away with laundry detergent and magazine subscriptions built around a "quartz-accurate" microchip? And, of course, "chronometer" is just a pretentious word for watch in this case. In other words, the brochure never really says that this *is* a fine watch at all!

EXERCISE 5-4

A. Explain what's really meant by these puffed up job titles.

1. Hallmark Greeting Cards makes "social expression products."

2. auto dismantlers and recyclers

3. North American Van Lines is now North American Relocation Services.

4. executive snack route consultants

5. nail technicians

6. From a supermarket advertisement: "part-time career associate scanning professionals"

B. Various government agencies employ code names for their operations. For example, U.S. efforts to force Iraq out of Kuwait were dubbed Operation Desert Storm, and the removal of Panamanian strongman

Manuel Norrieaga was labeled Operation Just Cause. Associated Press writer Ernest Sandler reports that Eric Berryman, a spokesman for the Immigration and Naturalization Service (INS), claimed that "There isn't a real logic to this. [The code name] could be anything. It could be your Aunt Matilda. It could be 'x, y, z.'" See if you agree with Berryman as you discuss the connotations and implications of these examples of actual code names:

CODENAME	ACTIVITY
Operation Gatekeeper	INS efforts to control illegal immigration at the California border
Operation Safeguard	INS efforts to control illegal immigration at the Arizona border
Operation Hold-the-Line	INS efforts to control illegal immigration at the Texas border
Operation Hot Chips	U.S. Customs campaign against illegally exported technology
Operation Ironhorse	INS efforts to control illegal immigrants traveling by train
Operation Buck Stop	Combined efforts to control smuggled currency

Source: *Redding Record Searchlight*, April 23, 1995

Gobbledygook

It is not always easy or necessary—or possible—to distinguish precisely among the various kinds of doublespeak. Indeed, there are probably more categories than we can imagine. But it helps to recognize the various sources from which doublespeak draws. As noted, jargon can be used as puffery. So can euphemism, as when *toilet paper* becomes *toilet tissue,* or when Chrysler euphemistically puffs up the fact that it's firing 5,000 workers by saying that it is initiating *a career alternative enhancement program.* When the U.S. Army, Navy, Air Force, and Marines invaded Grenada in 1983, they were called the Caribbean Peace Keeping Forces, clearly euphemistic puffery. Of course, the military action wasn't an invasion, anyway, it was a "predawn vertical insertion." (No kidding.)[10]

A kind of catchall doublespeak combines elements of euphemism, jargon, buzzwords, and puffery, and goes by Stuart Chase's delightful name *gobbledygook. Gobbledygook (or bureaucratese) is a way of attempting to overwhelm an audience with sheer volume and complexity of words and language.*

---

10. Lutz, *Doublespeak,* p. 7.

In gobbledygook, the bigger the words and longer the sentences are, the better. During the 1988 presidential campaign, then-candidate Senator Dan Quayle explained the need for a strategic defense initiative this way:

> Why wouldn't an enhanced deterrent, a more stable peace, a better prospect to denying the ones who enter conflict in the first place to have a reduction of offensive systems and an introduction to defensive capability? I believe this is the route the country will eventually go.[11]

In 1986, during the investigation of the *Challenger* space disaster, the associate administrator of NASA was asked if the performance of the space shuttle had been holding its own or improving with each launch. He answered in gobbledygook:

> I think our performance in terms of liftoff performance and in terms of orbital performance, we knew more about the envelope we were operating under, and we have been pretty accurately staying in that. And so I would say that the performance has not by design drastically improved. I think we have been able to characterize the performance more as a function of our launch experience as opposed to it improving as a function of time.[12]

Lutz points out that passages such as the above may appear to be jargon, but are in fact gobbledygook laced with jargon. As we'll see in the next chapter, when deception or manipulative persuasion, rather than communication and demonstration, are the arguer's primary intention, we often encounter more than one source of confusion. It's as if our potential deceivers throw in anything that might trick us. Thus, do not be discouraged if you seem to spot more than one form of doublespeak in a passage, or if a passage may be both, say, euphemism and puffery.

Since all forms of doublespeak have the same purpose—to obscure, bury, deceive, evade responsibility, and impress—they will often overlap. It is worth making an effort to distinguish among forms of doublespeak at this stage of your studies in order to sharpen your critical thinking skills. The more precise you can be in analyzing obscuring misuses of language, the better protected you will be.

EXERCISE 5-5 *

Analyze the following examples of doublespeak. Indicate, *if possible,* whether these are euphemisms, jargon, buzzwords, puffery, or gobbledygook (or a combination). Try to give a clear restatement of what each most likely means. In

---

11. Lutz, *Doublespeak,* p. 5.

12. Lutz, *Doublespeak,* pp. 5–6.

cases of pure gobbledygook this may not be possible. Don't think so much in terms of giving *the* right answer as in providing a clear, cogent explanation for your answers and interpretation. Note: these are all real-life examples.

1. P. W. Botha, Premier of South Africa, denied that South Africa violated a sovereignty agreement with neighboring Mozambique, saying that South Africa's actions were "technical violations."

2. Augusto Pinochet, dictator of Chile, imposed stricter control on Chileans saying, "It is precisely in order to safeguard democracy that today more than ever it is necessary to be inflexible."

3. Dear Stepmother: There must be a special place in heaven reserved for people like you, but I hope you don't have to wait too long for your reward. Bless you for your generous, understanding heart. (From Dear Abby, November 20, 1981)

4. Surgeons talk about "skin incursions."

5. Doctors jokingly refer to doing a "wallet biopsy."

6. "We've overdone teaching the academics and ignored the need for vocational training. I think the universities have to get more into the practical aspects of teaching graduates how to do something while they are in attendance, so that when they leave, they already have done what they are hoping to do for the rest of their lives. I call it an action oriented curriculum." (Jerry Falwell, quoted in *Nutshell*, Fall 1981, p. 38)

7. In 1972, the Ford Motor Company was required to recall 423,000 Torino's and Mercury Montego's for what Ford, in a letter to dealers and owners, called "mechanical deficiencies," which could cause rear axle bearings to "deteriorate." Ford added, "Continued driving with a failed bearing could result in disengagement of the axle shaft and adversely affect vehicle control."

8. "In other words, feediness is the shared information between toputness, where toputness is at a time just prior to inputness." (From a 1966 U.S. Office of Education research report)

9. "I will not stand by and see those of you dependent on Social Security deprived of the benefits you've worked so hard to earn. You will continue to receive your checks in the full amount due." (President Ronald Reagan, July 27, 1981)

10. Airlines have added a new category of flight, *direct;* they do not always inform passengers that *direct* does not mean "nonstop." An airline lawyer has denied that the airlines are misleading passengers, asserting, "It's just a question of semantics."

AMBIGUITY AND ARGUMENT

Obscurity (intentional or otherwise) isn't the only problem that haunts sloppy language. Ambiguity also poses problems for arguments. Obscure or *vague* language differs from *ambiguous* language.

Suppose, for example, someone says, "Mike is a wealthy man." Although we know what is meant, we do not know exactly how much money or property Mike has because the term "wealthy" is *vague. A claim is obscured when vague terms are used to substantiate it, when it lacks specificity sufficient to verify it.* We cannot determine the truth value of claims until any vague terms they may contain are clarified. Relative terms can be vague if used out of context: "She's happier now." Terms that refer to degrees often need clarification. We cannot evaluate an argument until we know what its premises and conclusion assert; we must therefore attempt to clarify any vague claims before proceeding with our analysis.

Ambiguity is a special form of language misuse that results in flawed and inadequate arguments. *A term is ambiguous if it has more than one possible meaning in a given context.* We should not confuse ambiguity with vagueness. The "front of the room," for example, is vague but it is not ambiguous. It has only one meaning, even though the demarcation of the area denoted by "front of the room" may be unspecified. Let's distinguish a case of ambiguity for contrast.

"John and Mary dove into the pool where he kissed her on the bottom." The humor in this statement in part rests on its ambiguous nature. It has two possible meanings, but it is still far from clear. It may be telling us that John and Mary smooched underwater—or it may have an "X-rated" meaning. That's why people usually laugh or groan on hearing it. Since two meanings are possible, this statement is ambiguous. In most cases, ambiguity is a result of either unclear reference ("If I told you that you had a beautiful body would you hold it against me?"), or faulty grammatical construction (as in the John and Mary example).

Remember, in order to evaluate an argument we must know what its premises and conclusion assert. Ambiguous claims make this impossible—they have no

© Grimmy Inc., Distributed by Tribune Media Services. Reprinted with permission.

single, obvious meaning. Let's take a look at some forms of ambiguity that result in commonplace errors of reasoning caused by careless language usage.

QUESTIONABLE PREMISES AND AMBIGUITY

Sometimes arguments appear to be cogent when they are not. When we mistake a flawed argument for a cogent one, we may have succumbed to a *fallacy*. Generally speaking, *a fallacy is an error in reasoning.*

Informal fallacies are commonplace errors in reasoning that result from careless language usage or inattention to subject matter. Informal fallacies can be especially persuasive because they often "feel" as if they are cogent.

Although there is no universally agreed-upon classification of informal fallacies, one commonly used classification is that of *questionable premises. A premise is questionable when it is used to establish the truth of a problematic claim before its own truth value has been clearly and independently established.* Any premise whose truth value has not been established will fail to meet the reasonableness criterion for cogency. Vague and ambiguous premises are always questionable because their multiple possible meanings prevent us from knowing *which one precise meaning* the arguer intends.

Questionable premises always result when premises are framed in ambiguous, vague, or poorly constructed language. Two interesting sources of questionable premises are equivocation and amphiboly.

Equivocation

When we confuse the separate meanings of a word, using it in varying senses in the same context, we are using the word *equivocally.* For example, the word *laws* may refer to human-made laws, which prescribe how people should behave. It may also refer to scientific laws, which describe how things in the physical universe operate. When we confuse the varying meanings of *laws,* using it in both senses within the same context, we are using the word equivocally.

Equivocation occurs when the same word or phrase is used to mean more than one thing in a single context, or when a word or phrase is used in an odd, unexpected way without clarifying its unusual meaning. When an equivocation occurs in an argument, the argument will contain at least one questionable premise. Consider this example:

> **All laws have a lawmaker.**
> **The laws of gravitation and motion are laws.**
> _____
> **Therefore, the laws of gravitation and motion have a lawmaker.**

This argument contains an equivocation. For the first premise to be true, *laws* must be intended as human-made laws. But *laws* in the second premise refers to scientific laws. Human-made laws are prescriptive: They prescribe proper human behavior. Scientific laws are descriptive: They report or describe how things function, but they do not say how things *ought to* function. So *laws* is being used in two separate senses within the context of one argument. That's why we can say this argument contains equivocation.

Equivocations often arise in the use of relative terms. A relative term is one in which meaning depends on some point of reference. Words such as *small, big, bright, tasty,* and *smooth* are relative terms. As noted earlier, relative terms used out of context are vague. Their meanings can vary according to what they're describing. Here's a humorous argument that equivocates on the relative term small:

> Since a buffalo is an animal, a small buffalo must be a small animal.

Don't buy one for a house pet. What "small" means relative to an animal is hardly what it means relative to a buffalo.

Beware of equivocation in advertisements. For example, a cigarette manufacturer tries to persuade you to smoke a brand because "It's only natural." What does "natural" mean here? That the cigarette contains "natural" ingredients? That everyone is smoking this cigarette? That smoking this cigarette is as "natural," say, as eating or sex?

Often such ambiguity is intentional. An ad for an MG sports car, for example, once showed a young couple tightly fitted into a two-seat sports car. The ad read, "MG. Big enough for two. Exciting enough to breed a generation of sports car enthusiasts." The appeal intentionally equivocates on the word *breed,* mixing sexual and nonsexual meaning. Clever and amusing, and probably harmless enough, if you take "safety measures."

But sometimes intentional equivocations can really mislead. Suppose you pass a newspaper vending machine and see a headline that reads "PRESIDENT TALKS OF WAR." You insert your quarter and quickly start scanning the paper for news about some international conflict you inferred the nation was about to get embroiled in. It turns out that the "war" is on poverty or disease or slums. "Duped again," you think, discarding the paper, and with it what could be information on an important issue, though not as sensational as "blood and guts." The equivocation has led you to an erroneous conclusion and also to a subsequent course of action.

Amphiboly

Sometimes a statement is ambiguous because its very structure is flawed. *An amphiboly is a statement with more than one meaning because of ambiguous, incomplete, or disorganized grammatical construction.* "Leslie told her mother she was a fool." Who's the fool? Did Leslie tell her mother that her mother was a fool? Or did she tell her mother that she (Leslie) was a fool? Both meanings are possible because of the faulty structure of this sentence. To dissolve the ambiguity, we must do more than change a word or expression, as is the case with equivocation. We must actually restate the sentence.

THE FAR SIDE   By GARY LARSON

"Fuel ... check. Lights ... check. Oil pressure ...
check. We've got clearance. OK, Jack—let's get
this baby off the ground."

The Far Side © 1990 Farworks, Inc. Used by permission of Universal Press Syndicate. All rights reserved.

In the mid-1970s, one of Jimmy Carter's campaign slogans was "Carter—a leader for a change." Here, the amphiboly was deliberate. Its purpose was to catch our attention, to make us chuckle, and ultimately, to encourage us to think about and vote for Carter. The possible desired meanings included these: "Carter—a leader who will bring about change" or "Carter—it's about time we elected a leader" or "Let's change leaders—elect Carter." An unexpected and humorous meaning, which no doubt disconcerted Carter's campaign advisors, was something to this effect: "Carter's finally acting like a leader." That's the problem with amphibolies; we can't always anticipate the ways others will interpret them. Consequently, any argument that contains an amphibolous premise will be fallacious because it contains a questionable premise.

It's tempting to confuse equivocation and amphiboly. In most cases, equivocation does not involve the major grammatical confusion found in amphiboly. In an *equivocation,* the ambiguity is caused by an unexpected or unusual meaning being given to a *particular word* or *phrase.* What can, and does, sometimes happen is that an amphibolous construction can confuse us so that we do not know which meaning to apply to a term or which terms to stress. *The rule of thumb is that if the only way to avoid the ambiguity is to restate the entire sentence, it is an amphiboly.* That is, if we have to add punctuation, move entire phrases or

Reprinted with special permission of King Features Syndicate.

clauses around, add words, or otherwise perform "major surgery" to clarify a passage's meaning, it is an amphiboly.

The differences between equivocation and amphiboly are easier to identify if we remember that although they are both ambiguous, we distinguish between them based on the *source of ambiguity*.

STUDY HINT

In cases of equivocation, the substitution of a word or phrase dissolves the ambiguity.

As a general rule, no modification of grammar or syntax is necessary for equivocation. If such modifications are necessary, the ambiguity is an amphiboly.

Note: Ambiguity caused by misuse or improper placement of pronouns (he, she, it, they) should be treated as amphiboly, not equivocation.

EXERCISE 5-6

All of the following contain ambiguous language. Identify the source of ambiguity (equivocation or amphiboly) as specifically as possible. Restate in unambiguous fashion (if there is enough context). Occasionally, more than one reasonable diagnosis is possible. If so, explain why.

1. Abraham Lincoln wrote the Gettysburg Address while riding on a train on the back of an envelope.

2. When I saw I could not avoid a collision, I stepped on the gas and crashed into the other car.

3. And he went out from Pharaoh in hot anger. (Exodus 11:8 RSV)

4. The problem with coed swimming is that the boys often outstrip the girls.

5. Mr. Richard Lowry visited the class yesterday and lectured on destructive pests. A large number were present.

6. Zimbabwe Rhodesian guerrilla leaders demanded Monday that a Commonwealth peacekeeping force of several thousand men—one with teeth—be sent to enforce a cease-fire in the war against their forces. (Cited by Richard Lederer in *Fractured English*)

7. LAWYER: Tell us, doctor, how many autopsies have you performed on dead people.
DOCTOR: All my autopsies have been on dead people.

8. No wonder nobody comes here—it's too crowded. (Yogi Berra)

9. Jimmy Pea pleaded not guilty, not guilty.

10. In Rome they love artichokes more than anything else.

11. "Study predicts number of elderly to explode in 50 years." (Newspaper headline)

12. "Shasta County Office of Education is accepting applications for Special Education Teachers, 1 severely handicapped, & 1 learning handicapped . . . to start 12-1-92." (Classified ad in the *Redding Record Searchlight*, November 20, 1992)

13. "The World's Largest Van For Its Size!" (Ad slogan for Volkswagen Eurovan)

14. "Anderson was . . . abducted by terrorists in March 1985. . . . He was released last year by his captors, and has written a book, "Den of Lions," about his ordeal with his new wife, Madelaine." (Quoted in *New Yorker*, August 23, 1993)

15. Commenting on the controversy surrounding nude bowling, a spokeswoman for the bowlers said that her critics "had their minds in the gutter."

Composition

The fallacy of composition is an argument that erroneously attributes characteristics of the parts of a whole to the whole itself. "Since I can lift up each individual part of my car," I claim, "I can therefore lift up the whole car." Of course, I can't. The mistake is in assuming that a property of parts of a whole is also a property of the whole itself. Again, someone might argue. "Because each chapter of the book is an artistic masterpiece, the book itself must be a masterpiece." Not necessarily; taken as a whole, the book may be far less than an artistic masterpiece, even though each of its chapters is brilliant. Simply because each member of a choir sings well doesn't mean that the choir as a unit will sing well.

THE BORN LOSER reprinted by permission of Newspaper Enterprise Association, Inc.

Division

The fallacy of division is the reverse of the fallacy of composition. *The fallacy of division is an argument that erroneously attributes to the parts of the whole the characteristics of the whole itself.* Thus, "The United States is a rich nation. Therefore, every American is rich." Scratching around for movie money, you'd not likely swallow that argument. The mistake, of course, is in assuming that a property of the whole unit is also a property of any part of the unit. In fact, what is true of the whole is not necessarily true of its parts any more than what is true of the parts is true of the whole. Because a choir is ready for a performance doesn't mean that "Perfect Pitch" Petersen, a member of the choir, is also ready.

STUDY HINT

In composition, the conclusion is about the whole and the premises are about its parts.

In division, the conclusion is about the parts (or a part) and the premises are about the whole.

The quickest way to distinguish composition from division is by examining the conclusion. If it is about the *whole*, the fallacy is *composition*. If the conclusion is about a *part*, the fallacy is *division*.

SUMMARY

This chapter dealt with the connection between logic and language. We learned how closely connected language is to what we think and perceive. We learned how language reflects thought and influences experience. We distinguished between objective and subjective connotation. Subjective connotations are especially powerful and can persuade without argument.

Next we turned to a common misuse of language known as doublespeak. Doublespeak is a widespread hindrance to clear thinking, which deliberately distorts, inflates, and obscures the truth to create some advantage for its user. By concealing more than it reveals, doublespeak makes determining truth difficult or impossible. We studied five of its most common sources (though there are many more):

1. A euphemism is an inoffensive or positive word or phrase used to avoid facing or acknowledging a harsh, unpleasant, or distasteful reality. Examples include "passing away" for dying, or "fibbing" for lying.

2. Jargon is specialized, technical language of a trade, profession, or membership, such as that of doctors, lawyers, educators, auto mechanics, firefighters, police officers, and so on.

3. Buzzwords are vague words and phrases that create an impression of action, dynamism, and vitality but that are devoid of content (i.e., they mean nothing). Examples include "exciting," "tax reform," "democracy," and "marvelous."

4. Puffery is the use of obscure, technical, or complex words and grammar for the purpose of inflating the content of a claim. For example, referring to students as "educational consumers."

5. Gobbledygook (or bureaucratese) is a catchall term for language used to overwhelm an audience with sheer number and complexity of words and grammar. In gobbledygook, the bigger the words and longer the sentences are, the better.

We've seen how careless use of language can pose serious problems of both communication and reasoning. As we continue our study of logic, we will also see how fallacies usually "travel in packs." That is, often, one ambiguity will accompany others, or one error in reasoning will accompany others. It is important to us as clear thinkers that we insist on sufficient clarity and precision to make clear analyses of the cases that we consider. We've learned that failure to do so may result in a fallacy of questionable premise, an argument containing a premise that fails to meet the reasonableness criterion for cogency. With effort and experience, we find ourselves "fine-tuned" for spotting the following fallacies of questionable premise, which result from careless, incorrect, and vague language use:

1. *Equivocation:* An argument that confuses the varying meanings of a word or phrase.
   Example: Good steaks are rare these days, so don't order yours well done.

2. *Amphiboly:* A statement with more than one meaning because of ambiguous, incomplete, or disorganized grammatical construction.
   Example: I love candy more than you.

3. *Composition:* An argument that attributes to a whole characteristics of the parts.
   Example: Since I can lift up each individual part of my car, I can lift up the whole car.

4. *Division:* An argument that attributes to the parts of a whole the characteristics of the whole itself.
   Example: The United States is a rich nation. Therefore, every American is rich.

Summary Exercises

1. Read the labels on a variety of products. How clear are they? Are the technical terms helpful? Try to find the meanings of some of the technical terms printed on the labels. How does knowing what they really mean affect your attitudes toward these products?

2. What, if any, conclusions can you draw about our culture from the fact that most of our common euphemisms concern sex, death, and bodily functions?

3. Collect your own real-life examples of doublespeak and share them with your logic class.

4. Logicians sometimes illustrate how subjective connotations can alter our perceptions of the same thing, event, or characteristic, with a humorous declension of terms along this pattern: "He is pig-headed, you are obstinate, I am firm." "She is cowardly, you are cautious, I am smart." Construct a few of your own.

5. Discuss the ramifications of referring to your teachers by first name only, last name only, Mr., Mrs., Ms., or a title such as Professor or Doctor. Will it make any difference to a class? Explain why or why not.

6. What's the best way to answer someone who dismisses a clash over terms such as *black, gay, Ms.,* and so on, as "only a matter of semantics"? Explain.

7. Doublespeak is found in many (most?) advertisements and political speeches. Compile a list of five or six examples and analyze them.

8. Comedians love "word play." Have some fun and reinforce what you've learned about language at the same time by identifying five or six jokes that involve concepts covered in this chapter. Here's a shopworn starter: "Take my husband. Please."

ADDITIONAL EXERCISES*

A. Analyze the following real-life examples for the presence of doublespeak. When possible indicate whether they are euphemisms, jargon, buzzwords, puffery, or gobbledygook (or a combination). Try to give a clear restatement of what they most likely mean. In cases of pure gobbledygook this may not be possible. Explain your answers.

1. From a sign: "Open 24 hours a day. Hours: 9 AM to Midnight, Sundays 12 to 6."

2. Nursing II "focuses on the care of clients throughout the life cycle who have basic alterations in health status." (Course description from Rutgers University)

3. Chemical dependency

4. In 1982, Supreme Court Justice William Rehnquist experienced severe withdrawal symptoms when the dosage of his sleeping medication was cut back. His doctor said that the drug had "established an interrelationship with the body, such that if the drug is removed precipitously, there is a reaction."

5. "When taken as directed, the tablets offer virtually 100% protection. . . ." (From Eli Lilly pamphlet, accompanying birth control pills)

6. Ford once advertised their LTDs with the slogan "Ford LTD— 700% quieter."

7. Inventory shrinkage

8. "Notice to consumer: The equipment described within this Service Guide may or may not be identified as either standard or optional." (From *1986 Taurus/Sable Do-It-Yourself Service Guide*)

9. When he was running for president, Nelson Rockefeller was asked to explain his position on the Vietnam War. He replied: "My position on Vietnam is very simple. And I feel this way. I haven't spoken on it because I haven't felt there was any major contribution that I had to make at the time. I think that our concepts as a nation and that our actions have not kept pace with the changing conditions. And therefore our actions are not completely relevant today to the realities of the magnitude and the complexity of the problems that we face in this conflict."

   Asked what that meant, Rockefeller responded: "Just what I said."

10. "This notice assures you that the second (corrected) tax statement we sent to you is accurate. . . . The original statement we sent to you understated your beginning balance of retirement contributions.

The second statement corrects this error. . . . We are sending this notice to all annuitants who received accurate corrected copies because some annuitants were sent corrected copies by mistake." (Letter to certain taxpayers from U.S. Civil Service Commission)

11. **"AN OPEN LETTER TO SEARS CUSTOMERS:** You may have heard recent allegations that some Sears Auto Centers in California and New Jersey have sold customers parts and services they didn't need. We take such charges very seriously, because they strike at the core of our company—our reputation for trust and integrity.

    We are confident that our Auto Center customer satisfaction rate is among the highest in the industry. But after extensive review, we have concluded that our incentive compensation and goal-saving program inadvertently created an environment in which mistakes have occurred. We are moving quickly and aggressively to eliminate that environment." (From ad run nationwide June 25, 1992)

12. Referring to a net loss of $19.9 million, a 1991 press release for SHL Systemhouse, Inc., stated: "SHL Systemhouse Inc. today released its financial results for the fiscal year ended Aug. 31, 1991, which reflect provisions to reposition itself for profitable growth and to consolidate business functions to achieve operational synergies."

13. A June 1994 ad for "The Early Listener" wireless earphone system contained this: "And if your equipment is not quite so high-tech, and your TV is not outfitted for cable or speakers, The Easy Listener's mini-microphone picks up sound and brings it through the headset."

14. From a May 30, 1994, ad for Rayovac reusable batteries: "Introducing the best-performing battery in all of creation."

15. "Suicide is usually the result of a lack of perspective to see all the alternatives and possibilities for action that life has to offer. People who consciously think and act in a *pro*-life way will never consider a premature voluntary death, unless unbearable pain renders further living meaningless." (Josef Haid, *On The Side of Life*, Germany: Asama AG Publishers, p. 123.)

B. Identify any sources of ambiguity you find in the following passages. If there are more than one, so indicate. You may find it helpful to try to restate unclear passages and discuss their sources of confusion.

1. During a tense period in the Civil War, Abraham Lincoln was rudely awakened by a character hoping to take advantage of the fact that the head of customs had just died: "Mr. President, would it be all right if I took his place?" "Well," Lincoln supposedly said, "if it's all right with the undertaker, it's all right with me."

2. Sports reporter Dan Jenkins told the story of a football player who didn't need drugs to get psyched up to play. When asked how he was always able to get up for the game, he replied: "Coach just comes by and knocks on the door."

3. A woman phoned the Whitney Museum of American Art to ask if her husband could bring his camera. "Is picture-taking allowed?" she asked. She was asked to repeat the question and she did. "No," came the reply, "You have to leave the pictures here."

4. "Workmen swept snow from the seats of 20,000 spectators." (Cincinnati *Post and Times-Star*)

5. John Johnson lives with his wife, his high school sweetheart, and three sons.

6. "Enraged, Achilles Hector shall subdue." (*The Iliad*)

7. "Seeing that the eye and hand and foot and every one of our members has some obvious function, must we not believe that in like manner a human being has a function over and above those particular functions?" (Aristotle, *Nicomachean Ethics*)

8. In a Northern California community some years ago, a young man was involved in a fatal automobile accident. His girlfriend, who was a passenger in the car he was driving, was killed when the vehicle swerved off the road and hit a power pole. The young man was charged with reckless driving because of the excessive speed at which he was traveling on a road well known for its dangerous curves. An uproar ensued when his lawyer argued—and won a significantly reduced sentence for his client—that the young man was not "driving" since at the moment of impact he was talking to his girlfriend and not looking at the road, and since his hands were not on the steering wheel. (This is a true case.)

9. "One afternoon in the hospital operating room where I am a nurse, I heard one of our nurse anesthetists trying to put a patient to sleep. Now I want you to breathe in and out," she intoned, "in and out, slowly in and out."

   The patient opened her eyes and said, "Is there any other way?" (Contributed by Ann Quezada to "All in a Day's Work,"® *Reader's Digest*, August 1990)

10. Crown Camera in Redding, California, gives each customer a nickel to pay for the parking meters out front. The nickel is taped to this message: "CROWN CAMERA APPRECIATES YOU . . . please park on us next time."

11. "I've never been qualified for anything I'm good at." (Sonny Bono, R—Cal., in *The Economist*, May 2, 1992.)

12. For too long, men have messed things up! It's time to give women the opportunity.

13. "When a friend loses a loved one, flowers from the FTD® Remembrance® Collection say you care."

14. Referring to the 1991 Los Angeles riot triggered by the first Rodney King verdict, a congresswoman said: "Well, if you call it a riot, it sounds like it was a bunch of crazy people who went out and did bad things for no reason. I maintain it was somewhat understandable, if not acceptable. So I call it a rebellion." (Reported by Joe Klein, *Newsweek*, February 22, 1993)

15. In 1990, the U.S. Government introduced a new category of workers: "involuntary part time."

CHAPTER 6

Inattention to Subject Matter

Good, too. Logic, of course; in itself, but not in fine weather.
ARTHUR HUGH CLOUGH

This chapter is about arguments which violate the relevancy criterion for cogency. *A fallacy of relevance is an argument that attempts to demonstrate its conclusion by appealing to logically irrelevant premises.* Irrelevant premises often arise when arguers rely on emotion, diversion, or assumption in order to try to establish the truth of conclusions. In many instances, failure to pay close attention to the subject matter of an argument—the issue—results in accepting as relevant premises which have no logical bearing on the conclusion. Recognizing some of the common fallacies of relevance will help us identify the subject matter of arguments. Failure to recognize the subject matter of an argument prevents us from being able to determine whether or not the relevancy criterion is being met. A useful way to organize common violations of the relevancy criterion is to divide fallacies of relevance into three categories: reliance on emotion, reliance on diversion, and reliance on assumption.

RELIANCE ON EMOTION

Both reasons and emotions are, of course, inescapable and valuable tools for making choices. But there are times when our emotions can interfere with our ability to think clearly, much to our detriment and even to our sorrow.

An emotional appeal is an attempt to persuade without logical reasons. In other words, *an appeal to emotions is a deliberate attempt to evoke an emotional response to get someone else to accept a conclusion, to adopt a belief, or to act in a certain way.* It is often easier to influence another's feelings than it is to change his or her mind. Under certain conditions, we can change a person's thinking by first changing how he or she feels about something. We are often more susceptible to emotional appeals than we are to reasons.

It's worth especially noting that fallacies are difficult to spot when emotions cloud our thinking. Note, however, that as clear and critical thinkers we are concerned with the *logical* adequacy of arguments, not their *psychological* "relevance" or persuasiveness. In other words, arguments can be highly persuasive because of various emotions they stimulate—hostility, fear, enthusiasm, pity, lust, and so on—even though they are logically flawed. We may be overcome by the *feeling* of logical justification. An argument's logical adequacy, however, is not determined by how we feel about it.

STUDY HINT
Logical v. Psychological Relevancy

The intensity with which a belief is held does not reflect the reliability of the belief. Sincerity is of limited evidentiary value. Psychological relevancy is not the same as logical relevancy. Neither truth value nor cogency are functions of the sincerity, integrity, or intelligence of the arguer or the critic.

Whenever others deliberately attempt to persuade us by using factors of which we are unaware, we are being manipulated, not reasoned with. And this is the *desired* effect of a fallacious appeal to emotions. Feelings are used *in place* of reasons—where reasons are appropriate. Used this way, feelings weaken our ability to think carefully and clearly. We'll begin our study of six of the more common fallacious appeals to emotions with one of the most common forms: arguments directed "at the person" rather than at the issue.

Personal Attack

Often, in argument, we attack the arguer instead of the argument. That's like rejecting an argument because it is written in pencil rather than typed, or because the speaker has a speech impediment. Neither factor has any bearing on the argument.

Whenever we attack a person instead of his or her argument, we commit a form of the fallacy known as *personal attack*. Historically, this fallacy has been known as the *argumentum ad hominem,* or *ad hominem* for short. *Ad hominem* is Latin for "to the man," and because not all personal attacks are directed at men, we shall use the inclusive term *personal attack. A fallacious personal attack is an argument that claims to be a refutation of an opponent's argument when it in fact attacks the opponent.* The personal-attack fallacy comes in many forms, and we'll look at three of them: character assassination, circumstantial, and *tu quoque.*

Character Assassination

Character assassination is a form of personal attack in which the arguer's personal failings or problems are cited as evidence against his or her argument. Former President Richard Nixon, for example, has had a tarnished reputation from his earliest political activities through the Watergate scandals of the 1970s. Nixon was also an effective innovator of foreign policy. Although he continued to speak and write on political matters after his resignation from office, some people automatically rejected whatever he said because of his past reputation and conduct. Whatever Nixon's character, his advice on specific political matters should have been evaluated on its own.

Rejecting a claim by hurling personal insults at an opponent may sway an audience's emotions, but it does nothing to shed light on the argument in question. Insults and charges need not be true to be effective, as we witness far too frequently in dirty political campaigns. Sadly, character assassination often works. And, even more sadly, it can produce tragic consequences.

A particularly vicious example of character assassination is found in the case of French film actress Jean Seberg. In the 1960s, the FBI wanted to discredit Seberg because of her expressed sympathy toward the Black Panthers, a black political group. So the FBI circulated the lie that the baby Seberg and her husband were expecting actually had been fathered by a member of the Black Panthers. The FBI believed that widespread circulation of this story would damage Seberg's moral reputation to such an extent that no one would take her views seriously. From the FBI's perspective, the manufactured character assassination of Seberg had the additional advantage of harming the Black Panthers' reputation as well. Of course, even if the claim were true, it would be *logically irrelevant* to the cogency of the political arguments of the Black Panthers or of Jean Seberg.

As it turned out, Jean Seberg was the biggest loser in the ugly skullduggery. According to her husband, she was thoroughly traumatized by the rumor, so much so that she attempted to take her life every year on the birthday of their child. In the fall of 1979 she succeeded. Shortly thereafter, the FBI admitted it was all a lie and said it didn't do that sort of thing anymore.

It's important not to confuse the fallacy of character assassination with legitimate considerations of personal character. When assessing *individuals* for employment, political office, college admissions, enlistment into the armed services, and the like, we are wise to consider a variety of relevant personal factors: honesty, dependability, capability, and so forth. As we noted in Chapter 1, when evaluating political candidates, it can be difficult to determine what personal factors are relevant to the qualities needed to succeed in the office being sought. In such cases, we must employ our best critical thinking skills to determine the truthfulness (reasonableness) of both the accusations and the responses made to them, as well as for deciding on the relevancy and sufficiency of the charges. Raising questions about a political, academic, or employment candidate's personal character does not—of itself—constitute character assassination. Character assassination occurs when issues of character are irrelevant to the matter under scrutiny.

"And I'd like to ask my mud-slinging opponent if
he's been faithful to that moose he married."

Drawing by C. Barsotti; © 1996 The New Yorker Magazine, Inc.

Circumstantial Personal Attack

A second, more subtle form of personal attack is known as the *circumstantial personal attack. A circumstantial personal attack is an argument that rejects an opponent's argument solely on the basis of possible bias due to some aspect of the opponent's personal life.*

Examples of circumstantial personal attacks might include rejecting Robert Redford's views on recycling solely because he's an actor, or rejecting Whoopi Goldberg's arguments concerning the need for critical-care facilities for people with AIDS just because she's an actress. In either example, the arguments offered by Redford or Goldberg might be ignored or hastily dismissed.

Just as we must be wary of appealing to false authority, we must also guard against what can be thought of as a "reverse" of the false authority fallacy. False authority occurs when we uncritically accept someone's argument based on their fame or expertise in an irrelevant field. A common form of circumstantial personal attack occurs when we dismiss an individual's argument because he or she belongs to a particular group. For example, some people might dismiss anything a priest says about abortion because he is Catholic and the Catholic Church condemns abortion.

A particularly subtle and ironic form of circumstantial personal attack occurs when professionals reject the opinions of others in the same field based solely on where they graduated from, where they work, or what areas they specialize in. For example, male logicians might reject arguments made by feminist philosophers, or feminist philosophers might reject arguments made by men. It is all too common to encounter subtle prejudice based on the status of one's degree or institution. An argument concerning teaching practices made by a community college instructor might not be accorded the respect the same argument would get if presented by a Harvard or UC Berkeley professor.

The subtlety of such often unrecognized circumstantial personal attacks comes, say, from the seemingly reasonable induction that professors at important universities have to meet higher standards of employment and research than do community college instructors. Although this may be true—generally—it is not relevant to the analysis of this argument. In fact, the community college instructor might well argue that he or she has more relevant teaching expertise than his or her university counterpart. General practice physicians sometimes experience similar forms of circumstantial personal attacks from specialists.

While we must always demand relevant expertise, we must be sure that it is truly relevant. Women are not the only persons qualified to analyze women's issues, neither are members of ethnic minorities the only ones qualified to address issues of discrimination. Whenever we uncritically reject others' arguments *only on the basis of their membership in a group,* we are in danger of committing a circumstantial personal attack. Because this particular fallacious argument is not usually abusive, it often goes unrecognized as a form of personal attack.

A very common form of this appeal involves citing the *possibility* of personal or financial interest as a sufficient reason for rejecting a person's arguments. Rejecting a teacher's argument for an increased allotment of funds for education *because* he or she is involved in education is a common example; so is arbitrarily rejecting your father-in-law's suggestion that you should apologize to your spouse *because*—as your spouse's father—he *might* be biased in his or her favor. A particularly childish version of the circumstantial personal attack seems to be a staple of many of our politicians who summarily reject arguments made by "liberals" or "conservatives"—depending on the attacker's political orientation.

Notice that the appeal of this form of circumstantial attack comes from the observation that people are often biased, and that people do favor what's to their advantage. The fallacy occurs when we go beyond being cautious and taking possible arguer bias into account, and uncritically assume its presence. Further, an individual's personal motives for asserting an argument are always logically irrelevant to the argument's cogency. The most such motives can tell us is: be wary. They are not part of the argument itself.

There's an even more important reason to be wary of this and all forms of personal attack: The argument may be cogent even when the arguer is immoral, biased, or means us no good. Our task as logical thinkers is to look for good evidence and truth. Even if the professor in the above example will double her salary if the education budget is increased, increasing it might be the wise choice. If we are not careful, we will always arbitrarily reject claims of innocence or reasonable requests for money or aid. Suppose jurors arbitrarily reject a defendant's argument in favor of innocence on the mere basis that it is in his interest to claim innocence. How could innocent people ever argue in their own behalf?

STUDY HINT

Reminder: Cogency is an objective quality of arguments. It is part of the public dimension of argument. The character, motives, and behavior of the *arguer,* on the other hand, are part of the personal dimension of argument. Although they can and do influence what arguments we make and accept, they remain irrelevant to an argument's cogency.

Tu Quoque

The tu quoque personal attack is an argument that rejects advice or criticism solely on the grounds that those giving it don't follow it. This is a most common fallacy. Here's an example: "How dare you tell me not to smoke. You do." This form of personal attack is referred to as the *tu quoque* fallacy from the Latin for "you also." It's often informally expressed by such phrases as "Look who's talking!" or "You've got no room to criticize." The *tu quoque* fallacy is often used as a way to justify ourselves in the face of criticism or advice. In such instances, it occurs when an arguer rejects an opponent's advice by arguing that the opponent has said or done things just as bad as the arguer is being accused of.

The force of this fallacy probably derives from a general distaste for hypocrisy and self-righteousness. We may assume that anyone giving advice ought to "practice what they preach." Perhaps they should. But that's a moral and psychological issue, not a logical one. From the standpoint of rational self-interest, we are best served by analyzing the quality of the advice given and the argument used to support it, not the arguer's ability or willingness to follow it. *Tu quoque* arguments sometimes refer to past behavior: "Don't tell me to study, Pop. Grammy said that you nearly flunked high school." If the advice to study (or any other advice) is good, a reasonable person will attempt to heed it—regardless of its source.

Notice how all forms of personal attack involve confusing an issue by introducing logically irrelevant emotions and beliefs. We must not confuse our personal annoyance or dislike of the arguer with the argument. This is not always easy, but it is necessary if we wish to be good thinkers.

Sticking to what's logically relevant seems to be especially difficult when our sense of moral outrage is involved or when we perceive others as "getting away with something." Two close cousins to the *tu quoque* result from just this confused sense of moral indignation. Let's see how.

Two Wrongs Make a Right

The fallacy of two wrongs make a right is an argument that attempts to justify what is considered wrong by appealing to other instances of the same or similar action. For example, Wilma scolds B.J. for ripping the funnies out of the paper before she's had a chance to read it. B.J. replies that Wilma tears the sports section out of the paper before he gets a chance to read it. The fact is two wrongs *don't* make

The Far Side © 1993 Farworks, Inc. Used by permission of Universal Press Syndicate. All rights reserved.

a right. When we argue to the contrary, we're introducing a premise that's irrelevant to the conclusion. We imply that we are innocent of wrongdoing or that our wrongdoing is justified.

The "wrong" actions of past political administrations do not mitigate the misconduct of present ones. Defenders of Washington, D.C. Mayor Marion Barry argue that he should never have been convicted of using illegal drugs because, in the first place, the authorities were wrong to set up a "sting."

When Zoë Baird's 1993 nomination for U.S. attorney general was withdrawn because she failed to pay Social Security and employment taxes for an undocumented domestic worker, Baird argued that the regulations covering domestic workers were unrealistic and foolish—in other words, wrong. When students or their parents justify lying on financial aid applications because they believe "it's unfair to count parents' income," they are also using two-wrongs reasoning. Perhaps a better approach in such circumstances would be to challenge the specific laws and regulations seen as wrong in a more direct manner in the proper forum.

The years 1993 and 1994 saw other candidates for high office derailed for failing to pay Social Security taxes for domestic helpers. Like Baird, most of these candidates invoked the two-wrongs-make-a-right fallacy, adding that virtually no one paid such taxes for domestic workers. In other words, what they did was merely common practice.

Common Practice

The common-practice fallacy is a variation of the two-wrongs theme that attempts to justify wrongdoing on the basis of some practice that has become commonly accepted. For example, when Roscoe was new to the job, he was taken aback to see Sweeney take company tools home with him for his personal use. One day he asked him about it. Sweeney said, "Oh, that's one of the *perks* of the job." By "perks," of course, Sweeney meant perquisites, fringe benefits, as it were. Since it was a practice that most of the other workers followed, Sweeney didn't see anything wrong with it. Yet a short time afterward, management issued a memo forbidding the common practice.

One of the issues raised during Senate hearings to confirm Justice William Rehnquist's appointment to the position of chief justice of the United States Supreme Court centered on the fact that Rehnquist once owned property whose deed contained a clause forbidding sale or transfer to blacks and members of other minorities. This raised the question of whether or not Rehnquist was bigoted. Some of Rehnquist's defenders pointed out that at the time, over twenty years before, many parcels had such riders, and many decent people owned property with the same conditions. Thus, they argued, even though Justice Rehnquist was a lawyer who could be expected to understand the legal language of this proviso, what he did should not be held against his appointment since it was "common practice for the time."

Have you ever had to fill out a form in triplicate, perhaps even in quadruplicate? Maybe you couldn't see the reason for it and asked somebody. If you were told, "That's just how we do things here," you were being given a common practice appeal. Possibly four separate offices or departments needed copies of what you'd signed. If so, that would be a logically relevant reason. But "That's just how we do things here" is logically irrelevant; it's a common-practice appeal.

Years ago, Regimen, manufacturers of weight-reducing tablets, was charged by the Justice Department with deliberate misrepresentation and falsehood in advertising its product. In fact, the U.S. attorney general charged that Regimen's was "one of the most brazen frauds ever perpetrated on the public, mostly women.[13] Regimen's reply: "Thousands of other advertisers and agencies are doing the same kind of thing."[14] No matter how common the practice, misrepresentation is misrepresentation—hence, the irrelevancy of Regimen's defense.

Mob Appeal

You've probably noticed how many commercials and advertisements involve music, little sketches of lifestyles, and so on. Commercials for major burger chains

---

13. Samm Sinclair Baker, *The Permissible Lie* (New York: World, 1968), p. 24.

14. Ibid.

often have themes, for example. In one, a shy, white-haired older man flirts with an older woman. In another, practically everyone eating is black. In a third they're teens. In some, a single man or woman takes several kids out to eat. In others, people of all ages, races, and sizes happily eat together. Occasionally a handicapped person appears. What's going on?

Each of these theme ads, and thousands like them for countless products, is attempting to advance a conclusion by appealing to the deepest emotions, beliefs, and values of a group or individual. They are appealing to a fallacy known as the *argumentum ad populum,* but which we shall refer to as *mob appeal. The fallacy of mob appeal is an argument that attempts to persuade groups or individuals by arousing their deepest emotions, beliefs, and values.*

Don't be confused by the name. The fallacy was first identified before the advent of mass media. When great debates took place in front of large audiences (the mob or *populum*), debaters attempted to manipulate the audience's feelings. We've all noticed the phenomenon of *crowd infection,* when, say, one person coughs in a quiet church and a half-dozen others follow suit. Television shows sweeten comedies with laugh tracks on the theory that we're more likely to laugh if others laugh. (Incidentally, isn't "sweeten" an interesting example of doublespeak?) A "mob," or physically assembled audience, is sometimes easier to sway than one individual. The original *ad populum* attempted to turn the audience from thinking individuals into a reacting "mob" by appealing to its collective sense of justice or patriotism or other deeply felt belief.

STUDY HINT

Despite its name, the mob-appeal fallacy is also aimed at individuals.

We see present-day mob appeal in virtually every political campaign or ad in such words and phrases as "my fellow Americans," "common decency," "this great land of ours," "God given," often accompanied by flag waving and stirring patriotic music.

In fact, some of the greatest oratorical movements in American history resorted to mob appeal. Here's William Jennings Bryan opposing gold as a monetary standard in his famous "Cross of Gold" speech:

> We care not upon what lines the battle is fought. If they say bimetalism is good, but that we cannot have it until other nations help us, we reply that, instead of having a gold standard because England has, we will restore bimetalism, and then let England have bimetalism because the United States has it. If they dare to come out in the open field and defend the gold standard as a good thing, we will fight them to the uttermost. Having behind us the producing masses of this nation and the world, supported by the commercial interests, the laboring interests and the toilers everywhere, we will answer their demand for a gold standard by saying to them: You shall not press down upon the brow of labor this crown of thorns, you shall not crucify mankind upon a cross of gold.

Mob appeal, however, need not appear only in speeches. Beware of it in advertisements, where generally every attempt is made to associate a product with things that we can be expected to approve of strongly: patriotism, status, sexual gratification. Also, pictorial ads can be most effective in appealing to our deepest feelings. For example, there's no counting how often a picture of the White House or the Capitol has been used as a background for an ad. The daughter of a former U.S. president has even appeared in one such ad—for an automobile.

In his successful 1988 bid to become president of the United States, George Bush's campaign rallies often included a stirring rendition of the best-selling song "I'm Proud to be an American" sung by Lee Greenwood, the popular country singer who had the original hit. Bush's Democratic rival, Massachusetts Governor Michael Dukakis, countered with Bruce Springsteen's "Born in the USA," sung by the "Boss" himself. Both campaigns were using mob appeal, selling a vague sense of a lifestyle, of values. Four years earlier, Ronald Reagan's campaign included a short filmed look at the then-president's "lifestyle"—complete with Reagan touring his ranch in a four-wheel-drive vehicle and wearing jeans, boots, and a cowboy hat. In 1992, Ross Perot adopted the Patsy Cline hit "Crazy" as his theme song to counter accusations that his behavior during his on-again-off-again presidential campaign was "crazy." Bill Clinton and Al Gore kicked off their campaign against George Bush and Dan Quayle by touring the countryside on a bus, and frequently appearing in casual clothes—thereby creating a stark contrast with the more conservative and formal style of their opponents. The Clinton-Gore theme song was the 1970s Fleetwood Mac hit "Don't Stop Thinking About Tomorrow."

Mob appeal can backfire when the target audience recognizes it for what it is. For example, famed trial lawyer F. Lee Bailey became a brief subject of ridicule for a miscalculated use of the mob appeal when, during the notorious O. J. Simpson trial, he informed the court in a very dramatic tone that he and a potential witness had spoken "Marine to Marine."

As you become sensitized to the mob appeal, you will discover that it occurs in everyday conversation, court rooms, advertisements, and political speeches. Emotional appeals are powerful and useful motivators to action. They can evoke worthy feelings of compassion, empathy, courage, righteous indignation, and so forth. But emotional appeals should not be used to substitute for cogent reasoning when issues warrant careful, rational scrutiny.

Bandwagon Appeal

One common variant of mob appeal is directed at our desire to be popular, to be "just folks," a regular person. *Bandwagon mob appeals invoke inclusive feelings of belonging to a group.* In the examples cited earlier, Bush, Dukakis, Perot, and Clinton invoked bandwagon appeals in their choice of campaign songs and singers. Broad appeals to "the workingman and workingwoman," the "moral majority," the "silent majority," the "average guy and gal," are examples of appeals to "jump on the bandwagon."

One component of bandwagon mob appeals is a sense of basic values. The Motel 6 chain runs a series of radio ads by Tom Bodett. Bodett speaks in what might be called a "country accent." He sounds "folksy," not stuffy, not sophisticated. Accompanied by fiddle and guitar music, he stresses the no-frills nature of Motel 6: clean sheets, nothing fancy, just a basic place to get a good night's rest at "decent" prices. He closes with, "We'll leave the light on." The entire focus and tone of the ad campaign is cozy, safe, warm, welcoming, personal. The reality is that every word Bodett utters, the pace at which he speaks, the music, and his accent are carefully chosen by sophisticated advertisers for a multimillion-dollar corporation.

The very same product is often sold differently on various radio stations, for example. On a country-music station, any music in the background is likely to be country, and the announcers will have a country way of "talkin'" to "regular folks" like "us." On a rhythm-and-blues station, the music and the announcer both change. The use of songs from old television shows and films is designed to evoke nostalgic feelings and a sense of identification with one's particular generation or a favored lifestyle. And on it goes.

Ads for denture creams contain older spokespeople than ads for jeans or sports motorcycles. Ads for touring motorcycles show neatly dressed middle-aged couples—because they buy more touring bikes than do teenagers. Ads for cafe racer motorcycles show slim young daredevils rocketing along empty country lanes. Virtually any ad with a celebrity in it contains a mob appeal.

Snob Appeal

Sometimes we don't want to be part of the crowd and there's a mob appeal aimed at just those times. *The snob-appeal version of mob appeal invokes feelings of superiority and exclusivity.* In contrast to the bandwagon appeal which says, in effect, "Everybody jump aboard," the snob appeal is aimed at "those few who appreciate and deserve the very best."

Snob appeals are usually easy to recognize. An ad for a luxury car simply stated, "You've finally made it." Ads for audio components that appeal to those willing to pay a little more because they truly appreciate quality are snob appeals. Pitches like "Sure it costs a little more, but I'm worth it" and "If you have to ask how much it costs, you can't afford it" are both snob appeals. Appeals with "rare," "exclusive," "limited edition," and the like contain a snobbish element.

Some years ago, J.C. Penney ran a clever reverse-snob snob-appeal ad campaign for its Plain Pockets Jeans. At a time when name-brand jeans were at the height of their popularity, the Penney's campaign was aimed at those individuals who thought of themselves as wise enough and secure enough not to need name brands on their pockets. This clever *reverse-snob snob appeal* occurs when no-frills is sold as a way of being superior, of being beyond succumbing to the pressure to be in style. In other words, this kind of appeal is directed at our snobbish pride in not being snobs!

Sometimes the line between bandwagon and snob appeal blurs. Commercials for light beers that involve famous macho celebrities doing silly things are clever mixes of both appeals: couch potatoes and nonmacho types can laugh *at* the exaggerated macho strutting; macho types can laugh *with* their good-natured famous counterparts. Bandwagon appeals like the Tom Bodett commercials for Motel 6 noted above might contain a tinge of snobbery in the implied notion that Motel 6 customers are too smart to be seduced into wasting money at "highfalutin" motels; they have their values straight.

The point is that bandwagon and snob appeal both invoke a sense of identity with a group, and this can easily involve two conflicting desires: to be part of the crowd while remaining a special individual. In any case, the presence of either desire is never logically relevant to accepting a mob appeal's conclusion. Who to vote for, what brand to buy, and other decisions, should not be made just on the basis of some vague identification with a lifestyle or values associated with a person or product.

STUDY HINT
Mob Appeal

The lifestyle element of mass market advertisements should always be viewed as a form of mob appeal. The locale, music, clothing, physical appearance, race, gender, age, accent, and activities of the characters in ads are evoking the mob appeal. Celebrities, sexy settings, vignettes (like the Taster's Choice couple and the adventures of the Round Table Pizza man) are common forms of this widespread technique.

Pity

The fallacy of pity is an argument that arouses compassion to advance a conclusion. A good example occurred just the other day when Speedy was pulled over for speeding in his new sports car. When it became obvious he was getting a ticket, he said to the officer: "Oh, c'mon, will you? One more ticket and I'll lose my insurance." Recognizing the irrelevancy of Speedy's appeal to pity, the officer replied, "You should have thought of that before you sped."

Appeals to pity frequently arise in the courtroom when defense attorneys are backed against a wall. Then there's often talk of the defendant's misspent youth, deprived childhood, neglectful parents, and so forth. Here's an example involving perhaps the most famous defense attorney of all time, Clarence Darrow. In this instance he's defending Thomas Kidd against the charge of criminal conspiracy. In addressing the jury, Darrow says:

> I appeal to you not for Thomas Kidd, but I appeal to you for the long line—the long, long line reaching back through the ages and forward to the years to come—the long line of despoiled and downtrodden people on the earth. I appeal to you for those men who rise in the morning before daylight comes and who go home at night when the light has faded from the sky and give their life, their strength, their toil to make others rich and great. I appeal to you in the name of those women who are offering up their lives to this modern god of gold, and I appeal to you in the name of those little children, the living and the unborn.[15]

---

15. Quoted by Irving Copi in *Introduction to Logic,* 4th ed. (New York: Macmillan, 1972), p. 78.

THE FAR SIDE   By GARY LARSON

"Wait! Spare me! . . . I've got a wife, a home,
and over a thousand eggs laid in the jelly!"

The Far Side cartoon by Gary Larson is reprinted by permission of Chronicle Features, San Francisco, CA. All rights reserved.

Despite the effectiveness of such an appeal, the question is still whether the defendant is guilty of the crime. In that light, this appeal, though psychologically persuasive, is logically irrelevant to the question. We should quickly add, however, that the line between relevance and irrelevance is often blurred. Sometimes what appears to be an appeal to pity actually is an attempt to demonstrate that a defendant's will was so constrained that the person didn't freely choose to commit a crime.

Salespeople are fond of appeals to pity, particularly in selling life and health insurance. It's not surprising. After all, if a pitiful picture is painted of a provider's children scratching around for food and clothes in the absence of the provider, the person's likely to take out some life or health insurance. The beauty of such an appeal is that it makes a person live with guilt *before the fact*. The pitches for purchasing a "preneed" burial plot work the same angle. It's tough for people to live with the guilt of making their loved ones scurry around making funeral arrangements for them, so why not arrange for all that "before the time comes"?

In that way people can presumably just sit back and enjoy your funeral. These examples also contain appeals to fear, discussed below.

Controversy has surrounded appeals to pity in ads and films used by some anti-abortion and animal rights groups. One group mails out graphic photographs of baby harp seals being killed for their fur. One especially disturbing photo shows a cute little baby seal, its large dark eyes staring lifelessly out of its bloodied white face. The contrast of the blood against the white fur is effective. This flyer counts as an example of an appeal to pity because the picture is the first thing the reader encounters. The feeling is raised *before* any argument is encountered. An anti-abortion campaign in a major midwestern city consisted of large, white billboards with a small bloody handprint and the word "please," in dripping, blood red in the lower right-hand corner.

Regardless of our beliefs, we have to be wary of using emotional appeals—no matter how effective they are. Appeals to emotion can inhibit rational discourse and almost guarantee confrontation. Further, they can encourage an atmosphere of nonreason. Even when successful, emotional appeals carry a price. The price is the instability of any change of heart unaccompanied by a change of mind.

Fear

The fallacy of fear is an argument that uses the threat of harm as evidence for a conclusion when in fact such a threat is not at all evidence. Also known as "swinging the big stick," the appeal to fear is summed up in the adage "might makes right." Of course, might doesn't make right; that's the whole point.

Thus the lobbyist who says to a politician "The best reason for supporting my proposal is that I represent 2 million people" is using fear to persuade. How many people the lobbyist represents is logically irrelevant to the merits of the proposal, although emotionally it's most relevant to the politician's future. That's precisely why the lobbyist makes and gets away with such appeals.

Appeals to fear are widely used by those who support mandatory testing of federal employees for drugs—and by those who oppose such testing. The former appeal to our fears regarding drug-impaired individuals in crucial jobs: air traffic controllers, military personnel, police officers and firefighters, and so forth. Their opponents appeal to our fears of a *1984*-type world in which a "Big Brother" government pries into our very bodies. Appeals to fear are widespread in discussions of AIDS or the purported dangers of rock and roll. Proponents of increased military spending appeal to our fear of being defenseless against attack from other countries.

Such appeals are often used to exert pressure on average people in their everyday work lives. Thus, a male boss might expect sexual favors from a female employee as a condition for employment or promotion. A doctor might demand gratuities from a neighborhood pharmacist in exchange for sending patients to that pharmacy. A teacher might be pressured not to join a union under threat of being denied tenure or getting unattractive assignments. New workers at a job might be told "to clam up" or "don't rock the boat" if they want to "get ahead."

In all cases, the appeal is to fear, which although emotionally persuasive, is logically irrelevant to the positions being advanced.

STUDY HINT

The appeal to fear is committed by the arguer, not by the person being threatened.

Appeals to fear are especially distasteful when they do not stop at threatening their victim, but add insult to injury by pretending that the victim is involved in a rational, civilized discussion. In an especially powerful scene in Mario Puzo's novel *The Godfather,* young Vito Corleone has a pleasant, civilized conversation with a man he wants to sign a contract. Sipping espresso, speaking softly and courteously, always addressing his guest as *Signor,* Corleone points out that they have a "problem." He then makes his case for the *Signor* to sign the contract. On the table near Corleone, in full sight of the frightened *Signor,* is a pistol. At the end of his case, Corleone points out that he knows his "guest" is a "reasonable man." He then gives this "reasonable man" one minute to make up his mind, uttering the now-famous line, "I am making you an offer you can't refuse." The offer? "In one minute I am going to have either your signature or your brains on this contract. Which shall it be?"

Obviously, the mere presence of a pistol evokes fear, even if it is never mentioned. The Latin name for this fallacy is *argumentum ad baculum.* The *baculum* was a rod of authority carried by Roman officials. So the fallacy is the "argument from the rod." Over the years, the *ad baculum* became known as "the argument with a stick" or "swinging a big stick." The point is that just carrying the stick is enough to make rational deliberation difficult or impossible for the person being bullied.

In everyday examples of the appeal to fear, a certain tone of voice, posture, or other behavioral cues can substitute for showing the rod, stick, or pistol. Friends and relatives can give very clear signals that the stick is out without verbalizing a threat. There are many ways to accompany an argument with a threat. Crying in the middle of a discussion may disorient or embarrass your companion, in effect coercing him or her to go along with your suggestions just to prevent a scene. You need not actually cry; the threat of crying may be enough. You might only need to show the stick by getting red in the face, or getting just a bit misty-eyed. Being a poor sport in order to convince someone to do what you want can be a form of appealing to fear. In this case, the threat is fear of loss of affection or of a ruined occasion.

Appeals to fear are difficult to resist when something important to us is threatened. Indeed, there are times when the rational course of action may be to yield to significant threats. This can only be determined on a case-by-case basis. If we remain aware that yielding to force is not the same thing as accepting the conclusion of a fallacious argument, we have not succumbed to the fallacy.

EXERCISE 6-1 *

Identify the fallacies in the following passages from among personal attack (specify which form), mob appeal, pity, and fear. If you think that some form of ambiguity is also present, identify it.

1. RAQUEL: How about joining me in my aerobics workout? I have Jane Fonda's new exercise tape.
   DEBBIE: Are you kidding? I won't watch anything she's in—not even an exercise video.
   RAQUEL: Why not?
   DEBBIE: Because back in the '60s and '70s she was opposed to the Vietnam War, she's antibusiness in her support of migrant workers and secretaries, and now she is Mrs. Ted Turner. Hey, face it, she's anti-American.

2. Political brochure: "You and I are about to reach a crossroads in county government. We can choose a path that will lead us into more of what we have experienced in the last few years, or we can choose a new direction, a new agenda, with new and creative solutions to the complex problems we face today. The choice is yours.
   "It is difficult to find people willing to do their very best nowadays, people who will choose the right path, the honest path, even if it hurts. We need more people willing to help . . . people committed to giving their all . . . people willing to go the extra mile, just because it's right!"

3. JAN: I think it's only fair that members of oppressed minorities get special treatment for jobs and things.
   DEAN: Well, you're a woman; of course you can't be objective. After all, everything you think is biased according to your experiences as a woman.

4. A U.S. senator arguing for Senate ratification of the Strategic Defense Initiative: Any red-blooded American, who places his country's interest above all else, as he should, would vote for this. Why? Because it prevents the most powerful nation on Earth, the United States of America, from becoming a second-rate power.

5. Mother to son: Oh, don't worry about me, dear. Go out on your date. I'll be all right. After all, I've got the TV to keep me company.

6. Father to daughter: Be home by eleven tonight, or you can forget about next weekend at the beach.

7. MEG: Driving as fast as you did on such slick pavement is really dumb.
   PEG: Oh yeah? I suppose you've never driven that way.

8. FRED: You know, I really have to laugh when Congress asks the Pentagon how much money the military needs.

JUDY: Why do you say that? Who would be in a better position to know than the Pentagon?

FRED: Are you kidding? As representatives of the military, everybody in the Pentagon is naturally going to want as much money as they can get.

9. Commercial: "You're in a strange city. Suddenly someone snatches your wallet. Your traveler's checks are inside it. What will you do now? What will you do? . . . American Express—never leave home without it."

10. Union leader: Of course, you'll have to vote your consciences on whether to strike. But just let me say this. All loyal members would see their duty and not cower to the thought of what management might do to them. . . . Okay, let's pass out the ballots!

11. Student to teacher: I know I earned a C in the course. But if I don't get an A, my GPA isn't going to be high enough to get me into medical school. How about giving me the A?

EXERCISE 6-2

1. Mob appeal is present in virtually every radio and television commercial. One currently widespread trend is the use of well-recognized music to enhance a product's appeal. This may be classical, country and western, rock, jazz, blues, or whatever. The producers of such ads hope that we will identify their products with the lifestyle, values, or positive personal feelings we associate with the selected music. Thus there is a built-in identification factor at work. Collect five or six examples of these "musical mob appeals." What special values do you think they are trying to sell? Do they work? If so, why? If not, why not? To what extent has the clever use of music influenced your own attitudes toward a product?

2. Political figures also use music to create an image. This, too, is a form of mob appeal. Can you recall some widely used songs that are of special appeal in the political arena? Can you identify three or four especially effective uses of music in a political campaign? Describe.

3. Under what circumstances, if any, are personal traits relevant to an individual's argument? Explain and justify your answer.

4. The appeal to pity can be persuasive because most of us believe that compassion is a virtue. Under what circumstances might "pity" be a legitimate consideration?

5. In 1990, fourteen-year-old Gina Grant pled no contest to killing her alcoholic mother with 13 blows of a candle holder, and trying to make it look like her mother had committed suicide by sticking a knife in her mother's neck and placing the dead woman's hand around the handle. Gina served six months in jail. (Grant's father had died of cancer in 1987.) Five years later, Grant, now a straight-A student, was accepted for

early admission to Harvard. Her high school teachers and Harvard admission committee members were impressed by the orphaned Grant's tale of overcoming an abusive childhood. When an anonymous writer informed Harvard of the details surrounding Grant's mother's death, Harvard withdrew its acceptance offer, for, among other reasons, Grant's failure to fully disclose the nature of her role in her mother's death. Explaining the omission, Grant said, "I deal with this tragedy every day on a personal level. It serves no good purpose for anyone else to dredge up the pain of my childhood." Was Grant making a fallacious appeal to pity by emphasizing the fact that she is an orphan with a troubled past, or was she providing relevant evidence of her strong character and impressive abilities? Do you think that an applicant's criminal history is a relevant character consideration for admission into college?

6. In the 1950s, household products such as bleaches, detergents, refrigerators, food stuffs, and the like, were often sold on television by well-dressed women in evening gowns, with tightly permed hair, wearing jewelry and high heels—they looked like Mrs. Cleaver, Beaver's mom. After thirty years of the civil rights movement, the Vietnam War, Watergate, and a public debate over sex roles, such ads seem naive and silly. What types of people are now used in commercials? Discuss some of the ways in which advertisers keep up with lifestyle and value changes in order to make the most powerful mob appeals they can.

7. The issue of when to resist a threat and when to give in is complex. It involves an assessment of basic values and priorities. When is principle more important than expediency? When is expediency a sufficient justification for giving in to a threat? Discuss this important issue.

RELIANCE ON DIVERSION

As we've seen, fallacious emotional appeals can interfere with critical-thinking skills. They can also distract us so that we become concerned with secondary or peripheral, logically irrelevant, issues before we've adequately analyzed logically prior and more significant considerations. In a sense, most fallacies of emotion involve some element of diversion from logically relevant concerns. There is also a class of fallacies that more directly involves diversion and distraction.

Let's first take a look at the most basic fallacy of diversion, the infamous red herring.

Red Herring

A form of distraction, the fallacy of red herring is the introduction of a logically separate and irrelevant issue into a discussion for purposes of diverting scrutiny away from the issue being evaluated. The story is told that dog trainers used to teach hunting hounds to follow a trail by dragging the fresh carcass of a rabbit, bird, squirrel, or other prey through a field. This track was allowed to grow cold overnight. The next morning, a smoked "red" herring, which had been allowed to "ripen," was dragged over the original trail. The young dog was then set off on the original trail. When he came to the scent of the red herring, he would be distracted by the fresher, stronger odor—and his trainer would put him back on the scent of his original prey.

We don't have such trainers, and so we often resort to and take off after all sorts of red herrings. Consider what happened when B.J.'s geography teacher asked him to remain after class to discuss his declining grades. B.J. was ready for her. "Ms. Roe," he said, "I'm glad you asked me to stay. I've been meaning to ask you about the San Andreas fault. I'm fascinated by this, but I'd like to know more about it. Can you recommend any good books on it?"

Of course, B.J. may or may not be telling the truth. The point is that he has deliberately attempted to distract Ms. Roe from the original issue (B.J.'s declining grades) with a red herring—and a flattering one at that because it appeals to Ms. Roe's love of geography and geology. Most of us quickly recognize the concept of the red herring, for changing the subject is a nearly universal instinct when the subject is in some way difficult or threatens us in some way.

Appeals to flattery (which some logic texts treat as a specific fallacy) are also commonly used as red herrings. Let's see how they work.

Fred's just come in the door when he realizes that he forgot to buy milk—and Wilma was very emphatic about needing milk for breakfast. Just as she is about to ask him about the milk, he rushes up to her, takes her in his arms, and says, "Gosh, you're pretty. Sometimes I forget how pretty." Sadly for Fred, Wilma knows most of his tricks, and answers, "I'll be even prettier when I know I have enough milk for breakfast. Did you buy it?"

When we are confronted by red herrings, the best thing to do is to refuse to be tempted by the new issue, no matter how appealing it may be, until we have resolved the initial one. Changing the subject is not a fallacy, but changing the subject to distract others from a weakness in our position is.

Here's a more subtle example of red herring. In charging a business executive with embezzlement, a prosecutor quotes harrowing statistics about white-collar crime. His statistical barrage may influence a jury, but it is irrelevant to establishing the guilt of the defendant. The alarming statistics only support the assertion that white-collar crime is a serious, widespread social problem and divert attention away from the real issue.

STUDY HINT

A red herring is always a *logically* separate issue.

Ridicule

A common form of diversion is the appeal to *ridicule, an attack on an idea or argument that relies strictly on cutting humor or abuse.* Sarcasm and ridicule often accompany personal attacks and mob appeals. They are especially effective when strong prejudices or stereotypes are invoked. But as British novelist Graham Greene's *Monsignor Quixote* reminds us, "Laughter is not an argument. It can be a stupid abuse." And yet the substitution of the sarcastic rejoinder or the cruel retort are unfortunately both prevalent and effective—especially in front of an audience.

For example, a member of the British Parliament named Thomas Massey-Massey introduced a bill to change the name of Christmas to Christide. He reasoned that *mass* is a Catholic term. Since Britons are largely Protestant, they should avoid the suffix *mass* in *Christmas*. Thus, he proposed "Christ-tide," whereupon another member suggested that Christmas might not want its name changed. "How would you like it," the member asked Thomas Massey-Massey, "if we changed your name to Thotide Tidey-Tidey?" The bill died in the ensuing laughter.[16]

Here's another example. When, at the post–World War I Versailles conference, French leader Clemenceau heard Woodrow Wilson propose the so-called Fourteen Points, Clemenceau supposedly reacted, "Fourteen Points! God Almighty had only ten!" Clearly Clemenceau was being more than amusing. Like the member of Parliament, Clemenceau was being contemptuous. Neither one, of course, enjoins the issue. Instead humor and ridicule are relied upon to demolish the opponent's proposal.

We note, however, that no amount of ridicule can substitute for a logically cogent critique of an argument. Sarcasm and ridicule may or may not reflect wit; they do not, in and of themselves, substitute for reasoned analysis and argument.

Straw Argument

The fallacy of a straw argument occurs when a weakened imitation of an opponent's argument is attacked instead of the opponent's original argument because the imitation is easier to refute. The weakened imitation is known as a straw argument. The name of this fallacy is particularly revealing of what it accomplishes. In effect, it sets up a "straw," which is easy to blow over. Of course the "straw" is not the original argument at all. But that's the whole point. The original was much harder to assail than the straw argument. Having set up the straw argument, the arguer is then in a position to "blow it over." And if we're not careful, we may erroneously conclude that the original argument has been demolished.

For example, many critics of laws guaranteeing equal rights for women argue this way: "If these laws pass, we'll have to draft women into the army. This will weaken our military posture and jeopardize the security of our country. And I, for one, don't want a militarily weak nation." Notice what's going on here. The original issue was equal rights for women. The straw issue is military strength. It's probably a lot easier to get people to support a position in favor of military strength than against equal rights for women. Thus, the original issue—

---

16. See S. Morris Engel, *With Good Reason,* 5th ed. (New York: St. Martin's Press, 1994), p. 201.

equal rights for women—has been cleverly altered into an issue about military strength. And thus, the straw argument.

A particularly fine example of the successful use of the straw argument fallacy can be seen in the so-called Princeton plan,[17] a plan adopted by Princeton University in the fall of 1970 whereby the university would schedule no classes for a short period before the congressional elections of 1970, thus enabling students to campaign for candidates if the students so wished. Princeton officials sponsored the plan in the aftermath of our invasion of Cambodia in June 1970. That incident touched off considerable protest throughout the country, especially on college campuses. The Princeton administration thought that its plan would help defuse any further unrest, even violence, that might erupt during election time among students who believed they were being excluded from the electoral process. The immediate reaction to the plan among other colleges was quite favorable. For a time it appeared that many other institutions would adopt it.

At this point, Senator Strom Thurmond of South Carolina attacked the plan. In fact, he asked the Internal Revenue Service to investigate how it would affect the tax-exempt status of educational institutions that adopted it.

In the aftermath of Thurmond's warning, the American Council of Education cautioned member institutions to be careful about engaging in any "political campaign on behalf of any candidate for public office." Under tax laws, an institution may lose its tax-exempt status for engaging in "partisan political activity."

The Princeton plan was not, of course, advocating partisan political activity. It was merely releasing students to campaign for whomever they wished, if in fact they cared to campaign at all. Thus, Senator Thurmond had associated the original Princeton plan with partisan political activity and the dire implications for tax-exempt institutions that adopted it. In brief, a marvelous straw argument had been created, plus an appeal to fear attached (the threat of losing tax-exempt status).

And it worked; very few institutions adopted the Princeton plan. For whatever reason, they failed to see that giving students released time to campaign was not to engage in partisan politics. Failing to see that, the institutions rejected the Princeton plan on the basis of a straw argument that Senator Thurmond had created.

Red herring and straw argument are sometimes confused. A red herring, remember, introduces a *logically separate issue* in order to divert attention away from the original issue. Its purpose is similar to a straw argument in that both fallacies avoid confronting a difficult argument by going after a less formidable one. But there are differences between the two fallacies. Red herrings often divert attention to more pleasant or trivial issues. This diversion often includes trying to involve an opponent in a prolonged discussion of the red herring, hoping that he or she never gets back to the original issue. Straw argument, by contrast,

---

17. See Howard Kahane, *Logic and Contemporary Rhetoric*, 2d ed. (Belmont, Calif.: Wadsworth, 1976), pp. 53–55.

attempts to thoroughly demolish the *original issue*. It does not, as a rule, aim at prolonging the issue; rather it seeks to finish it off once and for all.

A straw argument weakens the opponent's case; it does not change the issue. What may be confusing is that it does change the *argument*. That is, straw argument weakens the evidence supplied for the original conclusion, most commonly by altering the scope of the conclusion. Making an argument's conclusion stronger or broader has the same effect as weakening its premises. Evidence that is sufficient to support a tentative or modified conclusion will be insufficient to support a strong, unqualified, universal one. Here's an example of how that works:

Original Argument

Premises: You've been doing poorly in school lately, and your last chance to save your scholarship is your term paper, due Monday. This is the last weekend left to work on your term paper.

Conclusion: Therefore, you must stay home *this weekend in order to finish your term paper.*

Straw Argument

Premises: You've been doing poorly in school lately, and your last chance to save your scholarship is your term paper, due Monday. This is the last weekend left to work on your term paper.

Conclusion: Therefore, you can *never* go out on weekends.

As presented, the straw argument is obviously unreasonable. That's its function: to be easily refuted. You might wonder how anyone could ever be taken in by it. The straw argument is often sneaked in as a "restatement" of the original. An irate student might, for instance, shout back at the parent making the original argument: "What! I can't go out weekends! That's unreasonable." Notice that the student's version of the parent's conclusion is stronger than the original conclusion. It constitutes a straw argument because its sole purpose is to render the original case unreasonable.

If the parent and student move on to a general discussion of family policy regarding studying, going out, dating, and so forth, the clever student will also have introduced red herrings into the interaction. When an opponent fails to recognize a straw argument, he or she may be distracted into disputing or discussing other issues. In the case of the Princeton plan, for example, a "natural" red herring would be delving into the general issues of tax exemption for educational institutions, free speech, academic freedom, and so on.

It might surprise you to learn that straw arguments are very common. They can be difficult to recognize when we lack adequate background knowledge of an issue because—without adequate background knowledge—we will be unaware of the most plausible and important arguments available. To avoid being deceived by a straw argument, be alert for the presence of *vague attributions* in argument. As the name implies, *a vague attribution credits an argument to a very general source, making it impossible to track down the purported original argument.* Here are some common examples of vague attributions: "the liberals," "the conservatives," "the fundamentalists," "the secular humanists," "the feminists," "the Communists."

Vague attributions tend to crop up in summarizations or paraphrases of an opponent's position. It is quite possible that the arguer invoking them sincerely believes that "they" really do advocate the paraphrased position. Indeed, "they" may. But to be sure that we are not succumbing to our own or others' imagined or distorted straw arguments, we should insist on specific attributions that can be verified.

When our emotions are strong, when our convictions leave no room for doubt, we run the risk of inadvertently viewing our opponent's views as less reasonable than they really are. Recast through our own filters, we tend to subvert positions we dislike intensely by not noticing qualifiers like "often," or "sometimes," or "in this kind of case." In their stead, we *hear* "always," "without exception," or "in every case." Without meaning to, we almost instantaneously create straw versions of others' arguments when we alter qualifiers in this manner.

This is why we must be very careful when summarizing or paraphrasing others' positions in our own words. The safest course is to cite the exact argument as our opponent presents it. When that is not possible, we must practice the *principle of charity* in our reconstructions of arguments. *The principle of charity is the rule that whenever two possible interpretations of an argument are equally likely, we should choose the one that most strengthens the argument.* This is especially important when we have intense feelings of dislike for the argument. (The principle of charity is explained in detail in Chapter 8.)

As noted earlier, "fallacies like to travel in packs." That is, once an arguer's purpose shifts from seeking truth through cogent arguments to persuasion at any cost, he or she is free of the constraints of good reasoning *and* honest communication. It should not be surprising, then, that fallacious cases contain more than one fallacy. If fear won't work, perhaps snob appeal will; if these both fail, maybe a *tu quoque,* or red herring. The point is, in real life, bad arguments are like unhealthy people: they usually have more than one problem. We would not be surprised to learn that a woman with the flu had both a headache and a stomachache, or that an overweight man suffered from both shortness of breath and bad knees.

When the limits of cogency are abandoned or subordinated to the demands of persuasion, expect to find more than one fallacy.

STUDY HINT

Straw argument distorts a single conclusion. Red herring is the introduction of a logically separate issue.

EXERCISE 6-3 *

Identify any of the fallacies (red herring, ridicule, straw argument, two wrongs, or common practice) you spot in the following passages.

1. There's been some criticism of this administration's support of the Stealth Bomber. It has been alleged that the technology is flawed. Let's study the issue. We can begin by pointing out that the defense industry is among the largest providers of jobs in this country. Imagine what would happen if we failed to provide funds for these jobs. Let's see some of the ways in which we all benefit economically from a healthy defense industry. . . .

2. MOM: I don't want you going to the movies tonight. It's a school night, and besides, you have an important algebra test in the morning.
STUDENT: What! You're telling me that I can't go to the movies on weeknights? That's unreasonable.

3. Ms. Norman argues that a woman has a right to decide what happens inside of her own body, and that the state has no business interfering in her right to abortion on demand. I say that we cannot stand by and simply allow pregnant teenagers to use abortion as a morning-after form of birth control, and Ms. Norman is wrong when she demands that right.

4. ANGRY TEACHER: Well, young lady, why did you kick Jenny?
ANGRY PUPIL: She kicked me first, and you said we're not supposed to kick.

5. PUSHER: Here, try some of this crack. It'll really get you loaded.
PAL: No, man, drugs are illegal.
PUSHER: C'mon, it's okay. Everybody here does drugs, even the cops.

6. INTERVIEWER: Tell me, Slats, do you ever feel guilty for getting paid so much money to put a basketball through a hoop?
SLATS: Look, everybody in the league with my ability gets paid as much.

7. FRED: Fudging on your taxes isn't anything to feel ashamed about. The tax structure in this country is unfair. It taxes us regular folks unfairly. In effect, it cheats us because it favors the wealthy. So a little padding of deductions here and there is just tit for tat.

8. BARNEY: Yeah, Fred! Besides, the IRS expects us to fudge. Nobody files a completely honest return. The system's built around a little good-natured cheating.

QUESTIONABLE PREMISES AND ERRORS OF ASSUMPTION

Recall that cogent arguments establish the truth of problematic claims by offering as evidence unproblematic ones. Sometimes, we are not sure whether or not the premises of an argument ar true, and we *tentatively* accept them for purposes of initial analysis. In this way, we reason along the lines that *if* these premises turn out to be true, *then* we can accept the conclusion as also being true. Eventually, however, we need to move beyond merely *assuming that* premises are true (unproblematic) and *determining whether* they are true.

A special class of arguments is uncogent because its premises *assume,* rather than establish, a key aspect of the conclusion. In these cases, the arguments themselves "assume too much." Such arguments rely on questionable premises, which we first studied in Chapter 5: *A premise is "questionable" when it is used to establish the truth of a problematic claim before its own truth value has been clearly and independently established.*

In Chapter 5, we learned about premises that are questionable because lack of clarity prevents us from establishing a precise meaning, and, hence, prevents us from determining their truth value. In this section, we shall learn about arguments that are incapable of independently establishing their conclusions *even if the premises are true.* These arguments violate the sufficiency criterion for cogency in a special way. Here's a simple example of this type of questionable premise:

> **Yesterday was Sunday.**
> **Tomorrow is Tuesday.**
> **The day before yesterday was Saturday.**
> **Therefore, today is Monday.**

You may have noticed each premise of this argument is merely another way of expressing the conclusion. In other words, the premises and conclusion are simply different ways of saying the same thing. Any argument whose conclusion is merely another form of its premises provides insufficient evidence for its conclusion.

If we treat this example as a deductive argument, it is *trivially valid,* since the truth of the premises logically guarantees the truth of the conclusion *because each premise is the conclusion.* But if the conclusion needs proving, then simply saying it in a different way fails to provide independent support for its truth. Simply *repeating* a problematic claim does not count as *establishing* it as true. Such a maneuver *assumes* what needs to be *proven.* A trivially valid argument like the one in this example will always fail to meet the sufficiency criterion for cogency because it relies on one or more questionable premises.

Put differently, *any argument that presumes as true key assumptions that must first be independently verified in order to establish its conclusion violates the sufficiency criterion for cogency.*

Most fallacious reliance on assumption is more subtle than the preceding example. But the result is the same: an argument that in effect "cheats" by treating as an assumption something that has not as yet been proven true. This may be a disguised version of the conclusion, as we saw in our example, or it may be a questionable, highly problematic claim. Beginning an argument with "Since scientists have clearly demonstrated that women's thinking is not linear and logical . . ." is also an example of basing an argument on a questionable premise.

In order to better protect ourselves against errors of assumption, we'll take a brief look at six of the most common: begging the question, circular reasoning, loaded epithets, complex question, dismissal, and invincible ignorance.

Begging the Question

The fallacy of begging the question is an argument that uses some form of its own conclusion as part of the evidence offered to support that very conclusion. The so-called question being begged is actually the conclusion. It might help to think of this fallacy as conclusion begging: Instead of offering independent evidence capable of supporting the conclusion, a begged question merely asserts a crucial factor necessary to support its conclusion and then refers back to its own assertion as if it had been proven. We can do this in a number of ways.

The common element in each of the following fallacious strategies is that an aspect essential to proving the conclusion is "begged." Thus, since the proof of the conclusion depends on this essential aspect, the conclusion itself is begged. Here are three of the more common ways in which this occurs:

1. Using equivocated terms in the premise and conclusion
   Example: Abortion is immoral because it's wrong.

In example 1, it is essential that we establish whether or not abortion is "wrong" *before* we can determine whether or not it is immoral. If "wrong" is used to mean "morally wrong," the premise "Abortion is wrong" means "Abortion is morally wrong," which, of course, is simply an equivalent way of saying "Abortion is immoral"—which is the premise! So this argument fails to *establish* its conclusion. It merely asserts it twice, once as its own questionable or problematic premise.

2. Assuming as a premise a more general form of the conclusion
   Example: Smoking marijuana is wrong because taking drugs is wrong.

Example 2 also fails to *establish* its conclusion. In this case, the premise *already includes* the conclusion, so if we accept the problematic premise we have also accepted the conclusion. If taking any kind of drug is wrong, then certainly smoking marijuana is wrong, because it is a drug. But is it wrong to take drugs in general? The obvious answer is "no." What this argument requires is evidence that it is wrong to take one specific drug, marijuana. As in the case of example 1, example 2 fails to provide independent proof sufficient to support its conclusion. It merely asserts the same point twice: once as part of a sweeping general claim and once more specifically as the conclusion.

3. Using a questionable premise to support a favored conclusion
   Example: Abortion is wrong because it's murder, and murder is wrong.

In example 3, the crucial issue is whether or not abortion is murder. *If* abortion is murder, it is wrong, because murder, by definition, is morally and legally wrong in our culture. The very term *murder* is only applied to the taking of human life when such an action is judged as morally or legally wrong. Since the concept of "wrong" is implicit in that of murder, to say that "abortion is murder" is essentially the same as saying "abortion is wrong." This argument reduces to "Abortion is wrong because abortion is wrong." What we have, then, is an "argument" only in a most trivial sense. As we have seen, when the premise and conclusion are logically the same, the argument is *trivially valid;* the truth of the premise entails the truth of the conclusion because it *is* the conclusion!

We see that in each of these examples, independent, sufficient proof for the truth of the conclusion is lacking. In its place we find only repetition and equivocation, so that the premises and conclusion are essentially the same. Rather than making a case, begged questions merely assert their conclusions twice: once as the conclusion and once disguised in a questionable premise. If you feel like gasping, "Whew! We're just going in circles," go ahead; you are absolutely correct. We are going in circles. In fact there's even a form of question begging known as circular reasoning.

Circular Reasoning

Circular reasoning is a more elaborate form of begging the question in which questionable premises are presented as a series of two or more steps. The example on page 152 is elaborate enough to be classified as circular reasoning. Another common pattern of circular reasoning can be represented as follows:

> *A* is true because *B* is true.
> *B* is true because *C* is true.
> <u>*C* is true because *D* is true.</u>
> *D* is true because *A* is true.

At first glance, it seems unlikely that anyone would be taken in by such thinking, since as the name implies, "it goes in circles." But consider a specific instance of this pattern:

> Lying is wrong (*A*) because it's immoral (*B*).
> Lying is immoral (*B*) because it's something we should not do (*C*).
> <u>Lying is something we should not do (*C*) because God forbids it (*D*).</u>
> God forbids lying (*D*) because lying is wrong (*A*).

The fallacious quality of all circular arguments is due to the fact that in one way or another they always assume too much, taking as given some essential claim that requires separate verification. Thus they are actually assertions of a claim to truth rather than demonstrations of it.

Loaded Epithets

The technique of loaded epithets uses questionable labels to advance a favored conclusion. In everyday terms, loaded epithets are name-calling. They beg the question via connotations.

An epithet is a word or phrase used to express some quality or characteristic of an object. An epithet is usually an adjective. Let's consider a few examples of epithets used to persuade without offering justification. A philosophy professor might announce, "And now class, let's take a look at Nietzsche's obviously juvenile moral philosophy." If this announcement is made before any discussion of Nietzsche, it is an example of using a loaded epithet ("obviously juvenile") in a way that advances the conclusion that Nietzsche's moral philosophy is juvenile without having to prove that it is, and which can be expected to bias subsequent analysis of it.

Expressions that "lead" us in the direction the arguer prefers are especially dangerous: "It's *obvious* to any *knowledgeable* observer that this position is *clearly ludicrous,* but we'll look at it anyway." Terms with strong emotive charges like *reasonable, ludicrous, ridiculous, idiotic,* and so forth, can often subtly (or not so subtly) color our perceptions of an issue by seducing us into accepting a position whose truthfulness is unproved.

Loaded epithets can be very effective. Carefully chosen for their subjective connotations, they can irretrievably alter our attitude toward something *before* we have a chance to investigate it. Once our attitude is tainted, we may never again look at the issue in question without bias. At any rate, well-chosen labels can and do substitute for argumentation and clear reasoning in too many cases.

"What do you think of the president's silly arguments about South Africa?" Are they silly? *Labeling* them so should not substitute for *showing* that they are. "Those godless humanists are at it again." A term like *godless* can have a very powerful effect—without any real reasoning to accompany it. So can the use of a word like *propaganda.*

Some years ago, a film titled *If You Love This Planet,* produced by the National Film Board of Canada, won an Academy Award for best short subject. The film dealt with the effects of nuclear war. Not liking the film's viewpoint, the Reagan administration, through the Justice Department, won a Supreme Court decision upholding its right to label the film (and two others that dealt with acid rain) propaganda. In so ruling, the Court said *propaganda* is a neutral term. Is it?

You have probably gotten the point. When questionable labels and name-calling are used to advance conclusions instead of reasons, we have in effect assumed these conclusions.

Complex Question

Sometimes an unestablished assumption is hidden in a question. When this occurs, it is a complex question. *The complex question is a way of wording a question so that it assumes an answer to an unstated prior question.* A not-so-humorous example is found in the old vaudeville question "Have you stopped beating your husband (or wife) yet?" No matter how you reply, the implication is you are or were a spouse beater. The reason is that the questioner *assumes* that you are currently beating your spouse or have in the past. This sneaky maneuver is known by many names: loaded question, trick question, leading question.

Complex questions attempt to coerce us into "answering" unasked questions in a way favored by the asker. Thus they are biased or loaded. "Are you still an alcoholic?" implies that you are now or once were one. In all fairness, however, the case that you are (or are not) an alcoholic should be made before this deceptive, leading, and loaded question is answered.

"When are we going to get married?" is really two questions, the first of which is "Are we going to get married?" If I want to marry you, I will try to "trick" you into assuming an affirmative answer to the unasked question.

You can easily imagine the impact of complex questions in the courtroom. Let's suppose a prosecutor asks a murder defendant: "Tell me, Mr. Smith, what did you do with the knife after stabbing your ailing wife to death with it?" or "Who helped you manufacture your flimsy alibi for your whereabouts the night of the crime?" If it has not been previously established that Smith did in fact stab his wife or did in fact manufacture an alibi *and* with someone else's help, such questions are presumptive. (Note, too, the added presumptiveness of the loaded epithets *ailing* and *flimsy*.)

We also want to be cautious of all forms of circular reasoning in propaganda. For example, a proponent for increased tariffs on imported cars might begin a position paper or speech with this loaded question: "Why do increased tariffs on imported automobiles strengthen the U.S. economy?" Do they? If this has not been established, the advocate is leading us toward accepting a conclusion before the point has ever been demonstrated. Or a poll might ask, "How should we moderate our support of Israel to facilitate negotiating with the Arab coalition involved in the war with Iraq over Kuwait?" We will say considerably more about this kind of leading question when we study biased questions in polls and surveys later in our study.

Dismissal

The technique of dismissal offers an attitude of indignation or superiority as the sole evidence in an argument. It assumes innocence without demonstrating it. Dismissal begs the question via attitude. Many times we have heard a public figure respond to charges of misconduct with an indignant shrug: "I cannot believe that anyone would take these charges seriously. I refuse to stoop to the level of my accusers. I will not dignify such charges with a response." During the House of Representative check-bouncing scandal of 1992, a California congresswoman who had bounced hundreds of checks referred to her "oversight" saying, "I have a wart, okay?"

An attitude is not a reasoned case. Simply acting hurt and indignant cannot substitute for a well-reasoned attack on a position or for a well-reasoned defense of one.

A professor asks a student taking an exam, "What's that you have there?" The student gathers up his books, including the suspicious notes the professor alluded to, huffily heads for the door, and announces, "I've never been so insulted. How could you think that *I* would cheat? Well, if you don't trust me any more than that, I'm not going to show you what I have here!" Slam goes the door!

A mother has reasons to suspect that sixteen-year-old Becky is using illegal drugs. One day she presents her reasons for being suspicious to Becky and asks for an explanation. Becky begins to cry (pity) and then blubbers, "Oh Mom! You've hurt my feelings! I can't believe you'd just accuse me like that. You've really upset me. If you're going to think something like that about me, I refuse to stoop to your suspicious level. I won't discuss this any more!"

Dismissal occurs when an issue is brusquely swept aside—rather than confronted. No amount of indignation can substitute for clear thinking. Our public figure, our indignant student, and poor suffering Becky all have one thing in common: They have brushed aside claims that warrant consideration. Other names for dismissal are pooh-poohing an argument and shrugging off an argument.

Dismissal is classified as a fallacy of assumption because the shrugger's case is *assumed*—it is *not supported by reasons.*

Willed Ignorance

One of the most frustrating fallacies of assumption occurs when we simply latch on to a point of view for any number of reasons, and then hang on to it for dear life. In other words, we adopt a rigid point of view in which we uncritically accept an idea, regardless of contradictory evidence.

The fallacy of willed ignorance is an argument that insists on the legitimacy of an idea or principle despite contradictory fact. Truth is begged via closed mindedness. To illustrate: In recent years, Joe and Amy have engaged in a number of discussions about the wisdom of national health insurance. Joe has reached the point where he doesn't even want to discuss the issue any more because no matter what he says, Amy inevitably replies, "I don't care what you say about national health insurance, when the government starts meddling in private enterprise like that, no good can come of it."

In effect, Amy insists on the legitimacy of her position no matter what facts or points Joe might raise. But such insistence is irrelevant to the issue at hand, which is whether such a program is effective. Amy must demonstrate that it is ineffective. Simply to insist on the correctness of her position, no matter what, is to commit the fallacy of willed ignorance.

A clear warning of the possible presence of this fallacy is the phrase "I don't care what you say" or some variation of it such as "All that's well and good *but* . . ." or "Be that as it may. . . ." Frequently what follows is a rejection of the opponent's position, not through justification but willed ignorance. Thus someone argues, "I don't know why everybody is so upset about this war. War is natural!" Or "Sure I know they look like tomatoes and feel like tomatoes and taste like tomatoes—even better than tomatoes! But they're hydroponic; they're not the 'real thing.' So they can't be any good for you." When faced with someone who's bent on willed ignorance, perhaps the best thing for us to

Reprinted with permission of the artist.

do is fold our tents and slowly steal away. And quickly! The reason's obvious: We're faced with someone whose mind is made up and who doesn't want to be confused with the facts—the ultimate form of begging the issue.

EXERCISE 6-4

Identify the errors of assumption in the following passages. Choose from among these: willed ignorance, begging the question, loaded epithets, complex question, circular reasoning, and dismissal. If you think that more than one is present, explain.

1. "... and, no, I did not read the obscene books in question. I don't have to stick my head in the garbage can to know that it contains garbage." (passage from a letter to an editor)

2. How do you know that you can trust me, Dealin' Doug? Well, for one thing, I would never cheat you, and you can rely on that because you have my word on it.

3. Why do you think this is such a wonderful textbook?

4. Item number 4 on our agenda is the stale old proposal to restructure the income tax. It's not worth our time to hash it over yet another time. Let's go on to item 5.

5. TROUBLED HUSBAND: I'm worried about our marriage. You've been staying out till the wee hours of the morning for weeks. You won't say where you've gone. I'm worried that you're having an affair. Where do you go? What do you do?
   TRANQUIL WIFE: Me? Fool around? That's ridiculous. I'll see you later.

6. Shall we go out to a nice restaurant and have a fine dinner or stay home and split the tiny amount of greasy leftover roast—you know the roast you said was overcooked?

7. UPTON: Black people are just not as bright as white people.
   SINCLAIR: Oh? What about Dr. Samuels? He's got a Ph.D.
   UPTON: He's not a typical black. He doesn't count.

8. JOYCE: What do you think of *Rambo XII*?
   GERARD: I don't. I never see Stallone films. I don't care what anybody says, I know they're violent junk!

9. What is it about me that's so lovable?

10. BERNIE: What do you think about "workfare," the idea of having people on welfare work for their money?
    TOD: Frankly, it reeks of socialism.
    BERNIE: How so?
    TOD: C'mon! It's obviously socialistic. It's the sort of socialistic thing you expect to find in Sweden.

11. RICH MAN: You know, people who make their own fortunes are superior to poor people.
    RICH WOMAN: How do you know that?
    RICH MAN: Because if we were not superior we wouldn't be able to make so much money.

12. JEFF: Putting money into space exploration is a waste of time. Nothing of real benefit to us here on Earth has come from all that wasted time and money.
    JAN: Oh? What about weather satellites?
    JEFF: They don't count. Whatever's come from space exploration doesn't matter. It's still a waste of time and money.

13. OLD HIPPIE: I am proud that I refused to be drafted during the Vietnam War. In good conscience I could not raise my hand against another human being.
    YUPPIE: I suppose you wouldn't have fought in World War II against the Nazis.
    OLD HIPPIE: That's a stupid thing to bring up. By the way, what do you think about economic sanctions against South Africa?

14. WORRIED PARENTS TO ELOPING TEENS: But how will you support yourselves?
    TEENS: Don't worry; we'll do it.

15. Everything happens for a purpose. If there were no purpose, nothing would happen.

16. PREACHER POPOVER: I can heal you if your faith is strong enough.
    SAD SINNER: But Preacher, my ulcer is as bad as ever.

PREACHER POPOVER: See! There's your proof of what I say! Your faith is not strong enough.

SUMMARY

This chapter dealt with a number of fallacies of relevance, which are arguments containing premises that are logically irrelevant to their conclusions or to the purpose of demonstrating their conclusions. The irrelevancy arises out of a reliance on emotion or diversion. This chapter also covered errors of assumption and related forms of questionable premise that violate the sufficiency criterion for cogency. A premise is "questionable" when it is used to establish the truth of a problematic claim before its own truth value has been clearly and independently established.

Reliance on Emotion

1. *Personal attack:* an argument that claims to be a refutation of an opponent's argument when it in fact attacks the opponent. The personal-attack fallacy comes in many forms, and we looked at three of them: character assassination, circumstantial, and *tu quoque.* Character assassination is a form of personal attack in which the arguer's personal failings or problems are cited as evidence against his or her argument. A circumstantial personal attack is an argument that rejects an opponent's argument solely on the basis of possible bias due to some aspect of the opponent's personal life. The *tu quoque* personal attack is an argument that rejects advice or criticism solely on the grounds that those giving it don't follow it.
   Example of character assassination: rejecting former President Richard Nixon's comments on foreign policy based solely on his tarnished reputation relating to the Watergate scandals of the 1970s.
   Example of circumstantial personal attack: rejecting Robert Redford's views on recycling solely because he's an actor.
   Example of tu quoque personal attack: "How dare you tell me not to smoke. You do."

2. *Two wrongs make a right:* an argument that attempts to justify what is considered wrong by appealing to other instances of the same or similar action.
   Example: arguing that Marion Barry should not be convicted of using cocaine because the government was wrong to set up a "sting" in the first place.

3. *Mob appeal:* an argument that attempts to persuade groups or individuals by arousing their deepest emotions, beliefs, and values. The chapter identified two common forms of mob appeal, *bandwagon* and *snob appeal.* Bandwagon mob appeals invoke inclusive feelings of belonging

to a group. The snob-appeal version of mob appeal invokes feelings of superiority and exclusivity.

Example of bandwagon: political ads relying on such words and phrases as "my fellow Americans," "common decency," "this great land of ours," "God given," often accompanied by flag waving and stirring patriotic music.

Example of snob appeal: "If you have to ask how much it costs, you can't afford it."

4. *Pity:* an argument that arouses compassion to advance its conclusion.
   Example: Clarence Darrow's defense of Thomas Kidd.

5. *Fear:* an argument that uses the threat of harm as evidence for a conclusion when, in fact, such a threat is not evidence at all.
   Example: the lobbyist who justifies a position by reminding the legislator how many constituents he or she represents.

Reliance on Diversion

6. *Red herring:* a form of distraction, the fallacy of red herring is the introduction of a logically separate and irrelevant issue into a discussion for purposes of diverting scrutiny away from the issue being evaluated.
   Example: asked to remain after class to discuss his declining grades in geography, B.J. said, "I'm glad you asked me to stay. I've been meaning to ask you about the San Andreas fault. I'm fascinated by this, but I'd like to know more about it. Can you recommend any good books on it?"

7. *Ridicule:* an attack on an idea or argument that relies strictly on cutting humor or abuse.
   Example: the case of the member of Parliament named Thomas Massey-Massey.

8. *Straw argument:* a straw argument occurs when a weakened imitation of an opponent's argument is attacked instead of the opponent's original argument because the imitation is easier to refute. The weakened imitation is known as a straw argument.
   Example: the Princeton plan.

Errors of Assumption

9. *Begging the question:* an argument that uses some form of its own conclusion as part of the evidence to support that very conclusion.
   Example: "Smoking crack is wrong because taking drugs is wrong."

10. *Circular reasoning:* a more elaborate form of begging the question in which questionable premises are presented as a series of two or more steps.
    Example: "Lying is wrong because it's immoral. It's immoral because it's something we should not do. It's something we should not do because God forbids it. Therefore, God forbids lying because it is wrong."

11. *Loaded epithets:* use of questionable labels to advance a favored conclusion.
    Example: "And now let's take a look at Nietzsche's obviously juvenile moral philosophy."

12. *Complex question:* a way of asking a question that assumes an answer to an unstated prior question.
    Example: the prosecutor who asks the murder defendant, "Tell me, Mr. Smith, what did you do with the knife after stabbing your ailing wife to death with it?"

13. *Dismissal:* offers an attitude of indignation or superiority as evidence in an argument. It assumes innocence without demonstrating it.
    Example: responding to an accusation that warrants a response by merely announcing, "I refuse to dignify that with a response."

14. *Willed ignorance:* an argument that insists on the legitimacy of an idea or principle despite contradictory fact.
    Example: "I don't care what you say about national health insurance, when the government starts meddling in private enterprise like that, no good can come of it."

Summary Exercises

1. Letters to the editor of your local paper are fertile sources of fallacies. Find an example of each of the three forms of personal attacks.

2. A number of television commercials use appeals to fear to encourage us to buy their products. Such products as traveler's checks, smoke detectors, locks, diet and health foods, and life insurance are especially prone to this fallacy. Spot two or three of them. Are the fears they raise legitimate? Is there a way to advertise such products without fallaciously invoking fear? If so, how? If not, why not?

3. Does the two-wrongs fallacy apply to arguments supporting capital punishment? Justify your opinion with your own fallacy-free argument.

4. What are some steps we might take to protect ourselves from fallacious and manipulative appeals to emotions?

5. Can you think of situations in which the "rational" thing to do might be to submit to a fallacious argument? Discuss.

6. In a speech made in the aftermath of the May 1995 terrorist bombing of the federal building in Oklahoma City, President Bill Clinton denounced what he termed the "self-styled militia" that advocate violence. Analyze this passage from President Clinton's commencement speech to the 1995 graduating class of East Michigan State University for evidence of mob appeal:

   > It is one thing to believe the federal government has too much power and to work to reduce it. It is quite another to break the law of the land and threaten to shoot officers of the law if all they do is uphold it.

If you appropriate our sacred symbols for paranoid purposes and compare yourselves to colonial militias who fought for the democracy you now rail against, you are wrong. . . . What you've [Clinton's Michigan audience] seen and heard is not the real Michigan. This is the real Michigan in this stadium today. It's the astonishing revival of the automobile industry. . . . Real Michigan is Kellogg's Corn Flakes and the best cherries in the world. (*Redding Record Searchlight*, May 6, 1995)

If you think that the President used mob appeal, do you think he was justified? Is mob appeal always fallacious?

7. Evaluate this passage from Mark Price's response to the President's remarks quoted in question 6:

I would say, sit down with some members of the Michigan Militia, talk to them man to man. We are working men of the community, and we love the Constitution of the United States and will defend it against all enemies, foreign and domestic. (*Redding Record Searchlight*, May 6, 1995)

Does it affect your analysis to know that Price is a spokesman for some militia groups?

ADDITIONAL EXERCISES*

Identify any fallacies, deceptive techniques, or errors of assumption you can find in each of the following passages. There may be more than one. Explain your choices. (If you spot any fallacies from Chapter 5, identify them also.)

1. Gauguin's paintings can't be very good. After all, he deserted his wife and family for a life in Tahiti.

2. Don't listen to Bowman when she talks about raises for police officers. She's a cop.

3. PROFESSOR: Why do you say that my teaching methods are ineffective? DEAN: Because the students say so—and they're the ones who pay the bills and keep us employed.

4. It's clear that the universe must have an order and purpose. Look around you: There is order and purpose in the human body, in nature, in the clockwork regularity of the stars, even in molecules and crystals. So surely the entire universe has order.

5. *"Don't risk letting a fatal accident rob your family of the home they love—on the average more than 250 Americans die each year because of accidents.* What would happen to your family's home if you were one of them?" (Ad for Colonial Penn Life Insurance Company)

6. An anti-abortion film called *The Silent Scream* contains ultrasound images of a twelve-week-old fetus being aborted. As the fetus draws away

from the probes of the abortionist's suction tube, it appears to open its mouth and utter what the narrator describes as a "silent scream." The narrator talks about the "child being torn apart," and so forth.

7. My fellow representatives, as you consider this new tax reform bill, please keep in mind that changes in it will fall squarely on the shoulders of the middle class. And the middle class is the largest single bloc of voters in this country. Do not be persuaded by the arguments of the poor: They rarely vote. It would be unwise to alienate the middle class—we must not anger those who elect us.

8. SKIP: Preacher Caldwell says we shouldn't take drugs.
ROCK: Don't listen to him. He drinks coffee, and caffeine is a drug.

9. Do you think it's wise to turn down a date with a professor? Don't forget who determines your grade.

10. You know, Professor, I think you might want to consider raising my grade, what with all the concern there is on this campus about sex between students and faculty. I mean, not that we're doing anything wrong, but what if people get the idea that we are? You wouldn't want me to leave here upset, would you? Who knows what people might think upset me?

11. I wouldn't trust Mack's advice on what kind of car to buy—he's a Chevy dealer.

12. Your honor, I know that my client was driving under the influence of alcohol. He's admitted it freely. But, your honor, he was just depressed over getting fired. He was worried about his young wife and two tiny children, one a mere babe in arms. Who will feed them? Who will clothe them? Who will comfort them if my client goes to jail? Look at that woman and those two little children, your honor. Can you deprive them of their daddy?

13. Sure, the so-called right thing to do is to love your neighbor. But they didn't have AIDS in the time of Jesus. I'm sure he didn't mean for us to jeopardize our own children's health by letting a child with AIDS attend school. What if your child has to sit next to him? What if he coughs on your daughter?

14. During a tax hearing, California Assemblyman Richard Floyd, D–Hawthorne, became impatient with a witness. The apparently exasperated Floyd demanded, "Do you think people are too damn dumb to throw out [officeholders] who vote for excessive taxes?" "You're living proof of that," replied Assemblyman Ross Johnson, R–La Habra. (Reported in the *Sacramento Bee*, October 5, 1986)

15. A picture of a shabbily dressed child holding an empty bowl accompanies this caption: "Poor little Maria! Will she go to bed hungry again tonight?" (Generic ad for various charities claiming to feed starving children)

16. " 'The Emotional Strain and Overspending Was Terrible,' . . . is a common statement after the funeral . . . *but there is a better way.*" (Opening lines in a mailer for National Memorial Plan. Note: the passage set in single quotation marks was printed in blue ink; the body of text was in black, and in much larger type than the rest of the text.)

17. "Nobody likes a phony. That seems to be especially so for folks like us who live in small towns. Maybe that's because our lives are simpler, purer than living in the city. I don't know. All I do know is that we should be able to depend on our state senators. That's why I'm so disappointed in Senator X. He took money from special interest groups and used it to pay his wife and then lived off of it. I think that's wrong; Senator X thinks it's all right. My name is _____, and that's why I'm running for the state senate." (Paraphrase of political radio commercial)

18. In 1974 Charles Evers, then mayor of Fayette, Mississippi, was indicted by the grand jury in Jackson on charges of evading payment of more than $53,000 in federal income taxes. In August 1974, he responded to the charges by saying, "They've tried everything else. Tried shooting me, starving me and breaking me, and they missed. Now they're trying this." (Quoted in Ronald Munson's, *The Way of Words*, 1976, p. 305)

19. I know $30,000 might seem like a lot of money to renovate my office. But, then, I am president of this company, and most executives of large companies spend more than that.

20. Cutting in on a man who was talking about drugs, *Today Show* host Bryant Gumbel asked: "Why should we care what you say—you're a junkie, right?" (*Washington Post*, January 4, 1986)

21. Judith Becker, a behavioral scientist at Columbia University, was a member of the Meese Commission on Pornography. During a discussion over what constituted being a "victim of pornography," she asked, "What exactly is a victim of pornography?"
    "Someone who has been raped," one member responded.
    "That is a victim of the crime of rape," another member answered.
    "Someone whose father or brother abused her."
    "That's a victim of incest."
    After more than an hour of wrestling over this, Becker finally concluded that "a victim of pornography [is] someone who sustains a paper cut while turning the pages of a sex magazine."
    (Carol Tavris, *Redding Record Searchlight*, July 12, 1986)

22. I don't trust all this talk about AIDS being difficult to catch through casual contact. Don't forget, most of the organizations saying this are full of gay people.

23. WAYNE: I'm in favor of legalized gambling.
    NEWTON: There are some strong reasons against legalizing it.
    WAYNE: Yeah, but anyone who's opposed to legalized gambling is not worth listening to anyway.

24. During a debate with William F. Buckley, novelist Norman Mailer said: "Mr. Buckley, you want me to lie down on the railroad tracks, tie my hands to the rails, and wait until the engine of your logic gets around to riding over me?"

25. Referring to an opponent for union leadership, John L. Lewis said: "There isn't any mincing, lakadaisical, pink-pantied gigolo going to dethrone John L. in his own convention!" (*Time,* September 25, 1944)

26. Benedict Spinoza, a famous seventeenth-century rationalist, was excommunicated from his synagogue as a heretic. This is a quote from a letter he received: "Miserable man and worm upon the earth that you are, ashes and food for worms, how can you confront the eternal wisdom with your unspeakable blasphemy? What foundation have you for this rash, insane, deplorable, accursed doctrine?"

27. In *Hendon's Life of Lincoln,* William Hendon mentions a law case in which Abraham Lincoln had an opponent by the name of Judge Stephen T. Logan. Logan was well known for the care with which he dressed. At his final summation to the jury, Lincoln said: " 'Gentlemen, you must be careful not to permit yourselves to be overcome by the eloquence of the counsel for the defense. Judge Logan, I know, is an effective lawyer. I have met him too often to doubt that; but shrewd and careful though he may be, still he is sometimes wrong. Since this trial has begun I have discovered that, with all his caution and fastidiousness, he hasn't knowledge enough to put his shirt on right.' Logan turned red as crimson, but sure enough, Lincoln was correct, for [Logan] had donned a new shirt, and by mistake had drawn it over his head with the pleated bosom behind. The general laugh which followed destroyed the effect of Logan's eloquence over the jury—the very point at which Lincoln aimed." (New York: World Publishing Co., 1965, p. 288)

28. "The religions of mankind must be classed among the mass delusions of this kind. No one, needless to say, who shares a delusion ever recognizes it as such." (Sigmund Freud, *Civilization and Its Discontents*)

29. "Erich von Daniken, whose distinctions include a jail term in his native Switzerland for embezzlement, widely popularized the notion that no mere human beings could have constructed the pyramids of Egypt, the statues of Easter Island, and other feats of preindustrial engineering. They must, therefore, have been made by extraterrestrial visitors." (L. Sprague de Camp, "Little Green Men from Afar," *Humanist,* July/August 1976)

30. "Creationists tend to appeal to authority—to neat, easy solutions to complex questions. Such arguments tend to be attractive to the frustrated, the needful, and the alienated." (Laurie R. Godfrey, "Science and Evolution in the Public Eye," *Paranormal Borderlands of Science,* Kendrick Frazier, ed.)

31. "I do it because I do it, because that's what I do." (Werner Erhard, quoted by Martin Gardner in *Science: Good, Bad and Bogus*)

32. From a *Newsweek* October 5, 1992, report on the increase of HIV-AIDS among non–drug using heterosexuals: "P_____ G_____, a trustee for the National Community AIDS Partnership, was infected with the AIDS virus in the mid-1980s. But she has only recently decided to tell the dozen or so men she has slept with that she is HIV-positive. Acknowledging that it was wrong not to tell them sooner, she rationalizes the omission. 'Being involved with men who are married helps,' she says. 'They aren't being honest; why should I be honest with them?'"

33. From a commercial for videotapes of the 1950s TV series *The Honeymooners:*
    RALPH: I only buy what's necessary.
    ALICE: You call $15 for a bowling ball necessary?
    RALPH: How am I supposed to bowl without a bowling ball?

34. Responding to evidence that he had employed an undocumented nanny, senatorial candidate Michael Huffington responded: "Who among us has not broken the law?" (*Redding Record Searchlight*, October 28, 1994)

35. Responding to charges that he sexually harassed more than fifteen women over a 24-year period, Oregon Senator Bob Packwood said that he has been a leading advocate of women's rights. He added: "I recognize that my personal conduct has been at variance with these beliefs—not because my convictions are not genuine but because my conduct was not faithful to my convictions." (Associated Press, December 10, 1992)

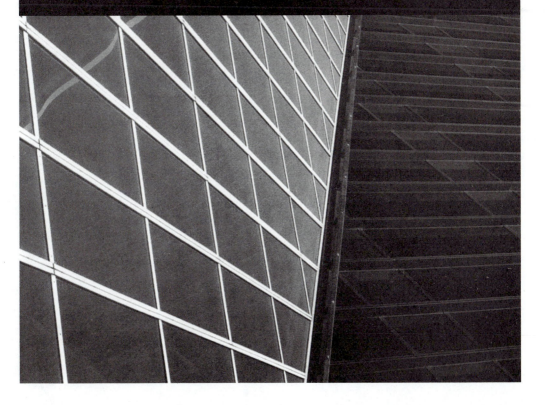

PART THREE

DEDUCTIVE ARGUMENTS

CHAPTER 7

Categorical Syllogisms

I readily own, that all right reasoning may be reduced to Aristotle's forms of syllogism.

JOHN LOCKE

Some logical arguments contain premises that are intended to provide conclusive support for their conclusions. Such arguments are called deductive arguments, and are the concern of this part of our study. *A deductive argument is an argument whose premises are intended to provide conclusive support for its conclusion.* In this chapter, we will study a special kind of deductive argument called a *syllogism* and the six rules which tell us *with logical certainty* whether or not the argument's form is valid.

VALIDITY

Validity is a formal property of deductive arguments. *A deductive argument is valid when it is impossible for its premises to be true and its conclusion false.* Put another way: *A deductive argument is valid when the relationship between the premises and conclusion is such that* **if** *the premises* **were all** *true, then the conclusion would* **have to be** *true.* Let's look at two examples:

A.
        All chairs are red.
        Aretha Franklin is a chair.
        Aretha Franklin is red.

and

B.
        All humans are mortal.
        Aretha Franklin is human.
        Aretha Franklin is mortal.

You might be inclined to say that B is good but A isn't. In a way you're right because A has false premises and the premises of B are true. And we know that a cogent argument can never have false premises. On the other hand, both arguments are "good" in the sense that their premises do provide conclusive *logical* support for their conclusions—that is, *sufficient* grounds. So, from the viewpoint of *logical deductions*, these arguments are equally good. Both are *logically* airtight. How can they be? How can an argument containing all false propositions be logically airtight?

It's possible because validity is a *formal*, not a *factual*, characteristic of deductive arguments. *If* all chairs really were red, and *if* Aretha Franklin really were a chair, then Aretha Franklin would *have to be* red. In other words, these two premises are relevant and sufficient to establish the conclusion. Since validity is basically a function of the quantity of evidence, and since the evidence here is *conclusive*, the argument is formally correct. It is valid. Of course it is not a cogent argument because it contains premises which are known to be false. In other words, it does not offer *reasonable* evidence for concluding that Aretha Franklin is red. But it is nonetheless a valid argument.

STUDY HINT

A deductive argument is cogent if and only if it is valid and contains only true premises.

When analyzing the validity of a deductive argument, we initially ignore the truth value of the premises by treating them *as if they were true*. If, based on this assumption, the premises provide conclusive support for the conclusion, the argument is valid. Having determined that an argument is valid, we may then test it for cogency by determining the truth of each premise. If all premises in a *valid* deductive argument are actually true, then the conclusion must be. In some cases we will immediately recognize the falsity of one or more premises. This tells us that the argument lacks cogency because the premises are unreasonable. But remember, arguments that aren't cogent still may be valid.

Before we can hope to evaluate deductive arguments, we must become familiar with the *form* in which they appear. One of the most common types of deductive argument is the syllogism. *A syllogism is a deductive argument containing two premises and a conclusion*. In this chapter we'll study one of the most common expressions of the syllogism: the standard-form categorical syllogism. The basic building block of this kind of syllogism is the *categorical proposition*.

CATEGORICAL PROPOSITIONS

Propositions, as we know, are statements that are either true or false. Certain kinds of deductive propositions relate two classes, *a class being a group of things having a common property or characteristic*. The proposition "All apples are fruits" relates the class *apples* with the class *fruits*. *Apples* is that class of things sharing the common characteristic of being an apple; *fruits* is that class of things sharing the common characteristic of being a fruit. In speaking of classes, Aristotle, "the father of logic," used the word *category*. So naturally enough, *any proposition that asserts that one class is included in whole or in part within another class* (such as the proposition "All apples are fruits") *is referred to as a categorical proposition*.

The statement "All apples are fruits" asserts that the whole class *apples* is included within the class *fruits*. Propositions of similar form are "All mothers are females"; "All humans are vertebrates"; "All dogs are carnivores." Sometimes a class is composed of several words, as in: "All *U.S. Presidents* are *persons who are at least thirty-five years old*" and "All *children too old to qualify* are *spectators for this event*." And of course, some categorical propositions are blatantly false: "All giraffes are animals of prey"; "All swimmers who wear caps are women"; "All things that fly are birds." But in studying deductive validity, as we just noted, we're not concerned with the factual truth of an argument's premises but with the argument's form. It's an argument's *form* that ultimately determines whether or not the argument is *valid*.

All the propositions we've mentioned so far take the form "All something is something." If we merely substitute *S* for the first *something,* or class term, and *P* for the second *something,* or class term, we have a form that reads: "All *S* is *P.*"

EXERCISE 7-1 *

A. Name completely the classes that are being related in the following propositions.

1. All Californians are citizens.

2. All baseball players are athletes.

3. All those breaking the law are criminals.

4. All newspapers that suppress news are inadequate sources of information.

5. All commercials that rely solely on persuasive techniques to communicate are vehicles of noninformation.

6. All nonvoters are citizens who should not complain when things don't go as they'd wish.

7. All nonparticipants in the finals held over the weekend in Washington are nonenrollees in next year's competition, to be held on July 4 at a yet-to-be-designated city.

B. Can you name completely the two classes being related in the following propositions?

1. No police officer is a thief.

2. Some police officers are thieves.

3. Some police officers are not thieves.

4. No nonpolice officer is a thief.

5. No nonpolice officer is a nonthief.

6. Some nonthieves are not police officers.

7. Some nonpolice officers who are chronically complaining about the lack of law and order are themselves violators of the law.

8. No police officer who takes the oath seriously and does the best he or she can is a person who must ever fear a charge of noncompliance with the law.

Propositional Form

When we speak of a proposition's form, we refer to the manner in which the proposition speaks of its classes. The form "All *S* is *P*" is the form of any proposition that relates one class to another in exactly this way.

Each member of the statement "All *S* is *P*" is performing a job. The *all* is telling us *how many* of *S* we're talking about. For this reason, *all* is said to quantify or to be the *quantifier* of this form. Here *all* speaks of *S* in a universal way; that is, it includes every single *S*. Because *is* links or couples the *S* and the *P*, *is* is said to be the *copula* of the propositional form.

Notice that *is* is affirmative. We speak of a form as having quality; *the quality of a proposition indicates whether the proposition is affirmative or negative.* In this instance *is* obviously affirms something between *S* and *P*; therefore, this particular form, All *S* is *P*, is *affirmative*.

What about *S* and *P*? We already know they stand for classes. *But if we define the subject as whatever appears between the quantifier and the copula, S represents the subject as well. And if we define the predicate as whatever follows the copula, P represents the predicate.* So we can see that *S* and *P* represent not only class terms but also the *subject* and *predicate* of the proposition itself.

Because we can put any proposition of this type into the form "All *S* is *P*," we may call this form *standard*, which is to say it's a conventional designation of all propositions that speak of their class terms in this way. "All *S* is *P*," then, simply says that every member of the class *S* is included within the class *P* (that is, "All apples are fruits"; "All humans are vertebrates"; "All mothers are females"). Since the quantity signified by *all* is *universal*—it includes every member of the *S* class—and since the quality of the proposition is *affirmative*—it affirms something of the subject class—this standard-form categorical proposition ("All *S* is *P*") is called a *universal affirmative*.

Aristotle observed four ways to relate the same subject and predicate of a categorical proposition. We've spoken of one; now let's consider the other three.

Consider the proposition "No apples are fruits." This relates the same subject and predicate as the proposition "All apples are fruits," but it relates them in a different way. Likewise, we could say "No humans are vertebrates" or "No mothers are females." We could represent such propositions symbolically as follows: "No S is P," in which S and P again signify class terms as well as subject and predicate of the given proposition. Like the universal affirmative, "No S is P" also says something about every member of its subject class. The quantifier *no* really means that every single member of the S class (apples) is excluded from the P class (fruits). Thus its quantity is certainly universal. Since "No S is P" is denying membership of one class within another, its *quality* is *negative*. So we can conclude that *"No S is P" is a universal negative* standard-form categorical proposition.

We can speak of the same subject and predicate in still another way. This time we'll not speak of all the members of a class but only of some; thus, "Some apples are fruits." Unlike the two standard-form universal propositions we spoke of, this form—"Some S is P"—does not speak of its subject term universally. The proposition says that there exists at least one particular instance of the subject and it will be found within the predicate class. In other words, "Some S is P" is affirming *partial* membership of S within P. Is it affirmative or negative? Affirmative. Such a propositional form that *affirms particular* membership of the subject within the predicate we call, appropriately enough, a *particular affirmative* standard-form categorical proposition.

As we saw, we can have both universal negative and universal affirmative propositions. Likewise, we can have particular negative as well as particular affirmative propositions. This is the fourth standard way of expressing a relationship between a subject and predicate class. The proposition "Some apples are not fruits" is an example of a particular negative proposition. As was true of the particular affirmative, this propositional form—"Some S is not P"—talks about some but not all members of the subject class. This is why we call it a particular proposition. Rather than affirming partial subject class membership within the predicate class, this form denies it. We call a proposition that denies partial membership of one of a class within another a *particular negative* standard-form categorical proposition.

These, then, are the four standard-form categorical propositions:

All S is P—universal affirmative (*A*)
No S is P—universal negative (*E*)
Some S is P—particular affirmative (*I*)
Some S is not P—particular negative (*O*)

In each, the S and P stand for subject and predicate and for class terms. The *all* and *no* mean that every member of the class is being referred to; the *some* means that at least one existing member of the class is being referred to. For simplicity we refer to the four standard forms by these letters: *A* (universal affirmative), *E* (universal negative), *I* (particular affirmative), and *O* (particular negative). These letter designations come from the Latin words *affirmo* ("I affirm") and *nego* ("I deny"), *affirmo* supplying the *A* and *I* and *nego* the *E* and *O*.

Since we are dealing with the form—and not the content—of the propositions at this stage, we should take advantage of this simplification. *Every single A, E, I, or O type proposition will have the preceding form.* No matter how long and complicated the class terms may be, the basic form remains the same. For example, the proposition "All students with short hair, but without moustaches, who have gone to college for one semester, but whose GPA is between 2.3 and 3.4, with one older brother and two younger sisters, whose last name begins with *M* are dismissed" is a basic *A* proposition. The subject term begins after the quantifier (*all*) with the word *students* and ends with *M*, before the copula (*are*).

STUDY HINT

Practice reducing categorical propositions to standard form by keying in on the quantifier and copula.

Whatever falls between the quantifier and copula is always the subject. Whatever comes after the copula is the predicate.

A good way to familiarize yourself with the four forms is to underline the quantifier and copula of a proposition. This will immediately isolate the subject and predicate.

EXERCISE 7-2

A. Name the subject and predicate terms of the following propositions; circle the copula and underline the quantifier; indicate their quantity and quality.

O 1. Some women are not members of the women's liberation movement.

2. No desirable leader is a coward.

A 3. All business people are rugged individualists.

4. All educators for capital punishment are nonhumanitarians.

E 5. No Christian is a believer in abortion.

6. Some students are either arts or science majors.

7. Some candidates who are not heavily financed are not potential pawns of big-money interests.

8. No one who believes in premarital sex is a nonsponsor of premarital cohabitation.

I 9. Some ecologists are nonopponents of offshore drilling.

10. No father who cares about his child's welfare is one who'd take his child to an X-rated film!

11. Some patients exhibiting all the symptoms of schizophrenia are manic-depressives.

12. No companies doing business in the Middle East are secure firms.

13. Some feathered things that fly are not birds.

14. Some stockbrokers who work for E. F. Hutton are not partners in companies whose securities they recommend.

15. All physicians who are licensed to practice in this state are medical school graduates who have passed special qualifying examinations but are not necessarily internists.

16. Some politicians who are not highly respected by the people are, without doubt, honest people.

17. No serious musician—stereotypes notwithstanding—is a dullard whose interests lie in nothing more than what's contained in a musical score.

18. Some women, despite what men say, are workers who are capable of outperforming their male counterparts.

19. No thing that is long lasting and productive of great long-term pleasure is an object that we should treat in a cavalier fashion.

20. Some occasions of intense suffering, though seemingly pointless, are opportunities for the growth that is necessary to achieve maturity.

B. Give the letter and name of each of the preceding propositions.

Distribution

There's one other point to note about the standard-form propositions—*A, E, I, O*—and that concerns the question of their *distribution*. When a proposition speaks *universally* of one of its terms it talks about every single member of that class, or *distributes* that term. *A proposition distributes a term if it refers to all members of the class designated by that term.* An *A* proposition ("All *S* is *P*") distributes its subject term because it speaks universally of *S*. Do you think it distributes its predicate? If it does, *S* and *P*, with respect to distribution, are being spoken of in the same way. In a proposition that handles its subject and predicate in the same way—distributes both or does not—the subject and predicate can be interchanged with no loss of logical meaning. Is "All fruits are apples" the logical equivalent of "All apples are fruits"? Obviously not. Let's use a diagram to see why not.

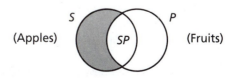

The preceding circles represent all members of both the *S* and the *P* classes. Since the propositional form claims that every instance of *S* is also an instance of *P*, let's indicate that the class of *S* without *P* is empty. We do this by shading out the appropriate area. The diagram now shows that "All *S* is *P*," as in "All apples are fruits." But is every instance of *P* an instance of *S*? No. Some portion of *P* exists apart from *S*: Some fruits are not apples. So *an A proposition distributes its subject but does not distribute its predicate.*

In speaking of *E* propositions ("No *S* is *P*"), we saw how they distribute their subject terms, that is, exclude every member of the subject class from the predicate class. Does an *E* proposition distribute its *P* term? Is "No fruits are apples" the logical equivalent of "No apples are fruits"? Yes, these are equivalents. The following diagram illustrates the point.

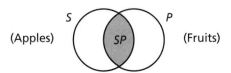

The circles again represent all members of both the *S* and *P* classes. The diagram shows that the class *SP* is empty, as the proposition "No *S* is *P*" prescribes. We see that *S* and *P* have no members in common (the shaded area *SP* is unoccupied), that every member of each class excludes every member of the other. For this reason "No apples are fruits" has its equivalent in "No fruits are apples." We are speaking of the classes in the exact same way. *In an E proposition, we are distributing both* S *and* P.

The particular affirmative position, *I*, obviously does not distribute its subject term because it speaks of *some*, not *all*. It says that there exists at least one member of the subject class that is a member of the predicate class. This is the meaning of *some: There exists at least one member.* But it also says only some members of the predicate class are members of the subject class. In other words, it doesn't distribute its predicate either; it speaks of its predicate in the same partial terms that it speaks of its subject, as the following diagram illustrates:

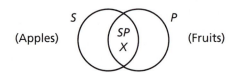

The form "Some *S* is *P*" claims that at least one member of the *SP* class exists. *X* represents the existence of this one member. Notice that only part of each circle is excluded from the other, which illustrates that neither term is spoken of universally. Since the subject and predicate are spoken of in precisely the same way, that is, as undistributed terms, we can interchange them and have a proposition equivalent to the original. So "Some apples are fruits" is logically equivalent to "Some fruits are apples." In other words, both propositions share the same portions of the interlocked circles shown.

Finally, in discussing the *O* form, "Some *S* is not *P*," we saw that the *S* term is spoken of particularly; therefore *O* propositions do not distribute their subject terms. A superficial look at an *O* proposition suggests that the *P* term is undistributed as well. But is it? Actually, in the proposition "Some *S* is not *P*," aren't we saying that *every member of the P class will exclude the particular members of the S class of which we're speaking*? In other words, "some *S*" is excluded from *all* of *P*; there is "some *S*" that is not identical with *any* member of *P*; every instance of *P* will exclude "some *S*." This is perhaps difficult to grasp. A good way to see it is, again, with the help of a diagram.

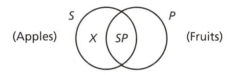

The diagram illustrates what "Some *S* is not *P*" is really saying. It says there exists at least one member of *S* (*X*) that is excluded from *P*. In other words, *every* instance of *P* will exclude the particular member of *S* that falls outside it ("some *S*"). Again, "some *S*" is always outside the *entire* class *P*. To see this in an actual proposition, consider "Some females are not mothers." If we try to interchange the subject and predicate here, we do not come up with an equivalent to the original proposition. Instead, we come up with "Some mothers are not females." This shows that the terms are not being spoken of equally: One is being distributed, but the other is not. (It is only by chance that many propositions, such as "Some males are not politicians," seem to produce an equivalent when we interchange the subject and predicate terms: "Some politicians are not males." This should impress on us the importance of *form*, not content, in determining the validity of a deductive argument. Distribution is vital in proving arguments valid.) The terms in ***boldface*** are always distributed—and only those terms—according to the following pattern:

A: All **S** is P.
E: No **S** is **P.**
I: Some S is P.
O: Some S is not **P.**

STUDY HINT

In determining subject, predicate, and distribution in standard-form categorical propositions, the key factor is *where* the term occurs and *not what* it says.

The following chart will help us master what we've discovered thus far about standard-form categorical propositions.

CATEGORICAL PROPOSITION	DESIGNATION	QUANTITY	QUALITY	DISTRIBUTION
All S is P	A	universal	affirmative	subject only
No S is P	E	universal	negative	subject and predicate
Some S is P	I	particular	affirmative	neither subject nor predicate
Some S is not P	O	particular	negative	predicate only

EXERCISE 7-3 *

Name the form of each of the following propositions and what it distributes.

1. Some children are lovers of ice cream.

2. No revolutionary is a believer in the status quo.

3. All men in combat are soldiers under extraordinary pressure.

4. All noncombatants earning combat pay are shameless individuals.

5. Some film projectionists are not members of a union.

6. Compared with foreign automobile manufacturers, some American automobile manufacturers, despite various pressures, are reluctant observers of the public interest.

7. Some nonmartial arts are not exercises that are lacking in physical courage.

8. All students, some of whom are under twenty-one, are advocates of more tax money spent on education.

9. Some colors of the rainbow are not hues seen anywhere else.

10. Some lives are tragedies that we write, direct, and star in.

The Simplified Square of Contradiction

If we compare the diagrams for each of the four standard-form categorical propositions, we observe an interesting pattern. *A* propositions assert that the class of *S* and *not-P* is empty, while *O* propositions assert that the class of *S* and *not-P* contains at least one member:

All *S* is *P*.

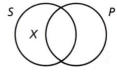

Some *S* is not *P*.

Comparing the diagrams for *A* and *O* propositions, we see immediately that both cannot be true at the same time. We also see that *A* and *O* cannot both be false at the same time. The class of things that is S and *not-P* must either be empty or not empty.

In technical terms, we can say that A and O propositions are *contradictories*. *Two propositions are contradictories if the truth of one implies the falsity of the other,* **and** *if the falsity of one implies the truth of the other. In other words, propositions are contradictories if they have opposite truth values.* For example, if the A proposition "All mothers are female" is true, a corresponding O proposition "Some mothers are not female" must be false.

We also see that E and I propositions are contradictories. E propositions assert that the class of things that is both S and P is empty, while I propositions assert that the very same class contains at least one member:

No S is P.   Some S is P.

For example, if the E proposition "No apples are blue" is true, then the I proposition "Some apples are blue" must be false.

We can construct a pattern resembling the four corners of a square that represents contradiction:

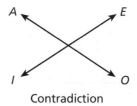

Contradiction

The square represents a set of *immediate inferences* that can be drawn based on what is known or assumed to be true for a given standard-form categorical proposition. If an A proposition is assumed true, we can immediately deduce that its corresponding O proposition is false. If an A proposition is assumed false, we can immediately deduce that its corresponding O proposition is true. The relationship holds in both directions, and we can just as easily make inferences based on the truth or falsity of O propositions. If an O proposition is assumed true, we can immediately deduce that its corresponding A proposition is false. If an O proposition is assumed false, we can immediately deduce that its corresponding A proposition is true. E and I follow an identical pattern. We can simplify contradiction as follows:

A is true = O is false	A is false = O is true
E is true = I is false	E is false = I is true
I is true = E is false	I is false = E is true
O is true = A is false	O is false = A is true

Existential Import

The particular interpretation we have given to the four standard-form propositions is based on a system of logic described by a nineteenth-century logician named George Boole. It is often referred to as Boolean logic.

In Boolean logic, we do not interpret *A* and *E* propositions as asserting the existence of anything. That is, they lack what is known as *existential import. A proposition has existential import if it asserts the existence of at least one thing.* For example, "All Olympian gods are Greek" can be true in two cases: (1) Olympian gods exist and they are Greek, or (2) no Olympian gods exist. Both possibilities are consistent with the proposition's essential meaning: "If there are Olympian gods, they must be Greek." Thus *A* propositions are neutral regarding the existence or nonexistence of their subjects. The same is true of *E* propositions. "No mothers are male" could be true if (1) mothers exist, and not one of them is male, or (2) no mothers exist.

By contrast, *I* and *O* propositions are understood to claim that something exists, since, as we have seen, *some* carries existential import. *Some* is taken to mean "At least one." "Some *S* is *P*" means "At least one *S* exists, and it is also *P*." Thus, "Some apples are red" can be true under only one set of circumstances or interpretation: at least one apple exists and it is red. "Some *S* is not *P*" is taken to mean "At least one *S* exists which is not *P*." Similarly, "Some mothers are not male" can be true under only one set of circumstances or interpretation: At least one mother exists and she is not male.

Universal propositions, *A* and *E,* by contrast, are ambiguous in the sense that they each can support two distinct interpretations. Thus, just because it is true that "All students who flunk logic are those who fail the final," we cannot validly infer that, therefore, "Some students who flunk logic are those who fail the final." The second proposition makes a stronger claim than the first: It asserts that at least one student flunked logic and failed the final. The first proposition, by contrast, merely sets down a conditional relationship between its subject and predicate. It says that any student who flunks logic will also have failed the final. But the *condition* will hold even if no one flunks logic.

Similarly, we cannot validly infer from "No unicorns are zebras," that "Some unicorns are not zebras." "No unicorns are zebras" can be true if there are unicorns which are other kinds of horses than zebras. It can also be true if there are no unicorns of any sort.

To simplify this important aspect of the Boolean interpretation of standard-form categorical propositions, *we cannot validly infer particular propositions from universal ones.* (In Part Four on induction, we'll study the conditions under which we can draw universal generalizations from particular instances. This can only be done inductively, however, not deductively.)

STUDY HINT

A and *E* propositions do not assert existence, but *I* and *O* propositions do.

Obversion, Conversion, and Contraposition

Within the constraints of the Boolean interpretation of existential import, *obversion*, *conversion* (for *E* and *I*), and *contraposition* (for *A* and *O*) are valid *equivalent inferences*.

Both obversion and contraposition involve a special kind of negation known as the *complement* of a term. The word "complement" derives from "that which completes." *The complement of a term consists of everything that is not that term.* For example, the complement of the class of "red" is "non-red" or "not-red." The complement of "heroes" is not "cowards," which is simply the "opposite" of heroes, but the more inclusive term "non-heroes," which includes flowers, bicycles, logic books—*everything* that is not included in the class "heroes."

Obversion consists of changing the quality of a proposition and replacing the predicate with its complement. To obvert the universal affirmative proposition "All thinking machines are computers," we first change the quality from affirmative to negative, resulting in the universal negative proposition "No thinking machines are computers." Next, we replace the term "computers" with its complement, "noncomputers," giving us: "No thinking machines are noncomputers." Applying the same steps, we can use obversion to infer that if "No thinking machines are computers" then "All thinking machines are noncomputers." Similarly, if "Some thinking machines are computers" then "Some thinking machines are not noncomputers." Lastly, if "Some thinking machines are not computers," it follows by obversion that "Some thinking machines are noncomputers."

STUDY HINT
Obversion

1. Change the quality of the proposition to be obverted.

2. Replace the predicate with its complement.

Contraposition consists of switching and complementing both the subject and predicate. Under the Boolean interpretation of existential import, contraposition is valid for *A* and *O* propositions, but not for *E* and *I*. The contraposition of "All mothers are females" is "All nonfemales are nonmothers." The contraposition of "Some students are not happy folks" is "Some unhappy folks are not nonstudents."

STUDY HINT
Contraposition (valid for A and O)

1. Replace the subject with the complement of the predicate.

2. Replace the predicate with the complement of the subject.

Conversion consists of switching the subject and predicate of a proposition with each other. Conversion is valid for *E* and *I* propositions, but invalid for *A* and *O*. "No logic students are infants" implies that "No infants are logic students." Similarly, "Some flowers are popular gifts" implies that "Some popular gifts are flowers." Reversing the subject and predicate in corresponding *E* and corresponding *I* propositions retains the meaning and truth value of the original proposition.

STUDY HINT

To convert a proposition, simply switch the subject and predicate with each other. Conversion is valid for *E* and *I*, but invalid for *A* and *O*.

EXERCISE 7-4

What additional propositions can you validly deduce if the following are assumed to be true?

1. No one who will be admitted is under twenty-one years old.

2. Some *S* is *non-P*.

3. All logic students who study diligently are likely to be happy in later years.

4. Some peaches are not sweet.

5. All unicorns are horses with magical horns.

6. No unicorns are horses with magical horns.

7. Some industrialized nations are on the brink of collapse.

8. No *non-S* is *non-P*.

9. Some plastic products are not recyclable.

10. All *A* propositions are true.

We've learned what a standard-form categorical proposition is and the forms that it can take. We're now ready to turn to the deductive arguments containing such propositions.

Since syllogisms often appear in deductive arguments, we must find out what a syllogism is, how we can construct one, and what role the syllogism plays in argument. Again, our goal is to be able to distinguish the valid deductive argument from the invalid one, the one whose premises logically imply its conclusion from the one whose premises do not. In short, we'll learn to recognize and use correct deductive reasoning. Of course, correct deductive reasoning alone does not guarantee truth, but it *can* guarantee true conclusions *if* our premises are actually true, as this argument illustrates:

> All mothers are females.
> Some students are not females.
> Some students are not mothers.

Here both of our premises are actually true and we have reasoned correctly from those premises to our conclusion. Our argument is valid, our conclusion true; the argument is cogent. But if our reasoning is invalid, no amount of true premises will *guarantee* true conclusions:

> All mothers are females.
> Some students are females.
> Some students are mothers.

Here again both our premises are true, but we have reasoned incorrectly from those premises to a conclusion. Our argument is invalid and our conclusion, although it might be true, doesn't logically follow from our premises.

Both of these deductive arguments are syllogisms. *Like all syllogisms they contain two premises and a conclusion.* Because these syllogisms contain only categorical propositions, they are called *categorical syllogisms.*

STANDARD-FORM CATEGORICAL SYLLOGISMS

To understand what a standard-form categorical syllogism is, let's consider this argument:

> All illegal drugs are hazards to health.
> All forms of cocaine are illegal drugs.
> All forms of cocaine are hazards to health.

This is a categorical syllogism. From it we can note a number of things that are characteristic of arguments like these. First, a categorical syllogism contains three categorical propositions. Second, the syllogism has *exactly three terms—illegal drugs, hazards to health, and forms of cocaine.* Third, *each of the terms appears in exactly two of the propositions.* Fourth, *the propositions are in a certain order—the conclusion coming last and the premises coming first.* We can specify even further the order of the propositions when we realize that the *predicate term* of the conclusion (*hazards to health*) is called the *major term* of a syllogism, and the *subject term* of the conclusion (*forms of cocaine*) is called the *minor term.* The premise containing the major term is called the *major premise;* the one with the minor term is the *minor premise.* (The term common to both premises is called the *middle term;* here it's "illegal drugs.") Like this one, a categorical syllogism should always appear in this order: major premise, minor premise, conclusion. These then are the defining characteristics of any standard-form categorical syllogism: (1) It consists of three categorical propositions; (2) it has exactly three terms; (3) each of its terms appears in exactly two of the propositions; and (4) it appears in the order of major premise, minor premise, and conclusion. To determine the validity of such an argument, we must know about its form.

We can summarize what we've learned thus far about syllogistic form as follows:

1. The conclusion determines the major and minor terms of a categorical syllogism.

2. The *major term* is always *the same term as the predicate* of the conclusion.

3. The *minor term* is always *the same term as the subject* of the conclusion.

4. The *middle term is not in the conclusion but is common to each premise.*

STUDY HINT

Look to the conclusion to determine the major and minor term. Once we have identified the components of the syllogism, determining its form is a matter of mechanics.

EXERCISE 7-5 *

In the following syllogisms (1) state the three terms; (2) state the major and minor terms; (3) state the major and minor premises; and (4) order them correctly. Assume that the last statements in 1 through 5 are the conclusions. You will need to spot the conclusion in 6 through 10.

1. All political candidates are seekers of offices.
   Some political candidates are Republicans.
   Some Republicans are seekers of offices.

2. No true sportsman is a cheater.
   All cheaters are dishonest persons.
   No dishonest person is a true sportsman.

3. Some animals are not endangered species.
   All endangered species are precious creatures.
   Some animals are not precious creatures.

4. Some epicureans are lovers of wine.
   Some epicureans are lovers of women.
   Some lovers of wine are lovers of women.

5. All pollutants are disease carriers.
   All cigarettes are disease carriers.
   All cigarettes are pollutants.

6. All men are equal citizens and all equal citizens are persons entitled to due process.
   Therefore all men are persons entitled to due process.

7. Some countries are belligerents and no belligerents are peace lovers. It follows that some countries are not peace lovers.

8. No sprinters are slow runners because no slow runners are members of the track team, and all sprinters are members of the track team.

9. Since some TV programs are bores and all bores are wastes of time, some TV programs are wastes of time.

10. Some airlines are poor means of transportation, for all airlines are expensive enterprises and some expensive enterprises are poor means of transportation.

Form

A syllogism's form consists of its mood and its figure. The mood of a syllogism is the order in which the propositions occur when the syllogism is in standard form. We determine the *mood* of a standard-form categorical syllogism by noting the order of the standard-form categorical propositions it contains. In our sample syllogism,

> **All illegal drugs are hazards to health.**
> **All forms of cocaine are illegal drugs.**
> **All forms of cocaine are hazards to health.**

the order is *AAA*, that is, the major premise is an *A* proposition, the minor premise is *A*, and the conclusion is *A*.

The figure of a syllogism is determined by the location of the middle term, the middle term being the term that appears in both premises. There are four and only four possible figure arrangements for the middle term. We can represent these as follows:

FIGURE 1		FIGURE 2		FIGURE 3		FIGURE 4	
M	P	P	M	M	P	P	M
S	M	S	M	M	S	M	S
S	P	S	P	S	P	S	P

In Figure 1, the middle term appears as the subject in the major premise and predicate in the minor premise. The middle term, *illegal drugs,* in the preceding argument occupies this position; so the argument is in Figure 1. In Figure 2, the middle term appears as the predicate of the major premise and minor premise. In Figure 3, the middle term appears as subject of major and minor premises. And, in Figure 4, the middle term appears as the predicate of the major premise and subject of the minor premise.

As we study this chart we see a basic pattern emerge for identifying each of the four figures. If we draw a real or imaginary line connecting the middle terms in each figure, we see the following.

FIGURE 1	FIGURE 2	FIGURE 3	FIGURE 4
M＼　P	P　Ｍ	Ｍ　P	P　／M
S　＼M	S　Ｍ	Ｍ　S	M／　S
S　　P	S　　P	S　　P	S　　P

Combine a syllogism's mood and figure and you have its form. The form of the preceding syllogism, therefore, is *AAA-1.* The following categorical syllogisms also have form *AAA-1:*

> All vertebrates are creatures with spines.
> All humans are vertebrates.
> _____
> All humans are creatures with spines.

> All identical medications are drugs producing the same results.
> All aspirin are identical medications.
> _____
> All aspirin are drugs producing the same results.

> All persons with needs are potential thieves.
> All consumers are persons with needs.
> _____
> All consumers are potential thieves.

All these arguments are valid. In fact any syllogism in *AAA-1* form is valid. There are 256 possible forms; only fifteen are valid. Knowing that a syllogistic form is valid, we know that any argument of the same form is also valid. Likewise, knowing that a syllogistic form is invalid, we know that any argument with that form is invalid.

But before we can test a syllogism for validity, we must first be able to identify its form. One of the most important steps in this process, no matter which method of testing we ultimately use, is correctly identifying the conclusion of the syllogism. If this crucial step is missed, any subsequent analysis will be futile.

Spotting the Conclusion

In testing a syllogism, we must be sure that we have correctly identified its form. That is, we must be sure that we correctly arrange the syllogism in the standardized way: major premise, minor premise, conclusion. Initially, it is easy to confuse the order of the premises or to misidentify the conclusion. To guard against this error, concentrate on finding the conclusion.

There are usually a number of signals, or clues, that can aid us in this task. For example, consider the *grouping* of the propositions. In the syllogism "All apples are red. All apples are sweet fruit, and all sweet fruit is red," we notice that one proposition is isolated from the other two. This is our signal that it is the conclusion. (Note that such an arrangement not only isolates one proposition but also groups the other two together, suggesting that they share some common feature.)

We should also look for *signal words.* For example, the same syllogism might be expressed this way: "Since all apples are sweet fruit, and since all sweet fruit is red, all apples are red." Here, the two premises are identified by the signal word *since. As a general rule, signal words always precede—but not always immediately—the propositions they signal.*

If the syllogism were presented as "therefore, because all sweet fruit is red, all apples are red, for all apples are sweet fruit," we must use both grouping and signal words to unpack it. The structure of this syllogism might be simplified like this:

Therefore, because <u>(Premise)</u>, <u>(Conclusion)</u>, for <u>(Premise)</u>.

Simplified in this way, we see that two of the propositions are identified by the premise indicators *because* and *for,* and that a premise comes between the conclusion and its signal.

Study the following ways in which the very same argument can be presented:

Example 1: <u>All apples are red</u> since <u>all sweet fruit is red</u> and <u>all apples are sweet fruit</u>.
Form 1: <u>(Conclusion)</u> since <u>(Premise)</u> and <u>(Premise)</u>.

Reminder: Signal words precede what they identify. In Example 1 above, the premise signal *since* identifies at least one premise; the conjunction *and* tells us "here's another." This is reinforced by the grouping of the propositions such that one is isolated from the other two; it's the conclusion.

Example 2: Because <u>all sweet fruit is red</u>, <u>all apples are red</u>, since <u>all apples are sweet fruit</u>.
Form 2: Because <u>(Premise)</u>, <u>(Conclusion)</u>, since <u>(Premise)</u>.

Example 3: Since <u>all sweet fruit is red</u> and <u>all apples are sweet fruit</u>, <u>all apples are red</u>.
Form 3: Since <u>(Premise)</u> and <u>(Premise)</u>, <u>(Conclusion)</u>.

Example 4: <u>All sweet fruit is red</u>, and <u>all apples are sweet fruit</u>. So <u>all apples are red</u>.
Form 4: <u>(Premise)</u>, and <u>(Premise)</u>. So <u>(Conclusion)</u>.

The presentation of any argument must somehow convey the logical relationships of its propositions. Rest assured that if there is an argument, there *must be* some way of isolating either the premises or conclusion. The above examples illustrate some typical patterns in which syllogisms occur. The key in all cases is to pay attention to grouping, punctuation, and signal words. Using all the information available, we can correctly distinguish the premises of a syllogism from its conclusion with accuracy. *Identification of the conclusion is the first important step in testing syllogisms for validity.*

STUDY HINT
Determining Syllogistic Form

To identify the form of a standard-form categorical syllogism, follow these steps:

1. Identify the conclusion of the syllogism.

2. Find the predicate of the conclusion, and then find the premise that contains the same term.

3. List that premise (the major premise) first.

4. List the remaining premise next. (If the syllogism is truly standard form, this premise will contain the same term as the subject of the conclusion.)

5. List the conclusion last.

6. Give the letter names of the premises and conclusion in standard-form order (major premise, minor premise, conclusion). This identifies the *mood*.

7. Find the pattern created by the middle term in each premise, and identify it according to the information on *figure* from above.

8. *Combine mood and figure to get form.*

EXERCISE 7-6 *

A. For each of the following syllogisms, identify the conclusions using grouping, punctuation, and signal words as your guides. Then rewrite the syllogism in standard form.

1. Some animals are objects of worship since all cows are animals and some objects of worship are cows.

2. Some Republicans are not opponents of deficit spending since no opponents of deficit spending are Keynesians and some Republicans are Keynesians.

3. Because no biologist who believes in Darwinian evolution is a literal interpreter of Genesis, no literal interpreter of Genesis is a college graduate, since all biologists who believe in Darwinian evolution are college graduates.

4. Since all toothpastes with fluoride are cavity fighters and some peppermint toothpastes are cavity fighters, some peppermint toothpastes are toothpastes with fluoride.

5. All males interested in females only for sex are male chauvinists, and all male chauvinists are persons insecure in their sex role. So some men interested in females only for sex are persons insecure in their own sex role.

6. Some nonparty members are nonvoters, for all nonparty members are officers and some officers are nonvoters.

7. All married persons are consumers, so since some individuals are not married persons, some individuals are not consumers.

8. It follows, because no one signing a living will is a believer in suffering for suffering's sake, that no one signing a living will is a theist, for all believers in suffering for suffering's sake are theists.

B. Give the mood and figure for the syllogisms in 7-6 A.

C. Using S = minor term, P = major term, and M = middle term, construct standard-form categorical syllogisms for each of the following forms. Here's a sample, using *IAI*-2:

$$\frac{\begin{array}{l}\text{Some } P \text{ is } M.\\ \text{All } S \text{ is } M.\end{array}}{\text{Some } S \text{ is } P.}$$

Now you try:

1. *AAA*-3	6. *AEA*-2
2. *III*-2	7. *EEE*-1
3. *IOE*-4	8. *EEE*-2
4. *IOE*-1	9. *EIO*-3
5. *OIE*-1	10. *IAI*-4

RULES OF VALIDITY

There is a quick, efficient method of proving the validity of a standard-form categorical syllogism. It involves applying six simple rules of correct deductive reasoning. An argument that violates any one of these rules is invalid. If it does not violate any of them, it is valid.

Rule 1: *A valid standard-form categorical syllogism must contain three, and only three, class terms, each being used in the same sense throughout the argument.* Any syllogism having more than three terms commits the *fallacy of four terms*.

Look at this argument:

Any fast runner makes a good halfback. Since Smith is a good long-distance runner, Smith is a good halfback.

Fast runner, a good halfback, Smith, a good long-distance runner—four terms. This argument commits the fallacy of four terms; it's invalid.

It's not likely that anyone would ever argue in such a blatantly invalid way. But the fallacy can occur in more subtle ways. Consider this argument:

> Unlikely things happen all the time. But what happens all the time is likely. So, unlikely things are likely.

The fallacy, and the amusement, of the argument can be found in its equivocal use of the phrase *all the time.* In the major premise ("what happens all the time is likely"), *all the time* means "usually," "ordinarily," or "generally." But in the minor premise ("unlikely things happen all the time"), *all the time* means "frequently," as in "frequently enough to be alert to them." So the fallacy of four terms can occur when a term is used equivocally. Here's another example:

All instances of a government's financing abortion clinics are instances of a government's officially supporting abortions.
No government should be an instance of a government's officially supporting abortion.
___
No government should be an instance of a government's financing abortion clinics.

After a quick first look, this argument may appear to be *AEE-2*, which happens to be a valid form. But be careful. The phrase *officially supporting* in the middle term, "instances of a government's officially supporting abortions," seems equivocal. In the minor premise it carries the meaning of taking an official position *in favor of* abortion. But in the major premise, *officially supporting* means "providing the financial wherewithal" to establish abortion clinics and making them available to those who may wish their services. Looked at this way, the argument commits the fallacy of four terms.

Consider this example from the brilliant philosopher David Hume's *A Treatise of Human Nature:*

> Since morals . . . have an influence on the actions and affections, it follows, that they cannot be deriv'd from reason; and that because reason alone, as we have already prov'd, can never have any such influence.

We can set up Hume's argument as follows:

> No acts of reason are influences on actions and affections.
> All moral sentiments are influences on actions and affections.
> ___
> No moral sentiments are things derived from acts of reason.

If we're not careful, we might take this to be an *AEE-2* form, which we just said is valid. But look again. The major term of the conclusion, "things derived from acts of reason," is not the same major term that appears in the major premise. There the term is "acts of reason." So the premises provide no basis for Hume's conclusion. What he could have implied, of course, was that "No moral sentiments are *acts of reason.*" But when he sneaked in "*things derived from* acts of reason," he committed the fallacy of four terms; after all, there's nothing in his premises that precludes moral sentiments being *derived* from acts of reason.[18]

Some logicians prefer to exclude this rule, since, by definition, any syllogism containing four terms is not in standard form. Technically, this is correct; standard-form syllogisms are defined as containing exactly, and only, three class terms. But the use of equivocal language is common enough, we think, to warrant inclusion of this rule, with the reminder that arguments that violate it are not *standard-form* syllogisms; they only appear to be. Thus, if an apparently standard-form syllogism commits the fallacy of four terms, you need not analyze it for violations of any other rules of validity.

Rule 2: *In a valid standard-form categorical syllogism, the middle term must be distributed in at least one premise.* Consider this *AII-2* argument:

> All mothers are females.
> Some students are females.
> Some students are mothers.

Although the premises and the conclusion are true, the argument is invalid. In this example the minor premise includes some students within *some females.* But since the major premise is not speaking about *every female,* we don't know whether the *particular ones spoken about in the minor premise* are the same ones *spoken about in the major premise.* So we cannot conclude that "Some students are mothers."

Compare the preceding *AII-2* argument with

> All mothers are females.
> Some students are mothers.
> Some students are females.

This *AII-1* form does not commit the error that *AII-2* does. In its minor premise it includes *some students* within the class *some mothers.* And the major premise speaks of *all mothers.* So we know that everything said of *all mothers* also applies to *those students who are mothers.* Thus, the premises entail the conclusion, making the syllogism valid.

Let's consider this argument.

> Some astronauts are engineers.
> Some astronauts are scientists.
> Some scientists are engineers.

This argument, an *III-3* form, assumes that the very same astronauts who are scientists are also engineers. But should it? Maybe the engineers it's talking about

---

18. See Gerald Runkle, *Good Thinking: An Introduction to Logic* (New York: Holt, Rinehart and Winston, 1978), pp. 152–53.

exclude the scientists it's talking about. Therefore, the premises do not logically guarantee the conclusion, and the syllogism is invalid. If, on the other hand, the argument read

> **All astronauts are scientists.**
> **Some astronauts are engineers.**

we could validly conclude

> **Some engineers are scientists.**

Why is *AII*-3 valid whereas *AII*-2 and *III*-3 are invalid?

In each of the two invalid syllogisms, the invalidity occurred because the middle term was not spoken of universally in at least one premise. In other words, the middle term wasn't distributed at least once. When a syllogism fails to distribute its middle term at least once, it commits the *fallacy of the undistributed middle*. This always produces an invalid argument. Thus, again,

> **Some females are vertebrates.**
> **All mothers are females.**
> **Some mothers are vertebrates.**

Although the premises and conclusion are true, this argument is invalid—it does not distribute its middle term. Thus, the form *IAI*-1 is invalid.

Rule 3: *No valid standard-form categorical syllogism may distribute in its conclusion any term not distributed in its premises.* Consider this argument:

> **All mothers are females.**
> **Some students are mothers.**
> **All students are females.**

The conclusion obviously overstates the premises, saying more than the evidence allows. The same holds true for this argument:

> **All milk-giving animals are mammals.**
> **Some cats are milk-giving animals.**
> **All cats are mammals.**

The conclusion speaks of *all cats*. Although the conclusion is true, the premises do not allow us to speak of *all cats* but of only some. What about this argument?

> **All doctors are college graduates.**
> **Some doctors are not golfers.**
> **Some golfers are not college graduates.**

It's a little harder to see the flaw here. But remembering that *O* propositions distribute their predicate terms, we see that this conclusion is speaking of *all college graduates.* But the major premise doesn't speak of *all college graduates.* Therefore, the argument is invalid.

So in concluding more than their premises allow them to, arguers commit fallacies called *illicit major* and *illicit minor* terms. *Illicit major means that the predicate is distributed in the conclusion but not in the major premise; illicit minor means that the subject is distributed in the conclusion but not in the minor premise.* In the first example given, about mothers, this *AIA*-1 form commits the fallacy of illicit minor term, as does the next one about cats, an *AIA*-1; the final example, *AOO*-3, commits the fallacy of illicit major term.

Rule 4: *No valid standard-form categorical syllogism may contain two negative premises.* The reason for this rule becomes clear when we look at some illustrations beginning with this *OOO*-1 argument:

> Some females are not mothers.
> Some politicians are not females.
> Some politicians are not mothers.

As tempting as such a conclusion may be, we cannot logically draw it because the subject, *politicians,* and the predicate, *mothers,* are excluding from their classes the middle term, *females.* As a result, the premises allow us no way to relate the classes *mothers* and *politicians* as the conclusion attempts to do. In other words, the premises don't show that these two classes have a common bond since it's impossible to know whether they are excluding the same females. A logical analogy will point up the error:

> Some politicians are not females.
> Some mothers are not politicians.
> Some mothers are not females.

Again, the conclusion must relate the classes *mothers* and *females.* But the minor premise excludes from the class *mothers* every instance of politician. The major premise excludes every instance of the class *females* from the particular politicians it's addressing. The classes *mothers* and *females,* then, share no basis for a relationship. Hence, no valid conclusion is possible.

In brief, whenever the premises of a syllogism are both negative, no valid conclusion can be drawn. *If we draw a conclusion from two negative premises we commit the fallacy of exclusive premises.*

Rule 5: *If either premise of a standard-form categorical syllogism is negative, its conclusion must be negative.* Consider these premises:

> No mothers are males.
> Some males are politicians.

Logically, the only conclusion we could draw here is the negative one:

> Some politicians are not mothers.

The major premise excludes the class *mothers* from the class *males.* The minor premise, on the other hand, includes part of the class *males* within part of the class *politicians.* The only possible relationship that could exist between *politicians* and *mothers,* then, is one of exclusion, in which some politicians are excluded from the class *mothers.* In other words, the conclusion must be a negative one. Whenever either premise of a syllogism is negative, the conclusion must be negative. An affirmative conclusion can only follow from premises in which the middle term includes one term (*S* or *P*) and is itself part of another (*S* or *P*), that is, from affirmative premises. When we exclude this middle term from either premise, we force the conclusion to exclude, or to be negative. *Whenever we draw an affirmative conclusion from a negative premise, we commit*—appropriately enough—*the fallacy of drawing an affirmative conclusion from a negative premise.* The corollary is this: *If the conclusion to an argument is negative, one of its premises must be negative as well.*

Rule 6: *No valid standard-form categorical syllogism with two universal premises may have a particular conclusion.* According to the Boolean interpretation of particular propositions, *I* and *O, some* means that there exists at least one member (*exists* taken to mean in the past as well as the present). We can say, then, *some* has *existential import:* It makes a comment about existence. *No* and *all,* on the other hand, carry no such meaning; they make no comment about existence at all. Thus, "All trespassers are persons who will be prosecuted" does not in itself imply the existence of any trespassers. But if we said "Some trespassers are persons who will be prosecuted," we would be logically implying the existence of at least one trespasser. What if someone says, "No lawbreaker is a good citizen"; does this imply the existence of a lawbreaker? No, it doesn't. But "Some lawbreakers are not good citizens" does logically imply the existence of at least one lawbreaker. Consider this argument:

> No lawbreakers are good citizens.
> All speeders are lawbreakers.
> ———————————————
> Some speeders are not good citizens.

The argument is invalid. It's invalid because the conclusion makes an existential claim that its premises just do not allow; the conclusion states that there exists at least one speeder, but the premises don't contain any such implication. The argument is said to commit the *existential fallacy. Any syllogism whose premises consist of universal propositions* (A *or* E) *and whose conclusion is a particular proposition* (I *or* O) *commits the existential fallacy and is thereby invalid.*

Summarizing, the six rules and their accompanying fallacies are

Rule 1: A valid standard-form categorical syllogism must contain three, and no more than three, terms; otherwise it commits the fallacy of four terms.

Rule 2: A valid standard-form categorical syllogism must distribute its middle term at least once; otherwise it commits the fallacy of undistributed middle term.

Rule 3: A standard-form categorical syllogism must not say more in its conclusion than its premises allow. If it distributes its major term (*P*) in the conclusion but not in the major premise, it commits the fallacy of illicit major term; if it distributes its minor term (*S*) in the conclusion but not in the minor premise, it commits the fallacy of illicit minor term.

Rule 4: A valid standard-form categorical syllogism must not contain two negative premises; otherwise it commits the fallacy of exclusive premises.

Rule 5: A valid standard-form categorical syllogism must not draw an affirmative conclusion from a negative premise; otherwise it commits the fallacy of drawing an affirmative conclusion from a negative premise.

Rule 6: A valid standard-form categorical syllogism must not draw a particular conclusion from two universal premises; otherwise it commits the existential fallacy.

So much for standard-form categorical syllogisms. At the beginning of our study of the syllogism, we mentioned that the categorical syllogism is only one kind of syllogistic argument and that there are two other kinds as well. These are easy to handle, but they do occur frequently enough for us to be alerted to them. So in Chapter 9 we'll take up validity as it applies to disjunctive and conditional syllogisms. But before that, we must consider the important topic of argument reconstruction.

EXERCISE 7-7 *

*A. Determine the validity of the following syllogisms by means of rules and their fallacies. If a syllogism breaks a rule, identify by name the broken rule and the fallacy. Give the form of each syllogism.

1. No refined foods are nutritional foods. So no white flour is a nutritional food because no refined foods are white flour.

2. Some people who believe in astronaut-gods are gullible readers and all gullible readers are fans of the book *Chariots of the Gods?*; therefore, some fans of the book *Chariots of the Gods?* are people who believe in astronaut-gods.

3. Some extrasensory experiences are not just the products of imagination because some products of imagination are things explained through sense data, and no things explained through sense data are extrasensory experiences.

4. Some professors are not idealists and all professors are college graduates. Therefore some idealists are not college graduates.

5. Since some ministers are not happy men, some ministers are not alcoholics, for no alcoholics are happy men.

6. All good teachers are good administrators because all good teachers are compassionate individuals and all compassionate individuals are good administrators.

7. It follows that some Americans are coffee lovers from the facts that some Americans are not tea lovers and no tea lovers are coffee lovers.

8. All horses are quadrupeds; so, because some horses are faster runners than humans, some quadrupeds are faster runners than humans.

9. Some inventors are people who know how to make money, for all inventors are imaginative individuals and all imaginative individuals are people who know how to make money.

10. All missionaries are altruists and some altruists are women. Thus, some missionaries are women.

11. No professional athletes are welfare recipients because no professional athletes are low-income earners, and all welfare recipients are low-income earners.

12. Some politicians are persons of integrity. Thus some entertainers are politicians, for some entertainers are persons of integrity.

13. All victims of injustice are members of oppressed groups, so, because all blacks are members of oppressed groups, all blacks are victims of injustice.

14. It follows that some American Indians are not exponents of the traditional account of American history because no American Indians are people dealt with fairly in American history books, and no one dealt with fairly in American history books is an exponent of the traditional account of American history.

15. Some explosives are chemicals, from which it follows that some purchasable items are not chemicals because no explosives are purchasable items.

16. Some wealthy people are millionaires because some millionaires are possessors of large sums of money and all possessors of large sums of money are wealthy people.

17. Some persons without sin are ones who should cast the first stone. So no person is one who should cast the first stone because no person is a person without sin.

18. Some newspapers are not true accounts of what's happened, for all true accounts of what's happened are complete and accurate sources of information, and some newspapers are not complete and accurate sources of information.

19. Because some movies are films for adults, some movies are not films for children, as no films for adults are films for children.

20. All roads are ways that lead to Rome and all roads are potential dead ends. Thus, all ways that lead to Rome are potential dead ends.

B. Test the validity of these forms:

1. *AAA*-4	11. *OAO*-2
2. *IOO*-3	12. *EAO*-1
3. *AII*-4	13. *IAA*-3
4. *OAO*-2	14. *OEO*-4
5. *EOO*-1	15. *AAA*-3
6. *OAI*-1	16. *IOO*-1
7. *AEE*-2	17. *EEO*-3
8. *OIO*-3	18. *AEE*-4
9. *IOI*-1	19. *AEO*-4
10. *IAI*-3	20. *EIO*-3

VALIDITY AND THE COGENCY CRITERIA

The premises of a deductive argument logically support its conclusion if the argument conforms to all six rules. Failure to satisfy these rules results in invalidity. An invalid argument, we know, is never cogent. Invalid arguments, by failing to conform to these rules, always lack sufficient evidence (the third criterion of cogency) to support their conclusions.

In the case of the first rule, however, it's probably clearer to view the problem as a lack of either reasonableness or relevancy owing to the problems of linguistic confusion that the rule addresses. For example, arguments that commit the fallacy of four terms may appear to be reasonable or relevant but only when the same word or phrase is used to mean two different things. For example, consider the argument:

> **All acts the state condemns are wrong.**
> **All wrong acts are against the law of God.**
> **All acts the state condemns are against the law of God.**

As it stands, the argument's premises appear to be reasonable and relevant to the conclusion. But are they? If we dissolve the ambiguity of the word "wrong," the argument's true form becomes obviously unreasonable:

> **All acts the state condemns are *illegal*.**
> **All *immoral acts* are against the law of God.**
> **All acts the state condemns are against the law of God.**

Stated more clearly, these premises establish no logical connection between the major and minor term because the argument lacks a bridge or middle term. If we try to make a connection by redefining "wrong" as "immoral" in both premises, the first premise becomes unreasonable: "All acts the state condemns are immoral." If we take "wrong" to mean "illegal," the second premise is unreasonable: "All illegal acts are against the law of God."

The remaining formal fallacies are ones of insufficiency of evidence. For example, when the middle term of a standard-form categorical syllogism is not distributed, the most the argument can establish is that the conclusion *might* be true, but "might" fails to conform to the definition or structure of validity, which calls for *conclusive* support. A deductive argument that can only establish its conclusion as a possibility or probability—and not as absolutely certain—fails to meet the sufficiency criterion.

Again, a standard-form categorical syllogism that distributes a term in the conclusion but not in a premise in effect reasons from "some" to "all." But since valid deductive arguments claim to establish their conclusions with absolute logical certainty, any deductive argument which asserts something about every member of a class in its conclusion must base that claim on a premise which asserts something about every member of the same class. Otherwise, the conclusion overstates the premises. In deductive arguments, "some" is *insufficient* for concluding "all."

By the same token, two negative premises fail to provide sufficient evidence for any conclusion in standard-form categorical syllogisms because they, in effect, deny any common relationship from which a conclusion can be drawn. And syllogisms that draw affirmative conclusions from negative premises or commit the existential fallacy always conclude more than their premises warrant. In the former instance, the conclusion overextends the major term. In the latter, since particular propositions are true only when at least one member of the subject class exists, they cannot be deduced from universal premises because they say nothing about existence.

STUDY HINT

Conformity to the six rules does not ensure that an argument is cogent. Violation of a single rule, however, guarantees that an argument is invalid, which in turn makes it noncogent.

SUMMARY

In this chapter we learned that validity is a formal characteristic of deductive arguments. A deductive argument is an argument whose premises are intended to provide conclusive support for its conclusion. A deductive argument is cogent if and only if it is valid and contains only true premises. The premises of invalid deductions fail to provide conclusive support in their conclusions, and thus are insufficient to support them.

This chapter also dealt with the categorical proposition and the standard-form categorical syllogism. A categorical proposition is a statement that relates two classes. A standard-form categorical proposition is one that relates two classes in one of four ways, as the following symbolic expressions designate: "All S is P"; "No S is P"; "Some S is P"; "Some S is not P." Each of these forms has quantity and quality: quantity pertaining to whether it's universal or particular, and quality pertaining to whether it's affirmative or negative. When a proposition speaks universally of a term, it's said to distribute it. For simplicity, these propositions are referred to by the letters A, E, I, and O.

We learned that two propositions are contradictories if the truth of one implies the falsity of the other, and if the falsity of one implies the truth of the other. A and O propositions are contradictories, as are E and I propositions.

Propositions that assert the existence of at least one thing are said to have existential import. According to Boolean logic, I and O propositions have existential import, but A and E propositions do not. Within the constraints of the Boolean interpretation of existential import, obversion, contraposition (for A and O), and conversion (for E and I) are valid equivalent inferences. Obversion is the immediate inference that consists of changing the quality of a proposition and replacing the predicate with its complement. The complement of a term consists of everything that is not that term. For example, the complement of the class of "red" is "non-red" or "not-red." Contraposition is the immediate inference that consists of switching and complementing both the subject and predicate. Under the Boolean interpretation of existential import, contraposition is valid for A and O propositions. Conversion is the immediate inference that consists of switching the subject and predicate of a proposition with each other. Conversion is valid for E and I in Boolean logic.

The categorical proposition is the building block of all syllogisms. In particular, it constitutes one kind of syllogism: the standard-form categorical syllogism, which consists of three categorical propositions. It has exactly three terms that appear in exactly two of its propositions, and it appears in the order of major premise, minor premise, and conclusion. The major premise of a categorical syllogism is the premise containing the major term—the predicate of the conclusion. The minor premise is the premise containing the minor term—the subject of the conclusion. The remaining term of the syllogism, the one that occurs in both premises, is the middle term.

Every standard-form categorical syllogism has form: mood and figure. Its mood is the order in which it appears when properly arranged (major, minor, conclusion); mood is designated by the letters of the propositions.

The figure is the position of the middle term in the premises: figure 1, middle term in the subject position of the major premise and the predicate position of the minor premise; figure 2, middle term in the predicate position of both premises; figure 3, middle term in the subject position of both premises; figure 4, middle term in the predicate position of the major premise and subject position of the minor premise.

To analyze any standard-form categorical syllogism correctly, we must accurately represent its form. The first step in so doing is to identify the conclusion. We do this by looking for signal words and grouping.

The quickest and simplest way to determine validity is to use the following rules and fallacies:

Rule 1: A valid standard-form categorical syllogism must contain three, and only three, class terms, each being used in the same sense throughout the argument. Any syllogism containing more than three terms commits the fallacy of four terms.

Rule 2: In a valid standard-form categorical syllogism, the middle term must be distributed in at least one premise. A syllogism that fails to do this commits the fallacy of the undistributed middle term.

Rule 3: No valid standard-form categorical syllogism can distribute in its conclusion any term not distributed in its premises. A syllogism that distributes its predicate in the conclusion but not in the major premise commits the fallacy of illicit major term; a syllogism that distributes its subject in the conclusion but not in the minor premise commits the fallacy of illicit minor term.

Rule 4: No valid standard-form categorical syllogism can contain two negative premises. A syllogism that does commits the fallacy of exclusive premises.

Rule 5: If either premise of a standard-form categorical syllogism is negative, its conclusion must be negative. A syllogism that violates this rule commits the fallacy of drawing an affirmative conclusion from a negative premise.

Rule 6: No valid syllogism can draw a particular conclusion from two universal premises. A syllogism that does this commits the existential fallacy.

Summary Exercises

1. What is the mood of a standard-form categorical syllogism with a universal affirmative minor premise, a particular negative major premise, and a conclusion that only distributes its predicate?

2. What is the figure of the syllogism described in question 1 if the major premise distributes the middle term and the minor premise distributes the minor term?

3. What is the figure of a standard-form categorical syllogism if the minor term is the predicate of the minor premise and the major term is the predicate of the major premise?

4. Using the rules, determine for yourself which of the possible 256 combinations of mood and figure are valid. (This is not as time-consuming as it may appear. For example, we know that any syllogism with two *E*

premises commits the fallacy of exclusive premises, so *EEA, EEE, EEI,* and *EEO* are invalid moods from just that one rule. Since the moods themselves are invalid, each figure is also invalid. Thus, *EEA*-1, *EEA*-2, *EEA*-3, and *EEA*-4 are all invalid. Ditto for the other three *EE* syllogisms. We have just eliminated four moods × four figures, or sixteen forms. This is a problem of logical organization.)

ADDITIONAL EXERCISES*

A. Following are fifteen propositions. Give their form, tell what they distribute, and state their contradictory form.

1. No spoiled children are candidates for self-reliance.

2. Some careless husbands are inattentive lovers.

3. All predators are animals of prey.

4. Some futile affairs are tragedies.

5. All the students are biology majors.

6. Some candidates for self-reliance are snobs.

7. Some predators are not threats to life.

8. No students are males.

9. No inattentive lovers are romantics.

10. All wars are tragedies.

11. Some spoiled children are snobs.

12. No careless husbands are romantics.

13. Some threats to life are not animals of prey.

14. Some wars are futile affairs.

15. No biology majors are males.

B. Assume that propositions 11 through 15 in A above are conclusions to arguments that include as premises propositions 1 through 10. Construct the appropriate syllogism for each conclusion, name its form, and test its validity.

C. Determine the validity of the following syllogisms. Identify the rule(s) violated for all invalid syllogisms. Give mood and figure for 11–20.

1. Since no barbers are qualified to practice medicine, all those qualified to practice medicine have been to college because no barbers have been to college.

2. Since some apples are fruits and some apples are red objects, some red objects are fruits.

3. If some women are college graduates, and all college graduates are high school graduates, then some high school graduates are women.

4. Some professional organizations that charge dues are not organizations worth belonging to. Some organizations worth belonging to are elite clubs. Consequently, some elite clubs are not organizations worth belonging to.

5. Some Chevrolets are overpriced lemons, and some overpriced lemons are selling like hot cakes, so some Chevrolets are selling like hot cakes.

6. If we assume that no signs of forced entry were present at the scene of the crime, we can conclude that the defendant is innocent.

7. All horses are quadrupeds. No humans are horses. Thus no humans are quadrupeds.

8. All horses are quadrupeds. No horses are human. Thus no quadrupeds are human.

9. All flour fit for consumption is ground. All places on which houses are built are ground. Therefore all places on which houses are built are fit for consumption.

10. All Communists are atheists. No atheists are good citizens. So some Communists are not good citizens.

11. *AEE*-3

12. *IOE*-2

13. *OOI*-1

14. *IOI*-2

15. *AAA*-4

16. *AAA*-3

17. *AEA*-2

18. *EAA*-2

19. *IAI*-3

20. *EIO*-4

CHAPTER 8

Reconstructing Arguments

The mass of mankind will never have any ardent zeal for seeing things as they are.

MATTHEW ARNOLD

It's commonplace to refer to the premises of an argument as assumptions—what the arguer takes or assumes to be true. And, in the case of deductions, assumptions ideally provide conclusive support for the conclusion. The tricky thing about assumptions, though, is that they're not always expressed. Sometimes they're merely implied, that is, not stated. In fact, in everyday life, when we use the word *assumption*—as in "I'm not sure I accept the assumptions behind your argument" or "Aren't you assuming an awful lot?"—we typically mean what's *implied,* not what's expressed.

If we take the word *assumption* to mean "an implied premise," it's a safe bet that most of the arguments we encounter are built on assumptions. For example, suppose someone says, "You shouldn't eat that apple because all the apples from that bag are sour." Clearly the speaker assumes "That apple is from that bag." Likewise, should someone argue, "Some of these students must be juniors because they're taking American literature," the speaker must be assuming that "All students taking American literature are juniors." The ability to see precisely what is being assumed in any argument is crucial. Determining validity depends on it. And we'd better be accurate in our reconstruction, otherwise we'll misrepresent the argument.

How do we know what's being assumed in abbreviated arguments? That's what this chapter is about. It concerns techniques for correctly reconstructing arguments when they come in incomplete form. A major problem concerns what is openly expressed in an argument. Rarely do real-life arguments contain statements that appear in standard propositional form. Indeed, they almost always contain statements expressed in ordinary, everyday language and syntax. If we're to evaluate ordinary-language arguments, we must know how to translate ordinary-language statements into standard propositional form. So we'll deal with that subject before going on to consider argument reconstruction.

TRANSLATING CATEGORICAL PROPOSITIONS INTO STANDARD FORM

All the deductive arguments we've dealt with thus far have been clean ones; they've neatly fallen into syllogistic form. Most arguments, however, contain propositions that at first glance don't resemble any of the standard propositional forms. Take these propositions, for instance: "The New York Mets defeated the Boston Red Sox in the World Series," "Mature people don't insist on having things their own way all the time," "A vandal broke the lock," "Not all people believe in an 'open' universe." Could you recognize these as *A, E, I,* or *O*? They are. And if we are going to insert them into a standard-form categorical syllogism, they need to be translated into those forms. We'll consider seven variations the standard-form categorical proposition often takes and show how these can be rendered into standard form. These variations will be propositions that

1. contain a singular reference;
2. contain adjectival phrases;
3. lack the verb *to be;*
4. have irregular quantifiers;
5. lack subject and predicate terms;
6. use *only* or *none but;*
7. consist of two statements, one affirmative, the other negative.

But first let's look at arguments that appear to have more than three terms but actually don't.

Arguments with Logical Equivalencies

What if you were evaluating the validity of this argument?

All humans are vertebrates.
Women are humans.
Therefore women are creatures with spines.

At first glance you might judge this argument to be invalid because it seems to contain more than three terms. But two of the terms mean the same thing—*vertebrates* and *creatures with spines.* Simply by replacing one with the other, we can produce a standard-form syllogism.

All humans are creatures with spines.
Women are humans.
Therefore women are creatures with spines.

Now what about this argument?

> **No human is a nonvertebrate.**
> **All snakes are nonvertebrates.**
> **All humans are nonsnakes.**

Not only do we appear to have four terms—*human, nonvertebrate, snakes,* and *nonsnakes*—but we also seem to have an affirmative conclusion following from a negative premise. But two of the terms—*snakes* and *nonsnakes*—are merely complements. We can eliminate one of the complements by restating one of the propositions in terms of its logical equivalent.[19] Thus, the logical equivalent of "All humans are nonsnakes" is "No humans are snakes." The syllogism now has three terms and a negative conclusion drawn from a negative premise. Since the syllogism commits no fallacy, it is valid. So whenever we find an argument appearing to have more than three terms, we should look for synonyms and complements. We should then eliminate one of the synonyms and employ a logical equivalent to eliminate the complement.

STUDY HINT

If an argument appears to have more than three terms,

1. identify any synonyms and complements;

2. eliminate one of the synonyms (if present); and

3. employ a logical equivalent to any complement.

Now let's consider the seven kinds of propositions that don't appear in standard *A, E, I,* or *O* form.

Propositions Containing Singular Terms

Sometimes a proposition takes this form: "Clinton is a U.S. president." Because it speaks of an individual, such a proposition is called *singular.* The proposition "This Harley-Davidson runs well" is another singular proposition. *Singular propositions affirm or deny that a specific individual is in a class. The individual is considered the sole occupant of its class.* So, since in mentioning the individual we are really speaking of the whole class, we consider singular propositions to be universal propositions *A* or *E.* The first two singular propositions then are

---

19. We do this through the process called *obversion:* changing the quality of a proposition and substituting the complement of its predicate for the predicate itself. Thus, "Some *S* is *P*" obverts to "Some *S* is not non-*P*," "Some *S* is not *P*" obverts to "Some *S* is non-*P*," and so forth. See Chapter 7.

universal affirmative and therefore *A* form. If the singular proposition is negative, its form is *E*. Thus the argument

> All U.S. presidents are male.
> Maya Angelou is not a U.S. president.
> Maya Angelou is not a male.

has the mood *AEE*.

STUDY HINT

Treat propositions containing singular terms as universals (*A* or *E*).

Propositions Containing Adjectival Phrases

In addition to arguments containing synonyms, complements, or singular propositions, some arguments appear with adjectival class terms. Thus,

> All fast runners are team members.
> "Toes" Larsen is really fast.
> "Toes" Larsen is a team member.

To get the minor premise into standard propositional form, you can change the adjective into a noun: "'Toes' Larsen is a fast runner." Consider this argument:

> What's obsolete and decrepit is an eyesore.
> All the buildings are obsolete and decrepit.
> Therefore all the buildings are eyesores.

Translating the adjectives into class terms, we get

> All obsolete and decrepit objects are eyesores.
> All the buildings are obsolete and decrepit objects.
> All the buildings are eyesores.

STUDY HINT

Change adjectival phrases to nouns.

Propositions Lacking the Verb *To Be*

The problem of converting adjectival phrases into noun class terms can be solved by using a form of the verb *to be* (*is, are, was, were, have been, has been, should be, will have been,* and so on). What's the simplest way to translate such a proposition as "Some men lust after their neighbors' wives" into standard form? Simply insert, *immediately after the subject,* a phrase consisting of (1) a form of the verb *to be,* (2) an appropriate class term, and (3) the relative pronoun *who* or *which;* then finish the proposition. This proposition becomes "Some men *are persons who* lust after their neighbors' wives." "All persons who defend themselves have fools for lawyers" becomes "All persons who defend themselves *are persons who* have fools for lawyers" (or simply "persons with fools for lawyers").

Propositions Containing Irregular Quantifiers

Sometimes the quantity of a proposition is not designated by the standard quantifiers *all, no,* and *some.* Thus, "Anyone present heard him make the remark"; "Everyone is late"; "Whoever votes is a citizen"; "Anything you bring to the picnic we'll appreciate." *Any, everybody, whoever, anything,* and similar words mean *all,* and we should handle them accordingly. Some confusion may arise, however, regarding the indefinite article *a.* In "A man is a vertebrate," the article *a* obviously means all humans are vertebrates; therefore, it should be considered a universal quantifier, making this proposition an *A* form. And "A snake is not a vertebrate" obviously means *no* snake is a vertebrate. But *a* can also mean "some," as in "A ball came crashing through the window" or "A question interrupted his speech." Because the *a* refers neither to every member of a class nor to singular members, these uses of *a* should be considered particular quantifiers, thus making their propositions particular ones. The two preceding propositions, then, are *I* form. (Remember: *Some* means at least one.) What about "A ball did not crash through this window"? This is *O.*

The article *the* is similar to *a* in this respect, but significantly differs in that *the* is always a universal quantifier. For example, the proposition "The lion is a carnivore" obviously speaks of all lions; so *the* functions as a universal quantifier, making the proposition *A* form. On the other hand, "The lion escaped from the St. Louis Zoo" refers, not to all lions, but to this singular lion. Still *the* serves as a universal quantifier, making this proposition, like singular ones, *A* form.

STUDY HINT

A can be a universal or particular quantifier. *The* is *always* a universal quantifier.

Propositions Lacking Subject or Predicate Terms

Some propositions begin with *wherever* or *whenever,* as in "Wherever there's smoke, there's fire" and "Whenever the means are outrageous, we must resist them." In addition to providing the quantifier *all* in such propositions, we must also provide a class term to complete its sense. Since *wherever* suggests a place, the word *place* itself becomes a convenient term to substitute for *wherever* and like terms; and since *whenever* suggests time, the word *time* is convenient to substitute for *whenever* and related words. Thus, in standard form, the preceding propositions become "All *places* there's smoke are *places* there's fire" and "All *times* the means are outrageous are *times* we must resist them."

Similar to *wherever* and *whenever* are *where, unless, never,* and *when.* Consider this proposition: "The Draculas will not come to a party unless blood pudding is being served." Translated into standard form this becomes "All *times* the Draculas come to a party are *times* that blood pudding is being served." We handle syllogisms containing such words by translating the propositions in which the words appear into standard form.

Since the baby cries whenever the phone rings, the phone mustn't be ringing because the baby is quiet.

Translated, this argument becomes

All times the phone rings are times the baby cries.
This time is not a time the baby's crying.
Therefore this time is not a time the phone is ringing.

The argument is valid. It is an *AEE*-2, a valid syllogistic form.

Propositions Using *Only* and *None But*

Sometimes categorical propositions specify the members of a class they're speaking about, as in "Only sophomores are entitled to a free bus ride." The use of *only* here restricts those entitled to a free bus ride to a special group known as *sophomores.* Such a proposition is said to be *exclusive.* Exclusive propositions can be deceiving; this one *seems* to be speaking universally of *sophomores* and thus appears to translate as "All sophomores are students entitled to a free bus ride." But this misrepresents the meaning of the sentence. The word *only* is really specifying *sophomores* within a larger unmentioned group, probably *students.* To translate this exclusive proposition faithfully, we should show that any instance of a student who is entitled to a free ride is an instance of a sophomore. Simply put, this means, "All those (students) entitled to a free bus ride are sophomores." Consider this example: "Only men are priests of the Roman Catholic Church." Does this mean that all men are priests of the Roman Catholic Church or that all priests of the Roman Catholic Church are men? Obviously the latter. So the *only* in an exclusive proposition is actually distributing the *apparent* predicate.

In translating an exclusive proposition into standard form, then, it's necessary to interchange the *apparent* subject and predicate and then treat the proposition as a universal one. Thus, "Only those younger than eighteen cannot vote" becomes "No voter is one less than eighteen years old." Similar to *only* is the phrase *none but,* as in "None but the most needy will be fed." This becomes "All those who will be fed are those who are most needy."

Look on the translation of exclusive propositions as consisting of three steps. First, drop the "only" or "none but." Second, translate what remains into standard form. Third, interchange "subject" and "predicate." What remains is the proper translation. Let's apply this procedure to the statement "Only nitwits pay attention to these talks." Thus

Step 1: Nitwits pay attention to these talks. (Drop "only.")

Step 2: All nitwits pay attention to these talks. (Translate into *A* or *E* form.)

Step 3: All persons who pay attention to these talks are nitwits. (Interchange subject and predicate.)

The error that students usually make in translating exclusive propositions is to end the translation at Step 2. Make sure that having completed Step 2, you then interchange "subject" and "predicate." That provides the correct meaning of the exclusive proposition. Consider, for an additional example, this statement: "None but the brave deserve glory." Applying the three steps, we get

Step 1: The brave deserve glory. (Drop "none but.")

Step 2: All brave persons are persons who deserve glory. (Translate into *A* or *E* form.)

Step 3: All persons who deserve glory are brave persons. (Interchange subject and predicate.)

STUDY HINT

When translating exclusive statements:

1. Drop *only* or *none but;*

2. Translate what remains into *A* or *E;* and

3. Interchange "subject" and "predicate."

Propositions Containing Two Statements: Affirmative and Negative

The quantifiers *almost all, only some, not quite all, all but,* and the like, often introduce propositions that need translation into standard form. Such phrases really imply *two* statements, not one. They are called *exceptive* propositions.

Take for example the statement "We grant that almost all the students' demands are justifiable." This statement means that some of the demands are justifiable and that some of the demands are not justifiable. The statements differ in quality, and a difference in quality may affect the validity of a syllogism. Thus

All demands that are justifiable are ones the university should meet.
Almost all the students' demands are justifiable.
_____
Some of the students' demands are ones the university should meet.

Now, translating the minor premise, we could have either "Some of the students' demands are not justifiable" or "Some of the students' demands are justifiable." Let's test each:

> **All demands that are justifiable are ones the university should meet.**
> **Some of the students' demands are not justifiable.**
> **Some of the students' demands are ones the university should meet.**

This *AOI*-1 syllogism draws an affirmative conclusion from a negative premise, and is therefore invalid. But notice what happens when we use the other implied meaning:

> **All demands that are justifiable are ones the university should meet.**
> **Some of the students' demands are justifiable.**
> **Some of the students' demands are ones the university should meet.**

This syllogism commits no fallacy. Therefore, the original syllogism, as demonstrated by this *AII*-1 form, is valid.

So in dealing with exceptive premises, we must test both *implied statements to determine the validity of the syllogism. If at least one of the implied statements helps entail a valid version, the original argument is considered valid.*

Now consider this argument:

> **All but the stubborn are willing.**
> **No one willing is present.**
> **No one present is stubborn.**

The major premise is actually composed of two propositions: "No stubborn person is a willing person" and "All nonstubborn persons are willing persons." Let's try each in the syllogism.

> **No stubborn person is a willing person.**
> **No willing person is a person present.**
> **No person present is a stubborn person. (*EEE*-4)**

This argument is invalid because of its exclusive premises. But before declaring the original syllogism invalid, we must test its other version:

> **All nonstubborn persons are willing persons.**
> **No willing person is a person present.**
> **All persons present are nonstubborn persons. (*AEA*-4)**

Notice that we used a logical equivalent of the original conclusion to ensure three terms in the syllogism. Having done that, we proved that the syllogism even in this form is invalid because it draws an affirmative conclusion from a negative premise. Therefore the original argument is invalid.

The phrase *not quite all,* as in "Not quite all the members were on time," introduces an exceptive proposition. We can handle this just as we did *almost all,* that is, by converting it into two propositions, one beginning *some are* and the other beginning *some are not.* In the argument

> **Everyone on time received an award.**
> **Not quite all the members were on time.**
> **Some members received an award.**

we can translate the minor premise into "Some members were persons on time" or "Some members were not persons on time." Substituting the second, we get

> **All persons on time were persons who received an award.**
> **Some members were not persons on time.**
> **Some members were persons who received an award. (*AOI*-1)**

This argument draws an affirmative conclusion from a negative premise and is therefore invalid. But what about using the other implication of the "not quite all" proposition?

> **All persons on time were persons who received an award.**
> **Some members were persons on time.**
> **Some members were persons who received an award. (*AII*-1)**

This argument commits no fallacy and is therefore valid. Thus the original argument is valid.

Now let's consider the case of an exceptive proposition serving as the conclusion.

> **All Republicans are registered voters.**
> **Some Republicans are businesspersons.**
> **Not quite all voters are businesspersons.**

Remember what we said about deductive arguments: The premises must entail, or logically guarantee, the conclusion. An exceptive conclusion implies either "Some *S* is *P*" and "Some *S* is not *P*," or "No *S* is *P*" and "All non-*S* is *P*." These are the only possible translations of exceptive propositions. So when we draw an exceptive conclusion from two standard-form premises, at the least we will commit either the fallacy of drawing an affirmative conclusion from a negative premise or a negative conclusion from an affirmative premise. So in the preceding argument, the premises can't logically entail *both* conclusions: "Some registered voters are businesspersons," and "Some registered voters *are not* businesspersons." *We can conclude that any syllogism whose premises are standard form and whose conclusion is exceptive is an invalid syllogism.* Of course, if a syllogism contains both exceptive premises and an exceptive conclusion, it can be valid if it entails *both* conclusions.

These methods, then, enable us to deal with propositions that do not appear in standard form. But what about propositions that are missing, that remain partially or fully unstated? Most arguments we encounter, in fact, come in this incomplete (abbreviated) form. How do we handle such arguments? We will consider this next.

STUDY HINT

In dealing with exceptive *premises,* always test both implied statements, and if one of them produces a valid argument, the argument is valid.

If a syllogism contains standard form (nonexceptive) premises and an *exceptive conclusion,* it is always invalid.

EXERCISE 8-1 *

A. Translate the following propositions into standard form and label *A, E, I* or *O.*

1. Flowers are fragrant.

2. Onions are not sweet.

3. Many a party-goer awakens to regret "the night before."

4. Not every opportunity lost is a catastrophe.

5. Nothing is both educational and frivolous.

6. If it says "Government Approved," you can feel safe.

7. Only the best teams play in the title game.

8. Not quite everything that's green is grass.

9. Not everything that's green is grass.

10. "You can be sure if it's Westinghouse."

11. Not all mammals are nonhumans.

12. "Let he who is without sin cast the first stone."

13. Only the good die young.

14. He who defends himself has a fool for a lawyer.

15. Some nonvoters are not noncitizens.

16. None but the eager volunteer.

17. Not all that glitters is gold.

18. None think the rich happy but the rich themselves.

19. To know her is to love her.

20. I go where I want.

B. Translate the following arguments into standard form; then test for validity.

1. All countries wanting war are threats to world peace. No threat to world peace is a member of the UN. So no member of the UN is a belligerent country.

2. Since some males are not chauvinists and some sexists are proponents of the Equal Rights Amendment, some proponents of the Equal Rights Amendment must be men.

3. Not all the victims were adults. Some of the dead were musicians. So some of the adults must have been musicians.

4. Smith must be a college graduate because he can apply and only college graduates can apply.

5. Whenever the president can't explain something he's done, he attributes it to national security. I guess he's at a loss again because he's attributing the wiretapping to national security.

6. None but the brave should volunteer for hazardous duty. Nothing personal, Jones, but you shouldn't be volunteering—you're a coward!

7. The competition for places at medical schools is fierce because there are so few places available, and the competition is never easy when there aren't many places available.

8. Since nothing relevant is immaterial and some relevant things are interesting, some immaterial things are uninteresting.

THE ENTHYMEME

An enthymeme is an argument in which a premise or conclusion is suppressed or missing. In the argument "Since I'm riding in a car I'll get sick," the major premise remains unstated. How do we know it's the major premise that is unstated? Basically, by asking ourselves, "What is the speaker assuming in order to draw the conclusion?" To see this argument more clearly, we can use what we've already learned to put it into standard form:

> (All occasions I ride in a car are occasions I get sick.)
> This is an occasion I'm riding in a car.
> _____
> This is an occasion I'll get sick.

Since the unstated premise, in parentheses, contains the predicate of the argument, it is the major premise. *An enthymeme suppressing its major premise is called a first-order enthymeme.* Another example is "He must be guilty. He has the gun." The conclusion is obvious: "He must be guilty." Since the stated premise does not contain the conclusion's predicate term, the missing premise must; this makes the missing premise the major premise and the enthymeme first order. The reconstructed argument appears:

> **(The person with the gun is the guilty person.)**
> **He is the person with the gun.**
> **He is the guilty person.**

Sometimes the minor premise is missing, as in the argument "Jefferson must have been a male because all U.S. presidents have been males." The stated premise, "All U.S. presidents have been males," contains the predicate of the conclusion; therefore it is the major premise. The minor premise must therefore be missing. *An enthymeme suppressing its minor premise is called a second-order enthymeme.* The reconstructed argument reads:

> **All U.S. presidents have been males.**
> **(Jefferson was a U.S. president.)**
> **Jefferson must have been a male.**

Another example of a second-order enthymeme is this argument: "Anyone who wasn't present for roll call has been marked absent. So Casper has been marked absent." Since the predicate of the conclusion, "Casper has been marked absent," appears in the stated premise, the missing premise must be the minor premise, thus making this argument a second-order enthymeme. The reconstructed argument reads:

> **All persons not present for roll call are persons marked absent.**
> **(Casper is a person not present for roll call.)**
> **Casper is a person marked absent.**

Sometimes an enthymeme suppresses its conclusion, as in the argument "Anyone who voted is a citizen, and Jean voted." The conclusion is obvious: "Jean is a citizen." *An enthymeme suppressing its conclusion is called a third-order enthymeme.* Another example would be "Where there's smoke there's fire. There's smoke pouring out of that store!" The conclusion? "The store is on fire!"

The premises and conclusions were omitted from the preceding arguments because they were obvious, too obvious to be stated. That's often why in writing and speaking we do not always state an argument in complete form. Sometimes, however, the reason is that the unstated premise or conclusion is offensive, crass, impolite, or plainly absurd. Take, for example, this first- and third-order enthymeme ad:

Star athletes drink milk.

The purpose of such a message is to persuade us to buy and drink milk. As is true of all ads, the implied conclusion would have us do something: "Milk is a liquid you should drink." If we rewrite but preserve the meaning of the stated premise, we can see the subject of the conclusion in it: "Milk is a liquid star athletes drink." So it's the major premise that remains unstated. Stating the major premise and subsequently the whole argument, we get:

> **(A liquid that star athletes drink is a liquid that you should drink.)**
> **Milk is a liquid that star athletes drink.**
> _____
> **(Milk is a liquid you should drink.)**

Pretty absurd, isn't it? Here's another ad enthymeme:

> Bayer brings fast headache relief.

Again, a premise and conclusion go unstated. The conclusion would have us buy Bayer; so we can safely reconstruct the conclusion to read, "Bayer is the aspirin you should buy." Since the stated premise contains the subject of the conclusion, we are again missing the major premise. Reconstructing it and the whole argument we get:

> **(An aspirin that brings you fast headache relief is an aspirin you should buy.)**
> **Bayer is an aspirin that brings you fast headache relief.**
> _____
> **(Bayer is an aspirin you should buy.)** (Spot the concealed evidence here?)

At times an enthymeme can take twists, as in:

> **All models are attractive women.**
> **Attractive women have good figures.**
> **No woman with a good figure is shy.**
> _____
> **No model is shy.**

This argument actually consists of two enthymemes, not one. A multiple argument such as this is a *sorites*. We'll see what a sorites is in the next section.

EXERCISE 8-2

Complete the following enthymemes, name their order, and test their validity.

1. Some books are thrillers, so some thrillers must be mysteries.

2. Not all advertisements are geared to inform, which means that some ads warrant scrutiny.

3. Whatever threatens privacy is serious. That's why subjecting people to polygraph tests as a condition of employment is so serious.

4. Knowledge is power and education means knowledge.

5. Only ambitious people succeed in politics. As a result, the country is run by self-serving individuals.

6. You know that I would be there if there was any way I possibly could, but I can't be there.

7. It's better to be talented than lucky. Talent you can control, luck you can't.

8. I only do what I want to do—and I don't want to do that.

9. Women are smarter than men because women control most of the wealth in this country.

10. This is one of the best books ever written. It's sold more than a million copies.

11. Eating less and exercising more increases a person's lifespan. Everyone wants a long lifespan.

12. Midge Malone can't be as incompetent as some people say. Bill Gates picked her for vice-president of his new Internet service.

13. Pornography is an evil influence on teenagers. We should ban all Judas Priest records.

14. Robby must be brilliant; brilliant people don't talk about silly things.

15. I'm sorry, Jimbo, but we have to conclude you're the killer. The killer's the only one strong enough to throw the body out the window.

16. Eddie's up to no good. He's poking around the tool shed again.

17. A unified Germany is a dangerous thing. Any country powerful enough to dominate Europe is a dangerous thing.

18. Affirmative action quotas should be prohibited since all forms of discrimination should be prohibited.

19. If you think I'm going to swallow that line of B.S. then I'm the woman in the moon.

20. There's no rest for the wicked, so I bet you're exhausted.

THE SORITES

The preceding argument actually consists of two arguments:

> **All attractive women are persons with good figures.**
> **All models are attractive women.**
> **(All models are persons with good figures.)** (*AAA*-12)

> **No woman with a good figure is a shy person.**
> **(All models are women with good figures.)**
> **No model is a shy person.** (*EAE*-1)

An argument like this one, which states one or more premises and a main conclusion but conceals conclusions in between, is called a sorites. Let's look at another sorites:

> All persons who climb mountains are physically fit.
> No one physically fit is a chronic smoker.
> Only chronic smokers develop respiratory problems.
> No mountain climber develops respiratory problems.

To conclude that "No mountain climber develops respiratory problems," as these premises do entail, we have to construct two syllogisms, not one. Thus:

> No physically fit person is a chronic smoker.
> All mountain climbers are physically fit persons.
> (No mountain climber is a chronic smoker.) (*EAE*-1)

Not stated in the original argument, this conclusion is now used by the speaker as the minor premise for the second syllogism:

> All persons with respiratory problems are chronic smokers.
> (No mountain climber is a chronic smoker.)
> No mountain climber is a person with respiratory problems. (*AEE*-2)

How do we know when a sorites is valid? By testing the validity of every syllogism it contains. The first syllogism above is *EAE*-1 and the second is *AEE*-2. Since both are valid, the sorites is valid. *All reconstructed syllogisms must be valid for the sorites to be valid.*

Sometimes a sorites can become quite involved, having many premises and a conclusion. For example:

> All mountain climbers are physically fit.
> No one physically fit is a chronic smoker.
> All respiratory diseases develop in chronic smokers.
> Lung cancer is a respiratory disease.
> All persons with lung cancer die soon.
> Some persons who die soon are reckless persons.
> Some reckless persons are not mountain climbers.

How many syllogisms would you say are needed to reconstruct this sorites? Let's see.

1. No physically fit person is a chronic smoker.
   All mountain climbers are physically fit persons.
   (No mountain climber is a chronic smoker.) (*EAE*-1)

2. All persons with respiratory diseases are chronic smokers.
   (No mountain climber is a chronic smoker.)
   (No mountain climber is a person with a respiratory disease.) (*AEE*-1)

3. **All persons with lung cancer are persons with a respiratory disease.**
   (No mountain climber is a person with a respiratory disease.)
   _____
   (No mountain climber is a person with lung cancer.) (*AEE-2*)

4. **All persons with lung cancer are persons who die soon.**
   (No mountain climber is a person with lung cancer.)
   _____
   (No mountain climber is a person who dies soon.) (*AEE-1*)

5. **(No mountain climber is a person who dies soon.)**
   Some persons who die soon are reckless persons.
   _____
   Some reckless persons are not mountain climbers. (*EIO-4*)

Is this sorites valid? It is only if *each* of its five syllogisms is valid. The fourth syllogism, *AEE*-1, contains an illicit major term thus invalidating the sorites.

We can now generalize about the sorites. Before testing the validity of any sorites, we should

1. Put all its propositions in standard form.

2. Make sure each term appears twice.

3. Make sure that every proposition except the last one (the conclusion) has a term in common with the proposition that immediately follows it.

What have we learned from discussing the enthymeme and sorites? Simply that what remains unstated in an argument is often crucial. Such assumptions aren't always crucial from the viewpoint of the persons arguing since they're interested in persuading us, and unstated premises and conclusions often help them do this. Unstated propositions are more frequently crucial from the viewpoint of the reader and listener, who are the targets of persuasive techniques. If we are to protect ourselves from being manipulated, we must be able to see an argument for what it is. This involves not only the ability to recognize an enthymeme or sorites when we see one—that's relatively easy—but also the skill of reconstructing the argument into a manageable syllogistic form. This is not always easy. But it's a vital skill to master.

To illustrate, consider this passage:

> Furthermore, those governments that condone acts of terrorism and blackmail within their borders are themselves no better than terrorists. The reason is obvious: None but terrorists would give aid and comfort to acts of terrorism. So let there be no mistaking the United States' resolve on this point: The United States will hold the new revolutionary government accountable for the terrorists' actions.

Editing out the strictly rhetorical, which is perfectly all right to do since what is strictly rhetorical doesn't advance the logic of the argument, we see that there are essentially three propositions here:

1. Governments that condone acts of terrorism and blackmail within their borders are terrorists.

2. Countries that give aid and comfort to acts of terrorism are terrorists.

3. The new revolutionary government is a group that the United States will hold accountable.

This argument is actually a sorites, which we may construct as follows, noting once again that statements in parentheses are unexpressed premises:

Countries that give aid and comfort to acts of terrorism are terrorists.
(Governments that condone acts of terrorism and blackmail within their borders are countries that give aid and comfort to acts of terrorism.)
Governments that condone acts of terrorism and blackmail within their borders are terrorists. (*AAA*-1)

Governments that condone acts of terrorism and blackmail within their borders are terrorists.
(The new revolutionary government condones acts of terrorism and blackmail within its borders.)
(The new revolutionary government consists of terrorists.) (*AAA*-1)

(Terrorists are groups the United States will hold accountable.)
(The new revolutionary government consists of terrorists.)
The new revolutionary government is a group that the United States will hold accountable. (*AAA*-1)

Here we have a sorites consisting of three arguments, each in the valid *AAA*-1 form. So the argument is valid. You'd likely admit that reconstructing this argument wasn't the easiest thing in the world to do. Look at some of those assumptions. How do we know that the arguer is making them? Have we misrepresented him or her? Answering these questions is important not only from the aspect of faithfully reconstructing what someone says but also from the view of critically analyzing it. If our reconstruction is accurate, the major premise of the final argument states that *all* terrorists are groups that the United States will hold accountable. Now that assumption warrants scrutiny. Does the arguer have in mind *any* act of terrorism, occurring in *any* country, aimed at *any* goal? In Ireland, say? In South Africa? In Bosnia and Rwanda? If our reconstruction is accurate, these are legitimate, indeed pressing, concerns that the arguer's assumption invites and that concerned citizens should raise.

So the skill of argument reconstruction is no frivolous one. Much is at stake. That's why the rest of this chapter is devoted to it. We won't be able to exhaust the subject, but we can provide useful techniques for reconstructing and cataloguing some common pitfalls.

EXERCISE 8-3 *

Translate each of the following sorites into standard form. Test for validity.

1. **No one who studies logic is stupid.**
   Anyone who is dull makes a bad writer.
   Stupid persons are dull.
   No one who studies logic makes a bad writer.

2. Only the brave are rewarded.
Some who are not promoted are not females.
Some who are rewarded are females.
_____
Some who are not promoted are not brave.

3. None but the ambitious need apply.
No one not applying should expect a check.
Smith's not ambitious.
_____
Smith shouldn't expect a check.

4. Some who should know better tread on thin ice.
A dog doesn't really know better.
Anyone treading on thin ice is bound to drown.
_____
No dog is bound to drown.

5. All my brothers are athletes.
All persons prone to diabetes are overweight.
No athlete is overweight.
All who must take insulin are persons prone to diabetes.
_____
No brother of mine must take insulin.

RATIONAL RECONSTRUCTION AND VALIDITY

The expression *rational reconstruction* refers to the process of exposing the logical (hence, "rational") structure of an argument for purposes of analysis. We do this when we encounter arguments couched in extraneous rhetorical devices, or which for some reason or other are confusing and incomplete. We may, for example, have to translate statements into standard form or infer implied premises and conclusions.

Since our purpose is to *analyze* the argument as it is made—and not to *create* the argument ourselves—we must take care not to change it for the worse. To do so would be to generate a straw argument, the refutation of which is unhelpful since it does not touch the original argument in any way. Further, as rational individuals, we seek the truth—not merely the defeat of an opponent's position. Indeed, as we've seen, an essential characteristic of being rational is a willingness to accept the conclusions of the best available arguments—even when they conflict with our personal preferences.

It is tempting and all too easy to unwittingly weaken an argument in the process of reconstructing it if we violate the guidelines discussed so far. One way to decrease the likelihood of this is to rely on the principle of charity.

Principle of Charity

The principle of charity in rational reconstruction is the rule that whenever two possible interpretations of an argument are equally likely, choose the one that most strengthens the argument.

Before we can analyze an argument, we must *see* it clearly—without distortion caused by our own biases. We must guard against hasty interpretation of only a fragment of the *intended* argument. We must also guard against an unconscious desire to defeat an opponent, because often such a desire interferes with our search for truth. We must make deliberate efforts to be fair and charitable in analyzing and reconstructing arguments.

Why should we do this? In the first place, we assume that others—just as we do—attempt to reason well. Thus, the author of an argument can, in general, be assumed to have intended a cogent argument. If an argument is presented in a fragmented, vague, or ambiguous manner, we must select the most likely interpretation *consistent with* what is given. Since most of us intend to reach true conclusions derived from cogent arguments, we are warranted in assuming that the best of the reasonable interpretations is the intended one.

Additionally, in some cases, we will spot ways to *improve* an opponent's argument. This means that even though he or she has failed to present a worthwhile argument to support a particular claim, we are aware that one exists. Although we may proceed to refute our *opponent's argument as presented*, we have not really refuted the *best argument* on that issue (the one most likely to be cogent). We have bested our *opponent* without thoroughly analyzing the *issue*. But remember that cogency is part of the public dimension of argument. If we are only concerned with defeating an opponent, we are engaged in persuasion and rhetoric, not demonstration.

Although technically we have not created a straw argument, the effect is the same: We are refuting an inferior argument while ignoring a more compelling one of which we are aware. This does not mean to suggest that we must do others' thinking for them. Our obligation is really to our own search for truth. In those cases in which two or more equally plausible interpretations of an argument are possible, we are on safer ground when we choose the better. In so doing, we diminish the chances of distorting the argument in favor of our own beliefs and we diminish the chances of overlooking the truth in that particular case.

Three Steps to Rational Reconstruction

Since most of the research dealing with argument reconstruction has focused on the standard-form categorical syllogism, we will concentrate on that argument form.

To call any syllogism incomplete or fragmented means that it leaves one or more of its premises or its conclusion unexpressed. An incomplete categorical syllogism is what we have previously termed an enthymeme. First- or second-order enthymemes are fragments that have not expressed their major or minor premises respectively, and a third-order enthymeme is a fragment that has not expressed its conclusion. The challenge of argument reconstruction therefore consists in making these missing parts explicit.

Missing premises usually test our reconstruction skills far more than missing conclusions. That's why we're going to focus on reconstructing first- and second-order enthymemes in this discussion.

The theory behind reconstructing missing premises in categorical syllogisms is direct enough. To begin, consider this form stripped of its quantity and quality:

$$
\begin{array}{cc}
P & M \\
M & S \\
\hline
S & P
\end{array}
$$

As you know, the middle term, M, is the bridge term in any categorical syllogism. It provides the link between S (minor term) and P (major term), which in turn logically entails a relationship between S and P as expressed in the conclusion. By definition, an enthymeme, in not expressing the middle term twice, does not provide an explicit bridge for relating S to P.

For example, in enthymematic form, the preceding complete form would appear as either

$$
\begin{array}{cc}
\textit{First order} & \textit{Second order} \\
\hline
\text{(unexpressed)} & \begin{array}{cc} P & M \end{array} \\
\begin{array}{cc} M & S \end{array} & \text{(unexpressed)} \\
\hline
\begin{array}{cc} S & P \end{array} & \begin{array}{cc} S & P \end{array}
\end{array}
$$

In each of these fragmented forms, the stated premise provides no explicit justification for asserting a relationship between S and P in the conclusions. In the first-order version, the P term isn't even mentioned in the evidence (premise), and in the second-order version, the S term isn't expressed in the evidence. Therefore there are no explicit grounds for accepting either version. Reconstructing such arguments therefore consists of restoring these terms in a way that allows one to *infer* a logical relationship between S and P. And the only way to do this is with the help of the bridge term, M.

If we are reconstructing a first-order enthymeme, then, we are expressing a premise that connects P to M. If we are reconstructing a second-order enthymeme, we are expressing a premise that connects S to M.

In reconstructing into standard form a fragmented argument that has left a premise unexpressed, follow these three steps:

1. Determine the conclusion of the fragmented argument and any stated premise(s).

2. Determine the middle term of the fragmented argument.

3. Reconstruct the missing premise by relating the middle term with the argument's predicate (in the case of a missing major premise: first order) or subject (in the case of a missing minor predicate: second order).

Let's see how this procedure works with a simple argument: "Sam is a student, so he is a participant." (1) What's the conclusion here? "He is a participant." The stated premise is "Sam is a student." (2) Since *Sam* (*he*) is the subject and *participant* is the predicate, *student* must be the middle term. (3) Since the major premise is missing, we must reconstruct the major premise by relating the middle term, *student,* with the major term, *participant.* Thus, "All students are participants." We can now reconstruct the whole argument:

> (All students are participants.)
> Sam's a student.
> _____
> Sam's a participant. (*AAA*-1)

But not all arguments are this simple. Consequently, a number of pitfalls await us in reconstruction. We must be careful. Following the preceding three steps will help us avoid these pitfalls, but even more is required.

In reconstructing fragmented arguments, it's vital to preserve the spirit and intent of the original argument. We have called this the *principle of charity.* Often we have to make judgments about the spirit and intent of an argument. For example, in the simple preceding argument, technically we had a choice between reconstructing the missing premise as we did or reconstructing it as "All participants are students." But this reconstruction would have resulted in an invalid *AAA*-2 argument. When we have such a choice, we should reconstruct the premise that entails validity.

Of course people can and do use enthymemes that, when reconstructed, are invalid. So we must be careful. Sometimes all possible relevant reconstructions result in invalidity. Suppose, for example, someone argues, "The Russian president can't be a capitalist because only capitalists believe that the means of production should be privately owned." This argument affords two possible reconstructions:

> All who believe that the means of production should be privately owned are capitalists.
> (No Russian president believes that the means of production should be privately owned.)
> _____
> The Russian president can't be a capitalist.

The form here is *AEE*-1; it's invalid because of an illicit major term. The other possible reconstruction is:

> All who believe that the means of production should be privately owned are capitalists.
> (No person who believes that the means of production should be privately owned is a Russian president.)
> _____
> The Russian president can't be a capitalist.

The form here is *AEE*-3, which is invalid, again, because of an illicit major term. Since invalidity results either way, we are justified in calling this argument invalid.

The point is that in reconstructing we should give the arguer the benefit of the doubt when, not knowing for sure what the arguer's assumption is, we have a choice between a reconstruction that entails validity and one that does not.

However, when no possible reconstruction that's relevant entails validity, we should consider the argument invalid. Having made these general remarks, let's take a closer look at the process of rational reconstruction.

Four Things to Do in Reconstruction

There are at least four things we can do to help provide accurate reconstructions. We can make sure that the reconstructed statements are (1) relevant, (2) self-supporting, (3) appropriately strong, and (4) contextually accurate. Ignoring even one of these will invite a straw argument.

Relevant Reconstruction

We can consider an unstated premise as an assumption speakers don't make explicitly but use to help entail a conclusion. As such, it must be directly related to the rest of the argument. It's crucial that we remember this requirement if we're to avoid misrepresenting the original argument.

For example, suppose someone argues, "He married mostly for sex; his marriage won't last long." What's the missing premise here? What's being assumed? We're apt to list among the possibilities "Anyone who marries just for sex is unwise"; "The person is not interested in a long marriage"; "People should marry for reasons other than sex"; "Sex is a temporary value; something more enduring is necessary to preserve a marriage"; and so on. The arguer may very well agree with any one of these statements, may even consider them to be the assumptions underlying his or her premises. But they are *not* the assumptions that lead *directly* to the conclusion of this argument. That's why being clear about the conclusion of an argument is the key to uncovering its unstated premise. Unless we consider *where* an argument goes, we're likely to reconstruct irrelevant premises.

Using the three-step method of operational reconstruction, let's first locate the conclusion: "His marriage (is one that) won't last long." The stated premise is "He married mostly for sex." Next, we can determine the middle term by putting the stated premise into standard form: "His marriage is a marriage entered into mostly for sexual reasons." Since *his marriage* is the subject of the conclusion, the minor term, it can't be the middle term; and since we know that the predicate, the major term, is *one that won't last long,* the middle term must be *a marriage entered into mostly for sexual reasons.* Reconstructing the major premise, we now get "All marriages entered into mostly for sexual reasons are ones that won't last long." Since this premise contains the middle term and the predicate of the argument, we know it must be relevant. Reconstructing the entire argument, we get:

(All marriages entered into mostly for sexual reasons are ones that won't last long.)
His marriage is a marriage entered into mostly for sexual reasons.

His marriage won't last long. (*AAA*-1)

Let's consider another argument: "Any time the superpowers are talking to each other increases the chances of world peace. The very fact that the Economic

Summit took place at all signals hope for world peace." Let's assume that one of these statements is intended as the conclusion but that we're not sure which. How can we decide?

We can usually find the conclusion in such cases by inserting the phrases *it follows that* and *for the reason that* before the propositions, each in turn. As we know, *it follows that* signals a conclusion; *for the reason that* indicates a premise. So one possible version of this argument is "(It follows that) any time the superpowers are talking to each other increases the chances for world peace, (for the reason that) the very fact that the Economic Summit took place at all signals hope for world peace." Here, we leap to a generalization from one event. As a result, the generalization does not follow, and if we grant the arguer any intelligence, it cannot be the conclusion of the argument. But there is another possible version of this argument: "(It follows that) the very fact that the Economic Summit took place at all signals hope for world peace, (for the reason that) any time the superpowers are talking to each other increases the chances of world peace." This argument makes more sense, and following what we have learned about rational reconstruction and the principle of charity, we should consider it to be the one the arguer intended. Having determined the argument's probable conclusion, we can now go about reconstructing the unstated premise.

We can restate the conclusion as "The Economic Summit is an occurrence that increases the chances for world peace." Since the predicate of the conclusion, *an occurrence that increases the chances for world peace,* is suggested in the stated premise, the stated premise must be the major premise. Since the subject of the conclusion, *the Economic Summit,* does not appear in the stated premise, the unstated premise must be the minor premise. There's still one term to be accounted for: *any time the superpowers are talking to each other;* this must be the middle term. We can fairly substitute *an occurrence of* for *time.* Notice how this information forces us to reconstruct a relevant assumption. The reconstructed argument thus appears:

All occurrences of the superpowers talking to each other are occurrences that increase the chances for world peace.
(The Economic Summit is an occurrence of the superpowers talking to each other.)
The Economic Summit is an occurrence that increases the chances for world peace.
(*AAA*-1)

By making the minor premise, the unstated one, adhere strictly to the *content* of the stated premise and conclusion, we have made it directly relevant to the argument. Having reconstructed the argument, we should now make one last check of each step of the reconstruction to make sure that we have retained the spirit and intent of the original fragmented argument.

Self-Supporting Reconstruction

In addition to ensuring that the assumption we reconstruct is relevant to the fragmented argument, we should also be certain that it is self-supporting. *A self-supporting premise is one that the arguer does not state (even indirectly) in the fragmented argument but is one taken for granted (assumed) as helping to entail the conclusion.* If we merely reconstruct what the arguer is already expressing, we don't provide an additional premise to entail the conclusion.

Take, as an example, this argument:

> Because TV violence is portrayed in graphic detail, it contributes to real-life violence.

That TV violence is portrayed in graphic detail does not—in and of itself—demonstrate that TV violence contributes to real-life violence. A missing premise is needed to link the idea of TV violence portrayed in graphic detail, *M*, with TV's contribution to real-life violence, *P.* Here are two candidates for the missing premise:

> **Candidate 1:**   Any violence portrayed in graphic detail contributes to real-life violence.
>
> **Candidate 2:**   Any TV violence portrayed in graphic detail contributes to real-life violence.

Each of these premises helps the expressed premise entail the conclusion. Is one preferable?

Although both premises are relevant, they clearly differ in the breadth of their claims. Candidate 1 in effect asserts that *anything* that portrays violence in graphic detail contributes to real-life violence. Candidate 2 connects only TV violence to real-life violence. Although Candidate 2 sticks closer to the argument's content, it really just repeats the argument without illuminating it. Anyone who argues, "Because television violence is portrayed in graphic detail, it contributes to real-life violence" obviously believes that the expressed premise leads to the expressed conclusion. That's how arguments and reasoning work: Premises entail conclusions; if the premises are accepted as true, a conclusion's supposed to follow logically. All Candidate 2 does, then, is make explicit what is implied about the nature of arguments and the reasoning process. Candidate 2 is, in effect, merely an expression of the general principle that leads any arguer from any premise to any purported conclusion: "If you accept my premise, you logically must accept my conclusion." But Candidate 2 doesn't tell us anything about the reasoning behind the argument; it doesn't show *how* the arguer moved from stated premise to conclusion. If we fill in the missing premise with Candidate 2, we can still ask, "But *why* does television violence contribute to real-life violence?" Candidate 2 doesn't come near answering that question—but that is precisely what the reconstruction must answer if it is to help entail the conclusion.

Of the two possibilities, Candidate 1 is preferable *because it does not merely repeat* what is already explicit in the argument. It *illuminates;* it *shows* how the arguer moved from expressed premise to conclusion. It answers the question of why TV violence contributes to real-life violence.

Appropriate Strength of Reconstruction

In determining a missing premise, choose one that is strong enough to help entail the conclusion but not stronger. Strong enough—but not too strong. There are good reasons for this advice.

If the reconstruction is not strong or general enough, it won't help provide conclusive support for the deduction. On the other hand, if it's too strong, it will misrepresent the argument; it will say more than the *arguer* intended. Either way, the reconstruction would be inadequate to the task of correctly completing the argument.

To understand this guideline, consider this argument:

Since Frances is a police officer, she probably favors collective bargaining.

The missing premise must connect "police officers," the middle term, with "people who probably favor collective bargaining," the major term.

The word *probably* in the major term is significant in distinguishing the asserted class from "people who *definitely* favor collective bargaining" and from "people who *may* favor collective bargaining." Since the stated premise—"Frances is a police officer"—does not express this likelihood, it's crucial that the reconstructed premise does. *In a valid argument, the conclusion cannot contain more than is given in the premises.* In this argument, likelihood must be introduced in one of the premises if it is to be entailed in the conclusion.

Thus, "All police officers are people who probably (or likely or typically or generally) support collective bargaining" reflects the notion of probability called for by the conclusion. On the other hand, to reconstruct the missing premise as "All police officers are people who support collective bargaining" is too strong. It calls for a stronger conclusion—"Frances is a person who (definitely) supports collective bargaining"—than the one stated. But to express the missing premise as "All police officers are people who *may* (or might or sometimes do or possibly) support collective bargaining" is too weak to support the *probably* in the conclusion.

In reconstructing missing premises, then, we need to be especially sensitive to words in the conclusion that imply certainty, probability, or possibility. We want to be sure to reconstruct missing premises that accurately reflect the degree of likelihood or certainty expressed in the conclusion—no more and no less. Missing premises need to reflect appropriate statistical conditions to be accurate.

Contextually Accurate Reconstruction

Thus far we've learned to be careful to make our reconstructed premises relevant, self-supporting, and strong. Our final note of caution concerns the context of an argument. *The context refers to the personal as well as the rhetorical dimension of an argument. The personal dimension of an argument includes such things as who voices it, where, when, and why—in short, the complexity of circumstances under which the argument was made.* These can prove vital in accurate reconstruction.

As an illustration, consider this simple argument, voiced by a judge in a beauty contest. Ordinarily this judge bases her decision on physical beauty alone. But in this contest, the beauty of the finalists is of comparable merit, so she's still left with the problem of deciding the winner. The finalists are asked to show any talents they have; after they do so, the judge announces to the audience, "The beauty of these finalists I've adjudged equal. What's made up my mind in this case is talent. The singer, finalist number three, is the winner." How would you reconstruct this argument?

The judge's conclusion is obvious: "Finalist number three is the winner." What about the premises? It might be best here to derive the unstated assumption before using the given ingredients to reconstruct the stated premise. What's the judge assuming? We might at first think, "Any finalist who sings should win a beauty contest." But it's more likely that she means that *in this particular case* singing has decided the contest for her. Does the context indicate that the judge feels a beauty-contest winner must have singing ability? Hardly. Perhaps she means, "Talent *must* be a factor in all beauty contests in which the beauty of the finalists is of comparable merit." But such an assumption would lead to the conclusion that talent must be a factor in *this* contest, not that finalist number three is the winner, the conclusion of this argument. The context seems to demand an assumption of this sort: "The most talented finalists should win this beauty contest, in which the beauty of the finalists is of comparable merit." Someone might argue that the judge says nothing of "talents" but only of singing. But again, inspect the *context. Under these circumstances* doesn't it make better sense to assume that the judge regards singing as simply one talent and that she would consider other talents? In other words, judging from the context, we show little sense in reconstructing such a narrow assumption as "The finalist who sings the best should win this beauty contest, in which the beauty of the finalists is of comparable merit."

Let's reconstruct the argument in standard form, using our more likely assumption:

(The most talented finalist should be the winner of this beauty contest in which the beauty of the finalists is of comparable merit.)
The finalist who sang, number three, is the most talented finalist.
_____
Therefore, the finalist who sang, number three, is the winner of this beauty contest. (*AAA*-1)

Let's now look at a simple example of how *rhetorical* surroundings, language, can affect an argument's reconstruction. "I'd prefer the cheaper car if it weren't so small," Joe tells a car dealer. The implied conclusion here is "I don't prefer the cheaper car." Would it be fair to say that Joe is assuming, "Any inexpensive car is one I prefer, as long as it's not small"? We certainly can view this premise as relevant and self-supporting enough to find its way into the argument:

(All cars that are inexpensive but not small are cars that I prefer.)
This car is inexpensive but small.
_____
Therefore, I do not prefer this car. (*AEE*-1) (Can you explain why?)

But before reconstructing the argument in this way, let's consider the context of the statement. When Joe says, "I'd prefer the cheaper car if it weren't so small," he's deciding on the basis of a comparison; the word *cheaper* gives that much away. But our reconstruction ignores this fact. The standard of comparison is a larger and more expensive car. What Joe means, then, is that in having compared the two cars, he'd prefer the cheaper one if it were not so small. In other words, as far as he is concerned, the difference between the two cars that makes him shy away from the cheaper one is that the cheaper one is so small. Does this mean that he would take any larger car for the same price? No, only one that meets the qualities of his standard of comparison, which is the bigger and more expensive car implied in the statement. So we'd faithfully serve Joe's argument by reconstructing the following premise:

All cars that are not so small and have the characteristics of car X but are cheaper are the cars that I prefer.

We can then use this premise and our conclusion to formulate the argument:

(All cars that are not so small and have the characteristics of car X and are cheaper are cars that I prefer.)
Car Y is not a car that is not so small and has the characteristics of car X and is cheaper.

Therefore, car Y is not a car I prefer. (*AEE*-1)

EXERCISE 8-4 *

Reconstruct the following fragmented arguments. Be certain the reconstructions are relevant, self-supporting, appropriately strong, and contextually accurate. Are the arguments cogent (that is, valid and free of informal fallacies)? Where necessary, use the parenthetical information.

1. Dogs are not ruminants, because they don't chew the cud.

2. Jacques Pení is the largest-volume furniture mart in America. You know you'll get the best deal there on new furniture.

3. Ad for Winston cigarettes: "Winston tastes good like a cigarette should."

4. Inasmuch as all voters are citizens, some of the people leaving the polling station probably aren't voters.

5. The Senator has something to hide. After all, only people hiding something refuse a polygraph test.

6. LULU: Government spending may contribute to inflation.
   LOLA: Why do you say that?
   LULU: Because government spending helps the employment situation.

7. Not all persuasive devices are reliable. Plenty of them are invalid arguments.

8. "In 1777 Washington and Lafayette may well have planned strategies over a glass of Martell." (Ad for Martell brandy, *not* for the American Historical Society or Alcoholics Anonymous)

9. That meat must be very good. The label says "U.S. Certified Grade A."

10. Ad for Waistlets gum: "Lose ugly bulges. Be more feminine."

11. It must have rained today, for the game was postponed.

12. "Yon Cassius has a lean and hungry look . . . such men are dangerous."

13. Ad for Salem cigarettes: "It's only natural."

14. California State Senator Clare Berryhill (opposing unemployment compensation for farmworkers): "California has already done more for farmworkers than any other state."

15. Maria can't be employed here. Her name isn't listed in the employment directory.

16. Not all people benefit from exercise. So I'm not going to start jogging without first consulting my physician.

17. JACK: Uh-oh, it must be tax time again.
    DEL: Why's that?
    JACK: Pop's groaning.

18. The president never expresses an opinion unless asked to. He must be very wise or very empty-headed.

19. Poker players are thinkers, simply because they're people.

20. George Bernard Shaw: "Liberty means responsibility. That is why most men dread it."

SUMMARY

This chapter concludes our treatment of converting propositions into standard form and reconstructing abbreviated deductive arguments. In handling the non-standard-form argument with more than three terms, we learned ways of handling synonyms and complements. Also, we can now convert into standard-form propositions that

1. contain a singular reference;

2. contain adjectival phrases;

3. lack the verb *to be;*

4. have irregular quantifiers;

5. lack the subject and predicate terms;

6. use *only* or *none but;* and

7. consist of two statements—one affirmative, the other negative.

Before we discussed the abbreviated argument, we learned that the best way to determine the conclusion and premises of an argument is through the context of the argument—the argument's rhetorical and physical surroundings.

Signal words are helpful but can be misleading, because they don't always indicate arguments.

The abbreviated or fragmented argument is called an *enthymeme*. A first-order enthymeme, we saw, suppresses its major premise; second-order, its minor premise; and third-order, its conclusion. Often a string of enthymemes appear together, their conclusions suppressed except for the last one. Such an argument is called a *sorites*. A sorites is valid only if each argument it contains is valid.

Finally, we considered the important subject of reconstruction and validity. View this discussion as cautionary and advisory. We suggested a three-step method that's helpful in reconstructing fragmented arguments:

1. determine the conclusion;

2. determine the middle term; and

3. reconstruct the unstated assumption by relating the middle term with the subject (in the case of a missing minor premise) or the middle term with the predicate (in the case of a missing major premise).

In reconstruction, it's important to produce statements that are: (1) relevant, (2) self-supporting, (3) appropriately strong, and (4) contextually accurate. Throughout this section on reconstruction, we emphasized one thing above everything else: fidelity to the spirit and intent of the original argument. Only conscious commitment to this principle of charity can help us avoid misrepresenting arguments.

Summary Exercises

Reconstruct self-test: Answer the following questions for yourself. Then check your answers by referring to the text.

1. Whenever we find an argument appearing to have more than three terms, we _____ .

2. For propositions containing singular terms, the individual is considered _____ .

3. Treat adjectival phrases as _____ .

4. Give an example of a proposition in which the article *a* means "some."

5. When dealing with *only* and *none but*, we follow these three steps: (1) _____ , (2) _____ , and (3) _____ .

ADDITIONAL EXERCISES

Reconstruct the following argument fragments and determine whether or not they are valid.

1. Not every man with a ponytail is a radical. Grampa has a ponytail.

2. I have children, your honor. You should not send me to jail.

3. *Any* student who disrupts class must be expelled. I'm sorry, Tony, but you must be expelled.

4. All Republicans are conservative, so don't try pretending you're a liberal.

5. The only way to win in the playoffs is with a good offense. The Seahawks don't stand a chance.

6. I've tried everything short of spanking that child. I've got to do something to control his lying.

7. Worried about your financial future? Don't worry a minute longer. Call Silverado Savings and Loan.

8. Don't vote for Roxy Rodriguez. She's having an affair with a married man. And anyone who has an affair is a cheat.

9. I don't think Ivana Trump should get half of Donald's money. After all, she signed a prenuptial agreement limiting her share in case of divorce.

10. If creatures from other galaxies are smart enough to cross space and discover that there's life on Earth, then how come they can't find a major world capitol?

11. Jamal's an interesting lecturer if you like hearing about his personal life a zillion times. I doubt if you'd like his class.

12. They say that depression is caused by an overactive mind and an underactive body. It's no wonder you're depressed.

13. They have no right to ban offensive language from the radio.

14. You really should give Scientology a try. John Travolta and Kirstie Alley are scientologists.

15. Clothes by Nicole. For those who want the best.

16. All cultures and eras have believed in God. There must be some reason. It can't be just wishful thinking.

17. "Janet? Is that you? Oh my! I was just telling Jerry that I ought to call you! You know what that means. . . ."

18. I *told* you if you lied one more time, I was going to tell Mommy. You're going to get it now.

19. If Don Hopes Hardware ain't got it, it don't exist.

20. There's no point in explaining this to you; it takes average intelligence to understand it.

CHAPTER 9

Additional Syllogisms

Though syllogisms hang not upon my tongue,
I am not surely always in the wrong!
'Tis hard if all is false that I advance—
A fool must now and then be right, by chance.

WILLIAM COWPER

As we saw in Chapter 7, having a "sense" about the validity of an argument is not very reliable. And just as Cowper's fool "must now and then be right, by chance," so, too, must he be wrong.

Even if we always can't be right, we have reduced the likelihood of being wrong by learning how to prove the validity or invalidity of standard-form categorical syllogisms. But not all syllogisms are standard-form categorical syllogisms, and thus don't lend themselves to the methods of proving validity. We've discussed so far methods that apply only to standard-form categorical syllogisms. Consider, for example, this argument:

If all syllogisms are standard-form syllogisms, we have adequate means available for proving their validity.
Not all syllogisms are standard-form categorical syllogisms.

We do not have adequate means available for proving their validity.

Is it valid? Perhaps we can figure that out if we think about it carefully. But there is a better, more efficient, way of analyzing such syllogisms than just trying to "figure them out." This better way is the subject of this chapter. (By the way, the syllogism in question is invalid. It is an example of a commonly committed fallacy, called *the fallacy of denying the antecedent,* which we will learn about as part of our study of nonstandard syllogisms.)

In this chapter we'll discuss two of the most common patterns of deductive reasoning—patterns we naturally use as part of our everyday reasoning. We will also reinforce and add to our understanding of the concept of logical form. We will learn to recognize the forms of three nonstandard syllogisms and also how to simplify them. In Chapter 8 we learned how to "translate" or reconstruct syllogisms in ordinary language into standard-form categorical propositions. With the completion of this chapter, we will have a firm grasp on the basics of deductive reasoning and a supply of some basic analytic tools for handy reference.

We'll begin with a look at an argument form we encounter almost daily: the disjunctive syllogism.

DISJUNCTIVE SYLLOGISMS

We often find ourselves choosing between alternatives which we express in propositions containing the word *or*, as in, "Either you're for me or you're against me," or "Would you like soup or salad with that tofu, sir?" Notice that the preceding sentence contains alternative examples. In the common understanding of these examples—assuming the second occurs in a restaurant—the choice is between one alternative or the other. Trying to have both is implicitly forbidden. But sometimes alternatives allow for choosing one or the other or both, as in "Is the student a scholar or an athlete?" Both alternatives are possible in this case.

These examples remind us that in English we use the single word *or* in two senses. For example, in a statement on a restaurant menu such as "Dinner includes soup or salad," *or* means clearly *either* soup *or* salad *but not both*. This meaning, termed the "exclusive sense of *or*," is clear to most of us from the context: in this case, the context of a restaurant menu. But in "All those eligible for welfare are unemployed *or* infirm," *or* is used in a "weaker" sense known as the *inclusive* sense. In this example of the "weaker" sense, the statement asserts that one could be either unemployed *or* infirm and allows for the possibility of being *both* unemployed *and* infirm. The inclusive *or* asserts that *at least one of the alternative statements is true*. Thus, "All those eligible for welfare are at least unemployed or infirm."

The alternative statements joined by the inclusive *or* are called *disjuncts. The statement including both disjuncts and the inclusive* or *is called a disjunction.* A disjunction is true if either of the disjuncts is true. This is another way of saying that a disjunction is true whenever *at least one* of its disjuncts is true.

STUDY HINT

The inclusive *or* asserts that at least one of the disjuncts is true.
A disjunction is false in only one case: when both disjuncts are false.

Recall that a syllogism consists of two premises and a conclusion. When a disjunction occurs as the premise of a syllogism, the syllogism is called a *disjunctive syllogism. Valid disjunctive syllogisms contain a disjunction as one premise, the negation of one of the disjuncts as the second premise, and the affirmation of the remaining disjunct as the conclusion*. The basic form of valid disjunctive syllogisms look like this:

Either *this* or *that*	Either *this* or *that*
not *this*	not *that*
that	this

Here's an example:

> **Either some students are scholars or they are athletes.**
> **Some students are not scholars.**
> **Then some are athletes.**

Notice that the second proposition negates (or denies) one of the disjuncts, and the conclusion affirms the other. Since to assert a disjunction is to assert that at least one of the disjuncts is true, we may validly infer such a conclusion if both premises are treated as being true. In our example, the conclusion "Then some are athletes" must logically follow. Let's look at another example:

> **Either the plane has crashed or it's been delayed.**
> **The plane has not been delayed.**
> **Therefore the plane has crashed.**

Here, too, the second premise denies one of the disjuncts and the conclusion affirms the other. This is the same logical pattern—or form—as the first example. It, too, is valid.

On the other hand, consider this argument:

> **Either the plane has crashed or it's been delayed.**
> **The plane has been delayed.**
> **Therefore the plane has not crashed.**

Notice that the second premise does not deny either disjunct; rather it affirms one of them. Is it possible for both disjuncts to be true? Yes—that's the meaning of disjunction. It allows for the possibility that the plane has been delayed *and* has also crashed: Our second premise is merely telling us that at least one of those two disjuncts is true. The meaning of disjunction, as defined above, only says that *at least one disjunction must be true*—it also always allows for the possibility that both might be. Consequently, the conclusion in this example does not follow from the premises with logical certainty—it goes beyond them. So this example is invalid.

Last, consider this example:

> **The senator is qualified to be either president or vice president.**
> **The senator is qualified to be president.**
> **Therefore she's not qualified to be vice president.**

As we've already noted, affirming one of the disjuncts does not deny the other. The conclusion, because it does not necessarily follow from the premises, is invalidly drawn. This argument, too, is invalid.

Using p and q to represent any two propositions, let's contrast the basic form of valid and invalid disjunctive syllogisms:

valid disjunctive syllogism	invalid disjunctive syllogism
Either p or q	Either p or q
not p	p
Therefore, q	Therefore, not q

EXERCISE 9-1 *

Determine the validity of the following disjunctive syllogisms.

1. There's either a fuel shortage or the government is lying.
   There is a fuel shortage.
   Therefore the government is not lying.

2. Either the general is guilty of obstructing justice or he's a patriot.
   The general is no patriot.
   Then the general is guilty of obstructing justice.

3. The United States either supports the Iraqis or the Kuwaitis in the Middle East.
   The United States supports the Iraqis.
   Therefore, the United States does not support the Kuwaitis.

4. Whether we like it or not—and we probably don't—we must either become energy self-sufficient or resign ourselves to international blackmail.
   We must not resign ourselves to international blackmail.
   Hence we must become energy self-sufficient.

5. The matter of the universe will continue to expand to extinction, or it will begin to contract, in which case another "big bang" will eventually occur.
   The matter of the universe will continue to expand.
   So the matter of the universe will not begin to contract and thus another "big bang" will not eventually occur.

6. Either all S is P or no S is P.
   Some S is not P.
   It follows that no S is P.

7. Either some S is P or some S is not P.
   No S is P.
   Therefore some S is not P.

8. Either all S is P or some S is P.
   Some S is not P.
   So some S is P.

9. Either no S is P or some S is not P.
   No S is P.
   Then some S is not P.

CONDITIONAL SYLLOGISMS

We sometimes express the conditions under which something will occur in "if . . . then" form as in, "If I have time, I'll drop your suit off at the cleaners," or "If you love me, you'll be nice to my dog." "If . . . then" statements assert a conditional relationship only. They do not promise or guarantee that those conditions will be met. I may not have time to drop your suit off at the cleaners, or you may not love me.

Certain "if . . . then" statements are called *conditionals, hypotheticals,* or *implications. We'll call the statement that occurs between* if *and* then *the antecedent of the conditional, and we'll call the statement that follows* then *the consequent.* This is a special kind of conditional known as a material conditional. (Other kinds of conditionals are logical, definitional, causal, and decisional. We are concerned only with material conditionals.)

Let's see how a material conditional statement is true by considering the following example: "If it's raining, the game is canceled." This conditional is true provided that "the game is canceled" is not false at the same time that "it is raining" is true. *A conditional statement is true if and only if the consequent is not false and the antecedent true.* Every conditional statement—whatever else it may mean—asserts this relationship: It denies that its antecedent is true and its conditional false. Although this may seem odd, remember that we are talking about only one type of conditional statement, the *material conditional* as logicians call it.

Conditional statements can occur as the premises of arguments. Consider the following syllogism:

If we begin recycling efforts immediately, we have a good chance of saving the environment.
We begin recycling efforts immediately.
We have a good chance of saving the environment.

This argument form is called a *mixed-conditional syllogism.* It is "mixed" because it contains a conditional premise and a second, simple premise. If we look carefully at this argument we notice that the second premise affirms the antecedent of the conditional premise and the conclusion affirms the consequent. This form is valid. Such arguments are said to be in the *affirmative mood;* they are commonly referred to by their Latin name: *modus ponens. Any time the second premise of a mixed conditional syllogism affirms the antecedent of the conditional premise and the conclusion affirms its consequent, the syllogism is valid.*

There's a fallacy that superficially resembles *modus ponens:*

> **If we begin recycling efforts immediately, we have a good chance of saving the environment.**
> **We have a good chance of saving the environment.**
> ————————————
> **We begin recycling efforts immediately.**

Even if this conclusion is, in fact, true, it does not *logically follow* from the premises. Consider a very simple instance of the same fallacious pattern:

> **If my car is out of gas, it will not start.**
> **My car will not start.**
> ————————————
> **My car is out of gas.**

Even if the conclusion is, in fact, true, the argument upon which it is based is flawed. *Based only on the information provided in the premises,* the conclusion "my car is out of gas" is too strong for the premises. Other factors may account for my car's not starting: bad battery, failed ignition, and so forth. A deductive argument is valid only when the premises entail the conclusion—a condition not met by these last two examples of mixed-conditional syllogisms. Any argument of this form is invalid because the form commits *the fallacy of affirming the consequent.* Compare *modus ponens* to affirming the consequent:

modus ponens:	*fallacy of affirming the consequent:*
If *antecedent* then *consequent*	If *antecedent* then *consequent*
antecedent	*consequent*
consequent	*antecedent*

Simplified further, we get:

modus ponens:	*fallacy of affirming the consequent:*
If p then q	If p then q
p	q
q	p

STUDY HINT

Modus ponens is always valid; affirming the consequent never is.

Besides *modus ponens,* another valid form of mixed-conditional syllogism—*modus tollens*—denies the consequent as its second premise and denies the antecedent as its conclusion. Here's an example:

If we begin recycling efforts immediately, we have a good chance of saving the environment.
We don't have a good chance of saving the environment.
We're not beginning recycling efforts immediately.

We can compare the forms of *modus ponens* and *modus tollens* as follows:

modus ponens:	*modus tollens:*
If *antecedent* then *consequent*	If *antecedent* then *consequent*
antecedent	not *consequent*
consequent	not *antecedent*

Simplified:

modus ponens:	*modus tollens:*
If *p* then *q*	If *p* then *q*
p	not *q*
q	not *p*

To help see that *modus tollens* arguments are valid, consider this simple instance:

If my car is safe to drive, then it has good brakes.
My car does not have good brakes.
My car is not safe to drive.

Just as we have to be wary of confusing *modus ponens* with the fallacy of affirming the consequent, we must be careful not to confuse *modus tollens* with the fallacy of denying the antecedent. Here's an example of the *fallacy of denying the antecedent:*

If my car is safe to drive, then it has good brakes.
My car is not safe to drive.
My car does not have good brakes.

Based only on the premises, the conclusion "my car does not have good brakes" does not follow. The conditional relationship asserts only that it is not possible for the antecedent to be true and the consequent false. In other words, the occurrence of the antecedent guarantees the occurrence of the consequent. This relationship only goes in one direction. We cannot, for example, reverse the antecedent and consequent and retain the original conditional relationship. "If my car is safe to drive, then it has good brakes" is not equivalent to "If my car has good brakes, then it is safe to drive." Yet this is exactly what the fallacy of denying the antecedent assumes. Compare *modus tollens* and the *fallacy of denying the antecedent* to see how these clearly differ:

modus tollens:	*fallacy of denying the antecedent:*
If *antecedent* then *consequent*	If *antecedent* then *consequent*
not *consequent*	not *antecedent*
not *antecedent*	not *consequent*

Simplified:

modus tollens:	*fallacy of denying the antecedent:*
If *p* then *q*	If *p* then *q*
not *q*	not *p*
not *p*	not *q*

Pure Conditional Syllogism

Sometimes, a conditional syllogism contains only conditional propositions, for example:

> If Lisa has nightmares, then Nicky wakes up.
> If Nicky wakes up, then Lina goes bonkers.
> If Lisa has nightmares, then Lina goes bonkers.

Since the syllogism contains only conditional propositions, we call it a *pure* conditional (or hypothetical) syllogism. Note three things about this particular argument that make it—and any argument with the same form—valid:

1. the consequent of the first premise is the same as the antecedent of the second premise;

2. the antecedent of the first premise is the same as the antecedent of the conclusion; and

3. the consequent of the second premise is the same as the consequent of the conclusion.

We can use the following abbreviated arguments to represent the form of valid pure conditional syllogisms. (1, 2, 3, *X*, *Y*, and *Z* represent any statements whatsoever.)

If 1 then 2	If *X* then *Y*	If 1 then *Z*
If 2 then 3	If *Y* then *Z*	If *Z* then *X*
If 1 then 3	If *X* then *Z*	If 1 then *X*

Any *pure* conditional syllogism of this form is valid; if it does not follow this form it is invalid.

Using p, q, and r, we can represent the basic form of the pure conditional syllogism as follows.

pure conditional syllogism:

If p then q
If q then r

If p then r

EXERCISE 9-2 *

Determine which—if any—of the following conditional syllogisms are valid.

1. If the vice president was not guilty of wrongdoing, he would not resign from office.
   The vice president did resign from office.

   Therefore the vice president was guilty of wrongdoing.

2. If there's life in outer space, it's superior to us.
   If it's superior to us, it will contact us.

   If there's life in outer space, it will contact us.

3. If a thing precedes itself, it is its own cause.
   A thing cannot precede itself.

   Thus a thing is not its own cause.

4. If this is Brussels, today is Tuesday.
   Today is not Tuesday.

   Therefore this is not Brussels.

5. If a president is impeached, then no one benefits.
   A president is impeached.

   Then no one benefits.

6. If the witness is either the criminal or the criminal's accomplice, he'll lie.
   The witness is neither the criminal nor the criminal's accomplice.

   Therefore, he'll not lie.

7. If Joanne knows what she's talking about, I'm a monkey's uncle. And since I'm obviously not a monkey's uncle, Joanne doesn't know what she's talking about.

8. If taxes rise, consumer purchases decline. If consumer purchases decline, the economy suffers. If taxes rise, the economy suffers.

9. If the president knows what he's doing with this Gulf War thing, I'm not your wife. Since you're my husband, the president doesn't know what he's doing with this Gulf War thing.

10. If Harry goes to town on payday, he'll come home broke. Harry comes home broke, so we can conclude that he goes to town on payday.

THE DILEMMA

Most of us have probably found ourselves "between a rock and a hard place," faced with "choosing the lesser of two evils." There are times when we'd like to avoid either of the only alternatives open to us. Perhaps you've waited until the last minute to prepare for your Cosmetology 1A final. You've planned to study this weekend—and then the boss calls and says you have to work overtime or be fired. You need the job to pay for next term's tuition, but if you fail Cosmetology 1A you won't be allowed back in school anyway. You've got a dilemma.

In logic, a dilemma is a very specific argument form. *A dilemma is a syllogism that contains a conditional and disjunctive premise, and either a simple statement or a disjunction for its conclusion. A simple dilemma contains a simple statement for its conclusion; a complex dilemma contains a disjunction for its conclusion.*

To illustrate a simple dilemma, let's look at the structure of a simple dilemma many students feel themselves confronted with:

If I don't go to the party with my best friend and have fun, I'll feel guilty; if I don't stay home and study, I'll feel guilty.
Either I go to the party or I study.
Therefore I'll feel guilty.

If we let *p, q,* and *r* stand for any of three different propositions, we can represent the form of a valid simple dilemma like this:

$$\text{If } p \text{ then } q \text{ and If } r \text{ then } q$$
$$\frac{p \text{ or } r}{q}$$

We notice that a simple dilemma combines two instances of *modus ponens:*

$$\begin{array}{ccc} \text{If } p \text{ then } q & & \text{If } r \text{ then } q \\ p & \text{and} & r \\ \hline q & & q \end{array}$$

Any argument of this form is valid.

Now let's look an example of a complex dilemma:

If I get married, then I lose my freedom; if I stay single, then I am lonely.
I either get married or stay single.
Therefore I either lose my freedom or I am lonely.

The basic form of this argument—and of any valid complex constructive dilemma—is

$$\text{If } p \text{ then } q \text{ and if } r \text{ then } s.$$
$$\frac{\text{Either } p \text{ or } r.}{\text{Either } q \text{ or } s.}$$

Any complex constructive dilemma of this form is valid; otherwise it is invalid.

STUDY HINT

Simple dilemmas contain simple statements as conclusions: complex dilemmas contain disjunctions as conclusions.

Dilemmas and Cogency

Our example of a complex dilemma illustrates an important point: The frustration we so often feel when confronted with an apparent dilemma is usually compounded by the fact that most of the dilemmas we encounter in our daily dealings are valid. So we often feel the frustration of being "caught on the horns of a dilemma." In fact, you may have noticed that the everyday use of the term *dilemma* is almost entirely confined to circumstances in which someone seems to be confronted with an inevitably unattractive outcome. There are times, as we'll see, when the inevitable isn't at all bad; but generally the dilemma poses an undesired and unpleasant conclusion.

The very sense of frustration and inescapability we feel in the presence of a valid dilemma makes the dilemma a powerful tool in making a case. We are understandably often reluctant to take difficult action. Consider the case of a state legislator trying to convince the governor to increase the education budget. If our legislator can formulate his case as a dilemma, he will have effectively limited the governor's options. This may compel the governor to see things his way. Let's see how.

The legislator might, for example, argue that there are only two places in the budget left to cut: welfare or education. Having gotten this far, our legislator makes his case: "The registrar of voters reveals that there are 200,000 registered voters on welfare. Four million registered voters have children in school. If you cut funds from welfare, you risk alienating 200,000 voters. If you cut funds from education, you risk alienating 4 million voters. You must either cut funds from welfare or education. Therefore, you must alienate either 200,000 voters or 4 million voters."

Although the legislator's dilemma may not be cogent, it is valid. If he has presented it in a persuasive manner, the governor may very well feel there are only these two alternatives. That's what the legislator hopes. When simple and complex dilemmas deviate from valid form, they present no problem of rebuttal. We simply can dispose of them as being invalid. But what about dilemmas that are valid? What can we do to avoid being impaled on the horns of simple and complex dilemmas?

As is true of any valid argument, before accepting it as cogent we should examine its premises for truth. There are two ways to challenge the truth of dilemmas. One is to take the dilemma by the horns; the other is to escape between the horns. Let's illustrate what we mean by focusing on the student's argument.

By "taking the dilemma by the horns," we mean attacking the truth of the conditional premise. Respecting the student's dilemma we can ask, Why are studying and having fun mutually exclusive? Can't studying *be* fun? In fact, the best kind of learning takes place when we're enjoying what we're studying—when we're "having fun." The point is that if we successfully attack one of the conditionals (by perhaps showing that it is a false-cause fallacy or a hasty conclusion, discussed in Chapters 11 and 13), we destroy the dilemma it sets up.

On the other hand, rather than attacking the conditional proposition, we might *"escape between the horns" of the dilemma by attacking the disjunction.* Thus, perhaps we can be both studious and idle. Surely there are times when the mind must turn away from intense work to restore itself for more work. Undoubtedly, a healthful combination of study and idleness—rest and relaxation—is the best guarantee of success. Reasoning in this way, we in effect contend that the disjunction poses a false dilemma, an either/or situation where, in fact, none exists. If our contention is correct, we destroy the disjunction and the dilemma with it.

Taking a dilemma by the horns or escaping between the horns are the best ways to refute a dilemma. There is a third way, however, that is marvelously entertaining, though usually inadequate to the task.

The Counterdilemma

A counterdilemma is a dilemma whose conclusion is opposed to the conclusion of the original. Ideally the counterdilemma should contain the same premises as the original dilemma. A celebrated lawsuit between the ancient Greeks Protagoras and Eulathus provides a classic example of such a counterdilemma and how rhetorically devastating it can be.

Protagoras was a fifth-century BC teacher who specialized in pleading cases before juries. Eulathus was his student. Lacking the required tuition for his training, Eulathus arranged with Protagoras to defer payment until he, Eulathus, won his first case. Unfortunately for Protagoras, Eulathus delayed going into practice after he finished his training. Fed up with waiting for his money, Protagoras decided to sue his former student for the tuition. At the beginning of the trial, Protagoras posed his case in the form of a dilemma:

> If Eulathus loses this case, then he must pay me (by judgment of the court); if he wins this case, then he must pay me (by terms of the contract). He must either lose or win this case. Therefore Eulathus must pay me.

What could be harder to imagine than Eulathus's avoiding the horns of this dilemma? As unpromising as his situation seemed, Eulathus was nonetheless up to it; evidently he had learned his rhetorical lessons well. He offered the court a counterdilemma:

> If I win this case, I shall not have to pay Protagoras (by judgment of the court); if I lose this case, I shall not have to pay Protagoras (by the terms of the contract, for then I shall not yet have won my first case). I must either win or lose this case. Therefore, I do not have to pay Protagoras!

Notice that the beauty of Eulathus's counterdilemma is that its conclusion explicitly denies the conclusion of Protagoras's dilemma. Genuinely to rebut a dilemma requires such an explicit denial in the conclusion. When it occurs, the counterdilemma is most effective. But rarely do we come across such counter-dilemmas. More often than not, the counterdilemma, although enormously crowd pleasing, logically does nothing to refute the dilemma.

To illustrate an entertaining but logically inert counterdilemma, let's again dip into Greek history. An Athenian mother who was attempting to persuade her son not to enter politics is said to have argued:

> If you say what is just, men will hate you; and if you say what is unjust, the gods will hate you; but you must either say the one or the other; therefore you will be hated.

To which her son replied:

> If I say what is just, the gods will love me; and if I say what is unjust, men will love me. I must say either the one or the other. Therefore I shall be loved!

Although such a counterargument is extremely clever and bound to win many debating points, its conclusion is not an explicit denial of the dilemma's conclusion. Recall the Protagoras-Eulathus debate. Protagoras's conclusion was "Eulathus must pay me." Eulathus's conclusion was "I do not have to pay Protagoras." These two statements are incompatible; to accept one is to deny the other; one is the contradiction of the other. But believe it or not, the Athenian youth's conclusion, "I shall be loved," is *not* incompatible with his mother's conclusion, "You will be hated." The reason is that the mother is, in effect, concluding, "You will be hated by men or by the gods." And the son, in effect, is concluding, "I shall be loved by the gods or by men." Since the son could end up being hated by men and loved by the gods, or hated by the gods and loved by men, the conclusion of mother and son are perfectly compatible. The son has not refuted his mother's argument. He'd be much better served to attack the horns of its dilemma or try to escape between its horns. And thus we all would when faced with a dilemma.

But daily, as politicians and advertisers prove, we are taken in by flashy rhetorical devices. And the counterdilemma can be one of them. Not only can the counterdilemma win over an audience, it can even convince arguers that their shrewdly constructed dilemmas are unsound. Consider this example:

Lloyd thought he had Dean right where he wanted him. He had loaned Dean 20 dollars to bet on a horse, and according to their agreement, Dean either owed him 20 dollars or a share of the winnings. Maybe so. But with uncommon deftness, Dean counterattacked. He posed a counterdilemma of essentially this form:

If the horse wins, then I don't owe you the 20 dollars (for in that event, I'd owe you a share of the winnings); if the horse loses, then I don't owe you a share of the winnings (because obviously there would be no winnings).
Either the horse wins or loses.
___
Either I don't owe you the 20 dollars or I don't owe you a share of the winnings.

And then, with a flourish of his hand, he added, "Either way we're even." Whereupon Lloyd did what any rational person would do under the circumstances: He threatened to rip Dean's beard off if he didn't get his money back.

EXERCISE 9-3 *

Refute the following either by taking the dilemma by the horns or by escaping between the horns. Construct a counterdilemma for each original dilemma.

1. If the speech is just informative, it will bore me; if it is just entertaining, it will not educate me.
   The speech will be either informative or entertaining.
   Therefore the speech will either bore me or not educate me.

2. If there is a God, he will reward me for my virtuous deeds; if there is no God I will sleep a peaceful, uninterrupted sleep.
   There is either a God or there is not.
   Thus I will either be rewarded for my virtuous deeds or I will sleep a peaceful, uninterrupted sleep.

3. If she rejects me, I'll be crushed; if she accepts me, I'll be terrified.
   She'll either reject me or accept me.
   I'll be either crushed or terrified!

4. If the United States modifies its Middle East position, it will offend a good many American Jews; if the United States does not modify its Middle East position, it will jeopardize its fuel supplies in Arab countries.
   The United States must either modify its position in the Middle East or not.
   As a result, the United States will either offend a good many American Jews or jeopardize its fuel supplies in Arab countries.

5. If I study my logic tonight, then I will not get to go to the movies; if I don't study my logic tonight, I will worry.
   I either study my logic tonight or I don't.
   I either don't get to go to the movies or I worry.

6. If I vote, then I must choose between two evils. If I don't vote, then I am not a good citizen.
   Either I vote or I don't.
   So I either choose between two evils or I am not a good citizen.

7. If I pay my rent, then I can't pay my utilities and they will be turned off. If I don't pay my rent, then I will be evicted.
   I either pay my rent or I don't.
   I am either evicted or they turn off my utilities.

8. If I get married, I lose Midge; if I don't get married, then I lose Louise.
   Either I get married or I don't.
   I lose either Midge or Louise.

9. If I tell the truth, you will be angry with me; if I lie, I will be angry with myself.
   I either tell the truth or I lie.
   One or the other of us is angry with me.

10. **If I keep this old clunker, I must spend a fortune on repairs; if I buy a new car, then I must spend a fortune on payments and insurance.**
    Either I keep this old clunker or I buy a new car.
    _____
    Either I spend a fortune on repairs or I spend it on payments and insurance.

SUMMARY

In this chapter we learned how to recognize some common deductive syllogisms. We learned that:

A disjunction is a compound proposition that asserts that at least one of its disjuncts is true. The alternatives that compose a disjunction are called disjuncts. A disjunction is true if either of its disjuncts is true, and it is true if both of its disjuncts are true. The only time a disjunction is false is if both of its disjuncts are false.

Valid disjunctive syllogisms contain a disjunction as one premise, the negation of one of the disjuncts as the second premise, and the affirmation of the remaining disjunct as the conclusion. The basic form of *valid* disjunctive syllogisms looks like this:

$$\text{Either } p \text{ or } q$$
$$\underline{\text{not } p}$$
$$q$$

Invalid disjunctive syllogisms look like:

$$\text{Either } p \text{ or } q$$
$$\underline{p}$$
$$\text{not } q$$

We also learned about hypothetical or conditional propositions and syllogisms. A hypothetical proposition is a compound proposition that asserts a conditional relationship between two other propositions, expressed in "if . . . then" form. The proposition that occurs between *if* and *then* is called the antecedent of the conditional, and the proposition that follows *then* is known as the consequent. A hypothetical proposition is true if and only if the consequent is not false when the antecedent is true. The only time a hypothetical proposition is false is when the antecedent is true while the consequent is false.

Modus ponens and *modus tollens* are two forms of valid mixed-conditional syllogisms. When the second premise of a mixed-conditional syllogism affirms the antecedent of the conditional premise and the conclusion affirms its consequent, the syllogism is a valid instance of *modus ponens*. When the second premise of a mixed-conditional syllogism denies the consequent of the conditional premise and the conclusion denies its antecedent, the syllogism is a valid instance of *modus tollens*.

We can illustrate the form of *modus ponens* and *modus tollens* as follows:

modus ponens:	*modus tollens:*
If *antecedent* then *consequent*	If *antecedent* then *consequent*
antecedent	not *consequent*
consequent	not *antecedent*

We distinguished between two fallacies that superficially resemble *modus ponens* and *modus tollens*. Structurally they compare as follows:

modus ponens:	*fallacy of affirming the consequent:*
If *antecedent* then *consequent*	If *antecedent* then *consequent*
antecedent	*consequent*
consequent	*antecedent*

modus tollens:	*fallacy of denying the antecedent:*
If *antecedent* then *consequent*	If *antecedent* then *consequent*
not *consequent*	not *antecedent*
not *antecedent*	not *consequent*

We can also illustrate these argument forms using the variables p and q:

modus ponens:	*modus tollens:*
If p then q	If p then q
p	not q
q	not p

modus ponens:	*fallacy of affirming the consequent:*
If p then q	If p then q
p	q
q	p

modus tollens:	*fallacy of denying the antecedent:*
If p then q	If p then q
not q	not p
not p	not q

Lastly, we studied two kinds of dilemma. A dilemma is a syllogism that contains a conditional and disjunctive premise, and either simple or compound statement for its conclusion. A simple dilemma contains a simple statement for its conclusion; a complex dilemma contains a disjunction for its conclusion.

A valid simple dilemma looks like this:

If p then q and if r then q
p or r
q

A valid complex dilemma looks like this:

> If p then q and if r then s
>
> p or r
> _____
>
> q or s

We learned to refute dilemmas with counterdilemmas, as well as to take a dilemma *by the horns* by attacking the truth of its conditional premise. We learned to *escape between the horns* of a dilemma by attacking the disjunction.

ADDITIONAL EXERCISES

Determine the validity of the following. Identify any fallacies that may be present. Name the form of each argument.

1. The president either forgot that he promised no new taxes, or he lied. He didn't lie, so he must have forgotten.

2. If secular humanism is a religion, then it should not be taught in public schools. But secular humanism is taught in public schools, so it must not be a religion.

3. If I study for my logic final, then I'll lose my sweetheart. If I lose my sweetheart, then my life's empty and futile. If I study for my logic final, my life's empty and futile.

4. If I go to the movies, then I enjoy myself; if I stay home, then we have fun together. I'm either going to the movies or I'm not, so I'll either enjoy myself or we'll have fun together.

5. God either exists or I'm a fool. God exists. Therefore I'm not a fool.

6. If you think Snipes is a better actor than Stallone, then I'm a nitwit, and I ain't no nitwit!

7. If you love me, then you give me gifts. You give me gifts, so I know that you love me.

8. If I love you, then I want to marry you. But I don't love you, so I don't want to marry you.

9. If it rains, the crops will die; if it doesn't rain, the stock will die. Either the crops will die or the stock will die, since it either rains or it doesn't.

10. If this is question 10, then we're through with this exercise. We're not through with this exercise, so this isn't question 10.

PART FOUR

INDUCTIVE ARGUMENTS

CHAPTER 10

Inductive Reasoning and Generalizations

He who begins to count begins to err.

OSKAR MORGENSTERN

In Part Three we learned that a deductive argument is one whose premises are intended to provide conclusive support for the conclusion. By contrast, *an inductive argument is one whose premises are intended to provide some, but not conclusive support, for the conclusion.* In an inductive argument, the conclusion is likely or probable but never logically certain; for example, "Employee Brown has arrived on time for work the last thousand days. Therefore, he'll probably arrive on time today." There's nothing certain about this conclusion. We can easily imagine some event or condition that will disprove the conclusion. Brown may be ill or have had an accident or overslept. The evidence stated in the premise in and of itself does not necessitate the conclusion. It does, however, make the conclusion probable or likely. Thus, the word *probable* must be used or understood before the conclusion of any inductive argument. So when one argues, "Since many drug addicts who come through the courts admit that they started on pot, pot probably causes hard-core drug addiction," one is arguing inductively.

STUDY HINT

Inductive reasoning is concerned with degrees of likelihood, not logical certainty.

Inductive arguments can grow better or worse as new evidence comes in. They are *justified* when they have "enough good evidence" to support their conclusion.

As with deductive arguments, inductive arguments may be well constructed or poorly constructed. We shall term a well-constructed inductive argument *justified*, as opposed to *valid*, which characterizes correct deductive arguments. *An inductive argument is justified when its premises, if assumed true, lend its conclusion a high degree of probability.* A poorly constructed induction can be termed "unjustified."

The most basic kind of inductive argument has a generalization for its conclusion. *A generalization is a statement that covers many specifics.* Here are some examples: "When people use seat belts, deaths from traffic accidents decrease"; "If detected early enough, many cancers can be cured"; "Apple trees grow better in Washington State than in Florida." Each of these examples cover the specific instances of wearing seat belts, early detection of cancer, and growing apple trees in Washington and Florida. *The most basic type of inductive argument is one whose conclusion is a generalization.*

It is easier to identify bad induction than it is to give a precise set of rules that guarantee good induction (as we were able to give six rules to guarantee the validity of standard-form categorical syllogisms in Chapter 7). We can, however, identify obviously bad inductive arguments (one's that aren't justified) as well as provide an outline of general principles for good induction by studying examples of typical patterns of cogent inductive reasoning. From these we can draw general guidelines for avoiding common errors of induction.

Let's begin with a quick look at induction and the sufficiency criterion.

INDUCTION AND THE SUFFICIENCY CRITERION

Recall that a valid deduction may not be a cogent argument because the notion of validity refers only to the logical or evidentiary relationship between premises and conclusion, not the truth or reasonableness of the individual premises. The same idea must be kept in mind with respect to "justifiedness." To call an inductive argument "justified" simply means that the premises—*when they are assumed true*—provide strong support for the conclusion. Might the premises actually be false? They might, indeed, just as with deduction. Thus every *cogent* induction is justified (as every cogent deduction is valid). But not every justified induction is cogent (no more than every valid deduction is cogent).

Now notice that when we ask of an inductive argument, "Is it justified?" we are in effect asking: "Do the premises offer *sufficient* support for the conclusion?" Since by nature an inductive argument offers *some,* but not *conclusive,* support for its conclusion, the central evaluative concern in inductive logic is the sufficiency of evidence to support the conclusion. In other words: "How much evidence is needed to justify an inductive conclusion?" This is a very important question because, remember, only justified inductions can be cogent inductions. (Of course, to repeat, a justified induction may not be cogent. Its premises, for example, may be untrue and thus unreasonable. Still, the probabilistic nature of induction makes the sufficiency criterion the problematic one.)

In general, an inductive argument is *justified* when its premises—if assumed true—provide "enough good evidence" to support the generalization offered as its conclusion.

How many times do you have to burn your hand on something hot to conclude that touching hot things hurts? How many people do you have to hire from a certain trade school to reasonably conclude that its graduates are well qualified? In other words, when are inductive generalizations justified? When are they not? Induction is problematic by its very nature, and so we can only provide general—inductively based—guidelines for good inductive reasoning.

STUDY HINT

In general, inductive arguments are justified when their premises—if assumed true—provide "enough good evidence" to support their conclusions. Whether or not justified, inductive arguments are cogent depends on whether or not the premises actually are true (reasonable).

Consider these two inductive arguments:

I ate watermelon on the Fourth of July and my nose broke out in a rash.
I ate watermelon at my sister's birthday party on July 6 and my nose broke out in a rash.
I ate watermelon on August 11 at Midge's anniversary dinner and my nose broke out in a rash.
I *must* be allergic to watermelon.

I ate watermelon on the Fourth of July and my nose broke out in a rash.
I ate watermelon at my sister's birthday party on July 6 and my nose broke out in a rash.
I ate watermelon on August 11 at Midge's anniversary dinner and my nose broke out in a rash.
I *might* be allergic to watermelon.

The conclusion of the first argument, you'll likely agree, expresses greater probability than the conclusion of the second. The first argument's conclusion asserts that the arguer *must* be allergic to watermelon. That's a pretty strong claim to rest on only three instances. Further, the argument fails to consider and isolate other variables that have a bearing on developing a rash: Was the arguer wearing sunscreen? A wide-brimmed straw hat? Was the arguer taking medication? How closely did the development of the rash follow eating watermelon? Did it always follow eating watermelon? How long did the rash last? The premises may offer *some* evidence, but seemingly not enough to justify the high probability expressed in the conclusion.

The conclusion of the second argument is put differently. It only claims that the arguer *might* be allergic to watermelon. The premises do seem to provide enough support for this qualified claim.

One of the complicating factors with induction arises from the fact that generalizations vary in strength. For example, "Bob almost never wants Mexican food," expresses a higher degree of probability than "Every now and then Bob doesn't want Mexican food." This complicates the analysis of inductive arguments, because we are not always attentive to the way we frame our generalizations.

For example, does the statement "Teachers prefer students who write neatly" mean *all* teachers, *most* teachers, *many* teachers, *some* teachers, or *a few* teachers? Usually we can tell from context, but even then a certain lack of precision may remain. What percentage of teachers is meant by the statement "Most teachers prefer students who write neatly"? 80 percent? 60 percent? Technically, "most" could be as few as 50.001 percent.

So, the point at which an inductive argument provides enough good evidence varies with the nature of each argument, and specifically with the conclusion. Changing a single word or phrase in the way the conclusion is expressed can quantitatively affect whether or not the premises are *numerically adequate* to support the conclusion.

Sufficiency and Quality

But "sufficiency" means more than quantity—it also refers to the *quality* of the evidence offered to support the inductive conclusion. In the watermelon example, we noted that no mention was made of other possible causes or contributors to developing a rash. Simply multiplying more of the same kind of evidence will not, in this form of argument, be enough to support the first conclusion, expressed in terms of the highest probability ("I *must* be allergic to watermelon"). In addition to being "enough," the premises must also be *thorough* if the argument is to be cogent. They must include all other relevant factors which can affect the likelihood of the conclusion being true. The first argument would be strengthened by the addition of premises such as these: "I had on a sunscreen each time I ate watermelon"; "These are the only three times I have eaten watermelon in the last few years"; "These are the only three times I have had a nose rash"; and so on.

An inductive argument satisfies the cogency criteria when its premises are reasonable, relevant, numerically adequate, and thorough. An inductive argument that meets the sufficiency criterion is not automatically cogent. The premises of a cogent inductive argument must also be reasonable to help ensure that they report facts (true statements). They must be relevant to the conclusion, as well. Inductive reasonableness and relevancy are more complex than deductive reasonableness and relevancy because induction often involves causal connections and expert knowledge.

Even these simple examples point up the evaluative problems that induction raises. Since the premises of an inductive argument are intended to provide some, but not conclusive, support for the conclusion, inductive arguments are *relatively* strong or weak. They're *relatively* strong or justified when the premises make it unlikely that the conclusion is false; they're weak or unjustified when the premises fail to do this. But still we're left wondering exactly when this is so—under what conditions we can call an inductive argument relatively strong and justified. Although, as we just saw, it's impossible to so generalize the "rules of justifiedness" as to apply to every inductive argument in precisely the same way (in the way we can the "rules of validity"), we can identify some common errors in inductive reasoning—inductive fallacies—in whose presence an induction is not justified. Becoming aware of these errors not only will help us spot unjustified (and, therefore, noncogent) inductions, but also deepen our understanding of what's meant by "enough of the right kind of evidence." In order to flush out these matters, we need to take a close look at one particular kind of generalization, the inductive generalization.

STUDY HINT

Inductive arguments are cogent when their premises are reasonable, relevant, thorough, and numerically adequate. Inductive arguments that meet the sufficiency criterion are not automatically cogent.

INDUCTIVE GENERALIZATION

An inductive generalization is an inductive argument whose conclusion expresses a pattern or principle derived from its premises. It works as follows. On the basis of some cases known through experience, one draws an inference that applies to the whole collection of cases. Thus, having observed that some crows are black, I conclude that all crows are black. Or having observed that some basketball players are taller than 6 feet, I infer that most basketball players are taller than 6 feet, or that 99 percent of them are. Notice that in each case the generalization is based on observing a connection between two things—between crows and the color black, between basketball players and a height in excess of 6 feet. Having observed this connection on several or many occasions, I generalize that in the future the same connection will hold. The next crow I see probably will be black; the next basketball player probably will be taller than 6 feet.

So, in forming inductive generalizations, we start with specifics and end with a statement that will apply to similar specifics in the future. By so doing, we hope to avoid past mistakes; we exercise greater control over our lives and actions.

Naturally we don't always go through the entire process of forming inductive generalizations. Often we accept other peoples' generalizations. For example, you needn't go through the process of learning that foul-smelling, discolored meat is spoiled and not safe to eat. That generalization was formed long ago and passed on to us. But of course, we do form generalizations of our own. In form- ing our generalizations, it's important to ensure that we've observed enough relevant specifics before generalizing. Thus, if you observed a couple of teachers at college being indifferent to their students' needs, you shouldn't immediately generalize that all teachers, or even most teachers, at the college are similarly indifferent. You simply wouldn't have enough specific instances of teacher indif- ference to form so sweeping a conclusion. You'd be guilty of a faulty generaliza- tion. We'll talk more about this later in the chapter when we discuss fallacies connected with generalizations.

Before we do so, let's look again at two of our examples of inductive gen- eralizations: "All crows are black" and "Most basketball players are taller than 6 feet." Notice that in one we have used the word *all;* in the other we've used the word *most.* This suggests that generalizations can take two principal forms: the strong generalization and the weak generalization.

Strong Inductive Generalizations

A strong, or universal, inductive generalization is a statement that asserts that something is true of all members of a class, for example, "All humans are verte- brates"; "All voters are citizens"; and "Every instance of human decapitation re- sults in death." In each statement a property is attributed to every member of a class. Sometimes, of course, a universal quantifier such as *all* or *every* or *any* is not stated but is implied. Thus, "Humans are vertebrates" and "Voters are citi- zens" imply that we're speaking of every human and every voter.

Again, suppose you have a barrel of coffee beans. After mixing them up, you remove a sample of beans, ensuring that the sample is drawn from different parts of the same barrel. Upon examining the beans, you find that they are all grade A. You conclude, "The beans in the barrel are grade A." If you mean *all* the beans, then you have made a strong generalization. Incidentally, you could write your inductive generalization as follows:

The beans in the observed sample are grade A.
Therefore the beans in the barrel are grade A.

Your premise states information about the observed beans in the barrel; your conclusion is a statement about all the beans in the barrel. It's a universal generalization.

Sometimes a universal generalization doesn't universally affirm membership of one class of things within another; it denies it. Thus, "No human can remain underwater very long without oxygen" and "Men cannot bear children" are uni- versal generalizations because they deny of *all* members of a class some property, characteristic, or attribute. In other words, no member of the class "human" will be found within the class of "things that can remain underwater very long with- out oxygen"; no member of the class "men" will be found within the class of "humans who bear children."

Weak Inductive Generalizations

A weak, or particular, inductive generalization is a statement that asserts that something is true of some members of a class. For example, "Nello's Ristorante serves good food," "As a rule, the younger two people are when they marry, the more likely they are to be divorced in five years," and "Students who come to class prepared do better than those who don't" are all examples of the kinds of generalizations usually meant to assert only that something is true of some members of a class.

We must be careful not to confuse weak generalizations with strong ones. Often we will mistake a weak generalization for a strong one by overlooking such key qualifiers as *usually, often, most of the time, rarely, as a rule,* and the like. Thus, when a sociology professor points out, "College graduates tend to make more money than high school dropouts," she might encounter this reaction: "But Miss Vargas, that's not true. My grandfather dropped out of school in the third grade, and he's a multimillionaire." Or a psychology teacher might carefully assert, "Most violent criminals were physically abused as children," only to hear this kind of objection: "Excuse me, Dr. Reich, but it's just not true. My cousin Bernie was physically abused as a child and he's a saint."

Generalizations involving human behavior and moral principles are often of the weak, or particular, form. They assert patterns ranging in degrees of probability from "rarely," or highly improbable, to "almost always," or highly probable. But they are not meant as universal statements.

Here, as we have so often seen, we must rely on context and signal words to help us out. We must be especially careful when qualifiers are implied but not stated, as in "Students who are prepared for class do better than those who are not" and "Republicans are richer than Democrats." In both cases, treating the statements as universal is probably incorrect. They are only meant to identify what the speaker asserts is a general pattern, which is sometimes true, perhaps even almost always true—but *almost* always is logically distinct from always.

If we fail to recognize that difference, we will be unable to analyze inductive arguments intelligently. And to analyze inductive arguments intelligently, we must also become aware of the uses of statistical generalizations, which are a particular form of weak generalization.

Statistical Generalizations

A statistical generalization is a statement that asserts that something is true of a specified percentage of a class. Being weak, statistical generalizations never speak of every member of a class, but only of some. "Seventy-five percent of the voters favor a reduction in property taxes," "Over half the fruit in this vineyard is rotten," "A large number of students today are majoring in business"—all qualify as statistical generalizations.

Back to our barrel of coffee beans. Suppose you notice that 80 percent of all the beans in the sample drawn are grade A. You conclude that 80 percent of the beans in the barrel are grade A. Your inductive generalizations might be written:

Eighty percent of the beans in the observed sample are grade A.
Therefore 80 percent of the beans in the barrel are grade A.

Your conclusion is a statistical generalization. It asserts that something is true of a percentage of the beans in the barrel, not of every bean in it.

In both the strong and weak generalizations, we assert something about all or a percentage of the class members on the basis of enumeration, that is, observing some members of the class. For this reason, such generalizations are often referred to as inductions by enumeration.

Induction and Strong Generalizations

You might wonder how any inductive argument can ever adequately support a conclusion which is a strong generalization.

Technically, justified induction requires the implicit or explicit acknowledgment of probability. In the example of the coffee beans, the most reasonable interpretation of the conclusion is "All beans are probably grade A," or "Virtually all beans are likely to be grade A." If the arguer asserts, *without qualification,* that based on his or her sample, *all* beans *are* grade A, then the argument fails to meet the sufficiency criterion.

We must not confuse the relationship of an inductive argument's premises to its conclusion with the nature of the conclusion itself. Strictly speaking, universal knowledge is beyond human experience. We will never know for certain that "All decapitations result in death." As fantastic as it seems, it is *possible* that some disembodied, decapitated head exists without anyone's knowledge. Not *likely,* but still *possible.* We can never know for certain that "All crows are black" because we can never be sure we've sighted every crow.

Strong inductive generalizations are *provisionally true.* They are true so far. The more confirming instances we record, the higher the probability becomes that they are true without qualification. If we do not allow for the provisional nature of strong inductive generalizations, we will confine strong generalizations to statements that are true by definition or based on identity: "All bachelors are males," or "$A = A$." If we insist that all strong generalizations be verified with absolute certainty, we will no longer be able to infer causal connections or universal patterns.

Whenever we encounter strong inductive generalizations, we should understand them to mean that "All X are probably Y," or "Probably no X are Z."

Inductive generalizations, or inductions by enumeration, always consist of conclusions that go beyond their premises. Based on observed instances, we form a judgment about the unobserved. As a result, generalizations can yield false conclusions despite the truth of their premises. In other words, even though the premises of an inductive generalization describe an actual state of affairs (a true proposition), its conclusion may not describe an actual state of affairs. Thus, maybe the next crow you observe will *not* be black; perhaps only 60 percent of the beans in the barrel are grade A. This possibility of error in inductive generalizations shouldn't be surprising, however, for it's the characteristic of all inductive arguments that their conclusions are at best probable, never certain.

POSSIBILITIES AND PROBABILITIES

One widespread misconception concerning what is or is not "reasonable" involves confusing *possibilities* with *probabilities*. When we fail to distinguish what is possible from what is probable, we run an increased risk of accepting highly unlikely claims.

The controversial 1994–1995 case of *California vs. Simpson* (the "O.J. Simpson case"), brought this issue—if not the distinction itself—to national attention. In this, as in other legal cases, lawyers for both sides argued about whether or not it was "possible" to do something in a specified period of time or under certain conditions. They wrangled over the "likelihood" that blood or fiber evidence pointed to guilt or innocence for the defendant, and so forth. Yet much of the media commentary regarding the trial, as well as the trial arguments themselves, clouded over the important distinction between what is merely *possible* and what is *probable*.

The possibilities-probabilities issue confronts us when we face all sorts of decisions: "Is it possible for a 60-year-old couch potato atheist to be happily married to a 20-year-old fundamentalist jogger?" "Is it possible to get an A in logic by studying only twelve minutes a week?" "Is it possible that you'll get a Fedex package tomorrow informing you that you have inherited millions of dollars from your third grade teacher?" The answer to every one of these questions is "Yes—it is *possible*." Of course, what's merely possible is a far cry from what's likely or probable.

Good inductive reasoners are not seduced by what's merely possible. They demand that inductive arguments be based on reasonably plausible evidence. The standard of evidence is higher for probabilities than it is for possibilities. Anything that can be imagined without contradiction is technically "possible." Consequently, the threshold of proof for simple possibilities is notoriously low.

When assessing inductive arguments, it helps to keep the following continuum in mind:

POSSIBILITIES			PROBABILITIES	
highly unlikely	somewhat unlikely	?	somewhat likely	highly likely
LOWER		STANDARD OF PROOF		HIGHER

We could, of course, add more segments to this continuum (very, very, very unlikely . . . etc.), but they're not necessary to illustrate our basic point. In the realm of induction, degrees of likelihood are unavoidable. Occasionally, the evidence for an inductive generalization or hypothesis (see Chapter 14) is so strong that we can accept it as "virtually certain." But no matter how strong the evidence is, we are wise to remind ourselves that we are dealing with degrees of probability. Any degree of probability carries more evidentiary force than mere possibility.

Our task, then, is to formulate reliable inductive generalizations, ones that are justified—probable. We must try to construct generalizations in such a way that we reduce the chances of false conclusions following from true premises. Of great help here is an awareness of the factors involved in formulating reliable generalizations.

EXERCISE 10-1 *

Classify the following generalizations as weak or strong. Support your choice with inductive reasoning.

1. Cigarette smoking causes lung cancer.

2. Women earn 59 cents to every dollar a man earns.

3. Sound deductive arguments are valid.

4. Wearing seat belts reduces the chance of serious injury from automobile accidents.

5. More men than women die from heart attacks.

6. Being overweight is a risk factor for high blood pressure.

7. Most AIDS victims are gay.

8. The best time to fish for trout is in the early morning.

9. Nine out of ten people surveyed report that Bufferin doesn't upset their stomachs.

10. According to a 1985 survey by Ann Landers, 72 percent of American women would trade sex for cuddling.

RELIABLE INDUCTIVE GENERALIZATIONS

In Chapter 11 we will deal thoroughly with statistical arguments as they apply to all forms of induction. Since what we say there will also apply to generalizations, we'll be brief here. It is sufficient to point to at least four factors to consider in determining the reliability of a generalization. Three of these deal with whether the sample is representative of the entire group. Specifically, it's important to consider whether the sample is comprehensive of the group, whether it's large enough, and whether it's random. The fourth factor deals with the margin for error in the generalization itself.

Comprehensiveness

In formulating or evaluating inductive generalizations, it's important to ensure that the sample that is the basis for the conclusion accurately reflects the nature of the entire group. A small sample from a well-shaken bottle of milk will indicate whether the entire bottle is sour. But an accurate estimate of the size and quality of tomatoes in a truckload requires samples taken from different parts of the truck, including some from the bottom. The reason: In transportation, the smallest tomatoes invariably fall to the bottom of the load. A sample taken only from the top (or bottom) of the truck will misrepresent the variety contained in the load.

When a class of things consists of subclasses, numerous samples of the subclasses are needed to ensure comprehensiveness. This is especially true when people constitute the samples. For example, before a generalization is justified about the merits of a drug, the public's opinion of TV programs, or the political preferences of persons under 30, considerable sampling must be done to account for the vast differences among the members of the class which is the subject of the generalization.

Take, for example, the generalization "College graduates make more money in a lifetime than noncollege graduates." Obviously, the class "college graduates" includes a vast number of individuals who differ from one another in a multitude of ways. In other words, the category of "college graduates" includes many subcategories: "college graduates who majored in business," "college graduates who attended Ivy League colleges," "college graduates who entered a field directly related to what they studied in college," "female college graduates," and so on. A sample that overlooks the many subgroups within the group termed "college graduates" misrepresents the group itself. Any conclusion it suggests, therefore, must be considered unjustified—*even if it turns out to be true.*

Size

Directly related to the comprehensiveness of the sample is the sample's size. Ordinarily, the more instances observed, the more reliable the generalization. The reason is that large numbers tend to follow fixed laws.

You can easily demonstrate this tendency by tossing a dime. The chances of heads coming up on any toss is one in two. If you want a sample to serve as the basis for this generalization, don't flip the coin just twice. Heads could easily come up on both occasions, or not at all. To form an accurate generalization, you must toss the coin many times—hundreds, even thousands of times. The more tosses you include in your sample, the closer to the one-in-two split you'll observe.

The size of any sample is tied directly to the size of the group and the number of subgroups within it. Usually, the larger and more diversified the group, the larger the sample should be to ensure that it represents the group. Again, the generalization about the financial fortunes of college graduates is a good example. Since the class of "college graduates," as we saw, consists of many different subgroups, a relatively large sample is needed to justify any conclusion. If, on the other hand, we were interested only in the finances of graduates of a specific college, a smaller sample would be acceptable.

Randomness

Randomness means that each member of the group has an equal chance of ending up as part of the sample. A sampling technique that lacks randomness yields an unrepresentative sample.

Again, suppose you want to form a generalization about the percentage of the students at your college who believe in God. To do so, you query every student who has classes with you. Here again, your sample would lack randomness because not every student had an equal chance of being queried.

Each of the preceding factors clearly deals with whether a sample accurately represents the group being generalized about. A sample can be unrepresentative by not being comprehensive, by being too small, or by lacking randomness. Even when a sample is comprehensive, large enough, and random, the generalization that follows it may be risky because of the breadth of its claim. This point is directly related to its margin for error.

Margin for Error

Be sensitive to the breadth of the claim made by any generalization. Ordinarily, the less specific the claim, the more reliable is the generalization. A less specific claim has a greater margin for error. That is, it requires a lower standard of proof than a more precise claim. For example, it is easier to justify the claim "Some students believe in God," than the claim "The vast majority of students believe in God." The greater the *allowance* for error in the generalization, the more reliable the generalization is. A simple example will clarify the point.

Let's return to your interest in finding out what percentage of students believe in God. This time let's restrict your curiosity to the students in your logic class, of whom, we'll say, there are 33. You want to find out what portion of this 33 believes in God.

To form your generalization, let's suppose you randomly sample 12 of your classmates. You find out that 10 believe in God; two don't. Thus, your sample indicates that those who believe in God outnumber those who don't by a ratio of six to one. As a result, it would be very safe for you to generalize, "The *majority* of students in my logic class believe in God."

The reason this is so safe a generalization is that your sample can accommodate a substantial margin for error, or variation, before your claim is falsified. Just think, of the remaining 21 classmates, only seven would have to believe in God to verify your generalization. In other words, even if the ratio of believers to nonbelievers flips from six to one to one to three, your generalization is still true.

Now, contrast such a generalization with this one: "Eighty-three percent of the students in my logic class believe in God." You based this, of course, on the original sample: 83 percent of the original 12 believed in God. But the margin of error for this generalization is considerably smaller than for the first, less-specific one about the majority. Remember that in generalizing about the majority, only seven of the remaining 21 students would have to believe in God to verify your generalization. But in the 83 percent generalization, a full 17 must believe in God to verity it ($33 \times .83 = 27.4$; $27.4 - 10 = 17.4$). Clearly, then, the majority generalization, because it makes a less specific claim, allows for a greater margin for error. It is the safer of the two, although both could be justified. (Of course, a generalization about more than 83 percent believing in God wouldn't even be justified.)

So the margin for error a generalization can tolerate is important in evaluating its reliability. The greater the margin for error, the more reliable the generalization. But keep in mind that a generalization that carries the tiniest margin of error may, notwithstanding, be *justified*. You'd be wise, however, to reduce the breadth of its claim to be on the safe side.

When we overlook the preceding four factors, we probably formulate unreliable generalizations.

EXERCISE 10-2 *

The following arguments are inductive generalizations. Identify premises and conclusions and criticize the arguments in terms of the four factors relative to their reliability.

1. I know a half-dozen college graduates who are making over 50,000 dollars a year in their jobs. That just goes to prove that college graduates are paid handsomely in their occupations.

2. BILL: I think our next class president is going to be Lydia.
   TONY: I think Myra has a much better chance.
   BILL: Myra? I just can't believe that a sizable number of our 7,500 student body even knows who Myra is.
   TONY: Are you kidding? The school paper just conducted a poll. They set up a booth over in the cafeteria last Wednesday afternoon. And guess what? Sixty-two percent of the 112 students they asked said they were voting for Myra.

3. Member of committee supporting tax levy for schools: I think the public is squarely behind this measure. After all, every member of the PTA and school board supports it.

4. To find out what percentage of their income a family of four spends for food, a sample is taken. Fifteen hundred phone calls are made to 1,500 different families. Of these, a thousand indicate that they spend at least 25 percent of their income on food. The conclusion is drawn that two-thirds of American families of four spend at least 25 percent of their income on food.

5. In every case of syphilis we have ever observed, a certain spiral-shaped bacterium called a spirochete has been present. This proves that a spirochete, and only a spirochete, is the cause of syphilis.

6. GEORGE: There's no question that farmers think that government is giving them the shaft.
RUTH: My father's a farmer and he thinks he's getting a pretty square deal.
GEORGE: Oh sure, you're always going to find the isolated exception. But a recent poll of farmers in the San Joaquin valley in central California reveals widespread discontent with government farm policies.

7. A jar contains a thousand jelly beans. After the jelly beans are thoroughly mixed, a handful of them is taken out. Twenty-eight of them are green, 27 red. It's concluded that (1) the jar contains only green and red jelly beans, and (2) that at least half are green.

8. ALYSON: All men are fickle.
AL: Honey, I have something to tell you.
ALYSON: Why, you didn't hear a word I said.
AL: I'm sorry, I have this other thing on my mind. What did you say?
ALYSON: I said that all men are fickle.
AL: Oh, come on now.
ALYSON: I mean it. Every guy I've ever dated has thrown me over for somebody else. . . . Now what is it you have to tell me?
AL: Well, I . . . uh . . . I've met somebody else.
ALYSON: See!

9. A man has a bucket of gravel. He notices the big, smooth rocks on the top. But he's no fool. He realizes that the ones below may not be big and smooth, so he gives the bucket a thorough shaking. Lo and behold, big, smooth rocks are still on top. That satisfies him—the bucket of gravel contains big, smooth rocks.

10. MADGE: You know, the courts are really too lenient in granting paroles.
MIKE: Why do you say that?
MADGE: Because a day doesn't go by when I don't read of some paroled convict who's committed a crime.
MIKE: Hmm, you have a point there.

11. Report to the Downtown Mall Association: The results of our report are based on a survey conducted the week of September 9 from 1 to 3 PM, M–F. Over 63 people answered our simple six-question form. Here, then, is our report on the attitudes of the typical mall shopper.

12. Mr. Boswell must be a great instructor. The results of his student evaluations are consistently excellent. Thirty-eight percent of the students responded, and over 50 percent of these responses rated Dr. Boswell excellent.

13. LEE: There's no point in asking if you want to go skating.
GAIL: Why do you say that?
LEE: I asked you to go twice this month, and both times you refused.

14. I demand that Dr. Boswell be fired. I've talked to a number of my friends, and they all think she's a lousy lecturer.

15. To Whom It May Concern: Enclosed please find the manuscript of my two-thousand-page saga. I know that it is a good book because I've let my friends and family read it, and they are unanimous in their praise.

16. Virtually every heroin addict ever studied has been found to have begun abusing drugs by smoking marijuana. Thus we see that marijuana usage always leads to heroin addiction.

17. Look, I'm tellin' ya, Fords are all lemons. I had two myself—both lemons. And my brother had one, a lemon. Trust me in this; I am giving you the benefit of my experience.

18. Ladies and gentlemen of the jury, how else can we explain the presence of this fiber at the scene of the crime? After all, chemical analysis shows that this fiber is identical to fibers in the jacket found in the defendant's car. And even though the defendant claims that this is not his jacket, let us ask ourselves: How likely it is that somebody else's jacket would be in his trunk? No, ladies and gentlemen, the conclusion is obvious: The only explanation for the presence of that fiber at the scene of the crime is that the defendant was wearing this jacket when he broke into the parlor that awful night.

19. I'm never going back to House of Steaks. The last time I was there I had to wait 20 minutes for my meal. Their service is horrible.

20. Boy, this Phish album will be just great. Every Phish album I've ever heard has been great, so this one will be too!

INDUCTIVE FALLACIES

Although we might consider numerous fallacies associated with simple inductive arguments, we'll restrict our discussion to four: hasty conclusion, anecdotal evidence, accident, and guilt by association. These are very common fallacies that have their roots in faulty induction. You may find them called by other names in different texts.

Hasty Conclusion

The fallacy of hasty conclusion is an argument that draws a conclusion based on insufficient evidence. Sometimes the insufficient evidence in a hasty conclusion takes the form of isolated cases, which a person uses to force the conclusion. For example, on the basis of having been "ripped off" by a used-car salesperson, you conclude, "All used-car salespersons are ripoff artists." The single, isolated case is not sufficient to warrant the conclusion. We could say that the sample in question, the isolated case, is too small to justify the inference. Suppose that someone argues that every member of the National Organization for Women is a socialist on the basis that a half-dozen of them are known socialists. The evidence here is not enough to support the conclusion; the sample is far too small. We sometimes call this error *leaping to a conclusion*.

An arguer would be guilty of a hasty conclusion if, on the basis of a handful of college and noncollege acquaintances, he or she concluded that people going to college to improve themselves financially stand a better chance of learning than those not so motivated. Obviously, people go to college for all sorts of reasons: for knowledge, for status, for social interaction, and so on. What motive is best for learning? No one knows. Certainly, such a tiny sample doesn't warrant that conclusion.

Sometimes the hasty conclusion results from basing an inference, not so much on isolated cases, but on exceptional ones. For example, someone argues, "Jones must have been an athlete at one time, for he's built so well" or "I bet Smith recently inherited a lot of money; otherwise he wouldn't have been able to afford that brand-new Mercedes." Although it's true that people with good builds often are or were athletes, and similarly, a recent inheritance sometimes explains the purchase of a new Mercedes, there are exceptions: Many people who have not recently inherited a lot of money also buy Mercedes. In both cases, the specific cases are related to the generalization in an unessential way. There is no logical or actual basis for assuming a connection. The conclusions are "hasty" because they are made without fully studying the circumstances used as premises.

Sherlock Holmes was at times guilty of the hasty conclusion. Take, for example, his conclusions about Dr. Watson, which Holmes formed immediately upon being introduced to him:

> Here is a gentlemen of a medical type, but with the air of a military man. Clearly an army doctor, then. He has just come from the tropics, for his face is dark, and that is not the natural tint of his skin, for his wrists are fair. He has undergone hardship and sickness, as his haggard face says clearly. His left arm has been injured. He holds it in a stiff and unnatural manner. Where in the tropics could an English army doctor have seen much hardship and got his arm wounded? Clearly in Afghanistan.[20]

Holmes turns out to be, of course, correct. But that's irrelevant. The question is, does the evidence warrant his conclusion? Certainly Watson could have a military bearing without ever having been in the military, let alone having been a military doctor. And certainly he needn't have acquired his tan in the tropics. And surely a "haggard face" doesn't always mean "hardship and sickness"; neither does holding the arm in a "stiff and unnatural manner" always result from an injury. Nonetheless, Holmes not only forms these hasty conclusions but also uses them as the basis for his final hasty conclusion: that Watson was in Afghanistan!

To sum up, there are at least three ways inductive reasoning can be "hasty." (1) We may reach a conclusion before we have enough instances on which to base

---

20. Arthur Conan Doyle, "A Study in Scarlet," *The Adventures of Sherlock Holmes* (New York: Berkley Publications, 1963), pt. 1, ch. 2.

it. When we do this, we, in effect, don't wait until we have a reasonable amount of evidence—thus, we are "hasty."

(2) We can be "hasty" by basing our conclusion on atypical, or exceptional evidence. A large quantity of unrepresentative evidence has the same effect as not having enough evidence. Overlooking key factors in a given circumstance can produce this kind of hastiness, as can zeroing in on selected atypical factors. Prejudices, stereotypes, and guilt by association are examples of basing conclusions on atypical or incomplete factors (often resorted to because the arguer lacks representative instances).

(3) When dealing with complex causal or factual arguments (see Chapter 13), care must be taken to analyze all relevant facets of the issue. Sometimes, what appears to be a straightforward causal link turns out to be a coincidental correlation or chance linkage. We see violations of this type of hastiness in popular medical journalism, when, on the basis of limited studies, mass-media medical reporters hastily proclaim first that coffee is deadly, then report maybe not; salt will kill you . . . or maybe not; olive oil is good for you . . . not exactly . . . perhaps. You get the picture.

Anecdotal Evidence

The fallacy of anecdotal evidence is a form of hasty conclusion that occurs when we attempt to refute a well-established generalization based solely on limited personal experience. Personal stories are called *anecdotes,* and anecdotes—of themselves—cannot refute more thoroughly established principles and generalizations.

The classroom is one of the most common breeding grounds for the fallacy of anecdotal evidence. Consider this not uncommon scenario:

> PROFESSOR VARGAS: As a general rule, the data suggests that the younger you are when you marry, the more children you have, and the less education you receive, the lower your socioeconomic status is likely to be.
> SOCIOLOGY STUDENT: That's not true! My uncle dropped out of school in the third grade, married my aunt when he was 15 years old, and had eight children before his twenty-third birthday—and he's rich and famous.

Since most generalizations are particular, or "weak," they have a large enough margin for error to tolerate individual counterexamples. The sociology student's rich and famous uncle is likely to be an exception to the sociological generalization expressed by the professor. In other words, the uncle's case is *exceptional,* not *representative.* The student's retort is clearly hasty in two ways, and probably hasty in all three ways: It is based on one instance (not enough); it is atypical; and unless the student has carefully studied socioeconomic class structure elsewhere, her or his remarks are only based on a brief, introductory-level look at this complex issue.

Whenever we jump to inductive conclusions based on our limited experience, we are reasoning anecdotally. Even if we have great instincts and turn out to be right, our reasoning is still fallacious. Limited personal experience is inadequate for refuting (or establishing) generalizations that reach beyond us. As interesting, inspiring, and informative as anecdotes can be, they cannot refute (or establish) dietary, medical, financial, psychological, and other such patterns and principles.

We must be careful to avoid giving too much importance to our own personal experience when constructing generalizations. Concluding that logic is boring because you have attended some boring lectures fails to take into account a number of relevant factors: Were the lectures typical of logic or the instructor? Was the instructor having some off days? Were you? Condemning soul food or country music because you don't like them are examples of the fallacy of anecdotal evidence. Arguing that Jerry Seinfeld is not funny because you watched an episode of his show and did not like it is another example of drawing a hasty conclusion based on insufficient anecdotal evidence.

Accident

The fallacy of accident occurs when an argument treats a weak generalization as if it were strong by overlooking the qualifications attached to a general rule. Let's start with a simple example. You discover that your neighbor has dumped six bags of garbage in your backyard. When confronted, she justifies her actions with the following argument: "Americans have a right to do whatever they want to with their own property. Those garbage bags are my property and I want to put them in your backyard." This argument overlooks the many conditions limiting the general rule "Americans can do whatever they want to with their own property."

This error in induction is called *accident* because it occurs when we apply a general rule to a case whose unique—"accidental"—features make it an exception to the rule. Put another way, this error involves failing to acknowledge the qualifiers attached to weak generalizations. "People should tell the truth," for example, probably does not mean that we should always tell the truth, no matter what. Suppose, for instance, that a deranged individual knocks on your door, demanding to see your child. If the individual were clearly under the influence of drugs, armed with a shotgun, and asked, "Is Jimmy here?" should you tell the truth? Many moral philosophers make a strong case that you should not. The general moral rule to tell the truth does not apply when one is confronted by, say, deranged people with loaded shotguns looking to kill people.

Jesus' admonition to consider the spirit of the law, not just the letter, can be interpreted as a caution against the fallacy of accident. If we treat all generalizations as strong ones, we fail to make important allowances for individual circumstances. A class rule never to leave during lecture probably is not meant to apply to cases of sudden nausea. Because it is often not possible to include every conceivable exception—or accidental circumstance—when we express generalizations, it is especially important that we do not confuse rules that are weak generalizations, meant to apply in certain circumstances, with strong ones, meant to apply without exception.

Guilt by Association

The guilt-by-association fallacy is a form of hasty conclusion in which people are judged guilty solely on the basis of the company they keep or the places they frequent.

For example, over the years, Frank Sinatra has had to defend himself against charges that he has underworld connections. Why? Because at least one or more persons of his acquaintance were involved in organized crime. Even if Sinatra did know such a person, that didn't mean that he himself was involved, as many of his critics intimated.

Those who prejudge by association assume that likes always attract likes, that birds of a feather always flock together. They use such generalizations as a basis for judging someone guilty by association. The way to help someone see the error involved in this fallacy, then, is to demonstrate that the generalization on which it is based is faulty. Likes don't always attract likes; birds of a feather don't always flock together. Seeing that, we should realize that association is not a sound basis for inferring guilt.

But clearly we often do judge others guilty by their looks or dress. Thus, a Brazilian soccer team once canceled a match in Lusaka, Zambia, when officials there demanded that the Brazilians cut their (the Brazilians') long hair. It seems the Zambians had a "mind-set" about long-haired people. Since the Brazilians had long hair, the Zambians judged them guilty by association with all the negative qualities they connected with long hair. Zambia and other African countries also assumed that those wearing short skirts or tight-fitting trousers are disreputable.

In all such cases, the arguer generalizes that because something is sometimes the case, it is always the case. Having formed such faulty generalizations, we then apply them to people, judging them guilty by association with the object of disdain: long hair, criminals, and so forth.

The guilt referred to in the phrase "guilt by association" is not always legal or moral guilt. It can include any condemnatory judgment. In this sense, guilt by association functions much like the circumstantial personal attack (Chapter 6). In the O.J. Simpson criminal case, for example, partisans for both sides claimed that witnesses and lawyers were "guilty" of racism for simply being on the opposing ("wrong") team. Stereotyping, prejudice, provincialism, and other defense mechanisms and errors in reasoning reinforce this type of hastiness.

STUDY HINT
Don't Confuse Guilt By Association
With Circumstantial Personal Attack

Guilt by association uncritically condemns an *individual*, whereas the circumstantial personal attack uncritically rejects an *argument* (see Chapter 6).

EXERCISE 10-3 *

Identify the fallacies in the following. Choose from hasty conclusion, accident, guilt by association, and anecdotal evidence. In all cases, explain.

1. JACK: I think Uncle Bill should be allowed to own that lot on Main Street.
   BETTY: But Uncle Bill has been declared insane.
   JACK: I know. But everybody has the right to own property.

2. STAN: I wouldn't trust any more union representatives.
   OLLIE: Me neither—not after seeing the last two we had put in jail for embezzling union funds.

3. MUDCAT: I just bet twenty bucks on the Wildcats in the big game today.
   MOOSE: I think you made a good bet, Mudcat. I've talked to every Wildcat, and they all say they're ready.
   MUDCAT: I knew it! As a team, the Wildcats couldn't be more prepared!

4. FRED: There's no doubt in my mind that our former U.N. Ambassador Andrew Young is anti-Israeli.
   MONA: Why do you say that?
   FRED: Well, because of that party he attended where there were people from the Palestine Liberation Organization. And you know how the PLO feels about Israel.

5. The sole purpose of an army is to defend its nation from aggression. So it follows that the sole purpose of any solider should be the same.

6. JUNE: I just know that Professor Macbeth must have studied drama.
   JODY: You mean because she wears so much makeup?
   JUNE: Don't be silly. Because she speaks so eloquently.

7. People should work for what they get. So this business of providing food stamps for those in need is really immoral.

8. New England is boring. I spent two weeks there last summer and found it quite dull.

9. JANICE: I think it was unconscionable of you to ask me to help you cheat on your logic test.
   JERRY: Oh yeah? Well, I'm sorry you don't have more appreciation for the Golden Rule.
   JANICE: The Golden Rule! You call cheating on a test living by the Golden Rule?
   JERRY: Sure. The Golden Rule tells us to do unto others as we would have them do unto us. Well, if our positions were reversed, I'd help you cheat. . . . You know, I really thought you were more moral than that, Janice.

10. STUDENT: Tell me, Professor. What can I do to improve my comprehension of this material?
    PROFESSOR: Plan to come to class on time; take careful notes; read the material twice.
    STUDENT: That doesn't work. I've tried it all week and I'm still confused.

SUMMARY

This chapter dealt with basic inductive arguments and generalizations. We learned that an inductive argument is one whose premises are intended to provide *some*—

but not conclusive—support, for its conclusion. The most basic kind of inductive argument has a generalization for its conclusion. A generalization is a statement that covers many specifics. Here are two examples: "When people use seat belts, deaths from traffic accidents decrease"; "If detected early enough, many cancers can be cured."

We defined an inductive generalization as an inductive argument whose conclusion expresses a pattern or principle derived from its premises. Thus, on the basis of some cases known through experience, we draw a conclusion that applies to a whole collection of cases, for example, "All the crows I've seen are black, therefore, the next crow I see will probably be black."

Inductive generalizations can be either strong or weak. A strong, or universal, inductive generalization is a statement that asserts that something is true of all members of a class. For example: "All voters are citizens." Weak, or particular, inductive generalizations are statements that assert that something is true of some members of a class. For example: "Students who come to class prepared do better then those who don't come prepared."

Statistical generalizations assert that something is true of a specified percentage of a class: "Seventy-five percent of voters favor a reduction in property taxes."

Four factors affect the reliability of inductive generalizations:

1. *Comprehensiveness:* Does the sample accurately reflect the nature of the entire group?

2. *Size:* Because large numbers tend to follow fixed laws, we can infer that, ordinarily, the more instances observed, the more reliable the generalization.

3. *Randomness:* Does each member of the group have an equal chance of ending up as part of the sample?

4. *Margin for error:* The greater the allowance for error in the generalization, the more reliable it is. In other words, less specific claims allow a greater margin for error than more specific claims.

In overlooking these factors we commit fallacies. Three fallacies are particularly noteworthy:

1. The *hasty conclusion* is an argument that draws a conclusion based on insufficient evidence, for example, Sherlock Holmes' conclusions about Watson. The hasty conclusion should be distinguished from the fallacy of composition.

2. The misuse of *anecdotal evidence* is a form of hasty conclusion that occurs when we attempt to establish or refute a generalization based solely on personal experience.

3. The *accident* is an argument that applies a general rule to a particular case whose special circumstances make the rule inapplicable, for example, arguing that because people, generally speaking, have a right to go where

they want, a convicted murderer should be permitted to leave prison at the prisoner's request.

4. *Guilt by association* is a form of hasty conclusion in which people are judged guilty solely on the basis of the company they keep or the places they frequent, for example, judging Frank Sinatra to be a criminal based on his friends.

Summary Exercises

1. Find a few examples of hasty conclusion. Fertile sources include prejudicial claims made about racial or gender characteristics and vague attributions such as "the humanists," "the fundamentalists," and so forth. The more sweeping such claims are, the more difficult they will be to justify.

2. Find some examples of accident involving moral and behavioral maxims (rules of conduct). Here's a case to start with:

> Bob and Ray are good friends. Bob has borrowed Ray's car with the promise to return it whenever Ray asks. Late one evening, Ray shows up obviously drunk, so drunk that he can barely walk or talk coherently. He demands the keys to his car. Bob hands them over without hesitation. Later, after Ray has been hurt in an auto accident that very night, Bob justifies giving him the keys by saying, "Well, we should always keep our promises."

Explain why Bob's attempt at justifying his action is a case of the fallacy of accident.

See if you can find other examples of accident involving moral or behavioral rules misapplied or taken too literally.

ADDITIONAL EXERCISES*

Identify the fallacies, if any, in the following passages. Choose from hasty conclusion, anecdotal evidence, accident, and guilt by association.

1. ANNA: I see you're on that liquid protein diet.
   ANDY: Yes, I'm really enthusiastic about it.
   ANNA: But haven't you heard that it can be really dangerous?
   ANDY: Oh, I don't know about that. After reading a book on liquid protein diets, I don't think they're all that dangerous.

2. FATHER: There's no way Suzy can learn in that school.
   MOTHER: Why not?
   FATHER: Because the classes are large and the school district's poor. And you know what that means.
   MOTHER: Sure, that the school can't provide an opportunity that could do justice to Suzy's ability to learn.

3. DALE: Roy, why don't you take an aspirin for that terrible headache?
   ROY: You know that nature's way is best, Dale. It's not wise to interfere with Mother Nature.

DALE: So you're just going to sit there and suffer?
ROY: I'm just going to let nature take its course because that's obviously best.

4. PAIGE: You say commercial nuclear power plants are safe. Why?
LEE: Because there are over 50 of them operating in the United States. Collectively they've produced 2,000 years of reactor operation. And there are more than 100 nuclear submarines operating in the U.S. Navy.
PAIGE: So?
LEE: So, none of these has ever injured or killed a member of the public. That proves without doubt that commercial nuclear power plants are safe.

5. "According to folk wisdom in many cultures, redheaded people tend to be a bit temperamental. An Israeli researcher believes there may be something to the ancient prejudice. At the Honolulu conference, psychiatrist Michael Bar, of Israel's Shalvata Psychiatric Center, reported a study showing that redheaded children are three or four times more likely than others to develop 'hyperactive syndrome'—whose symptoms include overexcitability, short attention span, quick feelings of frustration, and, usually, excessive aggressiveness.

Bar arrived at this conclusion after matching the behavior of 45 redheaded boys and girls between the ages of six and twelve against that of a control group of nonredheaded kids. Though the evidence was far from conclusive, Bar believes the study points to a genetic connection between red hair and hyperactive behavior." (*Time*, September 12, 1977)

6. Part of an ad used by the Kellogg Company to establish the nutritional value of "ready-sweetened cereals": "FACT: READY-TO-EAT CEREAL EATERS SKIP BREAKFAST LESS THAN NON-READY-TO-EAT CEREAL EATERS. In a study which surveyed the breakfast eating habits of 250 children, it was established that breakfast skipping occurred three times as often among noneaters of ready-to-eat cereal."

7. EVA: Barbados must be the island in the Western world where Europeans first landed.
ED: How come you're so sure?
EVA: Because the great explorer Thor Heyerdahl has successfully crossed the Atlantic in a papyrus raft and landed on Barbados.

8. Journalist Nicholas von Hoffman, on the television program *Sixty Minutes,* April 21, 1974, said he hoped President Nixon would not be impeached so that the electorate could reverse Nixon's 1972 mandate by turning every Republican out of office that November.

9. A congressional seat is on the line. An unpopular but important politician insists on campaigning for his party's candidate. Party officials do not want the politician to come to their state to campaign, but he does and the candidate loses. Party officials say that that proves the politician was a liability.

10. DEFENSE ATTORNEY: Now, your honor, you know as well as I that mothers love their children. Knowing that, how can you find my client guilty of callously abandoning her children?

11. MICK: I think it's terrible that a court sentences a man to five years in jail for stealing a loaf of bread to feed his family.
    BIANCA: Don't you believe that thieves should be punished?
    MICK: Of course I do, but—
    BIANCA: But nothing. The guy stole—now let him pay the price.

12. Judge Marvin Frankel's reaction to a politician's charge that "the time has come for softheaded judges . . . to show as much concern for the rights of innocent victims of crime as they do for the rights of convicted criminals": "One case I remember vividly was of an orchestra leader, a devoted father, whose first conviction was clearly going to be his last—a judgment shared by the prosecution as well as the probation officer and me—and whom no jury would have convicted in the first place if it knew he faced anything like five or ten years in prison." The judge inferred on the basis of this and one other similar example that leniency is necessary. (*Los Angeles Times,* May 20, 1973)

13. FRAN: I think students should be allowed to use their textbooks during examinations.
    EMIL: I'd sure go for that.
    FRAN: Sure, just think about it. A key function of a textbook is to provide students with information in a field. Well, when do we need the information more than on an exam?
    EMIL: I see what you mean. I'm going to ask Professor Emerson to let us use textbooks on the next exam.

14. MURRAY: You know, even if I thought she had something worth listening to, I'd tune out Goldie Hawn.
    BEA: But why? She often makes a lot of sense.
    MURRAY: Maybe so. But you know who she's dating? That arrogant Kurt Russell.
    BEA: Oh, I didn't know that. I'd better reconsider my opinion of her.

15. TYLER: Personally, I don't think we citizens have any right to decide whether or not our country goes to war.
    TRUDY: Are you mad?
    TYLER: No, just logical. Think about it—no citizen has a right to decide whether or not their fellow citizens should die, does he or she?
    TRUDY: Probably not.
    TYLER: Then it follows that we shouldn't have the right to decide such crucial matters as war and peace.

CHAPTER 11

Statistical Arguments

There are three kinds of lies—lies, damned lies, and statistics.

BENJAMIN DISRAELI

One of the most heated and controversial political campaigns in California's recent history was the 1986 election campaign for chief justice of the California Supreme Court. Opposition to the incumbent, Rose Bird, was intense, centering primarily on the fact that virtually every capital punishment verdict sent before the Bird court had been overturned. This led Bird's detractors to accuse her of being "prodefense." Surprisingly, however, the *California Journal* reported that "85 percent of Chief Justice Rose Bird's decisions tend to favor prosecutors," and *Time* magazine reported that Bird's "backers claim that she sided with the prosecution 90 percent of the time."[21]

At first glance, the case against Bird seemed especially compelling since it contained statistics, which many people equate with "hard data" or "facts." Indeed, one of the most common kinds of case appeals to statistics either directly, as in the Bird example, or indirectly through the use of expressions that less specifically imply statistics, such as "most of," "the majority of," or "a high percentage of." The respect we have for science and technology makes us especially vulnerable to statistical cases. They seem to be so precise, so clear, so rigorous. In order to evaluate statistical claims, we must learn how statistics are used in inductive arguments. Like other assertions used as evidence, statistical claims must be reasonable, relevant, and sufficient to establish any conclusions based on them. Statistics can be used both to reveal and conceal facts. Let's return to the Bird case to see how.

What were the "facts"? Was the Chief Justice inclined to "favor" either the prosecution or the defense? One way to answer this question is to consult the statistics.

---

21. Thomas Sowell, "Painting Bird as 'Pro-Prosecution' Is to Use Fine-Haired Brush Indeed," Scripps Howard News Service, October 16, 1986.

But there is a problem. If we consider *all* the petitions coming before any supreme court, virtually *every* supreme court is "proprosecution"—since most of the cases petitioning review are initiated by defendants. And because most cases are denied a hearing by most supreme courts, most decisions are "against" defendants—or "proprosecution." And so it was that Bird's opponents, citing only capital cases, were able to claim that the chief justice was "anti-victim" and "anti-law and order," whereas her defenders, using a database of *all* petitions presented to the court, were able to claim that her court was predominantly "proprosecution."

It's precisely this kind of statistical sleight of hand that confuses and frustrates so many of us and mocks good inductive process. Bird's supporters and her opponents both based their claims on statistical samples. And each faction, not surprisingly, chose the sample that best suited its purposes. But since we are often unaware of all of the relevant factors involved in statistical claims, most of us have fallen victim to the misuse or misunderstanding of a statistical sample.

One reason for our vulnerability to statistics is that ours is a fact-minded culture. Graphs, averages, trends, relationships—all feed our hunger for facts. When someone claims that "Violent crimes have increased 12.5 percent in the last six months" or "Zombie aspirin has been found 25 percent more effective in relieving pain than any other nonprescription analgesic," we listen. The language of statistics impresses us; it sounds authoritative. And the more precise the statistic, the more convincing. In a word, even the most absurd claims sound plausible when propped up with a statistic.

In one sense all inductive arguments rely on statistics since they base their conclusions on a number of observed specifics. But things like studies, polls, and surveys supposedly use statistics in precise, scientific ways to generate inductive conclusions. It's this use of statistics, and the common devices that rely on them, that concern us in this second chapter devoted to inductive reasoning.

We are considering this topic second in our look at induction to emphasize that statistics can be associated with any form of inductive conclusion: generalization, analogy, hypothesis, or cause. For example, someone might decide to buy an Aquarius compact car because it will have a high resale value. The belief about the resale value of the Aquarius is based on using statistics in an inductive argument: Statistically, the Aquarius has had a higher resale value than any other similar compact. Another person could argue that since a certain percentage of colds clear up after treatment with antihistamine pills, antihistamine pills can cure colds. This final example is, of course, also an illustration of how statistics can be used in causal reasoning.

By the time you complete this chapter, you'll have a good idea of how statistics are used in inductive arguments. More important, you'll know what to watch out for in statistical arguments, the common fallacies often committed by such arguments. Although we can't promise that you will never again be hooked by statistics, you will be a tougher fish to land.

STUDIES, SURVEYS, POLLS

"Two out of three doctors recommend Bayer," "By the year 2000 more women will be contracting lung cancer than breast cancer," "Eighty-four percent of Golden Lights' smokers switch from higher-tar brands and stay," "More people watch CBS in a given week than any other network," "Sixty-one percent of the American people believe the president is doing a mediocre or poor job," "Studies prove that saccharin can cause cancer." "By 2001 every person in the United States will personally know someone who has AIDS." Our world is alive with statistics. In the battle for our minds we may be the casualties. We must be careful.

Before considering the common fallacies associated with statistics, let's take a brief and admittedly superficial look at the usual spawning grounds for statistics: studies, polls, and surveys.

Studies

Probably there are no research studies that bombard us more on a daily basis than those associated with aspirin. Aspirin advertisers, regardless of the brand, continue to make claims for their product's superiority. Some even "back up" their claims by quoting "studies conducted by a major university." The makers of Bayer and Tylenol once took out full-page ads disputing, and supposedly refuting, the claims made by the other. It has reached the point that whenever a white-smocked individual with stethoscope appears on the TV screen pushing some brand of aspirin, some of us are tempted to launch into a profanity-peppered diatribe against misleading commercials. The upshot, of course, is that we're often left with, well, a splitting headache. It seems as if such commercials exist, not to offer relief, but to produce pain! And today, the producers of the various forms of over-the-counter "pain relievers" like Aleve, Advil, and Motrin have joined in, further confusing the statistical claims.

Our consternation is understandable. For one thing, tests independently conducted some years ago by Robert C. Batterman at the New York Medical College and Dr. G. A. Cronk at Syracuse University have shown that "there are no significant differences in speed of absorption, promptness of pain relief, or safety between plain and buffered aspirin.[22] In addition, the amount of food in the stomach and the user's emotional state determine absorption rate more than an antacid that may be in an aspirin. Obviously, until consumers know what the aspirin and non-aspirin companies' studies entail—including the mental and physical state of the subjects in the study—they're unwise to accept any product's claim on the basis of some authoritative-appearing individual.

The fact is that in the case of aspirins we're probably better served by reading a thirty-odd-year old report of a comparative study of Bayer Aspirin, St. Joseph's

---

22. The Editors of Consumer Reports, *The Medicine Show* (Mount Vernon, N.Y.: Consumers Union, 1972), p. 14.

Aspirin, Bufferin, and Excedrin in the December 1962 issue of the *Journal of the American Medical Association*.[23] There we learn *specifics* of the study and can thus evaluate the truth of the conclusion that no significant differences were found among the products in their effectiveness and speed in easing pain.

Cold remedies advertised on television and in magazines are another thing that can drive the concerned consumer right up the wall—especially when he or she has a cold. And rightly so. Cold remedies also make questionable claims based on dubious research. As sincere as much of the research may be, it's still difficult to diagnose accurately the cause of acute nasal and throat congestion. Neither is it any easier to determine the precise effect a person's mental state plays in relieving cold symptoms. And since very little is known and understood about the common cold, it's tough to forecast the course of a virus-induced cold. In short, no available evidence provides high-enough probability to justify some antihistamine claims that a particular product *causes* symptomatic relief. Indeed, in controlled clinical trials, antihistamines have been found only as effective as placebos (inert pills) in relieving cold symptoms. "Over the long haul, the antihistamines have proved of no real value against the common cold; furthermore, they produce in many users such side effects as drowsiness, dizziness, and headache.[24]

In 1995, two widely prescribed drugs used to decrease the production of stomach acid and protect against heartburn were finally released in over-the-counter (nonprescription) doses. Immediately, Tagamet and Pepcid waged a major media blitz, bombarding us with clever graphics and entertaining commercials—but no hard data, unless we asked. And most people don't ask.

What can we say, then, about the kinds of studies that are used to sell products? Before accepting their findings as justification for buying and using a product, we should satisfy ourselves on a number of points. These can be put in the form of questions:

1. Who were the subjects involved in the study?

2. For how long was the research conducted?

3. Who conducted the study—the company itself or some independent agency such as the National Institutes of Health, the Food and Drug Administration, the Federal Trade Commission, a nonpartisan university?

4. Who participated in the study—physicians, medical centers, hospitals?

5. To which stage of research does the claim refer—test tube, animal, human?

---

23. Thomas J. DeKornfeld, Louis Lasagna, Todd M. Frazier, "A Comparative Study of Five Proprietary Analgesic Compounds," *Journal of the American Medical Association*, 182 (Dec. 29, 1962) 1315–1318.

24. DeKornfeld, et al., p. 1319.

6. How was the study conducted? Were all the variables accounted for? What methods were used to establish causation between product usage and claimed results?

7. How extensive was the testing?

8. How many subjects were involved? What were their backgrounds? Were they always under control during the testing? How were they selected?

9. Were follow-up studies conducted? If so, for how long?

10. Did the subjects report side effects? If so, at what stages? Did they report cures or relief? How were their reactions different from those using conventional treatment or products?

EXERCISE 11-1

From your television viewing and from reading compile a list of ads that include or imply studies or findings. How many are documented? Write to an advertiser and ask for the specifics of a study. Include in your letter questions from the preceding list.

Polls and Surveys

We should ask similar questions of what can be another great source of unrepresentative generalizations: the poll or public opinion survey. So common have these become in our society that most politicians automatically include in their campaign budgets amounts for poll taking. For some time these figures have been staggering. Roll and Cantril pointed out in their fine, succinct work on the subject, that as early as the 1972 presidential election, candidates spent in excess of 1.5 million dollars just taking *polls*.[25] (Now, such a figure is not uncommon in *state* elections.) The money is often well spent, however; for despite criticism, polls, if properly conducted, are extremely accurate in their predictions. Of course they cannot predict with certainty the outcome of an election, but by using the inductive method together with careful statistical procedures, they can make highly probable predictions. Unfortunately people conducting polls do not always use careful procedures.

People harbor several misconceptions about polls and surveys, which sometimes make us more gullible, sometimes more skeptical, than we should be. First, many of us believe that the size of the group sampled *substantially* affects the accuracy of the poll. For example, we think that a poll or survey that reports how 1 million people feel about an issue is far more likely to be accurate than one that

---

25. Charles W. Roll, Jr., and Albert H. Cantril, *Polls: Their Use and Misuse in Politics* (New York: Basic Books, 1972), p. 31.

TABLE 11–1   Sample Size and Sampling Error

NUMBER OF INTERVIEWS	MARGIN OF ERROR (%)
4,000	±2
1,500	±3
1,000	±4
750	±4
600	±4
400	±5
200	±6
100	±11

Source: Roll and Cantril, *Polls,* p. 72.

reports how 100,000 people feel. Statistically, the margin of sample error, which is the numerical designation in percentage form of how inaccurate a poll may be, is identical in both cases, when the sample size is the same. So the size of the group may not be a significant factor. What is a factor is how *accurately* the sample represents the group.

A second misconception is that the group size must determine the sample size. Thus, for accurate results, we must draw a larger sample if we want to find out how 1 million people feel about an issue than we must if we want to find out the feelings of 100,000. As Table 11-1 indicates, sample size is a significant factor in polling but not as significant as many of us think. Statistical analysis shows that beyond a 1,500 probability sample, we reach a point of diminishing returns—the costs of additional interviews outweigh their advantages in accuracy. Of course, the difference between 100 interviews and 1,500 is significant. Nevertheless, people continue to be impressed by large numbers.

A third misconception about polling is that the interviewee or respondent must be handpicked to typify a group or subgroup member. Actually, the accuracy of the sample depends largely on the *randomness* of the sampling. As we saw in the chapter on generalization, *randomness means that each member of the group has an equal chance of being sampled*. When a poll or survey is conducted through a random sample, nothing but chance determines the instances selected.

But selecting purely random subjects isn't easy—or cheap. For example, if a television rating service interviewed every fifteenth person who passed the busiest corner of a city during school hours, it wouldn't be getting random subjects. Among other groups underrepresented would be children. If the television service wants purely random subjects, it will have to devise a way of making sure that *everyone in the population has an equal chance to be selected*. And that could end up being a lot more expensive than just spending a few hours on a street corner.

Just how closely a sample approximates pure randomness depends in part on the purpose of the sample. Consider the case of a local newspaper, for example, that predicts local election results on the basis of samples composed of every tenth name on an alphabetic roster of registered voters. Now that procedure is fairly close to random for predicting an election. Unfortunately, the paper uses the same technique for rating the popularity of television programs. What the paper fails to realize is that the directory, in excluding all people below voting age, excludes an important segment of the population: the television audience.

Another thing: A haphazard selection is not necessarily random. For example, suppose that your math teacher, Mr. Hrasta, occasionally likes to select a half-dozen students in the class to get an idea of how well the class as a whole has prepared an assignment. Hrasta does this by allowing his eyes to roam the room and selecting people. It all seems random enough, but it's not, and everyone in the class realizes this except Hrasta himself. Everyone knows that Mr. Hrasta is influenced by his moods: If he's feeling grouchy, he'll probably pick students who will be unprepared; if he's feeling good, he'll probably pick those who will be prepared. Mr. Hrasta does this subconsciously, not by design. Nevertheless, his sample is biased; it is not random but haphazard. One way to make the selection random would be to assign each student a number, put all the numbers in a hat, shake up the numbers, and then pick a half-dozen of them.

Of course, when you're dealing with large groups, ensuring randomness is not so simple. And as mentioned, it can be very expensive. Of great help in such cases is the so-called stratified sample. *A stratified sample is a sampling technique in which relevant strata within a group are identified and a random sample from each stratum is selected in proportion to the number of members in each stratum.* For example, if the local newspaper were genuinely interested in determining the popularity of television programs, it would establish relevant strata on the basis of the characteristics of people that could influence their program preferences, characteristics such as age, sex, educational level, and geographic region. Having established these strata, it would then randomly select persons from each stratum in direct proportion to the number of people within it. So three steps are necessary for a stratified sample: (1) Identify the strata within the population; (2) determine the number of instances in each stratum; and (3) randomly select the same proportion from each stratum.[26]

A final misconception worth noting relates to the so-called barometer areas, areas of the country that supposedly have so accurately reflected the whole population in, say, past elections that they can be taken as accurate barometers of how the country will vote: thus, "As goes Maine; so goes the nation." As Roll and Cantril demonstrate, however, the record does not justify such lofty assumptions. For example, if one had taken barometer counties Clay (Indiana), St. Francis (Kansas), Guilford (North Carolina), and Carroll (Tennessee), one would have predicted a Nixon victory over Kennedy in 1960. The forecaster could have pointed to the reliability of those counties in having forecast Republican percentiles within 1 percent in 1948, 1952, and 1956. But in 1960 these barometers were off by a whopping 10 percentage points. Obviously, the more barometric areas polled, the more accurate the forecast. But conditions change from election to election. No amount of barometer-area polling can account for the

---

26. See W. Edgar Moore, Hugh McCann, and Janet McCann, *Creative and Critical Thinking,* 2d ed. (Boston: Houghton Mifflin, 1985), pp. 119–120.

idiosyncrasy of each election. Only the stratified random sample has a good chance of doing this.

Having spoken generally of studies, polls, and surveys, let's now get specific. Let's look at some informal fallacies frequently associated with statistics.

STATISTICS AND FALLACIES

Although just about any of the informal fallacies that we've already discussed could turn up in a statistical argument, several warrant special consideration because they occur so frequently. We'll focus on six: the biased sample, equivocation, the biased question, the ambiguous question, the false dilemma, and concealed evidence.

The Fallacy of Biased Sample

The fallacy of biased sample is an argument that contains a sample that is not representative of the population being studied. We came across this fallacy earlier in discussing generalizations. Here we want to specify just how bias can creep into a sample. Three ways bear mentioning: (1) through the pollster, (2) through the sampling technique, and (3) through the respondent.

The Pollster

In guarding against a biased sample, the first thing to look out for is pollster bias. If the poll is one of the many so-called private polls we read about, be suspicious. The private poll is often conducted by an individual, group, party, or manufacturer whose vested interest in the findings can taint the poll's objectivity.

For example, the makers of Zest soap wished to find out what consumers thought of their product. Predictably enough, Zest found that consumers thought highly of its soap. The only problem with the survey was that the majority of people interviewed were Zest loyalists to begin with.

Similarly, Alpha Beta supermarkets used to sponsor a commercial that showed AB spokesperson Alan Hammel knocking on people's doors and soliciting their opinion about Alpha Beta. The opinions were, to say the least, most complimentary of Alpha Beta. The inherent pollster bias in such a sample needs no further comment; the lack of randomness couldn't be any more obvious than if a "warning" to that effect accompanied the commercial.

In brief, be suspicious of the results of surveys that support the positions of the very people who conducted the surveys. Because the investigator's objectivity is in question, the survey and its results must be in question as well.

The Sampling Technique

The sampling technique is the method or procedure used to select a sample. The most accurate techniques, as we've seen, are the random and stratified samples. When interviewers use other techniques, they introduce bias into the resulting statistics.

For example, in the aforementioned case of Zest, interviewers decided to use a sample of people who lived in Jacksonville, Florida, and who in general were loyal Zest users. This could hardly be considered an unbiased sampling technique. If Alpha Beta decides to feature only endorsements of their supermarket, thus giving the impression of consumer consensus of approval for AB, its sampling technique is biased.

A notorious *Literary Digest* prediction of the presidential election of 1936 was guilty of biased sampling technique in two ways. First, it sent ballots mainly to people listed in telephone books and city directories. In so doing, it introduced a decided socioeconomic bias into its sample: Only the relatively well-to-do had telephones in 1936. Second, the *Digest* counted *only* the ballots that were returned. Experience indicates that ballots or questionnaires voluntarily returned are likely to "load" the sample: Those with an interest in the result are more likely to go to the trouble of filling out and returning a ballot/questionnaire than those without such an interest. In 1990, the U.S. Census Bureau went to great lengths to avoid sampling bias in conducting the 1990 census. They hired interviewers who spoke Spanish, Japanese, Chinese, Italian, various Southeast Asian dialects, Navajo, and so on. They even went in search of the homeless.

Polls reporting the results of telephone interviews have their own problems, even though they are cheaper and quicker than the mail format and guarantee dispersion. First, it's often difficult to extract necessary personal information from someone during a telephone interview. Information about income, race, religion, and age is something few people are willing to disclose to a faceless voice on the other end of a phone. Yet such information may be crucial for stratification. The same reservation applies to answering controversial questions. People simply are less inclined to be open and candid with someone they cannot see. The most obvious drawback with the telephone poll, however, is the one the *Literary Digest* discovered: The interviewer cannot reach those without a phone—or a home.

Although the telephone is quicker and cheaper than polling by mail, important segments of the desired sample population may be over- or underrepresented. Certain low-income communities; some nonwhite communities; communities of immigrant groups who—though citizens—speak little English; rural pockets, especially in parts of the South; and so on, are likely to be underrepresented.

Even where stratification is properly performed, bias can creep in via interviewer selection of respondents. Suppose, for example, an agency wants to find out what people think of child-care centers. The agency decides that one of the strata within the population is the category "young mothers," let's say those between 18 and 30 years of age. Now it's important that the interviewer equally represent the various interests within this stratum. If, say, the interviewer questions only "young mothers" age 23, the sample is bound to overrepresent that group and underrepresent the others. Such a sample would lack randomness.

The Respondent

People who respond to polls (respondents) can bias a sample. Why? Blame it on human nature if you want, but people often tell us what they expect we want to hear and not what they *actually* think, prefer, or do. A classic example is seen in a house-to-house survey made some years ago purporting to study magazine readership. The question asked respondents was: "What magazines does your household read?" The replies indicated that a large percentage of households read *Harper's*, but not many read *True Story*—a forerunner of today's supermarket tabloids. This was odd, since publishers' figures clearly showed that *True Story* sold millions of magazines, whereas *Harper's* sold hundreds of thousands. When pollsters eliminated all other possible explanations, they faced an unmistakable conclusion: A good many respondents had lied. And those lies biased the sample and led to an erroneous conclusion.

A humorous footnote to this study occurred some time afterward when a worldly wise pollster set out again to determine people's reading preferences. The question asked respondents dealt with the kinds of books they usually read. An overwhelming number indicated that they read the classics: Shakespeare's plays, Dickens' novels, O. Henry's stories, and so forth. As a token of appreciation for their participation, the pollster offered each respondent a choice of any book from among a vast array of titles and subject matter, which included of course, many of the "beloved" classics. Curiously, the work most selected was hardly a classic, except perhaps in the field of ecdysiastism. Its title: *Diary of a Stripper*, authored by the most famous ecdysiast of all time, Gypsy Rose Lee. Thus, not in what people said, but in what they did, was to be found the naked truth.

The television program *Candid Camera* once went even further to show that people's responses can be highly misleading. As a stunt, a man pretending to represent a soft-drink concern asked respondents to sample two colas and to indicate which they preferred. A number of people had little trouble deciding, even going to lengths to detail why one was decidedly better than the other. In fact, the two colas were identical. This type of test has been conducted with brands of beer, ice cream, and other items, with similar results. The "Kona" coffee scandal of 1996 reaffirmed the powerful influence of expectation and perception on sensory experience when it was discovered that a major supplier of supposedly premier Hawaiian Kona coffee beans substituted less elite beans from other sources. For over ten years, coffee consumers and experts willing to pay a premium price for Kona beans failed to taste the difference.

EXERCISE 11-2 *

Examine for bias the sample used in each of the following arguments. Explain.

1. A poll is being conducted to determine whether the students at a college are for or against the construction of commercial nuclear power plants. A sample is taken in the library on a Wednesday between 8:00 AM and 9:00 PM. Every tenth person passing through the turnstile at the main entrance is asked his or her opinion. The results indicate that 61 percent of the students oppose the construction of commercial nuclear power plants, 37 percent favor it, and 2 percent have no opinion either way. The student government is thinking about using these findings as the basis for asking the administration to put the college on record as opposing the construction of nuclear power plants.

2. To predict the next election, candidate Smythe's forces take a survey. They phone at random 2 million registered voters. It is found that 1.5 million are expecting to vote for Smythe, in an election that figures to have a voter turnout of 50 million. Smythe's people are elated!

3. The Target Public Opinion Agency wants to find out how widespread coke snorting is among U.S. college students. To do so it uses a stratified random sample of 1,500 college students. The results indicate that a minority of students snort coke on a regular basis (at least once a week). In publishing its findings, Target editorializes that the incidence of cocaine use among U.S. college students is greatly exaggerated and uses its survey to back up its claim.

4. Ad for Ford Taurus: "63 percent of those who tested a Ford Taurus and a Chevy Lumina chose Taurus. Recently 50 Ford and 50 Chevy owners selected at random in the L.A. area rated both a Ford Taurus and Chevrolet Lumina for overall styling, interior and exterior features, roominess, trunk space, parking and driving under city, freeway and residential conditions. A total of 55 separate tests were performed. At the conclusion of these tests, all were asked: If they had to choose, which of these cars would they be more likely to buy? The answer? 63 percent, or nearly 2 out of 3, chose a Ford Taurus. See why at your Ford Dealer."

5. Harris Gallup has been hired by the Valley Shopping Mall Association to take a survey. The members want to know why the number of shoppers at the mall has been steadily declining for the last year. After determining that a survey of 350 shoppers is ample, and after careful preparation of a questionnaire, Harris Gallup tells his pollsters to be very sure not to interfere with the randomness of the sample. They are to set up a table with a big sign, "OPINION POLL," in the center of the main floor of the mall, Monday through Friday from 10:00 AM to 10:00 PM (the mall's weekday hours of operation), and they are to interview the first 350 people who randomly approach. Gallup was very careful to impress on his polltakers that they were in no way to encourage or discourage anyone from responding to the questionnaire. This approach seemed unbiased, random, and professional to the association. Was it? Explain why or why not.

6. In an effort to improve his teaching, Professor Stallone decides to sample his home economics class. He prepares a questionnaire with the help of Ms. Pascal, the college statistician. He then calls each of his students into his office—one at a time—and has them answer aloud the questions as he asks them. Professor Stallone is very careful to make sure that each student is interviewed.

7. Well-known pollsters Rowland Evans and Robert Novak have built a formidable reputation on, among other things, preelection polls. Typically, they poll 50 to 75 voters in "key" districts and then generate a statewide prediction. Howard Kahane reports the case in which they rated the

chances of Democratic State Senator Sander Levin to become the Governor of Michigan. They concluded that his chances were poor because only 42 percent of those polled in a key Democratic precinct favored Levin (36 percent favored his opponent; 22 percent were undecided). The entire sample consisted of 64 blue-collar workers living in the suburb of Warren, Michigan. (Howard Kahane, *Logic and Contemporary Rhetoric,* 4th ed. [Belmont, Calif.: Wadsworth], 1980, pp. 103–104)

The Fallacy of Equivocation

The fallacy of equivocation is an argument that uses a word or phrase in a way such that it carries more than a single meaning. Equivocation occurs frequently enough in statistics for us to consider it again here. Generally, the fallacy of equivocation in statistics takes one of two forms: verbal or visual.

Verbal

Often a statistic includes a word that equivocates; that is, it can be taken to mean different things. A good example is the word *average.*

For example, one reason Sweeney bought the home the family currently occupies was that the "average" income in the neighborhood impressed him and Wilma. Until the realtor mentioned the average income, the Sweeneys were indecisive about the purchase. But when the realtor casually said to Sweeney and Wilma one afternoon, "I don't know if you're aware of this, but the average income in this neighborhood is $55,000 per year," well, that did it. There was just enough snobbery in the Sweeneys to hook them with that bait.

Interestingly, a few years later Wilma joined a local taxpayers' committee that actively sought to curb the steady increase in property taxes. One of the committee's arguments was that the "average" income in the Sweeney's neighborhood was $25,000. Although Wilma went along with the committee, she couldn't help wondering about the disparity between the committee's "average" and the realtor's. When she told Sweeney about it, he simply said, "Somebody's lying."

Actually, as their daughter Slim was fast to point out, nobody was lying. "That's the beauty of statistics," she told her parents; "you can use them to do your lying for you." What Slim meant was that the word *average* was being used differently in the two instances.

The fact is that in statistics, *average* can carry one of three meanings: as the mean, median, or mode. The mean is an arithmetic average. You derive it by adding up the values of the items and dividing by the number of items. Thus, add up the incomes of all the people in the neighborhood and divide by the number of people. The result is the mean. That's the figure the realtor gave the Sweeney's.

The median is the figure right in the middle of all the items. Technically, in any distribution the median is the figure above which 50 percent falls and below which 50 percent falls. That's the figure the tax committee used.

To illustrate, let's consider just five incomes:

1. $180,000

2.   40,000

3.   25,000

4.   15,000

5.   15,000

Add all those figures, divide by five, and you get $55,000, the average taken as the mean. But the average taken as the median is the figure right in the middle, $25,000.

Actually, if the tax committee were dealing only with these figures, they'd be better served by claiming that the "average" income was $15,000. That would be the average taken as the mode. The mode refers to the figure in a distribution that occurs most frequently. Here it's $15,000.

When Slim pointed out to her parents these various uses of the word *average,* they decided to do a little investigating of their own. They acquired figures on the incomes of wage earners in their neighborhood. They learned that the disparity between the $55,000 and the $25,000 figures could be explained simply: The neighborhood included two millionaires, which boosted the total income of the neighborhood and thus the arithmetic average, the mean. Actually, everybody else in the neighborhood was making far less. All of which gave Sweeney pause. "This word *average,*" he mused, "it doesn't tell you much, does it?" No, it doesn't. When we find it in a statistic, we better find out in what sense it's intended. If we don't, then rest assured that on the *average* we'll be duped.

Statistical verbal equivocation arises with other words. For example, almost any claim containing a superlative—*best, finest, most*—is using the word equivocally, and perhaps even meaninglessly. Thus, Armour-Dial once advertised, "Dial is the most effective deodorant soap you can buy." Now you might take that as a claim to superiority over any other soap. But when pressed by the Federal Trade Commission (FTC), Armour-Dial insisted that the claim simply meant that Dial soap was *as* effective as other soaps. So why not say that? The fact is that even if Armour-Dial had said "as effective as," that wouldn't be much of an improvement; for the phrase "as effective as" is itself hopelessly obscure. "As effective as" in what sense—cleaning, perfuming, softening?

Weasel Words

And, oh yes, let's not forget "weasel words" in statistical equivocation. *Weasel words are words used to evade or retreat from a direct or forthright statement or position.* They are advertiser's buzzwords. They allow somebody to say something without really saying it. The weasel *help* is a good example. *Help,* of course, means "aid" or "assist" and nothing else. Yet, as one author has observed, "'Help' is the one single word which, in all the annals of advertising, has done the most to say something that couldn't be said."[27] What he means is that, since *help* is used to qualify, once it's used, almost anything can be said after it. Thus we're exposed to ads for products that "*help* us keep young," "*help* prevent cavities," "*help* keep our houses germ free." Just think about how many times a day you hear or read phrases like these: "*helps* stop," "*helps* prevent," "*helps* fight," "*helps* overcome," "*helps* you feel," "*helps* you look." Of course, *help* isn't the only weasel. Here are some others: *like, virtual* or *virtually, can be, up to* (as in "provides relief *up to* eight hours"), *as much as* (as in "saves *as much as* one gallon of gas"). Such words and phrases function to say what really can't be said because, in most cases, the statistical studies necessary to back up a specific claim just aren't available; if they were, rest assured that the advertiser would happily boast of them. Lacking hard data, advertisers—as well as those in other fields, of course—enlist the weasels to give the *impression* of substantial claim support.

Visual

Statistical equivocation need not come only in words. Graphs, charts, pictographs, and other visual aids used to represent statistical claims can also commit the fallacy of equivocation. If a picture is worth a thousand words, in statistics it may be worth considerably more.

Take, for example, the common two-axis graph, consisting of a vertical ascending linear scale and a rightward extending horizontal linear scale.[28] All sorts of trends and data are plotted on this most common visual aid. But be careful. The two-axis graph can be used to misrepresent.

To illustrate, let's represent a region's increasing unemployment in the course of a year (shown in Figure 11-1). Now this graph is clear enough. It shows what happened with unemployment, month by month through the year. The graph is in proportion. There's a zero line at the bottom for comparison. The 10 percent increase in unemployment during the year looks like 10 percent. In short, the unemployment picture is conveyed clearly, quickly, accurately, and unemotionally.

But suppose you wanted to alarm readers, convince them that the situation was very serious. If you did, Figure 11-1's chart wouldn't be nearly dramatic enough. Figure 11-2 is a more effective graph for that purpose. Notice that the figures and curve are the same. But by chopping off the graph we've changed its impression. The reader now sees an unemployment line that has climbed halfway up the chart in one year! What is actually a relatively modest rise now appears enormous.

You say you're still not satisfied? That you want something even more dramatic because you have an even bigger axe to grind? Very well. Simply alter the proportion between the vertical and horizontal axes by letting each mark up the

---

27. See Paul Stevens, "Weasel Words: God's Little Helpers," in *Language Awareness,* eds. Paul A. Eschhol, Alfred A. Rosa, and Virginia P. Clark (New York: St. Martin's Press, 1974), p. 156.

28. See Darrell Huff, *How to Lie with Statistics* (New York: W. W. Norton, 1954).

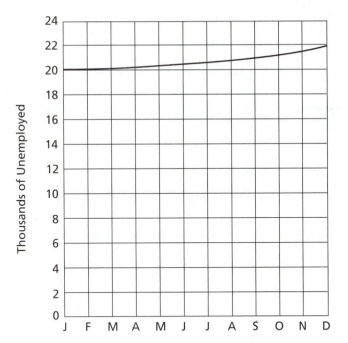

FIGURE 11-1

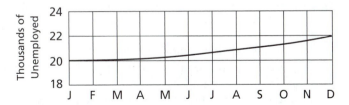

FIGURE 11-2

vertical line represent only one-tenth as many people as before: thus the graph shown in Figure 11-3. Now, that should produce a cardiac skip in the most lionhearted chest. In fact, this graph represents a subtle, visual way of editing "Unemployment rose 10 percent" into "Unemployment climbed a whopping 10 percent!" And the beauty of it is that the graph contains no words that might betray slanting. Indeed, it appears completely objective, unless of course you know what to look for and think about.

Technically speaking, such graphic distortions are a form of *equivocating on relative terms*. Bases of comparison get shifted. The standard of comparison is obscured by truncating or compressing the graph. Interpretation is served up with information. In short, the data the graph represents carry more than one meaning. In that lies the equivocation.

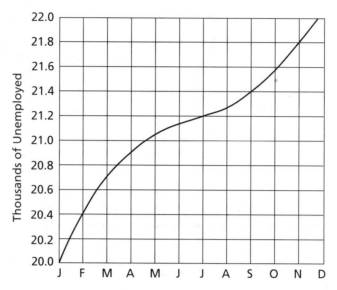

FIGURE 11-3

Other statistical visuals can equally mislead. The pictograph is a good example. Pictographs are little pictures used to present data: a picture of a man carrying a lunch pail to represent labor, a picture of a woman in a gingham dress to represent housewives, a picture of a barrel to represent amounts of oil. Imagine, in fact, a graphic that attempts to portray increasing American oil consumption since World War II by depicting a series of increasingly large barrels, one at each regular interval along a horizontal axis. Ambiguity arises when we interpret the pictograph. Do we compare the barrels' relative heights, areas, or volumes? Because we generally underestimate increases in areas resulting from increases in height and width and increases in volume resulting from increases in areas, we can easily downplay our increasing oil consumption. The point: Look skeptically on pictographs that change their lengths and widths while representing a single factor or that present three-dimensional objects whose volumes are difficult to compare.

EXERCISE 11-3

Are there any fallacies of equivocation in the following passages? If so, explain.

1. BONNIE: Wow! I feel a lot better after reading that article in *Self*.
   BART: I thought you might. I knew how you'd been struggling with those unresolved feelings of hostility toward your parents.
   BONNIE: And now this article says I'm perfectly normal!
   BART: That's what I've been trying to tell you—the average person feels the same way you do.
   BONNIE: That's exactly what the article says.

2. "Alka Seltzer: the best antacid you can buy without a prescription." (Ad for Alka Seltzer)

3. FERN: You know, the cavalier way that peoples' political freedoms are treated around the world is really outrageous.
STU: I guess you're talking about Russia, huh?
FERN: I'm talking worldwide. Did you know that in the past year the political liberties of 823.3 million people were violated?
STU: No, I didn't know that.
FERN: Then here, read this article. I think it's about time this country did something about this outrage.

4. BETH: Can I use your cellular phone?
BURT: Sure, if I had one.
BETH: No phone?
BURT: I just ordered one.
BETH: Well, lots a luck! Did you know it takes anywhere from 90 to 180 days to get a cell phone activated in this area?
BURT: Oh no!

5. WIFE: Well, you're running true to form—having a drink before dinner.
HUSBAND: What's that supposed to mean?
WIFE: According to the latest survey, more middle-aged men have at least one drink before dinner than any other age group of males or females.

6. Every 90 seconds a woman gives birth in America: We've got to find that woman and stop her!

7. There's no more effective analgesic on the market today.

8. You'll be surprised at how well it works.

9. MOE: Why're you so depressed, Larry?
LARRY: I just got my Archeology 1A midterm back—I got an F.
CURLEY: Oooooo! Ooooooo! That's awful!
LARRY: Yeah, I'll say. But I'm not alone; over half of the class flunked.
MOE: Hey! Don't feel so bad then; you got an average grade.

10. JERRY: I object to my children studying Einstein.
JIMMY: Why? He was a genius.
JERRY: That's what I mean. He was deviant, abnormal.

The Fallacy of Biased Question

The fallacy of biased question is an argument based on the answer to a question that is worded to elicit a predetermined reply. For example, suppose a pollster asks respondents this question: "Should the United States continue to spend millions of dollars annually on foreign aid while neglecting needed domestic problems?" The results: 77 percent "no," 23 percent "yes." You'd be unwise, however, to accept this conclusion because the question that generated it is biased. It is worded to elicit a predetermined reply, in this case "no." Such questions are commonly termed *loaded* or *complex.*

Consider this example of a biased question. It was part of a "survey" purportedly to determine how people felt about reinstating the death penalty. The question read: "Should we reinstate capital punishment, or continue to allow the potential murderer and rapist to operate without even the threat of death?" Psychologically, a respondent is made to feel that a "no" reply is a vote for murder and rape. The question is calculated to elicit a "yes" reply.

Sometimes a biased question can result when alternatives aren't clear. Consider, for example, this question: "A proposal has been made in Congress to use American soldiers to stabilize conditions in Rwanda. Would you like to have your representative vote for or against this proposal?" Without a follow-up question, the results can be misleading. Those responding "no" to this question might change their minds when subsequently asked: "Some people say that the United States has a basic humanitarian obligation to provide food, clothing, and other supplies to the thousands of sick and starving Rwandan refugees presently confined to relocation camps. Do you agree or disagree?"

Question bias can result from the substitution of one word for another. For example, here are several questions that the makers of Alamo Brand pet food once asked respondents in a "Pet Owner's Opinion Study." Observe how using the word *that,* instead of *whether* or *if,* biases the questions.

1. Did you notice that Alamo Brand looks meatier than the dry dog food you have been using?

2. Did you notice that Alamo Brand has a meatier feel than the dry dog food you have been using?

3. Did you notice that your dog preferred and enjoyed Alamo Brand more than his usual dry dog food?

4. Did you notice that your dog appeared more contented and satisfied after eating Alamo Brand?

Are they serious? Apparently so. The respondent was asked to return the survey to Manufacturers Marketing Research Services in Chester, Pennsylvania. And just to confound matters, Alamo promised to conduct a follow-up study based on the responses to this questionnaire! As they put it: "Based upon the responses to this questionaire [sic], we are going to choose a select group of consumers for a 30 day Use and Opinion Study of ALAMO BRAND. The purpose of this study will be to see if consumers notice an improvement in their dog's general condition and health when they feed [sic] ALAMO BRAND for a long enough time. If you are selected for this study, would you agree to give us your opinions?" The worst part of this sort of thing is that we all continue to suffer through the annoying ads and commercials such "studies" generate.

The Fallacy of Ambiguous Question

Just as unreliable in statistical arguments as the biased question is the ambiguous one. *The fallacy of ambiguous question is an argument based on a question that contains a vague or equivocal key word or phrase.* "Do you think it's a good practice for a woman to be paid less for doing the same job that a man does?" Well, probably that depends on what is meant by "a good practice." From the viewpoint of employers, or maybe even men, it might well be "a good practice." From the viewpoint of women, it wouldn't be. Again, the question "Do you think it's possible that we'll discover intelligent life in outer space by the year 2000?" is ambiguous. Does the interviewer mean empirical, technical, or logical possibility? The respondent has no way of knowing; indeed, the interviewer may even mean "likely" or "probable," and not "possible" at all. And what—precisely—is meant by "intelligent"? The problems with such questions are twofold. First, the respondent doesn't know which meaning is intended. Second, the pollster has no way of knowing that all the respondents understood the question in the same way. Hence, any conclusion drawn from an ambiguous question is fallacious.

EXERCISE 11-4 *

Are any of the following survey questions biased or ambiguous? If so, which questions? Explain.

1. Do you favor more educational programs on television?

2. Should the United States support the Israelis in its dealings with the Arab countries?

3. Many people believe that we are spending far too much on national defense. Do you agree?

4. Do you usually have a ready-to-eat cereal for breakfast?

5. Do you think the United States should accept Russian influence in Cuba?

6. Do you think the government should ration gasoline?

7. To which class do you feel you belong: white-collar, blue-collar, or some other?

8. Which of these questions is less biased? Why?

   a. Do you think most manufacturing companies that lay off workers in the slack periods could avoid layoffs and provide steady work right through the year?

b. Do you think most manufacturing companies that lay off workers in the slack period could avoid layoffs and provide steady work right through the year, or do you think layoffs are inevitable? [29]

The Fallacy of False Dilemma

The fallacy of false dilemma is an argument that erroneously reduces the number of possible positions or alternatives on an issue. To argue, for example, that one should either support our government's policies or leave the country is to commit a false dilemma. There is ample middle ground, alternatives, between these two extremes. A bank commits a false-dilemma fallacy when it suggests, "A logical alternative to the stock market: MADISON SAVINGS AND LOAN." The bank implies that there are just two ways to invest: either in the stock market or in Madison Savings and Loan.

Of course there are times when such either-or choices are appropriate. One of Aristotle's three laws of thought is *the law of the excluded middle:* A thing is either *A* or not *A*. Thus, the object before you is either a book or not a book. It can't be both. Similarly, a question such as: "Is the flower in your hand a rose or not a rose?" poses a genuine dilemma, not a false one. Surely the flower either is a rose or not a rose. Notice that the question did not ask, "Is the flower in your hand a rose or a carnation?" Unless it had been established previously that the flower was, in fact, only one or the other, that question would be a false dilemma; the flower might be neither one.

The false dilemma is a ploy. Arguers use it when they wish to eliminate your range of choices and thereby lead you to a predetermined conclusion. In this sense, a question that poses a false dilemma is a variation of the biased question. Statistics frequently have as their source results generated by a false dilemma.

For example, a poll that asks, "Are you for or against the women's liberation movement?" creates a false dilemma. You may be indifferent to the women's liberation movement. (Of course the question is ambiguous as well: Just what constitutes being "for" or "against"?) Here's another false dilemma question: "Do you think the United States should support the Arabs or the Israelis in the Middle East?" Maybe you feel the United States should "support" neither or perhaps both equally. It's true that most polls do provide a "no-opinion" choice, but the trouble with this category is that it's hopelessly ambiguous. After all, in addition to those who genuinely have no opinion are those who have an opinion that wasn't listed and those, perhaps logicians, who refuse to answer such a fallacious question. All are treated as having "no opinion," which surely must qualify as the fallacy of hasty conclusion.

---

29. Quoted in S. L. Payne, *The Art of Asking Questions* (Princeton, N.J.: Princeton University Press, 1951). Question **a.** elicited far more affirmative replies than **b.**, although the questions are essentially the same.

EXERCISE 11-5 *

Are the following examples of genuine or false dilemmas?

1. Directions for an essay exam: Write an essay titled "Captain Ahab—Fanatic or Idealist?"

2. Poll question: Do you favor or oppose a tax cut?

3. Political commentator on the 1979 seizure of the American embassy in Tehran by Iranian students: The entire episode goes to prove that the United States is a paper tiger. Otherwise we would have exercised our military muscle to free the U.S. citizens being held hostage. The fact that we didn't demonstrates that we no longer have the will to stand by our principles. And it also shows something else: In a real showdown we will put our material interests, oil in this case, before the lives of Americans abroad.

4. Ad for Vivarin tablets: "Coffee, Tea or Vivarin?"

5. Ad for Subaru: "At Mercedes Benz, they engineer a great car, without regard for price. Subaru engineers a great car, with great regard for price. . . . Subaru and Mercedes, two of the finest engineered cars around. One sells for 8 times the price of the other. The choice is yours."

6. SALLY: Well, the evidence is in. Business leaders continue to discriminate against women on the job.
   SAM: Why do you say that?
   SALLY: Because the results of a study prove it. Look, a thousand business leaders were picked at random and asked: "If you had to choose between a male and a female for a job with your firm, and the two happened to be equally qualified, which would you choose—the male or the female?" And guess what? Sixty-eight percent said they'd choose the male.

7. Following are questions from a course evaluation designed by the instructor: The best thing about this course is (a) the instructor, (b) lectures, (c) the tests, (d) weekly practice quizzes, (e) a–d are equally effective.
   The worst thing about this course is (a) time it meets, (b) day it meets, (c) book, (d) room, (e) none.
   What grade would you give this instructor? (a) A, (b) B, (c) not sure.

8. Christ was either a madman or who he said he was. (Paraphrase of C. S. Lewis's oft-quoted assertion)

The Fallacy of Concealed Evidence

Recently the Sweeneys were victimized by a "numbers game." It seems they were in the market for an automatic fruit juicer. In their shopping, they came across one that claimed to extract 30 percent more juice. That sounded pretty good, so they bought it. Only afterward did they find out that the manufacturer meant 30 percent more juice than the old-fashioned hand-reamer juicer. Since the Sweeneys had never intended to buy such a juicer, the advertised claim was totally irrelevant for their purposes. This kind of hidden or suppressed information constitutes one of the most common, and potentially dangerous, fallacies often associated with statistics: the fallacy of concealed evidence.

The fallacy of concealed evidence is an argument that presents only facts that are favorable to its conclusion while suppressing relevant but nonsupportive facts. Before showing this fallacy in a statistical context, let's see how widespread its use is in nonstatistical contexts.

Nonstatistical

One of the most dramatic examples of nonstatistical concealed evidence concerned a product called Pertussin Medicated Vaporizer.[30] Between 1968 and 1973 18 persons apparently died from inhaling its contents. Some deaths resulted from product abuse; some did not. On July 2, 1973, a decade after the product first appeared on merchants' shelves, the Food and Drug Administration removed Pertussin from the market.

In that 10-year interim, anyone reading the can's label read nothing alarming about the product's contents. On the contrary, Pertussin spray supposedly built "a roomful of relief" from colds and hay fever. The directions called for spraying the contents on handkerchiefs, in rooms, and even on pillows and sheets. "Repeat as often as necessary" and "safe even in the nursery" made the unsuspecting shopper even more confident of the product's merit. Pertussin even had the blessing of *Parents* magazine (an appeal to authority), its seal indicating that the spray had been tested by the FDA. It had not. Even the most suspicious consumer was reassured by the harmless ingredients listed: menthol and oil of eucalyptus. In short, consumers seemed safe in buying and using this product. They might have reasoned that any medicated vaporizer containing the ingredients Pertussin claimed it did was versatile enough to be used on handkerchiefs, in rooms, and even on pillows and sheets; had been proved effective; and was moderately priced and a product they should buy. As it turned out, such an argument was tragically uncogent. Evidence had been concealed.

A couple of ingredients and related facts about them went unmentioned on the can. First, the manufacturers made no mention that menthol and eucalyptus made up only 12 percent of the total ingredients. The remaining 88 percent consisted of propellants and solvents. Neither did the manufacturers mention that the propellants and solvents were about equally divided between fluorocarbons and trichloroethane, which tend to upset the heartbeat and depress other vital activities such as breathing. The combination proved fatal, and a tragic example of how dangerous concealed evidence can be. As Daniel Webster once

---

30. For the related facts, see the *Los Angeles Times,* July 2, 1973, p. 1.

noted, "There is nothing so powerful as the truth, nothing so dangerous as a half-truth."

From our discussion in Chapter 1, we know that a proposition is either true or it is not; it cannot be half true and half untrue. But we include that term *half-truth* because the term's popular connotation is that of an incomplete picture or omission of pertinent facts, details, or information. Understood this way, *half-truth* becomes a useful term, suggesting the common characteristic of all the fallacies of concealed evidence: They result from relying on incomplete or inaccurate evidence.

To generalize correctly we need *all relevant facts*—not just some of them. We've already touched on the information explosion and how difficult it is for us to obtain certain knowledge, even under the best of conditions. But added to this difficulty is the fact that we must often evaluate highly technical and specialized claims and act on these evaluations, in many cases for our physical survival.

The most common examples of concealed evidence are in advertising. Because most of us have so little knowledge of the product, we can't begin to detect the fallacy in the appeal. Many advertising executives nevertheless insist that the primary purpose of advertising is not to sell a product but to educate the public. Certainly many ads do do this. Mounting evidence, however, contradicts the claim that this is generally the case. In fact, one very influential advertising president, David Ogilvy, admitted, "Surely it is asking too much to expect the advertiser to describe the shortcomings of his product."[31] This is little more than a defense of concealed evidence. In *The Permissible Lie,* Samm Sinclair Baker, who spent many years in advertising, made the point more forcefully:

> Inside the agency the basic approach is hardly conducive to truthtelling. The usual thinking in forming a campaign is first, what can we say, true or not, that will sell the product best? The second consideration is, how can we say it effectively and get away with it so that (1) people who buy won't feel let down by too big a promise that doesn't come true, and (2) the ads will avoid quick and certain censure by the Federal Trade Commission.[32]

In defending concealed evidence, advertisers often like to say that the public is too smart to be duped, that it's impossible to "put one by" as sophisticated an audience as a product is likely to find in contemporary America. This may be so. But at a gathering of the American Marketing Association in the spring of 1973, Seymour Lieberman—president of Manhattan-based Lieberman Research, Inc.—reported that "deceitful ads can be far more persuasive than promotions that tell the simple truth."

> Lieberman enlisted the aid of the Kenyon & Eckhardt agency to create one deceptive and one truthful television commercial for each of six fictitious products. A panel

---

31. David Ogilvy, *Confessions of an Advertising Man* (New York: Atheneum, 1963), p. 158.

32. Samm Sinclair Baker, *The Permissible Lie* (New York: World, 1968).

of 100 largely middle-income consumers watched the truthful commercials and another group of the same size, income and education level saw the dishonest versions. Both sets of commercials used the same actors, and except for the misleading bits, the same language. Yet in four of the six tests, the cheating commercial placed well ahead of the honest promotion in coaxing the audience into a buying mood. More people were persuaded to buy the mythical Pro Gro plant fertilizer when the commercial stressed that it contained protein—*though protein is of absolutely no help to plants*. A bunion remedy, D-Corn, drew more buyer interest when it was touted as having four times as much methylglyoxal as its competition; yet *no evidence was offered to support the notion that increasing the amount of methylglyoxal might be in the least beneficial.*[33]

The sample used in this test is hardly large enough to provide conclusive findings. Neither is the evidence we've provided sufficient to conclude that the advertiser is primarily motivated by a desire to sell, not to inform.

But we neither desire nor intend to indict the advertising industry. We only want to be alert to those areas in which concealed evidence in argument constitutes a real and present threat to life and limb. Consumerism is one of those areas, a vital one. What the advertiser "forgets" to tell you in the interest of preserving the persuasiveness of the argument or demonstration usually falls under the heading of *concealed evidence*. This evidence, of course, would make the stated or implied conclusions less forceful and, in some cases, highly improbable.

The whole area of labeling is rife with concealed evidence. For example, the so-called feminine deodorant sprays, which have mushroomed into a multi-million dollar annual sales industry, never mention that the products are unnecessary. (Any gynecologist will verify that normal daily cleansing is much more hygienic than any cosmetic application.) Neither does the label mention the undesirable side effects that such products cause: itching, burning, blistering, and urinary tract infections. The Food and Drug Administration has finally proposed the following warning on all such products:

> CAUTION—For external use only. Spray at least eight inches from skin. Use sparingly and not more than once daily to avoid irritation. Do not use this product with a sanitary napkin. Do not apply to broken, irritated or itching skin. Persistent or unusual odor may indicate the presence of a condition for which a physician should be consulted. If rash, irritation, unusual vaginal discharge or discomfort develops, discontinue use immediately and consult a physician.

Even with this warning, the mind boggles at the millions of cans already sold without this information.

With many of us conscious of our weight, concealed evidence also turns up in the selling of low-calorie foods or diet-control products. Some diet aids claim to suppress appetite. For example, some ads claim that bulk-producing products taken before meals allegedly swell in the stomach (by absorbing water), thus

---

33. *Time,* May 14, 1973, p. 96. Italics added to show concealed evidence in the first case and a questionable claim in the second case.

suppressing appetite. Unfortunately, most of these products contain methylcellulose, originally sold to relieve chronic constipation. Consequently, rather than swelling the stomach, such products quickly pass into the small intestine. But even if this mass does inhibit hunger contractions, as advertised, it does nothing to curb appetite. Appetite is a learned way of behaving, associated with a complex network of pleasurable physical and psychological feelings. It's appetite, not hunger, that causes obesity. Hunger is caused by normal, natural stomach contractions signaling the body's need for food; satisfying these signals hardly ever causes obesity. Then there are those products that would persuade us to purchase diet aids by using "before" and "after" photos. Often, however, the photos have been as touched up as the centerfold of *Playboy*.

The year 1996 saw the addition of a fifth over-the-counter pain reliever, ketoprofen, to the already heavily advertised market for competing pain relievers aspirin, acetaminophen, ibuprofen, and naproxen. The manufacturers of two new brands of ketoprofen chose the same theme to introduce their products: "*Actron*. It's so small because it's so powerful," and "New *Orudis KT*. The potent medicine for pain." According to a May 1996 *Consumers Report* analysis of pain relievers, while it may, indeed, require fewer milligrams of ketoprofen to achieve pain relief comparable to quantitatively larger doses of the other products, the differences among all products are nearly "meaningless" for many consumers. For others, high blood pressure, kidney disease or damage, age, sensitivity, and other factors play a role in choosing the most appropriate product. As far as the new kid on the block is concerned, until ketoprofen becomes available in generic form, it will cost more than its competitors.

The same report reveals another case of concealed evidence, this time involving a full-page ad by the manufacturer of *Advil* claiming that in some doses *Tylenol* can harm your liver if you typically consume three alcoholic drinks a day. The makers of *Tylenol* countered that anyone drinking that much on a daily basis should consult a physician before taking any pain reliever. What's concealed? Although the *Advil* ad is correct in its claim that liver damage has been linked with consumption of alcohol and acetaminophen (*Tylenol*), it conceals the clearly identified risk of gastrointestinal bleeding associated with the use of the other pain relievers, including ibuprofen (*Advil*).

APPLES TO ORANGES   One of the most common and difficult-to-spot forms of concealed evidence conceals or disguises the exact nature of a comparison. This amounts to "comparing apples to oranges." Ads for deodorants compare apples to oranges when they make claims like this: "Sweet Smell roll-on deodorant offers more protection than UpClose pump deodorant and Harmony aerosol deodorant." If you are already suspicious of the phrase "more protection," you are on the right track. "More protection" is notorious advertising doublespeak (see Chapter 5). Does it mean "stronger protection"? "longer-lasting protection"? Not in this case. In this kind of claim, various brands of deodorant formulas are not being compared at all; the comparison is among *methods of application— which have nothing to do with deodorant compounds in this case*. What's being concealed from the consumer is the general pattern that roll-on applicators are more efficient "deodorant delivery systems" than either pump or aerosol "systems" for the simple reason that pumping or spraying results in product loss due to drifting and dripping in the air. With a roll-on ball, most of the deodorant that does not attach to the skin remains on the ball for subsequent application. So in this kind of claim, what we really have is "apples (roll-on) to oranges (pump-on) to plums (spray-on-via-propellant)."

An even slicker form of apples-to-oranges pitch can be found in comparisons between large-ball roll-on deodorants and standard-ball deodorants: "Powerhouse Roll-on Plus provides more protection than Soso Regular Roll-on and Hohum Basic Roll-on." In this type of ad, the formulations and properties of the deodorants themselves is not at issue—the size of the applicator ball is. Obviously, a larger-diameter sphere will cover more rolling area than a smaller sphere. Thus, what the ad is really saying is: "The larger (wider) of two roll-on balls will cover a wider swath of skin per distance rolled than will a smaller (narrower) ball." "More protection" only means more product applied per swipe—not stronger or longer-lasting protection.

In the area of nutrition, manufacturers compare apples to oranges when they alter the portion sizes of the "regular" version of a product in order to inflate (puff) the health benefits of their "low-calorie," "low-fat," and "low-salt" versions of that products. Thus, four of one company's "regular" cookies might constitute a "serving," whereas only two of their *smaller* "low-fat" cookies might be counted as a serving. "Regular" microwave popcorn might come in 3.5 ounce packets while the "low-fat" variety comes in 3.0 ounce packets. The 0.5 ounce difference is easily overlooked by busy consumers. In such cases, even if the number of portions does not change, the actual amount of popcorn per serving is reduced.

Note, too, that in our health conscious era, the number of "servings" listed on "regular" products is often ridiculously high. Who do you know who eats one cup of *popped* popcorn? Who gets 8 servings out of one nine-inch cheese cake? Who eats four potato chips or one-third of a candy bar? Whether we should eat more modest amounts or not, increasing the number of servings in such circumstances amounts to concealing evidence. See for yourself how common this practice is by checking out the number of servings on "healthier" versions of such products as microwave popcorn, cookies, cheese, yogurt, bread, and the like.

With errors of concealed evidence or half-truths, then, the conclusions seem to follow from the evidence, but we should not be persuaded to accept those conclusions. The reason is that we don't have all the relevant evidence, the whole truth. To put it another and more precise way, such arguments omit evidence bearing directly on the conclusions they're trying to force. As a result, the arguments are not *cogent*. And an uncogent argument should never persuade us.

Statistical

Turning to the statistical uses of concealed evidence, let's consider a simple example. Some years ago it was reported that the number of deaths chargeable to steam railroads in one year was 4,712. If you were around then, you might have considered that as ample reason to stay off trains. But if you'd taken the time to investigate what the figure was all about, you would have learned that nearly half of those victims were people whose automobiles had collided with trains at crossings. And the great part of the remainder were killed while jumping on or off moving trains illegally. In fact, of the 4,712 people killed, only 132 were passengers on trains. (Even that figure doesn't mean much until you know how many passenger miles trains traveled that year.)[34]

Look for statistically concealed evidence in the profit pictures that large corporations try to paint. For example, a big company might report that in a given year it made only one cent in profits out of every sales dollar. Sounds fair enough. After all, to replace a two-dollar typewriter ribbon, the company would lose the profit on two hundred sales dollars. Makes you feel guilty about making "typos," doesn't it? But the truth is that what a company reports as "profits" is only a fraction of the overall profit picture. Hidden depreciation, special depreciation, reserves for contingencies—all make up the part of the profit picture that goes unreported.

Appeals for rate increases for everything from utilities to insurance often rely on concealed evidence. An insurance company, for example, might argue that it's paid out 3 billion dollars more in claims than it has collected in premiums over the past eight years. Sounds like reason enough for a rate increase, doesn't it? Well, don't be so sure. Remember that the profit standing of an insurance company is hardly determined by subtracting claims from premiums. After all, premiums don't lie buried in an office vault somewhere. They're banked and invested, whereby they generate additional income. So before believing that the increase is justified, find out the total income and total expenditure, because that will reveal true total profits.

Sometimes, because statistics conceal evidence, we feel we're getting something for nothing. For example, a supermarket once advertised a price reduction on over 7,500 products.[35] What it didn't report was that its *original prices* were for the most part higher than prices in competitive chain markets. Beware of this kind of "prices slashed" advertising. It may be concealing evidence.

In "Selling It," the August 1990 issue of *Consumer Reports* stated that it found two different sized packages of *Knorr's Leek Soup* for sale. The smaller box cost $1.39. So did the larger one. The smaller box contained enough dry soup mix to make four 8-ounce servings. The larger contained enough to make only three servings. The larger box was a ploy to conceal the evidence of a 33 percent price increase. In the same issue, *Consumer Reports* described an ad in an Illinois newspaper which pictured what it called the "Commander's Tower." The Tower pictured was a wooden jungle gym with a slide, climbing rope, pole, and ladders. It was advertised for $98, which looks like a fair price for such a sturdy set. Then you notice it says, "$98 plus wood!" Next, your eyes turn to a long list of

---

34. Huff, *How to Lie with Statistics,* p. 79.

35. See *Accurate Pricing Book,* Marketing Service Corporation, Central Valley, Calif., September 1, 1972.

products sold separately: the pole, roof, ladders, slide, climbing net, and so on. *Consumer Reports* noted that a call to the store revealed that $98 buys only the plans and the "hardware." What's in the photo cost $650. Concealed evidence is one of the most common, destructive fallacies in wide use.

As the saying goes, "The more things change, the more they stay the same." The "Selling It" section of the November 1996 edition of *Consumer Reports* noted that T.G.I. Friday's restaurants' patrons could earn points each time they paid their checks. Prizes were awarded at different point levels. Everyone began with 500 points, and 10 points were awarded for each dollar spent (plus occasional "bonus point" offers). As of November 1996, customers needed to spend $75 to "earn" an appetizer, $100 to receive a certificate good for sweatshirts, $3,650 to get a jacket, watches, or other such item—and $24,950 to "win" a cruise. That's quite a cruise, to say nothing of tasty $75 appetizers or $100 sweatshirts.[36]

The same "Selling It" column included another item concerning dry soup mixes, this time Lipton's. According to the report, in May of 1996, Lipton chicken soup mix with extra noodles cost 20¢ more than regular Lipton chicken soup mix with noodles—$1.19 compared to 99¢. The extra-noodles version weighed 0.4 ounce more, or 4.9 ounces compared to 4.5 ounces for the regular version. In both versions, noodles are listed first among ingredients. The instructions on the extra-noodle mix call for adding 3 cups of water per packet of mix. The regular mix calls for 4 cups of water. So, the extra-noodle mix increases the mix total by less than 9 percent while decreasing the water by 25 percent. Of course less water per mix results in less watery soup—what Lipton's called "extra noodles."

A final word about concealed evidence. Obviously, before we are able to detect the concealed evidence fallacy, we must know what it is that an argument is suppressing. This means that we, as practical logicians, must constantly be expanding our repertory of information in economics, politics, consumerism, history, nutrition, medicine, science—indeed in every field imaginable. Otherwise, we're just asking to be duped and ripped off. Think about it—think about the times we've wondered about the usefulness of all those "other" courses, the ones outside our majors that we must take in college. Forget about all the high-blown justification for those courses. Think of them in terms of simple survival. The person who knows nothing about politics, consumerism, history, science, and so on, stands a greater chance of perishing financially, emotionally, intellectually, even spiritually, than the one who keeps informed of these and other fields. So when a college curriculum requires us to take courses outside our major field, it's not punishing us; it's protecting us. End of sermon.

EXERCISE 11-6

1. The fallacy of concealed evidence is often present in textbooks. Choose one of the following subjects from American history. Then consult an

---

36. *Consumer Reports*, November 1996.

American history textbook and see if the author has omitted information incompatible with the impression he or she is trying to create.

a. Native Americans

b. people of color

c. women

d. U.S. presidents

e. wars and the need for them

2. Pretend that you've just attended a party and that you're about to transcribe what you witnessed. First, write precisely what you saw. Then write an account that by omitting pertinent information misrepresents what occurred.

3. Document three cases of advertising that conceal evidence for the purpose of persuading.

4. For the next two weeks, read two newspapers. Do you find that they report the same event differently? Is concealed evidence involved?

5. Carefully read the speeches and comments of leading politicians for the next two weeks. How many times do you catch them concealing evidence to persuade? (Undoubtedly there will be some students who lack sufficiently masochistic tendencies to do this exercise.)

6. Fallacies of ambiguity are often used to conceal evidence. For example, some years ago Ocean Spray Cranberry Juice ran a campaign in which they touted the fact that their cranberry juice contained "more food energy" than orange juice. "Food energy," it turned out, meant calories. Find two or three current examples in your local supermarket of fallacies of ambiguity used to conceal evidence.

7. *Consumer Reports* has a feature called "Selling It," which carefully scrutinizes products and claims. This is an excellent source of examples of concealed evidence. Find three or four cases of concealed evidence from recent editions of the "Once Over" column.

SUMMARY

This chapter dealt with statistics. Statistics can be associated with any form of inductive argument: generalization, analogy, hypothesis, or cause. The usual spawning grounds for statistics are studies, polls, and surveys. Before accepting the results of a study, you should satisfy yourself on a variety of questions dealing with who conducted and participated in the study and the methods used.

The same applies to polls. Polls can be reliable when proper sampling procedures are followed. The accuracy of any sample depends largely on randomness, which means that each member of the group has an equal chance of being sampled. Selecting a purely random sample can be difficult and expensive. Of great help is the stratified random sample, a sampling technique in which relevant strata within the group are identified and a random sample from each stratum is selected in proportion to the number of members in each stratum.

Three steps are necessary in using a stratified random sample: (1) Identify the strata within the population, (2) determine the number of instances in each stratum, and (3) randomly select the same proportion from each stratum.

A number of fallacies are associated with the improper use of statistics: biased sample, equivocation, biased question, ambiguous question, false dilemma, and concealed evidence.

The fallacy of biased sample is an argument that contains a sample not representative of the population being studied. Sample bias can originate with the pollster, sampling technique, or respondent. An example of pollster bias is Zest marketers selecting only Zest loyalists to find out what people think of Zest soap. An example of sampling technique bias is *Literary Digest*'s sample consisting of people listed in telephone books and city directories and its counting *only* returned ballots. An example of respondent bias is people telling the pollster what they think the pollster wants to hear and not what they actually believe or do, as in indicating what magazines they prefer.

The fallacy of equivocation, discussed in Chapter 5, can take two forms in statistics: verbal and visual. An example of verbal equivocation in statistics is the ambiguous use of the word *average*. An example of visual equivocation in statistics is a two-axis graph that not only conveys information but an interpretation as well; as when, in presenting unemployment statistics, an illustrator so compresses the graph that it conveys alarm along with statistical information.

The fallacy of biased question is an argument based on the answer to a question that is worded to draw a predetermined reply, for example, "Should the United States continue to spend millions of dollars annually on foreign aid while neglecting needed domestic problems?"

The fallacy of ambiguous question is an argument that contains a vague or equivocal key word or phrase, for example. "Do you think it's a good practice for a woman to be paid less for doing the same job that a man does?"

The fallacy of false dilemma is an argument that erroneously reduces the number of possible alternatives or positions on an issue, for example, "Should the United States support the Israelis or the Arabs in the Middle East?"

The fallacy of concealed evidence is an argument that presents only facts favorable to its conclusion while suppressing relevant but nonsupporting facts. Concealed evidence takes a nonstatistical as well as statistical form. An example of nonstatistically concealed evidence is Pertussin failing to mention the potentially dangerous ingredients in its medicated vaporizer. Comparing apples to oranges is a common strategy of evidence concealers. Comparing the size of competing deodorants' roller-balls under the guise of comparing the deodorants themselves is an example of comparing apples to oranges. An example of statistically concealed evidence is a company's report of its profit picture that conceals such profits as hidden and special depreciation and reserves for contingencies. Of all the informal fallacies, concealed evidence is potentially the most harmful. To detect it, one must have a vast repertory of information, which suggests a solid reason for practical logicians to school themselves in as many fields of knowledge as they possibly can.

Summary Exercises

1. Products are often sold "below list price." For example, compact discs and cassette tapes often sport stickers showing, say, a $14.95 list price and—in bolder print or different colors—"Our Price: $9.95." Find out (if you can) what "list" the famous list price refers to. Do many stores sell at list price? Try to find out.

2. Similar to the "list price" in question 1 is the notorious phrase "Nationally Advertised at $X—Now Only $Y." Pick a product you are suspicious of, and try to find out what is behind the claim "Nationally Advertised at. . . ."

3. Words such as *natural, organic, artificial, lite* or *light* and so on are often used ambiguously. Find three or four examples of concealed evidence in health-oriented claims.

4. One way to raise prices without appearing to do so involves leaving the dollar amount constant but decreasing the amount of product. Recent examples: Coffee sold in 13-ounce containers virtually indistinguishable from previous 16-ounce ones—at the same price; candy products becoming thinner and lighter—while the cardboard backing remains the same size—thus creating the illusion that the amount of candy is constant; spray deodorants decreasing from 12 ounces to 10 ounces, while the can and box remain exactly the same size (in one case, the package even said "NEW!"—meaning *less!*). Find a few current examples from among products with which you are familiar.

5. Speaking of satisfaction surveys, many colleges conduct instructor evaluations based on surveys taken of students currently enrolled in an instructor's courses to evaluate his or her teaching. What do you think of such evaluations? Are these biased samples or not? What factors need to be considered in evaluating such surveys? Have you ever taken or avoided a course based on student evaluation results? If so, what factors were most important in your decision? In your opinion, are such evaluations generally reliable? Discuss.

ADDITIONAL EXERCISES*

Identify the fallacies, if any, in the following passages. Choose from biased sample, equivocation, biased (or ambiguous) question, false dilemma, and concealed evidence. In all cases explain.

1. Test question: Is Freud's libidinal drive explanation an oversimplification of human motivation or an adequate explanation of it?

2. MORTON: Did you know that it's safer to take a trip across country than to drive into town for a movie?
   MEL: I didn't know that.
   MORTON: Amazing, but true. Half of all auto accidents occur within five miles of the driver's home.

3. Gallup Poll question: "In politics, as of today, do you consider yourself a Republican, Democrat, or Independent?"

4. WYATT: I think it'd be unconstitutional to restrict an American's right to own a handgun. And plenty of Americans would agree.
   ELLEN: Oh, come on now. How do you know how many Americans would agree?
   WYATT: Are you kidding? A survey was just conducted that backs up what I'm saying.
   ELLEN: Is that a fact? Who conducted it?
   WYATT: The American Rifle Association.
   ELLEN: I rest my case.

5. RELUCTANT AUTO BUYER: I don't know. The sticker price doesn't seem like such a deal to me.
   SALESPERSON: Okay, tell you what I'm going to do. I'm going to slash three hundred bucks off the sticker price. How's that?
   RAB: Now you're talking.

6. "The extra strength non-aspirin in Datril 500 worked better than 2 leading prescription pain relievers." (Ad for Datril 500)

7. TONI: I'm definitely going on Dr. Linn's high-protein diet.
   JULIE: I don't blame you. It's the quickest way ever to lose weight. And much safer than fasting.

8. Gallup Poll question: "How would you describe yourself—as very conservative, fairly conservative, middle of the road, fairly liberal, or very liberal?"

9. "Incredible. Almost 50 percent of America's children don't get their recommended daily allowance of vitamin C. That's why I'm glad my whole family loves the fresh taste of TANG Instant Breakfast Drink. It gives us a full day's supply of vitamin C." (Florence Henderson, ad for TANG)

10. Administrators at Hudson State College are interested in determining why Hudson graduates attended Hudson and what factors contributed to their successful completion. So they devise a questionnaire, which they send to their graduates. Among the questions asked is this one: "How important does each of the following items appear to you now that you have graduated? (PLEASE CHECK EACH ITEM THAT APPLIES.)" The respondents are asked to react to the items as follows: Not Important, Important, Very Important, No Opinion/Not Applicable. Here are some of the items: writing emphasis, logic course, math course, science courses, behavioral science courses, humanities courses.

11. Gallup Poll question: "Many states have tenure laws, which means that a teacher cannot be fired except by some kind of court procedure. Are you for giving teachers tenure or are you against tenure?"

12. In advertisements and free audiotapes, Dr. Joel Wallach, B.S., D.V.M., N.D. is described as a "Nobel Prize nominee—medicine." One ad for a free seminar by Wallach says, "Dr. Wallach reveals the hidden keys to how 5 modern cultures around the globe consistently enjoy active lives of 120 to 140 years old. Dr. Wallach has been involved in biomedical research and clinical medicine for over 30 years. His research in comparative medicine is based on more than 17,500 autopsies. Dr. Wallach was a nominee for the Nobel Prize of medicine for his stunning discoveries in the prevention of Cystic Fibrosis." (*Redding Record Searchlight,* July 24, 1996)

13. "Dear Ms. _____ :

    "If you sign your name to anything. If you own a piece of property. If you drive a vehicle. If you hire anyone to do any kind of work. If you have pets. If you allow the neighborhood kids to play in your yard or let the deliveryman walk on your sidewalk . . . you put yourself and your savings at risk.

    "It's sad, but true. In today's complex times, every new day brings with it the chance that something may happen to put you in the middle of a very costly legal dispute.

    "The odds, in fact, are almost frightening.

    "According to American Bar Association statistics, if you are an average law-abiding American citizen, *you have a 37% chance of having a legal problem during the next 12 months!*

    "Simply stated, there's a better than 1-in-3 possibility of you needing an attorney very soon. . . ." (Letter to Chemical Bank credit card holders promoting prepaid legal services)

14. STU: What a fraud!
    JAY: What are you so hot about?
    STU: You remember that "winner-take-all" tennis match on TV last spring?
    JAY: Sure. That was great. I hope they televise something like that again this year.
    STU: Oh, yeah? Well, what if I told you that it wasn't a winner-take-all proposition at all?
    JAY: What?
    STU: That's right—everybody who participated got handsomely paid for it.
    JAY: Why, if I had known that I wouldn't have watched it.

15. "Why do doctors recommend Tylenol more than all leading aspirin brands combined? The reason is simple. Tylenol reduces pain and fever as effectively as aspirin but is far less likely to cause side effects. What are some of the common aspirin side effects? Heartburn, nausea, and

allergic reactions are just a few. But perhaps the most common aspirin side effect is stomach bleeding." (Ad for Tylenol)

16. Gallup Poll question: "Do you know what the metric system is?"

17. "*Fact:* Ready-to-eat cereals do not increase tooth decay in children.
    Fact: Ready-sweetened cereals are highly nutritious.
    Fact: There is no more sugar in a one-ounce serving of a ready-sweetened cereal than in an apple or banana or in a serving of orange juice.
    Fact: The per capita sugar consumption in the United States has remained practically unchanged for the last 50 years." (Part of a two-page ad titled "A Statement from Kellogg Company on the Nutritional Value of Ready-Sweetened Cereals")

18. "The American Funeral: Useless tradition for the dead . . . or useful therapy for the living?" (Ad for Clark Metal Funeral Vaults)

19. RON: Smoking pot definitely leads to heroin addiction.
    ROY: Oh, I don't know.
    RON: Figures don't lie. A report by the U.S. Commission of Narcotics on a study of 2,000 narcotics addicts in a prison shows that well over two-thirds smoked marijuana before using heroin.
    ROY: Hmm, I guess I can't argue with that.

20. "When you start an IRA or Keogh retirement program at Glendale Federal, you'll get an immediate substantial deduction. But that's only part of your tax relief. For example, IRA, the Individual Retirement Account, can earn *tax-sheltered* interest of 7.75 percent a year. So if you were to contribute the allowable $1,500 each year, you would have:

AFTER	WITH A TAX-SHELTERED PLAN	WITHOUT A TAX-SHELTERED PLAN	EXTRA MONEY FOR RETIREMENT
10 years	$25,548	$15,758	$7,790
20 years	$74,670	$44,098	$30,571
30 years	$185,653	$95,067	$90,586"

(Ad for Glendale Federal Savings and Loan Association)

21. Gallup Poll question: "There's always much discussion about the qualifications of presidential candidates—their education, age, race, religion, and the like. If your party nominated a generally well-qualified man for president and he happened to be black, would you vote for him?" (Do you think that Gallup should have asked this other question to put the results of the preceding one in proper perspective?: "How likely do you think it is that your party will nominate a black for the presidency sometime in the next twenty years?")

22. "150% Raise for Redding Council Studied" (This headline in the Redding, California, *Record Searchlight,* November 4, 1986, is for an article about an increase in city council salaries from $200/month to $500/

month; the last pay increase for the council was $150 to $200 in January 1977.)

23. A 2-ounce jar of *Royal Kona* freeze-dried instant coffee sold for $7.34 in October 1985. (Hint: What does that cost per pound?)

24. "A vigorous lifestyle puts extra demand on your body. So if you play golf or tennis or swim, walk, jog or bike, you should know about our formula." (Ad for Activitamins)

25. "Over 33⅓% Larger!" (Copy on wrapper of 0.78-ounce candy bar)

26. "S-10 Blazer's always open for adventure, now in a new 4-door model. Bigger than ever before. With 25% more cargo room, and 100% more doors." (Ad for Chevy Blazer S-10)

27. **"NORTHWEST BEATS THE TOP FIVE US AIRLINES IN ON-TIME PERFORMANCE. YOU COULD SAY WE'VE ARRIVED.** The latest results have arrived. And so have we. For the sixth straight month, Northwest has finished ahead of the top five U.S. airlines in on-time performance. And because of service like this, more people are choosing to fly with us than ever before. So why waste time with anyone else? Call your travel agent or Northwest . . ." (This ad for Northwest Airlines includes, in small print, the following: "Source: Department of Transportation Air Travel Consumer Report, 1990. © 1990 Northwest Airlines, Inc.")

28. "40% MORE PROTEIN FROM A GOLDEN GRIDDLE PANCAKE BREAKFAST. If you want your kids to have a nutritious breakfast that's also delicious, give them a hearty Golden Griddle breakfast of pancakes with Golden Griddle Syrup, orange juice and milk. IT CONTAINS 40% MORE PROTEIN THAN A TYPICAL BREAKFAST OF ORANGE JUICE, COLD CEREAL, AND MILK." (Ad for Golden Griddle Pancake Syrup)

29. "Anacin-3 is 100% aspirin-free, more effective than the pain reliever doctors recommend most, pharmacists recommend most, and hospitals use most.

    "In fact, you can't buy a safer, more effective aspirin-free pain reliever than Anacin-3." (Ad for Anacin-3)

30. "In general, do you favor increasing or decreasing the present defense budget, or keeping it the same as it is now?" (Harris and Associates survey question quoted in *Public Opinion Quarterly,* February/March 1985)

CHAPTER 12

Analogical Arguments

Comparisons are odorous.

WILLIAM SHAKESPEARE

The conclusions of inductive arguments always go "beyond" their premises. Indeed, that's induction's most important—and problematic—feature: It helps us increase our store of knowledge and learn from our experiences by identifying patterns, connections, and similarities. A common form of inductive reasoning attempts to derive new information from knowledge of similarities between two things. These comparisons are called analogies, and arguments based on them are known as *analogical arguments.*

Many cases take the form of analogies: "I'm going to see the next Sinbad film because I like what he does"; "We've got to stop Hussein's aggressive moves early, or we'll have another Hitler on our hands." Both examples compare something known (the first arguer's initial reaction to Sinbad films and the second's knowledge of how nations ignored Hitler's early acts of aggression) to something else (a new Sinbad film, Saddam Hussein's acts of aggression). Not all analogies are arguments, however. Sometimes they are descriptions, as when the poet Robert Burns says, "O, my Luve's like a red red rose / That's newly sprung in June: / O my Luve's like a melodie / That's sweetly play'd in tune." Analogies are also used to explain things, as when somebody says, "Thinking is like swimming. Just as in swimming our bodies naturally float on the surface and require great physical exertion to plunge to the bottom; so in thinking it requires great mental exertion to force ourselves away from the superficial surface down into the depths of weighty problems." Here a comparison is made between thinking and swimming to make the point about the effort involved in deep thinking more comprehensible. Both the descriptive and the explanatory use of analogies are nonargumentative analogies.

An analogical argument is an inductive argument that uses known similarities that two things share as evidence for concluding that the two things are similar in additional ways. The two things compared in analogies are known as *analogs.* The basic form of analogical arguments looks something like this: "If entity *A* has characteristics *w, x, y,* and *z;* and if entity *B* has characteristics *w, x,* and *y;* then entity *B* would probably also have characteristic *z.*" Thus we can see that any analogical argument extends what is known to be true about members of one class to new objects standing outside that class. In other words, analogical arguments are another form of inductive generalization.

Note, too, that all arguments have an analogical component. In the case of deductive arguments, the analogical component is that all arguments sharing a specific form are valid—or invalid. For example, any argument, regardless of its content, that has the form *modus ponens,* is valid. In the case of inductive generalizations, the analogical component is that the object of the generalization is similar to the instances upon which it is based. To simplify even further, induction always involves both assumptions and demonstrations of similarity, or analogous relationships.

THE VALUE OF ANALOGICAL ARGUMENTS

We routinely rely on analogical arguments. Consider this example. Wally's just graduated from high school and is waiting to enter community college in the fall. He's trying to figure out how much time to allow for homework so he can look for a job that won't involve so many hours in which he falls behind in school. One day Wally discusses this with his friend J. R. J. R.'s a year older than Wally, and has completed two semesters of general education courses at the local college.

In high school, J. R. got As by studying three hours a week. In college, J. R. discovered that he had to study six hours a week to get As. The two friends then compare J. R.'s experience in high school to Wally's. They note that they had almost identical grade point averages, and that they took many of the same classes from the same teachers. Using this information, J. R. and Wally draw a comparison between J. R.'s need to study twice as hard in college as he did in high school, and the number of hours Wally will *probably* have to study when he gets to college. They conclude that for Wally—as well as for J. R.—college will take twice as much studying as high school did.

Wally and J. R.'s reasoning rests on two analogies: (1) between their high school experience and (2) between J. R.'s high school and college experience. From these they conclude that, based on the similarities between their high school experiences, a similarity will also exist between their college experiences.

How good are these arguments? Actually, they are not very good since they lack thoroughness: How many units is J. R. taking in college and will Wally take the same number? Is J. R. working? If so, how many hours? What courses is J. R. taking? Is Wally planning to take the same courses? Will Wally be able to get the same instructors? Are Wally and J. R. equally motivated to go to college? And so on.

Most analogies are not good ones. But as difficult as it can be to construct cogent analogical arguments, it is often worth the effort. One of the most fruitful— and controversial—contemporary uses of analogical reasoning is in the area of medical research. When medical researchers experiment with animals, they do so based on their assessment of the similarities between an animal's nervous system, digestive tract, mucous membranes, and so on, and a human's. These similarities are used as the basis for testing drugs, cosmetics, and so forth, on animals. To the extent that the animal's reactions are analogous to a human's, researchers can evaluate products. Those who object to animal experimentation as cruel sometimes argue that cell cultures and other nonanimal alternatives offer enough relevant similarities to provide researchers with the same—or even higher—quality evidence as animal research. Part of the dispute, then, is over what constitutes a sufficient analogical relationship.

To see how analogical arguments can provide valuable insights, even suggest a viewpoint, consider the evolution of scientific knowledge about the atom. The earliest problem scientists faced was figuring out how the atom's positive and negative electric ions were arranged so that atoms could exist as stable entities and not simply fly apart. Experiments by English physicist Ernest Rutherford indicated that the atom's positive charge was highly concentrated. So Rutherford and, later, Niels Bohr suggested that the atom was analogous to the solar system. An atom, they said, is like a miniature solar system. Just as the sun is in the center of the solar system, so all of the positive charge is in the center of the atom. Similarly, just as the planets orbit the sun, so electrons move around the center of the atom while carrying the negative charge.

In effect, then, Rutherford and Bohr saw the solar system as a model for the atom, arguing that the structure of the atom is analogous to the structure of the solar system. Even today this model is used in elementary discussions of atomic physics.[37]

In fact, the history of science is studded with examples of how instructive analogical reasoning can be. The classic illustration perhaps is Archimedes' discovery that a body immersed in fluid loses in weight an amount equal to the weight of the fluid it displaces. Supposedly the discovery occurred while Archimedes was trying to help solve a problem for King Hieron. It seemed the king wanted to know what metals had been used in his crown. But he didn't want to destroy the crown by melting it down to find out. Archimedes solved the problem by using an analogy. Having observed that the water in his bath rose as his body displaced it, the brilliant Greek mathematician reasoned by analogy that a certain weight of gold would displace less water than silver of the same weight, because gold was smaller in volume. He tested the crown, and found that it was, in fact, made of impure gold.

A similar example of analogical reasoning underlay Copernicus's revolutionary theory of a sun-centered universe. Boating near the bank of a river one day, Copernicus is said to have been struck by the illusion that the bank, and not his boat, was moving. Could a similar illusion produce the common belief that the sun moves around a stationary Earth? The thought intrigued Copernicus. Subsequently, he went on to overturn our understanding of the universe.

---

37. See Ronald N. Giere, *Understanding Scientific Reasoning,* 3rd ed. (New York: Holt, Rinehart and Winston, 1991), pp. 23–24.

These examples notwithstanding, even when analogies are good, they don't prove anything. They must be tested and proved. Recall that Benjamin Franklin, having observed a number of resemblances between electric sparks and lightning, wondered if lightning possibly could be a form of electricity. But he didn't stop there. He saw this insight as an explanation, a hypothesis, that needed to be tested and proved. Of course he subsequently did just that. He conducted a test with his kite-and-key experiment. It proved that lightning was, indeed, electric. The analogy itself *proved* nothing.

EXERCISE 12-1 *

Indicate whether the following are argumentative or nonargumentative uses of analogy. Explain your answers.

1. It's so hot today you could fry an egg on the sidewalk.

2. A family is like a nation. Both consist of individuals related by blood, culture, and interests. And just as a nation is best governed by an elected head, so is a family. Let the family members decide who will govern it.

3. BRAD: Have you heard Willie Nelson's latest LP?
   BELLE: I don't have to to know I'll like it. He's never done an LP I haven't liked.

4. "The bees have only one king, the flocks only one head, the herds only one teacher. Can you believe that in heaven the supreme power is divided and that the entire majesty of that true, divine Authority is broken up?" (Prudentius)

5. Instructor: I have no doubt that the vast majority of students will pass this test. They've passed the last three tests I've given, haven't they?

6. "In nearly all of the non-Communist world, socialism, meaning public ownership of industrial enterprises, is a spent slogan. Like promises to enforce the antitrust laws in the United States, it is no longer a political program but an overture to nostalgia." (John Kenneth Galbraith, *The New Industrial State*)

7. "One of the pleasures of science is to see two distant and apparently unrelated pieces of information suddenly come together. In a flash what one knows doubles or triples in size. It is like working on two large but separate sections of a jigsaw puzzle and, almost without realizing it until the moment it happens, finding that they fit into one." (John Tyler Bonner, "Hormones in Social Amoebae and Mammals," *Scientific American,* November 1969)

8. "The objections which have been brought against a standing army, and they are many and weighty, and deserve to prevail, may also at last be brought against a standing government. The government itself,

which is only the mode which the people have chosen to execute their will, is equally liable to be abused and perverted before the people can act through it." (Henry David Thoreau, "On the Duty of Civil Disobedience")

9. "We are seeing the end of our adolescence. In its reincarnation as guardian advisor and donor to half the world the United States is emerging from its teens. A certain glow begins to fade. The hard, gray thoughts of maturity take possession and there is some danger of the cynicism that is itself immature." (Eric Sevareid, *This is Eric Sevareid* [New York: McGraw-Hill, 1964])

10. "We have waited for more than 340 years for our constitutional and God-given rights. The nations of Asia and Africa are moving with jetlike speed toward gaining political independence, but we still creep at horse-and-buggy pace toward gaining a cup of coffee at a lunch counter." (Martin Luther King, Jr., "Letter from Birmingham Jail")

11. "One of the most popular [explanations for student revolt]—too many students still live in an adolescent stage of parent rejection, and if a university insists on maintaining its role of parental substitute, it must be prepared to face rebellious offspring." (Bill Ward, "Why Students Revolt," *The Nation,* January 25, 1966)

12. "Father was always a bit skeptical of this story, and of the new flying machines, otherwise he believed everything he read. Until 1909 no one in Lower Binfield believed that human beings would ever learn to fly. The official doctrine was that if God had meant us to fly He'd have given us wings. Uncle Ezekiel couldn't help retorting that if God had meant us to ride He'd have given us wheels, but even he didn't believe in the new flying machines." (George Orwell, *Coming Up for Air*)

13. "If a single cell, under appropriate conditions, becomes a man in the space of a few years, there can surely be no difficulty in understanding how, under appropriate conditions, a cell may, in the course of untold millions of years, give origin to the human race." (Herbert Spencer, *Principles of Biology*)

14. "Amidst all the earnest wringing of hands, nobody is so impolite as to point out that the taking of stands against drugs is like taking a stand against death, communism, or the rain." (Lewis H. Lapham, *The Sacramento Bee Forum,* September 21, 1986)

15. "Accepting the claims of astrology is much like accepting the laws pertaining to property rights and slavery set up over three thousand years ago by the rulers of Babylon, and using their theories of medicine as well, for that is when the rules that are still used by modern astrologers today were devised." (James "The Amazing" Randi, *Flim-Flam!* [Buffalo, N.Y.: Prometheus Books, 1982])

ANALOGICAL ARGUMENTS AND THE COGENCY CRITERIA

An analogical argument is no stronger than the basic relationship between the two things upon which it rests.

Cogent analogical arguments must provide reasonable, relevant, and sufficient evidence for their conclusions. The points of comparison must be true—that is, they must meet the reasonableness criterion. They must also be relevant. A simple example illustrates what happens when these two criteria are not met: "Since my new car is the same shade of red as my old car, I can expect to get the same kind of great performance from the new that I got from the old one." Clearly, a car's color is not relevant to its performance. The implied premise that a car's performance is a function of its color is unreasonable. When comparing an older car to a new one in terms of performance, color is also irrelevant.

As with any other kind of induction, the sufficiency of the evidence to support the conclusion of an analogical argument is the key evaluative problem. In evaluating an analogical argument, we're really interested in determining how strong the connection is between the analogs. Three different factors affect the sufficiency of analogical arguments: (1) the number of entities involved in the comparison; (2) the number of relevant likenesses between the entities; and (3) the number and nature of differences between the entities. We'll consider each.

Number of Entities Involved

Ordinarily, the more instances upon which an analogical argument is based, the greater the likelihood of its conclusion. This point is obvious when you recall what we said about generalizations: Ordinarily, the larger the sample, the more representative of the class it is. The more courses Wally and J. R. have based their analogies on, the stronger the analogies become.

Number of Relevant Likenesses

The greater the number of relevant likenesses among the instances upon which an analogical argument is based, the more likely its conclusion. The fact that Wally and J. R. took many of the same courses from the same teachers strengthens their primary analogy. This factor is actually an extension and refinement of the first. It protects us from constructing an analogy based on a large number of only marginally similar instances.

Number and Nature of Differences

Frequently, things being compared differ in a number of aspects. Certain kinds of differences actually strengthen an analogy; others weaken or destroy it.

The greater the number of strengthening differences between analogs, the stronger the analogy. The smaller the number of weakening differences (disanalogies), the stronger the analogy. Strengthening differences in J. R. and Wally's first argument include the fact that they took various courses different semesters. This minimizes the likelihood that their similar experiences in high school came from studying together or even cheating together. Consider J. R. and Wally's second argument, based on a comparison of J. R.'s high school and college experiences. If they know other students who report an increase of approximately 100 percent in study time from high school to college, their comparison between high school and college will be strengthened.

But if they discover no pattern between average high school and college study time among even a half-dozen students, these *disanalogies* will effectively destroy that analogy. Other examples of possible disanalogies or weakening differences might include learning that J. R. has been taking the maximum number of units possible on a pass-fail basis—something that Wally's pre-med major prohibits. It may turn out that J. R. is taking six units less per term than Wally plans. Obviously, the more disanalogies uncovered, the weaker the argument becomes.

EXERCISE 12-2 *

A. Evaluate the following analogical arguments in terms of the criteria previously explained. Identify any criteria violated by answering these questions: a) What's being compared? b) In what ways are the things being compared alike? c) In what ways are they different? d) What's the analogical conclusion? e) Is the argument strong or weak?

1. Children are very much like puppies—they have to be trained and taught how to behave. Otherwise, they'll grow up to be wild and troublesome.

2. Of course limiting property taxes will result in the curtailment of many social services. But that can't be helped. Remember: If you want to make an omelet, you must break some eggs.

3. A college education is like the foundation of a house. Both must be solid and adequate to support what will rest on it. And just as you'd not think of laying a foundation without regard to the structure it must support, you should not commence a formal education without knowing what it is you want to do with your life.

4. People shouldn't be any more critical of advertisements than they are of poetry. Just as a poem deals in fantasy, hope, and promise, so does the well-crafted ad. In fact, the purpose of the ad, like the poem, is to go beyond reality and offer illusion. So the next time you criticize an ad as foolishly unrealistic, ask yourself if you'd say the same of your favorite poetry.

5. "If you cut up a large diamond into little bits, it will entirely lose the value it had as a whole; and an army divided up into small bodies of soldiers loses all its strength. So a great intellect sinks to the level of an ordinary one, as soon as it is interrupted and disturbed, its attention distracted and drawn off from the matter in hand: for its supe-

riority depends upon its power of concentration—of bringing all its strength to bear upon one theme, in the same way as a concave mirror collects into one point all the rays of light that strike upon it." (Arthur Schopenhauer, "On Noise")

6. "Sentiment is all right up in the part of the city where your home is. But downtown, no. Down there the dog that snaps the quickest gets the bone. Friendship is very nice for a Sunday afternoon when you're sitting around the dinner table with your relations, talking about the sermon that morning. But nine o'clock Monday morning, notions should be brushed aside like cobwebs from a machine. I never took stock in a man who mixed up business with anything else. He can go into other things outside of business hours but when he's in the office, he ought not to have a relation in the world—and least of all a poor relation." (Dan Drew, founder of Drew Theological Seminary)

7. Where are wars won or lost? On the gridiron, that's where. For the gridiron is a battlefield where the many learn to function as a single, well-oiled fighting machine. It's where a man learns to sacrifice self for the good of the team and to endure pain, even perform with it. And mostly the gridiron is where men learn to hold on to what's theirs, even if it's only a few inches of mud. Sure, football may be brutal, perhaps barbarous. But what's war—a Sunday-school picnic?

8. Sex is just as natural as eating. And just as we don't regard an appetite for variety in diet as strange or unnatural, why should we consider any less normal a desire for a variety of lovers?

9. Americans have become energy junkies. We need our energy fix on a regular basis and we're willing to pay anything for it. That's why the Arabs can so successfully taunt, insult, even blackmail us. They're our neighborhood pusher, and as long as they can satisfy our addiction, we'll do their bidding.

10. "If the nature of the work is properly appreciated and applied, it will stand in the same relation to the higher faculties as food is to the physical body. It nourishes and enlivens the higher man and urges him to produce the best he is capable of. It directs his free will along the proper course and disciplines the animal in him into progressive channels. It furnishes an excellent background for man to display his scale of values and develop his personality." (J. C. Kumarappa, *Economy of Permanence*)

B. Each of the following analogical arguments is followed by several additional premises. Indicate whether the premises would strengthen, weaken, or have no effect on the conclusion. In all cases use the criteria for evaluating analogies.

1. On two separate occasions you have bought a pair of shoes at Naturalizer. The shoes wore exceptionally well. So now that you're in the

market for another pair of shoes, you infer you'll again get a good pair at Naturalizer.

    a. Suppose you'd bought shoes there on four occasions, rather than three.

    b. Suppose a number of your friends also had bought shoes there that wore well.

    c. Suppose that two sweaters you'd bought there also wore well.

    d. Suppose that you expect to get a full three years' wear from your new shoes, although the others lasted only two years.

    e. Suppose you expect to get at least a year's wear from your new shoes, again assuming the other two pairs wore well for two years each.

2. The first three films by Woody Allen you saw were comedies situated in New York, starring Allen and Diane Keaton. When you hear that Allen has come out with another film, you assume it's a comedy situated in New York and stars Allen and Keaton.

    a. Suppose that the film, unlike the others, was made after the off-the-screen Allen–Keaton romance had cooled off.

    b. Suppose that you merely infer that the film is a comedy.

    c. Suppose you read that Allen had spent considerable time in California during the time the film was shot.

    d. Suppose that you merely infer that there is a female lead.

    e. Suppose you infer that the film is a comedy situated in New York and stars Keaton but not Allen.

3. Several of Myron's relatives, including his mother and father, have died of heart disease. Myron is therefore convinced that at some point he, too, will develop heart disease.

    a. Suppose that Myron smokes, but none of his relatives did.

    b. Suppose that Myron is the only member of his family ever to be consistently underweight.

    c. Suppose Myron jogs two miles a day, whereas his relatives were sedentary.

    d. Suppose Myron prefers the diet of his parents.

    e. Suppose Myron is the only college graduate in his family.

    f. Suppose Myron merely infers that he probably has a tendency to develop heart disease.

4. Stella has taken three philosophy courses and found them very stimulating and worthwhile. So she enrolls for a fourth, fully expecting to enjoy and profit from it.

   a. Suppose her previous philosophy courses were in ethics, epistemology, and religion.

   b. Suppose all her previous courses had been taught by the same professor who is scheduled to teach the present one.

   c. Suppose Stella had found the three previous courses the most exciting intellectual experiences of her collegiate life.

   d. Suppose the three previous courses were in general ethics, business ethics, and medical ethics, whereas the present one will be in metaphysics.

   e. Suppose the three previous courses had all met at 10 AM, and the present one is scheduled to meet at 7 PM.

   f. Suppose Stella expects the course will prove to be the most enriching of any course she'll take in college.

FAULTY ANALOGY

The fallacy of faulty analogy occurs when an analogical argument overlooks relevant, weakening differences between the things compared. Like other forms of induction, analogical arguments are relatively strong or relatively weak depending on whether or not they meet the cogency criteria. When evaluating analogical arguments, it is especially important to make sure that no relevant, weakening differences between the things compared are ignored. Since even strong analogies never *prove* anything, we must take special care not to be persuaded by weak or faulty analogies.

Questionable analogies are often used as a substitute for cogent argument, as in this example from a letter to the editor attempting to compare reading what the author judged to be "heathen books" with allowing children to play with guns: "If we allow children to read *The Wizard of Oz* and Mark Twain's *Letters to Earth*, we might as well put guns to their heads and let them shoot themselves." In order to evaluate this analogy, we must ask certain questions concerning the two things compared: books and guns.

How similar is reading *The Wizard of Oz*, or any book, to a child playing with a loaded gun? Books and guns have different natures and functions. Books inform and convey information, among other things; guns do not. Guns are designed to shoot things; they are physically dangerous. Books are not. The kind of damage caused by an accident with a gun cannot be compared to an "accident" with a book (whatever that might mean).

Here's another example from an essay titled "On Suicide," by the great Scot philosopher David Hume: "It would be no crime to divert the Nile or Danube from its course, were I able to effect such purposes. Where then is the crime of turning a few ounces of blood from their natural channel?" Is suicide really like altering the course of a river? Is suicide nothing more than "turning a few ounces of blood from their natural channel"? Altering the course of a river does not destroy it; suicide destroys its victim. Suicide victims have friends and families who often suffer greatly; rivers do not. Rivers are not people; blood is not water. When we ask—*and answer*—these questions, we identify serious weakening differences between suicide and altering the course of a river. Hume's analogy is faulty.

Faulty comparisons are often used to create immediate, intense emotions. Consider this one: "Reducing welfare benefits amounts to depriving innocent children of food and drink. What kind of person can push a crying, starving child away, while dining on plentiful gourmet fare?" Rarely are we given any extended justification to support such questionable analogies.

EXERCISE 12-3 *

Identify the analogies in the following passages and determine whether they are reliable or faulty. Explain.

1. JAY: I think student government is not only a waste of time but can actually be counterproductive.
   JAN: But shouldn't students have a say about what goes on at their school?
   JAY: Look, I've seen what's happened in houses where parents let their kids run things their own way.

2. TED: You know, this whole multibillion dollar bailout of the savings and loan industry by the federal government is a real ripoff.
   PAT: Why do you say that?
   TED: For one simple reason. Imagine what the government's reaction would be if I asked it to subsidize my antique business because I mismanaged it.
   PAT: It'd probably tell you to get lost.
   TED: Exactly.

3. TRISH: All this talk about reducing foreign aid—I think it's downright irresponsible.
   TOM: "Irresponsible"? That's pretty strong, isn't it?
   TRISH: I don't think so. You'd call a parent who wouldn't care for his or her children irresponsible, wouldn't you? By the same token, if we don't take care of the less-fortunate nations of the world, we're being irresponsible.

4. BUDDY: I'm convinced that Venus is habitable.
   BERTHA: I doubt it.
   BUDDY: Think about it for a minute. Venus is roughly the same radius

as Earth. And it has approximately the same mass. You can't say that about any other planet in our galaxy.

BERTHA: So, you're saying that since there's life on Earth, there probably is life on Venus?

BUDDY: Right.

5. GEORGE: I'm convinced that the mind really can produce physical changes in the body.

GINGER: Oh that's ridiculous. Does the smoke from a locomotive have any influence on the movement of a train?

GEORGE: Well, no, but—

GINGER: Well, then, there's your answer.

6. PHILLIP: Cigarette?

MORRIS: No thanks.

PHILLIP: What! You've given up smoking?

MORRIS: You said it. Yesterday I took a good look at my fingers. They're yellow! Can you imagine what my lungs must look like?

PHILLIP: Wow!—I never thought of that. Pass me that ashtray, will you?

7. STUDENT LEADER: I think it's time colleges started paying students for high scholastic achievement.

DEAN OF STUDENTS: Paying? As in dollars and cents?

STUDENT LEADER: You said it. Business gives its top people bonuses and commissions doesn't it? And look at the performances it gets out of them.

8. DISILLUSIONED TEACHER: I've had it. No more teaching for me. I'll pump gas first.

COLLEAGUE: Oh come now. You're just a little discouraged today.

DISILLUSIONED TEACHER: A little discouraged? The hell you say! I'm desperate! What I do every day in the classroom is tantamount to casting real pearls before real swine.

9. COMMUNITY COLLEGE BOARD MEMBER: I think we should start charging students tuition.

COLLEGE PRESIDENT: I'm unequivocally opposed to that. Why it would be like charging for withdrawing books from the library.

COMMUNITY COLLEGE BOARD MEMBER: Is that so? Well, I make my children pay for their toys and treats. And believe me, they appreciate them all the more because they have to pay for them. I think that's pretty clear evidence that we should start charging tuition.

10. CARMEN: You're not going to put that saccharin in your coffee, are you?

CARL: Sure, I'm on a diet.

CARMEN: But don't you realize that saccharin has caused cancer in laboratory rats?

CARL: Really! Pass me the sugar, will you?

SUMMARY

In this chapter we learned about inductive analogies and analogical arguments.

We learned that an analogical argument is an inductive argument which uses known similarities that two things share as evidence for concluding the two things are similar in additional ways. The two things compared in analogies are known as analogs. The basic form of analogical arguments looks something like this: "If entity A has characteristics w, x, y, and z; and if entity B has characteristics w, x, and y; then entity B would probably also have characteristic z."

We learned that cogent analogical arguments must meet the criteria of reasonableness, relevancy, and sufficiency. We noted that even when the reasonableness and relevancy criteria are met, the sufficiency criterion requires that analogies must meet the following requirements: (1) comparison based on enough similar entities to establish a clear similarity; (2) enough relevant likenesses to establish a fundamental similarity between the analogs; and, (3) the nature and number of any dissimilarities, and that sound analogical arguments must meet the same criteria as any other inductive generalization.

The stronger the connection between the things compared in an analogical argument, the stronger the argument. Four specific factors affect the cogency of analogical arguments: (1) the number of instances involved in the comparison; (2) the number of relevant likenesses between entities; (3) the number and nature of relevant differences between the entities; and (4) the strength of the conclusion relative to the premises. If the number of significant differences between analogs, known as disanalogies, is great enough, the analogy is weakened or destroyed. The fallacy of faulty analogy occurs when an analogical argument rests upon a questionable analogy. Violating any of the criteria discussed above for establishing strong analogies produces a faulty analogy. Although analogies can provide valuable insights and viewpoints, especially in science, in the last analysis, even good analogies prove nothing.

Summary Exercises

1. Give an example of a faulty analogy and explain why it is faulty by specifically listing weakening differences between the things compared.

2. Give an example of an analogy that you find both reliable and useful.

3. Discuss and explain what's meant by saying that "analogies never prove anything."

ADDITIONAL EXERCISES

One of the most common sources of analogies is speculation about the origins of the universe, life, and God. Consider the following:

1. In 1953, Stanley Miller, a biochemist at the University of Chicago, provided the first empirical evidence for the possibility that organic life

could evolve from inorganic matter. Miller tried to replicate conditions as they would have been early in the Earth's formation. He put methane, ammonia, and hydrogen into a glass container. As the chemicals were mixed with steam coming from boiling water, they passed through glass tubes and flowed across electrodes that were constantly emitting a spark. At the end of a week, the gases were separated from a soupy liquid. Upon analysis, this liquid was shown to contain organic compounds and amino acids—building blocks for organic matter and life forms. In the decades since Miller's experiment, many of the necessary components in living organisms have been produced in laboratory conditions thought to mimic conditions during various stages of the Earth's development. Many people see this as evidence that life evolved without Divine intervention. Carefully analyze the analogical argument upon which this conclusion rests.

2. Perhaps the most famous analogical argument is the "argument from design" used to prove the existence of God. One popular version is based on eighteenth-century Anglican William Paley's watchmaker analogy. Paley compared the universe to a watch, pointing out that the existence of a watch always implies the existence of a watchmaker. The universe, Paley argued, contains much more complexity than the finest watch. Thus, he continued, its creator must be at least as much greater than a watchmaker as the universe is greater than a watch. His contemporary, David Hume, summarized the general form of such arguments this way:

> Look round the world: Contemplate the whole and every part of it: You will find it to be nothing but one great machine, subdivided into an infinite number of lesser machines, which again admit of subdivision to a degree beyond what human senses and faculties can trace and explain. All these various machines, and even their most minute parts, are adjusted to each other with an accuracy which ravishes into admiration all men who have ever contemplated them. The curious adapting of means to ends, throughout nature, resembles exactly, though it much exceeds, the productions of human contrivance—of human design, thought, wisdom, and intelligence. Since therefore the effects resemble each other, we are led to infer, by all the rules of analogy, that the causes also resemble, and that the Author of Nature is somewhat similar to the mind of man, though possessed of much larger faculties, proportioned to the grandeur of the work which he has executed.[38]

Analyze this version of the argument from design.

3. Now analyze this analogy offered as a refutation of the argument from design:

> Now, if we survey the universe, so far it falls under our knowledge, it bears a great resemblance to an animal or organized body, and seems actuated

---

38. David Hume, *Dialogues Concerning Natural Religion*, Pt. XI. (Yes—*that* David Hume.)

with a like principle of life and motion. A continual circulation of matter in it produces no disorder; a continual waste in every part is incessantly repaired; the closest sympathy is perceived throughout the entire system; and each part or member, in performing its proper offices, operates both to its own preservation and to that of the whole. The world, therefore, I infer, is an animal; and the Deity is the *soul* of the world actuating it, actuated by it.[39]

4. Discuss the problems of arguing from analogy in relationship to the origins of the universe, life, and the existence of God.

5. "Scuba diving, roller skating, jogging and tennis are all part of today's life-style that's full of life. A style that is shared by the sporty and efficient Chevy Monza." (Ad for 1980 Chevy Monza)

6. INTERVIEWER: Your honor, do you think you can fairly rule on motor accidents when, in fact, you yourself have never driven a car?
   JUDGE: Certainly. Remember, I also try rape cases.

7. "There is absolutely no reason for . . . any . . . presidential candidate to apologize for raising the matter of Chappaquiddick vis-à-vis Senator Kennedy. To the contrary Chappaquiddick is as much a part of Senator Kennedy's background as is the date of his birth. Considering its implications it merits serious discussion and consideration." (Letter to *Time*, November 5, 1979, p. 5)

8. "Let no one belittle coaching experience in preparation for a position as college president. As coach, you must win or leave. I suggest this is similar to the president's position." (McNeese State University athletic director Jack Doland on the occasion of being elected the university's new president)

9. "A judge once said: 'The death penalty is a warning, just like a lighthouse throwing its beams out to sea. We hear about shipwrecks but we do not hear about the ships the lighthouse guides safely on their way. We do not have proof of the number of ships it saves, but we do not tear the lighthouse down.'" (J. Edgar Hoover, then-director, FBI)

10. I am the father of two daughters. When I hear this argument that we can't protect freedom in Europe, in Asia, or in our own hemisphere and still meet our domestic problems, I think it's a phony argument. It is just like saying that I can't take care of Luci because I have Lynda Bird. We have to take care of both of them and meet them and we have to meet them head on." (Lyndon B. Johnson when president)

11. "It can run a mile cheaper than you can. The Rabbit Diesel runs a mile, and burns about 1.4 cents worth of fuel. Compared to that you're a

---

39. Ibid.

guzzler. If you weigh 150 pounds, you'd burn around 90 calories per mile. Figure that as a mere fourth of a fast-food cheeseburger, and comes to about 18 cents. Fact is, if you were a car, you couldn't afford *you*. So, don't walk. Run for a Volkswagen Rabbit Diesel." (Ad for Volkswagen Rabbit Diesel)

12. Fundamentalist Muslim defense of state executions of those convicted of adultery, prostitution, or homosexuality: "If your finger suffers from gangrene, what do you do? Letting the whole hand and then the body become filled with gangrene, or cutting the finger off? . . . Corruption, corruption. We have to eliminate corruption." (*Time,* October 22, 1979, p. 57)

13. Apartment tenant commenting on landlords' "no children allowed" policies: "When I first moved into this complex, the ages of the tenants varied from twenty-one to thirty-five. Then the older generation moved in and most of my friends said how the place was going to pot. Well, today do you know that the place is a better one because of them? That's why I think it would not be bad to allow children here. I think it would be a better place because of them." (*Sixty Minutes,* January 22, 1978)

14. Spokesperson for the Golden Empire Transit District explaining why residents should be willing to subsidize the district's transportation service: "GET provides a service the same as police and fire departments do. Think of it this way; how often do you need the fire department or police, on the average? Sometime the average person is going to need a transit system that serves his needs . . . especially if the energy crunch becomes real enough to force people to consider riding the buses all the time."

15. Political commentator about to evaluate a freshman senator's first year in office: The senator has been in Congress for some nine months. Since this is the normal human gestation period, it is time to see what new policies he has given or is about to give birth to and to grade these policies.

16. Former Los Angeles Police Chief Ed Davis defending capital punishment as disallowing the murderer from murdering again: "It's like shooting a rabid dog—you don't kill it as a warning to other dogs. You kill it so innocent people will be protected." (Editorial, *Bakersfield Californian,* November 2, 1977)

17. In an article titled "The Linguistic Gap between Men and Women," sociolinguist Deborah Tannen discusses how different language patterns can create communication difficulties between men and women. Tannen asserts that men and women learn different ways of communicating, which though not better or worse, are different enough to create problems. She illustrates this with the following analogy: "Whenever linguistic habits differ, each person is likely to make the other feel manipulated

simply in an attempt to get comfortable in the situation. For a nonverbal analog, imagine two people who have slightly different senses of appropriate distance between conversants. The one who feels comfortable standing farther away keeps backing off to adjust the space, but the conversational partner who expects to stand closer keeps advancing to close up the space, so they move together down the hall until one is pinned against a wall." (*Sacramento Bee Forum,* October 26, 1986)

18. "The proposed economic sanctions against South Africa, now being bruited about in Congress and the media, bear comparison to the sprinkling of holy water on money received in plain brown envelopes from the purveyors of munitions and pornography." (Lewis H. Lapham, "End Paper," *San Francisco Chronicle's World,* July 27, 1986)

19. "X-rated movies are boring. Generally it's a novelty buy. But it's like peanut butter—a little goes a long way." (Arthur Morowitz, *Sunday Punch,* October 19, 1986)

20. "An astronomer is somebody who can tell you about faraway worlds that are hostile to human safety and well-bein'. In that sense, he's like a Washington correspondent." (Oxnard N. Thorpe, quoted by Richard K. Morse, *Sunday Punch,* October 19, 1986)

21. President Reagan suggesting a way to pacify those who object to the sight of oil rigs off their beaches: "Maybe we ought to take some of those liberty ships out of mothballs and anchor one at each one of the oil platforms between that and offshore, because people never object to seeing a ship at sea." ("Reagan Supports Watt Stand," *Santa Barbara Evening News Press,* August 5, 1981, p. A21)

CHAPTER 13

Cause

To know truly is to know by causes.

FRANCIS BACON

Cases often contain causal claims. For example, a case for quitting smoking because "You'll get cancer," is likely to rest on current scientific claims linking smoking to lung cancer. In other words, the case is built on claims that smoking *causes* lung cancer. A case for studying more often because "Your grades reflect your study habits," most likely depends on a *causal connection* between study habits and grades. Cases involving causal arguments are numerous and often involve important issues. Consequently we need to know a little bit about causation in order to evaluate the cases. In this chapter we'll learn how to evaluate causal inductive arguments from a logical perspective. In complex, technical cases, we will probably need to defer to experts. But, as we'll see, a basic understanding of causal arguments can help us distinguish cogent, plausible causal claims, from insufficient, unreasonable, or irrelevant claims.

We make causal claims daily, even though we don't necessarily use the term *cause* itself. Such terms as *make, prevent, produce, lead to,* and the like, can and often do imply causal connections. There are literally thousands of such expressions and terms, all of which carry the idea of causation.

Such terms become part of what are called causal statements or causal hypotheses. *Let's define a causal statement as a statement that asserts a relationship between two things, such that one is claimed to effect the other.* Thus, "Vitamin C prevents the common cold," "Smoking causes cancer," "Penicillin can cure syphilis," "Melatonin cures insomnia"—all are causal statements or hypotheses asserting causal relationships.

Naturally, we'd be pretty foolish to accept or formulate a causal statement without reasons, that is, without causal arguments. *A causal argument is an argument that attempts to support a causal statement.* Causal arguments are another common form of inductive reasoning, and these abound. Just think about the countless commercial and public service messages you've seen, causal arguments

FRANK & ERNEST ® by Bob Thaves

I FORGET WHAT THE TV COMMERCIAL CALLED IT, BUT YOU SPRAY IT ALL OVER YOU AND SUDDENLY YOU'RE IN A TUXEDO WITH A VERY ATTRACTIVE WOMAN.

MEN'S TOILETRIES

© 1996 by NEA, Inc.   THAVES 7-15

E-mail: FandEBobT@AOL.COM

FRANK & ERNEST reprinted by permission of Newspaper Enterprise Association, Inc.

about anything from toothpaste to nuclear energy. In your reading you come across causal arguments that relate to economics, politics, education, the arts—every field.

So, given the centrality of causal argument in our lives, we should take a close look at this form of inductive reasoning. That's what this chapter aims to do. We're going to find out what a good causal argument consists of and consider some common informal fallacies associated with causal reasoning. But before we do that, we must look at this slippery idea of causation so that we understand more precisely what a causal statement is asserting.

THE IDEA OF CAUSE

As we just saw, *a causal statement is a statement that asserts a relationship between two things, such that one is claimed to effect the other.* A simpler way to say this is that a causal statement is one that reduces to the claim that *A* causes *B*. But just what does it mean to say that *A* **causes** *B*—that the use of marijuana leads to heroin addiction, that cigarette smoking causes lung cancer, that oral contraceptives cause fatal blood clots? There is perhaps no more elusive a question in the philosophy of science.

An important point in understanding cause is that a connection often exists between cause and control.[40] And a sound causal argument recognizes this connection. In the case of disease, for example, the control interest is obvious: extermination of the disease. In general, a causal statement implies an interest in control. "Vitamin B_1 can prevent beriberi" implies that we have an interest in *controlling* that disease. Further, any attribution of cause depends on what we know at a particular time. What we assign as cause also is influenced by our own individual interests.

---

40. See Perry Weddle, *Argument: A Guide to Critical Thinking* (New York: McGraw-Hill, 1978), pp. 162–65.

STUDY HINT

Any causal statement generally implies an interest in control.

To illustrate how idiosyncratic interests affect our attribution of cause, let's take the case of Pete's being late for a very important project-planning meeting at work. Pete was detoured from his normal route because a fire had cordoned off traffic. As a result, he arrived in the plant parking lot at 8:55, five minutes before the meeting. Now, ordinarily, this would be ample time for him to park and be punctual. But his usual parking place was occupied. That didn't surprise Pete because everyone in his section knew that unless they arrived by 8:45, they'd have to park in a remote area of the lot; the nearest parking spots were always occupied by that time. Had traffic not been detoured, Pete would have been in the lot by 8:45. As it turned out, he didn't even find a parking space until 9:00. He arrived at the meeting five minutes late.

Even before he got there, Pete knew what he was in for. Supervisor Severer was a stickler for punctuality. No excuse for tardiness ever satisfied him. Sure enough, when Pete walked in late, Severer jumped all over him. Pete claimed that he couldn't find a parking space. Severer insisted that it was poor planning on Pete's part that *caused* him to be late. "You should have given yourself more time!" the supervisor told a red-faced Pete.

Who was right—Pete or the supervisor? Well, it's not a matter of right or wrong. It's a question of one's interest, or viewpoint. In one sense, you could say that Pete's tardiness was caused by the lack of a parking space. We might call that the *proximate cause* of his tardiness. In the view of many at the meeting, that represented a true and complete statement of cause. And they told Pete as much afterward. But obviously that cause didn't wash with Severer. In an attempt to calm him down, Pete explained to him about the fire and detour. And rightly so, for in another sense, these were the causes of his tardiness as well—what might be called *remote causes,* as distinguished from the proximate cause.

Where there is a causal sequence of several events, say A causing B, B causing C, C causing D, and D causing E, E can be regarded as the effect of any or all of the preceding events. The *nearest* of them, D, is considered the proximate cause; the others are considered more and more remote. Thus, A is more remote than B, B is more remote than C, and so on.

STUDY HINT

The *proximate cause* is the one "nearest" the effect. Any other causes are *remote causes.*

The remote causes that Pete added to his initial proximate-cause explanation didn't impress Severer. He insisted that the tardiness was caused by Pete's failure to take extra efforts to be on time for this important meeting. And in a sense Severer was also right, for this was a still more remote cause. Pete knew about the importance of the meeting. What's more, he knew how finicky Severer was about punctuality. He should have given himself more time, just in case an emergency arose. But he didn't, and, yes, *as a result,* he was late. The point is simple but important: *causes are not discrete.* Different interests and viewpoints frequently suggest different causes in a causal sequence or chain of several events.

So causation is associated with control and diverse interests. To understand the idea of cause is to recognize control and interest as integral parts of it. Because of this connection, it's not surprising that we entertain many causal concepts that accommodate the degree of control we wish to exercise and the interests we have. Let's look at some of these concepts.

CAUSAL CONCEPTS

As we just saw, what makes the idea of cause so elusive is that cause may have different meanings under different circumstances. It's convenient to view causal statements, and supporting arguments, as possibly involving four different relationships between cause and effect. These relationships are generally termed *necessary, sufficient, necessary **and** sufficient,* and *contributory.* Although in some ways similar, these four relationships are different enough to be considered separate causal concepts.

Necessary Cause

*A necessary cause is a condition that **must** be present if the effect is to occur.* Thus, if in "A causes B" the term *causes* implies a necessary condition, then A must be present for B to occur. In other words, in the absence of A, B cannot occur, or simply "If no A, no B." In this sense, electricity is a necessary cause for light in a bulb; without electricity the light will not occur.

Sufficient Cause

*A sufficient cause is any condition that, **by itself,** will bring about the effect.* Thus, if in "A causes B," the term *causes* implies a sufficient condition, then when A is present, B will always occur. In other words, the presence of A is always enough to bring about B, or simply "If A, then B." In this sense, a tripped circuit breaker is a sufficient condition for a light to go out. If the circuit breaker trips, the light will go out. But of course, a tripped circuit breaker is not a necessary condition for the light to go out; because should the circuit breaker not trip, the light could still go out, perhaps because the power company turned off the current when you failed to pay the electric bill.

Necessary and Sufficient Cause

A necessary and sufficient cause is any condition that must be present for the effect to occur and one that will bring about the effect alone and of itself. Thus, if in "*A* causes *B*," the term *causes* implies a necessary and sufficient condition, then *B* will occur *when and only when A* occurs. In other words, *A* and only *A* is enough to bring about *B*.

Instances of a single necessary and sufficient condition are understandably rare, but they do occur. Far more common are occasions of several necessary conditions that, taken together, constitute a sufficient condition and sometimes a necessary *and* sufficient condition. For example, taken together, current, bulbs in working order, correct current for the bulbs, and satisfactory wiring constitute a necessary and sufficient condition for an electric light to burn.

Contributory Cause

A contributory cause is a factor that helps create the total set of conditions, necessary or sufficient, for an effect. Thus a violent storm can be a contributory cause to your room's suddenly being pitched into darkness. A violent storm can help create the conditions that cause the lights to go off. But obviously the light may go off without a storm; and the lights may remain on in the presence of a storm. So to say that *A* is a contributory cause of *B* is to say that *B* is more likely to occur when *A* occurs than when *A* does not occur. The lights in your room are more likely to go off in the presence of a violent storm than in its absence.

Usually we speak of contributory causes when we wish to emphasize the complexity of a problem. Thus, in discussing the cause of the fall of the Roman Empire, historians often cite a number of contributory causes: the rise of Christianity, moral decay, economic chaos, and so on. Of course speaking of contributory causes doesn't rule out the possibility of focusing on one chief or sole cause. Thus, while mentioning the nexus of contributory causes to explain the fall of the Roman Empire, some historians have concentrated on the rise of Christianity, others on economic disorder. Once again, then, we are reminded of the role that one's interests and viewpoint play in the attribution of cause.

The danger in formulating any causal argument is the same danger we observed previously in discussing analogy and generalization: observing only the instances that confirm the causal hypothesis and ignoring violations of it. For example, a person might take notice only of those instances that confirm the hypothesis that vitamin C can prevent the common cold and ignore those instances that disconfirm it or tend to suggest that it may be just a contributory cause. In the same vein, another danger is to focus on a single cause, when in fact there are many contributory causes that account for a phenomenon. Failing to recognize and appropriately deal with the elusiveness of the whole idea of cause, we overlook these dangers and commit fallacies. We must look at these fallacies. But before we do, let's try to illuminate the problem of establishing probable causation. Let's try to devise some method of determining that *A* is the probable cause of *B*.

EXERCISE 13-1 *

Is the relationship of the items in the left-hand column to the items in the right-hand column that of necessary cause, sufficient cause, necessary and sufficient cause, or contributory cause, or is it noncausal?

1. no sleep   fatigue

2. overeating   illness

3. deciding to raise your hand   raising your hand

4. writing an essay   reading that essay

5. bullet penetrating the heart   death

6. SlimFast   weight loss

7. unscrewing a light bulb   no light

8. friction   heat

9. infection   fever

10. fear   increase in adrenaline

11. sexual intercourse   sexual pleasure

12. mature female   child

13. oxygen   fire

14. capital punishment   fewer capital offenses

15. smoking   cancer

16. college education   earning potential

METHODS FOR ESTABLISHING PROBABLE CAUSE

In evaluating any causal argument, we face two tasks. One is to determine whether a relationship between *A* and *B* actually does exist; the other is to determine whether the relationship is that type of causal relationship claimed to exist.

For example, Helon's college offers a number of television courses. One is called "The Long Search," a marvelous journey into the world's religions. Here's how the course is set up. "The Long Search" consists of about fifteen one-hour TV segments on different religions. Students enrolled in the course are expected to view the programs and complete reading assignments in conjunction with them. The only time the class ever meets as a group is for the final examination.

Helon's college offers a review session one week before the final. Students are invited, but not required, to attend this review. In the literature it mails to enrollees, the college claims that those who attend the review are more likely to perform better on the exam than those who don't attend. In effect, the college is claiming a causal relationship between review attendance and exam performance.

If we're to deal with such claims intelligently, the first thing we must do is to determine whether a relationship between review attendance and test performance does in fact exist. We might do this by monitoring the performance of review attenders over several terms. If, as a group, they perform better than those who don't attend the review, we have reason to suspect a relationship between attendance and performance. But this is *not* enough evidence to infer a causal relationship. The better performance could be caused by any number of things: Maybe the students who turned out for the review watched the programs more faithfully and did the assignments more conscientiously than the others; perhaps these students are better test takers to begin with; possibly review attenders could be superior students overall. The point is that considerably more is needed to establish a causal relationship.

Suppose the college randomly selected students enrolled in "The Long Search" and gave only these students the review. In each of several terms, this group as a whole outperformed those who didn't get the review. Assuming that the college *controlled relevant variables,* it would now be justified in inferring a *contributory* causal relationship between review attendance and test performance. But it would not be justified in claiming a *necessary* relationship.

In short, in formulating and evaluating causal arguments, we must judge whether the evidence establishes a relationship between a phenomenon and an alleged cause. In addition, we must determine whether the evidence establishes the relationship as the particular type supposed to exist. This is no mean undertaking. But the process is aided by several methods for establishing causal relationships. These methods are usually associated with the nineteenth-century English philosopher John Stuart Mill, who formalized them. Although philosophers of science point out certain limitations to Mill's methods, they need not concern us here. Mill's methods provide a basic introduction to essential features of causal relationships. We'll consider three: the method of agreement, the method of difference, and the method of concomitant variation.

Agreement

The method of agreement states that if two or more instances of a phenomenon have **only one circumstance in common,** *that circumstance is probably the cause (or the effect) of the phenomenon.* For example, suppose that in a particular section of the country a group of twelve people contract a lung disease. We wish to determine "the cause." We might begin our investigation by looking for any possible candidates for necessary conditions for contracting this lung disease. We collect basic information about our sample, which we represent on the table, using "yes" to signify the presence of the following potentially significant conditions: working in the local coal mine, living near the paper mill, or having a history of tuberculosis in the family:

CASE	MINE WORKER	PAPER MILL	TB IN FAMILY
1	yes	yes	yes
2	yes	yes	
3	yes		yes
4	yes	yes	
5	yes		
6	yes	yes	yes
7	yes		yes
8	yes	yes	yes
9	yes	yes	yes
10	yes	yes	yes
11	yes	yes	
12	yes	yes	yes

We see at a glance that the one common relevant antecedent condition is working in the local mine. Based simply on the method of agreement, we have a strong case for identifying that condition as the probable cause of this lung disease.

But our chart concerns only three variables. What if in addition to working in the mine all those with the disease also smoked? Is it working in the mine, smoking, or some combination of the two which causes this lung disease? We need to add another method to the method of agreement.

Difference

*The method of difference states that if an instance when the phenomenon occurs and an instance when it doesn't occur have **every circumstance in common except one**, and that circumstance occurs only in the former, then that circumstance is probably the cause (or the effect) of the phenomenon.* The essence of this method is the elimination of all except one difference between the instances when the phenomenon occurs and those when it doesn't. Thus, to resolve the lung disease case, we interview other inhabitants of the area who have every relevant factor in common with the victims save one: They don't work in the coal mine. We isolate a difference. If none of the other people in the area—including smokers—has the disease, we can conclude that working in the coal mine is an indispensable part of the cause of the lung disease.

So using the method of agreement, we found that men having the lung disease shared two characteristics: They worked in the coal mine and they were smokers. Using the method of difference, we found that working in the coal mine was an indispensable part of the cause of the disease. Clearly, it is not a sufficient condition, for not every coal miner contracted the disease. Taken together with smoking, which itself may be an indispensable part of the cause, working in the mine *could be* a sufficient condition. Indeed, working in the mine and smoking might turn out to be a necessary and sufficient condition. But more investigation is needed.

At the same time, our conclusions may turn out erroneous. Perhaps something else is causing the disease, something that we haven't as yet detected. In other words, our causal argument is *probable, not certain.* For this reason, when it is appropriate, both the method of agreement and difference are applied in testing for cause; we want as much probability as possible. What's more, since in such cases we're really dealing with a hypothesis—a causal hypothesis—the factors for judging hypotheses come into play. Of particular relevance in this lung disease case would be testing the inferences that can be drawn from the hypothesis that working in the mine is an indispensable part of the cause of the lung disease. Thus, if we gave every miner an air-filtration mask and ensured it's use, we could at the least expect a marked decline in the incidence of the lung disease. Also, if the hypothesis is sound, we could expect to find an occurrence of this same disease among miners who work in substantially the same environment. Were these expectations borne out, the probability of our causal hypothesis would increase dramatically.

Joint Method of Agreement and Difference

As a rule, the methods of agreement and difference are combined in scientific and everyday efforts to identify causes and their effects. Let's see how they worked together helping AIDS researchers unlock one small piece of the complicated puzzle of what causes this horrible disease.

In the process of looking for the causes of AIDS, researchers discovered that AIDS inhibits a particular kind of white blood cell known as a granulocyte. The researchers thought that if they could find out why this inhibition occurs, they would be nearer to understanding the causes of AIDS. "Whatever inhibits the granulocytes appears to be in the blood serum, the liquid part of the blood, not the granulocytes themselves," researchers reported. They noted that if they removed inhibited cells from sick patients and placed them in healthy donor serum, the defect in the cells was corrected. "But," they added, "if we put healthy granulocytes in sick serum, they start acting sick."[41]

The effect being studied is the inhibition of granulocytes. Two factors are involved: the cells themselves and blood serum. In AIDS patients, both are diseased. By applying the joint method of agreement and difference, researchers were able at least to rule out the cells as the cause. To see how, consider three combinations of the relevant factors and what they produced:

A: sick cells + sick serum = inhibited cells
B: sick cells + healthy serum ≠ inhibited cells
C: healthy cells + sick serum = inhibited cells

---

41. The article from which these quotes are taken appeared in the *New York Times,* September 7, 1985. We are indebted to David Kelley's *The Art of Reasoning* (New York: W. W. Norton & Company, 1988), p. 278, for this example.

A represents the condition of AIDS patients. Comparing *A* and *B* is the method of difference. Sick cells placed in healthy blood serum are no longer sick. Comparing *A* and *C* is the method of agreement. Sick blood serum results in sick cells, whether or not the cells themselves are sick when isolated from the serum. By combining both methods, researchers determined that the cause—inhibited granulocytes—was in the blood serum, not in the cells themselves.

The method of agreement can be used to identify a sufficient cause for an event's occurrence, but—by itself—cannot show a necessary cause. Thus, using the method of agreement (*A* and *C*), the researchers learned that the presence of sick blood serum was sufficient to inhibit the normal action of certain white blood cells. But that did not tell them whether or not sick blood serum was necessary for this effect to occur.

Using the method of difference (*A* and *B*), the researchers isolated sick cells from sick serum. This showed that sick serum was *necessary* to produce sick cells. The method of difference can identify a necessary causal factor. But—by itself—it cannot identify *sufficient* causes. It showed researchers only that sick blood serum was necessary to produce this particular condition in granulocytes.

Combined, the method of agreement and difference showed that unhealthy blood serum causes a particular malfunction in certain white blood cells in people with AIDS. As researchers discover more apparent factors influencing blood cells, blood serum, and the entire immune system, they must continue to refine the connections between and among them. This is quite complex, since even the selection of the factors requires great care. The process of tracking the cause of something like AIDS is thus much more tedious and time consuming than the layperson can sometimes imagine.

Whether agreement or difference, or a combination, it's clear that *elimination is an integral part of establishing cause*. The application of these methods, then, demands the presence or absence of certain circumstances or the occurrence or nonoccurrence of a specific circumstance. But what if none of these is the case?

For example, how would we establish a causal connection between air pollution and lung cancer? Since fresh country air no longer exists, we'd be hard pressed to eliminate polluted air, as called for by the method of difference. By the same token, we couldn't use the method of agreement, since polluted air is common to all the instances of lung cancer involved; that is, no matter who we are or where we are, we breathe air that is to some degree polluted. We need another method.

Concomitant Variation

The method of concomitant variation states that whenever a phenomenon varies in a particular way as another phenomenon varies in a particular way, a causal relationship probably exists between them. For example, the faster you drive your car, the greater the distance you need to stop it; the faster you drive your car, the fewer miles per gallon of gas you get. In the case of lung cancer and polluted air, we might be able to show that there's a direct relationship between an increase in air pollution and an increase in lung cancer.

A direct relationship means that as one thing increases, the other increases proportionally; or as one thing decreases, the other decreases proportionally. Speed and safe following distance would be an example of two things that bear a direct causal relationship to each other. The opposite of direct relationship is inverse relationship. *An inverse relationship means that as one thing increases, the other decreases proportionally; or as one thing decreases, the other increases proportionally.* Speed and fuel efficiency would be an example of this kind of causal relationship, generally speaking.

Clearly, the method of concomitant variation is based on a repeated, regular connection between one phenomenon and another. The fact is that such a connection is an integral part of the idea of cause and naturally plays a significant role in all methods of establishing causal relationship. Such a connection is often called a *correlation*. Do correlations establish causes? This question naturally arises in any discussion of causation, but it's especially present when concomitant variation is relied on to establish cause. The reason is that concomitant variation more overtly deals with correlations than do the other methods. And there always exists the temptation to infer causation from a correlation. Although sometimes a correlation indicates a genuine causal factor, often it does not. The difference between a correlation and a causal relationship is something we must now look at very closely. Failing to distinguish them, we invite error into our causal reasoning.

CORRELATIONS AND CAUSES

It's important to distinguish causal connections from a special kind of noncausal statistical relation known as a *correlation*. (In Chapter 11 we looked at statistical claims.) Perhaps you've noticed that red cars get proportionally more speeding tickets than cars of other colors. Is there something about red cars that causes their owners to speed? Not really. Two more plausible explanations concern the cultural associations we have with red: fiery, daring, exciting, sexy. Thus a person who chooses a red car may have a temperament different from one who chooses a car of a less "exciting" color, say a tan or maroon one. It is also suggested that red cars are easier to spot than some other colors; they are more quickly noticed by traffic officers. This factor, combined with red's sporty image, may also account for the high percentage of tickets written for drivers of red cars. In other words, there is nothing about the color red that causes red cars (or their drivers) to speed; but there is a higher correlation between driving a red car and getting a speeding ticket than there is between driving a tan one and getting a speeding ticket.

To cite another example of a correlation: Historically some academic majors have been dominated by males, others by females. Even today, with more freedom of choice and sensitivity to gender discrimination, more females major in nursing than do males, and more males major in law enforcement. Are these statistical patterns reflections of a *causal* pattern? That is, does being a woman somehow "cause" one to choose nursing over law enforcement? Does being a man somehow "cause" one to prefer majoring in law enforcement over nursing?

Most likely both patterns reflect complex social habits, customs, and expectations. As powerful as these may be, strictly speaking, they are not causes. Men can—and do—become fine nurses, just as women can—and do—become excellent police officers.

Whenever we confuse statistical patterns with causal connections, we always lose some control over our environment. We may waste effort seeking ways to change something by concentrating on inessential, noncausal aspects associated with it. To cite one currently controversial and important example of the importance of distinguishing statistical patterns from causal connections, educators and legislators are struggling over the proper use of standardized tests as criteria for college admissions. The most famous such test is probably the Scholastic Aptitude Test (SAT). White students have tended—on average—to score higher on certain portions of the SAT than nonwhite students. This raises the question of test bias. Is there a cultural bias favoring white students? Some argue that there is. Others argue that the actual *cause* of this statistical pattern is not racial bias, but social and economic factors. That is, students from middle-class environments tend to do better on the SAT than students from economically disadvantaged groups—regardless of racial background. Because more white students come from the middle class than students from other ethnic backgrounds, proportionally more white students will score well—not because they are white, but because they are middle class. This issue is still being debated.

This example shows just how important it is not to confuse statistical patterns with causes. Whatever accounts for patterned differences in SAT scores needs to be clearly identified. In 1995, the Educational Testing Service of Princeton, New Jersey, "re-normed" the SAT by adding 100 points to each student's total score. "Re-norming" is a statistical adjustment. If indeed the test is biased, then it needs to be rewritten or discarded—not merely "renormed." If, on the other hand, the test is fair and accurately predicts an individual's chances of success in college, then the factors that account for different scores among various economic groups need to be corrected. The mere presence of a clearly identified statistical pattern does not entitle us to infer a causal relationship. Such clearly defined statistical patterns identify correlations, which may or may not indicate causes.

Technically, *a correlation is a systematic connection between two properties (variables) shared by a single group.* Correlations involve statistical information pertaining to the group in question, which is known as a *population*. For instance, in the red car example, the population consists of people getting speeding tickets. The two variables being correlated are driving red cars or driving tan cars.

Perhaps the simplest way to get a grasp on correlations is to take an extended look at an example. Suppose we want to know if there is any correlation between smoking cigarettes and gender.[42] Let's assume that 51 percent of adult male, and 34 percent of adult female Americans smoke. If we combine these two pieces of statistical information, we are asserting the existence of a correlation. We could

---

42. The chart and description in this section are based on material in Ronald N. Giere's superb *Understanding Scientific Reasoning*, 3rd ed. (New York: Holt, Rinehart and Winston, 1991).

Adult Americans

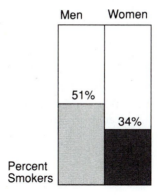

be specific and say that "Seventeen percent more adult American males smoke than do adult American females," or less specific, "More adult American males smoke than do adult American females," or simply, "The smoking rate is higher among adult American males than among adult American females."

We can represent this relationship graphically: Referring to the graph below, we see that comparing men and women to smoking rates, a higher percentage of men than women smoke. This is called a *positive correlation*. We might wish to express the identical correlation by asserting that a lower percentage of women than men smoke. This is called a *negative correlation*.

In order to get a clearer understanding of correlations, let's use A to represent any property the members of the population might have. In this example, then, A would represent being a smoker. Smokers would be As and nonsmokers would, naturally enough, be non-As. For convenience, we can represent the two categories into which we have divided the population (men and women) in terms of B. Those in one category are B, the remainder are non-B. In our example, we'll let B represent male and non-B represent female.

We can now say that B *is positively correlated with* A *if and only if the percentage of* Bs *among the* As *is greater than the percentage of* Bs *among the non-*As. Let's plug the variables from our example into this formula to see what we get: Being male (B) is positively correlated with smoking (A) if and only if the percentage of males (Bs) among the smokers is greater than the percentage of males among the nonsmokers (non-As). Since the percentage of males among smokers (51 percent) is greater than the percentage of nonsmoking males (49 percent), we see that the formula accurately represents positive correlation.

B *is negatively correlated with* A *if and only if the percentage of* Bs *among the* As *is less than the percentage of* Bs *among the non-*As. Given what we discovered when we substituted our variables in the formula for positive correlation, we know that being male is positively correlated with being a smoker. So, if we let B represent being female in the formula for negative correlation, we should get a confirmation of the formula for negative correlation: Being female (B) is negatively correlated with smoking (A) if and only if the percentage of females (Bs) among the smokers (As) is less than the percentage of females (Bs) among the nonsmokers (non-As). Since the percentage of females among the smokers (34 percent) is less than the percentage of nonsmoking females (66 percent), we obtain our correlation.

Should we wish, we could express the very same relationship in reverse, by saying that being female is positively correlated with not smoking. Conversely, this would mean that being male is negatively correlated with not smoking. For various reasons, negative statements, and double negatives especially, are often more difficult to understand than affirmative statements, so we have to be especially alert when dealing with negative statements when forming correlations.

If it should turn out that equal numbers of men and women smoke (and sadly recent trends indicate that, although more men have stopped smoking, more women are taking it up), then gender will have no correlation with smoking. The formula for this kind of relationship is: *B is not correlated with A if and only if the percentage of the Bs among the As is the same as the percentage of the Bs among the non-As.*

Notice that correlation is nothing more than a conjunction of two statistical relationships.[43]

It is important to understand that *correlation is not causation.* Giere cites the case of researchers at a state hospital affiliated with a major state university who began studying recovery rates of patients. One of the things they discovered was that patients who lived within 50 miles of the hospital had a higher recovery rate than those living farther away. Thus there was a positive correlation between recovering and living within 50 miles of the hospital. This led some people to conclude that living near a hospital was somehow beneficial to patients. Others refined this hypothesis a bit, and concluded that quick treatment was the key.

Both explanations probably had some merit. Quick and convenient access to medical care undoubtedly plays some role in recovery rate. After more careful analysis, however, the correlation was explained by the status of this particular hospital. Being associated with a major university, the hospital enjoyed a well-deserved reputation for providing state-of-the-art, sophisticated medical care unavailable at most nonteaching hospitals in the state. Consequently the most seriously ill patients from all over the state were brought to the university hospital. Less seriously ill patients were treated locally. Thus, the patients who traveled more than 50 miles to get to this particular hospital were—as a group—more seriously ill to begin with than those patients who went to the university hospital simply because it was nearby.[44]

Positive correlation, it turns out, is what's called a *symmetrical relationship*. In a symmetrical relationship, if *B* is positively correlated with *A,* then *A* is positively correlated with *B.* In our first example, if being male is positively correlated with being a smoker, being a smoker is also positively correlated with being

---

43. The strength of a correlation is ordinarily measured on a statistical scale ranging from -1 to $+1$, where 0 = no strength—no correlation at all. The formula for the strength of a correlation looks like this: *The strength of the correlation between **B** and **A** is the fraction of **A**s that are **B** minus the fraction of non-**A**s that are **B**.*

44. Giere, *Understanding Scientific Reasoning,* pp. 209–211.

a male. But causal relationships are *not* symmetrical relationships. Yes, increasing your speed *causes* you to get fewer miles per gallon; but getting fewer miles per gallon does *not cause* you to increase your speed. Again, decapitation is a *cause* of death; but death does *not* cause one to be decapitated. Similarly, being male does not *cause* one to smoke, *neither* does smoking *cause* one to be male. Putting the causal relationship abstractly: Where *A* causes *B*, *B* does not necessarily cause *A*. Clearly, then, when we assert a causal relationship, we are saying something quite different than when we assert a simple statistical correlation.

The thing that's confusing, and often leads us astray, is that causation inevitably involves a connection between two things. For example, if we say that cigarette smoking causes lung cancer, implied in that is that there is a connection between smoking and getting cancer. But the connection is not just a correlation that holds that there are, in fact, more cases of lung cancer among smokers than among nonsmokers. To assert a causal relationship between smoking and lung cancer is to say that there *would be* more cases of lung cancer in the population if everyone smoked than if no one smoked, other factors remaining constant. And that is an entirely different statement.

To sum up, *a correlation is a relationship between properties that exist in some actual population.* In contrast, a causal relationship is defined in terms of a connection between two *hypothetical* versions of the real population. Failing to distinguish between a correlation and a causal relationship, we can grossly distort Mill's method of concomitant variation. Notice that the method of concomitant variation says that *whenever* a phenomenon varies in a particular way as another phenomenon varies in a particular way, a causal relationship probably exists between them. That "whenever" is crucial. Implied in it is that hypothetical version of the real population just mentioned. For example, let's say that there is a positive correlation between taking vitamin C and cold prevention. If on the basis of concomitant variation, you assert a causal relationship between vitamin C and cold prevention, what you're saying is that if everyone in the population took vitamin C, there would be fewer colds than if no one took vitamin C. Such statements relative to disease are possible as, for example, with vaccinations and small pox or vaccinations and polio. But to conclude that vitamin C can prevent the common cold, exclusively on the basis of a positive correlation, is not at all a proper application of the method of concomitant variation. Indeed, to argue that way is to commit the fallacy of questionable causation.

In fact, there are several common fallacies associated with causal arguments. Now that we've deepened our understanding of cause and considered some of the ways of establishing probable causation, we'll take a look at these fallacies next.

EXERCISE 13-2 *

1. Illustrate through a hypothetical example how you'd establish probable causation in the following cases by using Mill's methods of agreement and difference.

   a. Food poisoning in a college cafeteria (a phenomenon, of course, that we all know is pure fantasy)

    b. A disproportionally large number of men to women enrolled in a philosophy course

    c. The failure of your car to start on a chilly morning

    d. Your occasional but recurring tendency to stutter, stammer, or be at a loss for words

2. Using capital letters (*A*, *B*, and so on) to indicate circumstances and small letters (*a*, *b*, and so on) to indicate phenomena, can you symbolically represent Mill's methods of agreement and difference?

3. Explain the difference between asserting a simple correlation and a causal relationship in the following cases:

    a. Christmas and an increase in suicides

    b. Violence on television and real-life violence

    c. The decline of membership in institutionalized religion and growing interest in the occult

    d. The women's liberation movement and an increasing number of working women

FALLACIES OF CAUSATION

Causal fallacies are arguments that assert that a particular circumstance produces (that is, causes) a particular phenomenon when there is, in fact, little or no evidence to support such a contention. For example, when the Borana tribe in Kenya witnessed the solar eclipse of June 30, 1973, they claimed it was caused by the white men who having landed on the moon, had learned the secrets of the heavenly bodies and were presumably tampering with them. Similarly, in Nigeria's Islamic Neth, emirs waged *jihad* (holy war) on single women because the emirs believed the women had brought on a drought in western Africa. These are two obvious examples of questionable causation.

Questionable causation inevitably pops up when we infer causation from correlation. A classic example is found in anthropology. Anthropologists studying a South Seas tribe found its members believed that body lice advanced good health. In fact, every healthy person had some lice; in contrast, most sick people didn't. Clearly, then, there was a positive correlation between having lice and being healthy. But the lice didn't promote health. Being healthy caused a person to have lice! After all, lice aren't dummies. They don't want to leach off sick, feverish bodies. That's why the ill didn't have lice whereas the healthy did.

In questionable causation we mistake what is not the cause of a given effect for its real cause. But taking for a cause what is not a cause may occur in a less general way.

Post Hoc Fallacy

The post hoc fallacy[45] *is an argument that asserts that one event is the cause of another from the mere fact that the first occurred prior to the second.* As an absurd example, suppose that after breaking a vase, a person fell and broke a leg. If we inferred that breaking the vase caused the accident, we'd be guilty of the post hoc fallacy. A more serious example is found in Egyptian history. Egyptians used to worship the ibis (a bird) because each year, shortly after flocks of ibis had migrated to the banks of the Nile, the river overflowed its banks and irrigated the soil. The Egyptians believed the ibis caused the floodwater, when of course both the birds' migration and the river's overflow were attributable to the change of season.

The basis for post hoc fallacies is understandable. Causes precede events. So it's tempting to causally associate events occurring near one another. But neither immediate temporal succession nor more remote temporal succession is sufficient for establishing a causal relationship. Simply because the Roman Empire declined after the appearance of Christianity does not demonstrate that Christianity caused the decline of the Roman Empire. By the same token, just because an individual's collagen disease abated after massive doses of vitamin C doesn't mean that vitamin C caused the remission of the disease. True, such occurrences

---

45. The fallacy's full name is *post hoc, ergo propter hoc,* which literally means "after this, therefore because of this." It's better known simply as the post hoc fallacy.

may suggest an association that should be further investigated. But temporal relationships alone are insufficient for establishing causal relationships, in the same way that correlations alone are insufficient for establishing causation.

Magical Thinking

The fallacy of magical thinking is an argument that uncritically attributes causal power to thoughts and words. Another name for magical thinking is appeal to superstition (*argumentum ad superstionem*). For example, in a fit of anger, little Nick hollers at his brother Harry: "I hope you break your neck!" Later that same afternoon, Harry falls off his bike and sprains his wrist. Nick is consequently consumed with guilt, believing that his angry words and thoughts somehow "caused" Harry's accident.

Psychologists sometimes refer to this pattern of thinking as "imminent justice." In other words: we assume an "instant accounting" for whatever we do or think, and that the act of thinking about it is sufficient to trigger its occurrence. So the magical thinker who in a moment of temporary rage wishes you were dead, feels somehow responsible when you do, coincidentally, die a short time later.

In the examples we've just seen, magical thinking is a variation of post hoc fallacy. But sometimes magical thinking occurs in other forms. Perhaps, as a child, your parents warned you to watch what you said "or else it might come true." Here, even though nothing has as yet happened, the fear that just saying or thinking something might have the power to cause its occurrence is still an instance of magical thinking.

The origins of this fallacy are probably rooted in our primitive past, in which shamans, witch doctors, priests, and priestesses claimed to be able to control nature through the utterance of secret, powerful incantations. Thus, we "knock on wood" as we say something positive to assuage ancient Celtic and Druid gods and demons thought to have lived in trees ("wood"), we cross our fingers, and so on.

Growing empirical evidence shows the importance of how we think to how we feel and even to physiological well-being. But these claims are based on careful, controlled observations; they do not attribute magical omnipotence to thinking or speaking. Whenever we *uncritically* attribute causal power to words or thoughts, we are guilty of magical thinking.

Slippery Slope Fallacy

The fallacy of slippery slope is an argument that objects to a position on the erroneous belief that the position, if taken, will set off a chain of events that inevitably will lead to an undesirable outcome. For example, many people oppose the legalization of marijuana primarily because they believe that such action will lead to the legalization of heroin and other "hard" drugs, which in turn will eventuate in America's becoming a drug culture. The fact is that legalization of marijuana does not *have to* lead to those things at all. The subsequent legalization of other drugs is a separate and distinct issue from the legalization of marijuana. What those holding this view fail to realize is that the legalization of marijuana is in no way a sufficient condition for the legalization of other drugs. Indeed, people who rely on slippery slope appeals don't understand what constitutes a cause. Whenever one can refuse, resist, or prevent *B* from occurring after *A,* then *A* cannot be said to produce *B* inevitably, inalterably, unequivocally.

Yet many celebrated arguments ignore this fact. A glaring example was the Vietnam War. How many times did we hear that if Vietnam went, Thailand would follow, then Burma, India, and so forth? But why a stand couldn't be taken at any one of these junctures—indeed, perhaps a strategically *better* stand—was never mentioned. Similarly, a U.S. vice-president once defended a state governor's refusal to meet with prisoners at their request during a prison riot by insisting that had the governor met with them and refused to surrender the state, the prisoners would have demanded that the president of the United States meet with them. Obviously, had that scenario occurred, the president simply could have refused.

Regardless of the desirability or undesirability of the final event, all slippery slope fallacies involve hasty conclusions because they fail to adequately consider the complex factors involved in causal chains. They are thus always based on questionable causes. Like post hoc and magical thinking, slippery slope oversimplifies what is in fact a complex set of circumstances. Oversimplification is not confined to these specific causal fallacies, but can occur in more general form. Let's see how.

Oversimplification Fallacy

The fallacy of oversimplification is an argument that treats a situation as if it involved only a few significant factors when in fact it involves a complex of many significant, interrelated facets. Consider this all-too-common example: You've just asked your logic instructor for tips on improving your grade. She responds with: "Well, it's really very simple. Just study more." Let's assume that in this case "more" won't help. You need a more detailed answer, such as: identify key concepts in the reading, take better notes, review your notes daily, ask questions in class. "Just study more" is too simple in this case (but not in every case!).

When we oversimplify our view of a situation, we deprive ourselves of enough information to make a reasonable analysis of it, and thus we deprive ourselves of any realistic chance of adequately dealing with it.

"The Republicans have caused our gross national debt." "The Democrats always cause inflation." Such statements are overly simplistic—and that is their appeal. They allow us the illusion of analysis without effort, and often encourage and reinforce stereotypes, prejudices, and faulty frames of reference.

Moore, McCann, and McCann point out that "Chronic oversimplifiers are easy to spot. They have a breezy, self-assured way of speaking and hold strong opinions on every subject. They are fond of such expressions as 'That's the situation in a nutshell'—as if any complex situation would fit into a nutshell."[46]

A dogmatic, overly exaggerated manner of speaking often accompanies oversimplification because, to the oversimplifier, everything is clear—too clear. "I don't see why the American people can't see that they're being lied to by the administration. All they have to do is use a little common sense." Expressions such as "all they have to do" or "it's simple, just . . ." are also warning signs. "My wife left me 'cause she didn't love me" may sound like an adequate explanation of a marriage's demise, but it usually isn't. To learn from such a tragedy, we need to delve more deeply into the myriad aspects that make up any marriage. "Losing weight's simple—just eat less and exercise more." To be helpful, such advice must dig deeper: It must deal with why it is so difficult to change dietary or behavior patterns, what food does that makes compulsive overeating addictive, and so forth.

One last class of examples here: hyperbolic (extremely exaggerated) claims. "That's my favorite movie of all time," uttered without reflection immediately upon leaving the theater, or, "It was all your fault that we went broke," and the like, almost always signal oversimplification, in addition to whatever other fallacies that may be involved.

We see, then, that many fallacious arguments include some faulty causal assumptions and claims. These may be present in addition, and as contributors, to other, more easily spotted fallacies.

EXERCISE 13-3 *

Explain whether or not the following passages commit the fallacies of post hoc, slippery slope, magical thinking, or oversimplification. Also see if you can spot any examples of confusing correlation with causation.

1. "Impeach the Press!" (Bumper sticker popular during times of intense domestic turmoil)

2. PHIL: That's the last time I'll leave that bedroom window open at night.
   PAT: But it's good to sleep in a roomful of fresh air.
   PHIL: Are you kidding? My throat's killing me!

3. INTERVIEWER: Three hundred people on board and all are killed but one—you. How do you feel about that?
   SURVIVOR: All I can say is it's a miracle.

4. JERRY: Of course we've been visited by astronaut-gods.
   ANNA: That's absurd.
   JERRY: Okay, know-it-all, how would you explain airstrips thousands of years old in primitive and remote areas of the Earth?

---

46. W. Edgar Moore, Hugh McCann, and Janet McCann, *Creative and Critical Thinking* (Boston: Houghton, Mifflin Company, 1985), p. 313.

5. CARRIE: You know, Don, you should get married.
DON: Really?
CARRIE: Sure. Married men on the average live longer than single men.
DON: So what?
CARRIE: So that proves that for men, marriage is more conducive to a longer life than bachelorhood.
DON: Okay, you've talked me into it. Let's get married.
CARRIE: Don't be ridiculous. Within a month we'd be fighting, within a year we'd be separated, and within two years I'd have all your money.
DON: Phew! I'm glad you mentioned that. I'd rather die young and rich than live old and poor.

6. MAURICE: So you're opposed to a national health insurance program, eh?
MILLIE: And if you had any sense you would be, too. Who wants to live in a country where all its institutions are socialized? And that's what's going to happen if we pass this thing.

7. MYRA: Oh, don't bother offering Fred another cup of coffee. He never has more than a single cup.
SUE: Oh really?
MYRA: Ever since the night he had two cups and didn't sleep a wink, he never has more than one cup after dinner.

8. In every single case I've ever investigated, men convicted of rape have had pornographic magazines in their homes. It's clear that pornography causes sexual violence.

9. RYAN: You know, I really think we should require foreign companies doing business in America to pay ransom for the return of kidnapped executives held hostage in their countries.
ROSS: Why is that?
RYAN: To ensure the safety of Americans currently held hostage there.
ROSS: Don't be foolish! The next thing, we'd have every radical group in the world kidnapping Americans and making outlandish demands. Once you give into any terrorists, you've set up a pattern of no resistance.
RYAN: Wow! I never thought of that.

10. I kept hoping you'd call. I sat here and thought, "Call me! Call me!" And you did! I guess I've got more psychic powers than I realized.

11. It's clear to me that Dr. Duck is a miracle worker. For days I had these awful headaches. Then I went to Dr. Duck. He gave me a few of his secret formula injections. In a couple of days, I felt better.

12. "If you [*sic*] could get rid of drugs [in the workplace], we'd be far ahead of other countries in productivity." (Ira Lipman quoted in Stanley Penn, "Losses Grow from Drug Use at the Office," *Wall Street Journal,* July 29, 1981, p. 27)

CAUSAL ARGUMENTS AND THE COGENCY CRITERIA

The assessment of causal arguments can be divided into two parts: (1) determination of causal relationship, and (2) evaluation of the argument. As with all induction, causal arguments present the ever-present problem of determining the *sufficiency* of the evidence offered to establish the likelihood of the conclusion. Though we often lack the expertise and specific knowledge to assess the quality of specific causal claims, we can nonetheless reject arguments that commit causal fallacies or that confuse correlations with causes. In other words, we can, once again, more easily recognize arguments that fail to meet the cogency criteria than we can establish simple, beforehand standards of sufficiency.

Relevancy sometimes plays a role as well. For example, in a post hoc argument, a person may conclude that walking under a ladder is bad luck because right after so doing he was hit by a car—the problem here isn't sufficiency but relevancy. In fact, every post hoc can be considered a violation of the relevancy criterion because the fact that some *A* preceded some *B* does *not* count as evidence for saying that *A* caused *B*. If time order was relevant, then *any* event that preceded *B* could be a relevant candidate for *B*'s cause.

On the other hand, in the cases of causal oversimplification or slippery slope, the problem lies plainly with the *sufficiency* of evidence. In other words, even if *A* is relevant to *B*, it doesn't *fully* account for it. To say that it does amounts to causal oversimplification or slippery slope—both violations of the sufficiency criterion.

SUMMARY

This chapter dealt with causation and causal argument. A causal argument is an argument that attempts to support a causal statement, that is, a statement that reduces to the claim that *A* causes *B*. In understanding the idea of cause it's important for us to remember that causes are not discrete; they are associated with control and various interests. This results in several concepts of cause. It's convenient to view causal statements, and supporting arguments, as possibly involving four different relationships: necessary, sufficient, necessary and sufficient, and contributory.

A necessary cause is a condition that must be present if the effect is to occur. Electricity is a necessary cause for light in a bulb.

A sufficient cause is any condition that by itself will bring about the effect. A tripped circuit breaker is a sufficient cause for a light bulb to go out.

A necessary and sufficient cause is any condition that must be present for the effect to occur and one that will bring about the effect alone in and of itself. A specific spirochete is a necessary and sufficient cause of syphilis.

A contributory cause is a factor that helps create the total set of conditions, necessary or sufficient, for an effect. A violent storm can be a contributory cause for your room's suddenly going dark.

The danger in formulating any causal argument is observing only the instances that confirm the causal hypothesis and ignoring violations of it. In evaluating a causal argument, we must determine (1) whether a relationship between A and B actually exists, and (2) whether the relationship is that type of causal relationship claimed to exist. Helpful here are Mill's methods of establishing probable causation, of which we discussed three: agreement, difference, and concomitant variation.

The method of agreement states that if two or more instances of a phenomenon have only one circumstance in common, that circumstance is probably the cause (or the effect) of the phenomenon.

The method of difference states that if an instance when the phenomenon occurs and an instance when it doesn't occur have every circumstance in common except one, and that the circumstance occurs only in the former, then that circumstance is probably the cause (or the effect) of the phenomenon.

The joint method of agreement and difference often enables us to identify both the necessary and sufficient cause of an event.

The method of concomitant variation states that whenever a phenomenon varies in a particular way as another phenomenon varies in a particular way, a causal relationship probably exists between them.

The subject of correlations naturally arises in connection with the method of concomitant variation, although correlations are an integral part of all causal statements and arguments.

Correlations do not necessarily imply causation. A symmetrical relationship can be generalized to any positive or negative correlation. But causal relationships are not symmetrical. Further, whereas a correlation is a relationship between properties that exist in some actual population, a causal relationship is defined in terms of a relationship between two hypothetical versions of the real population. Failing to distinguish between correlations and causal relationships, we often commit fallacies of causation, arguments that assert that a particular circumstance produces a particular phenomenon when there is, in fact, little or no evidence to support such a conclusion.

Another fallacy connected with causation is post hoc: an argument that asserts that one event is the cause of another from the mere fact that the first occurred earlier than the second, for example, the ancient Egyptians' belief that the ibis caused the Nile to overflow.

The fallacy of magical thinking is an argument that uncritically attributes causal power to thoughts and words; for example, you yell at your friend, "I hope you fall off your bike and break your neck!" Shortly thereafter she falls and sprains her wrist. You conclude that your wish caused her accident.

Still another causation-related fallacy is the slippery slope: an argument that objects to a position on the erroneous belief that the position, if taken, will set off a chain of events that ultimately will lead to undesirable action; for example, insisting that the legalization of marijuana will inevitably lead to the legalization of hard drugs and ultimately to the United States becoming a drug culture.

The last causal fallacy we studied was oversimplification: an argument that treats a situation as if it involved only a few significant factors when in fact it involves a complex of many significant, interrelated facets. Example: "The Democrats cause inflation."

Summary Exercises

1. "If one hundred police officers testify that every drug addict they arrested was found to have milk in the refrigerator at home, why can't we conclude that drinking milk leads to drug addiction?" (Carol Travis, "Porn Panel Report Doesn't Give Complete Analysis of Sexual Abuse," *Los Angeles Times;* reprinted in the Redding *Record Searchlight,* July 12, 1986)

2. Discuss Gaffney's First Law of Nomenclature (named in honor of Wilbur G. Gaffney of the University of Nebraska): "You become what your name is." Examples used to "support" Gaffney's Law include a linebacker named Quash, an offensive lineman named Heavyside, an animal psychologist named Fox. (Reported in Charles Osgood's column in *USA Weekend,* October 24–26, 1986)

ADDITIONAL EXERCISES

A. What are the explicit or implied conclusions in the following? Where appropriate, indicate which of Mill's methods are being used. Do you think the conclusions are strong? If they could be strengthened, explain how.

1. "It has long been assumed that a diet low in saturated fats (meaning mostly animal fats) can reduce the risk of cardiovascular disease. Direct evidence for this assumption, however, has been scarce. Such evidence is now provided by a study made at a veterans' hospital in Los Angeles. The study shows that the incidence of cardiovascular disease in a group of 424 veterans with a diet high in unsaturated fats for eight years was 31.3 percent, whereas a control group of 422 men with a normal diet high in saturated fats had a cardiovascular disease rate of 47.7 percent." ("Science and the Citizen" *Scientific American,* September 1969)

2. ABE: There's no question that the Democrats are the "war party."
   TOM: That's absurd!
   ABE: Is it? Wilson, a Democrat, was president when the United States got into World War I. Roosevelt was in charge when we entered World War II. And who was president when we sent troops to Vietnam? Kennedy—another Democrat! Now I ask you—what other conclusion can you draw but that American wars are caused by Democratic administrations?

3. MARIE: I sure wish I could get my coleus to grow.
   MATT: Have you tried talking to it?
   MARIE: What?
   MATT: I mean it. I have two coleuses. A month ago they were just about the same size and color and in the same state of health. Which stands to reason, because they're in the same room where they get

the same amount and degree of light. Well, for the past month I've been giving both the same amount of water and plant food, and I've been spraying them in the same way. The only difference is that I speak softly to one, but not the other.

MARIE: And now I suppose you're going to tell me that one's bigger, brighter, and healthier.

MATT: If looks are any indication, the one I talk to is—a full 8 inches longer, much brighter, and apparently thriving, compared to the other.

4. "The commissioners are convinced that many more inmates should be paroled. For prison experience unquestionably boosts the chance that an offender will break the law again. In one experiment, conducted by The California Youth Authority, a group of convicted juvenile delinquents were given immediate parole and returned to their homes or foster homes, where they got intensive care from community parole officers. After five years, only 28 percent of the experimental group have had their paroles revoked, compared to 52 percent of a comparable group that was locked up after conviction" ("Crime and the Great Society," *Time,* March 24, 1967, p. 21)

5. CHAD: All this talk about vitamin C preventing colds—I think it's a lot of bunk.

CAROL: Not me. I'm taking about 2,000 milligrams of it a day and I haven't had a cold all year.

CHAD: Big deal. There's nothing scientific about that. But let me lay this on you. Researchers recently carried out a mass experiment on 2,500 army conscripts. They were randomly divided, with half receiving 200 milligrams of ascorbic acid a day and the other half receiving placebos. And guess what—absolutely no difference was noted in the frequency or duration of colds or diseases of any description in the two groups!

6. "Aristotle believed a moving object could continue in motion only as long as something moved it. In the case of a projectile, air displaced by compression in front of the object came around behind it and pushed it along. The new medieval theory of 'impetus' insisted that a moving object continues to move until it is stopped by resistance: air has nothing to do with motion except insofar as it is a cause of friction. The anti-Aristotelian scientists of the fourteenth century used the rotary grindstone (a device that, as we have seen, was unknown to Aristotle) as a favorite nonspeculative proof of their position. The grindstone still turned for a time after the grinder's hand left the crank, but its motion, unlike the motion of a traveling projectile, displaced no air. Therefore the grindstone moved not by pressure of air but by impetus until the resistance of friction at the axle stopped it." (Lynn White, Jr., "Medieval Uses of Air," *Scientific American,* August 1970)

7. MAUDE: Don't tell me you're ordering a cheeseburger.
HARRY: Sure, why not?
MAUDE: Because meat contains large amounts of cholesterol and saturated fat, which stimulates the production of cholesterol. And cholesterol contributes to heart attacks.
HARRY: How do you know so much about all this?
MAUDE: I just read a study conducted on Seventh-Day Adventists. They don't eat meat at all, you know. Well, the study reports that Seventh-Day Adventist males suffered only 60 percent as much heart disease as other American males. And even where they did develop it, it was much later in their lives.
HARRY: Wow! . . . Hey, waiter! Cancel that cheeseburger, will you? I'll have the soybean burger with alfalfa sprouts on the side and a small plate of mash.

8. "Two ads were prepared, set in editorial style with no pictures, two columns, 100 editorial lines. The last paragraph a phone number. Ad number 1 differed from ad number 2 only in headline. Number 1's read, 'It's not the heat it's the humidity. New room coolers dry the air.' Number 2's headline read, 'How to have a cool home. Even on hot nights.' Number 1 was run one Friday in May in the local daily (circ. 400,000) and number 2 was run the following Friday. Number 1 produced 75 calls, number 2 produced 160 calls. Obviously number 2 was more effective at generating response." (Perry Weddle, *Argument: A Guide to Critical Thinking* [New York: McGraw-Hill, 1978], p. 187)

9. "It's not hard to demonstrate the key role that the love song plays in mating. Remove the male fly's wings and he will court with the same persistence as before, but his courtship is seldom successful. It is apparent that the male's wing display, at least, is a prerequisite to mating. Indeed, one species (D. obscura) sings no song and courts only by means of a silent wing display. This, however, is one of the few fruit fly species that will not mate in the dark. Since most species breed successfully at night, one must conclude that visual display alone is not enough to win female acceptance. The importance of sound to the female is also easy to demonstrate. Our colleague A. W. G. Manning has shown that when the antennae of a sexually responsive female are immobilized with glue, she ceases to be receptive." (H. C. Bennet-Clark and A. W. Ewing, "The Love Song of the Fruit Fly," *Scientific American,* July 1970)

10. MOTHER (to teenage daughter): Judy, I wish you wouldn't start smoking.
JUDY: Oh, I don't intend to, Mom. I know it's bad for your health.
MOTHER: It's not just that. I just read a study that links smoking to having sex.
JUDY: You're kidding!

MOTHER: Uh-uh. Two hundred and fifty boys and girls were interviewed at random. Fifty-seven percent of the boy smokers reported engaging in sexual intercourse, whereas only 23 percent of nonsmokers said they had. Of the girls, 31 percent of the smokers had had sex. Only 8 percent of the nonsmokers had.

JUDY: On the other hand, Mom, I'm inclined to think that the health hazards associated with smoking have been greatly exaggerated.

11. CITY COUNCIL MEMBER: Chief, every year you come before us and ask for more money to fight crime.

POLICE CHIEF: But, believe me Councilman, it's necessary.

CITY COUNCIL MEMBER: How can you say that? In 1978 we budgeted $30,000 for law enforcement and that year you reported a total of 200 crimes. In 1979, we gave you $35,000 and you reported 275 crimes. Last year we upped the ante to $40,000 and you have just reported that a whopping 380 crimes were committed!

POLICE CHIEF: What are you getting at?

CITY COUNCIL MEMBER: What I'm getting at is a *reduction* in your budget to $25,000.

POLICE CHIEF: You can't be serious!

CITY COUNCIL MEMBER: On the contrary. It's obvious to me that that's the only way we're going to reduce the annual crime rate in this city.

12. "Dew, the deposit of moisture on the outside of a cold glass, and the condensation of steam on the inside of a teacup all have one thing in common: air containing moisture is cooled to the point where it can no longer contain it all. This, then, is the cause of the phenomena: temperature dropping below the point of supersaturation." (Gerald Runkle, *Good Thinking: An Introduction to Logic* [New York: Holt, Rinehart and Winston, 1978], p. 255)

13. ANDY: Gimme a straight whiskey, will you?

BARTENDER: No water this time?

ANDY: No way. I've tried scotch and water, vodka and water, brandy and water, even whiskey and water—and every time I get kind of wobbly in the knees. No more water for me.

BARTENDER: Makes sense to me.

14. BILL: I think they should lower the speed limit to 40.

BUCK: That's pretty low. Lots of people favor raising it from 55.

BILL: I know, but don't you realize that traffic fatalities declined after the national speed limit was reduced to 55 mph?

BUCK: Yeah, but maybe cars or roads are safer or somethin'?

BILL: Naw! It's pretty clear: lower the speed limit, lower the death rate.

15. Sin causes punishment: AIDS is spread by homosexuals, and the Bible condemns homosexuality.

B. State the correlations which can be drawn in the following passages. Is there any reason to think that the correlation provides any support for a causal hypothesis? Explain.

1. The results of a nationwide poll indicate that 68 percent of females older than 18 favor the equal rights amendment, and 41 percent of males older than 18 favor it.

2. U.S. Census Bureau statistics indicate that in the 50-to-65-year-old age bracket five of every six divorced males marry for the second time; three of every four divorced women do.

3. A survey indicates that 57 percent of college students with below-average grades smoke pot; 21 percent of non-pot-smokers have below-average grades. Opponents of the legalization of marijuana claim that these figures prove that pot smoking causes one to get below-average grades. Others argue that getting below-average grades causes one to smoke pot. Is there reason to think that the correlation provides more justification for one causal hypothesis than for the other?

4. A study indicates that 52 percent of those earning in excess of $22,500 a year favor gasoline rationing, whereas 33 percent of those earning less than that figure favor gasoline rationing.

5. A study is conducted to find out whether people think that a government should give in to terrorist demands if that is the only way to save the lives of hostages. Eighty-eight percent of those who have been hostages say a government should; 11 percent of those who have never been hostages say it shouldn't.

6. A survey indicates that considerably more people who earn in excess of $30,000 a year believe that the United States should take whatever means necessary to secure enough industrial resources from Third World countries to ensure "the American way of life" than people making less than $30,000 a year.

7. Fifty-seven percent of "regular church or synagogue goers" are found to believe that at least some UFOs are extraterrestrial space travelers, as opposed to 21 percent of those who don't regularly attend a church or synagogue.

8. Teenage suicides often occur in clusters.

9. Various studies show that virtually all heroin addicts have smoked marijuana.

10. Records indicate that crime rates increase during periods of the full moon.

11. Records indicate that crime rates decrease during cold spells.

12. Male children of alcoholics are four times more likely to be alcoholics than are male children from nonalcoholic homes.

13. Every time I wash my car it rains.

14. A 15-year study of thirty celebrated American authors by University of Iowa psychiatrist Nancy C. Anderson finds that 80 percent were treated for mood disorders (compared with 30 percent of a control group), 43 percent experienced manic-depression (compared with 10 percent of the control group), 30 percent suffered alcoholism (compared with 7 percent of the control group), and two of the authors committed suicide. (Reported in *Psychology Today,* April 1987)

C. Identify the fallacies (post hoc, slippery slope, magical thinking, oversimplification), if any, in each of the following:

1. CRAIG: This bread you baked is great!
   JAN: It must be the sea salt. I ran out of regular salt for this batch.
   CRAIG: What a difference! You should use it all the time.

2. "Everybody I talked to there (in Vietnam) wants to know why they can't go in and finish it, and don't let anybody kid you about why we're there. If we weren't, those Commies would have the whole thing, and it wouldn't be long until we'd be looking off the coast of Santa Monica [at them]." (Bob Hope, quoted in Anthony J. Lukas, "This is Bob [Politician-Patriot-Publicist] Hope," *New York Times Magazine,* October 4, 1970, p. 86)

3. The women's liberation movement is partly responsible for the energy crisis because it's encouraged more women to enter the job market. This means more people are consuming energy on highways and at jobs than there used to be. (General Electric's energy systems manager John C. Fischer, in a speech to the National Academy of Science, January 29, 1973)

   Reactions to Fischer's remarks: "It's an incredible distortion. It's convulsive. We are becoming energy gluttons not because women are out working but because companies like G. E. are pushing energy-consuming appliances down our throats" (Ellen Zawell, head of National Consumer Congress). "The energy crisis started because of incredibly poor planning on the part of men" (Karen De Crow, author of *Sexist Justice*). "Women certainly have been wasteful. They have been taught to be ostentatious, to be the consumers. . . . But it's predominately [*sic*] a male-oriented values system. Women were taught to please men." (all quoted in the *Los Angeles Times,* January 30, 1974, p. 10)

4. Every millionaire in this city has blue eyes. Who would think the color of a person's eyes affects how much money they have?

5. If marijuana is legalized, then sure as shootin' heroin and cocaine are on the way.

6. PARENT: I hope there's not going to be any beer at that party tonight.
EIGHTEEN-YEAR-OLD SON: There may be. Why?
PARENT: Please don't have any, son. Taking the first drink is the surest way to end up an alcoholic.

7. While General Grant was handily winning battles in the West, President Lincoln received many complaints about Grant's drinking. One day a delegation told the President, "Mr. President, the General is hopelessly addicted to whiskey." To which Lincoln is said to have replied, "I wish General Grant would send a barrel of his whiskey to each of my other Generals!"

8. SAM: Did you know that a greater percentage of men in America smoke than women?
LIL: That just goes to show that being a male is a contributing factor to smoking.

9. MARSHALL: There's no question that if a person wants to be wealthy they should enroll in an Ivy League college.
LAVERNE: Why? Are they giving away bushel baskets full of money to jack up their enrollments?
MARSHALL: Almost. A study just released shows that twenty years after graduation, Ivy League graduates have an average income five times that of people who have no college education.

10. "I've always reckoned that looking at the new moon over your left shoulder is one of the carelessest and foolishest things a body can do. Old Hank Bunker done it once, and bragged about it: and in less than two years he got drunk and fell off the shottower and spread himself out so that he was just kind of a layer, as you may say; and they slid him edgeways between two barn doors for a coffin, and buried him so, so they say, but I didn't see it. Pap told me. But anyway it all come of looking at the moon that way, like a fool." (Mark Twain, *Huckleberry Finn*)

11. "Fascism thus repudiates the doctrine of pacifism—born of renunciation of the struggle and an act of cowardice in the face of sacrifice. War alone brings up to its highest tension all human energy and puts the stamp of nobility upon the people who have the courage to meet it. All other trials are substitutes that never really put men into the position where they have to make the great decision—the alternative of life or death." (Benito Mussolini, *Encyclopedia Italiana*)

12. "Is it really a coincidence that the height of the Pyramid of Cheops multiplied by 1,000 million corresponds approximately to the dis-

tance between the earth and sun? That is to say, 93 million miles?" (Eric von Daniken, *Chariots of the Gods*)

13. Letter to the editor on the subject of high apartment rents: "The high rents are the result of our officialdom neglecting to plan ahead, and just spending merrily, including pay raises and pensions for themselves, that resulted in these usurious property taxes. Now they want to use the apartment owner as a scapegoat to pacify the outraged senior citizens," presumably by controlling rents, limiting increases, and so on. (*Los Angeles Times,* December 1, 1977)

14. INTERVIEWER: Why do you think [rapes are up]?
    L.A. POLICE CHIEF ED DAVIS: I don't know. I'm trying to find out. I had a meeting with a bunch of policemen recently and I asked them how many had arrested rape suspects, and all of them had. How many of them had found any unusual quantity of pornographic literature in the rape suspects' homes? All of them had. Pornography gets into the hands of socially inadequate people who can't express themselves normally and be attractive, in love, or go through the courting routine and all that sort of thing." (*New West,* December 19, 1977)

15. "'Before he took B-15 he [her husband] could barely get up for his meals [because of a severe heart condition],' said Jaye Link, a 51-year-old Glen Cove, New York, widow. 'Two weeks after he started taking the vitamin pill he was completely changed.' Then Bill stopped taking the vitamins. Three months later he was dead— victim of a fifth heart attack. . . . Now Mrs. Link takes B-15 herself for arthritis. 'I take it constantly, three 50 milligram tablets a day,' she said. 'I have a slipped disc in addition to the arthritis. I tried everything under the sun to relieve the pain. But nothing else has worked.'" (*Globe,* September 11, 1979, p. 22)

16. RHETA: That chicken should taste a lot less oily than usual.
    ROB: Really? Why's that?
    RHETA: I used Wesson this time. You've seen their commercial, haven't you?
    ROB: The one where the actor returns the oil to the bottle after frying the chicken and the oil measures only a tablespoon less than it did to start with?
    RHETA: That's the one.
    ROB: Did you test it for yourself?
    RHETA: Not this time, but I intend to.

17. TRACY: I think it would be terrible if the state legalized gambling.
    TROY: But think about the revenue it would generate. That would really help out social services.

TRACY: Maybe. But do you want drugs, prostitution, and organized crime?

TROY: Well, no.

TRACY: Then you better think again about the merits of legalized gambling.

18. My wife left me because I wouldn't go to her mother's for Christmas; can you believe it?

19. After Baba Bubba touched my head I felt such a healing peace that I cannot doubt his holy powers.

20. "Order today: The Seven Magic Words to Guarantee Success! Learn the seven magic words to use to retrieve lost objects, to mend broken relationships, to get a job—and more!" (Ad for self-help cassette tape)

21. After his team lost the sixth game of the 1986 World Series, Dwight Evans said, "We've got to come back and win one ball game. Nothing more. It's as simple as that." (Lowell Cohn, *San Francisco Chronicle*, October 27, 1986)

22. "Rain is caused by high-pressure areas, cold front, warm, moist air and weekends." (Paul Sweeney in *The Quarterly*, in "Quotable Quotes," *Reader's Digest*, August 1990)

23. "I have always thought that anyone who sacrifices stuffing power by using chopsticks in a Chinese restaurant must be demented. I would use a tablespoon if I thought I could get away with it, but I know that the people I tend to share my Chinatown meals with, terrified that I would polish off the twice-fried pork before they had a chance to say 'Pass the bean curd,' would start using tablespoons themselves, and sooner or later we would be off on an escalating instruments race that might end with soup ladles or dorybailers." (Calvin Trillin, *American Fried: Adventures of a Happy Eater*, p. 61)

24. "The Human Life Amendment (and that is no euphemism) was introduced in response to the Supreme Court's unbelievable pronouncement that it is the law of the United States that unborn babies may be freely killed because they are incapable of 'meaningful life.'

"We do not know at this time whether the Court plans to pursue this reasoning to include paralyzed people, very old people, retarded people, or deformed people. But all such citizens might be described as being incapable of 'meaningful life.'" (Edwin A. Roberts, "An Amendment About Life," *The National Observer*)

25. "Sex educators loudly proclaim that there is no relationship between their methods and promiscuity. Yet the facts are disheartening, to say the least. At a time when youngsters know more about sex than

any preceding generation, we have more sex-related problems than at any other time in history. If the advocates of sex education as now taught consider this an endorsement of their approach, then I think they're more in need of 'instruction' than their childish charges." (Donna W. Cross, *Word Abuse*)

26. "Benjamin Fernandez, a Republican presidential nominee, was born in a converted boxcar in Kansas City, to Mexican immigrants, 53 years ago. When asked why he is a Republican, he says that when he was in college in California, someone told him the Republican party was the party of rich people. 'And I said, "Sign me up! I've had enough poverty."'" (George F. Will, *Washington Post*, August 23, 1979)

27. In 1990, Binney & Smith Inc., the makers of Crayola crayons, announced plans to replace eight pastel shades of color with brighter, bolder colors to accommodate what they identified as the changing tastes of the children of the 1990s. This upset many people. One of them was a New Yorker who objected to the removal of two favorite colors, raw umber and maize, and who faxed the following message to Binney & Smith Inc.: "If you remove them, what next will come? Burnt sienna? Periwinkle?" (Quoted by Pamela Mendel in *Newsday*, reprinted as "Crayola's Color Plan Protested," *Redding Record Searchlight*, July 26, 1990)

28. "**On guard.** Standing at a mirror in the restroom at the Phoenix airport, I got into a conversation with a woman next to me. I commented that I had all sorts of car troubles on the way there: I had difficulty starting the car in Gallup, N. M.; it finally died as we pulled off the interstate in Flagstaff, Ariz.; a mechanic there installed a new battery, but soon after, the car quit again. To top it off, I told her, when I called my husband at home, he told me our dishwasher was not working. Just then, a voice from the other side of the room broke in to ask, 'Miss—do you mind telling me what flight you're taking?'" (Contributed by Lola Poirer to *Reader's Digest*, August 1990)

PART FIVE

EVALUATING ARGUMENTS

CHAPTER 14

Sophistries and Pseudoscience

We must always follow somebody looking for truth, we must always run away from anyone who finds it.

ANDRE GIDE

It is the dull man who is always sure, and the sure man who is always dull.

H. L. MENCKEN

Scientific evidence enjoys a unique place in our society. It is generally accepted as the "court of last resort." That is, scientific proof is often viewed as being final, absolute, rock solid—certain. We know, however, that this is an oversimplification. Scientific reasoning is a combination of deductive inferences drawn from inductive generalizations. And like all forms of reasoning dealing with causes and effects, predictions, and general patterns, scientific reasoning results in probabilities, not absolute certainties.

We regularly draw generalizations from experience and use these to guide future choices. One of the most common kinds of everyday, practical reasoning, involves drawing tentative conclusions which help us organize and relate different ideas or events. We call this speculating or hypothesizing. That is, we offer initial explanations or predictions which we expect to confirm, modify, or reject based on more experience and evidence.

The term *hypothesis* is often used to mean any unproved or untested assumption. In a stricter sense, a *hypothesis is a tentative conclusion that relates and explains a group of different items of information*. For example, if you notice that your hair has become dry and brittle, you might begin to speculate on why. A natural place to start might be to survey any recent changes in your lifestyle which might affect your hair: new shampoo, changes in diet, stress, medication. If you identify a recent change, say in shampoo, you could hypothesize thusly:

"This new shampoo is probably causing my hair to become dry and brittle." You could easily test your hypothesis by switching back to your old brand. If this solves the problem, then experience will have verified your hypothesis. If not, you will need to construct another hypothesis or get professional advice. If you get advice, your doctor or cosmetologist will offer his or her own hypotheses—which must be tested against subsequent experience.

We hypothesize regularly: "Bob's probably been cranky lately because he's worried about the results of his English placement test; take my word, he'll be his old fun-loving self after he gets the results"; "I'll bet my grades will go up if I get more rest"; "Don't run your dishwasher unless you have it fully loaded, and watch: your water bill will go down." We test our hypothetical explanations with varying degrees of care and precision, depending on how important they are to us. Hypothesizing helps us go beyond merely generalizing about our own immediate experiences; hypothesizing helps us understand, explain, predict, and control events. It's a significant and familiar part of our everyday experience.

In the realms of social and medical science, the complex relation between the mind and body increases the number of possible factors involved in constructing appropriate hypotheses, and makes testing especially difficult. Yet the general public (and perhaps even some experts) continue to look to science for cures, gadgets, cheap fuel, clean air, the elimination of the ravages of old age, and so on. Even the most philosophical and religious among us tend to look to science for at least some of the keys to happiness and the control over the conditions necessary for it. Control comes from knowledge of cause and effect, and scientific reasoning is the most reliable way of determining causality.

PREDICTIVE POWER AND FALSIFIABILITY

When our hypothesizing concerns factual matters, it makes *empirical claims*. The word *empirical* comes from a Greek root that means "sense experience." *Empirical claims assert information about the sensible world*. The sensible world is the world we experience through our five senses: sight, touch, taste, hearing, and smell. Empirical claims describe or predict what sense experiences we will have when they are true or when they are false. This kind of predicting is part of our everyday experience; it's an informal way of hypothesizing. Let's look at two simple examples of empirical claims:

> *Practical Logic* weighs 7 ounces.
> The front cover of *Practical Logic* is yellow.

Both of the preceding sentences make empirical claims; they predict sense experiences involving the book you are reading right now. Note, however, that the authors of this book did not know *whether* or not these claims would be true when they wrote them, because the finished book had not been manufactured. But they did know *that* these two empirical claims would be either true or false—because they knew that such claims are *verifiable*.

If you are sighted, you already know whether the second claim was a reliable predictor of the sense experience of the cover's color—you have verified or refuted the claim that "The front cover of *Practical Logic* is yellow." If you are visually impaired or color blind, you will have to rely on others for verification or refutation. You are less likely to know *whether* or not this book weighs 7 ounces because most students don't weigh their books. You do know, however, *that* this book must either weigh 7 ounces or not weigh 7 ounces. In other words, you understand that the claim can be verified because it makes a falsifiable empirical claim. You know what steps are necessary to verify or falsify the claim that this book weighs 7 ounces.

An empirical claim is verifiable only if it is falsifiable in theory or in fact. A falsifiable empirical claim is subject to some test or experiment of disproof. If a claim is not falsifiable, it is non-empirical or unverifiable. In other words, its truth value is *unknowable*. (See "The Fallacy of Unknowable Fact" in Chapter 3.) When claims are verifiable they have *predictive power* or *empirical meaning. A claim has predictive power or empirical meaning only if we know what steps are necessary to verify **and** to falsify it.* In other words, if an empirical claim is not verifiable, it will lack predictive power.

Some philosophers refer to all unverifiable claims as "meaningless." To such philosophers, only empirical claims can be "meaningful." We recognize, however, that some individuals' most *personally meaningful* beliefs are expressed in non-empirical statements. Considerable confusion and, we think, unnecessary conflict occurs when we confuse personally meaningful non-empirical (unverifiable) claims with empirical (verifiable) ones. Here are two examples of unverifiable claims:

> Everything always happens for the best.
> I would have been killed in that accident if it weren't for my guardian angel.

These claims are unverifiable because we cannot even conceive of what steps to take to verify or falsify them.

You may be uncomfortable with the preceding examples because you've said and thought similar things, or because you know people who do. Unverifiable claims are quite common. When they involve cherished beliefs, scrutinizing them can be uncomfortable, to say the least. But we cannot become good critical thinkers if we do not hold ourselves to rigorous standards. Although we should not uncritically or maliciously attack ideas we do not like, we must not shy away from scrutinizing claims we personally cherish just because we cherish them.

Conflicting or inconsistent beliefs compete for our allegiance. Opinion polls show that more people believe in ESP than evolution. For starters consider: There are 20 times the number of astrologers in America than astronomers, and millions of people believe in astral projection, "channeling," healing properties of crystals, and the causal intervention of angels in our lives.[47]

---

47. See Thomas Gilovich's well-researched and intriguing work, *How We Know What Isn't So: The Fallibility of Reason in Everyday Life* (New York: The Free Press, 1991), Introduction.

By some estimates, Americans spend 10 billion dollars a year on quack medical cures. Included in that figure is an estimated three billion dollars on worthless cancer "cures," and at least one billion dollars on worthless AIDS cures.[48] In the realm of less serious conditions than AIDS and cancer, approximately 50 percent of all illnesses are "self-limited," that is, they are cured by the body's natural healing processes.[49] In other words, if the treatment doesn't kill us or make us sick, we'll recover no matter what kind of "cure" we are given.

It's clear that the stakes are high when it comes to acting on strongly held beliefs. We can jeopardize our very lives, waste hard-earned money or valuable time, and at the very least, diminish the quality of our lives when we accept bogus claims as legitimate, when we buy into unrealistic promises of health, wealth, and success. If we value truth and if we want to live the best lives possible, then we must be willing to test the more significant claims we encounter in our busy lives.

To begin, let's look at the "marketplace of happiness," and a special sort of trickster that thrives in it—the new sophist.

THE NEW SOPHISTS AND THEIR SOPHISTRIES

Does faith healing regularly occur in front of millions of viewers, as well-known television evangelists claim? Can we be "personally transformed" in a weekend? Is it possible for almost anyone to make a fortune with no experience and no money down? Can reading *Dianetics* help free us of past hangups? Can we really melt away tons of ugly fat while we sleep? Are there a few secret "power phrases" that will turn us into successful business dynamos? Can we improve our daily affairs by *Winning Through Intimidation?* Is "the government" secretly hiding proof of visits from extraterrestrials? Have the big oil companies bought up the patent to the 200-mile-per-gallon carburetor? Is the greedy medical profession hiding a cure for cancer in order to make lots of money treating it? Can Madame Rosa read your future in the Tarot deck? Can Mr. Lucky's astrological reading help you save your marriage?

These and related claims are the fertile province of cranks, con artists, pseudoscientists, and myriad salespeople, who offer us hope when we are discouraged, easy schemes when we are overwhelmed—instant fixes for our instant era. Unverifiable or unreasonable claims and the fraudulent characters who make them have certain basic characteristics that we can identify and then use to save ourselves from wasted time and money, from grief, from disappointment, from being used, even from an early death. All the time, money, and energy put into dishonest, unworkable, or truly harmful schemes are time, energy, and money that could be used more effectively to find reasonable and plausible solutions to our problems. If it sounds too good to be true, it usually isn't.

---

48. V. Herbert, Testimony before United States Congressional hearing, "Quackery: A 10-billion dollar scandal" (May 5, 1984), p. 88; "Preying on AIDS Patients," *Newsweek*, June 1, 1987.

49. Gilovich, p. 128.

Over the years, we have seen the rise of various systems, techniques, psychologies, therapies, and religions designed to offer a *quick fix, instant* enlightenment, *instant* gratification, the few *simple secrets (or keys) to success,* happiness, contentment, wealth, power, or health. Such claims are the special province of the "new sophists"—who are not really new at all.

This style of sophistry was identified in the West in Athens, in the fifth century BC, and remains essentially unchanged today. Sophists deliberately used flattery, mob appeals, all sorts of fallacies and persuasive devices, to advance any claim they chose, with no regard for truth. They would teach anybody anything if they were paid enough. They flattered their paying pupils and thrived on competition over who had the most disciples, who made the most money, and who had the most social connections. They believed in a dog-eat-dog world in which "it's not what you know but who you know." They curried favor with power and practiced as well as taught the arts of persuasion and manipulation. Sound familiar?

Because we are dealing with inductive reasoning here, we must judge each case on its own merits in light of the most likely evidence. Still, we can discern some general warning signs. The presence of one or more of these characteristics does not always indicate sophistry. We are wise, however, to be very careful in our scrutiny of any claims accompanied by the following:

1. There's *always* money required—usually up front.

2. Virtually anyone with the fee is accepted—without insistence on any special abilities or qualities—under the guise of being open and democratic.

3. Overly simple or overly complex language is used to manipulate and obscure, not to communicate straightforwardly.

4. The group is often centered on a "dynamic personality" who "discovered" the system but who is (or becomes) increasingly isolated, hostile, paranoid, and inaccessible.

5. An air of secrecy creates an aura of both elitism and paranoia in followers, which makes it difficult, if not impossible, to analyze claims or origins of either the leader or the doctrine.

6. There is often an escalating system: a hierarchy in which success at one level "entitles" you to advance to a higher one—always with a new fee attached.

7. The group is hostile to critical questions, favoring instead groupthink and groupspeak.[50]

8. There is widespread use of fallacies, especially personal attacks, in response to criticism.

---

50. For excellent literary treatments of groupthink and groupspeak see George Orwell's *1984,* Aldous Huxley's *Brave New World,* and Ira Levin's *This Perfect Day.* For a lucid philosophical treatment of the whole dynamic involved here, see, of course, Eric Hoffer's succinct classic *The True Believer.*

9. Often followers are isolated physically, emotionally, or intellectually by strictly controlling contact with unbelievers, censoring reading and friendships, and so forth.

Psychological Sophistry

Psychological sophistry tries to take advantage of the scientific aura of psychology without subjecting itself to the rigors of verification and falsifiability. Examples abound in certain kinds of self-help books and systems, on talk shows and in newspaper and magazine columns. Although experience is an important part of induction, we must be sure to scrutinize claims made by self-appointed experts, counselors, therapists and behaviorists who base their hypotheses on unspecified, undocumented, unverified "experience." We don't want to accept complex causal claims based solely on anecdotal evidence. Lack of data is often buried in a special kind of vague language which R. D. Rosen called "psychobabble."[51]

One of the hallmarks of this contemporary sophistry is extreme self-centeredness. Social scientists refer to this as the "egocentric point of view." What we find here is the substitution of exuberance for information, the substitution of feelings for reasons.[52] (See Chapter 4.)

Psychobabble is always an early warning sign of the possible presence of sophistry: In the case of much new sophistry, this means inappropriately personal sounding, overly warm, "open," "life-affirming" language coupled with an excessive emptiness of content and ultimately impersonal behavior. The psychological appeal of such talk is obvious; the practical value of it—except as a kind of personal expression—is not. When claims to knowledge are made, critical analysis is appropriate. And critical analysis requires verifiable claims and rational discourse, which psychobabble can never provide.

No claim is made by the new sophists that requires more than unreflective self-verification as a substitute for evidence—although a great deal of thought goes into creating the *impression* that meaningful claims are being made. By not actually saying anything meaningful, the sophist avoids the legal complication of having to substantiate the pseudoclaim—since no specific claim has been made. Thus, sophists are free to interpret their own words to their own advantage as circumstances require. Such empty claims allow their makers a perpetual escape clause: Sophists always take credit when we feel satisfied with their product. When we aren't satisfied, sophists always insist that the fault lies with us: *We* have somehow failed to try hard enough, to have enough faith, to think positively, and so forth. In either case, the system and the sophist appear to be beyond refutation—beyond falsification. The sophist has used circular reasoning in a way that makes

---

51. *Psychobabble* (New York: Atheneum, 1978), p. 51.

52. See Christopher Lasch, *The Culture of Narcissism: American Life in an Age of Diminishing Expectations* (New York: W. W. Norton, 1979).

© Tribune Media Services, Inc. Reprinted with permission.

it impossible to ever seriously criticize the system: The begged assumption is that all failures are ours. Thus, sophistic claims are not testable. This means that they are not falsifiable. If they are not falsifiable, they cannot be reasonable.

But not all of us seek personal transformation or enrichment. Some of us seek regular old "richment." We want to be wealthy, powerful, dynamic. We want to be *successful*. We need not fear. For us, there is another kind of sophistry.

EXERCISE 14-1

1. Analyze the following passage from a brochure titled "The Possible Human: A Journey of Personal and Social Transformation," a workshop with Jean Houston, Ph.D. (Jean Houston is the advisor whose relationship with Hillary Rodham Clinton came to public notice in 1996 with the revelation that Mrs. Clinton—under Houston's guidance—had imaginary "conversations" with Eleanor Roosevelt.) What kind of language usages can you find? Discuss in terms of the criteria for evaluating hypotheses and scientific methods referring to what you've learned about

sophistries, psychobabble, meaningfulness, and anything else from your logic studies that seems appropriate. What—specifically—is being said and promised?

> The premise of my teaching is that we cannot make the world work unless we are educated to do so. Most of us, unfortunately, are not being educated for the enormous complexity and challenge of our time. These educational workshops have been successful for so many people because we are providing them with an educational process whereby they develop dimensions of body, mind, spirit which gives them access to a far greater range of their own potentials. And with this they can deal creatively and even transformationally with problems, opportunities and challenges as these may arise. Thus, they can become change agents in their personal and professional lives—entrepreneurs of the possible, the ones who can, with the appropriate education, make a difference.

2. Werner Erhard, the controversial founder of EST (Erhard Seminars Training) is also associated with Transformational Technologies. Analyze his following comment about Transformational Technologies. What do you think he is really saying? Discuss in terms of what you've learned about sophistries, psychobabble, meaningfulness, and anything else from your logic studies that seems appropriate.

> What we intend that our work will do is to empower, facilitate and enable people to bring forth a new domain of possibility through which they will evolve on their own. Our work does not bring people to the end of that possibility but we intend it to bring them into a new possibility. So the work is a beginning rather than an end and it's true that people will come to new blocks in this new space of possibility.[53]

Success Sophistry

Success sophistries are chiefly concerned with selling us the secrets to quick, guaranteed success marked by money, power, and/or prestige. Although they may overlap with other kinds of sophistry, *success sophistries usually rely heavily on "powerbabble," a fusion of psychobabble, buzzwords, and puffery.* (See Chapter 5.) The chief function of this kind of language is to connote an aura of competency, power, and dynamism, a no-nonsense approach that "cuts to the heart of the matter and gets things done!"—without actually saying or doing much at all. Its style is usually overly simplified, nearly always vague, but "exciting."

---

53. Quoted in Mark Dowie's article, "The Transformation Game," *Image: The Magazine of Northern California,* reprinted in the *San Francisco Examiner,* October 12, 1986.

Some of the hallmarks of success sophistries include the following:

1. Promises of instant success

2. Simplicity almost anyone can follow

3. Use of power terms and language of dynamic action

4. Emphasis on money and social prestige

5. Promises of "secrets," "keys," "a few simple principles"—ways to manipulate other people or the marketplace

6. Stress on tricks and appearances more than development of substantive abilities

7. Unrealistic, absolute claims: "always," "inevitably," "without exception"

8. Demands for money—usually up front

One of the cleverest devices for getting money way up front is used by Barrie D. Stern at the end of *How To Be NUMBER ONE Instantly!*, a slim volume that introduces us to "skinetics," a way of "causing" others to become our allies by the use of an "effective" two- to four-second touch.

At the conclusion of the book, Stern says, "Quite a few people have asked me about legitimate businesses that they can get into where the use of skinetics can make them rich quickly."[54] Stern claims to have become rich by using skinetics in a business that "never goes out of style," a business resting on a very simple and "unique" way to get started for less than $200. This business requires no showroom, no stocking of merchandise. "You can make as much as $1,000 to $2,000 per night! Yes . . . per night! It's one of the few businesses that I know about that you can legally charge anyone as much as you want—the sky is the limit and you can never get into any kind of legal trouble!"[55]

This sounds too good to be true. But Stern was apparently writing a new book, which would cost $75 (the skinetics book, by the way, was only 64 pages long). Here's the truly clever part: We were told that because we had purchased the skinetics book, and because the business book, *How to Get into Almost Any Business You Want for $200 or Less!*, was not yet completed, we could reserve a copy for a "ten-dollar pre-publishing discount!" In other words, we were asked to send in $65 for an unfinished book. It would, we were promised, teach us " 'tricks' we've never seen or heard about before!"[56] (Like how to get people to pay $65 for an unwritten book?)

But perhaps you are more concerned with college. No problem; there are success sophistries for students, too. A flier for the Info/Quest Co. of Vancouver,

---

54. Barrie D. Stern, *How To Be NUMBER ONE Instantly!* (published by author, 1979), p. 62.

55. Ibid., p. 63.

56. Ibid., p. 64.

Washington, announces, "A Great G.P.A. Is Within Your Grasp! Guaranteed! 3 Power Packed Volumes. OVER 450 PAGES!—Guide to Better Concentration—How to Make Better Grades—The Exam Secret. Order Today! Only $10 postpaid."

How can anyone legitimately "guarantee" a "Great G.P.A." to any student who sends in $10? But is it actually a great grade point average that is being guaranteed? Or is the guarantee, rather, that a great GPA is "within your grasp," whatever that might mean. Perhaps we are being guaranteed that there are really 450 pages in the three "power packed" volumes? And what is a "power packed volume"? How come this "exam secret" is a secret? In other words, is anything specific being claimed, and if so, is it reasonable? There are, as you no doubt realize, countless ads for apparent sophistries dealing with business, personal health, or interpersonal success. They promise fantastic results for little or no effort or risk. They offer "guarantees" meant to suggest that the systems themselves are foolproof. Yet there is little *verifiable evidence* that such systems actually work.

Clearly, sales, interpersonal successes, breaking harmful habits, and the like require certain abilities. Some of these can be learned, but not all of them. Yet by stressing how "simple" their systems' requirements are, sophists imply that virtually anyone can succeed by using them. Many sophistic pitches use phrases such as "so simple almost anyone can follow this foolproof plan." Others, as we've seen, take great pains to encourage us that "no special education is needed," that results are "guaranteed," and so on. By implying guaranteed results, the success sophists tip their hands. In their breezy, overly confident way, they oversimplify some of the most complex, important, and frustrating aspects of our lives for one ultimate purpose: to sell us something.

They offer us something unreasonable—and out of confusion or need, we buy it. Yet with just a bit of clear thinking, we can usually see these "secrets" for what they are: twentieth-century snake oil. We'll close with a look at one of the most offensive species of sophistry: spiritual and psychic deception.

EXERCISE 14-2 *

Analyze and discuss the following for signs of success sophistry.

1. Miscellaneous items from a full-page newspaper ad: "California Millionaire Wants To Share The Wealth." A California millionaire only wants a check for $10 postdated 60 days. And his system, as he says, does *not* require "education," "capital," "luck," "talent," "youth," or "experience." What, then, does it require? "Belief. Enough to take a chance. Enough to absorb what I'll send you. Enough to put the principles into *action*. If you do just that—nothing more, nothing less—the results will be hard to believe. Remember—I guarantee it . . . soon you'll be making enough money to [give up your job]—I guarantee it."

2. From an ad for Helen Gurley Brown's book *Having It All:* "Let Helen Gurley Brown Show You How to Have It All! Love, Success, Sex, Money—even if you're starting with nothing. . . ." Ms. Brown also

states, "I'll scold you, support you, inspire you to become the best you can be—and that's enough to *guarantee* success. I promise!"

3. From an ad for Orgi-Nine: "New Pill Speeds Up Metabolism and Makes You Lose Weight Even While You Sleep!" We are cautioned, "As the pounds burn off, you should use good judgment and not let yourself become too thin."

4. Assess the comments from Jean Houston and Werner Erhard from Exercise 14–1 for signs of success sophistry.

Spiritual and Psychic Sophistry

Sophists exist in all areas of life. Some of the most unpleasant are found in religion, as has been demonstrated by James "The Amazing" Randi, a professional magician who publically debunks fraudulent healers and psychics.

Operating on the principle that "it takes one to know one," Randi believes that it takes a professional trickster to spot another professional deceiver. Hence, a magician can often spot what a layperson cannot. Martin Gardner, who coined the term pseudoscience, concurs, pointing out that according to magicians, scientists are actually among the easiest people for psychic frauds to deceive. "The thinking of a scientist is rational, based on a lifetime of experience with a rational world. But the methods of magic are irrational and totally outside a scientist's experience," Gardner says.[57] The habit of disciplined observation, which is so valuable under certain circumstances, is a liability when dealing with clever tricksters, for the typically trained scientist is very likely to look "where she's supposed to," meaning where the trickster wants her to look. A magician, on the other hand, is more likely to have the necessary background knowledge to look where she's not supposed to—at the source of the illusion.

Tricks of the Trade

Some of the common hedges against failure used by spiritual sophists might include:

1. Manifestations of spiritual or religious "powers" occur only before true believers or under conditions controlled by the sophist.

2. Circular, unverifiable explanations are offered whenever a manifestation of psychic or spiritual power appears to fail: The most common is a charge of lack of faith on someone else's part, never a failing of the sophist's "gifts" or "powers."

3. Healings are carefully limited to conditions unverifiable to the immediate audience: ulcers, asthma, leukemia, and so on—never the straightening of arthritically deformed joints, healing of burns, restoration of missing limbs, or the like, which are much harder to fake.

---

57. Martin Gardner, *Science: Good, Bad, and Bogus*, p. 93.

By permission of Johnny Hart and Creators Syndicate, Inc.

4. Vague or deceptive predictions are made.

5. Money is usually involved, even if it is called a "love offering" or a "good-faith gift." One subtle ploy involves demanding money as a form of "sacrifice" on the part of the follower. Bhagwan Shree Rajneesh had over one hundred Rolls Royces at his ashram in Oregon, claiming that they were "symbols" of the unimportance of possessions.[58]

Be especially wary of foolproof claims or any hypothesis which explains "too much." Remember that an adequate hypothesis must be falsifiable. If it is not, then it may beg the question. For example, when a psychic claims that a demonstration of psychic powers has been jinxed because someone in the room has "bad vibes," the psychic is begging the question of whether or not there is such a thing as psychic power.

In the hands of sophists, the hypothesis "There is psychic power," *explains too much*. That is, it explains both successful demonstrations and unsuccessful ones. In other words, it *predicts nothing*. The same tends to be true with astrological and metaphysical hypotheses. These are offered as after-the-fact "explanations": "Ah, now I know why I hate water. I drowned in a past life." Such sweeping hypotheses do not predict events. They fail to meet the reasonableness criterion for cogency.

When in doubt, ask yourself: What does this hypothesis predict? Can I verify it? Is it falsifiable? Does the hypothesis always have an answer to every challenge? If so, it explains "too much."

Electronic Wizardry

In 1986, psychic investigators James Randi, Paul Kurtz, Joseph Barnhart, and Philip Singer conducted surveys of various well-known, popular faith healers.

---

58. See Frances FitzGerald's article, "Rajneeshpuram, Parts I and II," in the "Reporter At Large" column of *The New Yorker,* September 22 and September 29, 1986.

Perhaps the most troubling item to come out of these investigations was Randi's discovery that the Reverend Peter Popoff was using a tiny, pink radio receiver inserted in his ear like a hearing aid to receive information sent to him on radio frequency 39.170 megahertz by his wife, Elizabeth.[59] Here is a sampling of what Randi's electronics expert, Alec Jason, recorded while Popoff was preaching in San Francisco: "Hello, Petey. I love you. I'm talking to you. Can you hear me? If you can't you're in trouble. 'Cause I'm talking. As well as I can talk. [Pause] I'm looking up names now."[60]

The "names," of course, were the names, street addresses, healing requests, and so forth, that Popoff's wife and assistant had gathered from cards filled out by audience members before the service. Elizabeth Popoff and Peter's assistant strolled among the faithful, matching cards with faces. Later, as Popoff publicly prayed and preached, Elizabeth would direct him from a van stationed outside the auditorium, using a television monitor to spot the people who'd filled in the cards.

And when Popoff asked if *he* had ever met these people before, they could honestly say no. His wife and assistant had met them instead. He had "plausible deniability." Thus, Popoff apparently deliberately concealed information to imply a false conclusion: Only divine knowledge could account for the remarkable accuracy of his claims.

In one of the most troubling of the recorded segments, Elizabeth laughingly says that they've got a "hot one"—referring to a prospect, an unfortunate woman with lumps in her breasts. According to Randi, there are recordings of Mrs. Popoff and a staff member laughing about the "big butts" of some of their temporary congregation, swapping recipes, and making small talk. What makes such callous deception especially reprehensible is that it occurs at the expense of desperate, seriously ill people, often seeking any last resort. We see graphically what can happen when unmet needs or powerful emotions dominate or block clear thinking.

Selective Cures
Randi also discovered that none of the healers studied ever attempted to heal anyone in a customized wheelchair or who exhibited any evidence of a severe physical disability. In fact, Randi and his crew discovered that some faith healers cart around their own wheelchairs and put elderly or tired persons in them before the service begins. Then, during the heated frenzy of the show, the healer rushes over to the person, grabs them, shouts something like, "Show these folks how you can walk!" and sends the excited or bewildered individual scurrying up and down the aisles. Here, again, we have what clearly amounts to deception.

Randi reports that some healers go so far as to have people demonstrate their faith in God's healing power by throwing away their medications—insulin,

59. James Randi, "Taking It on Faith," *Penthouse,* December 1986, p. 178.

60. Ibid.

digitalis, nitroglycerin tablets, for example. After the momentary excitement, most of these people find that they must return to their medications.

Concealing Wealth

As an additional element of deception, sophistic characters of all types can create the appearance of being nonmaterialistic by publicly reporting relatively modest salaries. As "nonprofit" legal corporations they need only report whatever portion of their income they pay themselves as "salary"—the rest can be buried in the corporation. So it is that "the church" or "the foundation" may be the technical owners of a fine house, a luxury automobile, even a sharp wardrobe, but only the sophist (and his or her family) has free use of them. Thus, although technically true that a given individual earns only a modest "salary," his or her real income may be astronomical. By equivocating on terms like *salary* and *own*, and speaking the literal legal truth to a general audience, which may be unaware of these legal distinctions, such characters can effectively conceal evidence of their true earnings.

Crossroads Pitch

A very common maneuver used by psychic sophists is a type of "reading" that we'll label the "crossroads pitch." Although there are variations, these usually follow a common theme: The psychic sees a vision, a dream, a spirit entity, or some other "psychic representation" of the person consulting them standing at a "crossroads." A typical reading might go like this: "I see a crossroads. One path is bumpy and heads downhill to a dark cloud. The other is steep and leads to a bright sun." If it's not a crossroads, it might be the bank of a stream or the foot of a mountain. The point is that it will involve *two clearly distinct choices.*

When are we most likely to seek psychic readings in earnest? Usually when we are confused, lost, or in need of assurance. It's a safe bet that *psychologically* the feeling of choice ("the crossroads") will strike a responsive chord. Then, if the psychic suggests that in the "near future" we will choose the sunlit, upward path, we feel more hopeful, confident, and pleased. We've been given just what we were looking for, told just what we hoped to hear. This simple, reassuring scenario may even have a placebo effect on our spirits, and our renewed self-confidence may then help us make better choices. But as clear thinkers, we do not want to settle for fallacious explanations of how the "reading" helped us.

Multiple Predictions

Another common way of "explaining too much" involves multiple predictions. To help understand this, consider a law of thought called the law of excluded middle: Either A is true or not-A is true, but not both (there is no middle possibility). Either it is Monday or it is not Monday. Note that the statement "Either it is Monday or it is not Monday" is true. Statements of this form (called *tautologies*) are always true. They are true by form or shape, not because they report facts. You can substitute any terms or statements you chose for A in the tautologous form "Either A or not-A," and always get a true statement. (You must of course use the same term for both substitutions.) In the preceding example we substituted "it is Monday" for *A*. Logicians call such tautologies *trivially true* to indicate that they only report a basic logical relationship, not new information or facts.

If a psychic predicts "It will rain tomorrow" or "It will not rain tomorrow," he or she is guaranteed to be "correct." But correct in a trivial way. We can rattle off thousands of such "predictions." So long as we retain the tautological form "Either *A* or not-*A*," we will always end up with a true statement. These statements are true by form. They are true as soon as we make them. In other words, they are not falsifiable predictions but merely tautologous pronouncements. Clever psychic sophists know better than to rattle these "pseudopredictions" off back to back. Instead, they make multiple predictions in different places and on different dates, and wait to see which half of the tautology occurs. The result is the same: a trivial truth. But the sophist loudly proclaims predictive ability and reminds us of the true half of the tautology, while hoping that we have forgotten the false one—if we even know of its existence.

A variant of this is to make scattered predictions that are not simply denials of each other. Many of these seem to be more along the lines of shrewd guesses and more ordinary nonpsychic assessment of current trends and events, much like a financial analyst might make stock market predictions. Examples of this approach include "psychic predictions" of natural disasters, economic or political trends, or divorce or marriage for celebrities.

Over 20 million people read the *National Enquirer* every week. In 1987, Jeanne Dixon made 13 predictions as part of the *Enquirer's* "10 top psychics" series. None of them came true, but Ms. Dixon remains famous and apparently successful. She is only one example of how little careful scrutiny is applied to verifying psychic predictions.

Remember that scientific reasoning involves the development of systematic knowledge. That includes repeatable observations and specific, falsifiable predictions. We must ask ourselves what being correct infrequently and without any apparent pattern means. Thus, even when psychic sophists can point to a list of accurate "predictions," we need to know the conditions under which they were made, as well as *how many wrong predictions are being hidden*. Further compounding our task of careful analysis is the vague nature of so many of these predictions.

Vague Prediction

Vague prediction involves disguised clichés, proverbs, and common sense. For example, a horoscope running near the Christmas/Hanukkah season might read, "GEMINI: Watch matters of health. Family member plays important role." Yet this would be good, basic, general holiday-time advice for most of us. It is common for summertime (meaning vacation-time) horoscopes to say something like this: "LIBRA: change of location a possibility. Expect variety. Secure possessions." Again, note that this is basic, "commonsense" advice for most people anticipating a vacation. With the advent of the inexpensive personal computer, random generation of such vague "advice" has become a simple matter.

"OF COURSE YOU DON'T BELIEVE IN ASTROLOGY. AQUARIANS NEVER DO."

Reprinted with special permission of King Features Syndicate.

Popular astrology books are likely to contain elaborate descriptions of the basic "type" associated with each of the twelve zodiac signs. These descriptions usually contain enough variety of traits, couched in inconsistent and general language, to accommodate the selective identification of most people. The very same "description" will probably have enough variety (that is, inconsistencies) to fit anyone. On page 1 we might read, "The typical Aquarian needs to be alone at times." Page 2 informs us that "Aquarians are well liked and enjoy the company of good friends." Page 3 tells us, "Don't ever try to pin an Aquarian down," whereas page 4 says, "When he makes up his mind on a course of action, the Aquarian is among the most reliable of sun-types." Add to this mishmash such qualifications as "usually" or "typically" and the complications of ascending and descending planets, signs, cusps, and so on, and you have plenty of ways of modifying any astrological charting to accommodate any individual. A high-tech variation can be found in the "900" numbers one can call to get "personal" horoscopes for $2.50 (or more) per minute. Roger Culver and Philip Ianna studied 3,011 specific predictions made by well-known astrologers, and discovered that only 10 percent were realized.[61] Yet true believers will insist that there is a much higher rate of accuracy. They may be able to convince themselves because vague claims are susceptible to whatever interpretation is most desired, and because we have the ability to selectively recall only what supports our beliefs, ignoring what doesn't. In fact, all that happens is that these claims are rendered unverifiable by explaining too much.

Causal Confusion

Note, too, the likely presence of causal fallacies. Many, if not most, "illnesses" and depressive moods are self-limiting, which means that we will recover from

---

61. Charles Downey, "Straightening Out the Mind Benders," *This World Magazine,* November 9, 1986, p. 9.

them in time without any treatment. So whether we consult a palmist, numerologist, "psychic surgeon," fortune-teller, or bank teller today, we will be "cured" in the future (if nothing else interferes). However, we might be inclined to *attribute* our recovery to some noteworthy, prior event, such as our visit to the sophist. The psychic or faith healer who lays hands on us Wednesday will most probably claim credit for "healing" us when our illness has run its natural course on Friday.[62]

We should not overlook those people claiming to be "cured" of self-diagnosed "cancers," "ulcers," and so forth. As impartial observers, we cannot be sure that there ever was any organic condition to cure. What is glaringly absent in most such cases is any body of carefully controlled studies that support these remarkable claims. But as sophists from ancient times to the present are quick to point out, *scientists have been unable to disprove the successful sophist's claims of faith healing or psychic healing*—which is, we know, an instance of the argument-from-ignorance fallacy. That a major reason for the lack of such scientific criticism can be traced to the healers' refusal to cooperate in the acquisition of data, observations, and controls is, of course, not pointed out.

To a certain extent, we are perhaps sometimes responsible for our own gullibility. This does not, however, diminish the responsibility of those who deliberately and with great care fabricate claims designed to promise more than they deliver, and who deliberately take advantage of a person's feelings of inadequacy, financial fears, confusion, or suffering. We are justified in holding these sophists accountable because a great deal of *careful reasoning* has gone into crafting their fraudulent promises in ways that protect them from legal prosecution or from public exposure. We can conclude, therefore, that these misleading claims are deliberate.

Our best protection is to think clearly for ourselves and to use what we've thus far learned (and will learn) in our logic studies. We should always look for the presence of fallacies, and we should always demand clarity of expression—especially when promises are made that affect our pocketbooks; our self-esteem; or our physical, mental, or emotional well-being. We must ask basic questions, using our own experience to test all claims where possible and consulting objective experts when our own knowledge and experience are inadequate guides.

Good thinking skills are at their most practical when the stakes are the highest.

EXERCISE 14-3

1. The Amazing Randi reports that he once pretended to be an "astro-graphologist" on a call-in radio show out of Winnipeg, Canada. Listeners were asked to send in their birthdates and samples of their handwriting

---

62. This is an example of a casual fallacy called post hoc: Based *solely* on the fact that event *A* precedes event *B*, we conclude that event *A caused* event *B*. Post hoc is explained in Chapter 13, which deals with the concept of cause.

during the week before Randi's appearance. During his appearance, Randi gave "readings" for three listeners, who were then asked to call in and evaluate their accuracy. Randi was judged to be quite successful, initially getting accuracy ratings of 9, 10, and 10, with 10 being the highest score. The 9 was changed to a 10 after the first listener objected when Randi said that he disliked hard work. The listener pointed out that he was a laborer and was accustomed to hard work. "But," Randi countered, "I said that you *disliked* hard work." "True," the listener said. "I guess you're right, I don't really *like* it." [63]

As Randi says, the most amazing thing about the whole experience is that he did not have any handwriting samples or birthdays with him. Instead, he read, word for word, three readings that had been given in Las Vegas months before by Sydney Omarr while on "The Merv Griffin Show." The readings were originally done for three members of Merv's audience. [64]

Analyze this incident using concepts you've learned regarding fallacies, persuasive language, psychic sophistries, and pseudoscience.

2. Some popular television evangelists announce what they call a "Word of Knowledge" about healings: "I see a tumor shrinking. I see someone with congestion clearing up now. I see a broken marriage being mended at this very minute." What do you suppose are the odds that in an audience of a million or more people someone, somewhere will fit these symptoms? If just a small percentage of those watching notice that their (self-limiting) diseases disappear and send in a note of thanks, our sophist has a batch of testimonials. (One percent of a million is 10,000, so the odds of hitting a few "predictions" are high.)

What steps could be taken to verify such claims? You might want to write politely to see if you can find any objective evidence supporting such claims for a particular healer. If you do, analyze whatever response you get.

PSEUDOSCIENCE

Pseudoscience, a term coined by Martin Gardner, *refers to a certain category of theories, systems, and explanations, which though claiming to be "scientific," in fact use only the trappings of genuine science and avoid the rigors of the checks and balances of the scientific method or the scrutiny of disinterested experts.* [65] Invoking a certain

63. James Randi, *Flim-Flam!* (Buffalo, N.Y.: Prometheus Books, 1982).

64. Ibid.

65. See Gardner's *Fads and Fallacies in the Name of Science* (New York: Dover Publications, 1950) and *Science: Good, Bad, and Bogus: A Skeptical Look at Extraordinary Claims* (Buffalo, N.Y.: Prometheus Books, 1981), as well as James Randi's *Flim-Flam!* for more detailed explanations and examples of this useful concept.

caricature of scientific language and method, pseudosciences have proven to be highly lucrative to their founders and highly durable. What, then, are the basic characteristics of the pseudoscientist?

1. "First and foremost of these traits is that [they] work in almost total isolation from their colleagues . . . isolation in the sense of having no fruitful contacts with fellow researchers."[66]

2. The pseudoscientist submits his or her work not to bona fide experts in the field but to the general public, though the public is not qualified to evaluate it.

3. The pseudoscientist speaks through organizations he or she has founded, thus avoiding genuine peer review and conveying an aura of professional expertise.

4. The pseudoscientist considers himself or herself to be a genius (most likely misunderstood and persecuted).

5. The pseudoscientist regards colleagues to be, almost without exception, "blockheads" (Gardner's term).

6. The pseudoscientist compares himself or herself to Galileo, Bruno, Pasteur, or other well-known, well-respected scientists whose work met initial hostility and resistance. The pseudoscientist repeatedly cites comparisons between his or her own case and historical cases of the persecution of true scientific genius, which was initially misunderstood. (This functions as a form of the fallacy of positioning.)

7. The pseudoscientist exhibits a strong compulsion to focus criticism on the greatest scientists and/or best-established theories of the day.

8. The pseudoscientist tends to write in a complex jargon often making use of phrases, terms, and locutions he or she has coined. This rhetoric can be quite persuasive, creating a beautifully crafted jigsaw puzzle of assertions. Clever use of circular reasoning, equivocations, and other persuasive tricks makes it difficult to refute pseudoscience by logic and authentic scientific evidence.

Isolation from the scientific community greatly diminishes the chances of a hypothesis being thoroughly and correctly tested. Appeals for consensus from groups of unqualified laypeople substitutes popularity for legitimate authority. Use of complex, often invented, language makes meeting the falsifiability and testability criteria for hypotheses virtually impossible. Claims must be presented in precise language in order to be verified.

Although we must take care not to slip into the error of dismissing every "isolated" theorist or iconoclastic thinker as a pseudoscientist, a little careful

---

66. Gardner, *Fads and Fallacies*, p. 8.

thought about the "scientific establishment" suggests that, *as a rule,* scientists do not "gang up" against each other. Galileo, for example, was persecuted for political and theological reasons by the church and by scientists who subsumed their science under what they believed were the demands of their faith. More important, it was scientists—*not laypeople*—who ultimately accepted Galileo's superior evidence. Throughout history, the ultimate validation of the misunderstood scientific genius has come from fellow scientists, as it must. As laypeople, we are usually not qualified to pass judgment on the scientific merits of such disputes. And this is to the advantage of the pseudoscientist, who would rather appeal to our sympathies, to our fears and hopes, and to our basic distrust of "the establishment" than to a qualified, objective jury of genuine scientific experts.

In our own times, various best-sellers have extolled the theory that ancient "astronaut gods" visited prehistoric Earth in "chariots of the gods." Other popular books identify an area off the Florida coast as the deadly "Bermuda Triangle." Invariably, their authors rely on the general public for validation of their claims—not qualified experts.

To illustrate the practical importance of relying on legitimate authority in our daily dealings, we'll consider a hypothetical case: If the owner of the corner health food store tells me that "natural vitamins" are better for me than "artificial" ones, but my doctor and my chemistry professor both say that there is no significant difference, how am I to know which assertion to act on?

I can ask myself, "What kind of stake does each party have in the answer? What qualifications and experience does each party have relative to this issue?" In this hypothetical case, the store owner has a financial stake in what he or she says, and no verifiable expertise in vitamins, nutrition, or chemistry—only his or her own testimony and sincerity. My doctor and chemistry teacher, on the other hand, don't seem to have any stake that would be likely to bias their claims to the point of invalidating them. Thus, for me—a *nonauthority* on chemistry, biochemistry, nutrition, and vitamins—to reject the consensus of two qualified, unbiased authorities on behalf of the claim of a single nonexpert with a financial stake in the claim is rather foolish.

If my astronomy teacher asserts that astrological claims are untenable because the original observations on which they are (still) based were erroneous, but my astrologer tells me that I shouldn't marry you because our "sun signs are incompatible," whom should I trust?

Of course reading my horoscope is easier and, perhaps, more fun than learning enough physics and astronomy to make an educated assessment of astrological claims. It is also easier than making a serious attempt at an accurate and honest assessment of our current relationship and our chances for a long and healthy marriage. Then, too, pseudoscience sometimes appeals to our desire to be in touch with the mysterious forces of the universe, a desire to be in touch with guaranteed "inside information," perhaps even a need to feel special.

Pseudoscience also seems to thrive in part because of our basic distrust of "the establishment." We all know of professionals who refuse to consider any new theories until absolutely forced to. Science is conservative—it must be as a way of demanding quality evidence that can withstand rigorous testing and evaluation. And let's not overlook the widespread desire for hope. Science does not always provide enough hope fast enough. And it rarely provides the invariable "guarantees" of the pseudoscientist.

So it is that claims for psychosurgery, instant healing by the laying on of hands, or some other psychic process appeal to us. We want guaranteed hope where science offers only the possibility of hope. We want "magic"—a quick, easy, guaranteed way of making hard choices: Enter astrology, Tarot, palmistry, myriad "readings," mood rings, Kirlian photography, and other ways—we hope—of quickly and easily understanding life and choosing well.

A special species of pseudosciences involves spiritual gurus, financial gurus, social gurus, and healing gurus—all those characters lined up to sell us happiness, success, wealth, or health. They're called *sophists,* and they're all over the place. And because some of them can do us great harm, we'd be wise to get to recognize the species.

EXERCISE 14-4 *

A. Discuss the following in terms of pseudoscience and any other logical fallacies and principles that may pertain.

1. From the back cover of Joseph H. Cater's book *Awesome Force,* "A Private Publication of Cadake Industries," we read,

> This book will astonish the scientific community and shock the world. . . . In this book you will find one of the original thinkers of the 20th century relate information that will stun the layman and also the scientist. . . . He defiles [sic] the orthodox scientist for keeping the status quo. . . . Not since Velikovsky has one man dared to reveal what orthodox scientists would like to bury under the rug.

We are also told that Cater, "disillusioned with academic physics," gave up his career in this field to develop "the awesome force"—"The Unifying Principles for All Physical and Occult Phenomena in the Universe." Cater says that "there is no known phenomena [sic] not taken in stride by these new ideas."[67] He says that his revelations can be expected to "make a shambles of currently popular, and universally accepted ideas of conventional science," adding that he is not likely to endear himself to the scientific community at large, and so on.[68]

In Chapter 1, Cater claims that the moon has a surface gravity much like Earth's, but that NASA has covered up that fact by using doctored television transmissions of moon landings. Cater claims that NASA slowed down the transmitted images so that objects appeared to fall slower than they really did, and so on. He also asserts that the astronauts' spacesuits do not really weigh the claimed 185 pounds,

---

67. Joseph H. Cater, *Awesome Force* (Winterhaven, Fla.: Cadake Industries), p. 9.

68. Ibid.

that the "research and evidence" indicate that the suits could only weigh 20 pounds or less.

2. When Simon & Schuster published the blockbuster diet book *Calories Don't Count,* it had not sent the manuscript to a single expert for evaluation. The original manuscript, written by Dr. Herman Taller, a gynecologist, was simply rewritten by a free-lance sports writer, Roger Kahn.[69]

3. The late Carlton Fredericks was a very popular nutrition guru on radio who used the title "Doctor." He was a Ph.D., not an M.D. His dissertation was from the New York University School of Education, based on a thesis discussing how his female listeners responded to his own radio broadcasts.[70]

4. Scientists rarely debate publicly with pseudoscientists. Isaac Asimov says that one reason scientists rarely win such debates is because they often take place in front of audiences who have only the sketchiest of scientific backgrounds.[71] Elaborate on Asimov's point. Are there any other factors you can think of that might actually put the scientist at a disadvantage when dealing with refutations of pseudoscience?

B. Analyze the following *Dianetics*[72] quotes in terms of the general characteristics of pseudoscience thus far covered and for any other fallacies and difficulties you find pertinent.

> For thousands of years Man has been looking for the answers to his own mind, what it is, how it affects him and what he can do about it.
>
> At last, here is a book, DIANETICS: THE MODERN SCIENCE OF MENTAL HEALTH which provides the answers to the problems of real happiness for every man, woman and child on this planet.
>
> THIS BOOK CAN CHANGE YOUR LIFE!
> PERHAPS YOU COULD BE HAPPIER!
> BUY THIS BOOK BY
> L. RON HUBBARD TODAY

SUMMARY

In this chapter, we have learned about empirical claims, the importance of falsifiability, pseudoscience, and sophistry. We've discussed some of their general char-

---

69. Gardner, *Science: Good, Bad, and Bogus,* p. 55.

70. Ibid., p. 54.

71. See his interesting, succinct essay, "Losing the Debate," in *The Roving Mind* (Buffalo, N.Y.: Prometheus Books, 1983), pp. 29–30.

72. L. Ron Hubbard, *Dianetics: The Modern Science of Mental Health* (Los Angeles: The Church of Scientology of California, 1950), front and back cover copy.

acteristics, applying what we've learned about scientific reasoning, knowledge, and legitimate authority.

Pseudoscience, a term coined by Martin Gardner, refers to a certain category of theories, systems, and explanations, which though claiming to be "scientific," in fact use only the trappings of genuine science while avoiding the rigors of the checks and balances of the scientific method or the scrutiny of disinterested experts.

The *"new" sophistry* refers to the deliberate use of fallacies, persuasive language, "powerbabble," manipulative techniques, and personal charisma to sell success, health, salvation, or well-being.

We identified three general categories of sophistry in terms of their primary areas of interest, noting that all three may overlap: psychological sophistry, success sophistry, and spiritual and psychic sophistry.

Summary Exercises

1. Scan a recent issue of one of the popular newspaper tabloids for examples of sophistry. Analyze your examples in terms of the list of characteristics covered in this chapter.

2. Why do you think sophistries and pseudoscience persist to the extent that they do today? Do you see this persistence as good, bad, or unimportant? Discuss.

ADDITIONAL EXERCISES

1. In April 1978, *Psychic News* reported that one Ingo Swann had made an "astral trip" to Mercury and Jupiter. Swann apparently described his "impressions" of these planets well before *Mariner 10* journeyed past Mercury and *Pioneer 10* past Jupiter. *Psychic News* quoted astronaut Edgar Mitchell as saying that Swann described things that were not known to Earth scientists until *after* the *Mariner* and *Pioneer* probes.

   When careful analysis was made of Swann's 31 claims, six were true and four were probably true, 11 were wrong, one was probably wrong, three were unclear, and four were obvious.

   When his errors were pointed out in conversation with a British Broadcasting Corporation producer, Swann claimed that travel by astral projection takes place at such great speeds that it disorients the astral traveler. Swann then said that he had probably shot past Jupiter into another solar system: He had described another planet, not Jupiter.[73]

   Discuss this incident.

2. In his book *Superminds,* popular British "science personality" John Taylor, a mathematical physicist at King's College in London, claimed that

---

73. Gardner, pp. 63–68.

controversial "psychic" Uri Geller could bend spoons, keys, and other metal objects. According to Gardner, Taylor has, however, been unable to actually see anything bend or to videotape any actual bending. The reason for this is what Taylor labels the "shyness effect": Bending is most likely to occur when no one is looking.

Among his many claims, Taylor asserted that hundreds of British "superkids" could duplicate Geller's psychic bending. He backed up this claim by giving children crudely sealed tubes containing a straight metal bar. The children took them home and returned with bent bars. Taylor was perplexed by the curious fact that bending did not occur when the children were given well-sealed tubes.[74]

Discuss this incident.

3. Discuss the following assertions, which are part of a full-page ad headed "FROM DEBTS TO RICHES, THE POOR MAN'S ROAD TO WEALTH"—A PROVEN METHOD TO ACHIEVE FINANCIAL FREEDOM!

"From Debts To Riches The Poor Man's Road To Wealth" will show you how you can achieve an income of up to $5,000.00 per month, just by spending a few hours per day following the easy to read instructions in my book. **In it YOU WILL LEARN:**

—How to PASS any credit investigation.
—How to WIPE OUT all of your DEBTS, if you so wish, and still MAINTAIN AAA CREDIT.
—How to achieve FINANCIAL SECURITY, and a life of luxury, in less than 90 days.
—How to raise all the CAPITAL you need.

To accomplish all of the things contained in "From Debts to Riches The Poor Man's Road To Wealth," **there are some things that you DON'T NEED.**

—You don't need to be a genius
—You don't need to have an education
—You don't need to sell anything
—You don't need to visit anyone
—And you don't need to even move out of home.

4. What at first glance appears to be an article with the dateline Peachtree City, Ga. is headed "HIDDEN HEALTH SECRETS DISCOVERED." In small print, we notice that it is in fact an advertisement. Here's a sampling from that ad:

Amazing New Discoveries Give You Perfect Health and Help You Feel Great. (Special)

---

74. Gardner, *Science: Good, Bad, and Bogus,* pp. 93–94.

FC&A, a nearby Peachtree City, Georgia medical publisher announced today the release of a new, $3.99 book for the general public: *"Hidden Health Secrets."*

Look At Some Of the Secrets
Revealed In This Amazing
New Book
—Secrets that may help protect against gallstones, diverticulosis, some types of cancer, hardening of the arteries, varicose veins and hemmorrhoids [sic]
—A little known secret that can pep you up without pills
—A vitamin that cuts allergy and asthma attacks in half
—This secret may keep you from losing your teeth
—Headache . . . a mineral that may be helpful to migraine sufferers
—Ways to combat the common cold

Discuss this "article" in terms of the material covered in this chapter and any other fallacies, ambiguities, and so on, that seem pertinent.

CHAPTER 15

Normative and Nonnormative Arguments

Come now, let us reason together.

ISAIAH: 1:18

This chapter is about one of the most difficult yet interesting and important aspects of argument in real life: values in arguments. The word *value* comes from the Latin root *valere,* which means "to be strong" or "to be worth." Value judgments, then, involve assessments of worth.

Many of the most important questions we face, as individuals and as a society, involve values and value judgments. Daily we must formulate and respond to discourse on issues that involve assessments of worth: Is paying $300 a month for a car *worth* the sacrifice? Is learning logic *worth* giving up television time? What is the *worth* of a fetus's life? Of a woman's? Since it is impossible to avoid making value judgments, we'd best learn to deal with them intelligently and critically.

Because arguments involving value judgments constitute a large and vital part of our lives, and because they raise unique problems of analysis, we're devoting this last chapter to them. The primary object of this chapter is to broaden the scope of our practical logic, to show how what we've thus far learned can and should be used in what is the most meaningful aspect of our lives: values and value judgments.

In a real sense, then, this chapter begins our commencement. It keynotes ways that we can bring our practical logic to bear on the bread-and-butter issues of life. Its intention, of course, is not to impart values or to present a theory of value. Rather the chapter aims to provide an outline of how we can start to deal intelligently with value arguments—an outline that's broad enough to entertain diverse values and value systems yet narrow enough for immediate use.

But before getting into this important and intriguing subject, let's draw together what we've covered thus far by presenting a handy method of argument evaluation. What we present will provide a basis for evaluating any argument, including those expressing values.

EVALUATING ARGUMENTS: THE BASIC PROCEDURE

In the preceding chapters we learned how to spot argumentative cases, what valid deductive procedure is, what justified inductive procedure is, how to recognize formal fallacies, what informal fallacies are and their great variety. We identified three criteria for cogent arguments: reasonableness, relevancy, and sufficiency. We learned that critical thinking involves evaluating arguments according to these basic criteria. Although we need not be conscious of the process we use when evaluating and analyzing arguments, it might prove helpful to ponder the basic components of critical argument analysis. The following four basic guidelines are offered as a framework for analyzing and evaluating arguments. Your instructor may wish to adapt these to his or her own coverage of the text. *And, as always, our background knowledge and personal experience play a vital role.*

1. Clarify meaning.

2. Identify basic structure (premises and conclusion): What is being concluded, and what evidence is offered? This may require filling in any missing premises.

3. Identify any fallacies: formal and informal.

4. Apply cogency criteria: Are premises reasonable? Relevant? Sufficient?

As we briefly elaborate on each of these steps, note that they need not always be applied in order or as completely distinct steps. You might, for instance, quickly spot exclusive premises or a fallacious personal attack when first encountering an argument. If so, then you may not need or wish to evaluate the argument further. If, on the other hand, an argument under scrutiny is not immediately clear, you can use the four basic steps to organize your analysis. At any step, you might discover a flaw which renders the argument not cogent. If so, then further analysis may not be necessary. Let's elaborate a bit on each of the basic evaluative procedures.

The first thing we must do is make sure that we clearly understand what is being claimed. We begin with a linguistic and contextual overview. At this stage, we apply what we've learned about context, intention, and language. We want to make sure that we understand what is *intended,* not just what is *said.* To do this fairly and thoroughly, we must consider the context in which the argument occurs and carefully scrutinize it for unclear or misleading language. With experience, we need not consciously delineate each of these concerns; rather, we develop a sensitivity to the nuances of argument.

Before even attempting to clarify meaning, read a passage all the way through. This will give you a feel for the argument as a whole. If you happen to disagree with the position advanced, don't allow your disagreement to color your interpretation. If you don't understand some words, consult a dictionary. Beware of the blocks to critical thinking in the passage itself and in your own reaction. Recall and use what you've learned about stress and clear thinking, defense mechanisms, and methods of distortion. (See Chapter 4.) Be alert for double-speak in the forms of: (1) obscure or ambiguous language, including jargon; (2) shifts in word meaning; (3) bias communicated by highly emotive words and loaded epithets; and/or (4) euphemism.

Next, identify the argument's structure. Recall that signal words such as the following are helpful in identifying premises and conclusions. (Chapter 2):

> **Conclusion signals:** then, therefore, consequently, it follows that (and so forth)
> **Premise signals:** since, because, for, insofar as (and so forth)

When an argument contains none of the above, ask yourself: What is being advanced? What is the arguer trying to demonstrate as true? The answer to these questions most probably is the argument's conclusion. Similarly, to locate premises in the absence of signals, ask yourself: What bases does the arguer give for drawing the conclusion?

If necessary, reconstruct the argument into some syllogistic form—standard-form categorical, disjunctive, conditional. (See chapters 7, 8, and 9.) This includes minor or "mini" arguments, consisting of premises and their support, as opposed to the main argument, which consists of main premises and a main conclusion.

Fill in missing premises whenever an argument is incomplete and its missing premise is not exactly obvious. An argument is incomplete when the stated premises are insufficient to logically entail the conclusion. In other words, the conclusion in a fragment argument (enthymeme or sorites) is asserting more than the expressed premises logically warrant. (See Chapter 8.)

After identifying the argument's structure, our next task is to determine if it commits any formal fallacies. Apply the six rules of validity in the case of standard-form categorical syllogisms. If the argument is a hypothetical or disjunctive syllogism, determine whether its form is valid or invalid.

In checking the argument for informal fallacies, be familiar with the many emotional and psychological appeals that we've studied. While these devices are psychologically persuasive, they are irrelevant, presumptuous, or confusing, and therefore, illogical.

FALLACIES AND DEFENSE MECHANISMS COVERED IN THE TEXT

The numbers in parentheses indicate the chapters in which the fallacies are discussed.

Defense Mechanisms

Denial (4)
Introjection (4)
Prejudging (4)
Projection (4)

Rationalizing (4)
Scapegoating (4)
Stereotyping (4)

Fallacies of Meaning

accent (5)
amphiboly (5)
buzzwords (5)
composition (5)
division (5)
doublespeak (5)

equivocation (5)
euphemism as doublespeak (5)
gobbledygook (5)
jargon as doublespeak (5)
puffery (5)

Fallacious Reliance on Emotion

bandwagon mob appeal (6)
character assassination (6)
circumstantial personal attack (6)
fear of force (6)

pity (6)
snob appeal (6)
tu quoque (6)

Fallacious Reliance on Diversion

humor and ridicule (6)
red herring (6)

straw argument (6)
two wrongs (6)

Fallacious Reliance on Assumption

begging the question (6)
complex question (6)
dismissal (6)

loaded epithets (6)
willed ignorance (6)

Fallacies Connected with Induction

accident (10)
anecdotal evidence (10)
apples to oranges (10)
biased sample (11)
concealed evidence (11)
false dilemma (11)
faulty analogy (9)

guilt by association (10)
hasty conclusion (10)
magical thinking (13)
oversimplification (13)
post hoc (13)
slippery slope (13)
statistical equivocation (11)

Fallacies of Authority

argument from ignorance (3)
popularity (3)
positioning (3)

provincialism (3)
traditional wisdom (3)
unknowable fact (3)

Formal (Deductive) Fallacies

affirming the consequent (9)	existential (7)
denying the antecedent (9)	four terms (7)
drawing an affirmative conclusion from a negative premise (7)	illicit major term (7)
	illicit minor term (7)
exclusive premises (7)	undistributed middle term (7)

COGENCY, KNOWLEDGE, AND TRUTH

Ultimately, we need to apply the cogency criteria, checking to see that the argument contains enough of the right type of evidence to support the conclusion. In the processes of clarifying meaning, identifying form, or spotting fallacies, we might discover that an argument violates one or more cogency criteria. *In such instances, we do not need to apply the cogency criteria as a distinct step.* If, however, an argument is valid or inductively justified in terms of reasonableness and relevancy, we still need to determine if it provides sufficient evidence for its conclusion. We must ultimately assess the reliability and quality of its truth claims.

Here we can call upon what we've learned about knowledge, truth, and belief. (See Chapter 3.) Can the premises be substantiated by publicly verifiable tests? The legitimacy of observations offered as evidence depends on (1) the physical conditions under which they were made; (2) the sensory acuity of the observer; (3) the background knowledge of the observer; (4) the objectivity of the observer; and (5) the corroborative testimony of others. (See Chapter 3.)

Having completed the preceding analysis, we are now in a position to give the argument an overall assessment. Does it have force? That is, does it meet the cogency criteria? Are we ready to go with the argument on balance, or against it? Has the arguer won us over? To answer questions like these, we must return to our basic four-step evaluative procedure, especially to steps 2 and 3. Are the argument's essential premises so flawed that they provide little or no support for the conclusion? Or are the flaws contained in premises not essential to the claim? Rendering an overall evaluation is an important part of the evaluative process, for—if nothing else—it keeps critical thinking from becoming a bloodless, abstract exercise. It allows us to *decide* whether or not to believe, to endorse, and possibly to act on a claim. It also gives us an opportunity, which we should take, to *show* how the argument could be improved. Finally, it allows us to *clarify* our own beliefs as we respond to the argument in a creative and constructive way.

Of course not every argument requires a complete application of these steps. Very brief arguments with glaring falsehoods, highly questionable assertions, or obvious fallacies can and should be disposed of quickly by identifying the problem and, on that basis, judging the argument unsound. Other more complex or less clearly inadequate arguments require more detailed evaluation. The basic four-part procedure constitutes a conceptual framework which is intended to ease, not tax, the task of analysis and evaluation. It is best to use these steps prudently, in light of your own rational skills and your instructor's counsel.

Now, let's look at some specimen arguments.

Argument 1: "I reject Ms. Wilcox's arguments in favor of affirmative action because she's a member of the women's movement and therefore cannot be objective in what she says."
Analysis: This argument relies on a personal attack and is, therefore, not cogent.

Argument 2: "The Association of Law Enforcement Officers has just completed a study that indicates that capital punishment is indeed a deterrent to crime. The findings of such a prestigious body compel any thinking person to accept the thesis that capital punishment truly is a crime deterrent."
Analysis: This argument relies on a false appeal to authority because the experts are not in agreement on the claim. Also, the research methods must be examined before the findings can be accepted. This argument is, therefore, not cogent.

Argument 3: "Since no one has disproved O.J. Simpson's claim that he is innocent, there is considerable reason to believe it."
Analysis: This argument relies on an argument from ignorance and is, therefore, not cogent.

Argument 4: "Smith must be an AMA member because she's a physician."
Analysis: "Reconstructed this argument reads:

> **(All physicians must be AMA members.)**
> **Smith is a physician.**
> _____
> **Smith must be an AMA member.**

The major premise is a faulty generalization: Physicians need not be AMA members; many aren't. Therefore this argument's not cogent.

Argument 5: "Only citizens are voters. So Jones is definitely a voter."
Analysis: Reconstructed this argument reads:

> **All voters are citizens.**
> **(Jones is a citizen.)**
> _____
> **Jones is a voter.**

There are no informal fallacies in the reconstruction. The form of the argument is *AAA*-2. It commits the fallacy of the undistributed middle term. This argument, therefore, is not cogent.

Argument 6: "The human race tends to increase at a greater rate than the individual's means of subsistence. Consequently the individual is occasionally subject to a severe struggle for existence."
Analysis: Reconstructed, this argument reads:

(Whatever tends to increase at a greater rate than its means of subsistence is occasionally subject to a severe struggle for existence.)
The human race tends to increase at a greater rate than the individual's means of subsistence.
_____
Consequently the individual is occasionally subject to a severe struggle for existence.

The syllogism is valid, the premises are reasonable and relevant, and the argument contains no informal fallacies. This argument is cogent.

> **Argument 7:** "That the sun will rise tomorrow is a hypothesis; and that means we do not know whether it will rise."
>
> **Analysis:** If *know* will be taken to mean "to know with certainty," then this argument is a sorites consisting of the following reconstructed arguments:

> (No hypothesis is certain knowledge.)
> **That the sun will rise tomorrow is a hypothesis.**
> _____
> **(That the sun will rise tomorrow is not certain knowledge.)**

(If that the sun will rise tomorrow is not certain knowledge, then we don't know whether it will rise.)
(That the sun will rise tomorrow is not certain knowledge.)
_____
Then we don't know whether it will rise.

There are no informal fallacies in these reconstructions. The form of the first argument is *EAE*-1, valid. The second argument, a hypothetical syllogism, affirms the antecedent (*modus ponens*) and is, therefore, valid. The premises are true, the argument contains no informal fallacies. This argument is cogent.

The preceding arguments have one thing in common: They contain statements that are *value neutral.* This means that their premises neither express nor are intended to express a value judgment. Contrast this argument:

> Hiring people by quota is unfair because it introduces nonjob-related criteria into the decision process.

Now the assumption behind this argument is "Whatever introduces nonjob-related criteria into the hiring process is unfair." This is obviously a value judgment. How do we evaluate it? How do we determine whether it's reasonable, whether it contains informal fallacies?

Again, consider this argument: "As the major economic instrument of production in our society, business is justified in intruding into ecosystems." The assumption here is "The major economic instrument of production in our society is justified in intruding into ecosystems." Again, the statement expresses a value judgment. How can we assess the reasonableness of this value claim? The question is obviously important because determining the cogency of the argument depends on it, not to mention the integrity of the environment. Nevertheless, with what we already know, we can still intelligently evaluate many arguments that make value claims.

An Extended Example

Let's consider a complex argument which, while containing value claims, can nevertheless be evaluated in terms of these four steps just presented.

Argument 8: "In the fury that continues to surround the debate about school prayer, it is sometimes forgotten that prayer is an essential part of religion. To permit school prayer is virtually the same as endorsing religion. What can be said, then, for religion? Not much, I'm afraid. Indeed, religion is dangerous. It has spawned numerous wars throughout history. Today it continues to sow the seeds of discontent and destruction in Bosnia, Rwanda, Northern Ireland, and the Middle East. It divides people by emphasizing their differences rather than their similarities. It breeds intolerance of people with opposing views. Is there any doubt, therefore, that the responsible citizen should oppose school prayer?"

First, we clarify meaning. "Prayer" and "religion" are ambiguous. We will take "prayer" to mean a spiritual communion with God or an object of worship and "religion" to mean an organized system of belief in and worship of that God or object of worship. "Virtually" is a weasel. Every assertion made about religion in this argument is an unqualified generalization. "Spawns," "breeds," and "sows the seeds" are emotive. The last sentence attempts to persuade by using language loaded with strong connotations.

Next, we identify the argument's form, spotting its conclusion and main premises.

Conclusion: The responsible citizen should oppose school prayer.
Premise: To permit school prayer is virtually the same as endorsing religion.
Premise: Religion is dangerous.

Second, we identify basic structure. The main argument consists of the aforementioned two premises and conclusion, which can be expressed as a fragment standard-form categorical syllogism (actually a sorites).

> **To permit school prayer is virtually the same as endorsing religion.**
> **Religion is dangerous.**
> ————————————————————————————
> **The responsible citizen should oppose school prayer.**

Both main premises are themselves supported, thereby forming two mini arguments within the main argument. Mini argument 1, again, can be expressed as a fragment standard-form categorical syllogism:

> **Prayer is an essential part of religion.**
> ————————————————————————————
> **To permit school prayer is virtually the same as endorsing religion.**

Mini argument 2 can be viewed as consisting of an inductive generalization. Thus:

> **It (religion) has spawned numerous wars throughout history.**
> **Today it continues to sow the seeds of discontent and destruction in Bosnia, Rwanda, Northern Ireland, and the Middle East.**
> **It divides people by emphasizing their differences rather than their similarities.**
> **It breeds intolerance of people with opposing views.**
> ————————————————————————————
> **Religion is dangerous.**

Of course, it's possible to consider each piece of support separately as constituting, together with "Religion is dangerous," a standard-form categorical syllogism, actually an enthymeme. But this seems to undercut the spirit of the argument, which is to have the four pieces of evidence taken as a set or cluster of support data for the generalization that "Religion is dangerous."

We now fill in missing premises. Mini conclusion "To permit school prayer is virtually the same as endorsing religion" follows from "Prayer is an essential part of religion," plus the unexpressed assertion "To permit an essential part of religion to be practiced in school is virtually the same as endorsing religion." The reconstructed mini argument 1, therefore, reads:

Prayer is an essential part of religion.
(To permit an essential part of religion to be practiced in school is virtually the same as endorsing religion.)

To permit school prayer is virtually the same as endorsing religion.

The main argument, which consists of the two main premises and conclusion, is a sorites that can be reconstructed as follows:

> **To permit school prayer is virtually the same as endorsing religion.**
> **Religion is dangerous.**
>
> **(To permit school prayer is dangerous.)**

> **(To permit school prayer is dangerous.)**
> **(The responsible citizen should oppose anything dangerous.)**
>
> **The responsible citizen should oppose school prayer.**

Third, we identify formal and informal fallacies. We discover that all syllogisms are valid, but contain several informal fallacies.

It's difficult to evaluate "Prayer is an essential part of religion" because "prayer" and "religion" are ambiguous. But if these terms are stipulated, then the assertion can be considered true on definitional grounds. However, the unexpressed premise of this mini argument, "To permit an essential part of religion to be practiced in school is virtually the same as endorsing religion," is ambiguous and misleading. "Endorsing" literally means "supporting." If the state allows school prayer and if prayer is an essential part of religion, then it could be argued that the state "supports" religion in the sense that it provides a constitutional basis for the practice of religion in the classroom. We will say considerably more about this unexpressed assertion in the next step when we consider informal fallacies.

Mini argument 2 contains a value judgment, "Religion is *dangerous*," that needs much support, which presumably is provided by the four pieces of data expressed. An evaluation of this support is, again, best left to the next step. The same applies to the unexpressed assertions in the main arguments "To permit school prayer is dangerous" and "The responsible citizen should oppose anything dangerous." In short, the only acceptable assertion at this point is "Prayer is an essential part of religion."

Returning to mini argument 1, we find "endorsing" loaded with *subjective connotations.* An example will illustrate. The state permits the publication and sale of pornographic materials. Can it be said, then, that the state "endorses" pornographic enterprises? Yes, but only if "endorses" is taken to mean "support," and "support" in turn is taken to mean providing a judicial basis for the manufacture and sale of pornographic materials. "Endorsing," however, also carries the subjective connotations of "approval" or "actively advancing the interests of." But the state does not endorse pornographic enterprises in either of these senses. In fact, if you read the Supreme Court rulings on pornography, you'll find that the justices who comment without exception express revulsion toward pornography. The court's "permission," then, is based not on approval, and certainly not on active support of the interests of pornographers, but on an interpretation of the constitutional right to freedom of expression. Therefore we'd be inclined to think that, at the very least, to say that the state "endorses" pornography is misleading. Similarly, it seems just as misleading to argue that permitting school prayer is tantamount to endorsing religion in the sense of approving of or actively supporting the interests of religion. For this reason we're calling "endorsing" *doublespeak.*

But even if the arguer insists that "permit" implies "endorse" and "endorse," in turn, implies "approval of" or "actively advancing the interests of," then we must be clear about what it is that's being approved or advanced. It isn't religion but individual freedom, specifically the opportunity for the individual to say (or refrain from saying) a prayer in a public classroom, so long as that practice does not conflict with the constitutional doctrine of church/state separation. Stated another way, if school prayer does not violate church/state separation, then there is no constitutional basis for restricting individual freedom to worship. Consider the pornography example again. If the manufacture and sale of pornographic material is permitted, what is being approved of and actively advanced is the individual right to freedom of expression. To say that what is being underwritten is the pornography industry is a distortion, a *straw argument.* It is as much a straw argument, in our judgment, to say that permitting school prayer is tantamount to endorsing (that is, approving or actively advancing) religion. And the straw lies in the subjective connotations of "endorsing."

Our judgment that the arguer has introduced a straw argument is supported by what follows in the argument: namely, an attack on religion. Having identified prayer with religion, the arguer then attempts to show why religion is dangerous. The diversionary tack here is to discredit school prayer by discrediting religion. Whether or not this strategy proves effective very much depends on the audience's perceptions of religion. But it's easier to "blow over" the straw religion, and with it school prayer, than it is to repudiate thoughtful arguments supporting school prayer on legitimate grounds: namely, by attempting to show how school prayer violates the doctrine of church-state separation.

In other words, even if religion is dangerous, so what? How does this address the school prayer issue? The arguer undoubtedly will point to the first syllogism in the sorites that is intended to identify prayer with religion and school prayer with endorsing religion. At this point we would reintroduce our criticism of that mini argument on the grounds of ambiguity, doublespeak, and straw argument.

But if we wanted to be saintly charitable, we could concede the legitimacy of mini argument 1, and then closely inspect mini argument 2. The mini premises of that argument are generalizations that need qualification. They are also half-truths (*concealed evidence*), for they omit to mention that religion also has contributed to understanding and human betterment, to the establishment and maintenance of social services (such as schools, orphanages, hospitals, and disaster relief agencies), and the formulation of humanity's highest ideals. Moreover, all are *causal oversimplifications*. Beyond this, in the context of the main argument, all these mini premises are *illegitimate appeals to fear* and *slippery slopes,* such that if school prayer is permitted, presumably those dreadful things associated with religion will inevitably follow.

As for the two unexpressed main premises that make up the sorites, "To permit school prayer is dangerous" is *vague*—Just what is meant by "dangerous"?—and "The responsible citizen should oppose school prayer" is a persuasive definition containing the *loaded epithet* "responsible."

Fourth, we apply the cogency criteria. Are the premises reasonable? relevant? sufficient? The premises and their support downplay by various appeals of omission, diversion, and confusion, namely half-truth, straw argument, fear, causal oversimplification, and loaded and vague language. When the premises and support are stripped of these ploys, they collapse, thus rendering the conclusion unwarranted. It seems that any compelling argument against school prayer must establish that permitting school prayer violates the doctrine of church/state separation and perhaps that this doctrine is worthwhile. The preceding argument doesn't do this, neither does it develop an alternatively compelling argument against school prayer. This argument fails to meet the cogency criteria.

EXERCISE 15-1 *

Determine the cogency of the following arguments, using the basic guidelines of analysis. Be alert for the sorites.

1. As there is no direct evidence against Frank, we can't prove him guilty. So we can be confident of his innocence.

2. Communists read the *Daily Worker*. The *Daily Worker* used to be Fred's favorite newspaper. You can draw your own conclusion.

3. There's no question that members of the Jonestown community were incapable of thinking for themselves. Why I remember one incident when a Jonestown member was told to beat a three-year-old. And sure enough, that's exactly what he did.

4. Clearly the teller didn't push the alarm button. For if she had, the police would have arrived within five minutes, in plenty of time to have caught the robbers.

5. Sarah must be a Christian because none but Christians believe in the doctrine of the Trinity.

6. As regards the Nazi leaders, it's obvious that justice has never been meted out because not quite all of them have been brought to trial for their crimes.

7. Students who study at all will study each of their courses equally or study some more than others—which means that students who study at all will either get low grades in all their courses or fail some of them. Not a pretty picture.

8. The professor said she didn't want anybody unprepared for class. But obviously she didn't mean me, because I'm not just anybody—I'm the student council president!

9. Not all moneymaking films are made by the Hollywood studios. After all, some pornographic movies are moneymakers.

10. The number of people in the United States turning to Eastern religions is increasing at an astonishing rate—which goes to prove that not everything that's exotic by our own standards is outside our grasp.

VALUES AND VALUE JUDGMENTS

People value all sorts of things: health, wealth, power, time, friendship, love, prestige, leisure time—the list is endless. Sometimes the values are quite specific: We value a particular object such as a family heirloom or a stray dog. Other times the value is more general: We value a successful business career. We can value something in and of itself, as perhaps we value pleasure or knowledge; or we may value something because it leads to other things, as perhaps we value money or power. However we choose to talk of value, one thing's for sure: A value—any value— is an assessment of worth. If we value something, we consider it to have worth. Specifically, we view it as good or bad, better or worse, ought to be or not ought to be.

Frequently we express values, that is, assessments of worth, in statements. For example, B. J. claims, "Simply Red is a sensational rock group." Wilma insists, "*Moby Dick* is a masterpiece." Sweeney says, "Cocaine should not be legalized." And Roscoe observes, "The state of the world is revolting." Each of these statements reports the worth that the speaker attaches to something. Such statements express our value judgments; they are ordinarily termed "normative statements," as opposed to "nonnormative statements."

Normative and Nonnormative Statements

Normative statements are assertions that express value judgments. Normative statements come in many varieties. In our study of logic we have encountered and formulated many normative statements. Technically speaking, every time we termed an argument "bad," we were expressing a value judgment. Indeed, our whole study of logic is based on a value judgment: that knowing and using the rules of correct argument, we stand a better chance of surviving and prospering than if we didn't know these rules.

But ordinarily we think of normative statements as expressing our values in ethics, aesthetics, and social and political philosophy. Thus, in ethics someone might claim, "I shouldn't lie," "Keep your word," or "Murder is immoral." In aesthetics, "Picasso is a great artist," "Beethoven's Fifth Symphony is his best," "Spike Lee's latest movies are flawed." In social and political philosophy: "Democracy is the best form of government," "Abortion-on-demand ought to be legalized," "The United States should evenly distribute its wealth among its citizenry."

In contrast to normative statements stand nonnormative ones, which are not intended to express value judgments. *Nonnormative statements are true or false assertions used to express matters of empirical or logical fact.* A statement expresses a matter of empirical fact when its truth can be determined by appeal-to-sense observations. "Water boils at 212 degrees Fahrenheit at sea level," "George Washington was the first U.S. president," and "Many citizens don't vote" are nonnormative statements of the empirical variety. A statement expresses a matter of logical fact when its truth can be determined solely by appeal to reason. Thus, "Squares have four sides," "The form AAA-1 is valid," and "X must be greater than Z, if X is greater than Y and Y is greater than Z" are nonnormative statements of the logical kind.

When an argument contains only nonnormative premises, it's a nonnormative argument. In applying our basic method for argument evaluation, we confined ourselves mostly to this kind of argument. But numerous arguments, even the most important we formulate and encounter, are normative arguments; that is, they contain a normative statement as a premise.

EXERCISE 15-2

A. Identify the following statements as either normative or nonnormative.

1. Stealing is wrong.

2. Shakespeare is the most effective dramatist in the English language.

3. Shakespeare wrote comedies, histories, and tragedies.

4. Oxygen deprivation can result in brain damage.

5. Education is the surest ticket to occupational success.

6. Sexism is a function of acculturation.

7. Trading weapons to Iran in return for American hostages is based on a narrow and short-term view of national best interest.

8. Sex without love is sin.

9. Never give a sucker an even break.

10. Honesty is the best policy.

11. Polygamy is illegal in California.

12. If two candidates are equally qualified for a job and one is a woman or member of a minority group, we should give the job to the woman or minority member.

13. Photography isn't really an art.

14. Our criminal justice system is a national disgrace.

15. In part, philosophy studies issues that science cannot fully answer.

16. Alcoholism results from a character flaw.

17. Birth control pills, which can cause blood clots, shouldn't be taken over a long period of time without medical supervision.

18. Let the government stay out of business.

19. Although the law is a guide to proper behavior, sometimes what's legal is not what's moral, and what's illegal is not what is immoral.

20. The cooler the light, the less energy it wastes.

B. Write two statements about each of the following, one normative and one nonnormative.

1. political parties

2. sex education

3. legalization of marijuana

4. advertising

5. American military preparedness

6. genetic engineering

7. pornography

8. active voluntary euthanasia

9. premarital cohabitation

10. lesbian/gay liberation

11. children with AIDS attending school

12. parental influence on textbook selection in grade school

13. the government's right to "lie" in the interest of national security

14. warning labels on rock albums

NORMATIVE ARGUMENTS

A normative argument is one that contains at least one normative statement as a premise. Here's an example:

> Selling crack cocaine to children is reprehensible.
> Smith sells crack cocaine to children.
> _____
> Smith does something reprehensible.

This is a normative argument because one of its premises, "Selling crack cocaine to children is reprehensible," is a normative statement. Here's another example:

> If ours is a just society, then women have equal opportunities.
> Women don't have equal opportunities.
> _____
> Ours is not a just society.

Again, a premise contains a normative statement: "if ours is a just society, then women have equal opportunities." A final example:

> Any movie with Eddie Murphy is worth seeing.
> *The Nutty Professor* stars Eddie Murphy.
> _____
> *The Nutty Professor* is worth seeing.

Here the major premise, "Any movie with Eddie Murphy is worth seeing," is a normative statement. The argument, therefore, is a normative one.

Now let's take the same issues these arguments deal with and see how they might appear in *nonnormative* arguments. Notice that none of the following arguments contains a normative statement as a premise:

> Selling crack cocaine to children is a felony.
> Smith sells crack cocaine to children.
> _____
> Smith commits a felony.

> If women can't vote, then our society doesn't give them a voice in the electoral process.
> Our society does give women a voice in the electoral process.
> _____
> Women can vote.

> Any movie with Eddie Murphy is usually popular.
> *The Nutty Professor* is an Eddie Murphy movie.
> _____
> *The Nutty Professor* will probably be popular.

The four step method for argument evaluation applies equally to normative and nonnormative arguments. But to make the best use of this method with normative arguments, it helps to be aware of peculiar, pertinent problems, and know how to deal with these problems.

EXERCISE 15-3 *

Identify the following as normative or nonnormative arguments. Reconstruct assumptions.

1. Reverse discrimination should be allowed because it can promote social justice.

2. Reverse discrimination sometimes occurs in the workplace. So it's clear that in some instances people are judged on criteria that are not directly job related.

3. Mercy killing seems advisable in cases of terminal disease, to save the patient and loved ones from heroic suffering.

4. "When in Rome, do as the Romans do" is a time-honored tradition. So we shouldn't restrict our multinational firms from bribing foreign officials when that's the accepted practice of that country.

5. American businesses often behave overseas differently from how they behave at home, as indicated by the admissions of Gulf and Lockheed to paying millions of dollars in bribes and "grease payments" abroad.

6. Given the fact that between 10 and 20 percent of American adults are homosexual, it's safe to say that America is a very sick society.

7. Inasmuch as art is a form of human expression, all art is in one way or other a statement.

8. As a taxpayer, I have a right to decide what my child reads in school, and if it goes against my personal beliefs, I have an obligation to protect my child from reading it.

9. We should always keep our promises. That's why I'm so upset to learn that the United States secretly sold arms to Iran.

10. The primary obligation of the United States is the protection of its citizens. That's why I'm so glad to learn that President Bush was willing to stand up to Saddam Hussein.

Is It Possible to Evaluate Normative Claims for Reasonableness?

To begin with, reconsider the normative argument:

> Selling crack cocaine to children is reprehensible.
> Smith sells crack cocaine to children.
> _____
> Smith does something reprehensible.

Now we know that this syllogism, like any other, is cogent if, and only if, both premises are true and the argument is valid. Since the argument's form is AAA-1, it's valid. As for the truth of its premises, we can easily ascertain the truth of the minor premise, "Smith sells crack cocaine to children," by determining whether this statement describes a state of affairs. But what about the major premise? What must be the case for the statement "Selling crack cocaine to children is *reprehensible*" to be true? Just what state of affairs do we measure this statement against, indeed any normative statement, to determine its truth?

Such a question clearly stimulates philosophical concerns about the nature of truth and normative statements. But it also provokes questions about argument evaluation that are downright practical. Just how do we evaluate the truth of value judgments? Indeed, can we logically speak of truth at all in connection with such statements? Some people believe that normative statements are essentially meaningless. Others hold that they make sense but that they can't be justified. Still others believe that normative statements make sense and can be justified but that their justification does not extend beyond the society in which one lives. Since so many important arguments we face and devise are normative ones, we must know how to deal with such arguments. Otherwise we'll remain unequipped to deal rationally with a significant, perhaps the most significant, aspect of human existence.

If you're still unconvinced of the importance of this issue, reflect on your bedrock assumptions about morality, religion, art, politics, government, sex, education, child rearing, law—on any human concern. You'll see that they all reflect value judgments. *Nothing goes untouched by values and value judgments.* And they inevitably inform the arguments that we and others compose and accept to direct our lives, to fashion our dealings with other people, to chart our national and international course, and so on. Thus, if we can't make logic "work" in these areas, we'll remain mentally impoverished to deal with life's momentous concerns. And on the personal and collective levels, there's ample and frightening evidence that many individuals and institutions are currently in that state of logical bankruptcy.

So assessing the truth of normative statements is of pressing practical concern. We must find out how to handle them. In fact, there are several things we can do to meet this challenge. But first let's briefly confess and explain our own assumptions here.

A main thesis of this chapter is that value judgments can be evaluated. Now that doesn't sound like much of a claim. But without getting into all the philosophical subtleties that enshroud it, rest assured that the claim is far from being "obvious" in a philosophical sense. Just to give you the thrust of contentious views, be aware that some insist that only things that can be "counted" or "measured" can be evaluated. Since normative statements make assertions that cannot be so quantified, such statements cannot be evaluated. In short, generally speaking, only nonnormative statements can be evaluated.

Now it's undoubtedly true that value judgments can't be weighed and measured with scientific precision. But it doesn't necessarily follow that they therefore cannot be evaluated at all. The fact is, as we've just seen, people can, do, and must evaluate normative statements constantly. Simply because we can't count on laboratory precision in our evaluations doesn't in the least make our task less trivial, surely not meaningless. Indeed, it could be argued that the inevitable inexactness of our evaluations make it even more urgent that we carefully consider just how we go about the evaluations.

Probably the key thing for our purpose is to recognize and acknowledge that values and value judgments crowd in on us. Like it or not we must accept some, reject others, probably keep an open mind about most. And this presupposes evaluation. We must weigh the reasons that count for a normative claim and the ones that count against it. When there are more of the right kinds of reasons for it, we consider it warranted, that is, reasonable. When there are more of the right kinds of reasons against it, we consider it unwarranted, that is, unreasonable. And we make up our minds accordingly.

It's in this sense of warranty, then—of more counting for a normative claim than against it—that we seemingly can connect truth with normative statements. At least for our purposes this seems a most efficacious way of speaking about evaluating normative statements, because reasonableness is one of the three cogency criteria. In brief, when we speak of evaluating normative statements, we have in mind a rational process that aims to determine whether there are more reasons for accepting a value judgment than for rejecting it. Now let's consider just how we can evaluate normative statements.

Language Clarification

The most important thing to do in assessing the reasonableness of normative statements is to *clarify their language*. Value words such as *good, ought, wrong, superb, should not*, and *inferior* are vague; they invite numerous interpretations. So if we're to avoid fallacies of meaning, and if we're going to determine whether a normative statement is reasonable, we must know how the argument intends its value words. Take these normative statements from ethics: "Abortion is wrong," "Mercy killing should be legalized," "Forced sterilization is evil." *Wrong, should be, evil*—each of these must be clarified before we can begin to evaluate the statements that contain them.

Value words can carry several meanings, only some of which we'll cover here. Generally speaking, the ordinary value arguments we encounter carry a meaning that can be translated into nonnormative form and then evaluated. Specifically, when appearing in ordinary normative arguments, value words usually carry the meaning of (1) personal preference; (2) social preference; or (3) conformity with a principle, standard, or law.

1. PERSONAL PREFERENCE.   It's possible that value words are intended as expressions of personal approval or disapproval. Take, for example, the normative statement "Abortion is wrong." It's possible that those claiming this are expressing only personal disapproval of abortion. Thus, "Abortion is wrong" is equivalent to "I disapprove of abortion." Likewise, "The *Mona Lisa* is a great painting" translates to "I like (or I think highly of) the *Mona Lisa*." And "Everyone should get a college education" would mean "I'm in favor of everyone's getting a college education." In each instance the value word is intended as an expression of personal preference. This allows a translation into a nonnormative form that no longer reports a value but merely a feeling. Such a translation is perfectly legitimate if that's the meaning the arguer intends, for then the person is not commenting about the nature or quality of the act or thing itself.

As for the reasonableness of such statements, having translated them, we need only ensure that they accurately report the person's feelings. If we realize that value words carry only this *autobiographical meaning* for some people, we can save ourselves much time and exasperation in fruitless debates over normative issues. Even more important, we can direct the discussion to a far more constructive plane.

To illustrate, suppose someone argues, "Abortion on demand should be legalized." You find out that by "should be" the person intends personal approval. So the argument reads, "I approve of abortion on demand being legalized." Now you're in a position to ask the person *why* he or she approves of it. It may be that the person knew of someone who was legally obliged to carry a fetus to term, which ultimately produced great hardship and suffering for everyone. The arguer's approval may rest largely on that one episode. If so, you're then in a position to spot the inadequate induction based on anecdotal evidence. Better still, the arguer may see the flimsiness of his or her own argument as it becomes subject to public scrutiny.

The point is that once you've established an autobiographical interpretation of the value words, you're in a position to pin the person down on what generated the preference. This is crucial, for as we stated earlier, we're ultimately interested in how much counts for the claim, how much against it. Thus, the only way we can evaluate the normative statement is to find out what supports it. And having established a personal-preference interpretation of value words, we can then find out what, if anything, supports the statement.

One other point, this one on a philosophical level: This personal-preference view raises a number of philosophical questions, which we're justified in asking. First, since normative statements presumably express only personal preference, does that mean that no acts are right or wrong, that no things are good or bad, in and by themselves? Second, does this view imply that something can be "right" for you and "wrong" for me under identical circumstances? Is this sensible? Third, doesn't this view imply that debating the merit of normative arguments is foolish because such arguments are merely expressions of personal opinion?

Such questions may seem irrelevant. But that's not so. After all, anyone who assumes that a value word is only the equivalent of an expression of personal preference takes a lot for granted. Surely the "taken for granted" should be introduced in evaluating whether more counts for the normative claim than against it.

2. SOCIAL PREFERENCE.   Frequently people don't mean that only they approve or disapprove of something when they use a value word, but that society does. In other words, value words can carry the meaning of social preference. Thus, "Abortion is wrong" may be interpreted as meaning "Society disapproves of abortion."

If a normative statement carries this meaning of social preference, our job of verifying it simplifies. All we need do is verify that a majority approves or disapproves of the view. Determine the majority view and we determine the truth of the statement.

But again, as is true of personal preference, having established a sociological bias, we can now ask trenchant questions about its assumptions. Thus, is nothing right or wrong, good or bad in or by itself? Can't the individual be right and the majority wrong? After all, the German theologian Dietrich Bonhoffer, having spoken out against Hitler, was imprisoned and later hanged. Was he wrong and the majority right? The nineteenth-century American writer and naturalist Henry David Thoreau refused to pay taxes to a government that, supported by the majority, sanctioned slavery. One day his friend and fellow artist, Ralph Waldo Emerson, came to visit him in jail. "What are you doing in there?" Emerson asked. "What are you doing out there?" Thoreau answered. Was Thoreau wrong? Was Emerson? Was Christ wrong? And just what "majority" do we have in mind anyway—the community? state? nation? world? Maybe the majority is within one's own ethnic group, sex, profession, or economic stratum.

These questions are not trivial. In equating value words with social preference, we invite profound questions about the highly controversial assumptions underlying that equation. At the very least, such a translation seems to beg for charges of irrelevant appeals to popularity and provincialism. So anyone confronting this kind of rationale has a perfect right to raise the forgoing questions. What's more, such persons shouldn't be discouraged and intimidated by charges of "nit-picking" and "hair-splitting." They are doing no such thing, and those who insist they are themselves are relying on irrelevant personal attacks to discredit the questioner.

3. CONFORMITY WITH PRINCIPLE, STANDARD, OR LAW.   In addition to translating value words into expressions of personal or social preference, we sometimes identify them with conformity to principle, standard, or law. For example, suppose someone says, "Sexism is wrong." They don't mean "wrong" in the sense of personal or social disapproval but in the sense of nonconformity with the principle of justice as fair play and giving to others what they deserve. Similarly, by "Abortion is wrong" one might mean that abortion doesn't square with the law of God. Likewise, in painting, someone might consider Rembrandt's *Night Watch* a "great" painting because it conforms with artistic standards of light, color, proportion, and harmony. Respecting the evaluation of such normative statements, all we need do is determine whether the statement actually does conform with the principle, law, or standard. If it does, we can treat the statement as provisionally reasonable; if it doesn't, we can reject it as unreasonable.

But again, and most important, having ascertained this interpretation of the value words, we're then in a position to raise important philosophical questions about its underlying assumptions. For example, what makes the particular standard or principle itself doubtless? Take justice, for instance. In the preceding example, someone took justice to be a principle of fair play or just desert. But why not consider justice as a principle of efficiency? Lots of people do. They consider what's fair as what produces the most happiness for the greatest number of people, even if certain individuals suffer. Similarly, if "right" means that something squares with the law of God, what if one doesn't believe in God, or at least not with the God whose law is intended? Can such people be moral? In a similar vein, standards of beauty, success, morality, and other things frequently vary from person to person. Often these differing standards conflict. What makes one standard more credible than another?

Again, these questions are anything but irrelevant. They cut to the foundational assumptions of a normative argument. So we should ask them; for if there's a serious doubt about the legitimacy of the principle, law, or standard, conformity to it might be inconsequential, nothing more than an appeal to traditional wisdom or provincialism.

As we indicated earlier, these are only a few of the interpretations people place on value words. Reading in specialty fields such as ethics and aesthetics will reveal more. The key thing to remember is that the meanings affect our assessment of the truth of normative statements and, ultimately, of the cogency of normative arguments. Faced with any normative argument, then, you should first find out just what interpretation of the value word is intended. Having done this, you should do other things to minimize the difficulty of evaluating the argument itself. Let's see what these are.

EXERCISE 15-4 *

Determine the value words in each of the following statements and indicate what possible interpretations can be placed on those words. In the light of each meaning, show how the truth of the statements would be assessed.

1. Needlessly inflicting pain is wrong.

2. Infanticide is evil.

3. A doctor ought never operate on people without their informed consent.

4. Poetry is the highest artistic form.

5. Hypocrisy is immoral.

6. The best form of government is the one that allows the most personal freedom.

7. Einstein's theory of relativity is the greatest scientific development of the twentieth century.

8. A government should not underwrite research dealing with *in vitro* fertilization.

9. No war is ever morally justifiable.

10. You should never disobey your parents or persons in authority over you.

11. To those who believe that presidential elections are determined by the economy, I say that's the kind of thinking that leads to moral bankruptcy. The key issue is character.

12. Communism is godless.

13. The women's liberation movement threatens the survival of the family as we've traditionally known it.

14. The ends justify the means.

15. That was a lousy movie.

Evaluation

Just as people can give a variety of interpretations for value words, they can give many reasons for their normative claims. We have just seen that the *key thing in ensuring the reasonableness or truth of normative statements is to clarify the meaning of the value terms*. Once we do this, we can ask for reasons to support that meaning. In so doing we are, in effect, acknowledging what we've already learned: that the strength of any argument, normative or nonnormative, depends on the strength of the premises offered in support of the conclusion. *Because normative statements, as we've seen, can't be weighed and measured with the precision that nonnormative statements frequently can, the need for support in normative arguments looms large*. Until we hear enough of the right kind of reasons for the normative premises, we're simply not in any position to intelligently stake out our own reaction to the argument.

For example, consider this case involving Anna. Anna worked in a day care center for over a year before she decided to take another job to supplement her income. Because it offered good money, and she was reasonably good at it, Anna decided to work nights as an exotic dancer at a local club. For several months, things went well. Then the manager of the day-care center found out. In the manager's view, working as an exotic dancer was an unsavory occupation. And since that job could reflect unfavorably on the day care center, the manager gave Anna an ultimatum: Choose one job or the other.

Now the manager's claim that working as an exotic dancer is an unsavory occupation is a normative statement. *Before* we can rationally respond to it, and to the argument it's in, we need reasons. Maybe there are compelling reasons for the judgment. But maybe there aren't; maybe the manager's imposing an idiosyncratic evaluation on something she really knows very little about. Whatever the case, the wisdom or folly of the judgment depends on justification, that is, offering enough evidence of the right kind.

But just what sort of evidence are we looking for in support of normative statements? In general, we're seeking reasons that would persuade objective, informed, rational people that the normative claim is beyond any reasonable doubt. Specifically, it seems reasonable to expect normative arguments in whatever field to satisfy at least these two criteria: (1) that what's offered in support of the normative premise is, in fact, a justification of it and not merely a pseudo-justification; and (2) that the purported justification meets the minimum adequacy requirements in the appropriate field.[75]

---

75. See Peter A. Facione, Donald Scherer, and Thomas Attig, *Values and Society: An Introduction to Ethics and Social Philosophy* (Englewood Cliffs, N.J.: Prentice-Hall, 1978), pp. 26–31.

1. PSEUDOJUSTIFICATION.[76]   We already know enough about correct and incorrect arguments to know that people frequently confuse all sorts of things with reasons. People appeal to emotions, irrelevancies, to presumptions, thinking they're giving reasons in the sense of justification for their claims. We've spent considerable time cataloging these informal fallacies. Indeed, a big step in our basic evaluative method is a consideration of informal fallacies. Recognition of these informal fallacies is no less important in evaluating normative arguments. In fact, it's probably more important; for the temptations to "fudge" on rational justification for normative arguments is greater than with the nonnormative because the former can't be carted into a lab and demonstrated as true to all but the soft-headed.

For some reason, far too complex to go into here, there's evidently a decided inclination to cast reason to the winds in dealing with normative claims, to substitute phony or pseudojustification for the real thing. For example, not too long ago at work, Sweeney heard a fellow worker confess that recently he had banged into a parked car in a parking lot and then left without leaving a note for the driver. What's more, the fellow insisted that what he did was right.

"Right!" Sweeney exclaimed. "How can you say something like that is right?"

"I was scared," the man said. "I wasn't carrying any insurance and I couldn't cover the costs—not with the wife sick and two kids in college."

And on he went, enriching his appeal to pity to the point where Sweeney was sorry he'd asked the fellow to justify his action. In fact, the person had substituted motivation for justification: he explained what had motivated him to do the act, but he did not offer justification for it. There's a big difference. *Giving motivation, when justification is sought, results in pseudojustification.*

Just as justification is confused with giving motivation, it can also be confused with rationalization. Recall that *rationalization refers to giving reasons for a choice after the fact, after we've already decided what to do.* To rationalize is to choose first and look for reasons later. When we rationalize, we endorse or reject reasons because they support or weaken a predetermined choice.

A local politician in Sweeney's town recently endorsed an "anti-smut" bill because, he said, "We must protect the young and vulnerable against the onslaught of pornography." He added that that was why he intended to vote for the bill. If the truth were known, the reason he endorsed the anti-smut bill is that he believes his endorsement will look good to his constituents. The public reason is sheer rationalization, nothing more than pseudojustification. Beware of rationalization in normative arguments and of the informal fallacies that often accompany it, especially inductive and causal fallacies, and concealed evidence.

So *providing one's motivation or rationalizations is not providing justification.* Neither is providing excuses. *Excuses, although relevant in assigning blame or praise, are irrelevant for justification.* Generally speaking, we don't hold people accountable for their actions when circumstances were beyond their control or when they had no other alternative for what they did or when their freedom to

---

76. See also Chapters 3 and 4.

choose was so constrained that they couldn't be said to have chosen freely. But a good excuse provides a reason we shouldn't be blamed, punished, or held accountable. It *does not alter* what we did.

To illustrate, a firm doesn't meet the Environmental Protection Agency's (EPA) air pollution standards within the time prescribed. Now there's no altering the fact that the firm didn't comply with the standard. But there may be reasons to exonerate the company from blame: Maybe the costs for the antipollution devices were more than the business could bear; maybe the time allotted was simply insufficient to complete the job; maybe any number of things. But none of these reasons, taken alone or together, can be considered justification. Indeed, when the EPA or government chooses not to prosecute or fine the firm, but to extend the deadline, it in no way condones what the firm did. It simply recognizes that there are compelling reasons to *excuse* the firm from blame.

When a responsible defense attorney argues that a client committed a technically illegal act under extreme stress or duress, he is not condoning the *action* but rather attempting to mitigate his client's *responsibility*. In one famous case some years ago, a woman was *not* sent to prison for burning to death her violently abusive husband, although she was placed on probation after being convicted of involuntary manslaughter. At the time, some people were outraged because they saw anything short of a severe prison sentence as condoning homicide as a way of dealing with spousal abuse. Sometimes the line between explaining a motive and excusing a specific individual's specific action, or condoning it, blur together. It helps if we distinguish justification from excusing in terms of individual responsibility.

In short, an excuse is not a justification for conduct but from accountability for the conduct. Similarly, to excuse someone is not to justify the person's behavior but to free the person from responsibilities. In introducing excuses where justification is called for, we introduce irrelevant reasons into our argument.

So the tendencies to confuse motivation, rationalization, and excuse with justification result in a variety of informal fallacies in normative arguments, especially ones concerning ethics. Be alert to these tendencies. Focusing on them will take you a long way toward clarifying normative claims and evaluating normative arguments.

EXERCISE 15-5

Following are ten situations. For each situation, give two examples of (1) giving motivation, (2) rationalizing, and (3) offering an excuse.

1. Every Monday morning Myra's late for work.

2. A teacher fails to return student exams on the next meeting of the class, which is one week after the exam is given.

3. A doctor raises her fees for an office visit.

4. The government limits wage and price increases to 7 percent.

5. A man makes copies of his favorite CDs for his girlfriend.

6. A wife has an extramarital affair.

7. A politician suddenly shifts his position and endorses a property-tax-limit initiative.

8. A consumer, already heavily in debt, purchases a new car.

9. A state government makes all its residents carry an identification card at all times.

10. The personnel director of an advertising firm asks female applicants about their marital status.

2. Minimum Adequacy Requirements.   In addition to expecting a normative argument to provide justification, not pseudojustification, we're certainly correct in expecting it to meet the minimum adequacy requirements appropriate in the field. To discern what this means, let's consider the case of a nonnormative argument. Suppose Dr. McGee, renowned astronomer, insisted that the expanding universe could be accounted for by something other than the big bang theory. Now Dr. McGee wouldn't be much of a thinker or scientist if she hadn't assembled as much factual support for her claim as she could. And her fellow scientists, as well as we ourselves, wouldn't be very rational if we didn't insist on such factual support for her remarkable claim. Indeed, those in and outside science take for granted the obvious need to support claims with factual data. Providing such support is, after all, a minimum requirement for any cogent argument, which is readily acknowledged and acted on in all nonnormative arguments.

But along comes a normative argument, and often rationality is put on a back burner. For some reason, many of us act as if a normative argument concerning, say, ethics or aesthetics or social philosophy is exempt from the minimal requirements for cogent argument. Well, it's not. We as much need *factual* support for claims such as "Prostitution ought not to be legalized" and "The government should take over the oil industry" as we admittedly do for "Vitamin C can prevent the common cold" and "Humans are innately aggressive."

Now let's dwell on those last two nonnormative statements for a minute. Suppose you asked the claimant, "Why do you think that vitamin C can prevent the common cold?" and suppose the claimant responded, "I just think so, that's all." Or suppose, in the second instance, the claimant "justified" the claim by saying, "Humans are innately aggressive because I feel that they are." Surely you'd tell these people to go peddle their papers elsewhere. Or if you were kinder, you might insist that the persons were begging the question and press them about why they feel as they do. And if they persisted in such circularity, you'd rightly dismiss their arguments as absurd.

When it comes to normative arguments, however, it's amazing how often we not only tolerate but also endorse arguments that have no more to recommend them than personal whim, prejudice, feeling, hunch, or fancy. Don't misunderstand. As we've already established, normative statements do indeed differ from nonnormative ones, and thus normative arguments differ from non-normative arguments. But they don't differ so radically that the minimal requirements of good reasoning and cogent argument don't apply to normative claims.

It's true that when a person expresses a value judgment, the person may be intending it strictly as an expression of personal preference. Thus, "Lying is wrong" could be interpreted as "I disapprove of lying" and no more than that. And "Picasso is a great painter" might be interpreted as "I really like Picasso" and no more than that. But *meaning isn't justification* any more than motivation, rationalization, or excuse is. Thus, if you ask a claimant, "Why is lying wrong?" and the claimant replies, "Because I disapprove of it," you won't be any more satisfied with that reply than the comparable ones given in "justification" of the nonnormative statements about the expanding universe and the aggressive human. The reason for your dissatisfaction is that you realize that you're asking for justification, but the claimant is giving you meaning or interpretation. As we saw, that's a nice first step. But now that you understand what the claimant means by the value word, you'll likely ask, "Okay, so *why* do you disapprove of it?"

At this point, it's mind boggling, and downright disconcerting, how many people take such warranted persistence as aggressive behavior and summarily dismiss the interrogator as a "real pain." And this from otherwise intelligent people! Don't allow yourself to be cowed. Explain that you realize that one can't expect the scientific confirmation for the value judgment that one could muster, say, for the nonnormative assertion that cigarette smoking is a contributory cause of lung cancer. You realize that you're not dealing with such a statement to begin with. But at the same time explain that you do expect, and the person should be able to provide, supporting facts that make an endorsement of the value judgment more reasonable than not. Surely that isn't being nit-picking or being a "real pain."

Unfortunately, it seems that in more cases than not, people simply don't have the supporting facts to substantiate their value judgments. As a result, in everything from sex to social justice, *opinion passes for justification*—and one opinion is thought to be as good as the next. Regarding nonnormative claims, no one would be so foolish as to make such an assertion that one opinion is as good as the next. But not so for normative claims. More often than not, opinion, not justification, charts our thinking and actions. Thus: I'm of the opinion that extramarital sex is good, so I am justified in engaging in it; I believe that marijuana shouldn't be legalized, so that justifies the claim that marijuana shouldn't be legalized; I think *Star Trek V* is the greatest science-fiction film ever made, so the issue is closed. Fallacies such as hasty conclusion, post hoc, willed ignorance, and provincialism should leap out at you from the snarls that constitute unreflective and cloudy normative claims. And don't be surprised to find such defensive reactions as projection, prejudging, stereotyping, and rationalizing also substituting for justification, as well as impairing judgment.

But there's more to it than just committing informal fallacies. At issue is a whole mindset that really has relegated the normative to the realm of the irrational. Think about the countless hours consumed on talk shows by people pontificating on some very important issues of the day. With rare and refreshing exceptions, these folks offer little more to support their barrage of value judgments than that they believe what they're saying, that they're of a certain opinion. Dietary habits, religious affiliations, child rearing, criminal justice, nuclear power, sexual preferences, government spending—nothing escapes the value judgments of some talk-show guests. The fact that these people rarely know what they're talking about is only one affront to rationality. Compounding this is that the talk-show host, in the vast majority of cases, doesn't require any more justification of the guest's claims than that the claims are "interesting," "provocative," or "controversial." Can you imagine some medical researcher's claims for a cancer cure receiving serious scientific coverage simply because they're "provocative"? And just to make matters insufferable, the studio audience is left to evaluate the claims largely on the provincial basis of its own approval or disapproval, like or dislike, of them. So is the television audience, except that its evaluation probably carries the additional bias of having been colored by the resounding studio applause that greeted popular claims.

How, you might wonder, can you avoid falling into the mindset that relegates normative issues to the irrational realm of defensive face saving, biased assertion, and indifference to rational discourse? Surprisingly, one of the best defenses against ignorance of all kinds is a genuine desire to know what's true and real. Now "true" and "real" are philosophically thorny terms, and the nature and possibility of unbiased reasoning is one of the hot issues currently debated in professional (and popular) philosophical circles. We certainly aren't qualified to settle that issue here, nor would we wish to. Our goal is more modest, namely, to suggest that even if you suspect that pure objectivity is beyond human ability, and that rationality is not sufficient to solve all problems, you can still agree with us that opinions vary widely in their quality. At the lowest level, we place unreflective, uninformed, *mere opinions*. At the highest level, we place informed, justified, clearly articulated opinions.

So, the first step in protecting yourself from settling for nonrational mere opinions is to value justification, clarity, appropriate experience and expertise. This seemingly simple step goes a long way toward mitigating ignorance, contention, inconsistency, and divisiveness, for it links all truth seekers via the domain of *rational discourse. Rational discourse is the giving and receiving of reasons according to commonly agreed upon standards of verification, for the purpose of distinguishing truth from falsehood, appearance from reality, and mere opinion from informed opinion.* If you want to get a quick snapshot of what happens when people fail to participate in rational discourse, just watch almost any "discussions" presented on TV talkshows. Notice what happens when the participants substitute volume, rudeness (interrupting, all talking at once), explosive language and gesturing, dogmatic attitudes, and repetition for respectful, objective, clear, and reasonable discourse. Do you think the participants in such "discussions" are seriously open to the possibility of error on their own part? Do people change their *thinking* after such encounters? If they do, on what justification?

But it needn't be like this—at least not for you. Like Candide, Voltaire's indomitable pragmatist, you can tend to your own garden. You can protect yourself from the onslaught of the inane. The fact is that there is generally available to anyone taking the time to consult it a vast array of intelligent, insightful, often profound scholarship in any field. And this scholarship, in many cases the distilled wisdom of the ages, represents a rich source of the rational support needed to ground value judgments.

So familiarize yourself with political philosophy, economics, and psychology; with ethics and aesthetics; and with the various arts—poetry, music, literature, and painting. This doesn't mean that you need to be an expert before formulating or responding intelligently to a value claim. But surely you must be informed, because if you're not, you stand no chance of meeting the minimum adequacy requirements appropriate in a field or of detecting when the arguments of others don't.

SUMMARY

This chapter sketched a basic method of argument analysis and evaluation. First, clarify meaning. Next, identify basic structure (premises and conclusion): What is being concluded? What evidence is offered? Fill in any missing premises. Then identify any fallacies, both formal and informal. Last, apply the cogency criteria: Are premises reasonable? relevant? sufficient? This method can be used with normative and nonnormative arguments alike. A nonnormative argument is one that contains only nonnormative statements, that is, true or false assertions that express matters of empirical or logical fact. In contrast, a normative argument is one that contains a normative statement as a premise. A normative statement is an assertion of a value judgment. Because normative statements can't be verified with scientific precision, they raise special problems in arguments. In encountering any normative statement, always determine how it's being used and what interpretation the value words are carrying. Having established the meaning, you can assess the statement for warrantability or truth. Similarly, in evaluating normative arguments, always ensure that the reasons being offered are indeed justification for the claim and not pseudojustification. Motivations, rationalizations, and excuses are pseudojustification, not justification. Normative arguments, like nonnormative ones, must meet the minimum adequacy requirements in the appropriate field. In brief, this means that they need factual support. Lastly, although there's no guarantee against error, we can maximize our chances of making justified normative claims by committing ourselves to standards of rational discourse.

Summary Exercises

1. See if you can spot two or three examples of apparently factual statements that are, in actuality, disguised value judgments.

2. Sportscasts contain myriad value judgments. Just for fun, make a list of a few from a typical game.

3. Commercials and advertisements—obviously—express value judgments as well as appeal to our current values. Some of these are widely noted:

youthfulness, being trim, sexuality, success, and so on. Identify some of the specific ways in which advertisers express and foster value judgments. See if you can find some less obvious ones than those listed.

ADDITIONAL EXERCISES

Use the basic method to evaluate the following arguments. In the case of normative arguments, indicate what you'd have to do to assess the truth of the normative statements.

1. "[T]he American government leaves business 'on its own.' A government that lets business alone is said to be a *laissez-faire* government." (Richard E. Gross and Vanza Devereaux, *Civics in Action*)

2. JESS: The United States needs trade and military help. That's why the United States needs the friendship of other countries.
   JANE: Sure. But the United States has forgotten something really important: that it must also help other countries. And that's precisely why we're losing some of our friends.

3. "Whatever triumph the TV-movie genre had scored over cinematic religiosity with [director] Franco Zeffirelli's remarkable *Jesus of Nazareth* in 1977 is vitiated by this three-hour film [*Mary and Joseph: A Story of Faith*]. The art with which Zeffirelli destroyed 'myth' is missing in this pedestrian and pretentious work." (Judith Crist, *TV Guide*, December 8–14, 1979, p. A-6)

4. ROGER: The best offense is a good defense.
   RUTH: No question about it. That's why a woman today has to take courses in judo and karate—so she can get ahead in the world.

5. "Under a government which imprisons any unjustly, the true place of a just man is also in prison." (Henry David Thoreau, defending his being in jail, in *Civil Disobedience*)

6. "[W]e must not regard what the many say of us: but what he, the one man who has understanding of just and unjust, will say, and what the truth will say. And therefore you begin in error when you advise that we should regard the opinions of the many about just and unjust, good and evil, honorable and dishonorable." (Socrates in Plato's *Crito*)

7. "It is true also of journeys in the law that the place you reach depends on the direction you are taking. And so, where one comes out on a case depends on where one goes in." (Glanvil Williams, *The Sanctity of Life and the Criminal Law*)

8. WYATT: Dali's work is bound to appreciate in value now that he's dead.
   PEARL: Is that why you're buying all his stuff now?

WYATT: Not quite. His work isn't only a good investment, it's pure genius.

9. "If I am mobilized in a war, this war is *my* war; it is in my image and I deserve it. I deserve it . . . because I could always get out of it by suicide or by desertion." (Jean-Paul Sartre, *Being and Nothingness*)

10. PROFESSOR: What if I said that I am thinking of a primate that shares food and is monogamous? What would you say?
STUDENT: I'd say you were thinking of a human, a gibbon, or a marmoset.
PROFESSOR: Why?
STUDENT: Because among primates only humans, gibbons, and marmosets share food and are monogamous.

11. "[Chief Justice Warren] Burger is not the only Justice on the Supreme Court who lacks a coherent, identifiable judicial philosophy. . . . 'There are no strong philosophical bents on this court,' says University of Virginia Law Professor A. E. Dick Howard. 'Most of them are independent pragmatists who take each case as it comes.'" ("Inside the High Court," *Time*, November 5, 1979, p. 64)

12. "If we can justify the infliction of imprisonment and death by the state 'on the ground of social interests to be protected,' then surely we can similarly justify the postponement of death by the state. The objection that the individual is thereby treated not as an 'end' in himself but only as a 'means' to further the common good was, I think, aptly disposed of by [Justice Oliver Wendell] Holmes long ago. 'If a man lives in society, he is likely to find himself so treated.'" (Yale Kamisar, arguing against a relaxation of euthanasia laws, in "Some Non-Religious Views Against Proposed 'Mercy Killing' Legislation")

13. "Evolution is a scientific fairy-tale just as the 'flat-earth theory' was in the 12th century. Evolution directly contradicts the Second Law of Thermodynamics, which states that unless an intelligent planner is directing a system, it will always go in the direction of disorder and deterioration. . . . Evolution requires a faith that is incomprehensible! Biblical Creation is the only sensible alternative." (Dr. Edward Blick, professor of aerospace, mechanical and nuclear engineering at the University of Oklahoma, in *21 Scientists Who Believe in Creation*)

14. "[O]ne of the distinct inconveniences or tragedies of human sexuality is that it endows us, and perhaps particularly the males among us, with a propensity to become exceptionally involved and infatuated with members of the other sex whom, had we no sex urges, we would hardly notice. That is too bad; and it might well be a better world if it were otherwise. But it is *not* otherwise, and I think it is silly and pernicious for us to condemn ourselves because we are the way that we are in this respect." (Albert Ellis, *Sex Without Guilt*)

15. "Young people can no longer get a bootlegged feeling of personal identity out of the sexual revolt, since there is nothing left to revolt against." (Rollo May, *Antidotes for the New Puritanism*)

16. "If a being suffers, there can be no moral justification for refusing to take that suffering into consideration, and, indeed, to count it equally with the like suffering (if rough comparisons can be made) of another being. So the only question is: Do animals other than man suffer? Most people agree unhesitatingly that animals like cats and dogs can and do suffer, and this seems also to be assumed by those laws that prohibit wanton cruelty to such animals." (Peter Singer, "Animal Liberation")

17. "'If you don't break your neck,' said Garnett, 'you'll be the laughing stock of the expedition when we get back to the base. That mountain will probably be called Wilson's Folly from now on.'

   'I won't break my neck,' I said firmly. 'Who was the first man to climb Pico and Helicon?'

   'But weren't you rather younger in those days?' asked Louis gently.

   'That,' I said with great dignity, 'is as good a reason as any for going.'" (Arthur C. Clarke, *The Sentinel*)

18. "Working at a paid job, any job, a woman is no longer just a family creature. . . . Hence, for women to work means relieving at least some part of their oppression." (Susan Sontag, *Partisan Review*, XL, 1973, 199)

19. "Experience indicates that purely voluntary efforts at self-regulation are not likely to be successful. There must be some enhancement mechanism by which violations of regulatory norms can be punished through collective action against the violator." (David A. Aaker and George S. Day, *Corporate Responses to Consumerism Pressures*)

20. "Keep up with the latest developments in alternative technology, environmental issues, holistic health, and human potential. . . . Listen in on conversations with humanistic innovators such as Margaret Mead, Frederick Leboyer, Daniel Ellsberg, Allen Ginsberg, Elisabeth Kübler-Ross, and Bucky Fuller. . . . Look into *New Age*, the monthly magazine for people who want to make a difference in the world." (ad for *New Age* magazine)

21. "When you join DSOC, you're joining people like Michael Harrington, Representative Ronald Dellums, Gloria Steinem, Machinists Union President Bill Winpisinger, Irving Howe, James Farmer, Joyce Miller, president of the Coalition of Labor Union Women, Harry Britt, San Francisco Commissioner, and Ruth Messinger, NYC Council Member. Most important you're joining thousands of people you'll want to meet and work with in the struggle for a just society." (Ad for the Democratic Socialist Organizing Committee)

22. "Global Corporations, with their worldwide network of subsidiaries, high technology and marketing systems, far outstrip the puny regula-

tory efforts of a government that considers corporate crime a minor nuisance at worst. Nothing short of a complete moral transformation of the corporate ethos will stop dumping [the practice of exporting products banned in the U.S.]." (Mark Dowie, "The Corporate Crime of the Century," *Mother Jones,* November 1979, p. 49)

23. "[A]ccording to modern physics, radio is our only hope of picking up an intelligent signal from space. Sending an interstellar probe would take too long—roughly 50 years even for nearby Alpha Centauri—even if we had the technology and funds to accomplish it. But radio is too slow for much dialogue. The most we can hope from it is to establish the existence (or, more accurately, the former existence) of another civilization." (Patrick Moore, "Speaking English in Space: Stars," *Omni,* November 1979, p. 26)

24. "Primroses and landscapes, he [the Director] pointed out, have one grave defect: they are gratuitous. A love of nature keeps no factories busy. It was decided to abolish the love of nature . . . but *not* the tendency to consume transport. For of course it was essential that they [the lower classes] should keep on going to the country, even though they hated it. The problem was to find an economically sounder reason for consuming transport than a mere affection for primrose and landscapes. . . . 'We condition the masses to hate the country,' concluded the Director. 'But simultaneously we condition them to love all country sports. At the same time, we see to it that all country sports shall entail the use of elaborate apparatus.'" (Aldous Huxley, *Brave New World*)

25. "We are asked to notice that the development of a human being from conception through birth into childhood is continuous; then it is said that to draw a line, to choose a point in this development and say 'before this point the thing is not a person, after this point it is a person' is to make an arbitrary choice, a choice for which in the nature of things no good reason can be given. It is concluded that the fetus is, or anyway that we had better say it is, a person from the moment of conception. But this conclusion does not follow. Similar things might be said about the development of an acorn into an oak tree, and it does not follow that acorns are oak trees, or that we had better say they are. Arguments of this form are sometimes called 'slippery slope arguments'— the phrase is perhaps self-explanatory—and it is dismaying that opponents of abortion rely on them so heavily and uncritically." (Judith Jarvis Thomson, "A Defense of Abortion")

26. "Language is the symbolic repository of the meaningful experience of ourselves and our fellow human beings down through history, and, as such, it reaches out to grasp us in the creating of a poem. We must not forget that the original Greek and Hebrew words meaning 'to know' meant also 'to have sexual relations.' . . . The etymology of the term demonstrates the prototypical act that knowledge itself—as well as

poetry, art, and other creative products—arises out of the dynamic encounter between subjective and objective poles." (Rollo May, *The Courage to Create*)

27. "There is one law only which, by its nature, requires unanimous consent; I mean the social compact: for civil association is the most voluntary of all acts; every man being born free and master of himself, no person can under any pretense whatever subject him without his consent." (Jean Jacques Rousseau, *The Social Contract*)

28. "Just as a modern European economist would not consider it a great economic achievement if all European art treasures were sold to America at attractive prices, so the Buddhist economist would insist that a population basing its economic life on nonrenewable fuels is living parasitically, on capital instead of income. Such a way of life could have no permanence and could therefore be justified only as a purely temporary expedient. As the world's resources of nonrenewable fuels—coals, oil, and natural gas—are exceedingly unevenly distributed over the globe and undoubtedly limited in quantity, it is clear that their exploitation at an ever-increasing rate is an act of violence against nature which must almost inevitably lead to violence between men." (E. F. Schumacher, *Small Is Beautiful: Economics as if People Mattered*)

29. "It is the belief of this writer that *ecology is a profoundly serious matter, yet most of the solutions suggested for environmental quality will have, directly or indirectly, adverse effects on the poor and lower income groups.* Hence, economic or distributive justice must become an active component in all ecology debates." (David R. Frew, "Pollution: Can the People Be Innocent While Their Systems Are Guilty?")

30. "Man is condemned to be free. Condemned, because he did not create himself, yet in other respects is free, because, once thrown into the world, he is responsible for everything he does." (Jean-Paul Sartre, *Existentialism and Human Emotions*)

Venn Diagrams

The Venn diagram method of proving syllogisms valid is certain and relatively simple and quick. With it, we construct circles to represent the class terms in a syllogism. The method is particularly helpful because it makes the syllogistic argument and the relation between class terms clearly visible. The adage "A picture is worth a thousand words" is literally true as applied to the Venn diagram, for we can actually see why a particular argument is valid or invalid. Many students, especially those who shy away from mathematics, often shudder at the thought of having to use any diagrams whatever. But when we keep in mind a few simple principles, the use of Venn diagrams becomes almost as simple as drawing circles with a dime. It's even fun. And for those who think the Venn diagram is completely strange, it might come as a surprise to learn that we've already used a modified Venn diagram to see how propositions distribute their terms. Let's now take a closer look at that diagram.

VENN DIAGRAMS

Consider the interlocking circles that we used before in speaking of distribution in Chapter 7:

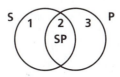

This diagram represents every instance of *S* and *P.* It also represents every instance of *SP*—where *S* and *P* come together. If we examine this diagram, we observe (1) that a portion of the *S* circle excludes a portion of the *P* circle, (2) that both *S* and *P* share a portion of the diagram, and (3) that a portion of the *P* circle excludes a portion of the *S* circle. We know we can represent (2) by placing *SP* where we have, or *PS* since they are equivalent (the same as 3 times 2 is the equivalent of 2 times 3). How in the diagram would you present (1) and (3)? To do this let's introduce the term *complement.*

    Complement means that which *completes.* If *S* represents a class, the complement of that class will be everything else it takes to complete the whole universe of things. Everything that isn't *S:* non-*S.* Taken together, *S* and non-*S* complete everything that is. So do *P* and non-*P.* Put another way: the complement of a term is everything that the term is not. What would the complement of apples be? Nonapples. And the complement of nonhouses? Houses. Non-S and non-P, for simplicity, are represented by the symbols $\bar{S}$ (read S-bar) and $\bar{P}$ (read P-bar). The complement of S, then, is $\bar{S}$ (S-bar); the complement of P is $\bar{P}$ (P-bar). And the complement of $\bar{S}$ is S; the complement of $\bar{P}$ is P. That's all the information we need to know how to fill in (1) that portion of the S circle that excludes a portion of the P circle and (2) that portion of the P circle that excludes a portion of the S circle.

Using what we know about a term's complement, we can make interlocking circles:

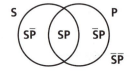

And notice that we can represent anything outside the circles by $\bar{S}\bar{P}$.

Let's now see what a proposition looks like on this diagram: "No mothers are males." This is an E form: No S is P. It's saying that no instance of a mother is an instance of a male. Applied to our circles, the proposition asserts that the portion of the circle signified by SP (mothers and males) does not have even one member. To show this on the diagram, let's shade in the portion of the circle marked SP. Thus, the diagram now appears as

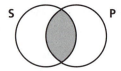

This simply means that where there is an S there is not P, and where there is a P there is not S. Since this diagram represents the *form* "No S is P," we can infer that the diagram represents *any E* proposition.

We can handle the other forms in a similar diagrammatic way. Let's consider the contradiction of E:I. "Some females are mothers" is an I proposition. This I proposition says that some of the members of S are included within the class P, and some of the members of P are included within the class S. S and P share a portion of the interlocking circles. Another way of saying this is that *there exists at least one member of the class* SP. So this time, rather than shading a portion of the circles to show that a class is empty, we should show that a class has at least one occupant. Let's signify this by placing an X in the appropriate portion of the circles. Thus

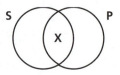

This diagram represents all I propositions.

What about the *A* proposition "All mothers are females"? This time the proposition says that every instance of *S* (mothers) includes an instance of *P* (females). Another way of stating this is that *S never appears without P* or that *S and non-P are incompatible.* Looking at our circles,

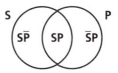

we see that we're talking about the area marked *S$\bar{P}$*. And we're saying that there can never be a member in that section. And on our diagram we show this by shading in the appropriate section to show that it has no membership. Thus

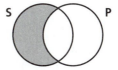

This diagram, then, represents all *A* forms.

Finally, we can do the same thing with an *O* proposition: "Some females are not mothers." This proposition says some members of *S* are excluded from *P*, that is, that sometimes an *S* is a non-*P*. Looking at our circles,

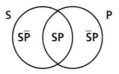

we see we're talking again about the area *S$\bar{P}$*. But this time, as is not the case with the *A* proposition, we are saying there is *at least one member of this class.* It is the denial of the *A* diagram, for *O* is the contradiction of *A*. We show this by placing an *X* in the appropriate section, indicating that it has at least one member. Thus

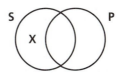

This diagram represents all *O* forms.

If the *P* comes before the *S* in a proposition—as we know in syllogisms it can, since the conclusion dictates what the *S* and *P* terms of the argument are—we adjust the diagrams appropriately.

The diagrams for propositions that reverse the order of *S* and *P* would be

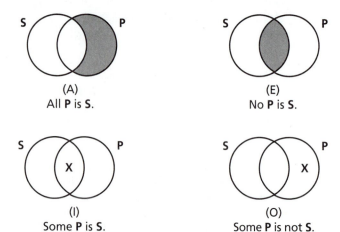

(A)
All **P** is **S**.

(E)
No **P** is **S**.

(I)
Some **P** is **S**.

(O)
Some **P** is not **S**.

Notice that the diagrams for "No *P* is *S*" and "No *S* is *P*" are the same, as are the ones for "Some *P* is *S*" and "Some *S* is *P*."

We have, then, the Venn diagrams, named after the nineteenth-century English mathematician John Venn. There are, in all, six different diagrams representing eight possible ways that a subject and predicate class can be related to each other in a proposition. Thus

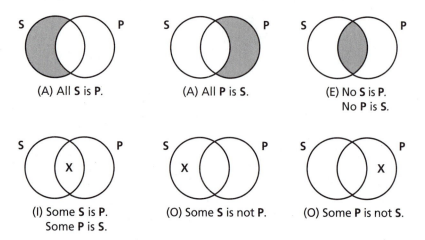

(A) All **S** is **P**.

(A) All **P** is **S**.

(E) No **S** is **P**.
No **P** is **S**.

(I) Some **S** is **P**.
Some **P** is **S**.

(O) Some **S** is not **P**.

(O) Some **P** is not **S**.

DIAGRAMMING SPECIFIC PROPOSITIONS

To diagram specific propositions, we simply use capital letters to symbolize the subject and predicate, making sure not to use the same letter to symbolize different categories on the same diagram. A good rule of thumb is to use the first letter from a significant word if the category has several clauses or modifiers. For example, to diagram the proposition "All logic students are happy people," we might let *L* stand for the subject "logic students," and *H* stand for the predicate "happy people." This reduces the proposition to "All *L* is *H*." To represent "All *L* is *H*" with a Venn diagram, we merely draw a basic A diagram, labeling the subject and predicate circles **L** and **H** rather than *S* and *P*:

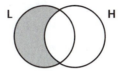

To diagram "Some advocates of school vouchers are not supporters of private schools," we can use the letter **A** to represent the subject class "advocates of school vouchers," and the letter **S** to represent the predicate class "supporters of private schools." (Note that in this case, *S* does not stand for the minor term, or subject of the conclusion.) Having decided what letters to use for the subject and predicate, we simply draw a standard O diagram, substituting **A** for *S* and **S** for *P*:

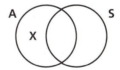

Notice that no matter how complex a given standard-form categorical proposition is, it can be reduced to its basic form and diagrammed on one of the eight possible diagrams.

STUDY HINT
Diagramming Specific Propositions

To diagram specific propositions, follow these steps:

1. Determine the form of the proposition (*A, E, I, O*).

2. Draw the appropriate Venn diagram for that form.

3. Select different capital letters to represent the subject and predicate of the proposition.

4. Label the diagram using the capital letters chosen to represent the subject and predicate.

EXERCISE A-1 *

A. Using capital letters to symbolize the subject and predicate, state the proposition in abbreviated form.

B. Give the letter names for each of the following propositions.

C. Diagram each proposition.

1. Some unhappy aardvarks are creatures who have been denied the pleasures of learning logic.

2. No trafficker in dope is an ethical person.

3. Some nonstudents are brilliant talkers.

4. No ethical person is a trafficker in dope.

5. Some strange odors are warning signs of danger or fire or decay.

6. All believers in psychic phenomena who are also holders of graduate degrees, but who have yet to achieve renown, are individuals frustrated by circumstances, yet possessing confidence in a benign future.

7. All believers in psychic phenomena who are not holders of graduate degrees are individuals frustrated by circumstances, yet possessing confidence in a benign future.

8. No sequestered jurors who are denied conjugal visits and medical leave are capable of rendering a fair verdict.

9. Some sodas are sweet.

10. Some sweeteners which are very popular are not very effective if they are not combined with natural ingredients.

DIAGRAMMING CATEGORICAL SYLLOGISMS

So far, we've been diagramming the relationship between two classes as expressed in a single categorical proposition. Standard-form categorical *syllogisms* express the interrelationships among three classes or terms: the major term, minor term, and middle term. We can diagram this interrelationship by adding a third circle to our Venn diagram. A helpful way to do this is to add the third circle so that it links the *S* and *P* circles—and thereby functions as a truly middle, or linking, term. To show this, we will need three letters to represent the three terms of the syllogism. Because the minor term of a standard-form categorical syllogism is also the subject of the conclusion, logicians use *S* to represent the minor term when referring to the structure of a syllogism. Because the major term is always the predicate of the conclusion, we use *P* to represent the major term. This leaves *M* as the logical choice to represent the middle term—the common term that links the minor and major term. The basic three-circle syllogism diagram looks like this:

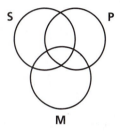

The addition of the third (*M*) circle to a Venn diagram can be confusing at first. The best way to learn to draw and interpret three-circle Venn diagrams is, of course, the practice-practice-practice method. But it helps to begin practicing with a clear grasp of exactly what the syllogism diagram consists of. By breaking the three-circle diagram into its component parts, we discover that it consists of three standard two-circle diagrams, overlaid one upon another as follows.

(1) *SP HORIZONTAL CONCLUSION DIAGRAM:* The area representing the *conclusion* is the portion of the diagram laid out on a horizontal *S-P* axis:

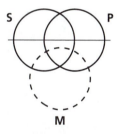

**IMPORTANT: LOOK BUT DO NOT TOUCH!
NEVER DIAGRAM DIRECTLY ON THE HORIZONTAL SP AXIS.**

(2) *SM DIAGONAL MINOR PREMISE DIAGRAM:* The *minor premise* is represented on the portion of the diagram created by the diagonal *S-M* axis:

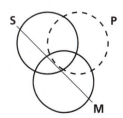

(3) *PM DIAGONAL MAJOR PREMISE DIAGRAM:* The *major premise* is represented on the portion of the diagram created by the diagonal *P-M* axis:

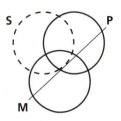

STUDY HINT

All diagramming takes place on the two diagonals.

Help familiarize yourself with the three-circle syllogism diagram by doing exercise Appendix-2 now.

EXERCISE A-2 *

The three-circle syllogism diagram form consists of seven segments:

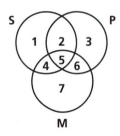

(1) Using S, P, M, and $\bar{S}, \bar{P}, \bar{M}$: (1) Write out what each segment represents in letters and bars. Example: segment $1 = S\bar{P}\bar{M}$.

(2) Label each segment to show what it represents. To start you off, we've already filled in segment 1 with $S\bar{P}\bar{M}$:

CRESCENTS AND ELLIPSES

Venn diagrams of individual standard-form categorical propositions consist of only two basic shapes: crescent-shaped semicircles and the elliptical shape created by the intersection of the *S*-circle with the *P*-circle. In other words, each diagram of a single proposition consists of two *crescents* (the subject and predicate semicircles), and one *ellipse* (the union of the subject and predicate circles):

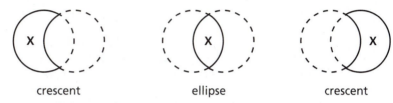

crescent   ellipse   crescent

By learning to recognize crescents and ellipses, we simplify the task of zeroing in on the appropriate segments to be graphed on the three-circle syllogism diagram. And since testing for validity requires that we *graph only the two premises,* our diagramming action will be confined to one of the two diagonals representing the minor premise (*SM*) and the major premise (*PM*).

Spotting Crescents And Ellipses

Let's practice looking for crescents and ellipses by diagramming individual propositions on three-circle diagrams. We'll refer to our numbered diagram throughout the following discussion:

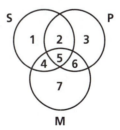

To diagram "All *M* is *S*," find the the *MS* crescent on the minor premise diagonal (segments 7 and 6), and shade it in. Because we list the subject first, *MS* tells us that *M* is the subject. Thus:

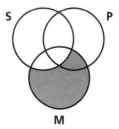

To diagram "All *S* is *M*," find the *SM* crescent on the minor premise diagonal (segments 1 and 2), and shade it in (*S* is the subject here):

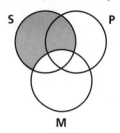

To diagram *either* "No *S* is *M*" Or "No *M* is *S*," find the *SM/MS* ellipse on the minor premise diagonal (segments 4 and 5), and shade it in:

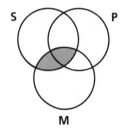

To diagram *either* "No *P* is *M*" Or "No *M* is *P*," find the *PM/MP* ellipse on the major premise diagonal (segments 4 and 5), and shade it in:

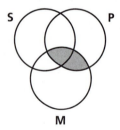

Diagramming Propositions With X

To diagram "Some *P* is not *M*," first find the *PM* crescent (segments 2 and 3) on the major premise diagonal. We notice that *PM* contains both segments 2 and 3. "Some *P* is not *M*" only tells us that the *X* goes *in* the 2-3 crescent—but *not* if it goes in 2 only, 3 only, or in both 2 and 3. We represent this ambiguity by putting the *X on the line inside the PM crescent:*

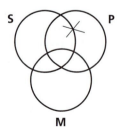

Similarly, if we wish to diagram "Some *M* is not *P*," we will need to show that X definitely goes *in* the *MP* crescent made by segments 4 and 7. But, as in the preceding example, we must be careful not to diagram a stronger claim than the individual proposition allows. So our diagram must put the *X in MP* but not specifically in either segment 4 or 7:

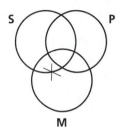

EXERCISE A-3

Graph the following propositions on a standard three-circle syllogism diagram.

1. All *M* is *S*.
2. Some *P* is not *M*.
3. No *S* is *P*.
4. No *M* is *S*.
5. All *S* is *M*.
6. All *P* is *M*.
7. Some *M* is *P*.
8. Some *P* is *M*.
9. Some *M* is not *P*.
10. Some *M* is not *S*.
11. Some *S* is not *M*.
12. All *M* is *P*.
13. No *P* is *S*.
14. No *S* is *M*.

USING VENN DIAGRAMS TO TEST FOR VALIDITY

You're probably wondering just how Venn diagrams can be used to *show* that a syllogism is valid or invalid. This method of testing for validity is based on the fact that if a standard-form categorical syllogism is valid, the two premises, "when added together," "produce" the conclusion. In more technical language, if the premises of a valid syllogism are true, the conclusion must be true also. Thus, *if by diagramming just the premises of a syllogism, we also get a clear diagram of the conclusion, we are assured that the argument is valid.* If we do not get a clear picture of the conclusion, we know that the argument is invalid.

STUDY HINT

When testing for validity, we assume that the premises are true. By the act of diagramming premises, we treat them *as if* they were true for purposes of analysis. We do not commit ourselves to asserting *that* they are true. If we discover that the argument is invalid, we know that it cannot be cogent. Validity does not guarantee cogency, however. A cogent deductive argument must have true premises. Determining truth is a separate matter from assessing validity.

To see how the Venn diagram method "pictures" validity, let's diagram this valid argument from Chapter 7:

> **All illegal drugs are hazards to health.**
> **All forms of cocaine are illegal drugs.**
> **All forms of cocaine are hazards to health.**

Before doing any diagramming, we must make sure that the argument is in proper standard-form order. We do this, recall, by identifying the conclusion (an easy task here!), and then determining the major and minor terms. We note that the form is *AAA*-1.

Having identified the major term (*hazards to health*), the minor term (*forms of cocaine*), and the middle term (*illegal drugs*), we're almost ready to begin diagramming. But before we do, we need to decide what letters to use to represent the three terms of this particular syllogism. Using key words from each of the three class term descriptions, the following choices seem appropriate:

$$S \text{ (minor term)} = forms\ of\ cocaine = \mathbf{C}$$
$$P \text{ (major term)} = hazards\ to\ health = \mathbf{H}$$
$$M \text{ (middle term)} = illegal\ drugs = \mathbf{D}$$

The next step involves drawing a three-circle syllogism diagram and labelling the *S, P, M* circles with the letters chosen to represent the specific class terms for this syllogism:

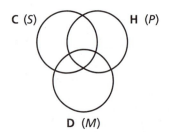

Now we're ready to *diagram just the premises*. (It is crucial *not* to diagram the conclusion directly. Doing so would render this procedure useless by picturing *all* syllogisms as valid!) Using letters, the major premise, "All illegal drugs are hazards to health," is abbreviated as "All **D** are **H**." We'll want to show this on the diagram by shading in the area represented by the **DH** crescent on the major premise diagonal. Following our convention, we know that **D** is the subject because it is listed first. Thus:

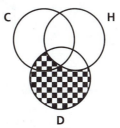

The minor premise is abbreviated "All **C** are **D**." The minor premise diagram must show that the area represented by the **CD** crescent is empty (shaded). Since **C** is the subject, we show:

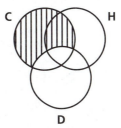

The complete diagram showing both premises looks like this:

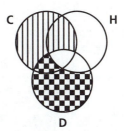

STUDY HINT
Never Directly Diagram The Conclusion

Do not directly graph the horizontal conclusion on the diagram. Only graph along the premise diagonals.

At this point, *if the syllogism is valid, the premises have already provided a graphic representation of the conclusion on the diagram.* In this syllogism, the conclusion is abbreviated as "All **C** are **H**." In other words, "**C** outside of **H**" is empty (shaded). If the syllogism is valid, the entire **CH** crescent must be shaded:

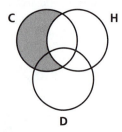

Key conclusion configuration
if "**C** outside **H**" is empty.

Does our completed diagram show this area as empty? Yes. In fact, it shows even more. But that's all right. When the premises of a syllogism contain more information than the conclusion draws, the syllogism is valid. *An argument is valid whenever the premises entail at least as much as or more than the conclusion claims.*

Let's compare our original completed diagram with the diagram that shows the key area that must be empty for the syllogism to be valid. Having used different styles of shading for the major and minor premises on the syllogism diagram makes it easier to see how each premise contributed to establishing the conclusion:

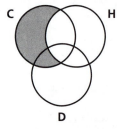

Key conclusion configuration
if "**C** outside **H**" is empty.

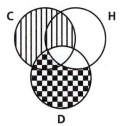

Completed diagram shows that
"**C** outside **H**" is empty (and more).

STUDY HINT

An argument is valid whenever the premises entail *at least or more than* the conclusion claims.

Now let's consider an *AAA*-2 variation of this argument:

> All hazards to health (H) are illegal drugs (D).
> All forms of cocaine (C) are illegal drugs (D).
> _____
> All forms of cocaine (C) are hazards to health (H).

The argument is already in standard-form order and we've previously determined the three terms, so we once again set up our basic diagram like this:

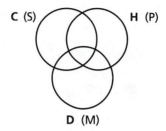

Simplified, the major premise reads "All **H** are **D**" or "**HD** is empty", which we diagram:

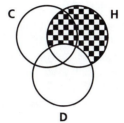

The minor premise, unchanged from the first argument analyzed above, is "All **C** are **D**." Its diagram must show that the area represented by the **CD** crescent (**C** outside of **D**) is empty (shaded):

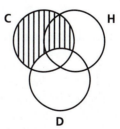

The completed diagram showing both premises looks like this (the solid black area shows where the information contained in the premises overlaps):

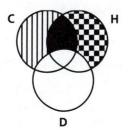

At this point, if the syllogism is valid, *the premises have already provided a graphic representation of the conclusion on the diagram*. In this syllogism, the conclusion, abbreviated "All **C** are **H,**" is the same as in the *AAA*-1 argument we just tested: "**C** outside of **H**" must be empty (shaded). If this *AAA*-2 syllogism is valid, the entire **CH** crescent will be shaded. Does our completed diagram show this? No. We can see this failure clearly by comparing the shaded area we are looking for with the completed *AAA*-2 diagram:

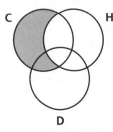

What the conclusion claims:
all "**C** outside **H**" is empty.

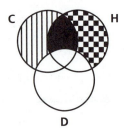

What the premises show:
some of "**C** outside **H**" is empty.

If we zero in on just the key crescent portion of the conclusion horizontal, and compare what this *AAA*-2 argument's premises actually entail with what the conclusion claims, we see that, like all invalid arguments, this one does not establish its conclusion:

Established
by AAA-2

Claimed
by AAA-2

To sum up: This *AAA*-2 argument is invalid because its conclusion claims more than its premises entail. And since validity is a formal property of arguments, we know that all *AAA*-2 syllogisms are invalid.

In Chapter 7, we learned six rules of validity for standard-form syllogisms. Whenever a syllogism fails the Venn diagramming test, we can be sure that it will also break one or more of these rules. Conversely, if a syllogism breaks one or more of the rules, it will also fail the Venn test. How does *AAA*-2 fare with the rules of validity? *AAA*-2 syllogisms commit the fallacy of the undistributed middle term.

Arguments With Two Particular Premises

Let's diagram an argument form containing only particular propositions, say *OOO*-2. Using *S, P,* and *M,* we first set up the syllogism like this:

$$\frac{\begin{array}{l}\text{Some } P \text{ are not } M.\\ \text{Some } S \text{ are not } M\end{array}}{\text{Some } S \text{ are not } P.}$$

The major premise (Some *P* are not *M*) means that "*P* outside *M* is not empty." In other words, the *PM* crescent on the the diagram requires an X. But in looking at our syllogism diagram, we see that this crescent contains two segments: $SP\bar{M}$ $\bar{S}P\bar{M}$. Since the premise does not tell us exactly where to put the X *within* the $P\bar{M}$ crescent, we must place it *on the line* between the two segments that make up the $P\bar{M}$ crescent:

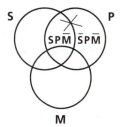

The minor premise (Some *S* are not *M*) means "*S* outside *M*" is not empty, so we should place an X in the area designated $S\bar{M}$. Again, however, this crescent is composed of two segments: $S\bar{P}\bar{M}$ and $SP\bar{M}$. So we must place the X *on the line inside* the portion of the *SM* crescent created by those two sections:

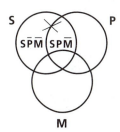

The completed diagram, combining the graphic representations of both premises looks like this:

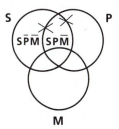

Is this argument valid? That is, does combining the two premises yield a clear (unambiguous) picture of what is asserted, or claimed, by the conclusion, namely that $S\bar{P}$ is not empty? There are, technically, three possible locations for the X when the conclusion is an O proposition. An X at any one of the three question marks would satisfy a conclusion that "Some S is not P":

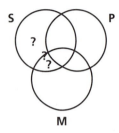

Zeroing in on the crucial area of the OOO-2 diagram, and comparing where we need an X with where we find an X, informs us that this argument does not establish its conclusion with logical certainty. What we have here is a logical "maybe," clearly not strong enough for validity. Because we only have an X *on* the inner arc of the subject crescent—and not definitively *inside* that crescent— we cannot tell whether the X belongs in or out of $S\bar{P}\bar{M}$:

Needed by *OOO*-2:
X at any one of ?s.

Established by *OOO*-2:
X *possibly* where needed,
but "possibly" is too
weak for validity.

STUDY HINT

Whenever an *X* falls inside of an area containing an unshaded line, put the *X on* that line.

Since the conclusion of *OOO*-2 is ambiguous, *OOO*-2 must break one or more of the rules of validity. The mood *OOO* commits the exclusive premises fallacy. *OOO* in the second figure distributes the major term in the conclusion but not in the major premise. Thus, besides committing the fallacy of exclusive premises, *OOO*-2 also contains an illicit major term.

Arguments Containing Mixed Premises

When a syllogism contains a universal and a particular premise, *always diagram the universal first*. That way you may eliminate the uncertainty of having an *X* "on the line," such as we just experienced in the case of *OOO*-2. Consider this argument:

Some humans (H) are vertebrates (V).
All humans (H) are mammals (M).
Some mammals (M) are vertebrates (V).

Since the argument is already in proper order, we can quickly identify the major term as **V,** the minor term as **M,** and the middle term as **H.** The form of this argument is *IAI*-3. Let's see if IAI-3 is valid. We begin, as always, by drawing and labeling three interlocking circles:

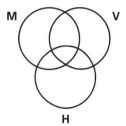

Next, we diagram the universal premise first (even though it's the minor premise): "All humans are mammals" or "All **H** are **M.**" We're already familiar with diagramming *A* premises, so we know that we must show that "**H** outside **M** is empty" by shading the **HM** crescent on the minor premise diagonal:

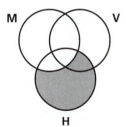

Shading the area designated as empty by the minor premise simplifies the task of diagramming the major premise. "Some humans (**H**) are vertebrates (**V**)" tells us that the elliptical shape created by the intersection of the **HV** circles is not empty. This means that we need to place an *X inside* that ellipse. On the three-circle diagram, the major premise ellipse consists of two smaller segments. Isolated, the major premise ellipse looks like this:

In order to be clearly and unequivocally *inside* of this area, the X must occupy one of the three places signified by question marks in this illustration:

We note that the universal minor premise of this *IAI*-3 syllogism asserts that the lower segment of the ellipse is empty:

This assertion rules out putting the X on the shaded line, since X *cannot* go into the empty area. Thus, the only place left to put the X is inside whatever portion of the ellipse remains unshaded:

Combining the universal minor premise with the particular major premise on one complete diagram gives us:

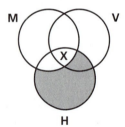

Is the argument valid? Do the premises entail the relationship claimed by the premises, namely that "Some **M** are **V**"? Yes. Once again, if we zero in on the key part of the diagram representing the conclusion circles, we get a clear picture of how that's so:

?s represent 3 possible positions for **X** if *IAI*-3 is to be valid.

X located at one of 3 possible positions for *IAI*-3 to be valid.

Diagramming this argument teaches us an important lesson in using Venn diagrams to test syllogisms for validity: *Whenever we have a universal and particular proposition as the premises of a syllogism, we should always diagram the universal first.*

STUDY HINT
Where To Put The X?

1. Diagram the universal premise if there is one.

2. Determine the basic area you will be putting an X in: subject crescent, or ellipse.

3. Find the corresponding area on the diagram.

4. Put the *X inside* the appropriate crescent or ellipse: If there is an *unshaded line inside* that area, put the X *on* it. If there is a *shaded line*, put the X *inside the unshaded subsegment* left within the main crescent or ellipse.

REVIEWING WHAT WE HAVE LEARNED

Let's review and simplify what we've learned about using Venn diagrams to test standard-form categorical syllogisms for validity. As you review, note how important it is to recognize the key shapes introduced in this Appendix: the subject crescent and the ellipse. Remember, too, that all of the active diagramming occurs on the minor and major premise diagonals.

Diagramming An A Minor Premise

The crosshatched areas below identify the only two possible minor premise diagrams for universal affirmative (*A*) minor premises. *Whenever the minor premise is an A proposition, shade the appropriate subject crescent on the diagonal:*

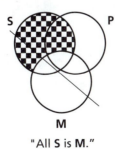

"All **S** is **M**."

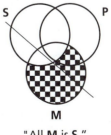

"All **M** is **S**."

A Minor Premises

Diagramming An A Major Premise

The crosshatched areas illustrated below identify the only two possible major premise *A* diagrams. Whenever the minor premise is an *A* proposition, shade the subject crescent like this:

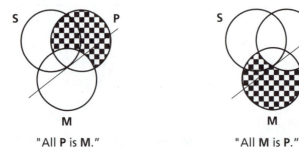

"All **P** is **M**."   "All **M** is **P**."

A Major Premises

STUDY HINT

In A diagrams, always shade the subject crescent. Although there are two crescents, *always work with the subject crescent.* It does not matter whether or not the subject circle is on the left, right, top, or bottom.

Diagramming An O Minor Premise

Whenever the minor premise is an *O* proposition, put an *X inside* the appropriate subject crescent on the diagonal. If the crescent is unshaded, put the X here:

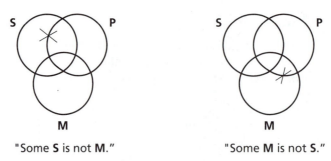

"Some **S** is not **M**."   "Some **M** is not **S**."

O Minor Premises

Diagramming An O Major Premise

Whenever the major premise is an *O* proposition, put an *X inside* the appropriate subject crescent on the diagonal. If the crescent is unshaded, put the *X* here:

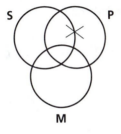

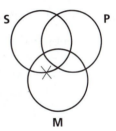

"Some **P** is not **M**."   "Some **M** is not **P**."

O Major Premises

STUDY HINT

In O diagrams, put an X inside the subject crescent. Although there are two crescents, we *always work with the subject crescent.* It does not matter whether the subject crescent is left, right, top, or bottom.

Diagramming An E Minor Or Major Premise

The minor and major premise portion of the diagram create only one ellipse each. *The crosshatched areas below identify the minor premise ellipse and the major premise ellipse. Whenever the major or minor premise is an E proposition, shade the ellipse like this:*

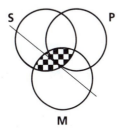

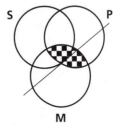

E Minor Premise   E Major Premise
"No **S** is **M**."   "No **P** is **M**."
"No **M** is **S**."   "No **M** is **P**."

STUDY HINT

In E diagrams, always shade the ellipse. Since there is only one ellipse per diagram, finding the right area to shade is simple.

Diagramming An I Minor Or Major Premise

The minor and major premise portion of the diagram creates only one ellipse each. *Whenever the major or minor premise is an I proposition, put an X **inside** the appropriate ellipse like this:*

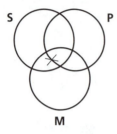

I Minor Premise
"Some **S** is **M**."
"Some **M** is **S**."

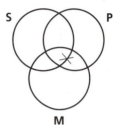

I Major Premise
"Some **P** is **M**."
"Some **M** is **P**."

STUDY HINT

In I diagrams, put an X inside the ellipse. Once again, there is only one ellipse; we simply make sure that we put the *X inside* it.

EIGHT STEPS FOR TESTING VALIDITY WITH VENN DIAGRAMS

1. Arrange the syllogism in standard-form order.

2. Draw three interlocking circles, one each for the major, minor, and middle term.

3. Label the circles with capital letters representing the three terms of the syllogism.

4. Because you want to see if the premises produce the conclusion, you must only diagram the two diagonal propositions—the major premise and the minor premise—one at a time (universals first). **CAUTION! DO NOT DIAGRAM THE CONCLUSION!**

5. Always use the subject crescent.

6. If there is an unshaded line inside an area where an *X* goes, put the *X* on that unshadezd line.

7. **STOP!** After diagramming both premises, stop.

8. **LOOK!** Determine whether the resulting diagram reflects the conclusion claimed by the syllogism. The conclusion portion of the diagram consists of the *SP* horizontal. If the syllogism is valid, this portion of the dia-

gram will reflect the conclusion *without ambiguity*. If the *SP* horizontal "could," "might," or "almost" shows or "suggests" what the conclusion asserts, the syllogism is invalid.

STUDY HINT WORTH REPEATING

All diagramming takes place on the minor and major premise diagonals. The conclusion is never diagrammed directly.

USING VENN DIAGRAMS TO "SEE" SYLLOGISTIC FALLACIES

Using Venn diagrams, we can actually "see" how arguments that violate the rules of validity fail. (These rules are discussed in Chapter 7) In this section, we'll conclude our look at Venn diagrams with a quick survey of examples of invalid arguments that break five rules individually and in combination.

Rule 2: *Any standard-form syllogism that fails to distribute its middle term at least once is invalid.* *III* (any figure) is the classic example of a syllogism that commits the fallacy of the undistributed middle term. Let's see why by diagramming *III*-1. (Note that the diagrams for *III*-2, *III*-3, *III*-4 will be identical):

Some M is P.

Some S is M.

Some S is P.

The diagram for *III*-1 shows only that "Some *S might be P.*" Clearly, this is not strong enough to establish the conclusion with deductive certainty:

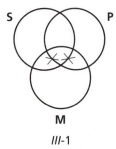

III-1

Rule 3: *Any term that is distributed in the conclusion, must be distributed in its premise.* Any syllogism that distributes its minor term in the conclusion but not in the minor premise commits the *illicit minor term* fallacy. Any syllogism that distributes its major term in the conclusion but not in the major premise commits the *illicit major term* fallacy. Consider *AOE*-1, which commits both fallacies:

All M is P.

Some S is not M.

No S is P.

For *AOE*-1 to be valid, the SP ellipse must be completely shaded in. The diagram of *AOE*-1 shows very clearly that this is not so:

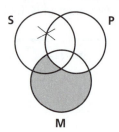

Rule 4: *A standard-form categorical syllogism with two negative premises is invalid.* Any syllogism with two negative premises commits the fallacy of exclusive premises. *EOE*-4 commits this fallacy:

> No P is M.
> Some M is not S.
> ―――――――――
> No S is P.

The diagram of *EOE*-4 pictures the syllogism's invalidity:

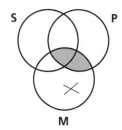

Rule 5: *A standard-form categorical syllogism with a negative conclusion must have a negative premise; if it does not, it is invalid.* Syllogisms that violate this rule commit the fallacy of drawing an affirmative conclusion from a negative premise. *IOI*-2 and *AEE*-3 both break Rule 5, and their respective diagrams expose their invalidity:

Some P is M.
Some S is not M.
―――――――――
Some S is P.

All M is P.
No M is S.
―――――――
All S is P.

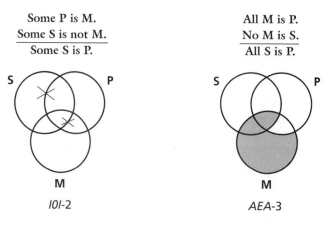

IOI-2   *AEA*-3

Rule 6: *In Boolean logic, if both premises are universal, the conclusion must be universal, and if both premises are particular, the conclusion must be particular.* Syllogisms that break this rule commit the existential fallacy. Venn diagrams make this very clear. It is impossible to derive an *X*ed conclusion from two shaded premises, which *AAI*-2, for example, tries to do. A quick glance at the diagram for this argument shows the structure of the existential fallacy (two universal premises combined with a particular conclusion). The diagram for *AAI*-2 contains no *X*:

All P is M.
All S is M.
Some S is P.

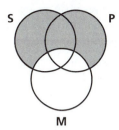

Incidentally, in Boolean logic it is also impossible to derive a shaded conclusion from two *X*ed premises. The following *IOA*-1 diagram illustrates the futility of this flawed argument form:

Some M is P.
Some S is not M.
All S is P.

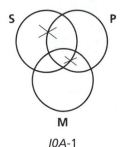

IOA-1

REINFORCING EXERCISES

A. Reinforce what you've learned by using Venn diagrams to confirm the validity or invalidity of the following syllogisms:

1. No professional athletes are welfare recipients because no professional athletes are low-income earners, and all welfare recipients are low-income earners.

2. Some politicians are persons of integrity. Thus some entertainers are politicians, for some entertainers are persons of integrity.

3. All victims of injustice are members of oppressed groups, so because all blacks are members of oppressed groups, all blacks are victims of injustice.

4. It follows that some American Indians are not exponents of the traditional account of American history because no American Indians are people dealt with fairly in American history books, and no one dealt with fairly in American history books is an exponent of the traditional account of American history.

5. Some explosives are chemicals, from which it follows that some purchasable items are not chemicals because no explosives are purchasable items.

6. Some wealthy people are millionaires, because some millionaires are possessors of large sums of money and all possessors of large sums of money are wealthy people.

7. Some persons without sin are ones who should cast the first stone. So no person is one who should cast the first stone because no person is a person without sin.

8. Some newspapers are not true accounts of what's happened, for all true accounts of what's happened are complete and accurate sources of information, and some newspapers are not complete and accurate sources of information.

9. Because some movies are films for adults, some movies are not films for children, as no films for adults are films for children.

10. All roads are ways that lead to Rome and all roads are potential dead ends. Thus, all ways that lead to Rome are potential dead ends.

*B. By means of a Venn diagram, test the validity of these forms:

1. *AAA*-4

2. *IOO*-3

3. *AII*-4

4. *OAO*-2

5. *EOO*-1

6. *OAI*-1

7. *AEE*-2

8. *OIO*-3

9. *IOI*-1

10. *IAI*-3

Logical terms are sometimes used with special meanings by different authors. The following definitions give the meanings that terms have in this book. This glossary is not intended to exhaust the logician's vocabulary, but to give the beginning student a simplified list of foundational terms. Each entry is followed by a chapter reference.

Abbreviated arguments   logical arguments that do not expressly state premises or conclusions. (See also enthymemes.) (1)

Accident (fallacy of)   argument that treats a weak generalization as if it were strong by overlooking the qualifications attached to a general rule. (10)

Affirming the consequent (fallacy of)   mixed-conditional syllogism in which the second premise affirms the consequent of the conditional, and the conclusion affirms the antecedent. (9)

Agreement (method of)   if two or more instances of a phenomenon have only one circumstance in common, that circumstance is probably the cause (or the effect) of the phenomenon; one of Mill's methods for establishing probable causation. (13)

Ambiguity   a word or phrase is ambiguous if it has more than one possible meaning in a given context. (5)

Analogical argument   inductive argument that uses known similarities that two things share as evidence for concluding that the two things are similar in additional ways. (12)

Analogy   comparison whereby we indicate in what respects two things are similar. (12)

Anecdotal evidence (fallacy of)   form of hasty conclusion that occurs when we attempt to refute a well-established generalization based solely on limited personal experience. (10)

Antecedent   statement that occurs between *if* and *then* in a conditional statement. (9)

Appeal to superstition (fallacy of)   see magical thinking. (13)

Apples to oranges (comparing)   form of concealed evidence in which the exact nature of a comparison is disguised or hidden. (11)

Argument (logical)   any group of propositions (truth claims), one of which is claimed to follow logically from the others. (1)

Argument from ignorance (fallacy of)   an argument that confuses a lack of proof with a refutation. (3)

Argumentum ad superstionem **(fallacy of)**   see magical thinking. (13)

Authority   an expert other than ourselves. (3)

Bandwagon   see mob appeal. (6)

Begging the question (fallacy of)   an argument that uses some form of its own conclusion as part of the evidence to support that very conclusion. (6)

Belief   a person's attitude toward a claim. (3)

Biased question (fallacy of)   argument based on the answer to a question that is worded to draw a predetermined reply. (11)

Biased sample (fallacy of)   argument that contains a sample that is not representative of the population being studied. (11)

Buzzwords   vague words and phrases that create an impression of action, dynamism, and vitality but that are devoid of content; that is, they mean nothing: a form of doublespeak. Examples include "exciting," "tax reform," "democracy," and "marvelous." (5)

Case   all of the elements used to persuade someone (including ourselves) of something. (1)

Categorical proposition   a proposition that relates two classes. (7)

Causal argument   an argument that attempts to support a causal statement; in evaluating causal arguments, it's necessary to determine whether a relationship between *A* and *B* actually exists and whether the relationship is the type of causal relation claimed. (13)

Causal fallacies   arguments that assert that a particular circumstance produces (causes) a particular phenomenon when there is, in fact, little or no evidence to support such a contention. (13)

Causal statement   statement that asserts a relationship between two things, such that one is claimed to effect the other. (13)

Character assassination   form of personal attack in which the arguer's personal failings or problems are cited as evidence against his or her argument. (6)

Circular reasoning   a more elaborate form of begging the question in which the questionable assumption is presented in a series of two or more steps. (6)

Circumstantial personal attack   an argument that rejects an opponent's argument solely on the basis of possible bias due to some aspect of the opponent's personal life. (6)

Class (category)   group of things having a common property or characteristic. (7)

Cogency   quality of an argument whose premises are reasonable, relevant, and sufficient to support the conclusion. (1)

Common practice (fallacy of)   variation of two wrongs make a right that attempts to justify a course of action perceived as wrong on the basis of the fact that it is widely practiced. (6)

Complement   the complement of a term consists of everything that is not that term. (7)

Complex question   an argument that in asking a question assumes an answer to an unstated prior question. (6)

Concealed evidence (fallacy of)   argument that presents only facts that are favorable to its conclusion while suppressing relevant but nonsupportive facts. (11)

Conclusion   the statement we are trying to prove is true by logical argument. (1)

Concomitant variation (method of)   whenever a phenomenon varies in a particular way as another phenomenon varies in a particular way, a causal relationship probably varies between the two; one of Mill's methods for establishing probable causation. (13)

Conditional statement   "if . . . then" compound statements asserting a special relationship known as "material conditional," "material implication," or "material hypothetical"; conditional statements are true if and only if the consequent is not false and the antecedent true. (9)

Conditional syllogism   syllogism containing a conditional statement as its major premise. (9)

Connotation (objective)   the collection of properties common to all (and only) those things to which a term refers; also known as a term's *intension*. (5)

Connotation (subjective)   moods, images, attitudes, and values commonly or individually associated with a term. (5)

Consequent   statement that follows *then* in a conditional statement. (9)

Contradictories   propositions with opposite truth values; the truth of one implies the falsity of the other, and the falsity of one implies the truth of the other. (7)

Contraposition   switching and complementing both the subject and predicate of a standard-form categorical proposition. (7)

Contributory cause   a factor that helps create the total set of conditions, necessary or sufficient, for an effect. (13)

Conversion   switching the subject and predicate of a standard-form categorical proposition with each other. (7)

Correlation   systematic connection between two properties (variables) shared by a single group; correlations don't necessarily imply causation; as distinguished from causal relations, a correlation is a relationship between properties that exists in some *actual* population and always implies a symmetrical relation, whereas a causal relation is defined in terms of a relationship between two *hypothetical* versions of the real population and never implies a symmetrical relation. (13)

Counterdilemma   a dilemma whose conclusion is opposed to the conclusion of the original dilemma; used in refutation. (9)

Critical thinking   the conscious and deliberate scrutiny of cases and arguments to determine whether or not they meet the criteria of reasonableness, relevancy, and sufficiency. (3)

Deduction   mode of reasoning that refers to arguments whose premises are intended to provide conclusive support for their conclusions. (1, 7, 8, 9)

Deductive argument   an argument whose premises are intended to provide conclusive support for its conclusion. (7)

Defense mechanism   a strategy designed to support a favored self-concept despite contradictory fact. (4)

Denial (psychological)   a defense mechanism that protects a favored self-concept by refusing to acknowledge the existence or nature of some unpleasant circumstance. (4)

Denotation   the collection or class of objects to which a term may correctly be applied; also called *extension*. (5)

Denying the antecedent (fallacy of)   mixed-conditional syllogism in which the second premise denies the antecedent of the conditional, and the conclusion denies the consequent. (9)

Difference (method of)   if an instance when the phenomenon occurs and an instance of when it doesn't occur have every circumstance in common except one, and that circumstance occurs only in the former, then that circumstance is probably the cause (or the effect) of the phenomenon; one of Mill's methods for establishing probable causation. (13)

Dilemma   a syllogism that contains a conditional and disjunctive premise, and either a simple statement or a disjunction for its conclusion. A *simple dilemma* contains a simple statement for its conclusion; a *complex dilemma* contains a disjunction for its conclusion. (9)

Direct relationship   as one thing increases, the other thing increases proportionally; or as one thing decreases, the other decreases proportionally. (13)

Disanalogy   in an argument from analogy, a significant, weakening difference between the things compared. (12)

Disjunction   a statement which is true whenever *at least one* of its disjuncts is true. (9)

Disjunctive syllogism   argument containing a disjunction as one premise, the negation of one of the disjuncts as the second premise, and the affirmation of the remaining disjunct as the conclusion. (9)

Dismissal (fallacy of)   an argument that uses the assumption of superiority to advance a conclusion; offers an *attitude* of indignation or superiority as evidence in an argument; assumes innocence without demonstrating it. (6)

Dissimilarities   in argument from analogy, significant strengthening differences between the things compared. (12)

Distribution   property of a standard-form categorical proposition which refers to all members of a class; the class so designated is said to be distributed. (7)

Doublespeak   term coined by William Lutz to refer to "language that pretends to communicate but really doesn't"; doublespeak deliberately distorts, inflates, and obscures the truth to create some advantage for its user. (5)

Drawing an affirmative conclusion from a negative premise (fallacy of)   invalid standard-form categorical syllogism which contains an affirmative conclusion and a negative premise. (7)

Emotive language   words or phrases which arouse moods and feelings. (5)

Empirical claim   assertion about the sensible word. (14)

Empirical meaning   see predictive power. (14)

Enthymeme   a fragmented argument; a first-order enthymeme suppresses its major premise; second order, its minor premise; third order, its conclusion. (8)

Equivalent inferences (Boolean)   obversion, conversion (for E and I), and contraposition (for A and O). (7)

Equivocation (fallacy of)   argument that confuses the varying meanings of a word or phrase; can occur statistically or visually. (5, 11)

Escaping between the horns of a dilemma   attacking the disjunctive premise of the dilemma. (9)

Euphemism   an inoffensive or positive word or phrase used to avoid facing or acknowledging a harsh, unpleasant, or distasteful reality; a form of doublespeak. Examples include "passing away" for dying, or "fibbing" for lying. (5)

Exclusive premises (fallacy of)   invalid standard-form categorical syllogism that contains two negative premises. (7)

Existential fallacy   based on Boolean interpretation of standard-form categorical propositions, invalid standard-form categorical syllogism that contains two universal premises and a particular conclusion. (7)

Existential import   property of a proposition that asserts the existence of at least one thing; under Boolean interpretation, *A* and *E* propositions lack existential import, *I* and *O* have it. (7)

Extension   see denotation. (5)

Fallacy   a type of argument that may seem to be correct but isn't. (3, 5, 6)

False authority (fallacy of)   an argument that violates any of the criteria for a justifiable appeal to authority. (3)

False dilemma (fallacy of)   argument that erroneously reduces the number of possible positions or alternatives on an issue. (11)

Falsifiable empirical claim   assertion about the sensible world that is subject to some actual or theoretical test or experiment of disproof. (14)

Faulty analogy (fallacy of)   an analogical argument that overlooks relevant, weakening differences between the things compared. (12)

Fear   an argument that uses the threat of harm as evidence for a conclusion when in fact such a threat is not evidence at all. (6)

Figure   determined by the position of a standard-form categorical syllogism's middle term; expressed as a number 1–4, as follows:

| Figure 1: $M\ P$ | Figure 2: $P\ M$ | Figure 3: $M\ P$ | Figure 4: $P\ M$ |
| $S\ M$ | $S\ M$ | $M\ S$ | $M\ S$ (7) |

Form (propositional)   the manner in which a proposition speaks of its classes; *A, E, I,* or *O.* (7)

Form (syllogistic)   in standard-form categorical syllogisms, mood and figure; in non-standard-form syllogisms, *modus ponens, modus tollens, dilemma, disjunctive syllogism, pure hypothetical syllogism.* (7, 9)

Formal fallacies   violations of the rules for correct deductive argument. (6, 7, 9)

Four terms (fallacy of)   invalid categorical syllogism containing more than three terms. (7)

Generalization   statement that covers many specifics. (10)

Gobbledygook (bureaucratese)   a catchall term for language used to overwhelm an audience with sheer number and complexity of words and grammar: a form of doublespeak. In gobbledygook, the bigger the words and longer the sentences are, the better. (5)

Guilt (psychological)   a feeling of discomfort which accompanies a perception of failure to act in accord with our own values. (4)

Guilt by association (fallacy of)   a form of hasty conclusion in which people are judged guilty solely on the basis of the company they keep or places they frequent. (10)

Hasty conclusion (fallacy of)   argument that draws a conclusion based on insufficient evidence. (10)

Humor and ridicule (fallacy of)   an attack on an idea or argument that relies strictly on humor or abuse. (6)

Hypothesis   a tentative conclusion that relates and explains a group of different items of information. (14)

Illicit major term (fallacy of)   invalid standard-form categorical syllogism which distributes its major term in the conclusion but does not distribute it in the major premise. (7)

Illicit minor term (fallacy of)   invalid standard-form categorical syllogism which distributes its minor term in the conclusion but does not distribute it in the minor premise. (7)

Indirect relationship   as one thing increases, the other thing decreases proportionally; or as one thing decreases, the other increases proportionally. (13)

Induction   mode of reasoning that refers to arguments whose premises are intended to provide some, but not conclusive, support for the conclusion. (10, 11, 12, 13)

Inductive argument   argument whose premises are intended to provide some, but not conclusive, support for the conclusion. (10)

Inductive generalization   inductive argument whose conclusion expresses a pattern or principle derived from its premises. (10)

Informative language   language that expresses cognitive meaning. (5)

Intension   see connotation (objective). (5)

Introjection   the defense mechanism by which we internalize the values, beliefs, and experiences of others. (4)

Jargon   specialized, technical language of a trade, profession, or membership, such as doctors, lawyers, educators, auto mechanics, firefighters, police officers, and so on; sometimes a form of doublespeak. (5)

Joint method of agreement and difference   practice of simultaneously using the methods of agreement and difference to identify causes and effects. (13)

Justification   property of an inductive argument whose premises, when assumed true, lend the conclusion a high degree of probability; also refers to the reasonableness and relevancy of the evidence offered to support a conclusion. (3, 10)

Knowledge   justified true belief. (3)

Loaded epithets   an argument that substitutes questionable labels for reasons to advance a favored conclusion. (6)

Logic   the study of the rules of correct argument. (1)

Logical argument   see argument (logical). (1)

Magical thinking (fallacy of)   a form of post hoc that uncritically attributes causal power to thoughts, feelings, and words; also known as appeal to superstition (*argumentum ad superstionem*). (13)

Major premise   in a standard-form categorical syllogism the premise that contains the major term. (7)

Major term   same term as predicate of the conclusion of a standard-form categorical syllogism. (7)

Margin of error   in a poll or study, the degree to which a statistical generalization may be inaccurate. (11)

Material conditional   see conditional statement. (9)

Material implication   see conditional statement. (9)

Middle term   term not in the conclusion of a standard-form categorical syllogism but common to each premise. (7)

Mill's methods   procedures for establishing probable causation: agreement, difference, joint method of agreement and difference, and concomitant variation; formulated by nineteenth-century English philosopher John Stuart Mill. (13)

Minor premise   in a standard-form categorical syllogism the premise that contains the minor term. (7)

Minor term   same term as subject of the conclusion of a standard-form categorical syllogism. (7)

Mixed-conditional syllogism   deductive argument containing a conditional statement as its first premise and a simple statement as its second premise. (9)

Mob appeal   an argument that attempts to persuade groups or individuals by arousing their deepest emotions, beliefs, and values. Two common forms of mob appeal are *bandwagon* and *snob appeal*. Bandwagon mob appeals invoke inclusive feelings of belonging to a group. The snob appeal version of mob appeal invokes feelings of superiority and exclusivity. (6)

Modus ponens   mixed-conditional syllogism in which the second premise affirms the antecedent of the conditional premise and the conclusion affirms its consequent. (9)

Modus tollens   mixed-conditional syllogism in which the second premise denies the consequent of the conditional premise and the conclusion denies its antecedent. (9)

Mood   order of a properly arranged standard-form categorical syllogism (major premise, minor premise, conclusion) expressed in terms of the letter designations of its premises and conclusion. (7)

Necessary and sufficient cause   any condition that must be present for the effect to occur and one that will bring about the effect alone in and of itself. (13)

Necessary cause   a condition that *must* be present if the effect is to occur. (13)

Negative correlation   a connection between properties that members of a group have, such that *B* is negatively correlated with *A* if and only if the percentage of *B*s among *A*s is less than the percentage of *B*s among non-*A*s. (13)

Nonnormative argument   argument that contains only nonnormative statements. (15)

Nonnormative statements   true or false assertions used to express matters of empirical or logical fact. (15)

Normative argument   argument that contains at least one normative statement. (15)

Normative statements   assertions that express value judgments. (15)

Objective claim   proposition whose truth value is independent of the unique knowledge, beliefs, and experiences of a specific individual. (3)

Objectivity   the quality of viewing ourselves and the world without distortion. (3)

Obversion   changing the quality of a standard-form categorical proposition and replacing the predicate with its complement. (7)

Oversimplification (fallacy of)   argument that treats a situation as if it involved only a few significant factors when in fact it involves a complex of many significant, interrelated facets. (13)

Particular inductive generalization   see weak inductive generalization. (10)

Personal attack   an argument that claims to be a refutation of an opponent's argument when it in fact attacks the opponent. Character assassination, circumstantial, and *tu quoque* are forms of personal attack. (6)

Persuasive language   language that aims to convince us of something. (5)

Pity (appeal to)   a fallacious argument that arouses compassion to advance its conclusion. (6)

Popularity (fallacy of)   an argument that tries to justify something strictly by appeal to numbers. (3)

Positioning (fallacy of)   an argument that tries to capitalize on the earned reputation of a leader in a field to sell something. (3)

Positive correlation   a connection between properties that members of a group have, such that B is positively correlated with A if and only if the percentage of Bs among As is greater than the percentage of Bs among non-As. (13)

Post hoc (fallacy of)   argument that asserts that one event is the cause of another from the mere fact that the first occurred prior to the second; full name: *post hoc, ergo propter hoc.* (13)

Predicate   whatever follows the copula (some form of the verb *to be*) of a standard-form categorical proposition. (7)

Predictive power (empirical meaning)   quality of assertions that can be verified *and* falsified in fact or in theory. (14)

Prejudice   a conclusion arrived at prior to pertinent experience or independent of evidence. (4)

Premise   statement claimed to support the conclusion of a logical argument. (1)

Principle of charity   rule of thumb followed in rational reconstruction that whenever two possible interpretations of an argument are equally likely, we should choose the one that most strengthens the argument. (8)

Problematic claim   claim whose truth is as yet unproven or whose truth is not yet known to the arguer's audience. (2)

Projection   the defense mechanism that attributes to others undesirable traits that we find in ourselves. (4)

Proposition   true or false statement. (1)

Provincialism (fallacy of)   an argument that views things exclusively in terms of group loyalty. (3)

Pseudojustification   giving motivation when justification is sought. (14)

Pseudoscience   certain category of theories, systems, and explanations, which though claiming to be "scientific," in fact use only the trappings of genuine science and avoid the rigors of the checks and balances of scientific methods or the scrutiny of disinterested experts. (15)

Public dimension of an argument   the objective properties of an argument's logic and content, and the objective criteria relevant to presenting and analyzing cases. (3)

Public verification   when a claim is subject to "public verification," almost anyone wanting to can verify it. (3)

Puffery   the use of obscure, technical, or complex words and grammar for the purpose of inflating the content of a claim: a form of doublespeak. For example, referring to students as educational consumers. (5)

Pure conditional syllogism   syllogism containing only conditional propositions. (9)

Questionable premise   premise used to establish the truth of a problematic claim before its own truth value has been clearly and independently established. (5)

Random sample   a portion of the population drawn in such a way as to ensure that every population member has an equal chance of being drawn. (11)

Randomness   designation given to a sample drawn from a population in such a way that each member has an equal chance of being drawn. (10, 11)

Rational discourse   giving and receiving reasons according to commonly agreed upon standards of verification. (1)

Rational reconstruction   process of exposing the logical (hence, "rational") structure of an argument for purposes of analysis. (8)

Rationalizing   the defense mechanism that presents bogus reasons as justification for a favored conclusion; giving reasons for a choice after the fact, after we've already decided what to do. (4, 14)

Reason   the capacity to draw conclusions based on evidence. (2)

Reasonableness   cogency criterion that is met when there is known good evidence for all of an argument's premises and no known evidence against them. (1)

Red herring   a form of distraction, the fallacy of red herring is the introduction of a logically separate and irrelevant issue into a discussion for purposes of diverting scrutiny away from the issue being evaluated. (6)

Reductio ad absurdum   counterargument that refutes an argument or claim by showing that it is absurd, contradictory, or generates an unacceptable result. (3)

Relevancy   cogency criterion that is met when the premises of an argument provide evidence directly related to establishing the conclusion as it is formulated. (1)

Scapegoating   the defense mechanism that singles out an innocent individual or group to blame for some undesired condition. (4)

Self-concept   the impression we have of the kind of person we are. (4)

Self-supporting statement   one that the arguer does not state (even indirectly) in the fragmented argument, but one taken for granted as helping entail the conclusion. (8)

Sensory acuity   the sensory abilities of the observer. (3)

Signal words (and phrases)   alert us to the possible presence of a premise or conclusion. (2)

Simplified square of contradiction   graphic representation of Boolean interpretation of contradiction showing A and O and E and I to be opposing (contradictory) corners of a square. (7)

Singular proposition   affirms or denies that a particular individual or entity falls within a class. (8)

Slippery slope (fallacy of)   argument that objects to a position on the erroneous belief that the position, if taken, will set off a chain of events that inevitably will lead to some other action. (13)

Snob appeal   see mob appeal. (6)

Sophistry ("new")   deliberate use of fallacies, persuasive language, "powerbabble," manipulative techniques, and personal charisma to sell success, health, salvation, or well-being. (14)

Sorites   a string of enthymemes. (8)

Statistical generalization   statement that asserts that something is true of a specified percentage of a class. (10, 11)

Stereotyping   occurs when we overlook an individual's unique qualities by viewing him or her only according to a rigid preconception. (4)

Stratified random sample   a sampling technique in which relevant strata within the group are identified and a random sample from each stratum is selected in proportion to the number of members in each stratum. (11)

Straw argument   attacking a straw argument occurs when a weakened imitation of an opponent's argument is attacked instead of the opponent's original argument because the imitation is easier to refute. The weakened imitation is known as a straw argument. (6)

Strong inductive generalization   statement that asserts that something is true of all members of a class; also known as universal inductive generalization. (10)

Subject   whatever appears between the quantifier (*all, no, some*) and the copula (some form of the verb *to be*) of a standard-form categorical proposition. (7)

Subjective claim   proposition whose truth value is dependent on the unique knowledge, beliefs, and experiences of a specific individual. (3)

Sufficiency   cogency criterion that is met when the premises of an argument, taken as a whole, provide enough evidence to support the conclusion. (1)

Sufficient cause   any condition that, *by itself*, will bring about the effect. (13)

Syllogism   deductive argument containing two premises and a conclusion. (7)

Taking a dilemma by the horns   attacking the truth of the conditional premise of the dilemma. (9)

Thesis proposition   in an extended argument, a statement of the main idea of the argument together with the author's attitude toward it. (15)

Traditional wisdom (fallacy of)   an argument that uses the past to justify claims made in the present. (3)

Truth   quality of a proposition that describes an actual state of affairs. (3)

***Tu quoque* personal attack**   an argument that rejects advice or criticism solely on the grounds that those giving it don't follow it. (6)

Two wrongs make a right   an argument that attempts to justify what is considered wrong by appealing to other instances of the same or similar action. (6)

Undistributed middle term (fallacy of)   invalid standard-form categorical syllogism that fails to distribute its middle term in at least one premise. (7)

Universal inductive generalization   see strong inductive generalization. (10)

Unknowable fact (fallacy of)   an argument that contains a premise that's unverifiable, either in principle or in a particular case. (3)

Vagueness   a word or phrase is vague if its meaning requires clarification in a given context. (5)

Validity   formal property of deductive arguments. A deductive argument is valid when the relationship between the premises and conclusion is such that *if* the premises *were all* true, then the conclusion would *have to be true*. (7)

Verifiable claim (empirical)   assertion with predictive power; see falsifiable empirical claim. (14)

Weak inductive generalization   statement that asserts that something is true of some members of a class; also known as particular inductive generalization. (10)

Willed ignorance   an argument that insists on the legitimacy of an idea or principle despite contradictory fact. (6)

To the student: In some exercises, only one answer can be correct. In others, a variety of correct answers are possible. Even when more than one answer is possibly correct, it does not follow that *any* answer is correct. Some answers are better than others, and some are, alas, plainly wrong. If you disagree with an answer, first double check and make sure that the answers you are using match the exercises. For instance, make sure that you're not confusing, say, answers from Exercise 2-1 with Additional Exercises, and so on. Then, rethink the problem. If you still disagree, consult your instructor.

CHAPTER 2   *Exercise 2-1*

1. No food is blue.
   All apples are food.
   _____
   No apples can be blue.

2. No one who is enjoying this exercise is thrilled by it.
   Some logic students are enjoying this exercise.
   _____
   No logic students are thrilled by it.

3. Anyone who can write a logic book is a genius.
   Anyone who can understand a logic book is a greater genius.
   Logic students can understand logic books.
   _____
   Logic students are smarter than logic book writers.

4. All trouble should be avoided.
   Some parties lead to trouble.
   _____
   Some parties should be avoided.

5. J.R.'s wearing a ring.
   _____
   J.R.'s married.

6. People should be paid comparable salaries for comparable work.
   Women are people.
   _____
   Women should be paid the same salaries as men when they do the same work.

7. Everything must have a cause.
   Nothing can cause itself.
   _____
   The universe must have a cause.

8. Everything must have a cause.
   God's something.
   _____
   God must have a cause.

9. All rocks are minerals.
   No minerals are tasty.
   _____
   Some rocks are not tasty.

10. First, rock music becomes more and more crude.
    Then it becomes satanic.
    Next, kids start listening to it.
    Then they commit suicide.
    _____
    Rock music leads to teen suicides.

11. If I marry Natasha, then Julie will be hurt.
    When Julie is hurt, she goes on the warpath.
    When Julie goes on the warpath, she is a terror to behold.
    I hate beholding terror.
    _____
    I had better not marry Natasha.

12. It's not fair to make U.S. taxpayers bail out savings and loan institutions that have failed due to greedy managers.

That's exactly what Congress is doing.
_____
What Congress is doing is not fair.

13. More than half of all automobile accidents involve drivers under twenty-five.
_____
Drivers under twenty-five are probably a greater driving risk than those older than twenty-five.

14. Smith only misses work when he is ill.
Smith missed work today.
_____
Smith must be ill.

15. The presidential candidate that Maine selects usually indicates the one who'll be elected.
_____
It's safe to say, "As Maine goes, so goes the nation."

16. Every class I've taken so far has an even male-female distribution.
_____
The student population of this college is evenly divided between males and females.

17. If the president stands for reelection, he'll surely be elected.
Anyone who thinks the president won't run again just doesn't understand politics or political ambition.
_____
It's clear who the next president will be: the present incumbent.

18. Sandy was either present or she knows someone who was present.
If she was present, she knows more than she's admitting.
If she knows someone who was present, she knows more than she's admitting.
_____
Sandy knows more than she's admitting.

19. The chances that there are atmospheric conditions similar to Earth's elsewhere in the universe are very high.
_____
Extraterrestrial life probably exists.

20. Any argument whose premises logically entail its conclusion is valid.
This argument's premises logically entail its conclusion.
_____
This argument is valid.

Exercise 2-2
Note: You may have other interpretations of these arguments. What's most important at this stage is that you learn to recognize logical structure, and that you make a case for your interpretation.

1. Only people wear hats.
(Bears are not people.)
_____
No bears wear hats.

2. T.R. is Eileen's sister.
(All sisters are women.)
_____
T.R. is a woman.

3. That's poison.
(You should not eat anything that's poison.)
_____
Don't eat that.

4. Yellowstone National Park is crowded.
(Mom doesn't like crowds.)
_____
Mom won't like Yellowstone National Park.

5. If Bill Clinton knows how to run this country, then I'm a monkey's uncle.
(I'm not a monkey's uncle.)
(George Bush does not know how to run this country.)

6. (No team can win the pennant that lacks power hitters.)

The Cubs lack power hitters.
The Cubs can't win the pennant.

7. (I won't go to any party that Polly goes to.)
If Polly's going to the party, then I'm staying home.

8. No one is allowed without a ticket.
You don't have a ticket.
(You are not allowed.)

9. (You should buy whatever's popular.)
This sold over 1,000,000.
(You should buy this.)

alternative:

(Whatever sells over 1,000,000 is good/desirable.)
This sold over 1,000,000
(This is good/desirable.)

10. Only the lonely [can] know how I feel.
(You're not lonely.)
You can't know how I feel.

11. Only another clown could've gotten close enough to murder Bozo the Clown.
(You're the only suspect who is a clown.)
You must have murdered Bozo the Clown.

12. You only hurt the ones you love.
(I don't love you.)
I can't hurt you.

13. Note: This is actually two arguments; the implied conclusion of the first is used as an implied premise in the second as follows:

If God can prevent evil, but doesn't, then He's cruel.
God is not cruel.
(God cannot prevent evil.)

If God would like to prevent evil, but can't, then He's not All-powerful.
(God cannot prevent evil. [This is the implied conclusion from the first argument.]
(God is not All-powerful.)

14. If there's an afterlife, I'll learn the mysteries of the universe.
If there's no afterlife, I'll sleep the dreamless sleep.
(There is either an afterlife or there isn't.)
Either I'll learn the mysteries of the universe or I'll sleep the dreamless sleep.

15. Chick's Cleaner uses only 100 percent natural ingredients.
Our competitors use artificial ingredients.
(You should not use products with artificial ingredients.)
(You should use Chick's Cleaner.)

Additional Exercise A.

1. Nonargument.

2. Argument
Premise: He was miles away when the crime occurred.
Conclusion: Jones cannot be the murderer.

3. Nonargument.

4. Argument
Premise: Our existence as an autonomous nation is at stake.
Conclusion: We must begin to develop alternative energy sources.

5. Argument
Premise: Most doctors want to set their own fees.
Conclusion: Doctors are natu-

ral opponents of socialized medicine.

6. Argument
Premise: Nobody will take advice but everybody will take money.
Conclusion: Money is better than advice.

7. Argument
Premise: Those who criticize and disrupt a nation are its enemies.
Conclusion: Political dissenters have no place in our society.

8. Argument
Premise: Those inside can't get out, and those outside don't want to get in.
Conclusion: There's no reason for a fence around a cemetery.

9. Argument
Premise: I've read enough of what you've written.
Conclusion: I know you'll understand what I'm going to say.

10. Nonargument.

11. Argument
Premise: I think.
Conclusion: I am.

12. Argument
Premise: We know that not all beliefs that societies and cultures hold are correct, and so forth.
Premise: Ethical principles are beliefs.
Conclusion: We know that not all ethical principles are correct, and so forth.

13. Argument
Premise: Statistics indicate that speeders have a greater chance of having accidents than those who don't speed.

Conclusion: It's unwise to exceed the posted speed limit.

14. Nonargument

15. Argument
Premises: We could put our extra money . . . Given our budget, we may need to use any money we try to save.
Conclusion: We'd better give up the higher interest rate and settle for quick access.

16. Nonargument

17. Argument
Premises: [T]here aren't enough teachers for required courses. . . .
Intermediate Conclusion: The more students they let into college, the more they lose.
Conclusion: They're letting too many students into college.

18. Argument
Premises: If you really loved me . . . But you won't go.
Conclusion: You don't really love me.

19. Argument
Premise: History indicates that nations divided against themselves don't last long.
Conclusion: Whether or not we survive depends on whether we can solve internal problems.

20. Argument
Premise: The ultimate . . . impulse to destroy.
Conclusion: We don't destroy . . . but to destroy.

21. Argument
Premise: If we can't defend ourselves . . . dead educated people?
Conclusion: We should . . . than on education.

22. Argument 1
Premise: It deters crime.
Conclusion: I'm all for capital punishment.

Argument 2
Premise: I can give you . . . prove it does.
Conclusion: Capital punishment deters crime.

23. Argument 1
Premise: But if the state . . . what they want.
Conclusion: Women should be allowed . . . abortion on demand.

Argument 2
Premise: That could lead . . . a vacation.
Conclusion: I don't think so (Women should not be allowed . . .)

24. Argument 1
Premise: Consumers are going . . . victimized.
Conclusion: There should be . . . advertisement.

Argument 2
Premise: Such intervention . . . free enterprise.
Conclusion: There should be . . . of advertising.

25. Argument 1
Premise: "A gentleman . . . his boots."
Conclusion: "He has been a fixture, therefore, all day."

Argument 2
Premise: "He has been a fixture . . . friends."
Conclusion: "You have been at your club all day."

(Note: In a chain of arguments, the conclusion of one argument may serve as a premise for another, as is the case here.)

Additional Exercise B.

1. The premises are reasonable and relevant, but not sufficient for the conclusion.

2. The premises are relevant, and if true sufficient. But the claim "All women need someone to nurture and care for" is questionable and fails the reasonableness criterion.

3. Premises are irrelevant and insufficient

4. Unreasonable and insufficient

5. The premise "It is always best to err on the side of caution" would not be accepted by all reasonable people, so the argument fails the reasonableness criterion.

6. Personal experience is always insufficient to support conclusions of such sweeping nature. It's also irrelevant in this case.

7. Irrelevant, unreasonable, insufficient

8. Cogent argument

9. Cogent argument

10. Premises are unreasonable

11. Premises are unreasonable and insufficient (they do not prove that only gay people have AIDS)

12. Unreasonable premise

13. Cogent argument if conclusion is taken to mean "If I pay my rent this month, I still won't be able to pay it next month, since I'll be fired by then."

14. Irrelevant, unreasonable, and insufficient

15. Irrelevant

CHAPTER 3   *Exercise 3-1*

A. 1. Belief

2. Knowledge

3. Knowledge

4. Belief

5. Belief

6. Knowledge if refers to inner sense of nausea; belief if refers to prediction regarding future health.

B. 1. Disagree. Any proposition *is* true *or* false, regardless of our knowledge.

2. Disagree. Meaningful propositions always require interpretation via context; this includes place and time. Only when a date is assigned to the words "The United States is made up of 48 states," do they acquire truth value.

3. Agree

4. Disagree, the proposition in the example is true (or false) for all persons, regardless of their ages.

5. Disagree; argument from ignorance

Exercise 3-3
1. Yes

2. No: no consensus; can't verify for self without appealing to additional authorities.

3. Yes: the statement asserts what many theologians believe and *not* that hell exists.

4. Yes: the statement asserts what the Bible claims and *not* that hell exists; there's probably consensus of biblical opinion that the Bible asserts this, although the opinion is far from universal.

5. Yes, if "cause" is taken in a contributory sense; that is, that together with oral bacteria sugar contributes to tooth decay; no, if "cause" is taken in the sense of necessary or sufficient by itself: that is, decay cannot occur in the absence of sugar, or the presence of sugar is enough to produce tooth decay.

6. No: violates all criteria for authority

7. Yes: an historical fact

8. No: no consensus

9. Yes: there is consensus to support

10. No: no consensus

11. No: no consensus

12. Yes, if "result" implies a contributory cause to crisis or a necessary cause; no, if "result" implies the sole cause.

13. Yes and no, as explained in 5 above.

14. Yes: a proven fact.

Exercise 3-5
1. Willed ignorance

2. Susan: provincialism
   Jim: unknowable fact

3. Unknowable fact

4. Provincialism

5. Unknowable fact

6. Provincialism

7. Provincialism

8. Provincialism

9. No fallacy—Carolyn only asserts a belief—not dogmatic enough to be ignorance.

10. Provincialism

11. Unknowable fact

12. Unknowable fact

13. Ignorance

14. Provincialism

15. May or may not be provincialism

Additional Exercises

1. Popularity

2. False authority, popularity

3. Legitimate authority

4. False authority

5. Traditional wisdom

6. Provincialism

7. Popularity

8. Positioning

9. Popularity

10. False authority

11. Traditional wisdom, popularity

12. Provincialism

13. Just an expression of opinion— it is not yet ignorance

14. Unknowable fact

15. Provincialism

16. Unknowable fact (also circular)

17. Provincialism

18. Provincialism: each expert ultimately sees the problem only in terms of his or her own bailiwick

19. Legitimate authority

20. Positioning

21. Popularity—or no fallacy, just an expression of an opinion

22. Positioning

23. Positioning

24. Traditional wisdom

25. Popularity

26. False authority

27. False authority, originally; Crawford may have become a legitimate authority through experience and education

CHAPTER 4   *Exercise 4-1*

Discussion and explanations will vary.

1. Projection, introjection

2. Projection

3. Introjection

4. Scapegoating

5. Scapegoating

Exercise 4-2

1. Denial; rationalizing

2. Rationalizing

3. Rationalizing (Note: Groucho was actually using ridicule and irony to make a point.)

4. Rationalizing

5. Stereotyping; prejudging

6. Rationalizing

7. Rationalizing

8. Denial

9. Rationalizing (also denial)

10. Denial; rationalizing

CHAPTER 5   *Exercise 5-2*

1. To die

2. To go to the toilet

3. Sexual intercourse

4. Pregnant

5. Old person

6. Toilet or lavatory

7. To fire an employee

8. To assassinate

9. Dead person or corpse

10. Menstrual period

11. To fire an employee

12. Poor worker; inadequate; one of the worst

13. Broke

14. Unmarried lovers; living together and having sexual intercourse

15. To steal

16. To use force to arrest a suspect

17. Lie

18. Rich

19. I'm disappointed.

20. Not very intelligent

Exercise 5-5

1. Technical violations = serious breaches of the agreement; euphemism.

2. Safeguard democracy = buzzword; inflexible = use of dictatorial force; euphemism

3. The writer wishes the stepmother would die and thinks she has been stingy and unloving; euphemism

4. Incisions or cuts; euphemistic jargon

5. Collecting a fee; jargon (informal)

6. Action oriented curriculum = buzzword for vocational education

7. Mechanical deficiencies = engineering and construction mistakes by Ford; deteriorate = fall apart; disengagement of the axle shaft = the axle could fall off the car; adversely affect vehicle control = cause an accident; jargon and gobbledygook

8. Huh? gobbledygook

9. On July 31, 1981, White House spokesperson David Gergen explained that Reagan did not mean that benefits would remain the same. He meant that he would determine who was "dependent," what counted as "earned," and what was "due."

10. The airlines are using jargon as doublespeak; the lawyer is using general doublespeak.

Additional Exercises
A. 1. Gobbledygook

2. Clients throughout the life cycle = patients; ambiguous as to whether "throughout the life cycle" means all ages or

from seriously to minimally ill; alterations in health status = become ill or injured; jargon

3. Jargon for being addicted to drugs or alcohol

4. The justice was addicted; jargon

5. *Virtually* is doublespeak, which means that the pills do not offer 100 percent protection.

6. General doublespeak; there's no way the average consumer (or student) could know what the Federal Trade Commission found out: Ford meant that the interior or the car was 700% quieter than its exterior!

7. Business jargon for losses due to theft

8. Gobbledygook

9. Gobbledygook, combined with jargon and buzzwords, doublespeak.

10. Jargon; gobbledygook

11. General doublespeak and euphemistic doublespeak; for instance: "our *incentive compensation* and *goal-saving program* inadvertently created *an environment* in which *mistakes have occurred.*"

12. General doublespeak; "synergies" may be a buzzword.

13. Wow! So "The Easy Listener's mini-microphone picks up sound and brings it through the headset"—what does this have to do with having cable or speakers? General doublespeak; puffery

14. Puffery (exorbitantly so); also unknowable fact

15. Meaningless doublespeak: "People who consciously think and act in a *pro*-life way will never consider a premature voluntary death, unless unbearable pain renders further living meaningless" (Note: this is a form of begging the question known as hedging or waffling. Here are two more examples: "I'll be there unless I don't make it" and "We'll have a test on Tuesday unless for some reason we can't." See Chapter 6 for more on question begging.)

B. 1. Equivocation

2. Equivocation

3. Equivocation

4. Amphiboly

5. Amphiboly

6. Amphiboly

7. Composition

8. Equivocation on "driving"

9. Accent

10. Amphiboly

11. Amphiboly

12. Amphiboly

13. "Loses a loved one" is a euphemism; "Remembrance Collection" takes advantage of positive, warm connotations

14. Equivocation on "rebellion"

15. Euphemism for being unemployed or underemployed against your will

CHAPTER 6   *Exercise 6-1*

1. Personal attack (circumstantial and abusive)

2. Mob appeal

3. Personal attack (circumstantial)

4. Mob appeal, fear

5. Pity

6. Fear

7. *Tu quoque* personal attack

8. Personal attack (circumstantial)

9. Fear

10. Mob appeal, possibly fear

11. Pity

Exercise 6-3

1. Red herring

2. Straw argument

3. Straw argument, ridicule

4. Two wrongs

5. Common practice

6. Interviewer creates a distorted view of playing basketball by characterizing it as "putting a basketball through a hoop"; this can be treated as humor or ridicule. Slats resorts to common practice.

7. Two wrongs

8. Common practice

Additional Exercises

1. Personal attack (abusive)

2. Personal attack (circumstantial)

3. Fear

4. Begging the question

5. Fear

6. Fear; pity

7. Fear; mob appeal

8. *Tu quoque*

9. Fear

10. Fear

11. Personal attack (circumstantial)

12. Pity; red herring

13. Fear

14. Humor/ridicule

15. Pity

16. Fear; accent

17. Personal attack (abusive); mob appeal

18. Pity

19. Common practice

20. *Tu quoque;* personal attack (abusive)

21. Humor/ridicule

22. Personal attack (circumstantial and probably abusive)

23. Personal attack (circumstantial)

24. Humor/ridicule; dismissal; personal attack (abusive)

25. Personal attack (abusive); loaded epithet

26. Personal attack (abusive); question begging; loaded epithets

27. Humor/ridicule; personal attack (abusive)

28. Question begging; ridicule

29. Personal attack (abusive); ridicule in title?

30. Question begging; personal attack (abusive); perhaps loaded epithet

31. Question begging

32. Two wrongs make a right

33. Question begging (and equivocation on "necessary")

34. Common practice

35. Question begging (maybe circular reasoning)

CHAPTER 7   *Exercise 7-1*

A. 1. Californians; citizens

2. Baseball players; athletes

3. Those breaking the law; criminals

4. Newspapers that suppress news; inadequate sources of information

5. Commercials that rely solely on persuasive techniques to communicate; vehicles of non-information

6. Nonvoters; citizens . . . wish

7. Nonparticipants . . . Washington; nonenrollees . . . city

B. 1. Police officer; a thief

2. Police officers; thieves

3. Police officers; thieves

4. Nonpolice officer; a thief

5. Nonpolice officer; a nonthief

6. Nonthieves; police officers

7. Nonpolice officers . . . order; violators of the law

8. Police officer . . . can; a person . . . law

Exercise 7-3

1. *I:* neither term

2. *E: S* (revolutionary); *P* (believer in the status quo)

3. *A: S* (men in combat)

4. *A: S* (noncombatants . . . pay)

5. *O: P* (members of a union)

6. *I:* neither term

7. *O: P* (exercises . . . courage)

8. *A: S* (students . . . twenty-one)

9. *O: P* (hues . . . else)

10. *I:* neither term

Exercise 7-5

1. *Major term:* seekers of offices
   Minor term: Republicans
   Middle term: political candidates
   Properly ordered as is.

2. *Major term:* true sportsman
   Minor term: dishonest person
   Middle term: cheater
   Properly ordered as is.

3. *Major term:* precious creatures
   Minor term: animals
   Middle term: endangered species
   Reverse first two statements.

4. *Major term:* lovers of women
   Minor term: lovers of wine
   Middle term: epicureans
   Reverse first two statements.

5. *Major term:* pollutants
   Minor term: cigarettes
   Middle term: disease carriers
   Properly ordered as is.

6. *Major term:* persons entitled to due process
   Minor term: men
   Middle term: equal citizens
   Reverse first two statements.

7. *Major term:* peace lovers
Minor term: countries
Middle term: belligerents
Reverse first two statements.

8. *Major term:* slow runners
Minor term: sprinters
Middle term: members of the track team
Proper order: No slow runners are members of the track team. All sprinters are members of the track team.
No sprinters are slow runners.

9. *Major term:* wastes of time
Minor term: TV programs
Middle term: bores
Reverse first two statements.

10. *Major term:* means of transportation
Minor term: airlines
Middle term: expensive enterprises
Reverse first and last statement.

Exercise 7-6

A. 1. Some objects of worship are cows.
All cows are animals.
Some animals are objects of worship.

2. No opponents of deficit spending are Keynesians.
Some Republicans are Keynesians.
Some Republicans are not opponents of deficit spending.

3. All biologists who believe in Darwinian evolution are college graduates.
No biologist who believes in Darwinian evolution is a literal interpreter of Genesis.
No literal interpreter of Genesis is a college graduate.

4. All toothpastes with fluoride are cavity fighters.
Some peppermint toothpastes are cavity fighters.
Some peppermint toothpastes are toothpastes with fluoride.

5. All male chauvinists are persons insecure in their own sex roles.
All males interested in females only for sex are male chauvinists.
Some men interested in females only for sex are persons insecure in their own sex roles.

6. Some officers are nonvoters.
All nonparty members are officers.
Some nonparty members are nonvoters.

7. All married persons are consumers.
Some individuals are not married persons.
Some individuals are not consumers.

8. All believers in suffering for suffering's sake are theists.
No one signing a living will is a believer in suffering for suffering's sake.
No one signing a living will is a theist.

B. 1. *IAI*-4

2. *EIO*-2

3. *AEE*-3

4. *AII*-2

5. *AAI*-1

6. IAI-1

7. AOO-1

8. AEE-1

Exercise 7-7

A. 1. Invalid, rule 4, exclusive premises, *EEE*-3

2. Valid, *IAI*-4

3. Invalid, rule 3, illicit major term, *IEO*-4

4. Invalid, rule 3, illicit major term, *AOO*-3

5. Invalid, rule 4, exclusive premises, *EOO*-2

6. Valid, *AAA*-1

7. Invalid, rule 4, exclusive premises; Rule 5, drawing an affirmative conclusion from a negative premise, *EOI*-1

8. Valid, *IAI*-3

9. Invalid, rule 6, existential fallacy, *AAI*-1

10. Invalid, rule 2, undistributed middle term, *IAI*-1

11. Valid, *AEE*-2

12. Invalid, rule 2, undistributed middle term, *III*-2

13. Invalid, rule 2, undistributed middle term, *AAA*-2

14. Invalid, rule 4, exclusive premises, and rule 6, existential fallacy, *EEO*-1

15. Invalid, rule 3, illicit major term, *IEO*-3

16. Valid, *IAI*-4

17. Invalid, rule 3, illicit major term, *IEE*-1

18. Valid, *AOO*-2

19. Valid, *EIO*-1

20. Invalid, rule 3, illicit minor term, *AAA*-3

Additional Exercise C

1. *EEA*-3. Invalid; fallacy of drawing an affirm. conc. . . . , exclusive premises

2. *III*-3. Invalid; undistributed middle term

3. *IAI*-4. Valid.

4. No form—not standard form categorical syllogism. (four terms)

5. *III*-1. Invalid; undistributed middle term

6. Not a standard-form categorical syllogism

7. *AEE*-3. Invalid; illicit major term

8. *EAE*-3, Invalid; illicit minor term

9. No form—not standard form. Equivocation on "ground"

10. *EAO*-1. Invalid; existential fallacy

11. Invalid; illicit major term

12. Invalid; illicit major and minor terms

13. Invalid; drawing an affirmative conclusion from a negative premise

14. Invalid; drawing an affirmative conclusion from a negative premise

15. Invalid; illicit minor term

16. Invalid; illicit minor term

17. Invalid; drawing an affirmative conclusion from a negative premise

18. Invalid; drawing an affirmative conclusion from a negative premise

19. Valid

20. Valid

CHAPTER 8   *Exercise 8-1*

A. 1. All flowers are fragrant things. (*A*)

2. No onions are sweet things. (*A*)

3. Some party-goers are persons who awake to regret the night before. (*I*)

4. Some opportunities lost are not catastrophes. (*O*)

5. No thing is both an educational and a frivolous thing. (*E*)

6. All things that say "Government Approved" are things you can feel safe about. (*A*)

7. All teams that play in the title game are the best teams. (*A*)

8. Some green things are grass (*I*) and some green things are not grass. (*O*)

9. Some green things are not grass. (*O*)

10. All things made by Westinghouse are things you can be sure of. (*A*)

11. Some mammals are not humans. (*O*)

12. The injunction seems to mean: Only those without sin should cast the first stone. Thus: All those who should cast the first stone are those without sin. (*A*)

13. All those who die young are good persons. (*A*)

14. All those who defend themselves are fools. (*A*)

15. Some nonvoters are citizens. (*I*)

16. All those who volunteer are eager persons. (*A*)

17. Some things that glitter are not things made of gold. (*O*)

18. All those who think the rich are happy are themselves rich. (*A*)

19. All cases of people knowing her are cases of people loving her. (*A*)

20. All places I go to are places I want to go to. (*A*)

B. 1. All belligerent countries are threats to world peace.
No threats to world peace are members of the United Nations.
_____
No members of the United Nations are belligerent countries. (*AEE*-4) *Valid*

2. Some men are not sexists.
Some sexists are proponents of the ERA.
_____
Some proponents of the ERA must be men. (*OII*-4)
Invalid: drawing an affirmative from a negative premise

3. Some of the dead were musicians.
Some of the dead were not adults.
_____
Some of the adults must have been musicians. (*IOI*-3)
Invalid: drawing an affirmative from a negative premise, and undistributed middle term

4. All applicants are college graduates.
Smith is an applicant.
_____

Smith must be a college graduate. (*AAA*-1)
Valid

5. All times the president is at a loss for words are times the president attributes something he's done to national security. This time is a time the president is attributing something he's done to national security.
This time is a time the president is at a loss for words. (*AAA*-2)
Invalid: undistributed middle term

6. All volunteers are brave persons.
Jones is not a brave person.
Jones is not a person who should volunteer. (*AEE*-2)
Valid

7. All cases of few places are cases of fierce competition.
Medical schools are cases of few places.
Medical schools are cases of fierce competition. (*AAA*-1)
Valid

8. Some relevant things are interesting.
No relevant thing is immaterial.
Some immaterial things are not interesting. (*IEO*-3)
Invalid: illicit major

Exercise 8-3

1. All stupid persons are dull persons.
No one who studies logic is a stupid person.
No one who studies logic is a dull person.
Invalid, Rule 3, illicit major

All dull persons are bad writers.
No dull person is a person who studies logic
No one who studies logic is a bad writer.
Invalid, Rule 3, illicit major

2. All persons rewarded are brave persons.
Some persons rewarded are females.
Some females are brave persons.
Valid

Some females are brave persons.
Some persons not promoted are not females.
Some persons not promoted are not brave persons.
Invalid, Rule 3, illicit major

3. All persons who apply are ambitious persons.
Smith is not an ambitious person.
Smith is not a person who applies.
Valid

No person not applying is one who should expect a check (or, all persons applying are ones who should expect a check).
Smith is not a person applying.
Smith is not a person who should expect a check.
Invalid, Rule 4, exclusive premises (or Rule 3, illicit major)

4. Some creatures who should know better are ones who tread on thin ice.
No dog is a creature who should know better.
No dog is a creature who treads on thin ice.
Invalid, Rule 3, illicit major

All creatures treading on thin ice are creatures bound to drown.

No dog is a creature bound to drown.

Invalid, Rule 3, illicit major

5. All my brothers are athletes.
No athletes are overweight persons.

No brother of mine is an overweight person.
Valid

All persons prone to diabetes are overweight persons.
No brother of mine is an overweight person.

No brother of mine is a person prone to diabetes.
Valid

All persons who must take insulin are diabetics.
No brother of mine is a diabetic.

No brother of mine is a person who must take insulin.
Valid

Exercise 8-4

1. (All cud-chewing animals are ruminants.)
Dogs are not cud-chewing animals.

Dogs are not ruminants.
Cogent

2. (The largest-volume furniture mart in America is the one where you'll necessarily get the best deal on new furniture.)
Jacques Pení is the largest-volume furniture mart in America.

Jacques Pení is the mart where you'll necessarily get the best deal on furniture.

Valid but: Major premise is a faulty generalization and a version of the appeal to popularity.

3. (If a cigarette tastes good like a cigarette should, you should buy it.)

Winston tastes good like a cigarette should.

You should buy Winston.

Valid but: Conditional premise is a hasty conclusion; both premises are ambiguous. Also, concealed evidence: Cigarette smoking contributes to disease.

4. All voters are citizens.
(Some of the people leaving the polling station are not citizens.)

Some of the people leaving the polling station are not voters.
Cogent.

5. (All people who refuse a polygraph test are people with something to hide.)
The Senator refuses a polygraph test.

The Senator has something to hide.

Valid but: Major premise is untrue, or, more kindly, a faulty generalization and conceals evidence (people often refuse polygraphs on principle).

6. (Whatever helps employment contributes to inflation.)
Government spending helps employment.

Government spending contributes to inflation.

Valid but: Major premise is questionable cause. "Helps" is ambiguous.

7. (All reliable arguments are valid arguments.)
Some persuasive devices are not reliable.

Some persuasive devices are invalid arguments.

Invalid: Illicit major.

8. (All liquors that Washington and Lafayette may have planned

strategies over are liquors worth buying.)

Martell Brandy is a liquor that Washington and Lafayette may have planned strategies over.

Martell Brandy is a liquor worth buying.

Valid but: Major premise is a false appeal to authority; both premises contain the weasel words "may have."

9. (Whatever meat is labeled "U.S. Certified Grade A" must be very good.)

That meat is labeled "U.S. Certified Grade A."

That meat must be very good.

Valid but: "Very good" is ambiguous. Also concealed evidence; even if "Grade A" in general indicates a high-quality meat, that doesn't mean that this specific package was examined and so judged. What's more, there are all sorts of ways that butchers misrepresent meats and packages. Also concealed is that meat, red meat, isn't necessarily healthful for us to begin with. False authority.

10. (All weight-control aids that help you lose ugly bulges and look more feminine are aids that you should buy.)

Waistlets Gum is a weight-control aid that helps you lose ugly bulges and look more feminine.

Waistlets Gum is an aid you should buy.

Valid but: Major premise is ambiguous ("aids," "more feminine"); faulty generalization; minor premise contains weasel word "helps." Most important, you should question statistical

procedures that presumably led to minor premise because of concealed evidence in almost all popular weight-control claims.

11. (All days the game is postponed are days it's rained.)

Today is a day the game has been postponed.

Today is a day it must have rained.

Cogent, providing major premise is true.

12. (All men with lean and hungry looks are ambitious.)

Cassius is a man with a lean and hungry look.

Cassius is ambitious.

Valid but: Major premise is ambiguous (what constitutes a "lean and hungry look"?) and a faulty generalization (hasty conclusion).

13. (All cigarettes that are natural are cigarettes you should buy.)

Salems are cigarettes that are natural.

Salems are cigarettes you should buy.

Valid but: Major premise is an appeal to popularity, a faulty generalization, and hasty conclusion. "Natural" is equivocal. Concealed evidence: Cigarette smoking contributes to lung disease.

14. (If California has already done more for farmworkers than any other state, then I should oppose unemployment compensation for farmworkers.)

California has already done more for farmworkers than any other state.

I should oppose unemployment compensation for farmworkers.

Valid but: Conditional premise is a hasty conclusion. More important, the statistics on which the minor premise rests conceal evidence: California *has* done more for farmworkers than any other state, but other states with farmworkers have done next to nothing to improve the lot of farmworkers.

15. All people employed here are people listed in the directory.
Maria is not a person listed in the directory.
_____
Maria is not a person employed here.
Cogent, provided major premise is true.

16. Some individuals don't benefit from jogging.
I'm one of those individuals.
_____
I won't benefit from jogging (from which it follows that I won't start jogging).
Valid but: Minor premise is hasty. Also, "benefit" needs defining; how many are "some"? Is the person in any position to *know* that he or she can't benefit from jogging?

17. Whenever Pop groans it's tax time.
This is a time Pop's groaning.
_____
This is tax time.
Cogent, providing major premise is true. If Pop groans on other occasions, the assertion is a faulty generalization.

18. (Anyone who never expresses an opinion unless asked to is very wise or empty-headed.)
The president is a person who . . . headed.
_____
The president is very wise or empty-headed.
Valid but: Major premise is a false dilemma and a faulty generalization.

19. (All people are thinkers.)
Poker players are people.
_____
Poker players are thinkers.
Valid but unsound. "Thinkers" is unacceptably ambiguous.

20. Liberty means responsibility. (Responsibility is something most people dread.)
_____
Liberty is something most people dread.
Valid but: "Most people" is ambiguous. So are "liberty" and "responsibility."

CHAPTER 9   *Exercise 9-1*

1. Invalid

2. Valid

3. Invalid

4. Valid

5. Invalid

6. Valid

7. Valid

8. Valid

9. Invalid

Exercise 9-2

1. *Valid—modus tollens*

2. *Valid*

3. *Invalid*—denies the antecedent

4. *Valid—modus tollens*

5. *Valid—modus ponens*

6. *Invalid*—denying the antecedent

7. *Valid—modus tollens*

8. *Valid*—pure hypothetical syllogism

9. *Valid—modus tollens*

10. *Invalid*—affirms consequent

Exercise 9-3

1. *I* = Speech is just informative; *B* = speech will bore me; *A* = speech is just entertaining; *E* = speech will educate me.

   (If *I* then *B*) and (If *A* then not-*E*)
   I or *A*
   _____
   B or not-*E*   *Valid*

   Counterdilemma: If the speech is informative, it will enlighten me; if the speech is entertaining, it will lift my spirits.
   The speech is either informative or entertaining.
   _____
   Either I will be enlightened or my spirits will be lifted.

2. *G* = there is a God; *R* = he will reward me . . . ; *S* = I will sleep.

   (If *G* then *R*) and (If not *G* then *S*)
   G or not-*G*
   _____
   R or *S*   *Valid*

   Counterdilemma: If there is a God, he will punish me for my transgressions; if there is no God, my life is meaningless.
   There is either a God or there is not.
   _____
   Either I will be punished for my transgressions or my life is meaningless.

3. *R* = she rejects me; *C* = I'll be crushed; *A* = she accepts me; *T* = I'll be terrified.

   (If *R* then *C*) and (If *A* then *T*)
   R or *A*
   _____
   C or *T*   *Valid*

Counterdilemma: If she rejects me, I'll be free; if she accepts me, I'll be loved.
She either accepts me or she rejects me.
_____
I'll be either free or loved.

4. *M* = U.S. modifies its Middle East position; *J* = U.S. offends many American Jews; *O* = U.S. jeopardizes oil supplies.

   (If *M* then *J*) and (If not-*M* then *O*)
   M or not-*M*
   _____
   J or *O*   *Valid*

   Counterdilemma: If the U.S. modifies its Middle East position, it will improve its relations with oil-rich Arab countries; if the U.S. does not modify its Middle East position, it will bolster its position with Israel.
   The U.S. either modifies its Middle East position or it does not.
   _____
   Either the U.S. improves its relations with oil-rich Arab states, or it bolsters its position with Israel.

5. *S* = I study; *M* = I go to movies; *W* = I will worry.
   (If *S* then not-*M*) and (If not *S* then *W*)
   S or not-*S*
   _____
   not-*M* or *W*   *Valid*

   Counterdilemma: If I study my logic tonight, then I will feel good about myself; if I don't study my logic, I will feel relaxed and refreshed.
   I either study my logic or I don't.
   _____
   I will feel either good about myself or relaxed and refreshed.

6. *V* = I vote; *E* = choose between two evils; *G* = good citizen.

(If *V* then *E*) and (If not *V* then not-*G*)

$\dfrac{\text{*V* or not-*V*}}{\text{*E* or not-*G*}}$ *Valid*

Counterdilemma: If I vote, then I am a good citizen; if I don't vote then I am making a symbolic statement.

I either vote or I don't.

Either I am a good citizen or I make a symbolic statement.

7. *R* = I pay rent; *U* = I pay utilities . . . ; *E* = I'm evicted.

(If *R* then not-*U*) and (If not-*R* then *E*)

$\dfrac{\text{*R* or not-*R*}}{\text{*E* or not-*U*}}$ *Valid*

Counterdilemma: If I pay my rent, then I'll improve my relationship with my landlord; if I pay my utilities, then I'll have light and heat.

I pay either my rent or my utilities.

I will improve my relationship with my landlord or I'll have light and heat.

8. *H* = I get married; *M* = I lose Midge; *L* = I lose Louise.

(If *H* then *M*) and (If not-*H* then *L*)

$\dfrac{\text{*H* or not-*H*}}{\text{*M* or *L*}}$ *Valid*

Counterdilemma: If I get married, I get to be with Louise; if I don't get married, I get to be with Midge.

I either get married or I don't.

Either I get to be with Louise or I get to be with Midge.

9. *T* = I tell truth; *L* = I lie; *Υ* = you are angry with me; *M* = I am angry with myself.

(If *T* then *Υ*) and (If *L* then *M*)

$\dfrac{\text{*T* or *L*}}{\text{*Υ* or *M*}}$ *Valid*

Counterdilemma: If I tell the truth, I will respect myself; if I lie, you will not be angry with me.

Either I tell the truth or I lie.

Either I respect myself or you are not angry with me.

10. *K* = keep old clunker; *R* = fortune on repairs; *N* = buy new car; *P* = fortune on payments

(If *K* then *R*) and (If *N* then *P*)

$\dfrac{\text{*K* or *N*}}{\text{*R* or *P*}}$ *Valid*

Counterdilemma: If I keep the old clunker, then I save a fortune on car payments; if I buy a new car, I save a fortune on repairs.

Either I keep the old clunker or I buy a new car.

Either I save a fortune on car payments or on repairs.

CHAPTER 10   *Exercise 10-1*

All weak except for 3.

Exercise 10-2

1. *Premise:* A half-dozen . . . in their jobs.

    Conclusion: College graduates . . . occupations.

    Unreliable: Sample too small; lacks comprehensiveness; lacks randomness.

2. *Premise:* Sixty-two percent . . . for Myra.

    Conclusion: Myra has a much better chance than Lydia.

    Unreliable: Lacks randomness.

3. *Premise:* Every member . . . supports it.

Conclusion: The public . . . this measure.
Unreliable: Lacks comprehensiveness; sample too small; lacks randomness.

4. *Premise:* One thousand . . . income in food.
Conclusion: Two-thirds . . . on food.
Unreliable: Lacks randomness; margin of error too small.

5. *Premise:* In every case . . . present.
Conclusion: The spirochete . . . of syphilis.
Unreliable: Margin of error too small because of "and only a spirochete."

6. *Premise:* A recent poll . . . farm policies.
Conclusion: There's no question . . . shaft.
Unreliable: Lacks comprehensiveness and randomness.

7. *Premise:* Eight of them are green, seven red.
Conclusion: The jar . . . of each.
Unreliable: Margin of error too small.

8. *Premise:* Every guy . . . somebody else.
Conclusion: All men are fickle.
Unreliable: Violates all criteria.

9. *Premise:* He gives bucket . . . still on top.
Conclusion: The bucket . . . rocks.
Unreliable: Lacks comprehensiveness.

10. *Premise:* A day . . . a crime.
Conclusion: The courts . . . paroles.

Unreliable: Lacks comprehensiveness; sample too small.

11. *Premise:* Over 63 people answered our simple six-question form.
Conclusion: Here . . . the typical mall shopper.
Unreliable: Lacks comprehensiveness and randomness; sample too small.

12. *Premise:* The results . . . excellent.
Conclusion: Dr. Boswell must be a great instructor.
Unreliable: Lacks comprehensiveness; sample too small.

13. *Premise:* I asked . . . you refused.
Conclusion: There's no point in seeing if you want to go skating.
Unreliable: Lacks comprehensiveness; sample too small.

14. *Premise:* I've talked . . . lousy lecturer.
Conclusion: Dr. Boswell should be fired.
Unreliable: Lacks comprehensiveness and randomness; sample too small.

15. *Premise:* I've let my family and friends . . . praise of it.
Conclusion: I know that it is a good book.
Unreliable: Lacks comprehensiveness and randomness; sample too small.

16. *Premise:* Virtually every . . . smoking marijuana.
Conclusion: Marijuana usage . . . heroin addiction.
Unreliable: Lacks comprehensiveness and randomness.

17. *Premise:* I had two . . . a lemon.
Conclusion: Fords are all lemons.

Unreliable: Lacks comprehensiveness and randomness; sample too small.

18. *Premise:* After all . . . be in his trunk.
    Conclusion: The only explanation . . . that awful night.
    Both: That the fiber came from the jacket is reliable; that the jacket is the defendant's is unreliable because it has a too small margin for error.

19. *Premise:* The last time . . . for my meal.
    Conclusion: Their service is horrible.
    Unreliable: Lacks comprehensiveness and randomness; sample too small.

20. *Premise:* Every Phish album . . . has been great.
    Conclusion: This Phish album will be just great.
    Reliable: If interpreted as a predictor of arguer's taste

CHAPTER 10   *Exercise 10-3*

1. Accident

2. Hasty conclusion

3. Hasty conclusion

4. Guilt by association

5. Division

6. Hasty conclusion

7. Accident

8. Hasty conclusion

9. Accident

10. Hasty conclusion

Additional Exercises

1. Hasty conclusion (also false authority)

2. Hasty conclusion (also accident if Suzy is the kind of person who can rise above the limitation of the school)

3. Accident (also traditional wisdom)

4. Hasty conclusion

5. Hasty conclusion (sample too small; lacks comprehensiveness; margin of error too small)

6. Hasty conclusion

7. Hasty conclusion

8. Guilt by association

9. Guilt by association, hasty conclusion

10. Accident

11. Accident

12. Hasty conclusion (also unknowable fact)

13. Accident

14. Guilt by association (also *ad hominem*)

15. Accident

CHAPTER 11   *Exercise 11-2*

1. Biased sample—sampling technique (time and place conducted)

2. Biased sample—sampling technique (telephone)

3. Good sample

4. Biased sample—pollster bias, respondent bias

5. Biased sample; lacks randomness—shoppers who for one reason or another have stopped shopping at the mall are not sampled; also overlooked are weekends, prime shopping time.

6. Biased sample—introduced by the conditions under which the interviews are conducted

7. Biased sample; lacks randomness

Exercise 11-4

1. "More" is ambiguous.

2. "Support" and "dealings" are ambiguous; so is "Arabs."

3. Biased, loaded

4. "Usually" is ambiguous.

5. "Accept" is biased; "influence" is vague.

6. Okay as is, although the question doesn't mean very much until "rationing" is defined.

7. The classes are ambiguous.

8. Option A does not exhaust the options.

Exercise 11-5

1. False dilemma

2. False dilemma

3. False dilemma

4. False dilemma

5. False dilemma

6. False dilemma—a third choice should be given: "No gender preference"

7. False dilemma

8. False dilemma: Who did *he say* he was?

Additional Exercises

1. False dilemma

2. Concealed evidence: Far more miles are driven within 5 miles of the driver's home than cross-country. (Thus also incomplete statistic)

3. False dilemma

4. Biased sample: pollster bias

5. Concealed evidence: Very few new cars ever sell for the sticker price.

6. "Better" is ambiguous.

7. Concealed evidence: In fact, the high-protein diet has been found very dangerous in many instances.

8. All terms are ambiguous.

9. Concealed evidence: The RDA is not necessarily a "full day's supply." How much of a vitamin a person needs varies greatly from person to person. RDA and MDR (minimal daily requirement) are essentially quantities needed to stave off disease associated with vitamin deficiency (e.g., beriberi, rickets). Further, no mention is made of ingredients in TANG, such as sugar, which may ultimately injure the consumer/child.

10. The question itself is ambiguous. It can mean (1) how important the subjects actually are to you now that you're graduated or (2) how important what you learned in these courses is to you now that you're graduated. The possible selections are ambiguous, and since different students

obviously take different logic or writing courses, any generalizations found on the basis of the questionnaire are very risky.

11. The opening sentence biases the question. Also the statement conceals evidence. Tenure laws also protect teachers from capricious and arbitrary dismissal; they in effect guarantee due process, although it's undoubtedly true that in some cases they have the effect of protecting the incompetent. The question suggests that tenure is a kind of privilege. Some would vigorously argue that it's a right.

12. Concealed evidence (by using equivocal language). What does "Nobel Prize nominee—medicine" mean? Who nominated Dr. Wallach? When? For exactly what? What does it mean to be "involved in" biomedical research and clinical medicine? What do the letters "N.D." stand for? Lastly, note that Dr. Wallach is a "D.V.M."—a Doctor of Veterinary Medicine—and the 17,500 autopsies were of animals. And so forth.

13. Concealed evidence—statistical. A 1-in-3 possibility of needing an attorney "very soon" (vague) is also a 2-in-3 chance of not needing one: the odds are twice as good that you will not need an attorney very soon. Why prepay for legal services you are more likely not to need? Also, the services provided do not cover all the costs and services that accompany major legal matters.

14. Concealed evidence

15. Concealed evidence: Abuse of Tylenol can cause liver damage. Also, recent research indicates that aspirin may be effective in reducing the chances of heart attack.

16. The word *know* is ambiguous here. It means "awareness of" or "familiar enough with to use."

17. Rife with concealed evidence. For example, studies conducted by Dr. Jean Mayer, a renowned diet authority, and endorsed by the Federal Trade Commission show that a heavy diet of presugared food, even when washed down with milk, contributes to tooth decay. The same studies reveal that even when fortified with milk, the total effect is one of inadequate nutrition. What's more, nutritional experts have questioned the methodology and evidence behind Kellogg's claim for the nutritional benefits of sugared foods. Of course, sugar contributes nothing to human nutrition save calories—no vitamins, no minerals, no proteins. A calorie of sugar contains no more energy than a calorie of anything else. In addition, the claim that there's no more sugar in an ounce of ready-sweetened cereal than in an apple, banana, or glass of orange juice is based on cereal containing 30.8 percent sugar. Many cereals contain far more sugar; worse, the refined sugar in a breakfast food seems more likely to cause cavities than the natural sugar in fruits. Finally, contrary to Kellogg's claims, sugar consumption has risen at least 13 percent

since 1960, with the consumption among children probably even higher.

18. False dilemma

19. Biased sample

20. Concealed evidence: You will pay taxes when you withdraw. The figures don't account for inflation that often accompanies withdrawals. False dilemma and penalties: There are more promising investments.

21. The second question is important in determining the degree of misrepresenting their views on the first question. If, for example, an overwhelming majority doesn't think its party will nominate a black, a decided absence of racism in the replies to the first is almost meaningless. We can all be tolerant in the abstract in reacting to a hypothesis, which in this case, would border on fantasy. In contrast, to really believe not only in the possibility of the hypothesis but also in the likelihood of it (that is, that the party will indeed nominate a black) compels us to face squarely and honestly whether we would be racists in the polling booth. This aside, respondent bias almost certainly will pollute this study: Very few of us even admit to ourselves we are racists, let alone express it openly in a poll.

22. Possible equivocal effect by saying "150 percent" rather than $300—the direction of bias (if any) depends on which seems better or worse to the intended audience.

23. Concealed evidence: $7.34/2 oz. = $58.72/lb.! Even granting that 1 oz. of freeze-dried coffee is the equivalent of many ounces of ground coffee, we're still talking about a pretty expensive cup of coffee.

24. Concealed evidence: Experts disagree regarding what—in fact—the recommended daily amounts of various vitamins are. Many claim that a healthy diet provides most of us with an ample supply. Over a certain amount, our bodies dispose of certain vitamins daily, so "megadoses" are often wasteful—if not dangerous. There appears to be little measurable effective difference between a wide range of vitamin brands, from inexpensive generic ones to high-priced brand-name ones. Note mob appeal, too.

25. Concealed evidence (equivocal, too); ask a science teacher to let you see and heft exactly what one-third of .78 ounces is; how big of a bite is it?

26. Ambiguous: What does it mean to claim that a "new" model is bigger than ever before? Concealed evidence and equivocation: "100% more doors," is just puffery for two more doors. And 25 percent more cargo room than what?

27. Concealed evidence: "on time performance" often refers to leaving the passenger gate—not to take off or arrival times. A plane that leaves the gate on schedule may sit for half an hour on the runway or circle overhead at its destination. "Service" is

ambiguous. Northwest may fly simpler, less-convenient schedules, and so forth.

28. Concealed evidence: Is the breakfast "typical"? According to what source? The fiber referred to comes from pancakes, not Golden Griddle Syrup.

29. Concealed evidence: verifiable claims refer to all acetaminophen-type products; most hospitals use Tylenol because it is provided at greatly reduced prices, not Anacin-3; claims are not unique to Anacin-3; vague and ambiguous—"more effective" is unspecified; equivocation on "pain reliever doctors recommend most" (aspirin).

30. Ambiguous; false dilemma

CHAPTER 12   *Exercise 12-1*

1. Nonargumentative

2. Argumentative

3. Argumentative

4. Argumentative

5. Argumentative

6. Nonargumentative

7. Nonargumentative

8. Argumentative

9. Nonargumentative

10. Nonargumentative: "horse and buggy"; argumentative: "the nations of Africa and Asia"

11. Argumentative

12. Argumentative

13. Argumentative

14. Argumentative

15. Argumentative

Exercise 12-2

1. Disanalogous

2. Disanalogous

3. Disanalogous—first, the foundation of a house presupposes a fixed, quantifiable unit that will rest on it. But a college education need not include any such presupposition. In fact, an inherent part of a college education is self-discovery, *including* the discovery of what one wants to do with his or her life. Further, unlike a house, which rests on a set, unchanging foundation, a college education may take unexpected directions and often is a dynamic, ever unfolding phenomenon full of novelty and surprise. Certainly we may talk of "laying a foundation" for this enterprise through education, but not a foundation that's analogous to the foundation of a house. In fact, such an analogy misleads by misrepresenting the nature of education and human experience.

4. Disanalogous—advertising generally differs from poetry in intention, function, and effect. The intention of advertising is to persuade someone to buy. It partially functions socioeconomically to generate a perception of needs, which consumers translate into product demand, which in turn increases productivity, sales, profit, and employment. The effects of advertising are likely legion: a blurring of the

distinction between what some have termed "true" and "artificial" needs; a whetting of consumer appetite; a quickening of the "immediate gratification" impulse; a heightening of expectations and demands among the least advantaged; and an increase in the frustration that arises from the "overselling" of a product (that is, when an ad promises more than a product can deliver).

5. Disanalogous—there are a multitude of weakening differences between intellects on the one hand, and large diamonds and armies on the other.

6. Disanalogous—people are neither "dogs" nor "machines"; moral sentiments, "notions," are not "cobwebs."

7. Disanalogous—historically the analogy between the playing field (the gridiron here) and the battlefield has been a popular one. And it has some merit. But there are clearly some striking differences between a field for play and sport and a field for war that weaken the analogy.

8. Disanalogous—several differences hold between the sexual and food appetites. Maybe the biggest relevant difference here is that sex involves more dimensions of the human personality than does eating. To view sex chiefly as an appetite analogous to our appetite for food is to disregard its complex physical, mental, and emotional facets. What's more, as used here, sex involves an *other*. This introduces a social, even moral, dimension that's generally absent in eating.

9. Disanalogous—"junkies" have an addiction to a drug, which means a psychological dependence on it, indicated by withdrawal symptoms if the drug is discontinued. Certainly we're not junkies in this sense. One might argue, however, that we do have a psychological dependence on things that consume energy, and thus indirectly on energy itself. But to so categorize this need as strictly psychological involves drawing a hasty conclusion, for the need has economic, political, social, even philosophical dimensions to it.

10. Given its qualifications and explanation, the analogy is very effective.

Exercise 12-3
1–9 are all faulty.

10. This one is bound to invite controversy. A human isn't a rat. But of over 30 agents known to cause cancer in humans, when given in high doses, all cause cancer in rats. Of course this doesn't necessarily mean that what causes cancer in rats will cause cancer in humans. But why assume saccharin is an exception? Some have pointed out correctly that the saccharin doses the rats were given in the experiments (7 percent of their diet) were far greater than any human would ingest (about 800 bottles of diet soda per day). Although this is true, by discovering what large doses do, one can roughly estimate

what conventional doses would do. But it's possible that below a certain dose an agent has no effect on anyone, that only after a threshold has been reached would the number of cancer cases begin to increase with increasing dosage. Before accepting this theory as likely, one should realize that no biological agent has even been shown to have such a threshold. Although saccharin may be the exception, there is no positive justification for believing it. So if we assume that the number of cases of cancer is roughly proportional to the dose, we can expect approximately 12,000 cases of bladder cancer in a population of 200 million people drinking less than one can of diet soda a day. This means any individual faces a chance of 6 in 100,000 of getting bladder cancer. Whether or not the person in the argument who refuses the saccharin is inductively justified is a separate question from whether the analogy between rats and people here is sound. It appears to be.

CHAPTER 13   *Exercise 13-1*

1. Contributory

2. Contributory

3. Necessary

4. Sufficient

5. Contributory

6. Noncausal

7. Sufficient

8. Sufficient

9. Contributory

10. Contributory

11. Contributory

12. Necessary

13. Contributory (some chemicals ignite in the absence of oxygen)

14. Probably noncausal, possibly contributory

15. Contributory

16. Contributory

Exercise 13-2

1. a. Suppose all the victims only shared the circumstance of eating the same salad dressing (agreement) and nonvictims shared every other circumstance with victims except having eaten the salad dressing (difference).

   b. Suppose that this is a section set up for nursing students and that every other nursing section shows the same female–male ratio (agreement) but no other section does (difference).

   c. Suppose that the only relevant characteristic on each occasion is a weak battery (agreement) and that on the occasions that the car has started the battery has tested out strong (difference).

   d. Suppose that the only circumstance that these occasions share is when you're speaking to a member of the opposite sex (agreement) and that you never have this difficulty when speaking to a member of your own sex (difference).

2. Agreement: ABC—abc
                    ADE—ade
   Difference: ABC—abc
                    BC—bc

A is the effect or the cause or an essential part of the cause of *a*.

3. a. *Correlation:* There are in fact more cases of suicides in the existing population among those for whom Christmas has meaning than among those for whom it does not.
Cause: There would be more suicides in the general population were Christmas to have a meaning for everyone than if Christmas had no meaning for anyone.

   b. *Correlation:* There are in fact more instances of violence committed by viewers of violent TV programs than by nonviewers of violent TV programs.
Cause: There would be more cases of violence committed if everyone watched violent TV programs than if no one watched them.

   c. *Correlation:* There is in fact a greater decline in institutional religion membership among those involved in cults than among those not involved in cults.
Cause: There would be a greater decline in institutional religion membership if everyone were involved with cults than if no one were.

   d. *Correlation:* There are in fact more working women among women sympathetic to the women's liberation movement than among women not sympathetic.
Cause: There would be more working women if all women were sympathetic to the women's liberation movement than if no women were.

Exercise 13-3

1. Oversimplification

2. Post hoc

3. Oversimplification

4. Oversimplification

5. Oversimplification (a correlation, perhaps, but not necessarily a causal connection); also, slippery slope

6. Slippery slope

7. Oversimplification

8. Oversimplification

9. Slippery slope

10. Magical thinking and post hoc

11. Post hoc

12. Oversimplification (the dogmatic nature of this assertion is what makes it problematic; with elaboration and in larger context there may be no causal fallacies—or there may be more)

CHAPTER 14　*Exercise 14-2*

1. Unreasonable guarantees; seems to imply that a strong desire is all that is required; overlooks such pertinent factors as ability and insight

2. Vague—"exciting"—promises; unreasonable guarantees

3. Oversimplifies complex problem; claim is at odds with scientific consensus; something for no effort.

4. Appeal to language of dynamic action *and* the language of success: We can become "entrepreneurs of the possible" and

"change agents" in our professional lives. Tone of the quoted passage implies more certainty than is reasonable: implied guarantee of success for "so many people."

Exercise 14-4

A. 1. Characteristic 1: Cater seems to have worked in isolation from colleagues as evidenced by amateurish writing style, use of private publisher.

Characteristic 2: refers to stunning "the layman . . ."

Characteristic 3: "[O]ne of the original thinkers of the 20th century . . ."

Characteristic 4: Cater claims that his revelations will "make a shambles of currently popular, and universally accepted ideas of conventional science . . ."

Characteristic 6: "Not since Velikovsky . . ."; says he is not likely to endear himself to the scientific community.

Characteristic 7: see Characteristic 4; "He defiles [sic] the orthodox scientist for keeping the status quo. . . ." (Do you think "defiles" was meant to be "defies"? Could this be an example of the infamous "Freudian slip"?)

2. Isolationism: avoids the scrutiny of disinterested experts; implies that money—not truth—was Simon & Schuster's main interest; Taller's motives are unknown; appeals to public, not to experts, for ultimate validation.

3. Lacks basic grounding in field; appeals to public rather than experts.

4. A scientist will not necessarily be adept at "working" an audience; a scientist will be limited by professional standards and restrictions; a pseudoscientist will not be constrained by the scientific method or other strict, independent standards of evidence; the public may mistake the pseudoscientist's dogmatic style and sweeping assertions as guarantees for reliable evidence; the scientist's professionally qualified assertions ("so it seems," "probably," "we need more testing to be sure") will pale beside pseudoscientific bombast.

CHAPTER 15 *Exercise 15-1*

1. Argument from ignorance

2. Guilt by association

3. Hasty conclusion

4. Unknowable fact

5. Cogent, providing Sarah believes in the doctrine of the Trinity, which is the unexpressed premise

6. "Justice" ambiguous

7. Faulty generalization

8. Equivocation

9. Valid, EIO-3, and probably uncogent since the suppressed premise is probably false.

(No pornographic films are made by the Hollywood studios.)
Some pornographic films are moneymakers.
Some money making films are

not made by the Hollywood studios.

10. Hasty conclusion; ambiguous ("turning to"); obscure ("astonishing rate")

Exercise 15-3

1. Normative; assumption: Whatever can promote social justice should be allowed.

2. Nonnormative; assumption: Any instance of reverse discrimination in the workplace, indicates that in some instances people are judged on criteria that are not directly job related.

3. Normative; assumption: Whatever saves patients and loved ones from heroic suffering in cases of terminal disease seems advisable.

4. Normative; assumption: In cases where a practice is accepted in a country, multinationals should be allowed to engage in it. (Bribery is such a practice.)

5. Nonnormative; assumption: Admissions of multimillion-dollar bribes and "grease payments" prove that American businesses behave differently overseas from how they behave at home.

6. Normative; assumption: When at least 10 percent of the American population is engaged in what is considered psychologically or physically unhealthful behavior, America is a very sick society.

7. Probably both; assumption: Whatever's a form of human expression is a statement.

8. Probably both; assumption: No one should be forced to pay school taxes unless schools only teach what does not offend the taxpayer.

9. Normative; assumption: Nations have similar obligations to those binding on individuals.

10. Normative; assumption: Selling weapons to Iran, in effect, protected United States citizens.

Exercise 15-4

NOTE: In all cases the value words will be interpreted in terms of the three perspectives: personal approval or disapproval, social convention, principle or law. The truth of the statements therefore would be determined on the basis of whether the statements were in accordance with these standards.

1. Wrong

2. Evil

3. Ought

4. Highest

5. Immoral

6. Best

7. Greatest

8. Should not

9. Morally justifiable

10. Should never

11. Moral bankruptcy; character

12. Godless

13. Threatens

14. Justify

15. Lousy

APPENDIX   *Exercise A-1*

A. 1. Some **A** are **C**. (**A** = aardvarks;
C = creatures)

2. No **T** is **E**. (**T** = trafficker; **E** =
ethical)

3. Some **N** are **T**. (**N** = nonstudents; **T** = talkers)

4. No **E** is **T**. (**T** = trafficker; **E** =
ethical)

5. Some **O** are **W**. (**O** = odors;
W = warning)

6. All **B** are **I**. (**B** = believers; **I** =
individuals)

7. All **B** are **I**. (**B** = believers; **I** =
individuals) NOTE: The same
letter can be used to represent different terms in different
propositions—so long as the
different propositions do not
occur in the same syllogism.
For example, both answers 6
and 7 in this exercise can use
B = believers. But should the
propositions occur together in
a syllogism, we would have to
distinguish between the believers described in 6 (believers
in psychic phenomena who are
also holders of graduate degrees, but who have yet to
achieve renown) and those described in 7 (believers in psychic phenomena who are not
holders of graduate degrees).

8. No **S** are **C**. (**S** = sequestered;
C = capable)

9. Some **D** are **S**. (**D** = drinks =
sodas; **S** = sweet) NOTE: Although no ambiguity occurs
when we use the same letter
to represent different terms

in different propositions (see
note to answer 7), we must
never use the same letter to
designate different terms in the
same proposition. One useful
rule of thumb is to find an associated term, such as "drinks"
is associated with "sodas." We
could have used "beverages,"
"pop," and "colas," also.

10. Some **S** are not **E**. (**S** = sweeteners; **E** = effective)

B and C

1. I:

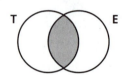

2. E:

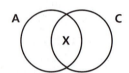

3. I:

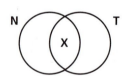

4. E:

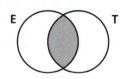

5. I:

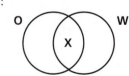

6. A:

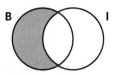

7. A:

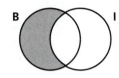

8. E:

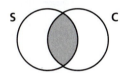

9. I:

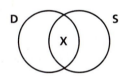

10. O:

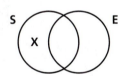

Exercise A-2

Seg. 1. = S P̄ M̄

Seg. 2. = S P M̄

Seg. 3. = S̄ P M̄

Seg. 4. = S P̄ M

Seg. 5. = S P M

Seg. 6. = S̄ P M

Seg. 7. = S̄ P̄ M

2.

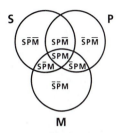

Reinforcing Exercise B.

1.

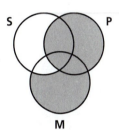

invalid

2.

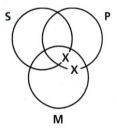

invalid

3.

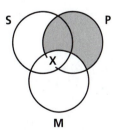

invalid

4.

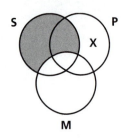

invalid

8.

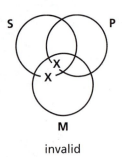

invalid

5.

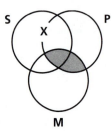

invalid

9.

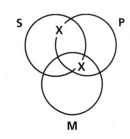

invalid

6.

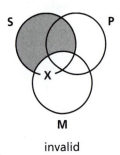

invalid

10.

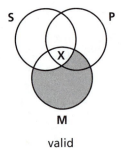

valid

7.

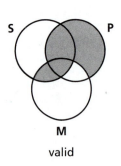

valid

Abbreviated arguments, 28–29
Accident, fallacy of, 272
Ad hominem fallacy. *See* Personal attack
Affirming the consequent, fallacy of, 240
Agreement and difference, joint method
    of, 339–340
Agreement, method of, 337–338
Ambiguity
    amphiboly and, 117–119
    argument and, 115–116
    equivocation and, 118–119
    questionable premises and, 116
    vagueness and 116
Ambiguous question, fallacy of, 297
Amphiboly, fallacy of, 117–118
Analogical arguments
    cogency criteria and, 319–320
    definition of, 314–315
    faulty analogy, 323–324
    number of entities, 319
    number or relevant likenesses, 319
    number and nature of differences,
        319–320
    value of, 315–317
Analog, 314
Analogy,
Anecdotal evidence, fallacy of, 271–272
Antecedent, 239
Apples to oranges, concealed evidence
    fallacy, 303–304
Arguable, what is, 51
Argument from ignorance, fallacy of,
    64–65
Arguments. *See also* Statistical arguments
    abbreviated, 28–29
    ambiguity and, 115–116
    analogical, 314–315
    belief and, 48–50
    as cases, 7–8
    causal, 331
    cogent, 11–15
    conclusion of, 8–10
    content of, 10–12

context and identification of, 21–23
critical thinking and, 45–47
deductive, 15, 171–172
definition of, 7
demonstration as function of, 29
evaluation of, 10
explanation as function of, 20, 29, 31
functions of, 29–32
inductive, 15, 255
knowledge and, 48
legal scope of, 33
logical form of, 10–12
moral scope of, 32–33
normative arguments, 406–419
objective properties of, 44
parts of, 8–10
personal dimension of, 79–92, 229
personal scope of, 32
political scope of, 32
premises of, 8–10
public dimension of, 44–45, 223
purpose of, 10
reasonableness of, 12
recognition of, 22–24
refutation as function of, 29, 31
relevancy of, 13–14
scope of, 32–34
signal words and phrases in, 23–24
sufficiency of, 14–15
truth and, 50–51
vague language and, 115–116
Argumentum ad baculum, 142
Argumentum ad hominem, 129
Argumentum ad populum, 136
Argumentum ad superstionem, 348
Aristotle, 95, 173, 174, 298
Arnold, Matthew, 205
Assertion, 7
Assumption. *See also* Premises
    definition of, 205
    fallacies of questionable, 151–158
Authority
    fallacies of, 67–71

Authority (*Continued*)
  reliability of, 55–56
  as source of knowledge, 54–55
Average, statistical, 290–291

Background beliefs, 15
Bacon, Francis, 331
Bandwagon, fallacy of, 137–138
Barnhart, Joseph, 378
Begging the question, fallacy of,
  153–154
Belief
  argument and, 48
  definition of, 48–49
  mere, 49
  truth compared with, 50
Biased question, fallacy of, 295–297
Biased sample, fallacy of, 286–288
Boolean logic, 182, 183, 196, 201
Brown, Edmund G. "Jerry," Jr., 109
Bryan, William Jennings, 136
Buzzwords, 109–110, 291, 374

Cases. *See also* Arguments
  apparent versus actual case, 6–7
  arguments as, 7–8
  definition of, 5
  logical evidence in, 6, 10
Categorical propositions
  with adjectival phrases, 208
  with affirmative and negative state-
    ments, 211–214
  copula of, 174
  definition of, 172–173
  distribution and, 177–180
  existential import and, 182
  with irregular quantifiers, 209
  lacking subject or predicate terms,
    209–210
  lacking the verb *to be*, 208–209
  with logical equivalencies, 206–207
  predicate of, 174
  quality of, 174
  quantity of, 174
  simplified square of contradiction,
    180–181
  with singular terms, 207–208
  standard-form of, 174–176
  subject of, 174

translation into standard form,
  206–214
using *only* and *none but*, 210–211
Categorical syllogisms
  figure of, 187–188
  identification of conclusion of,
    188–190
  major term of, 185–186
  middle term of, 185–186
  minor term of, 185–186
  mood of, 187–188
  standard-form of, 185–190
  sufficiency criterion and, 200
  validity of, 191–197
Causal arguments
  cogency criteria and, 352
  definition of, 331
Causal statements, 331, 332
Causation fallacies, 346
  magical thinking, 348
  oversimplification fallacy, 349–350
  post hoc fallacy, 347–348
  questionable causes, 346
  slippery slope fallacy, 348–349
  and sophistries, 382–383
Causal relationship
  direct, 341
  inverse, 341
Cause
  agreement method for establishing
    probable cause, 337–338
  concomitant variation method for
    establishing probable cause,
    341–342
  contributory cause, 335
  correlation compared with,
    341–345
  definition of, 331
  difference method for establishing
    probable cause, 338–339
  idea of, 332–334
  joint method of agreement and differ-
    ence for establishing probable
    cause, 339–340
  method for establishing probable
    cause, 336–341
  necessary and sufficient cause, 335
  necessary cause, 334
  sufficient cause, 334

Character assassination, fallacy
of, 130
Charity, principle of, 150, 222–223,
225, 227
Chase, Stuart, 112
Chuang-Tzu, 79
Circular reasoning, fallacy of, 154
Circumstantial personal attack, fallacy
of, 131–132
Claims
about emotions, 80, 128–129
empirical, 369
objective claims, 57
problematic claims, 19
subjective claims, 57
truth claims, 7
unproblematic claims, 19
Class, 172
Clough, Arthur Hugh, 128
Cogency
criteria for, 12–15
analogical arguments and,
319–320
causal arguments and, 352
dilemmas and, 245–246
and induction, 258–259
knowledge and truth, 396
psychological conviction and, 81
and validity, 199–202
Cogent arguments, 11–15, 79
Cogent explanations, 25–26
Common practice, 135
Complement, 183, 425
Complex question, fallacy of, 155–
156, 296
Composition, fallacy of, 120
Concealed evidence, fallacy of, 299–
306, 401
apples and oranges, 303–304
equivocation, 290–294
nonstatistical, 300–303
statistical, 304–306
Conclusion
of arguments, 8–10
of categorical syllogisms, 188–190
Concomitant variation, method of,
341–342
Conditional statement, 239
Conditional syllogisms, 239–243

Connotation
objective, 99
subjective, 99–101
Consequent, 239
Content of arguments, 10–12
Contextually accurate reconstruction,
229–231
Context and arguments, 21–23
Contradiction, 180–181
Contraposition, 183
Contributory cause, 335
Conversion, 183–184
Copula, 174
Correlation, 341–345
Counterdilemma, 246–247
Cowper, William, 235
Critical thinking, 45–48
Culver, Roger, 382

Deductive arguments, 15, 171–172
Defense mechanisms
chart of, 395
definition of, 83
denial, 87
introjection, 86
willed ignorance and, 84
prejudging, 89
projection, 85
rationalizing, 84, 88
scapegoating, 84–85
self-concept, 83–84
stereotyping, 89
Demonstration as argument,
29–30
Denial, 87
Denying the antecedent, fallacy of, 235,
241–242
Dianetics, 3
Diagramming. *See* Venn diagrams
Difference, method of, 338–339
Dilemma, 244–247
complex, 244
simple, 244
Discourse, rational, 4, 33, 141, 418
Disjunct, 236
Disjunction, 236
Disjunctive syllogisms, 236–239
Dismissal, fallacy of, 156–157
Disraeli, Benjamin, 279

Distribution, and categorical propositions, 177–180
Diversion, fallacies of, 142–150
Division, fallacy of, 121
Doublespeak, 102–112, 401

Emotional appeals
  bandwagon, 137–138
  character assassination, 130
  circumstantial personal attack, 131–132
  common practice, 135
  definition of, 128
  fear fallacy, 141–142
  mob appeal, 135–137
  personal attack, 129–133
  pity fallacy, 139–141
  rational discourse and, 141
  snob appeal, 138–139
  tu quoque, 133, 150
  two wrongs make a right, 133–135
Emotions and reasons, 6, 80–82, 141
Emotional needs, 83
Emotive language, 98–99
Empirical claims, 369
Empirical meaning. *See* Predictive power
Enthymeme, 215–217, 220
Epithets, loaded, 154–155, 401
Equivocation, fallacy of, 116–117, 118, 119, 290–294
Errors
  of assumption, 151–158
  interpretive, 53
Eulathus, 246–247
Euphemism, 104–106
Evaluation of arguments
  basic procedure for, 393–394
  content and logic in, 10–12
  examples of, 397–402
  normative arguments, 406–419
Evaluation of evidence, 59–61
Evidence
  anecdotal, 271–272
  evaluation of, 59
  fallacy of concealed evidence, 299–306
  necessary background knowledge in, 60
  evaluation of, 59–61
  objectivity in evaluation of, 61

physical conditions in evaluation of, 60
scientific evidence, 367–368
sensory acuity in evaluation of, 60
supporting testimony in evaluation of, 61
Evidentiary relationship, 19
Exceptive propositions, 211–213
Exclusive premises, fallacy of 195
Existential fallacy, 196
Existential import, and categorical propositions, 182
Explanations
  and arguments, 20, 29, 31–32
  cogent, 25–26

Facts and opinions, 51, 418
Fallacies
  accident, 272
  affirming the consequent, 240
  ambiguous question, 297
  amphiboly, 117–118
  anecdotal evidence, 271–272
  the argument from ignorance, 64–65
  of assumption, 151–158
  begging the question, 153–154
  biased question, 295–297
  biased sample, 286–288
  causation, 346–350
  character assassination, 130
  chart of, 394–396
  circular reasoning, 154
  circumstantial personal attack, 131–132
  common practice, 135
  complex question, 155–156, 296
  composition, 120
  concealed evidence, 299–306
  definition of, 116
  denying the antecedent, 235, 241–242
  dismissal, 156–157
  diversion, 142–150
  division, 121
  drawing an affirmative conclusion from a negative premise, 196
  emotional appeals, 128–150
  equivocation, 116–117, 118, 119, 290–294

existential, 196
exclusive premises, 195
false authority, 67–68
false dilemma, 298
faulty analogy, 323–324
fear, 141–142
four terms, 191–193
guilt by association, 272–273
hasty conclusion, 16, 269–271
illicit major and illicit minor
    terms, 195
inductive, 269–273
informal, 116
loaded epithets, 154–155
magical thinking, 348
mob appeal, 135–137
oversimplification, 349–350
personal attack, 129–133
pity, 139–141
popularity, 70–71
positioning, 68–69
post hoc, 347–348
provincialism, 63–64
red herring, 145–146
relevance, 128–129
ridicule, 146–147
slippery slope, 348–349
statistical, 286–307
straw argument, 147–150, 226
of traditional wisdom, 69–70
tu quoque, 133, 150
two wrongs make a right,
    133–135
undistributed middle term, 194
unknowable fact, 62–63
willed ignorance, 157–158
False authority, fallacy of, 67–68
False dilemma, fallacy of, 298
Falsifiability of empirical statements,
    368–370
Faulty analogy, fallacy of, 323–324
Fear, fallacy of, 141–142, 402
Figure, syllogistc, 187–188
Flattery, appeals to, 146
Form
    logical, 10–12, 172
    standard-form categorical proposi-
        tions, 174–176
    standard-form categorical syllogisms,
        187–188

Fragmented arguments. *See* Abbreviated
    arguments

Gardner, Martin, 377, 384
Gide, Andre, 367
Gobbledygook, 112–113
Groupspeak, 371
Groupthink, 371
Guild by association, fallacy of, 272–273
Hasty conclusion, fallacy of, 16,
    269–271
"Horns of a dilemma"
    escape between, 246
    taking by, 245
Hospers, John, 31
Human needs, 82–83
    emotional, 83
    physical, 82–83
Hume, David, 80, 192
Humor. *See* Ridicule, fallacy of
Hypothesis, 367–368

Ianna, Philip, 382
Ignorance
    fallacy of the argument from, 64–65
    fallacy of willed ignorance, 84,
        157–158
Illicit major and illicit minor terms, 195
Immediate inferences, 181
Implications, 239
Import, existential, 182
Inductive arguments, 15, 255
    analogical, 314–315
    justified, 256
Inductive fallacies
    accident, 272
    anecdotal evidence, 271–272
    cogency of, 258–259
    guilt by association, 272–273
    hasty conclusion, 269–271
Inductive generalizations
    comprehensiveness and, 265
    definition of, 256, 259
    induction and strong generalizations,
        262–263
    margin for error and, 266–267
    randomness and, 266, 284
    reliable inductive generalizations,
        264–267
    size and, 265–266

Inductive generalizations (*Continued*)
  statistical generalizations, 261–262
  strong inductive generalizations, 260
  weak inductive generalizations, 261
Inductive reasoning
  definition of, 255
  sufficiency criterion and, 256–258
Informal fallacies, 116
Informative language, 98–99
Intellectual maturity, 46
Intension, 99
Intention, 7
Interpretive errors, 53
Introjection, 86
Isaiah, 392

Jargon, 107–109
Judgmental errors, 53
Justification, 256

Knowledge
  argument and, 48
  authority as source of, 54
  cogency and truth, 396
  definition of, 48
  evaluation of evidence objectively and,
    59–61
  necessary background knowledge,
    60–61
  public verifcation of, 53
  reason as source of, 54
  senses as source of, 52–53
  sources of, 52–56
Kurtz, Paul, 378

Language
  amphiboly fallacy, 117–118
  buzzwords, 109–110, 291, 374
  clarification of, 409–412
  composition fallacy and, 120
  definition of, 95
  division fallacy, 121
  doublespeak, 102–112
  emotive language, 98–99
  equivocation fallacy, 116–117, 118,
    290–291
  euphemism, 104–106
  experience and, 96–98
  fallacies of ambiguity, 116–121
  gobbledygook, 112–113
  informative language, 98–99

jargon, 107–109
  objective connotation of, 99
  obscurity in, 115–116
  persuasive language, 98
  powerbabble, 374
  psychobabble, 372, 374
  puffery, 110–111, 374
  subjective connotation of, 99–101
  vague, 115–116
  "weasel" words, 291–292
Loaded epithets, fallacy of, 154–155
Locke, John, 19, 171
Logic, 4
Logical cogency, 81
Logical equivalencies, 206–207
Logical form, 10
Logical justification, feeling of, 129
Logical relationship, 19
Lutz, William, 102, 103, 113

Magical thinking, fallacy of, 348
Major term, 185–186
Margin for error, 266–267
Maslow, Abraham, 83
McCann, Hugh, 83, 349, 350
McCann, Janet, 83, 349, 350
Mencken, H. L., 367
Mere belief, 49
Merton, Thomas, 43
Middle term, 185–186
Minor term, 185–186
Mixed-conditional syllogisms, 239–242
Mill, John Stuart, 337
Mill's methods for establishing
    cause, 337
Mob appeal, 135–137
Modus ponens, 239–242, 244
Modus tollens, 240–242
Mood, syllogistic, 187–188, 240–242
Moore, W. Edgar, 83, 349, 350
Morgenstern, Oskar, 255

Necessary and sufficient cause, 335
Necessary background knowl-
    edge, 60
Necessary cause, 334
Needs. *See* Human needs
Negative correlation, 343–344
Nonarguments, 20–21
Nonnormative statements, definition
    of, 404

Normative arguments
  definition of, 406
  evaluation of, 413–415
  examples of, 406
  minimum adequacy requirements for,
    416–419
  pseudojustification and, 414–415
  reasonableness of, 407–409
  words and meaning in, 409–412
Normative statements, definition of, 403

Objective claims, 57
Objective connotation, of language, 99
Objective properties of arguments, 44
Objectivity, in evaluation of evidence,
  59–61
Obscure language, 115–116
Obversion, 183, 207
Opinions, and facts, 51, 418
Or. *See also* Disjunctive syllogism
  exclusive sense of, 236
  inclusive sense of, 236
Oversimplification fallacy, 349–
  350, 402

Pascal, Blaise, 3
Personal attack, fallacy of, 129–133
Personal dimension of arguments, 79–
  92, 229
Persuasive language, 98–99
Physical conditions, 60
Physical needs, 82–83
Pity, fallacy of, 139–141
Polls and surveys, 283–286
Pollster bias, 286
Popularity, fallacy of, 70–71
Population, and correlation, 342
Positioning, fallacy of, 68–69
Positive correlation, 343
Possibilities and probabilities,
  263–264
Post hoc fallacy, 347–348
Powerbabble, 374
Predicate, propositional, 174
Predictive power of empirical state-
  ments, 368–370
Prejudging, 89
Prejudice, 89
Premises
  of arguments, 8–10
  exceptive, 212

major, 185
minor, 185
questionable, 116, 151–158
Principle of charity, 150, 222–223,
  225, 227
Probabilities and possibilities, 263–264
Probable cause. *See* Cause
Problematic claims, 19
Projection, 85
Propositions. *See also* Categorical
    propositions
  definitions of, 7
  form of, 174–176
  as truth claims, 7, 50, 95
Protagoras, 44–45, 246–247
Provincialism, fallacy of, 63–64
Pseudoarguments, 21
Pseudojustification, 414–415
Pseudoscience, 377, 384–387
Psychic sophistry, 377–383
Psychobabble, 372, 374
Psychological conviction, 81–82
Psychological sophistry, 372–373
Public dimension of arguments, 44–
  45, 223
Public verification, 53
Puffery, 110–111, 374
Pure conditional syllogisms, 242–243
Pure hypothetical syllogisms, 242–243

Quality
  of categorical propositions, 174–176
  and sufficiency of induction,
    258–259
Quantifier, 174
Quantity, of categorical propositions,
  174–176
Questionable premises
  and ambiguity, 116
  and errors of assumption, 151–158

Randi, James, 377, 378, 379
Randomness, 266, 284
Rational discourse, 4, 33, 141, 418
Rational person, appeal to, 12
Rational reconstruction
  appropriate strength of reconstruc-
    tion, 228–229
  contextually accurate reconstruction,
    229–231
  definition of, 222

Rational reconstruction (*Continued*)
  principle of charity in, 150, 222–223,
    225, 227
  relevant reconstruction, 226–227
  self-supporting reconstruction,
    227–228
  steps in, 223–226
  validity and, 219
Rationalizing, 88, 414
Reason
  definition of, 30
  as source of knowledge, 54
Reasonableness
  of arguments, 12
  of normative arguments, 407–409
Reasoning, errors in, 6, 116
Reasons, and emotions, 6, 80–82, 141
Reconstruction, rational. *See* Rational
    reconstruction
Red herring, fallacy of, 145–146
Reductio ad absurdum, 45
Refutation as argument, 29, 31
Relativity of truth, 50–51
Relevance, fallacy of, 128–129
Relevancy
  of arguments, 13
  logical v. psychological, 13–14, 129
  personal, 80
Relevant reconstruction, 226–227
Reliable inductive generalizations,
    264–267
Respondent bias, 287–288
Ridicule, fallacy of, 146–147
Rosen, R. D., 372
Rules of validity, 191–197

Sampling technique, 286–287
Scapegoating, 84–85
Scientific evidence, 367–368
Self-concept, 83–84. *See also* Defense
    mechanisms
Self-supporting reconstruction,
    227–228
Senses as source of knowledge, 52–53
Sensory acuity, 60
Shakespeare, William, 314
Signal words and phrases, 23–24, 189
Simplified square of contradiction,
    180–181
Singer, Philip, 378

Singular propositions, 207
Slippery slope fallacy, 348–349, 402
Snob appeal, 138–139
Socrates, 44–45
Sophistries
  examples of, 370–372
  psychological sophistry, 372–373
  spiritual and psychic sophistry,
    377–383
  success sophistry, 374–376
Sorites, 218–221
Sowell, Thomas, 110
Spiritual and psychic sophistry, 377–383
Standard-form
  of categorical syllogisms, 187–188
  of categorical propositions, 174–176
  translating into, 206–214
Statement
  causal, 331, 332
  definition of, 7
  empirical, 368–370
Statistical arguments
  fallacy of ambiguous question, 297
  fallacy of biased question, 295–297
  fallacy of biased sample, 286–288
  fallacy of concealed evidence,
    299–306
  fallacy of equivocation, 290–294
  fallacy of false dilemma, 298
  nonstatistical concealed evidence,
    300–303
  polls and surveys, 283–286
  and pollster bias, 286
  respondent and, 287–288
  sampling technique and, 286–287
  statistical concealed evidence,
    304–306
  stratified sample, 285
  studies, 281–283
  verbal equivocation and, 290–291
  visual equivocation, 292–294
Statistical generalizations, 262–263
Stereotyping, 89
Stratified sample, 285
Straw argument, fallacy of, 147–150,
    226, 401
Strong generalizations, 260
Studies, 281–283
Subject, propositional, 174
Subjective claims, 57

Subjective connotation, of language, 99–101, 401
Success sophistry, 374–376
Sufficiency criterion
    of arguments, 14
    induction and, 256–258
    categorical syllogisms and, 200
    and quality of induction, 258–259
    questionable premises and, 152
Sufficient cause, 334
Supporting testimony, 61
Surveys, 283–287
Syllogisms. *See also* Categorical
        syllogisms
    conditional syllogisms, 239–243
    counterdilemma, 246–247
    definition of, 172
    dilemma, 244–247
    disjunctive syllogisms, 236–239
    mixed-conditional, 240
    nonstandard, 235–236
    validity of, 171–172, 191–197

Tautologies, 380–381
Thinking. *See also* Critical thinking
    fallacy of magical thinking, 348
Traditional wisdom, fallacy of, 69–70
Truth
    argument and, 48, 50
    beliefs compared with, 50–51
    cogency and knowledge, 396
    definition of, 50
    and induction, 262–263
    relativity of, 50–51
Truth claims, 7
Tu quoque, 133, 150
Two wrongs make a right, 133–135

Uncritical thinking, 47
Unknowable fact, fallacy of, 62–63
Unproblematic claims, 19

Vague attributions, 150
Vague language, 115–116
Validity
    categorical syllogisms and, 191–197
    and cogency, 199–203
    definition of, 171
    and conditional syllogisms, 240–242
    and the dilemma, 244–246
    and disjunctive syllogisms, 236–238
    and pure conditional syllogisms,
        242–243
    rational reconstruction and, 222–231
    rules of, 191–197
    testing with Venn diagrams, 435–445
    trivial, 152, 154
Values and value judgments
    definition of, 392
    evaluation of, 413–415
    normative and nonnormative state-
        ments, 403–404
    prevalence of, 392–393
    words and meaning, 409–412
Venn Diagrams
    basic form of, 425–428
    of categorical syllogisms, 430–432
    crescents and ellipses, 433–434
    eight steps for testing validity, 448
    of specific propositions, 428–429
    and square of opposition, 180–181
    testing for validity with, 435–445
Verbal statistical equivocation, 290–291
Visual statistical equivocation, 292–294

Weak generalizations, 261
"Weasel" words, 291–292
Willed ignorance, fallacy of, 84,
        157–158
Wittgenstein, Ludwig, 95

TO THE STUDENT

If we are to make *Practical Logic* a better book, we need to have your reactions and suggestions. We want to know what you like about the book and how it could be improved. Please answer the questions below and return this form to Philosophy Editor, c/o Harcourt Brace College Publishers, Inc., 301 Commerce St., Ste. 3700, Fort Worth, TX 76102. THANK YOU!!

Name _____

School _____

City, State _____

Course title _____

Instructor's name _____

Other required texts _____

1. In comparison to other textbooks, the reading level was:

    _____ too difficult _____ just right _____ too easy

2. Did *Practical Logic* succeed in clarifying important principles of logic? Can you give us an example or two?

    _____

    _____

    _____

3. Are there any topics covered in your course not covered in our book? What topics would you like added to *Practical Logic*?

    _____

    _____

    _____

4. Please rate each chapter on a scale of 1 to 6.

	Liked Least				Liked Best		Not Assigned
Argument and Cases	1	2	3	4	5	6	_____
Recognition, Function, and Scope of Arguments	1	2	3	4	5	6	_____
The Public Dimension	1	2	3	4	5	6	_____
The Personal Dimension	1	2	3	4	5	6	_____
Careless Language Use	1	2	3	4	5	6	_____
Inattention to Subject Matter	1	2	3	4	5	6	_____

	Liked Least				Liked Best		Not Assigned
Categorical Syllogisms	1	2	3	4	5	6	_____
Reconstructing Arguments	1	2	3	4	5	6	_____
Additional Syllogisms	1	2	3	4	5	6	_____
Inductive Reasoning and Generalizations	1	2	3	4	5	6	_____
Statistical Arguments	1	2	3	4	5	6	_____
Analogical Arguments	1	2	3	4	5	6	_____
Cause	1	2	3	4	5	6	_____
Sophistries and Pseudoscience	1	2	3	4	5	6	_____
Normative and Nonnormative Arguments	1	2	3	4	5	6	_____

5. Do any chapters need more explanation or examples? Which chapters and why?

   _____

   _____

6. Do any chapters need more (or fewer) exercises? Which chapters and why?

   _____

   _____

7. Did you use the glossary? How helpful was it? _____

   _____

   _____

8. Will you keep this book for your library? _____

9. Do you have any additional suggestions, criticisms, or comments about *Practical Logic*? _____